CM0079631

THE SECRET DOCTRINE

THE SECRET DOCTRINE:

THE SYNTHESIS

OF

SCIENCE, RELIGION, AND PHILOSOPHY.

BY

H. P. BLAVATSKY

AUTHOR OF "ISIS UNVEILED."

सत्यान्नास्ति परो धर्मः

"There is no Religion higher than Truth."

INDEX

PREPARED BY JOHN P. VAN MATER

1997

THEOSOPHICAL UNIVERSITY PRESS

PASADENA, CALIFORNIA

Theosophical University Press
Post Office Box C
Pasadena, California 91109-7107
1997

First Edition
Copyright © 1997 by Theosophical University Press

All rights reserved. No part of this publication may be reproduced for commercial or other use in any form or by any means, electronic, mechanical, photocopying, recording, or otherwise, without permission of Theosophical University Press.

The paper in this book meets the standards for permanence
and durability of the Council on Library Resources.

Library of Congress Cataloging-in-Publication Data

Van Mater, John P., 1917–
    The secret doctrine, the synthesis of science, religion, and philosophy, by H. P. Blavatsky.   Index / prepared by John P. Van Mater.
        p.   cm.
    ISBN 1-55700-003-4 (cloth : alk. paper)
    ISBN 1-55700-004-2 (paper : alk. paper)

    1. Blavatsky, H. P. (Helena Petrovna), 1831-1891. Secret doctrine—Indexes.   2. Theosophy—Indexes.   I. Title.

BP561.S4V36   1997
299'.934—dc21   97-35589
                                                                      CIP

Printed at Theosophical University Press
Pasadena, California

Introduction

OVER ONE HUNDRED YEARS AGO, in 1888, H. P. Blavatsky published her *Secret Doctrine*. Indeed it *was* an event, for these volumes disclose a description, inner and outer, of the structure and operations of the cosmos and the origin and evolutionary destiny of the kingdoms of nature. Much of its content would have been considered esoteric in former eras, part of the mystery teaching of the ancient schools of both East and West.

This wisdom has been known and taught in every age, in myth and legend, symbol and glyph, and comes down to us from out of the darkness of prehistory. Its substance or truth is also embodied in the various branches of learning, ancient and modern — religion, philosophy, science, literature, and art. Hence HPB, having stated certain principles, was able to illustrate, by referring to the world's literature, that what she was bringing forward has been part of the thought-life of all previous ages. This is no accident: every age has had its wise men, philosophers, artists, poets, who have speculated on cosmic and human life and described it in such a fashion that the universality of the secret doctrine or perennial philosophy may be seen on every hand by those who have the eyes to see it.

The Secret Doctrine is the most widely disseminated theosophical source book. Because of its encyclopedic range, indexing the *SD* has proved a complex and challenging task. My original instructions were: "Start by making your own index. Don't try to coalesce or combine the existing indices." Over the course of a number of years this phase of the project was completed. We then consulted an unpublished index to the *SD* compiled by Dr. Gertrude W. van Pelt — a longtime student with a penetrating and intuitive mind — and numerous valuable entries were gleaned. The indices prepared by Boris de Zirkoff and the United Lodge of Theosophists were also consulted, and further useful entries included.

Our entries are designed to be as straightforward and informative as possible, considering the wide range of subjects covered. Most subentries lead off with key words which are alphabetically arranged. In the course of compiling the index, it became apparent that many of the foreign terms used so widely by HPB are no longer spelled as they were by the scholars of her

time. To aid the reader we have listed all foreign terms and proper nouns as they are given by HPB, while adding modern spelling in brackets or — when alphabetizing requires — referring the reader to the modern spellings under which the terms are indexed. Exceptions to listing the modern spelling are Tibetan and some Egyptian terms, as well as other foreign words when there is doubt about transliteration. In subentries modern spelling is generally used, but underdots are omitted. To facilitate recognition and pronunciation of Sanskrit words, the TUP conventions are*:

c	is transliterated as *ch*	*r*	is transliterated as *ri*
ch	is transliterated as *chh*	ṣ	is transliterated as *sh*

For the convenience of the reader, many main headings, especially of foreign terms, are followed by definitions. Cited books whose titles are not given in the *SD*, are placed in brackets under the author. Also included are a list of abbreviations and an appendix of foreign phrases with translation.

A major guideline followed is that an index is *not* an interpretation. Its purpose is to point the reader to the essential material found in the book. If, for example, the word Lemuria is given, such entries are placed under that heading. The third root-race is often termed Lemurian; but where third root-race is given by HPB and not Lemuria, these references are under Root-Race–Third. In order to bring together all such similar entries or supplemental material, we have put "*See also*" after the main headings followed by one or more items. One may also consult terms in the subentries for additional references.

Many individuals have been involved in this project, and each and all have my hearty thanks and gratitude. Allow me to say in closing that I perceive the years spent on this task to have been a rare and inestimable privilege. It is still an ongoing enterprise, for I am sure that future students will revise, enlarge, clarify, and make more accurate the work already done, so that in time the index may become an increasingly useful tool for those following the ageless path of wisdom that HPB so magnificently sets forth.

— JOHN P. VAN MATER

May 8, 1996
The Theosophical Society
Pasadena, California

---

*Cf. Bruce Cameron Hall, *Sanskrit Pronunciation: Booklet and Cassette*, TUP, 1992.

Abbreviations

&	—	and	equiv	—	equivalent
Afr	—	Africa	Eur	—	Europe(an)
Akkad	—	Akkadian	evol	—	evolve(s),
Amer	—	American			evolution(ary)
antiq	—	antiquity (ies)	expl	—	explained
Arab	—	Arabian	fem	—	feminine, female
Aram	—	Aramaic	Finn	—	Finnish, Finland
arch	—	archaeology (ical)	fr	—	from
asc	—	ascend(ing)	Fr	—	France, French
astron	—	astronomy (ical)	ft	—	feet, foot
Bab	—	Babylonia(n)	FTS	—	Fellow of the TS
beg	—	beginning	geol	—	geology
betw	—	between	geom	—	geometry (ic, al)
BG	—	*Bhagavad-Gītā*	Ger	—	German(y)
bk	—	book	Gk	—	Greek, Greece
cent	—	central, century	Gnos	—	Gnosis, tic(ism)
ch	—	chapter	gt	—	great
Chald	—	Chaldea(n)	HPB	—	H. P. Blavatsky
Chin	—	Chinese	Heb	—	Hebrew
civ	—	civilize(d,ation)	Hind	—	Hindu, Hindi
comp	—	compared	hist	—	history (ian, ical)
conj	—	conjunction	Inst	—	Institute (ion)
cont	—	continued, continent	*IU*	—	*Isis Unveiled*
desc	—	descent(ding)	Jap	—	Japan(ese)
		describe(d)	kab	—	kabbalistic
dict	—	dictionary	Kab	—	Kabbala
dif	—	difference	lang	—	language
disc	—	discussed	Lat	—	Latin
div	—	division	lit	—	literature
ed(s)	—	editor(s)	masc	—	masculine
Eng	—	England (ish)	math	—	mathematics

mech	—	mechanical	*SD*	—	*The Secret Doctrine*
Mex	—	Mexico (an)	Sem	—	Semitic
ML	—	*Mahatma Letters to*	sing	—	singular
		A. P. Sinnett (2nd ed.)	Skt	—	Sanskrit
MS, MSS	—	manuscript(s)	Soc	—	Society
Mt	—	Mount(ain)	St	—	Saint, Street
n, nn	—	footnote(s)	Ste	—	Sainte
N	—	North(ern)	subst	—	substance
NE	—	Northeast	Swed	—	Sweden (ish)
no(s)	—	number(s)	symb	—	symbol(ize,ical)
NT	—	New Testament	Syr	—	Syria(n)
NY	—	New York	terr	—	terrestrial
orig	—	origin(al,ate)	theog	—	theogony
OT	—	Old Testament	theol	—	theology (ian,ical)
Pers	—	Persian	theos	—	theosophy (ical,ist)
philos	—	philosophy (er,ical)	thru	—	through
Phoen	—	Phoenician	Tib	—	Tibet(an)
pl	—	plural	trad	—	tradition
prop	—	proposition,	transl	—	translation (ed,or)
pseud	—	pseudonym	TS	—	Theosophical Society
pt	—	point, part	tx	—	text
Pyth	—	Pythagoras (ean)	univ	—	universe (al,ality)
q	—	quote(d,ing)	USA	—	United States
R	—	River	var	—	various
re	—	regarding	*VP*	—	*Vishṇu Purāṇa*
ref(s)	—	reference(s)	vs	—	versus
rel	—	religion (ous)	w	—	with
Rom	—	Roman	w/o	—	without
Russ	—	Russia(n)	W	—	West(ern)
S	—	South(ern)	wt	—	weight
SE	—	Southeast	yr(s)	—	year(s)
Sax	—	Saxon	*Zend*	—	*Zend Avesta*
Scand	—	Scandinavian	Zor	—	Zoroaster(rian)
sci	—	science			
SD	—	Secret Doctrine			

INDEX

A

Aam (Egy)
   electro-positive force, Tum I 674 &n
Aanroo, Āanru, Āaru, Āarru (Egy)
   Field of Amenti domain in realm of I 236n
   kāma-loka I 674 &n
   wheat gleaned in I 221, 236n; II 374 &n
Aarea (Tah) red earth
   man created out of II 193-4
Ab (Heb) the Father II 83
Ababel (Arab) "Father Tree," phoenix & II 617
Abacus, Pythagorean I 361
Abahu. *See* Abbahū
Abarbinel [Abrabanel, Abravanel], Isaac
   praises *Nabathean Agriculture* II 455-6
Abba (Heb), Father I 355
Abbā, Rabbi, re 5 lights & 7th II 625, 628
Abbahū, Rabbi
   on worlds created & destroyed II 53-4, 704
Abd Allatif ['Abd al-Latīf]
  —— [*Desc. of the Ancient Monuments*] II 362
Abdera, Democritus of. *See* Democritus
Abdi, Moham 4-letter God II 602
Abel. *See also* Cain, Hebel
   Cain &, male & female II 125, 127, 135,
      273n, 388, 469
   Chebel (Hebel) or, pains of birth II 125n
   first natural woman II 388
   Hebel or, female II 127, 135, 469
   separating hermaphrodite II 134
Abenephius
  —— *Liber de cultura Aegyptiorum* I 362
Aben Ezra, re Azāzēl I 441-2n
Ab Hati (Egy), animal soul II 633
Abhayam (Skt) no fear II 406
Abhimānin (Skt). *See also* Pitṛis
   father of 3 fires I 521; II 247
   Prometheus & II 521
Abhrayantī (Skt), a Pleiad II 551
Abhūtarājasas (Skt), incorporeal beings II 89
Abjayoni (Skt), "lotos-born" I 372
Aborigines. *See* Australian (Aborigines)
Abraham(s), Abram I 322, 422
   A-bra(h)m becomes II 139n
   fr Arba I 337n
   bosom of, or nirvāna I 568
   burning lamp of I 338n

   forefather of Jehovistic Jews I 578n
   God of, not Father of Jesus II 509
   God's covenant w II 508
   Hebrew number for II 40
   "no Brahmin" II 200
   pillars erected by II 472n
   recognized Phoenician god II 380
   Sarai (Sarah) wife of II 77, 174
   Saturn symbol I 578n
   story of, based on Brahmā II 77
   there were, before the Jews II 130
   fr Ur I 376; II 139n
Abrasax, Abraxas, Abraxax (Gnos)
   Basilidian supreme god I 350
   central spiritual sun II 214
   Garuda pictured as monster on, gems II 565
   Jevo genii antagonistic to II 541
   Mithra, IAO, or II 474
   as Priapus symb 4 Adamic races II 458
Abrayanti. *See* Abhrayantī
Absolute (the). *See also* Ain-sōph, Iᴛ, One,
   Parabrahm, Paranirvāṇa, Sat, Word
   Aʟʟ & universe not separate II 384n
   astral light lower aspect of I 196
   Being is Non-being I 54n; II 449n
   cannot create, be defined, or known II 34
   Causeless Cause I 569
   consciousness, motion I 51, 56
   Crookes' idea of I 581n
   Cusa's definition of II 158n
   devoid of attributes I 214, 420
   dhyāni-chohans cannot know I 51; II 34
   of East misunderstood I 496n
   everything other than, is illusion I 295
   evil rooted in I 412-13
   existence permanent I 39
   finite self-consciousness aspect of I 50n
   the "first" cannot be the I 14-15n
   how man is led to II 79n
   ideation & substance aspects of I 15, 326,
      329
   independent of numbers II 598
   kabbalists' I 214
   light is, darkness II 95
   mahāmāyā of II 446
   man can become one w II 78-9n

monad & jīva breath of I 247
monads rays of, principle II 167
monad's relation to I 135, 175
nature aspect of I 277n
never understood in West I 496n
Non-being is Absolute Being I 54 &n
One, Be-ness, Reality I 14, 54n, 290, 295
Parabrahm of Vedantins I 16
periodical manifestation of I 273
personified powers of I 350
reabsorption in, or paranirvāna I 135, 266, 636
Space the, ALL I 8
streams projected fr, life I 275
three aspects of I 43
two, impossible I 7, 412
Unity pulsating great heart II 588
universe issues fr I 88
unknown, essence I 273; II 240n, 728
Absoluter Geist (von Hartmann) I 50
Ab Soo [Apsu] (Chald)
  habitat of knowledge II 502
Abul-Faraj. *See* Bar-Hebraeus
[Abu'l-Fazl 'Allami]
—— *A'in-i-Akbari* ("Akbar's Institutes")
  Akbar's interest in various sects I xxivn
Abul Feda
—— *Historia anteislamitica* II 366
  names given initiates II 210n
Abul Teda. *See* Abul Feda
Abydos II 464
  Bes stands on lotus at I 385
  Osiris worshiped at I 437, 675
  table of, vindicates Manetho II 367
Abydos. See Mariette (Bey)
Abyss(es). *See also* Chaos, Great Deep
  arg, arca floating on II 313, 460
  ginnungagap (chaos) I 367, 427
  of Learning in Gobi II 502-3
  lower, of matter I 136, 195; II 235, 244
  Noot the celestial I 228
  of primordial creation (Berosus) II 65n, 715n
  watery, or Space I 346; II 53, 142n, 313, 503, 580, 653
Abyssinia
  Aryans reached Egypt thru II 746
  Bruce brings *Bk of Enoch* fr II 531
  once an island II 368
Académie des Sciences (*Comptes Rendus*) articles by Faye I 165, 496, 500, 505, 541n
Academy, The (journal)
  Petrie's letter to, re pyramid I 314
Accadia, Accadian(s). *See* Akkadians

Accident
  karma & I 643-4
  victims reincarnate quickly II 303
Achad. *See* Eḥād
Achaica [Achaia]. See Pausanias
Achar. *See* Aḥēr
Āchārya. *See* Bhāshyāchārya, N.
Achath. *See* Aḥath
Acherōn (Gk), & Helion II 357
Achilles
  heel of II 637
  shield of II 394
Achiochersus. *See* Axiokersos
Achiosersa. *See* Axiokersa
Achit or Anātman (Skt)
  Parabrahman, chit (ātman), & I 59n
Achod. *See* Eḥād
Achyuta (Skt) imperishable
  chyuta & II 47 &n
  "does not perish" I 18-19
  name of Vishnu I 19
  Purushottama, Brahmā or I 542
Ackerman, R. W., *Arth. Index* II 342n
Acosmism I 152
Acosta, José de
—— *Historia natural . . . de las Indias*
  immense stones at Cuzco I 209n
  seven Incas repeopled Earth II 141
Acquired Faculties, transmission of I 219
Acrania II 656
Acre of Earth, & Jared (Yared) II 597n
Acropolis, ever-burning fire of I 338n
Acropolis of Argos, 3-eyed colossus at II 294n
Actio in distans I 487-8, 491
Action(s)
  cause & effect II 73-4
  good, the only priests I 280
  karma-nemesis & II 305 &n
  mankind determines good & evil by II 512
  no independent I 566n
  will determines our I 639
Activity
  cycles of I 266; II 545
  forty-nine stages of II 747
  periods of I 62, 154-5
  rest &, law governing I 62
Actor, personalities are roles of II 306
Acts of the Apostles
  14:12 mistranslated II 481
  kosmic beings called elements I 338n
  Paul Hermes, Barnabas Zeus II 481
  quoted:
    God dwelleth not in temples I 327
    in him we live & move I 8

Holy Ghost as tongues of fire I 87, 379n
Ād, Ādi (Skt) first I xix; II 42-3, 452
Ad (Assyr)
  father or II 42-3
  Son(s) of I 207; II 42n
Ad-ad (Aramaean), the Only One II 42-3
Ad-ah, Sons of II 203
Adam(s), Admi, Adami
  animals & fowls preceded, (*Gen* 1) II 181
  animals came after, (*Gen* 2) II 1n, 181
  Aryans descend fr yellow II 426
  Assyrian, Chaldean II 42, 102
  became Cain & Abel II 124-5
  born of earth & fire II 4
  born of no woman II 125n
  chronology of II 71n
  coats of skin of II 202
  the coming II 100
  creation of II 86-7
  dark race II 5
  divine essence emanating fr, (*IU* q) I xlii
    [error, *see ML* page 45]
  driven fr Tree II 216
  earthly, & 7 angels II 112
  eating the fruit gave, wisdom I 404
  elohīm brought forth II 81, 134, 137
  elohīm expelled, fr Eden II 382n
  ethnology requires several I 323-4
  first & last II 513
  first divine androgyne II 124, 127-9
  five, & the races II 46n, 457, 503-4
  fourth or fallen II 457
  4004 bc I 323
  garment of light of II 112
  generative principle II 124-5n
  generic name II 454
  Gnostics on four II 458
  in God's image, male & female II 467
  had nephesh but no soul II 162, 456
  Heavenly, & 10 sephīrōth II 112
  Jah-Eve the original II 126
  Jod or Yōdh II 129
  Jupiter as Ham & II 270
  Kaimurath the Persian II 396-7
  last, a quickening spirit II 513
  -Lilith & chhāyā-birth II 174
  made perfect, joins dragon II 383-4
  Madim (Mars) is II 144n
  Naudin on II 119
  Noah, Jehovah &, same I 444
  Noah prayed before body of II 467
  not 1st man I 324
  Patriarch, & Kabiri I 642n
  primitive human race II 125

progenitor of human race II 467
"Prophet of the Moon" II 468
races of II 3, 46, 457
red II 43n, 124-5n, 144, 426
rib of II 46, 129, 193
Rishoun or II 315, 397
Samael & earthly II 112
second, septenary II 1-2n
Semites fr red II 426
separates into man & woman II 125, 129,
  134n, 135
serpent & I 404-5
sleep of II 181
solus, sexless 1st race II 134
Swedenborg called, a church II 42n
two faces yet one person II 134n
two races preceded II 394
white, black, red, etc I 323-4
Zohar on earthly II 44
Adam-Adami II 452-8
  Bible patriarch (Renan) II 454
  Brahmā-Virāj I 355-6
  earlier than Mosaic books II 43
  Elohīm-Jehovah I 355-6
  manifold symbol II 42
  personation of dual Adam II 456
Ad-am-ak-ad-mon
  became Adam Kadmon II 43
Adam & Eve
  apple, tree & II 354-5
  became matter II 273
  fall of II 62, 95n, 354-5
  Jehovah curses, then blesses II 410
  Jehovah is, blended II 125n, 128
  Ophis urges, to eat fruit II 215
  Tahitian II 193-4
  why Cain, Abel &, only humans II 286
Adamas (Gnos)
  archetype of 1st males II 3
  Ophite, or primeval man II 458
Adam-Eve
  androgyne 2nd race II 134
  Jehovah or II 127
Adam-Galatea, soul of, preexistent II 150
Adami
  Adam, Admi & II 4
  Aryan symbol II 452-8
  dark race II 5
Adamic Races, Man
  few million years old II 315
  pitris ancestors of II 91n
  pre- & post-, were giants II 289n
  Tree of Life, serpent & I 406-7

Adam-Jehovah
  symb generative powers II 43n
Adam-Jehovah-Eve
  bisexual creative deity II 125
Adam-Kadmon [Ādām Qadmōn] (Heb). *See
    also* Heavenly Man, 2nd Logos, Sons of
    Light
  Ad-am-ak-ad-mon became II 43
  Adam of *Genesis* 1 is II 129
  Ancient of Days & I 60
  androgyne I 98n, 215n, 246, 337, 355-6, 427,
    450; II 37, 129, 269n, 467, 537
  Athamaz, Tamaz, Adonis II 44
  Bath-Kol & I 137
  Bel & Noah preceded II 144
  circle w diameter is I 391
  collective name II 4, 234
  creative subordinate powers II 544
  Creator II 456
  Eve female portion of II 269n
  fecundates Earth I 240
  Fiat Lux of Bible I 246
  First Cause manifests thru I 214
  first triad of, unseen I 239
  host of elohīm II 112n
  Jah-Hovah mind-born son of II 126
  Jehovah & I 619n; II 269n, 537
  knew only Shekhīnah I 432
  leads prajāpatis, sephīrōth II 129
  Logos or I 99n, 214, 429; II 25, 234
  Lord is II 127
  made in image of God II 46n
  Manu-Svāyambhuva & II 128, 704n
  Philo calls, mind II 490
  prototype I 450
  quaternary or II 595-6
  Sacr-n'cabvah or II 467
  separates into male, female II 128
  Sephīrāh, Brahmā, Ādi-Sanat I 98
  Sephīrāh wife, mother, etc, of I 430
  Sephīrōthal Tree or I 352; II 293
  sexless II 37, 128, 595
  symbol of generative power II 124n
  synthesis of builders I 436-7
  ten sephīrōth I 391, 427, 432-3; II 1-2n, 544,
    704n
  Tetragrammaton I 99n; II 596, 601, 625n
  Tree of Knowledge II 4, 293
  Trinity in one I 432-3
  typifies water & earth II 124n
  vehicle of Ain-sōph I 179, 432
Adam of Dust
  earthly II 78-81, 86, 112, 458
  nephesh breathes into I 242n, 247

requires 2 middle principles I 247
  third Adam is II 457
  woman issues fr rib of II 129
Adam Rishoon, Rishoun [Ādām-Rishōn]
    (Heb) II 315, 397
Adams, John C. II 441
Adam's Earth
  mūlaprakriti I 10n
  unity of matter of kabbalists I 543n
Adan, mandrakes in city of II 27n
Adanari. *See* Ardhanārī
Ada-nāth. *See* Ādi-nāth
Adaptation(s)
  evidence of guiding process I 277-8
  factor in variation II 738
Ad-ar-gat (or Astartē, Syrian) II 42n, 43
Adbhitanya [Adbhutama] II 319
Adbhutam (Skt), impenetrable Rājah II 621
Adept(s) II 94. *See also* Arhan(s), Cis-
    Himalayan, Initiates, Mahātmas,
    Masters, Seers
  -astronomers II 699
  re Atlantis II 406
  can produce organic matter II 349
  can separate his upādhis I 158
  can transfer consciousness I 166
  concealed knowledge & I xvii, 156
  defined I 273
  dragons/serpents & I 404; II 94n, 210, 280n
  dwelt under pyramids II 351-2
  "euthanasia" of II 531
  in every age I 484
  few, know highest initiates I 611-12
  future mankind of II 446
  Galilean II 231
  -healer II 361
  India still has I 311
  initiation of II 215, 558
  jīvanmukta or high I 46n
  keeps personalities separated I 275
  knew of races on Mars, Venus II 699
  knowledge I 605; II 216, 700-1
  know occult properties of light I 516
  know their dhyāni-buddha I 573
  laws & duties of II 82
  lives of great, of Aryan race I vii
  manus, rishis & II 425
  maruts, nirmānakāyas & II 615
  master of occult sciences II 280n
  may read future in an elemental I 631
  moon mystery & I 179-80
  mountain abodes of II 494
  names given to II 210n, 211, 215
  Nebo starts new race of II 456

re nebular theory I 590-7
not influenced by genii I 295 &n
nursery for future human I 207
perceive the supersensuous I 489, 515, 582n
planes of consciousness I 701
power of, to change his form II 705n
preserve the wisdom-knowledge I xlv
rapport w higher globes II 701
records of I xxxiv; II 23
of right- & left-hand path I 417-19; II 211, 495, 501
Rudra-Śiva forefather of II 502n
seed for future II 228
seven classes of, (Row) I 574
śishta, holy sons of light or II 531
Śiva patron of II 282
solved mysteries of life, death II 451
spiritual intuition of I 46n
third, 4th, 5th races of II 210
visions of, checked I 273
war betw, & sorcerers I 417-20; II 384, 495, 501
re White Island II 407
wisdom imparted to II 636
Wondrous Being holds sway over I 207-8
won't give harmful information I 306
Adeptship
    seven degrees of II 614
    "War in Heaven" & II 380
Adhivāhikas (Skt) I 132
Ad-i, 1st speaking race II 452
Ādi (Skt) original I xix, 129; II 42, 452
Ādi-bhūta (Skt) I 129
    Kwan-yin or I 136
    primeval cause I xix
Ādi-buddha (Skt)
    Avalokiteśvara & I 110
    various names for I 571
Ādi-buddhi (Skt)
    not personal God or Creator I 635
Ādi-buddhic Monad
    manifests as Mahā-buddhi I 572
Ādi-budh (Skt), karma & II 48
Ādi-budha (Skt) I xix, 54n
Ādikrit (Skt), creator, Hari, or I 371-2
Ādi-nāth (Skt), Adam is II 452
Ādi-nidāna (Skt) I 98
Ādi Parvan. *See Mahābhārata*
Ādi-śakti (Skt)
    emanation of mūlaprakriti I 10
Ādi-sanat (Skt) I 31
    Ancient of Days, Brahmā or I 98
Ād-Īśvara (Skt), First Lord II 452

Aditi (Skt). *See also* Devamātri
    ākāśa or I 137, 332, 527n; II 42n, 613
    cosmic deep, Space I 53n; II 269
    Daksha son of, I 142, 623; II 247n
    Egyptian 7-fold heaven II 613
    Eve & I 355-6
    female Aranī (Vedic) II 527
    feminine Logos I 431
    Gaia (Gaea) II 65, 269
    higher aspect of nature II 65
    hydrogen, oxygen, or I 623
    light, sound, ether & I 431-2
    Mārttānda (Sun) 8th son of I 99, 448, 529, 553; II 210n
    Mother-space, Darkness I 99
    mūlaprakriti or I 430, 431
    point in disc or I 4
    -prakriti, spiritual-physical I 283
    Sephīrāh or I 354-6; II 43
    seven sons of I 72n, 434, 448, 553; II 210n
    sister or form of Diti II 613
    Sūrya son of, & Dyaus I 100-1
    Tiamāt, Sephīrāh or I 357
    Tiphereth issues fr II 214
    Vāch & I 137, 355-6, 431, 434; II 107
    Venus post-type of II 458
Āditya(s) (Skt)
    Adhivāhikas or, aid Jīva I 132
    allegory of the 8 or twelve I 100
    divine sacrificers, pitris or II 605
    gods in Vaivasvata cycle II 90
    highest dhyāni-chohans II 585
    Indra as II 382n
    life behind phenomena (Roth) II 489
    pitris' paternal great-grandfather II 248n
    seven planets or I 99-101 &nn
    twelve, of Vedic tridaśa I 71n
    various names for I 92; II 182, 585, 605
    Varuna, chief of II 65, 268n
Ādi-Varsha (Skt), Eden of 1st races II 201, 203
Ad-m, Admi II 4, 42n. *See also* Adam
Ad-on [Ādōn] (Heb)
    Lord of Syria II 42n, 43
    structures erected to II 541
Adonāi, Adoni, Adonīm (Heb)
    Aidōneus, Dionysius & I 463
    associated w Sun I 577; II 538n
    associated w Yaho-Iah II 129
    first sons of Earth II 452
    Jehovah made into II 465, 509
    Jews used, not Ehyeh or YHVH II 452
    Lévi's diagram of, & Enoch II 533
    name of Jao-Jehovah I 438; II 389

names of I 463
Satan's throne footstool of II 235
stellar spirit I 449
fr Syrian Ad-on II 43
Adonis
father of, became Apollo Karneios II 44
"First Lord" II 452
lunar god I 396
Mysteries of I 353; II 212
son, father, husband I 396
various names for I 353; II 44
worship of, & Osiris II 769n
Adrasteia (Gk), aspect of Nemesis II 305n
Advaita (Skt), Parabrahman of I 54n, 451
Advaita Vedānta (Skt)
von Hartmann approaches I 50
"I am myself God" I 636
one secondless Existence is I 54n
pradhāna called illusion I 62
prakriti & purusha II 598
roots of, & Buddhism identical I 636
triple aspect of Deity in II 597n
Advaita Vedantists, Advaitins
approach esoteric philosophy I 55
atheists, not atheists I 6, 8, 522
Buddhists in disguise I 636; II 637
doctrine of I 79n
Hegel & I 52n
initiates, yogins fr I 522
upādāna of I 55-6, 370n
Viśishta, & Parabrahman I 233n, 451
Advent, Second
of Christ, Enoch, Elijah II 531
Kalki-avatāra, paranirvāna & I 268
Adversary(ies) I 411-24; II 234-5. *See also*
Lucifer, Rākshasas, Rebels, Satan
of anthropomorphic god is Devil II 378
asuras, rudras & II 164
first, Nārada in Purānas I 413
has ever existed I 411
highest archangel became II 60
incarnated in man II 164
Jehovah II 387
Jews forbidden to curse II 477
lowest aspect of Lucifer II 162
origin of II 487
required by nature's harmony I 411
Satan as the II 60-1, 235-6, 243-5, 375-6, 387-90
Satan, or murderer II 389
Adversus Gentes. See Arnobius
Adversus Haeresis. See Irenaeus
Adv. Haeres. [*Panarion*] I 404. *See* Epiphanius
Adwaita. *See* Advaita

Adytum(a) I xxxvi, 426. *See also* Holy of Holies
Crookes approached I 626
Sanctum Sanctorum II 459-74
truths of I 117-18
Aeaea, Ulysses & Circe on isle of II 769n
Aed-en (Eden) II 42n
AEIOV, first 5 races II 458
Aelian(us), Claudius
—— *De natura animalium*
dragon's inner nature II 355
—— *Varia historia*
Aeschylus II 419n
Theophrastus [Theopompus] ref II 371, 760
Aeloïm, Les. See Lacour, P.
Aeneas, Apollo uses astral double of II 771
Aeneid. See Virgil
Aeolus, & the winds I 466
Aeon(s), Aiōn (Gnos). *See also* Angels
androgyne or 6th & 7th II 458
angelic beings & periods I 416
angels create 365 of I 350
beginning of I 612
Christ, Michael, chief of I 195n
emanation of dual II 569n
eternal & immutable I 63; II 488
everything created thru I 349
First Logos I 351
intermediate, & creation II 488
Lord of the Genii I 195
manus & I 442
Mikael 1st of II 381
motion during kalpas or I 116
rebellious, in *Pistis Sophia* II 604
sliding down of I 416-17
time oldest of, (Protogonos) II 490 &n
wrongly equated w Adam I 642n
Aerobes
first round devourers & I 258
live on "dead" tissues I 249n
men & animals swarming w I 260-1
Aerolites, Arago demonstrated II 784n
Aeronautics II 426-8
Aesar, Etruscan & Irish god II 114
Aeschylus
Father Bathybius & II 674
initiate II 419n, 524 &n
not understood by moderns II 524n
Prometheus older than Hellenes II 413
sacrilege of II 419
—— *Prometheus Bound*
Atlas supports the heavens II 763
dual character of myth II 523
karma-nemesis I 642-3
mindless, senseless man II 411

miserable state of humanity II 522
story summarized II 414
tortures of Prometheus II 412-13
trilogy of, lost II 414
untainted mind heaven's gift II 413
variously quoted II 411-22, 521-4
—— *Seven Against Thebes*
fourth generation heroes II 271
Aesculapius. *See* Asklēpios
Aesir, Aeser, Ases (Norse)
create world fr Ymir II 97
dhyāni-chohans or I 427
drove Turanian dwarfs north II 754
Odin father of I 427
parallels in other religions II 97
purified by fire II 99
ruled world preceding ours II 97
twelve, in Edda II 27
war w frost giants II 386
Aether I 330-2, 527 &nn. *See also* Ākāśa, Daivīprakṛiti, Elements, Ether, Protyle
ākāśa & I 76, 296n, 332, 343-4, 485; II 511
&n
on another plane I 487, 488n
astral light shadow of I 341
born of Erebos & Nux I 110
divine Idea moves the, (Plato) I 365
ether of science & I 13, 332, 460, 485-8, 508,
536
Father, (Plato) I 465
Father-Mother I 13, 76
fire &, or mind-consciousness I 216
fire in its purest form I 87
Fohat son of II 400n
four elements & I 141, 347, 460, 464
Homer silent re I 426
Lucretius re I 485-6
Magnes I 344
Magnus I 331
material, psychic, spiritual I 508
no, no sound I 536
Osiris, Zeus-Zen as II 130
Pater omnipotens I 331
personified as a god I 141
primordial chaos, creation & I 332
quintessence of energy I 508
seven principles of I 536
solar fire, Aith-ur or I 527
Spiller's incorporeal substance I 508
unseen space & veil of deity I 343
Aethereal Winds
impregnate divine egg I 365, 461
Aethiopians. *See also* Ethiopians
brought fr Indus to Nile II 418

Eastern, & pyramids II 429
one of three 5th race types II 471n
Aethiops, Ethiops River II 417-18
Aetna. *See* Mt Aetna
Affection, Devakī progenetrix of II 528
Affinity, Epicurus & Leucippus re I 2
Afghanistan, Afghans
Arabs fr II 200
older than Israelites II 200n
twelve tribes of I xxxiii; II 200n
Africa
appeared before Europe II 200, 368
Atlanteans fled to II 743-4
dolmens found in II 752
emerged in early Atlantis II 264, 368
European Neolithic plants fr II 739
future continents & II 404n
giants & dwarfs in II 754
Irish stones fr II 343
Lemurian portions of II 7
man originated in, (Darwinist) II 679-80
Neolithic man fr North II 716n
Nīla Mountain symb in Western II 403n
North, joined by Atlantis to Venezuela
II 791
NW, once part of Spain II 8n, 740, 793
not Atlantis or Lemuria II 263, 329
rose after Asia II 606n
serpent revered in II 209
South American fauna & II 792
submerged in 3rd race II 327
tall, fair-skinned race in II 754
African(s) II 168. *See also* Negro
crossed into Europe II 740
effects of isolation upon II 425
giants, dwarfs among II 433n
karma of, savages II 168
large cranial capacity of II 168n
offshoots of Atlanteans II 716n, 740-1
races dolichocephalic II 193n
some, cannot be civilized II 421n
some, "were not ready" II 162
worshiped idols II 723
Agadi (Akkad), capital of Sargon I 319n
Against Apion. See Josephus
Against Heresies. See Irenaeus
Agassiz, Jean Louis Rodolphe II 646
theosophists respect II 651
—— *Principles of Zoology*
budding among corals II 133
fauna evolves towards man II 170
man's multiple origins II 607n, 610-11
Agastya, Dattoli or II 232n

'Αγαθαὶ καὶ κακαὶ δυνάμεις (Agathai kai kakai dunameis, Gk). *See also* Appendix
Christ & Satan in Christianity II 497
good & evil forces [de Mirville] II 515
Agathodaemon, Agathodaimon (Gnos)
anathematized II 377-8
became Adversary, Satan II 60
Chnouphis or Chnoubis is I 472-3; II 210
&n, 377
Chnumis II 518
Clement knew secret of II 280n
coiled within Tiphereth II 214
endowed w divine wisdom II 210, 377
Gnostic savior or Priapus II 458
good serpent or Logos I 410
good spirit I 344
guardian of deceased I 410
Hermes, Seth & II 362
Kakodaemon & I 412
king of Egypt II 366
Mercury as II 28
number 700 & II 518
Seraph, fiery serpent I 442
Agathon, To Agathon (Gk) the Good
evil &, [de Mirville] II 515
intellectual quaternary & II 599
nous in close affinity w II 25
Age(s). *See also* Black Age; Brahmā, Age of;
Bronze Age; Cycle(s); Geological Periods; Golden Age; Ice Age; Iron Age;
Kali-Yuga; Silver Age; Yugas
among the ancients II 66
Earth's II 47, 66, 154
four, (*Opera et Dies*, Hesiod) II 270-1
four, of man I 377; II 198, 321
Great I 203; II 77
greatest conceit of our I 133
man's II 148
of our globe II 149n, 154
prehistoric II 67
of pygmies II 715n
races often alluded to as II 270-1
seven, of man II 117, 312n
three occult II 52n
Age and Origin of Man. See Pfaff, Dr F.
Aged, the, 1st-born Protogonos or II 703-4 &n
Agglutinative Languages
spoken by some Atlanteans II 199
stage in language development II 662
Āgneya (Skt), synonym of Krittikā II 550
Āgneyāstra (Skt) fiery weapon. *See also* Ashtar
Vidyā
mentioned in Commentary II 427
not edged weapons II 629n

sevenfold, & 7 priests II 630
Viśvakarma fabricated II 559
Wilson, Bawa re II 427n
Agni(s) (Skt) I 462; II 381-3. *See also*
Element(s), Fire
'Αγνός, Agnus Dei, or, (Kenealy) II 383
araṇī, pramantha &, (Vedas) II 101, 526-7
Aryan II 114
asura(s) in *Rig-Veda* II 92, 500
bhuranyu or II 520
dropped seed of Kārttikeya II 550
Garuda mistaken for II 565
identical w elohīm, cherubs II 85
ignis (Lat) fr II 101, 114
kāma identified w II 176
Kaśyapa & II 382
located in tail of tortoise II 549
maruts sons of, (*Rig-Veda*) II 613
Mātariśvan associated w II 413-14n
one of 49 fires II 57n, 85
one of Vedic Trimūrti I 90; II 114
seven friends, horses, heads of II 605
seven-rayed I 448
seventh tongue of black I 443
seven tongues of I 341
son of Lakshmī II 578
star in Ursa Minor II 612n
Vaiśvānara name of II 311n
Agni Abhimānin (Skt)
Brahmā's son II 247, 521
Agnibāhu (Skt), son of Priyavrata II 369n
Agnibhū (Skt)
Kārttikeya called II 382n, 550, 619
Agnibhuva. *See* Agnibhū
Agnīdhra (Skt), divides Jambu-dvīpa II 320
Agnihotris (Skt), knew soma powers II 499
Agniputra (Skt)
Titans-Prometheus-Kabirim II 363
Agniratha (Skt), weapon fr flying vessel I 563
Agnishvātta(s) (Skt) II 77-85
barhishads & II 77-9
completed egoic man II 79
fiery dragons or II 280n
fire-dhyānis, dhyāni-chohans II 91-2
incarnated in 3rd race II 91
-kumāras II 78, 361n
no astral body to project II 78-9
-pitris awakened man I 181; II 89, 280n, 525n
Prometheus or II 79, 411
saviors II 411-12
Sons of Fire I 86-7
triple set of II 89
Agni-Vishnu-Sūrya (Skt)
source of 7 planets or gods II 608

Ἁγνός (Hagnos, Gk)
  Agni or, (Kenealy) II 383
Agnostic(ism) II 589
  Faraday more an, than materialist I 507
  Janus-faced I 528n
  de Quatrefages an II 645
  Spencer an I 14
  veiled materialism of I 327
  Western psychology tends toward I 636
Agnus Dei (Lat) II 383
Agra-saṃdhānī (Skt) I 105
Agriculture
  Ceres taught man II 390
  improved by Huschenk II 396
  Kabiri taught man I 642n; II 364, 390
  man instructed in, (*Y-King*) II 374
  Osiris-Isis taught, (Basnage) II 366
Agrippa, Heinrich Cornelius I 611
  John Trithemius & I 453n
  MS on giants, shadows II 487
Agruerus (Phoen) II 142 &n
Ah (Pers), to be II 608
Aham (Skt), "I" I 78, 453
Ahamkāra (Skt) egoism, "I-maker"
  desires of, & our globe I 260
  "I-am-ness" I 452
  kāma-rūpa of II 241
  leads to every error I 536n
  Mahat, 5 tanmātras & I 256n; II 639
  manas springs fr I 334
  origin of elements II 616
  -rūpa, dhyāni-chohans near to I 197
  secret element in *VP* I 65-6
  spread of, in kali-yuga II 614
  triple aspect of I 335n, 452-3
A-hamsa, A-ham-sa. *See also* Haṃsa
  Brahma (neuter) is I 20
  esoteric meaning of I 77-8; II 465
Aham-ship (egoism) I 75
Ahan (Skt) day II 58
Aḥath (Heb) one (fem) I 129, 130n
Ahaz, King, Isaiah addresses II 492
Aḥēr (Heb), fallen angels II 508
Ah-hi. *See also* Ahi
  dhyāni-chohans, -buddhas I 37-8, 53
Ahi (Skt) snake, serpent II 181-2n
  -Vṛitra (Skt), Indra's battles w I 202;
    II 382, 384
Āhiyé II 468. *See* Ehyeh
Ahmed-ben-Yusouf Eltiphas. *See* Taifāshī
A'hoor [Āhōr] (Heb) II 538
Ahriman (Zor). *See also* Angra Mainyu, Satan
  brother of Ormazd II 283n
  devs ministers of I 577

dual nature of II 517
Fall & II 283, 516
made into a devil II 93
Michael conqueror of II 479
origin of II 490-2
shadow of Ahura Mazdā II 488, 490
Sons of Light are II 489
Typhon or II 93, 283 &n, 420, 516
Ahti, the Dragon (Finn) II 26
Ahu, Ain-sōph becomes, One I 113
Ahura (Zor)
  same as asura II 59, 92, 500
  sevenfold II 607
  thru, asuras restored II 61
Ahura Mazdā, or Ormazd (Zor) II 384-5, 420.
    See also Ormazd, Zoroastrianism
  Ahriman shadow of II 488
  Angra Mainyu black shadow of II 380
  Asura-Mazdā becomes II 92, 488
  connected w mānasaputras II 608
  defeats Ahriman, who falls II 516
  dual nature of, & Satan II 476
  Farvarshi, Ferouer or II 478, 480
  head of 7 Amesha Spentas II 358, 608
  instructs Yima II 291-2, 609-10
  light of the Logos II 233
  made Holy Tree II 97
  maker of material world II 291
  names of I 110; II 704n
  spiritual, purified man II 517
Ahura-Mazdāo II 92
Ai, King of, crucified II 558
Aidōneus (Gk), ident w Pluto I 463, 464
Ailanthus (tree), bisexual II 133
Aima, Aime ['Immă] (Heb) II 83
  Bīnāh or, woman w child II 384n
Ain, Aiōr, En (Heb). *See also* Ōr
  Macroprosopus II 626
  only self-existent I 214
Aindrī. *See* Indrāṇī
Aindriyaka (Skt) or Indriya Creation
  evolution of senses II 614
  Third Creation or I 446, 453-4
A'in-i-Akbari. *See* Abu'l-Fazl 'Allami
Ain-sōph [Ēyn-sōph] (Heb) I 429; II 233.
    See also Boundless, Unknowable
  Adam Kadmon vehicle of I 179, 214, 432;
    II 730
  alone above māyā I 54n
  becomes One, Echod, Eka, Ahu I 113
  beingless, sexless I 351
  Chaldean Anu I 357
  Chaos, Space, Void or I 109, 214, 343;
    II 126

concealed of the concealed II 111
does not create I 349, 353-4
emanates Shekhīnāh I 433n
endless No-thing I 214, 350; II 126
found now only in *Zohar* II 540
Gnostics knew esoteric meaning of II 386
how it can manifest I 214
Jehovah's name & I 335
kabbalists knew II 459
one infinite unity I 349
One though many forms in him II 290
Parabrahm I 391, 571; II 128, 553
pelican & I 80
sephīrōth & I 350, 614; II 39
should not be given form (Lévi) II 536
symbolized in pyramid I 617
unknowable, unnameable II 41, 128, 472
Zeroana Akerne & I 113
Aiōn. *See* Aeon
Aiōr. *See* Ain
Air (element) I 142; II 582
birth of I 250, 330, 447
fr, comes heat & fr heat water I 330
developed in 2nd round I 260
in early rounds I 252-4
ether & I 372-3, 534, 587
extinguishes fire at pralaya I 372-3
fluidic fire II 114
four elements & I 141, 216, 218n, 284, 461-5, 535-6; II 616
hydrogen generator of II 105
Indra, Vāyu or I 462
Lucifer, Prince of II 515
molecular separation of, (Keely) I 564
one of 7 natural elements I 616
pure, & continuous life I 260, 626 &n
in Pythagorean Kosmos II 599
St John, eagle &, (table) II 114
second to appear I 337, 365, 447
Sons of Rebellion in II 386
symbol of human soul II 113
third race lived in, water, fire II 220
touch is property of I 205, 372; II 107
universe fr water, fire & I 92 &n
Vāyu or, Vedic god I 462; II 114
Vishnu Purāna re I 521-2
wind, spirit & I 342
Air Vehicles. *See* Vimāna
Airy, Sir George B.
re bodies not under gravitation I 584n
Airyamā-ishyō (Pers)
prayer invoking Airyaman II 517
Airyaman (Pers)
divine aspect of Ahriman II 517

Airyanem Vaego, Airyāna-Varsedya
Asian birthplace of physical man II 416n
Eden or II 204
eternal spring of II 356
original Zoroaster born in II 6
polar land of gods II 291
Airy Bodies, Lords of II 75
Αἶσα (Aisa, Gk), is karma II 604-5n
Aish [Ĭsh] (Heb) II 561
Aitareya Brāhmaṇa II 500. *See also Taittirīya Brāhmaṇa*
Earth called Sarparājñī I 74; II 47
Fire is all the deities I 101
Io (cow), story of II 418n
Sun doesn't rise or set (Haug) II 155
Aitareya Upanishad, "This" in I 7
Aith-Ur, solar fire, aether I 527
Aja (Skt)
dragon in highest sense II 355
kāma is II 176, 578
Logos or II 69n, 355, 578, 602
Ajal II 376. *See* Azāzēl
Ajitas (Skt), refused to create II 90
Ajunta, built on labyrinth II 221
Ak, Ak-ad (Assyr), father-creator II 42 &n, 43
Akad. Vorles (Hist of Indian Lit). See Weber
Akarot (Skt) created II 253
Ākāśa (Skt) I 13 &n, 535-7; II 511-13. *See also* Aether, Astral Light
Aditi or I 527n; II 42n, 613
aether, astral light I 197n, 256, 331; II 511
anima mundi I 197n
aspect of Archaeus I 338n
celestial virgin & mother I 332
chaos or vacuity I 452
cosmic ideation I 326
differentiation of elements in I 452
Diti buddhi of II 613-14
dual aeons & II 569n
ether lower form of I 13n, 61, 76n, 97, 296-7n, 326
ether of the occultist I 515n
ether principle of I 526n
Father-Mother I 18
fifth universal principle I 13n
first matter may have been I 253
first to wake fr pralaya I 18 &n
Fohat & 7 principles of I 110
Holy Ghost, Sophia or I 197
Kant's primeval matter I 601-2
Keely & 5th & 6th principles of I 561
knowledge of, essential I 587
maruts & lower principles of II 615
matter on another plane I 487

Mother-Father of Logos II 400n
names for I 140
Nārāyana concealed in I 231
nirvāna &, (objectively) eternal I 635
not ether of science I 296n; II 511n
noumenon of ether I 137, 254-5, 534, 536
One Element, the I 140
pradhāna in another form I 256
primordial substance I 326
proceeds fr chaos I 536
Ptah is I 353
radiation of mūlaprakriti I 10, 35
septenary I 527n
sound & I 205, 255-6, 296n
Sound, Word, & I 256, 372
Space as I 534, 537; II 511-12
suns are kāma-rūpa of I 527n
supra-solar upādhi I 515n
waters of space I 457-8n
wrongly transl as aether I 332, 343, 485
Ākāśic
    nature of 1st dhyān-chohans I 82
    pralaya &, "photographs" I 18n
Akbar, Emperor
    A'in-i-Akbari & I xxiv &n
    sacred MSS hidden in reign of I xxiii &n,
        xxxiv
Āker (Egy), slays Apap II 213, 588n
Akhu (Egy) II 632 &n
Akibeel, taught portents II 376
Akkad, capital of Nimrod & Sargon I 319n;
    II 691
Akkadia(ns), Akkads
    fr Ak-ad (Assyr) II 42n
    Aryan instructors of Chaldeans II 202
    calendar of II 693
    creation story of II 53
    creative gods of II 54, 365
    earlier than Chaldeans I 650
    emigrants fr India I 392; II 202-3
    Genesis of I 357
    Great Deep of II 53, 477
    months derived fr zodiac I 649-50
    Moon called "Lord of Ghosts" II 139n
    Sargon of II 691
    seven-headed serpent of I 407
    taught emanation not creation II 54
Akki (Assyr), reared Sargon I 319-20n
Aksha (Skt), latitude II 402n
Akshonnati (Skt)
    elevation of pole II 401-2n
Akta (Skt), Agni as, suggests Christ II 101n
Alahim II 488. *See also* Alhim, Elohīm
Alais (France), meteorite w carbon at II 706

Al-ait, god of fire II 142n
Alaskan Peninsula II 327
Alaya [or Ālaya] (Skt). *See also* Anima Mundi
    alters during life period I 48
    Logos male aspect of I 58
    Universal Soul I 49
Albatross, magical properties I 362
Albertus Magnus I 581-2n
Alcamenes, three-headed statue by I 387 &n
Al-Chazari, Book of. See Ha-Levi
Alchemy (ists, ical) I 82n, 438
    alkahest of, & making man I 345
    angelic "Watchers" & numbers I 119
    artificial evolution by II 349
    Aryans learned, fr Atlanteans II 426, 763n
    athanor of I 81
    atoms were souls to I 567
    Bacon, Roger, protyle & I 581-2 &n
    celestial virgin of I 458n
    correlate sound & color I 514n
    creates ozone by sound I 144n, 555
    cube unfolded II 592-3
    Diocletian burned, books II 763n
    elements of I 141, 520; II 113-14, 592
    fire of I 81n; II 105-7, 113-15
    Frankenstein monster & II 349
    Inquisition & II 238
    "Mercury" radical *moyst* of II 542
    metaphors hide meaning I 520
    Mysterium Magnum & astral light II 511
    nature of hydrogen II 105-6, 113
    new, or metachemistry of Crookes I 622
    primordial substance of I 330
    renaissance of, in Egypt II 763n
    science & I 144n, 496
    sevenfold ether I 524n; II 594n
    spiritual secretion of I 509
    sun in ship on crocodile I 409-10
    swastika, sign II 99
    transmutations in nature II 170
    unity of matter I 543n
Alcyone, a Pleiad
    Alpha Draconis & II 432
    central point of universe II 551
    daughter of Atlas II 768
    Sun orbits, (Maedler) I 501
Aldebaran, in conjunction w Sun II 785
Aldobranda [Aldrovandus], Ulysses
    embalmed a dragon II 207n
Aleim (Heb)
    college of priests II 202, 215
    Tzyphon one of, (Lacour) II 216n
Aleph (Heb letter A)
    bull, ox, Taurus, etc II 551, 574

symbol of unity I 78
　of Taurus & Christ I 656
Aletae (Phoen)
　fire worshipers II 142n, 361
　Kabiri &, (Faber) II 360
　Titans in Sanchoniathon II 141-2 &n
Alētheia (Gk)
　angle of Gnostic square II 573
　breath of god I 2n
Aleutian Islands, America & Asia once connected by II 322n, 327
Alexander, Professor Stephen
　confirms nebular theory I 588
Alexander Jannaeus, slew initiates II 504n
Alexander Polyhistor, Berosus fragments in
　I xxvi; II 53, 54, 65n
Alexander the Great
　Berosus compiled history for I xxvi
　confused Nile & Indus II 417-18
　destroyed Magian works II 6n
　Greeks w, taught astronomy I 650
　went to Attock, not India II 418n
Alexandria. *See also* Neoplatonism, Ptolemy
　built 332 BC I 361 &n
　Gnostics of, & initiations I 416
　Greek astronomers at I 658
　Indian figures known to I 361
　initiates of, on number one II 574
　Platonist of, compiled *Pymander* II 267n
Alexandrian Library
　Caesar's burning of II 763n
　destroyed 3 times II 692
　MSS of, copied, destroyed I xxiii, xxxiv
Alexandrian School
　certain Church Fathers in I xliv
ἀλεξητήριοι (alexētērioi, Gk)
　tutelary gods (Seldenus) I 394
Alfuras, skulls of II 522
Algae I 177; II 712
Algebra II 555
Algeria, dolmens found in II 752
Alhim (Heb). *See also* Elohīm
　becomes Jahva-Alhim I 346
　light & II 37-8, 41
　π & numerical value of I 91, 114; II 38
Alhim-ness II 40
Ali (Alee) Beg, M.M. *See* Mitford, G.
Alkahest I 345
Alkaloids, in plants, animals, men I 261-2 &n
All, the. *See also* Absolute, Parabrahman
　Absolute, No-Thing I 73, 346, 629; II 553
　absolute thought opposes II 490
　Abstract I 15n
　Boundless I 109

Brahmā emanates out of I 7
ceaseless breath of I 75
circle is II 621
eternal, infinite I 8
Hermetic invocation to I 285-6
Oeaohoo or Rootless Root of I 68
one-voweled term I 20
Pan once was II 581
point in mundane egg I 1
precosmic "darkness" I 450n
ray of the Unknown I 106
That or II 158-9
Unit merged in I 330
universe not separate fr II 384n
unknown, unknowable II 272, 490
various names for II 553
Alla, Allah (Arab) II 601-2
Allahabad (India)
　built on earlier cities II 220-1
　lunar kings resided at I 392
All Be-ness, All-Being I 55
Allégories d'Orient. See Court de Gébelin
Allegory(ies). *See also* Fable, Legend, Myth
　allegory within an II 94
　ark & 7 rishis an II 139
　astronomical II 380
　based on reminiscence II 293
　Bible, now unveiled I 315
　bisexuality universal in II 125
　esoteric teaching uses II 81
　Fohat key to many I 673
　foolishly called fables II 103
　Garuda origin of other II 564-5
　of initiation & adeptship II 380
　interpretation of I 310; II 94n, 384, 765
　of Noahs, Vaivasvatas, etc II 314
　Purānas are history & I 520; II 253, 323
　record of real events II 235
　reject, based on creeds II 194
　seven, 10, 21 rishis, munis, etc II 259n
　of Soma & Tārā II 498-9
　symbolism &, in Mysteries II 124
　wisdom preserved in I 307, 466; II 235, 410
　years of patriarchs are II 426
　zodiacal, historical II 353
Allen, C. Grant II 686n
　exaggerations of, exposed II 687n
　man begins in Eocene II 288, 679, 690n
　Neanderthal skull II 687
　origin of cave man unknown II 740n
　Paleolithic man ape-like II 740
All-Father (Norse) II 100
　willed universe into being I 427
All-Force, inherent in the Monad II 110

Alligator II 753n. *See also* Crocodile
Alligator Mounds, not tombs II 752-3 &n
All in All, 7-voweled term I 20
Alm, Mohammedan symbol for virgin II 463
Almeh, Egyptian dancing girls II 463
Al-Orit II 361. *See also* Al-ait
Alorus-Adam of Berosus II 454
Alphabet(s) II 547n
    of Cadmus I xxiii
    Chinese I 307
    Egyptian I 267n, 307; II 581
    Hebrew I 114n; II 581
    Kabiri invented II 364
    Mayan I 267n
    occult meaning of I 94, 307; II 574
Alpha Draconis II 356. *See also* Pole Star
    Great Pyramid & I 407, 435; II 432
Alphonso [X], lunar tables of I 667n
Alps
    elevated greatly since Eocene II 727, 778
    formerly a sea bottom II 787n
    man saw rising of II 751 &n
Al-Taifāshī. *See* Taifāshī
Altar(s)
    horns placed near Jewish II 418n
    in our hearts I 280
    proportions of I 208-9n
    seven fires before Mithraic II 603
Alter und der Ursprung . . . See Pfaff, F.
Altruism, Altruistic
    intellect &, serve mankind II 163
    law of harmony depends on II 302n
    only palliative for life's evils I 644
Altyne-taga, Altyn-toga [Altyn-tagh Mts]
    ancient civilization in I xxxii
    hidden library in I xxiv
Am, or Om II 43. *See also* Aum
Amalthea (Gk)
    goat transformed into II 579
Amānasa(s) mindless (Skt) II 90-1
    defile future abodes II 191
Amazarak, taught sorcerers (*Enoch*) II 376
Amazons
    Aphides are like II 133
    prescribed circle-dance II 460
Ambā (Skt) II 551
    mother or, Aditi, ākāśa, etc I 460
Amber, Phaeton's sisters' tears II 770n
Ambhāmsi (Skt), chief of Kumāras
    four orders of beings I 458n
    Great Deep, chaos or I 459-60
Ambrose, St
—— *De mysteriis liber unus*
    re cardinal points I 123

Ambrosia
    flying dragon drank II 516
    Ūrdhvasrotas feed upon II 162
Amdo, Tsong Kha-pa born in I 108n
Amen, Ammon, Amon, Amun (Egy)
    concealed god I 366 &n
    Khnoom later becomes I 365
    Mout daughter, wife, mother of I 91n, 430;
        II 464
    Neith other half of Ammon II 135
    primeval source of light I 340; II 130
    Ptah & Ammon I 675
    ram-headed I 366; II 213n
    two mystic eyes of II 213
Ame no mi naka nushi no Kami (Jap) I 214
Amenophes [Amen-hotep] (Egy), King I 398
Amen-Rā, Amon-Rā (Egy). *See also* Rā
    immaculate incarnation of I 398-9
    Magna Mater & I 393
    secondary aspect of deity I 367
Amenthian Region [Amentian] (Egy) II 379
Amenti (Egy) afterworld
    Aanroo field domain in realm of I 236n
    forty [42] assessors, lipikas in I 104
    kāma-loka, Hel or I 463n
    man becomes pure spirit in I 365, 674n
    Osiris confers justice in I 312; II 481
    Osiris, "the defunct sun," enters II 580
    Soleil dans (Sun in) I 134n
    spiritual ego descends into II 558
    Thot scribe of I 385
America(s) I 297. *See also* Mexico, Peru
    Antipodes or II 446, 628
    Arjuna in II 214 &n
    Atlantis & II 34-5n, 147, 407n, 792-3
    called Atlanta II 221n
    cataclysm will destroy both II 445
    continent of, rose II 182, 406-7
    dolmens of II 752
    Europe &, joined by land in Miocene II 781
    fifth continent II 8
    flora of, & of Europe II 790-3
    future continents & II 404n
    giants in II 276n, 293
    gigantic ruins in North II 337-8
    Jambudvīpa & II 403 &n
    land connections w Asia, India II 322n,
        326-7, 781
    mission of, sowing seeds II 446
    mounds in, & Norway II 423-4 &n
    number 7 in II 34-5
    older than "Old World" II 407n, 446, 606n
    parturient symbol & I 390
    Pātāla or II 132, 182, 214n, 628

prophesied by ancients II 371
pyramids scattered over II 352
ruined cities in I 676
2nd continent & II 402
sixth & 7th subraces & II 444-6
submerged in Lemurian times II 327
two varshas of Pushkara or II 407
American(s). *See also* Indians
　almost a race sui generis II 444
　Basque language like ancient II 790
　European Tertiary &, flora II 727
　Nagals of, & Hindu Nāgas II 213
　Noah II 141
　number 7 among II 34
American Journal of Science
　Dana on European submergence II 324 &n
　glacial periods, floods II 141 &n
　Hunt, T. S., on ether I 495
　Lane, Homer, on heat I 84-5
American Naturalist
　[Skinner reference] I 322
　Todd on oscillations of Earth II 325
Amers, taught magic (*Enoch*) II 376
Amesha Spenta(s) (*Zend*) Beneficent Immor-
　tal(s) II 358, 517. *See also* Amshaspends
　Ahura Mazdā head of II 608
　rule over karshvars II 384-5
Ameyātman (Skt)
　of immeasurable wisdom I 422
Amilakha (Mongolian)
　animating human forms II 34n
Amitābha (Skt) I 356
　dhyāni-buddha of Gautama I 108
　O-mi-tu Fo II 179
　Teshu [Tashi] Lama, Gautama & I 471
　Tsong Kha-pa, Gautama & I 108 &n
Amita-Buddha (Chin)
　Gautama's celestial name I 108 &n
Ammianus Marcellinus
—— *Roman History*
　Brahmans of Upper India II 327
　passages under pyramids II 429
　spirits assist divinations I 395
Ammon. *See* Amen
Ammonites, Moloch Sun-Jehovah of I 397n
Ammon-Ra. *See* Amen-Rā
Amoeba
　division into two II 166, 661
　man not lineal descendant of II 259
　sexual & asexual II 116
Amon, Amon-Ra. *See* Amen, Amen-Rā
Amona (Heb) mother, Bīnāh or I 355
Amos, On. See Ambrose, St
Ampère, A. M., Law of I 512 &n

Amphian-Essumene [Amphain Essumen] (Gnos)
　androgynous Aeon II 458
Amphibia(n,s) II 656
　fishes, reptiles & II 256, 257
　forms of, fr 3rd round II 684-5
　healing of limbs of II 166n
　highest development in Oolitic II 258
　man descended fr, (Haeckel) II 656
Amphibious reptile
　human foetus resembles II 188
Amphiōn (Gk), Apollo &, as masons II 795
Amphioxus
　evolution of, to man (Haeckel) II 663
　man compared w II 370n
Amphitritē (Gk)
　goats sacrificed to II 579
　mother of Neptune's "ministers" II 578
　Poseidon became dolphin to win II 775
Ampsiu-Ouraan [Auraan] (Gnos)
　male & female Aeons fr II 569n
Amrita (Skt)
　beyond any guna I 348
　extracted fr "Sea of Milk" I 67
　latent in primordial chaos I 348
　ocean of immortality I 69 &n
　stolen by Rāhu II 381
Amsāmsāvatāra (Skt), Krishna called II 359
Amshaspend(s) [or Amesha Spenta] (Zor). *See
　also* Amesha Spentas
　archangels or, (Burnouf) I 437
　aspects of Logos I 429
　create world in 6 days II 488
　dual nature of I 235; II 476
　elements stand for I 339
　fight Ahriman, who falls II 516
　One becomes many or I 113
　Ormazd synthesis of I 127-8; II 358, 365n,
　　488
　refusal to create not pride II 92-3
　same as asuras, elohīm, etc I 113; II 92
　seven, or builders I 127-8
　ten or 7, & early man II 365
　Zarathustra called II 6n
Amun I 340; II 130. *See also* Amen
Amusement, creation of the world an II 53, 126
Amyot, Father J. J. M.
　saw Trinity in *Tao-teh-ching* I 472
An (Egy) Heliopolis I 674
　basin of Perséa in II 545
　Sons of Rebellion in Air [An?] II 386
Ana (Chald)
　astral light, anima mundi I 91
　Belita, Davikina & II 463
Anaces, Anactes [Anakes] (Gk)

confused w Aschieros, Kabiri II 106, 360
Anaerobes I 249n, 261
Anāgāmin (Skt), degree of initiation I 206
Anagram II 577-9
Anagraniyam [Aṇor aṇīyān] (Skt)
  "smaller than the smallest atom" I 357
Anaitia, Anaitis
  astral light or I 91-2
  Persian Moon-goddess I 395
Anak, Anakim [Anāq, Anāqīm] (Heb)
  giants II 336
  of Joshua II 340
  nephīlīm called sons of II 755
Analecta. See Brunck, R. F. P.
Analogy(ies). *See also* Correspondences
  in chemistry I 218n; II 627
  betw cosmos & man I 173, 177, 206, 227n,
    606; II 29n
  fr cosmos to smallest globe II 66
  dhyāni-chohans & II 700n
  false I 472
  guided ancient philosophers II 616
  guide to occult teachings I 173
  images on various planes II 268
  law in nature I 604; II 153, 699
  limitations of I 150
  logic of, & giants II 154n
  betw man & manvantara I 263n
  pralaya known by I 116n
  principles, rounds, races II 254n, 257, 684-5
  scientific corroborations I 585-6n
  seven rounds & 7-month embryo II 257
  seven turns of key of I 150-1
Ānandamaya-kośa (Skt), buddhi or I 157, 570
Anania, G. Lorenzo d'
  four-letter names of God II 602
Ananta, Ananta-Śesha (Skt)
  form of Vishnu II 505
  infinite time I 73 &n; II 49n, 98
  serpent of eternity I 73, 371, 407
  seven & 1,000 heads of I 407; II 381
  swastika on head of II 98, 99-100
  Vishnu rests on I 344; II 98, 381
Anarchist I 563
Anastasis (Gk)
  light of elohīm transmitted in II 514n
  resurrection & frog symbol I 385-6
Anātma[n] or Achit (Skt)
  quality of Parabrahman I 59n
Anatomy
  human & ape II 87n, 680-5
  man's, two million years ago II 287
  pineal gland II 295-7
Anatomy, Elements of. See Quain, J.

Anaxagoras (of Clazomenae)
  animated atoms of I 568
  chaos I 579
  elemental vortices I 117, 492, 623
  materialism of Democritus vs I 50
  nous of, acts w design I 50
  ordering & disposing mind of I 451, 595
  science has turned to I 586
  spiritual prototypes in ether I 331-2
Anaximenes (of Miletus)
  held universe evolved fr air I 77, 590
Ancestors. *See also* Pitris, Progenitors, Spirits
    of the Earth
  barhishads our II 77, 94
  breathed out 1st man II 86, 94-5
  common, of all races II 747n
  dual-sexed II 130
  Egyptian Moon-god 1st human I 227n
  lowest dhyānis I 224
  lunar I 160, 180-1; II 44-5, 75, 77, 102, 142n
  of man & apes I 190; II 185-90, 289, 443,
    683-5
  physical man progeny of I 224
  primitive, in *Popol Vuh* II 160
  rūpa & arūpa I 218-19n
  sixfold dhyāni-chohans or I 222n
  spiritual, of divine man II 81
  two types of I 241, 248; II 77
"Ancestral Heart"
  reincarnating principle (Egy) I 220
Anch. *See* Ānkh
Anchitherium
  Hipparion &, evolution of II 716
  three-toed, & modern horse II 735
*Ancient Faiths Embodied in Ancient Names.
    See* Inman, T.
Ancient Fragments. See Cory, Isaac
Ancient of Ancients
  At-tee'kah D'At-tee'keen or II 83-4
  White Head, 5th race or II 706
Ancient of Days
  Adam Kadmon vehicle of I 60
  Ādi-Sanat, Brahmā or I 98
  Ain-sōph, Shekhīnāh, chaos I 109
  ether concealed in II 83
  "Old Time" is I 459
  soul stands in presence of I 239
  swallowed all other fishes I 394
Ancients I xxxvii
  acquainted w evolution I 332
  alleged superstitions of I 466-70
  believed planets were living II 370
  cycles secret among II 396
  elements of I 342

esoteric architecture of I 208n
extraordinary knowledge of I 84, 96, 208n,
    574n; II 145, 252-4, 534-5
knew corporeal fr spiritual I 464
knew of & worshiped forces I 465, 509
knew of 7 moons I 179
linked religion, science, philos II 106, 107n
lived w animals now extinct II 206
lost arts of II 430-1
mystery gods of II 22-3
name for host of builders I 344
sevens of I 179, 204
spoke of more than 7 planets I 99-100, 152
    &n, 574n, 576; II 488-9n, 602n
subdivided their elements I 140-1
taught heliocentric theory I 117n, 441, 569;
    II 155
Ancient Stone Implements. See Evans, J.
Aṇḍakaṭāha (Skt)
    shell of Egg of Brahmā II 616
Andaman Islanders, descend fr Lemuro-
    Atlanteans II 195-6 &n, 721-2
Andes Mts
    man present during upheaval of II 745
Andhra Dynasty of Maghada [Magadha]
    II 220n
Andrews, Dr Thomas
    "critical temperature" II 136n
Androgyne(s), Androgynous I 354-6, 427, 450;
    II 37, 269n, 467. *See also* Lemuria, Root-
    Race-3rd
    Adam-Eve II 134
    Adam Kadmon-Sephīrāh I 98 &n, 215-16n,
        354-6, 427, 450; II 269n, 467
    Adam the 1st II 124-5, 128
    Adam the 2nd II 457, 503
    Adam the 3rd II 503
    Ada-nari as, symbol of 3rd race II 533
    angels & the dual light II 36-7
    creative gods are I 427, 437
    Darwin re II 118-19
    divine hermaphrodite II 124-30
    early man was II 2-3, 118n, 744
    early 3rd race was II 165, 172, 177, 197
    Eloha or II 60n
    elohīm were I 130n
    first gods were II 130
    of first 3 races I 444
    five, ministers of Chozzar II 577
    in *Genesis* 1 I 6n; II 124, 128
    gives birth to universe I 398
    Goat of Mendes (Lévi) I 253
    Iao, creator of man II 388
    Io, Jehovah & II 416n

Kwan Shai Yin & higher gods are I 72 &n
letter M & I 384
mammalia sprang fr, stock II 118-19
manifest beings become, gradually I 136n
Moon deity is II 66
Osiris-Isis divine II 366
Persian Tree & II 134
pineal gland, relic II 119
Plato re II 96, 133-4, 177 &n
radiations of the One are I 18
separate into male & female I 247; II 24, 134,
    147, 163, 171, 197-8, 201
serpent a dual II 214
fr sexless to bisexual or II 2-3, 132, 197
symbol for II 30
Virgo-Scorpio I 413
Anedots (Chald), 10 & 7, & early man II 365
Anemos (Gk). *See also* Pneuma
    anima (Lat) or soul & I 226n
    pneuma or spirit I 342
Anfänge zu einer . . . See Baumgärtner, K.H.
Angel(s). *See also* Archangel, Dhyāni-chohans,
    Fallen Angels, Lucifer, Sāraph
    act in space & time I 418
    aspire to become men (Lévi) II 377
    atom, soul, genius or I 107, 569
    avenging, & laws of life I 644
    Azāzēl a transgressing II 376
    cannot be propitiated I 276
    in chains (*Jude*) II 491
    cherub, seraph or I 363
    commanded to create, refused II 239, 242-3
    created 365 aeons I 350
    creations of II 41
    demons precede II 58
    dhyānis, devas, or I 206, 222 &n, 274; II 26
    Face, of the II 479
    fallen II 61, 103, 228-9, 268, 274-5, 390,
        475-505, 516
    fall into generation II 231n, 232, 282
    few, in Bible II 61
    fiery, sacrifice of II 243, 246
    first & secondary I 337
    four cosmic, & Ophite Faces I 127 &n
    gandharvas are Enoch's I 523n
    guardian I 222n, 644
    guardians of harmony I 644
    higher, assimilated all wisdom II 80-1
    incarnated in man II 283
    incorporeal essence of II 87
    initiates shall judge II 112
    intelligent forces I 234n, 287
    Kepler's I 498-9
    "Lords of the Zodiac and Spheres" I 577

lower, work of II 61, 96, 102
Lucifer gave man immortality II 388
man can transcend the II 111
man's spirituality eclipsed by mind I 189
messengers II 48, 61, 243, 359, 514n
Mikael, of Sun II 381
ministering I 92
Moloch, Muluk, Maluk, etc II 514n
-monad I 574n
-names key to Bible II 536
no disobedient II 487
no perfect II 162
obedient, story of II 242-3
oldest & highest cast down II 103
planetary, of Saturn group II 127
primitive spiritual, & Logos II 488
rebellious I 192-6, 418, 577; II 93-5, 237, 246-8, 280n
regents of worlds I 99
of Revelation II 565 &n, 618
rope of the I 90
rule cosmic elements I 604
rūpa, a quaternary group I 218n
St. Matthew-Angel Man II 114
Satan & II 234-8
self-conscious II 318n
serpent of *Genesis* was II 388
seven creative II 4
seven hierarchies of I 104, 230, 449
seven planetary rishis or II 318n
slaves of karma I 276
solar, & immortal ego II 88
superior or celestial men I 230, 276
under karmic law I 193-4
universal mind, father or II 492
Vossius on I 123n
watch over our world (Syrian) I 435
we do not worship I 499n
Angelic Heart, of dhyan-chohanic body II 91
Angelic Hierarchy I 129
Angelic Host I 119, 225
    dhyāni-chohans I 38
Angelic Virtues. *See* Virtues (Angelic Order)
Angel-Man
    Christ as II 115n
    St Matthew, Water &, (table) II 114
Angel of Death, Satan or, (*Talmud*) II 385
Angel of the Face
    Jehovah, Michael I 434n, 459; II 479-80
Angelology(ies) I 612
    Christian & Jewish II 61, 501
    Kabbala & Hebrew I 92
Ἄγγελος (Angelos, Gk), messenger II 48, 111
Angels of Darkness, Light

asuras, elohīm II 489
mythical enemy of Church I 457
three days' battle betw, (Milton) II 506
Angels of the Presence I 335
    seven, & lipikas I 104
    seven, or manus II 573
    virtues or aspects of God II 237
Angels of the Stars I 573
    Ōphanīm or I 117
    seven planets or II 358
Angelus Rector (Kepler) I 479
Anger
    desire &, (*Anugītā*) II 637
    passion of fools I 415-16
Aṅgiras (Skt)
    father of Brihaspati II 498
    one of 7 mind-born sons II 78
Āṅgirasas (Skt), deva instructors II 605 &n
Anglo-Saxons, mixed in America II 444
Angra Mainyu (Pers). *See also* Ahriman
    Ahura Mazdā defeats II 516
    aspect of Airyaman II 517
    shadow of Ahura Mazdā II 380
    Zarathustra appeals to II 385
Anguinum, made Rome tremble I 368
Aṅgula (Skt), finger's breadth I 289
Anī (Heb), personal pronoun "I" I 78
Anima (Lat). *See* Anemos
Anima, De [*Tractates de Anima*]. *See* Cordovero, Moses
Animae Procreatione, De. See Plutarch
Animal(s) (kingdom). *See also* Beast, Mammals, Sacred Animals, Vertebrates
    abyss betw man & II 81, 189
    acquire bones II 183
    almost individualized I 178
    ape fr man & I 185n; II 185, 187, 189, 262
    atrophied 3rd eye in II 296 &n
    bisexuality of higher II 659
    breeds strictly by genus, etc II 287
    change w each root-race II 697
    classes & orders of, in Purānas II 259n
    consciousness I 455; II 120
    creation precedes man I 455-6
    dwarfed during 3rd race II 329
    early man bred w II 184-5, 189, 191, 195, 201, 262, 267, 286
    ethereal, hermaphrodite II 299
    evolved fr man's tissues II 736n
    exchange of matter betw man & II 169-70
    first races of, androgynous II 118n
    forms fr 3rd round II 730
    genealogies give evolution of II 253-4

half-, half-human monsters II 192
higher principles dormant II 255, 267
human monad passed thru II 185-6, 254, 260
humans will never incarnate as I 185n
immortal soul latent in I 196-7; II 196n
irresponsible II 513
man &, compared II 299, 525n
man blind to consciousness of II 702n
fr man in 3rd round II 186-7
man knew of extinct II 206, 217-19
man never formed part of II 290
man preceded II 1, 155, 163, 168-9, 180, 186-7, 197n, 288, 289-90, 594n, 683-5, 736n
man storehouse of, seeds of life II 289-90
Maoben [Macben] symbolizes II 575
monad of II 103, 525n
monads human next manvantara I 184, 267
New & Old World, compared II 792
original sin & II 513-14
pilgrimage of, half-unconscious II 103
plants not physical before II 290n
fr primordial monsters II 186
procreation among, painless II 262
protista not an II 594n
sacred, & zodiac I 92, 442 &n; II 23, 181n
seasons of procreation w II 412n
seventh emanation of "Mother" & I 291
ternaries only II 575
two-sexed before man II 184, 262
unclean, of Bible I 355, 442n
unknown, described in Purānas II 254
use man's 3rd & 4th round relics II 290
Animal (man, ego, self, nature, soul)
brain alone "philosophizes" II 74
divine man dwelt in II 275
divine monad transforms II 377
fourth human principle (diag) I 153; II 596, 632-3
grossest part of man I 260
higher creators incarnate in II 98
inner god vs II 272
instinctual only II 103
kāma-rūpa or II 596
Lemuro-Atlanteans victims of II 285
Light of the Logos awakens II 42
lower manas descends into II 495-6
Lucianists' teaching re II 239n
nous reigns over II 110
passions of, a curse II 412-13
psychic being guided by II 413
selfish, sensual desires of II 496
sons of Mahat enlivened II 103

soul or Ab-Hati II 633
will be tamed II 268
Animalism, Animality
acme of, at mid-race I 610
curse of, chronic II 412
Animal Men
descended fr 3rd race I 650; II 192-3
Animal Spirits (Descartes)
nervous ether of Richardson II 298n
pineal gland & II 298
Anima Mundi (Lat) I 91, 296n; II 562. See also Astral Light, Ether, World Soul
Ādi-buddhic monad I 572
aggregate of life-atoms II 672n
ākāśa, alaya or I 49-50
aspect of Ptah I 353
astral light or I 59, 194, 196, 197n, 365n, 461
depths of spiritual soul II 573
dove was Christian I 402-3
feminine & evil w Gnostics I 194-5, 194n
Holy Spirit or I 402-3
Isis Unveiled on I 196-7
life principle or I 579; II 562
Mahā-buddhi, Mahat I 572
oversoul of Emerson I 48, 140
Plato & Anaxagoras taught of I 50
science does not teach I 49
septenary or 7-fold cross II 562
svabhavat I 98
Universal Soul, Alaya or I 48, 49, 58, 365n
various names for I 365n
Anima Supra-Mundi
human ego not separate fr I 130-1
Animate & Inanimate I 218n, 454; II 267
Aṇīyāṃsam Aṇīyasāṃ (Skt) II 46-7
many fr the One II 732
"most atomic of the atomic" I 542-3
name of Parabrahman I 357
Purushottama, Vishnu or I 542
Añjanā (Skt), Hanumān son of I 190
Āṅkh, Ank (Egy) II 546-8. See also Ansated Cross, Tau
Moses took; fr Egypt II 31
noose or ark symbol II 547
soul, life, blood II 600n
symbolized by ansated cross II 30-1
unites cross & circle II 546
vital force or Archaeus II 633
Ankh-te [-tie] (Egy) II 546-8
Anna (Chald), mother of Mary I 91
Annales de Philosophie Chrétienne
Quatremère on Chwolsohn II 453
de Rougemont on Chwolsohn II 454
de Rougé on Champollion II 367-8

de Sacy re *Enoch* II 533 &n
Annales des sciences naturelles
    man's age not in Bible (Lartet) II 690 &n
Annamaya-kośa (Skt)
    sthūla-śarīra in Vedānta I 157
Annapūrṇa (Skt)
    Anaitia, Devī-durgā or I 91
Annunciation, Gabriel w lilies I 379n
Annus Magnus (Lat)
    Aldebaran conjunction II 785
    periodic catastrophes & II 784
Ānochī (Heb), Ankh & II 31
Anointed(ing)
    Akta means, (Jolly) II 101n
    Christos the II 23
    "*Dii Termini*" symbols II 542
    Jehovah has become the II 234
Anoplotheridae II 735-6
Anouka [Anūhā]-Noah (Renan) II 454
Anouki. *See* Anukis
Anquetil de Perron [-Duperron], A. H. II 442
Ansamsavatara II 359. *See* Aṃśāṃśāvatāra
Ansated Cross (Egy)
    Ankh, life, Fall or II 30, 600n
    Ankh-te, circle & II 546
    on breasts of defunct mystics II 586
    cube unfolded (Skinner) I 321; II 542, 600n
    on Easter Island statues I 322
    human passions crucified on II 549
    Isis & I 366n
    parturient energy II 31n
    pāśa can be interpreted as II 548
    phallic symbol II 583
    on Philae bas-relief II 558
    placed on Calvary cross II 559
    symbol of female-male I 321; II 217, 548
    symbol of Venus II 30
    tau or I 657; II 30, 542
Anśumat [Aṃśumat] (Skt)
    nephew of 60,000 uncles II 570
Ant
    Haeckel traces civilization to II 650
    humans must be gods to I 133
    instinct of II 120
Antaeus, tomb of II 278
Antaḥkaraṇa (Skt) I 68n
Antarctic. *See also* Arctic, Hell, Pātāla
    called "Pit" II 357
    Circle & Lemurian continent II 324
    "ever-living" & "concealed" II 776
Anteaters II 789
Antelope II 577, 735
Antequera, Spain, dolmen at II 752
Anthropogenesis

fallen angels key to II 274
materialistic & occult II 157, 651
Stanzas of Dzyan on II 15-21
various systems of I 213-22, 308; II 83-5,
    168, 274, 797
Anthropogonie. See Haeckel, E.
Anthropography, mysteries of I 229
Anthropoid(s). *See also* Ape, Gorilla, Pithecoid
    born in mid-Miocene I 184n
    brain size of, & man II 193n
    bred in sin by Atlanteans II 195, 200, 286,
        679, 688, 689
    chasm betw man & II 189, 665n
    created by senseless man I 185n
    crossbreeding produced II 262, 286-8
    descended fr man II 185, 187, 287-8, 682
    fossil relics of man & II 675-80
    have degenerated II 676, 682
    human features of II 688n
    "human presentments" I 183
    Huxley re II 87n, 315n
    hybrids possible in 4th race II 195
    fr late Atlantean times II 193, 195
    man &, common ancestor II 646
    man preceded, in this round II 1
    monsters ancestors of II 184n, 201, 375
    none before Miocene II 688n, 690n
    none in "brighter" Atlantis II 679
    Pastrana species fr II 717n
    some, will be human in 5th round I 184;
        II 261-3
    third round ape-man & II 730
    unnatural, accidental creation II 261
    will die out in our race I 184
Anthropological Institute II 471n. *See also*
    Flower, W. H.
Anthropological Review
    Blake "On the Naulette Jaw" II 744
Anthropologists
    chronology of II 155
    dating of man by II 288
    failure of, re missing link II 287
    missing link of, in Stanzas II 184n
    physiological proofs of II 187
    proceed at random II 66-7
Anthropology II 67, 437, 645-55, 686
    dates of, differ fr Secret Doctrine II 794
    French school of II 288
    genesis of, begins at wrong end I 246
    modern, & occultism II 71
    occult, & human eye II 295
Anthropology. See Topinard, P.
Anthropomorphic(ism, ists) I 9n, 295n
    creator of exoteric Judaism II 40

element in old scriptures I 285-7; II 657
exalted ideas become II 38, 268n
first germs of II 227
folly of II 158, 304, 555
God a contradiction I 276, 295n, 499n
gods written in 4 letters II 601-2
Greek I 326
idol worship I 397
incipient stage of II 316
Jehovah I 619n
led to phallicism I 452n; II 273
led to sorcery II 503
materialistic age outcome of I 382 &n
medieval, & swastika II 99-100
powers, Atlantean worship of II 273
Secret Doctrine rejects, gods I 279
still backbone of theology I 3n
Viśishtādvaita philosophy is I 522
Anthropomorphized
  arcanum has become II 234
  Greeks, Nemesis II 305n
  Logos II 416
  powers, gods II 43
Ἄνθρωπος (Anthrōpos, Gk)
  Adam used in sense of I xliin
  son of Anthrōpos (Gnos) I 449
Ἄνθρωπος (*Anthrōpos*, work on occult
    embryology)
  germinal cell & 5-fold jīva I 224
Antichrist
  apex of kosmos for Catholics I 612
  Elijah, Enoch, Christ & II 531
  will be Satan incarnate II 229n
Antilles, seven II 35
Ἀντιμίμον πνεύματος (Antimimon pneu-
    matos, Gk), Buddhi or II 604, 605n
Antipodes
  America 5th continent at II 8
  regions of Pātāla or II 402, 407n, 446
Antiquitates Libyae. See Berosus
Antiquités Celtiques. See Cambry, J.
Antiquités Celtiques et Antediluviennes. See
    Boucher de Crèvecoeur de Perthes
Antiquités de France. See *Mémoires . . . par la
    Société des Antiquaires de France*
Antiquities. See Montfaucon, B. de
Antiquities of the Jews. See Josephus, F.
Antiquity. *See also* Ancients
  dwarfed by scholars I 676
  of man, science re II 70-1, 686-7
  truths of nature in I 285
Antiquity of Man. See Lyell, C.
Antiquity of Man Hist. Considered. See Raw-
    linson, G.

Anu (Chald)
  Ain-sōph or I 357
  Bel, Noah & II 144
  head of Babylonian gods II 139n
  Jehovah &, double sexed II 62
Aṇu (Skt)
  elemental atom, jīva I 567-8
  matter became, or atomic I 522
  name of Brahmā I 542
  primordial, or atom I 148, 357
Anubis (Egy)
  on Gnostic plates I 410
  Hermes, Mercury or II 28
  Horus or, dragon slayer II 385-6
Anubis-Syrius, or Michael II 481
Anugītā I 545n
  causes & agents of action I 534-5 &nn
  continues *Bhagavad-Gītā* (Müller) I 94n
  episode in *Mahābhārata* I 94n; II 495, 566
  fate of various beings at pralaya I 571-2
  forest, 7 trees, fruits, etc II 637-40
  life-winds in body II 496 &n, 566-70
  Mahat as ego-ism I 75
  Nārada (fire) the One Element I 101
  origin of speech & occult properties I 94
  Pistis Sophia in light of II 569
  Pratyāhāra, chapter VII re I 96
  seat abiding in the Self II 495
  seven priests (Aeons) in II 568, 569n, 628
  seven senses, principles I 87, 534; II 628
  smoke & fire II 567-8
  Tree of Life I 536
Anugraha (Skt), 8th Creation
  goodness & darkness in I 448
  Pratyayasarga Creation or I 456
Anukis (Egy)
  Ānochī in Hebrew II 31
  triadic goddess of Khnoum I 367n
Anūnnaki (Chald), angels of Earth II 248n
Anupadaka. *See* Aupapāduka
Anyāya (Skt) dishonesty I 377
Aour [Ōr] (Heb) I 76 &n. *See also* Aur
Apām-Napāt (Skt)
  Vedic, Avestan name of Fohat & II 400n
Apāna (Skt) II 566-9
  speech, prāna & I 94-5
Apap (Egy). *See* Āpep
Aparināmin (Skt), Purusha-pradhāna & I 582
Ape(s). *See also* Anthropoids, Gibbon, Gorilla,
    Homo primigenius, Missing Link, Root-
    Races 3rd & 4th
  anatomy of, & man II 87n, 287, 315n, 665n,
    666-8, 677-8, 680-5
  ancestry, linguistics against II 662

Atlanto-Lemurian sires of II 201n, 688 &n
begotten by mindless man I 190; II 189, 193,
    678, 689
brain of II 661, 682
catarrhine & platyrrhine II 171
chasm betw man & II 189, 665n, 729
degenerated man II 717
descended fr 3rd race man II 185, 262-3
differences among II 287
dog-headed, symbol of sun & moon I 388
egos of, compelled by karma II 262
extinct before 7th race II 263
Haeckelian man fr II 87n, 164-5n, 171
image of 3rd & 4th round man II 728-9
imitate man, not reverse II 676 &n
man &, common ancestor II 185, 189, 258,
    287-8, 634, 646, 674, 677-8
man indirect ancestor of II 289, 717
man not descended fr I 186, 190-1; II 87n
in Miocene strata II 690n
Neanderthal much superior to II 729
new forms will develop II 263
no development among II 682n
no missing link betw man & II 190, 720
origin of I 183-5, 190; II 185-90, 193,
    201 &n, 261-2, 689
de Quatrefages re II 646 &n, 666-7, 682
sacred in India I 185n, 190
scientists q re II 668-9
semi-astral in beginning II 689
tend toward male forefather II 201n
unnatural crossbreed I 183-5; II 201n, 261-2
"Απειρος (Apeiros, Gk) Boundless I 353, 426
Ape-like. *See also* Chhāyās
    forms evolved in 3rd round II 186-7, 688n,
        729
    lunar pitris emanate, forms I 180-1
    man, in 3rd round I 188-9; II 57n, 185, 187,
        261-2, 730
    more, men than men-like apes I 190
Ape-man
    Haeckel on II 193n
    of 3rd & 4th rounds II 730
Āpep, Apap (Egy). *See also* Apophis
    serpent or matter I 674
    slain by Aker II 213
    slain by Osiris-Horus II 588n
Apex
    Aristotle omitted, symbol I 615
    Monad, Father-Mother-Son or I 614
Apherides [Apharētides] (Gk) family of Aph-
    areus, Castor & Pollux II 122
Aphides (plant lice) II 133
Aphophis. *See* Apophis

Aphorisms of Śāṇḍilya I 7 &n
Aphorisms of the Bodhisattvas
    absolute knowledge & paranirvāna I 48
Aphorisms of Tsong Kha-pa. *See* Tsong Kha-pa
Aphrodite. *See also* Lakshmī, Śrī, Venus
    goddess of generative powers II 461
    sprang fr ocean I 380
    Venus-, & Argha II 461
    Venus-, & Mary I 458n
Apis (Egy) I 135, 657; II 418n
Apis pacis (Lat)
    bull deity of Hermoutis I 657
Apocal. Comm. *See* Cornelius à Lapide
Apocalypse. *See Revelation; also* Kenealy, *Book of
    God*
Apocatastasis (Gk) recurrences I 409, 650
Apocrypha(l, on)
    Book of Enoch declared II 454, 529, 531
    Book of Jude rejected as II 531
    Chaldean scriptures (Renan) II 456
    various, listed (de Rougemont) II 454
Apogee, of Moon I 666
Apollo (Gk) II 769-72
    Aesculapius I 353; II 106
    Agni, Michael, Mikael & II 381-5
    Arimaspi destroyed by II 769n
    Athene &, as birds II 771
    bisexual I 72n, 396
    born fr Leda's egg I 366; II 122
    closed up man's skin II 134, 177
    Diana &, Moon & Sun II 771 &n
    divine king of early nations II 774
    emotional, pomp-loving god II 383n
    father of Phoebe & Hilaeira II 122
    father, son, husband I 396
    god of hidden things (Ragon) II 796
    god of oracular wisdom II 106
    god of seers, punishes desecration II 770
    Helios as II 44, 106, 383
    heptachord (lyre) of I 167, 396
    Hyperborean II 7, 11, 769-71
    -Karneios, Sun-born II 44 &n
    Kārttikeya, Indra, Michael & II 382-3
    patron of number seven II 602, 772n
    -Python II 208, 379, 771n
    resurrected every 19 years II 770
    sends astral double of Aeneas II 771
    skeleton of giant killed by II 278
    southern II 769
    Sun or II 7, 44, 106, 211, 381, 771-2n
    swan associated w I 358
    torch of, aspect of Archeus I 338n
    various names for I 353; II 379, 770
Apollodorus, *Bibliotheca*

Berosus on monsters II 53
Deucalion, Pyrrha escape Deluge II 270
Dioscuri (Castor & Pollux) II 122
Hephaestus, Prometheus II 519
legend of golden apples II 770n
sons & daughters of Niobe II 771
Apollonius of Tyana
had key to characters at Gadir II 345n
met Buddhist nāgas in Kashmir II 211
Nuctameron of I 450
Apollonius Rhodius II 362
—— [*Argonautica*]
on rocking stones II 342 &n
Apollyon (Gk) II 229n
Apophis (Egy). *See also* Āpep
Michael slays I 459
slain by Horus II 380, 385, 588n
symbol of human passions II 588n
Typhon or II 380, 385
Apostle(s) I 87, 400, 649; II 115n
Append[ix] de Cabiris. See Cumberland, Bishop
Apperception
of ātman by buddhi I 177
Leibniz & I 179, 627, 629-31
in plants & minerals I 454-5
in 3rd order of elementals I 454
fr, to perception I 175, 179
Apple(s)
Apollodorus on golden II 770n
trees I 129n; II 97
tree, serpent & I 129n; II 354-5
Approaching End of the Age. See Guinness, H.
Apsarasas(es) (Skt). *See also* Nymph
gods & men II 211
Pramlochā & II 174-6
qualities & quantities II 585
Apsis(ides)
precession of equinoxes & II 330 &n
Apteryx, rudimentary wing of II 681
Apuleius, Latin text of Pymander II 491n
Aqua, Hydrargyrum, Natura & II 113
Aquarius
on Assyrian tablet II 353
Ganymedes is II 785
Hindu zodiac &, [Libra in tx, *see* Bailly] I 661, 663
man or, & Reuben I 651
Aqueducts, cement of ancient II 430
Aquinas, Thomas. *See* Thomas Aquinas
Aquitaine, bone caves of II 744
A.R. See Asiatic Researches
Arab(s) II 366
figures borrowed fr Hindus I 361
four-letter God of II 602

later Aryans II 200
Purānas speak of wars w II 406
revived astronomy in 9th cent I 658-9
twelve tribes of, & 12 signs II 200n
year had 6 seasons II 621
zodiac known among I 648
Arabia(ns)
Ak-ad or "Son of Ad" in II 42 &n
ancient wars in II 406
Aryans reach Egypt thru II 746
ate serpent heart & liver I 404
Mt. Sinai in II 76
seven holy fanes of II 603
winged serpents of I 362
Arabic
ancient records in II 431
Chaldean works transl into I 288
cifron or cipher in I 360-1
figures not oldest II 554
Nabathean Agriculture & II 452-3
Arachnida, scorpions highest group of II 257
Araea. *See* Aarea
Arago, D. François J.
named Sun's photosphere I 530
proved aerolites exist II 784n
Aral, Lake, Sea of II 204, 416n
Aramaean, "the only one" II 42 &n, 43
Arani, Araṇī (Skt) II 524-8, 524n
Catholic "vase of election" II 528
Devakī or, engenders fire II 527
gradual desecration of II 526-7
swastika & II 101 &n
Ararat
biblical mountain II 145
corresponds to body, Earth II 596-7
Hor-Jared or II 596
meaning of, & Deluge I 444
Arasa-maram, Banyan tree II 215
Arath (Aram), Ararat or II 597
Araucaria (pine genus) II 257
Arba-il [Arba'-ēl] (Heb) I 337 &n, 447
Arc, Ascending, Descending. *See also* Round
centripetal & centrifugal forces II 261
compared I 176-7, 232, 268; II 625n
man, fiery lives & I 263n
Ascending:
evolution spiritualizes in I 232; II 250
fifth, 6th races in II 300, 446
after mid-4th race II 308n
spirit over matter II 110, 180
three heavens are globes on I 250n
we are on I 641
Descending:
first, 2nd races on II 300

globes, rounds concrete in I 232
involution of spirit in I 416; II 180
some subraces still on II 301
stopped mid-4th round II 180
three "earths" or globes on I 250n
Arca, Arka II 460. *See also* Argha, Ark
Arcadians II 352
Arcane, derived fr *arca* II 463n
Arcanum(a) I 253n; II 282n
  magic & II 557
  phallicized II 233-4
  Sōd means II 212 &n
Arch. See Archaeologia
Archaeologia (London)
  Bel & dragon II 379
  Tooke on Tartars II 343
Archaeological Notes . . . See Rivett-Carnac
Archaeologist(s)
  dwarf antiquity I 676
  future, & present man II 722-3
  misdate N American mounds II 424n
Archaeology. See Archaeologia
"Archaeology of the Virgin Mother" I 393.
  See also Mirville, J. E. Marquis de
Archaeopteryx, betw reptile & bird II 183
Archaeus (Lat), Archaios (Gk)
  Anch [Ânkh] or, (diag) II 633
  attracts, repels other forces I 538
  Bourges, Richardson on II 654
  Father-Ether or I 51-2
  great, or astral light I 253-4n
  liquor vitae (Paracelsus) I 532 &n, 538
  names of various aspects I 338n
  nervous ether (Richardson) I 531-2
  self-moving I 670
Archagetos. *See* Archēgetēs
Archaic Dictionary. See Cooper, W. R.
Archaic Manuscript I 1-5; II 36-7
Archaic Records
  in Chaldean tablets II 3 &n
  concerning Atlantis II 425-33
  Egyptians preserved I 436
  historical proofs of II 354
  language of, symbolized I 23
  Stanzas & II 1
  will be found correct II 423
Archangel(s). *See also* Dhyāni-chohans,
    Michael
  abode of, in 7 great stars II 455n
  among highest deities I 116n
  Amshaspends or, (Burnouf) I 437
  anthropomorphous II 377
  architects I 16 &n
  archontes &, (Iamblichus) I 235

Christians call moon I 394
concept of, fr India II 584
conspire against fallen angels II 382n
dhyāni(-chohans) II 22, 242
doubles of I 235 &n
elements stand for I 339
first, called Lux (Lucifer) I 70-1
first differentiated egos II 242
Gabriel & lilies, lotus I 379n, 384; II 472
man compared w I 236, 277
Mercury ruled by I 435
Michael highest I 88, 437; II 94n
Milton q I 622
preside over constellations I 638
primordial flame I 88
rebellion of, as Fall II 62-3, 94n, 246
refused to create I 88; II 246
rule 2nd world of Syrians I 435
saptarishis or I 198
Satan the I 414; II 60
seven, or Virtues of God I 438
"Seven Spirits of the Face" II 115n
seven sublime lords I 42
sons of dark wisdom II 248
theological interpretation II 377
various equivalents of I 437
virgin-angels among II 246
wanted man to become a god II 246
work of II 242
'Αρχή (Archē, Gk)
  Egyptian ansated cross & II 547
  female generative power II 460
  rāsit or II 313, 460
Archebiosis
  fifth stage of evolution I 455
  Haeckel on II 164n
  primeval protoplasm I 542 &n
Archēgetēs (Gk), Sun-gods called II 463n
Archetypal Man (Proto-logos)
  Adam Kadmon I 443
  creative origin of all things I 443
  totality of prajāpatis I 356
Archetypal World, Universe I 177
  in diagram of planes I 200 &n
  svabhavat I 98
  three higher globes belong to I 152
  upper triad in I 213; II 2n
Archetype(s)
  Goethe's II 737
  Prometheus the, of humanity II 519
  symbols of the world of II 36
Archeus. *See* Archaeus
Archi-Ahas II 132
Archimedes, *Psammitēs*

taught heliocentric theory I 117 &n
Archis (Skt), certain pure souls I 132
Archisatrap of Sacred Militia II 479
Archistrategus, Michael as II 498
Architect(s). *See also* Builders, Deities,
    Masons
    conscious spiritual egos I 632
    creator, demiurgos I 279-80, 346, 380 &n
    dhyāni-chohans as I 16
    Dracontia called II 380
    fallen angels as II 516
    fashioners of worlds II 516
    higher dhyāni-buddhas I 267
    higher than creative deity II 43
    Law is the great I 199
    Logos I 279, 439-40
    Masonic I 613
    never touches a stone I 279
    of planetary chain I 128
    plural in number always I 440
    point in circle cause of I 426
    priest-, builders & I 209n
    rotary motion of spheres & I 442
    rounds, globes under I 233
    sephīrōth I 579n
    Uranus & Neptune as I 101-2
    Viśvakarman II 101n, 269n
    Watchers of the Seven Spheres I 53
Architecture(al)
    divine rulers cultivated I 208-9n; II 317,
    364
    ephemeral, of China II 311
    esoteric measurements in II 465
    Hindu, fr Greece (Fergusson) II 225
    Mars lord of, (Skinner) II 392
    taught at initiations I 208-9n
    taught man by gods II 366
    Vitruvius & I 208-9n
Archons, Archontes (Gnos) I 604
    astral light abode of I 196
    Iamblichus on I 235
Arctic. *See also* Hyperborean, Polar
    Region, Pole
    ancients knew the II 357 .
    Circle, lands around II 399n
    continents II 11-12, 398-9
    Persian legendary land & II 398-9
    Pole land of 1st race II 329
    sinking of Lemuria began in II 332
    yearly "day" & "night" of II 292
Arcturus, in *Job* I 647-8
Ardan, Eridanus, & Jordan I 392
Ardhanārī (Skt)
    hermaphrodite goddess II 31

symbol of 3rd race II 533
Ardhanāri-Īśvara I 392
Ardis, top of Mt Armon II 376
Ἄρης, Ἄρευς (Arēs, Areus, Gk), Mars II 392n
Ares of Paracelsus, dividing power I 284
Aretia. *See* Artes
Aretz [Erets] (Heb), Earth II 143-4n, 467
Arezahi (Pers), globe of Earth chain II 759
Arg, Arca. *See also* Argha, Ark
    female generative power II 416n, 460
    Parkhurst on II 313
Argeak, Argen [Argenk]
    Persian giant II 396, 398
Argha. *See also* Ark, Holy of Holies
    carries seed of life I 360
    crescent-shaped Moon II 462
    Hindu ark II 461
    linga, yoni, JHVH & II 473
    linked w Jehovah, Anu II 62
    Moon or ark II 142n, 145, 468
    navi-form, of Mysteries II 416n, 459
    sacrificial chalice II 461
    womb of terrestrial nature I 444
Arghya (Skt), libation cup II 416n
Arghyanāth (Skt), Mahā-chohan II 416n
Arghya-Varsha (Skt)
    became Āryā-varta (India) II 419
    Kalki-avatāra expected fr II 416n
Argians (Gk)
    Phoroneus father of, (Decharme) II 521
    termed Io the Moon II 416n, 463
Argolis (Gk), perpetual flame at II 519
Argonautica. See Apollonius Rhodius
Argonauts (Gk)
    Dulaure dates, at 6500 BC I 652
    moving stone left by II 345
    Samothrace flooded before age of II 4
Argos (Gk). *See also* Argus
    Arghya-Varsha is II 419
    Castor demi-hero at II 122n
    kingly race in II 416n, 418
    three-eyed statue at II 294n
Argua [Argha], or vehicle II 291
Argus, Argos (Gk). *See also* Argos
    Hermes & death of II 367
    Mercury as II 28
Argyll, Duke of. *See* Campbell, G.D.
Arhan(s), Arhat(s) (Skt), Arhatship
    Buddhist I xx, xxviii; II 339
    dhyānis became II 167
    discountenance hatha yoga I 95
    elements as viewed by I 249
    essence of fire, flame & I 6
    faces higher initiations I 206

of the Fire Mist I 207
of the 4 truths I 409
remodeled Bamian statues II 339
sat & asat of II 449
sees & feels 3rd eye II 294
seven planets show themselves to I 100
siddhis of I 97n
Sons of Will & Yoga ancestors of II 173
trans-Himalayan, Esoteric School I 157
Aria (Iran), Jews sought refuge in II 200
Ariadne's Thread
 analogy is II 153
 anthropologists & II 66-7
Aries
 Libra &, & Greek zodiac II 436n
 Mars & II 392 &n
 Volney re, & Libra I 658
Arimaspi(an), Arimaspes (Gk)
 Apollo destroyed II 769n
 Io visits II 416-17
 fr last Atlantean subraces II 774
 one-eyed Scythian race II 769n, 770
Arion (Gk), symb a cycle II 399n
Aristarchus of Samos
 taught heliocentrism I 117 &n
Aristobulus, supposed forgery of I 648
Aristophanes (Gk dramatist)
 describes Orphic Egg I 359-60
 —— [*Thesmophoriazusae*] (*Ar. Theism* in tx)
 definition of Moira & Fate II 604-5n
Aristophanes (in Plato's *Banquet*)
 ovoid, androgynous men II 96, 133-4, 177
Aristophyli [Aristophuloi] (Gk)
 Ptolemy called Afghans II 200n
Aristotle
 chaos is space I 336n
 dwarfed Pythagorean geometry I 615
 embryology, Weismann & I 223n
 Faraday used reflections of I 507
 God & direct creation II 159
 inductive method of I 153 &n, 481; II 573
 Leibniz' atoms & I 631n
 never initiated I 493
 privation, form, matter of I 59; II 489
 science &, against intuition I 279
 —— *De caelo*
 denies revolution of earth II 153
 stars & planets are living I 493
 taught Earth's sphericity I 117n
 —— *Metaphysica*
 numbers & ideas in I 361 &n
 stoicheia of I 123, 461
 water primal substance (Thales) I 345n
 —— [*De mundo*]

God & direct creation II 159
 —— *Physica*
 mind communicates motion I 595
Arithmomancy
 Pyth study of gods, numbers II 575
Arjuna, married Ulūpī & visited Pātāla
 (America) II 214 &n, 628
Arjuna Miśra
 Anugītā commentary II 567-8, 637-9 &nn
 material cause of words I 95
 Moon & fire constitute universe II 639n
 senses not independent I 96
 speech, mind & prajāpati I 94-5
Ark II 141-8, 459-63. *See also* Argha, Noah
 Astaroth or Venus shut up in II 145
 became phallic II 459, 467, 473, 518
 Chaldean II 141, 290
 contains germs of all things II 461
 Cosmas Indicopleustes on II 399
 Deucalion, Pyrrha escape in II 270
 divine spirit brooding over chaos II 313
 egg does not typify I 360
 emblem of Moon II 142n, 145
 female Noah one w II 463
 female principle or II 715n
 Ham stole 7 books fr II 612-13
 Holy of Holies or II 467-8
 man means II 291 &n
 Manu & 7 rishis saved in II 139, 715n
 Mazdean II 290-2
 meaning of II 460-3
 measurements of I 316; II 465
 Moses & Sargon placed in I 319 &n
 navis or womb II 139, 461
 Noah as Manu, Patriarch II 534, 597
 Noah's, & 4th race I 445; II 292, 467-8, 774
 of Salvation II 313
 śishtas preserved in II 307n
 of Vaivasvata Manu II 35, 69n, 290-1, 774
 womb of terrestrial nature I 444 &n
 Yima's II 610
Arkite Symbols
 ancient, source of *Genesis* II 143
Arkite Titans
 Ham, Shem, Japhet (Faber) II 343n
 seven listed by Orpheus II 142n, 143
Ark of the Covenant
 David danced before I 335; II 459-61
 generative symbol II 460
 Holy of Holies II 459-60
 Linga & Yoni of, (Jennings) II 473
 measurements of II 465
 Nave, Yoni, Mary, Eve or II 463
 number of II 40

Arm(s), multiple, symb subraces II 775-6
Ārmaita Spenta (Zor)
  spirit of Earth, materiality II 517
Armenia(ns) II 202
  Jews, Parsis &, Caucasian II 471n
  square hat of, priests & tau II 557
Armenian Tales, Fortunate Isles in II 398
Armon, Mt. *See* Mount Armon
"Army of the Voice" I 93-4, 96
Arnaud, on venoms, alkaloids I 262n
Arnobius (the Elder), *Adversus gentes*
  Manes, Mania II 143
  Mercury & Sol I 353
  talking stones, ophites II 342
[Arnold, Sir Edwin], *Light of Asia* II 229n
Ar(r)hētos (Gnos) I 446
Arrian, *Indica*
  Alexander, Indus & Nile II 417-18
Arte Chymiae, De. See Bacon, R.
Artemis (Gk)
  Diana, Isis, Juno or I 228-9
  Diana on Earth, Luna in Heaven I 387
  Dictynna, Anaitis or I 395
Artemis-Lochia (Gk), & conception I 395
Artemis-Soteira (Gk) [fem. of Sōter, savior]
  occult potencies of Moon I 396
Artes, Egyptian Mars II 143n
Artha (Skt), comprehension I 48n
Ar. Theism. See Aristophanes
Arth. Index. See Ackerman
Arthur, King. *See* King Arthur
Arts (Aretz) II 143-4n
Arts, the
  Aryan, fr 4th race II 426
  Atlantean, scientific I 464
  divine kings taught man II 201, 222, 317, 392
  initiated inventors of II 529
  Kabiri taught man II 364
  lost, of ancients II 430-1
  magic I 469
  Mars lord of, (Skinner) II 392
  Prometheus taught man II 413
  speech of ancients I 313
  taught to infant humanity I 208 &n, 267, 362; II 364, 572
  taught to 3rd race II 194
Artufas [Estufas] (Spanish)
  Pueblo initiation caves II 181n
Arūpa (Skt) I 53. *See also* Form, Rūpa
  cosmic pralaya &, world II 69n
  dhyān-chohans both rūpa & I 197
  dhyāni-buddhas fr, world I 571
  formless worlds or I 120, 200 &n, 436; II 69n
  four classes of, gods II 318n

incorporeal or, men II 194
monad all-potent on, plane II 110
rudras independent of, devas II 585
rūpa & I 89, 118, 122, 129, 197
subjective universe I 98
three classes of pitris are I 219n; II 91, 93-5
triad I 214
Arvāksrotas (Skt). *See also* Tiryaksrotas
  crooked digestive canals II 162
  man 7th Creation I 446, 456; II 162-3
Arvasthān (Skt), or Arabia II 406
Aryachatta [Āryabhata] (Skt)
  taught revolution of Earth I 117
  value of π & II 499n
Ārya Magazine, Aryan era in II 68n
Aryan(s) Race. *See also* Root-Race – 5th
  adept astronomers of II 699
  adepts I vii; II 495
  adepts vs Atlantean sorcerers II 384, 495
  allegories re II 82, 381, 383, 495, 576
  ancestors of Egyptians II 328
  Arabs are later II 200
  Arabs in Afghanistan II 200 &n
  Asiatics saw last of giant Atlanteans II 433
  Atlanteans preceded II 144, 352
  Atlanteans taught II 426
  born in the north II 768
  branches of II 106
  bull symbolizes II 533
  called 1st speaking race Ad-i II 452
  Carlyle q on II 470
  cataclysm will destroy II 445
  colonies fr Atlantis II 266n
  common religion before separation I xxix
  cosmogony II 23, 241, 500, 536, 603
  decimal system I 360-2
  descend fr yellow Adams II 426
  dvijas II 469
  early, Atlantean II 371 &n, 433n, 743
  early history of II 328, 395, 425-9, 609, 743, 768-9
  era, figures given II 68n
  Europeans & Christians latest I 425
  fifth race incorrectly called II 433-4
  Fohat key to, religions I 673
  height of, after 3rd subrace II 753
  Hindu, navigators before Phoen II 406
  Hindu, nearly 1 million yrs old II 470-1
  influence on Babylonian myth II 130
  initiated, view of Moon I 396
  Kabbala came fr I 376
  kali-yuga of I 644-5; II 147n
  knew mysteries of sound, color I 534
  knew of Earth's rotation II 154-5

languages II 199-200 &nn
magi emigrate to Sagdiani II 356
many colors of II 249-50
migrated to India II 609
mixed w 7th subrace Atlanteans II 743
Mysteries based on number ten II 603
Negroes, Mongols, & II 607n
neo-, of postdiluvian age II 356
Neolithic man &, invasion II 716n, 741
Peris or Izeds were II 394
philosophy older than Egyptian I 387
Rāma 1st divine king of II 495
rel concepts not just physiological II 526
root-race & 5th continent II 8, 10
second subrace of, built menhirs II 750
Semitic &, rel I 115n, 382-3, 444, 655;
    II 128, 142n, 200 &n
separated ⅔ million years ago II 425
sevenfold classification w II 34, 142n, 614
spiritual ancestors of II 165-6n, 318
spiritually higher than Greeks II 158
swastica mystical conception of II 99-100
symbols free of impure thought I 382-3
taught emanation, not creation II 54
tribes conquered Egypt II 746
Trojan ancestors were II 101
Veda theogony of II 450
war w Atlanteans II 384, 395, 495, 776
Western, in kali-yuga I 644-5
wisdom II 449-51
woman's status in early I 382
zodiac fr Sons of Yoga II 436n
Aryan Theosophical Society of NY I 630
Aryas (Skt). *See also* Aryans, Root-Race–5th
    forty-nine agnis (fires) of II 85
    prophecy re kali-yuga I 377
Ārya-Samāj (School) II 68 &n
Āryāsaṅga
    re Alaya I 48, 49
    pre-Christian adept I 49n
    rival of Nāgārjuna I 49
    school of I 69n, 158; II 637
    term Ādi-budha used by I xix
Āryāvarta (Skt) ancient India
    archangels trace back to II 584
    Arghya-Varsha & II 419
    Asuramaya astronomer of II 49
    primeval occultism of II 565
    Prometheus myth fr II 524
Aryo-Atlanteans II 433
Arzahi. *See* Arezahi
"As above, so below" I 177, 542; II 29n,
    699-700
Asam, Easam (Irish), to create II 114

Asaradel, taught motion of Moon II 376
Asat (Skt)
    mūlaprakriti or II 597n
    sat & II 449-50
Asathor (Norse), war of, w Jotuns II 386
Asburj, Ashburj, Az-burj (Mt)
    Sun sets at foot of II 403, 407
    survived Atlantis II 408
Ascending Arc. *See* Arc
Ascension Island, remnant of continent II 793
Ascetic(s). *See also* Daksha, Kumāras, Nārada,
    Rudras
    fruitless, & Nārada II 275n
    gods oppose II 78n, 174
    initiated, & 7th root-race II 275
Asch [Ush] (Skt), fire, heat II 114
Aschieros. *See* Axieros
Aschmogh. *See* Ashmogh
Ascidians II 119
Asclepiades, betyles, ophites II 342
Asclepias acida, soma juice fr II 498-9
Asclepios. *See* Asklēpios
Asclepios. See Kingsford, A., *Virgin of the World*
Ases. *See* Aesir
Asexual
    fr, to bisexual to sexual II 116, 132, 197
    first, second, races II 116
    primitive, forms remain II 133
    science on modes of repro II 658-9
Asgard (Norse) II 97
Asgard and the Gods. See Wagner, W.
Ash. *See* Ash Tree
'Āsh (Heb), Arcturus I 647-8
Asha [eshshā] (Aram) fire II 114
Ashburj. *See* Asburj
Asher. *See* Ehyeh asher Ehyeh
Asher [Āshēr] (Heb) son of Jacob
    Libra, the "balance" & I 651
Ashes, are passion (*Anugītā*) II 567
Ashmogh [Ashemaogha] (Zor)
    serpent w camel's neck II 205
Ashnagor (in Afghanistan)
    Isaguri, Issachar or II 200n
Ashṭadiśa (Skt)
    eight faces bounding space II 576-7
Ashtar Vidyā (Skt). *See also* Āgneyāstra
    extensive works on, lost II 427n
    vibratory force (vril) in I 563
    white & black forces used II 427
Ashtōreth (Sem)
    female aspect, Moon I 396; II 462
    Ishtar, Moon or II 145
    Queen of Heaven I 397n
Ash Tree, Ash-Wood

Jupiter made Bronze-age men fr II 772
　Melia or II 519-20
　third race created fr, (Hesiod) II 97, 181n,
　　520 &n
　Yggdrasil II 520
Asia. *See also* Central Asia, Lob-nor
　America & NE, once united II 322n
　ancient civ in I xxxii
　astronomy in I 658
　Chenresi protector of II 178
　cut off fr root continent II 401
　inland sea sacred island I 209; II 220
　Khamism fr Western I 115n
　Lemuria & II 327, 769n
　man originated in, (Darwin) II 679-80
　Neolithic man fr II 716n
　northern, as old as 2nd race II 401
　northern, "perpetual land" II 776
　Prometheus son of II 768
　refugees fr Atlantis in II 743
　rose after destruction of Atlantis II 606n
　Saturnine Sea north of II 777n
　Sons of Light in I xliii
　South, not man's origin (Haeckel) II 789
　trilithic & raised stones in II 346n
Asia ('Aσία, Gk)
　Prometheus son of II 768
Asia(tic World) ['Aśiyyāh] (Kab) II 111, 604
Asia Minor
　Accadians & II 203
　America, Europe coeval w II 8
　initiates of II 558
　priests of, knew of Atlantis II 371
　third Aryan subrace born in II 753
Asiatic Researches. See also Jones, Sir William;
　　Wilford, Col F.
　extravagant speculations in I 654
　Jones on:
　　Hindu trinity I xxxi
　　Nārada II 48
　Wilford on:
　　Brahmādicas II 142
　　divisions of Atlantis II 406n, 409
　　Great War I 369n
　　Hindu chronology I 654-5
　　Kai-caus II 403
　　King ı'т II 406
　　kumāras I 236; II 319
　　Meru & Atlas II 401n, 404
　　Nīla, Nile II 405 &n
　　White Devil II 147, 403
　　White Island II 402-3, 402n
　　Yudhishthira I 369-70
Asita (Skt), Saturn called II 29

Ask (Norse), Askr (Icel). *See* Ash Tree
Asklēpios (Gk). *See also* Ptaḥ
　embryonic stages known to II 259
　generic name, demi-god II 364
　Helius, Pythius, or II 106
　Hellenic Maitreya I 285-6
　"incorporeal corporealities" I 566
　Mercury is I 353; II 208, 211
　Roman Church makes, a devil II 208
　serpent & II 26n, 209
　son of Apollo II 106, 211, 770
　supernal gods of I 601
　various names for I 353
Aśoka (Buddhist emperor)
　grandson of Chandragupta II 550n
　inscription of (Piyadasi) II 50
　no rock temples before II 220n
Āsphujit (Skt), adopted Earth II 32
Asr (Egy), Osiris, aish & II 114
As Regards Protoplasm. See Stirling, J. H.
Ass II 287
Assam, Lemuria & II 324
Assessors, Forty, lipikas or I 104-5
Assur, Wilford sees, in Īśvara I 654
Assyria(ns)
　Ad, Ak-Ad in II 42 &n, 43
　antiquity of II 334
　armies called trees II 496
　bulls & cherubs of Jews II 115n
　chronology of, scholars on II 691
　evil spirits symbolized chaos II 386 &n
　initiate called cedar of Lebanon II 494
　invasion of Egypt I 311
　King Sargon's story I 319-20 &n
　Mysteries of, (Chwolsohn) II 452
　Nebo adored by II 456
　Perseus "son of, demon" II 345n
　priests took names of gods II 380
　recorded 27 myriads of years I 409, 650
　seven Adams or mankinds II 4, 102
　sevens in II 4, 35
　Shemites or II 203
　swastika found among II 586
Assyrian Cylinders, Tablets, Tiles I 269, 305,
　　390; II 226, 439, 477
　Babylonian creation in II 61
　Garden of Eden in II 202
　Moses' life on II 428
　twelve cantos of, & zodiac II 353
Assyrian Discoveries. See Smith, George
Assyriologists
　ignorance of II 4, 62, 104, 354
　say Nipoor center of black magic II 139n
Astaphoi, Astaphai(os) (Gnos)

genius of Mercury I 577; II 538n
stellar spirit I 449
Astaroth. *See* Ashtōreth
Astartē (Phoen)
    Ad-argat or, consort of Ad-on II 42n, 43
    goddess of generative powers II 461
    Hiram built temple to II 541
    Phoenician sailors prayed to I 468
    Venus-, & the Kadeshim II 460
    wife, mother & sister I 396
Asteria
    Apollo born on II 383, 773-4
    climate of, once a paradise II 773-4
    Hindu Hiranyapura II 383
    Nordenskiöld's discoveries & II 773 &n
    nymph, hides under ocean II 771n
Asterism(s)
    cyclic progress of II 253
    "fables" refer to II 585
    lunar, 7 rishis & kali-yuga I 378; II 550-1
Asterius, Pausanias saw tomb of II 278
Asteroids, influence of Earth on II 700
Asteropē (Gk) or Steropē, a Pleiad
    daughter of Atlas II 768
Aster't. *See* Astartē
Astoreth. *See* Ashtōreth
Astra (Skt) missile weapon II 629n. *See also*
    Āgneyāstra, Ashtar Vidyā
Astraea (Gk), goddess of justice II 785-6
Astrakhan (River), Io crosses II 416
Astral
    ancestors & primordial Adam II 46
    constitution cannot be excavated II 720
    devas inhabit, plane II 90
    Earth, in early ages II 250-1
    evolution merges into physical II 257
    fire & occult phenomena I 82n
    forms stored in Earth's aura II 684
    fourth state of matter II 737
    influences I 538
    man often evil genius I 639
    man 300 million years old II 251
    physical &, planes II 157 &n
    pineal gland & II 301
    pralayas &, "photographs" I 18n; II 660
    primeval, man II 688-9
    progenitors of early mammals II 684
    prototypes:
        become physical II 736, 738
        created I 282; II 68n, 186, 660
        shed by man II 684
        in space I 18n; II 660n
        fr 3rd round II 256-7
    records & lipikas I 104-5

relics of 3rd round II 712
sex first on, plane II 84
shadows II 46, 105, 110, 164, 186
Astral Body(ies). *See also* Body, Chhāyā, Linga-
    Śarīra, Nephesh, Shadows, Shells
    adepts live in II 499, 531
    agnishvāttas have no, to project II 78
    barhishads & II 79
    beasts have an II 196n
    becomes covered w flesh I 183-4; II 121
    body of kosmos I 167, 624n
    born before physical II 1
    breathed out II 86
    consolidation of II 653
    in diagram, table I 153, 157n, 242-3; II 596,
        632-3
    among Egyptians I 232n, 674n
    esoteric & profane sciences & II 149
    external form fr 175
    first race had no II 121
    kabbalists on I 234, 242-4
    māyāvic body II 241
    "missing link" in the II 720
    progenitors merged w their II 138
    sound & I 555
    Uraeus devours I 227, 674n
Astral Double(s). *See also* Bhūtas, Chhāyās
    became 1st human race II 183
    high adept can use II 771
    lunar pitris oozed out I 180, 248
    projection of I 234
Astral Fire or Fluid I 81, 82n, 93, 338n, 340-1,
    524n; II 188
Astral Light. *See also* Aether, Ākāśa, Anima
    Mundi, Ether
    above lowest prakriti I 255
    ākāśa & I 197n, 253-9, 296n, 326; II 511-12
    Ana, Anna, Chaldean heaven I 91
    anima mundi & I 59-60, 194-7, 365n, 461
    aspect of Archaeus I 338n
    bodies charged w I 526
    church turned, into Satan II 511
    cosmic soul II 113
    cosmic substance or matter I 326
    decrees of fate in II 236
    destiny of every man in I 104, 105
    divine, or One Element I 140
    dragon, serpent or I 73, 74n, 75; II 356
    entities in I 331n
    ether I 74n, 76 &n, 197, 326, 331n, 343, 524n
    evil on our plane I 73-4
    feminine w Gnostics I 194-5
    God & Devil II 512-13
    grand beings move in I 527n

great deceiver of man I 60
honey-dew or I 344-5
Isis Unveiled on I 194-7, 338n, 340-1
of kabbalists I 343
karma of humanity II 513
Lévi re I 196, 253-5, 254n, 259 &n; II 74,
    485, 511
life-principle of all I 196
limbus or I 353
lower ether I 331n
lowest of the 7 planes I 257
luminous zone (*Zohar*) II 409
Magic Head is, (*Zohar*) I 424
Nahbkoon [neheb-kau] or I 472
name coined by Martinists I 348
Nebelheim [Niflheim] I 367
not aether or ether I 296n
picture gallery, lipikas I 104-5
prince of the air & II 485
prototypes impressed in I 59, 63
shadow of aether I 341
sidereal light of Paracelsus I 255
soul of, divine & body infernal I 423-4
various names for I 140, 365n; II 511
vibratory motion of I 348
weird secrets of I 296-7
Astral Selves, Souls
    astral light furnishes I 196-7
    build physical tabernacle II 110
Astrolatry II 456
    astrology & II 23
    Chaldean II 622-3n
    exoteric Judaism, Christianity & II 41
    Gnostic, Zoroastrian, Christian I 402, 448
Astrology(er, ical). *See also* Horoscopy, Zodiac
    ancient mythology includes I 389n
    angel Barkayal taught II 376
    aspects of constellations II 179
    Brahman's life regulated by II 411n
    Chaldean II 622-3n
    college of, on Euphrates II 203
    conception, birth & I 228-9n
    definition of II 500n
    judicial I 575n, 647
    limitations I 642
    Makara in Hindu I 219
    Mercury in II 28
    origin of II 23
    Persian magic shield II 394
    on physical not spiritual plane II 631n
    prophecies I 646-7
    pyramid illustrates I 317n
    rationale of I 105, 532
    Scorpio & reproductive organs II 129

sign of Venus II 29-30
soul of astronomy I 645-7
star deals w personality I 572-3
Tritheim greatest, of his day II 512n
Astro-Magians of India II 612n
Astronomer(s). *See also* Asuramaya, Bailly
    adept, knew of Mars, Venus races II 699
    Garga oldest, of India II 49n
    modern, on Great Pyramid II 432
    record cyclic events I 646
    should be geologists (Faye) I 496
    two antediluvian II 47-51
Astronomiae. See Brahe, Tycho
Astronomical(ly)
    allegories II 45, 94 &n, 353, 380
    ancient, calculations II 620-1
    aspect of Vedic verse II 191n
    character of *Genesis* II 143
    influence of, phenomena II 73-4
    kalpa II 307n
    keys to theogony II 23
    key to symbolism I 363
    key to War in Heaven II 63
    Mackey on, dates of Atlantis II 407-8
    male gods become Sun-gods II 43
    occultism &, theories II 71
    phenomena & sexual religion II 274
    planets, many more in secret bks I 152n
    racial &, cycles II 49, 70, 330-1
    records began in Atlantis II 353
    Sun cosmic &, emblem II 208
    Sūrya Siddhānta oldest, work II 326
    symbols II 391n
    tables, ancient & modern I 658-9, 666
    Tārakā-maya full of, truths II 45
    truth concealed in legend II 93-4n
    Tyndaridae, symb of twin brothers II 122
Astronomie. See Francoeur, L. B.
Astronomie Ancienne. See Bailly, J. S.
Astronomie du Moyen Age. See Delambre, J.
Astronomy. *See also* Constellations, Nebular
        Theory, Planets, Precession, Stars
    all in scriptures based on II 77
    ancients knew, well I 650, 659-68; II 534-5
    archaic, & modern science I 203
    astrolatry confirmed by II 41
    astrology soul of I 645-7
    Aztecs' knowledge of I 322
    dead planets in occult I 149n
    divine kings gave early races II 29, 49, 317,
        366, 765-6
    Egyptian II 332, 435, 620, 631
    exoteric now II 124
    generation, conception & I 312

geology & II 71-2
has returned to Anaxagoras I 586
Hebrew, regulated by Moon II 75
Hindu I 658-68; II 253, 332, 551
inherited fr Atlantis II 426, 431
legendary teachers of II 765-6
light received by Venus II 29n
Moon, Earth II 64
mythology includes I 387, 389 &n
older, younger planets & II 251
Osiris-Isis taught, (Basnage) II 366
phenomena of, cyclic II 73-4
Purānic, a science II 253
pyramid & principles of I 317-18n
Śesha teacher of II 49n
taught man by gods II 366
theology &, connected I 320
unknown planets, globes I 163, 203, 576
Astronomy of the Ancients. See Lewis, G. C.
Astron. Poétique. See Hyginus, G. J.
Astro-Theosophic Chart. *See* Jennings
Asu (Skt) breath II 59, 500
Asura(s) (Skt) I 571. *See also* Agnishvāttas,
      Amshaspends, Angels, Dhyānis, Pitṛis,
      Sons of Brahmā, Suras, Vedhas
adversaries of gods II 45, 162, 164, 230, 500
Ahura same as II 59, 61, 92, 608
fr *asu* (breath) II 59, 500
Atlanteans & II 227n, 323
became, fr the Fall II 283
became inferior gods II 60
Brahmans distort meaning of II 92, 487
created fr "body of night" II 163
degraded into demons II 45, 500-1, 516
elohīm identical w II 487
esoterically & exoterically II 174, 227n, 230,
      232, 237 &n, 246-8, 283, 516
fallen angels II 500, 516, 525n
fire of I 521; II 57n, 106
first gods before "no-gods" II 248, 500
flames or, incarnate in 3rd race II 247-8
four mahārājas or I 126
four preceding manus & II 318n
gods of the secret wisdom II 500
highest dhyāni-chohans II 585
hurled to Earth II 93, 246-7
incarnated by implacable law II 487
incarnated in man II 164
Indra & I 202; II 378
kumāras, pitris & II 89, 106
nāgas &, used in creation I 348
origin of II 59, 490-2, 500-1, 571; II 59
rākshasas identified w II 163, 323
real jñānadevas (Gnana-devas in tx) II 90

rebellious or fallen gods II 162, 232
seven classes of I 218-19n; II 89-95, 164,
      318n, 489, 585
Sons of Light (Darkness) II 489
suras become I 412, 418, 422-3; II 57n, 59,
      92-3, 237, 500, 516
tempting demons II 174-5
three classes of I 218-19n; II 91-2
Titans II 525 &n
various names for I 92; II 92, 490, 500
Venus degraded into II 45
war of, (Tārakā-maya) I 418-23; II 45, 63,
      384n, 390, 497-501
Asura Devatās (Skt) II 248
Asuramaya
Atlantean astronomer II 47, 49-51, 67-8, 70,
      326, 436
based figures on Pesh-Hun II 49
Egy & Hindus have zodiac of II 436
giant sorcerer II 70
not derived fr Turamaya II 50
reincarnated in Ptolemy (Weber) II 326
Romaka-pura home of II 67
Tamil calendar based on II 67
used Nārada's records II 49
Asura-Mazdhā (Zor). *See* Ahura-Mazdā
Asura-Medhā. *See* Ahura-Mazdāo
Asura Viśvavedas II 92
Asurendra, a great asura II 487
Aśvamedha (Skt) Sacrifice, & Kapila II 570
Aśvattha (Skt). *See also* Tree of Life, Yggdrasil
Bo-tree of wisdom I 523
caduceus & I 549
forms new trunks, branches II 589
man's emancipation & I 536
symbol of life's illusions II 639
Tree of Life I 406-7; II 97
Tretāgni fires made fr I 523
Aśvins (Skt, Aswins in tx)
pitris, āngirasas, sādhyas II 605
two, of Vedic tridaśa I 71n
Atabulus (Lat), a hot burning wind (Sirocco)
diabolos, devil, Simoo(m)n II 385
Atabutos. *See* Atabulus
Atah. *See* Attāh
Atala (Skt)
Atlantis, White Island & II 322, 403, 408
one of 7 dvīpas (islands) II 402
Śankha-dvīpa called II 405n
Wilford mistaken re II 147, 402-4
At-al-as, divine sun II 361
Atash-[Ātas-]Behrām, Zor sacred fire I 338n
Atavism
law of I 261

man's stature & II 749
Athamas (Thomas) II 135
Athamaz (Tamaz)
    Adam Kadmon same as II 44
Athanor, astral fluid of alchemists I 81
Atharva-Veda
    adbhutam [*Rig-Veda*] II 621
    Agni & Kāmadeva II 578
    Kāma born first II 176
    Kaśyapa sprang fr time II 382n
    three rājamsi [*Rig-Veda*] II 622n
    time II 611-12
    watchers & guardians or lipikas I 104n
Atheism I 7 &n, 266
    anthropomorphism & II 555
    created by religion I 183
    idiotic, based on materialism II 158
    nihilism & II 651
    Secret Doctrine teaches no I 279
Atheist(s) I 644; II 653
    Advaitee occultists not I 6
    ancient, believed in gods I 611
    believers in karma not II 305
    Svabhāvikas called I 3
Athena, Athēnē (Gk). *See also* Pallas
    Apollo &, change into birds II 771
    Gladstone on II 770
    Prometheus &, create new race II 519
Athenaeum, The I 494; II 314, 647n
Athenaeus, *Deipnosophists*
    on Satan's name II 31n
Athenian(s)
    sacrifice to Boreas, etc I 467
    Swanwick re Zeus & II 411-12n
    Unknown God of I 327
Athens
    fossil monkeys found near II 723n
    Prometheus Bound & II 413
    submerged in ancient times II 270n
Athivahikas I 132. *See* Adhivāhikas
Athotis (Egy)
    built palace of Memphis II 334
Athtor I 346. *See* Hathor
Atizoë (Pers stone), magi consulted II 346
Atlantean(s) or 4th Race. *See also* Atlantis,
    Cainite, Daitya, Giants, Root-Race–
    4th, Ruta
    Andaman Islanders, Australians, Tasma-
        nians fr Lemuro- II 195-6, 721
    anthropoids in, expl II 185, 193, 201n, 286,
        679, 689
    apex of physical development I 609; II 319
    Aryan Asiatics saw last of II 433
    Aryan wars confused w, wars II 776

astronomical records kept by II 353
Asuramaya an II 47, 50, 67-8, 70
    bred w descendants of mindless II 286
    built great images II 331
    Cainites, sons of Ham II 146
    called the Great Dragons II 756
    cities of II 20-1
    civilization of, & Egy II 426, 429-31
    civilized & savage II 723
    colors of II 178, 227, 249, 433n
    completely human species II 227n, 266,
        715n
    continent in Eocene, Miocene II 693
    Cro-Magnon, Guanches, Basques, &
        II 678n, 740, 791
    Cyclopes belong to II 293
    Deluge not Chaldean or biblical II 4
    destruction of II 147n, 178, 350, 424-8, 494,
        533-4, 693, 742n
    devs (Pers) were II 394
    "divined the coming of floods" II 429
    dragon of *Revelation* &, magic II 356
    Druid priests descendants of II 756
    dwarfs among II 331, 433n
    Earth grosser in mid-, race II 250
    Easter Islands & II 224, 326
    eleven "Buddhas" of II 423n
    endured for millions of years II 263
    ethereal prototypes of II 9
    Europe rising during, peak II 722-3, 740-1
    fell into savagery II 743-4
    forefathers of apes II 201n
    giants II 9, 70, 93-4n, 146, 224, 227n, 232n,
        236, 265, 350, 433 &n, 753 &n, 756, 760
    gibborīm, rākshasas were I 415; II 273-4
    gravitated to South Pole II 274
    hierophants II 530
    highly civilized, intellectual I 189, 191, 192n;
        II 760
    incarnations of lunar devas II 495
    inhabited surviving islands II 326
    initiates taught Cyclopes I 208n
    invasions of Europe II 743-4
    Irish circular stones were II 343-4
    Isis Unveiled ref to II 496
    islanders perished II 395
    Jupiter belongs to, cycle II 270
    karma "bruised the heel" of II 411
    karma of, & 5th race II 302-3
    King of Tyre (*Ezekiel*) & II 492-3
    "land of bliss" of II 356
    language developed in I 189; II 198-200
    last of, mixed w Aryans II 444
    Lemurians & I 190; II 319-20, 333-4

libraries destroyed II 692
magic black & white I 192n; II 273
magic lang of, priests I 464
"mash-mak" force known to I 563
mated w animals II 286-7, 331, 689, 775
mid-, 29th kalpa II 249
Miocene destruction of II 693
moon, sun & I 397
mysteries secret after II 124
Noah was an, (Faber) II 265, 390
no anthropoids in brighter days of II 679
no fresh monads since mid II 303
now viewed as mythical II 761
one-third of, joined 5th race II 350
Paleolithic man was II 740 &n, 790
perished on Ruta & Daitya II 433
Peruvian colony offshoot of II 745
pioneers of 4th race not II 323
pride of II 271, 760
prototypes of Nimrods, Hamites II 272
Purānic accounts of II 140, 146-7 &n, 232n
pyramids, menhirs & II 352
rākshasas & asuras I 415; II 227n, 232n, 276, 323
records on prehistoric skins II 692
religion of II 273-4
rocking stones built by II 343-4, 347
Ruta & Greeks & Romans II 436
Ruta last large island of I 650
sacrificers to god of matter II 273
Sanskrit not spoken by I 23
satyrs among II 775
Senzar of, fr 3rd race I xliii
seven, divisions of Earth II 366
seven sacred islands not II 326
several humanities in II 433n
size of II 331, 760
skeletons may be discovered II 674
sleep never disturbed by dreams II 761
sorcerers, giants, & unholy destroyed I 419; II 93-4n, 350, 495, 636
sorcery of I 397; II 272 &n, 286, 371n, 493, 503, 772
Stone Age man & II 716n, 720-1
submerged in Miocene II 156, 395 &n, 433
superhuman powers II 760, 764
Telchines were Titans II 391
third eye atrophied II 302, 306
Titans, fallen angels, & I 417-19
Titans, Kabiri, & II 265, 390-1
Uranus(os) 1st king of II 762, 765
used magic against Sun II 762
went fr Sahara to Mexico by land II 424
"White Island," 7 kumāras & II 584

writing invented by II 439, 442
zodiacal records II 49
Atlantes (Gk). *See also* Atlanteans, Atlantis
Diodorus on II 762, 765
Herodotus on II 761-2, 771n
Titans &, (Faber) II 360, 765
Titans called II 360
Atlantic II 405, 408
continent possible (Huxley) II 780-1
great, flood II 353
huge Lemurian islands in II 327, 333
islands & New World flora II 322n, 791-2
Milky Ocean or I 419
Atlantic Islands, The. See Benjamin, S.G.W.
Atlantic Ridge(s) II 792-3
confirms horseshoe land bridge II 333
three long II 782
Atlantides (7 daughters of Atlas)
cursed the Sun II 407
historical II 761
Pleiades or II 768
symbols of subraces, 4th Race II 493
Atlantis. *See also* Atlanteans, Atlantes, Axis, Deluge, Root-Race–4th
adept re, before Plato's II 406
Africa & II 263-4, 314, 740, 761
alchemy born in II 763n
ancient writers describe II 767-8
art of II 426
astronomical allegory (Massey) II 353
astronomical evidence of II 407-8
Asuramaya's birthplace II 50, 67-8
Atlas & II 761, 763, 768
Bailly rejected submersion of II 265
broke into 7 pieces (dvīpas) II 405
cause of Deluge of II 349-50, 410, 427, 533-4, 636
Ceylon remnant of II 314
continents & kings before II 765
Cyclopean relics of I 208-9n; II 335-47, 742-60
destroyed by water II 316, 762
destruction of II 222-3, 313-14
divine dynasties of II 370-1, 773
Eocene height of II 710, 717
evidence for II 740, 780-2, 790-3
Ezekiel refers to II 494 &n
Faber re II 144, 264-5
Flood nearly wiped out II 309, 406n
flora evidence for II 322n, 727, 739
fourth continent I 369; II 8, 334, 606n
giants of II 275-6, 753, 777n
Hindu Aryans dwelt in II 406
histories of, destroyed II 763n

holy island black w sin II 371-2
Iranian folklore records II 393-4
Isis Unveiled on II 384
islands & continents of II 67, 220-4, 265, 322-3, 350
Latona-Niobe story & II 771-2 &n
lemming migrations & II 782
Lemuria & II 221, 266, 333
Lyell's "explanation" of II 787-8
Maligasima, "Maurigosima" II 365
man on, submerged (Gould) II 218-19
Mayas coeval w Plato's II 35n
moral depravity & sinking of II 786
mountain peaks of II 763
names for II 323-4n
Neptune divided, among sons II 406n
Noah & II 222, 265
northern & southern parts of II 371n
Northern Hyperborean II 770n
overlapped Aryan race II 433n
Pengelly re II 726-7
Phlegyae & II 144, 265, 365
Phrygian priests describe II 371
pithecoid skull & II 727
Plato's, coeval w Mayas II 34-5n
Plato's, in Hindu dress II 407-8
Plato's island/continent II 8, 141, 250n, 314, 323, 324n, 352, 370-1, 395, 743n, 761 &n, 767-8
postdiluvian (Bailly) II 265-6
Proclus re II 408-9
pyramids fr Plato's II 429
race of magicians II 222
remnants of II 222-3
"Romakapura" last of II 50, 67-8
Ruta, Daitya & I 650-1; II 314n, 433, 740
sacerdotal language of I xliii, 464
Śaka-, Śankha dvīpa, & Śankhāsura were II 322, 407-8 &n
sank end of Miocene II 8n, 10, 156, 314n, 395n, 433 &n, 693, 710, 740, 778
science denies existence of II 314, 429
secrecy re knowledge of II 763-4
seven islands of II 350, 408-9
sinking of, remnants II 124, 141, 250, 313-14, 332, 352, 395, 433 &n
Sons of Light, Darkness in II 772-3
submerged I 439n; II 140-1, 156, 266, 306, 310, 395, 606n, 693, 778, 786
subraces & 7 daughters II 768
survivors of, in Gobi II 371-2
Sweden as Plato's, (Rudbeck) II 402
Theophrastus [Theopompus] re II 371, 760
theory of, factual (Seeman) II 781

Thevetata king-demon of II 222
Vaivasvata & II 265, 310
war betw initiates & sorcerers I 419
White Island, Atala & II 67, 322, 403, 408 &n
Wilford's mistakes re II 402-9
Yudhishthira at sinking of I 369
Zarathustra fr early II 322-3
Atlantis: The Antediluvian World. *See* Donnelly, I.
Atlanto-Aryans
  first settled Egypt II 746
  Greeks, Romans, Egyptians fr II 436
  kings of Egypt II 750-1
  red Adams or II 426
Atlanto-Lemurians. *See also* Lemuro-Atlanteans
  religion of II 272
  sires of later anthropoids II 688n
  took mindless wives II 283
  Veda went forth to II 483
Atlantosaurus immanis II 218
Atlas. *See also* Niobe
  Atlantis named after II 765
  myth of II 762-3, 772
  Orion or, supports world II 277, 763, 791
  Pleiades daughters of II 618, 768
  symbol of 4th race II 493-4
Atlas, Mt
  Atlantes gave name to II 371, 761
  fables of II 493-4
  fourth race Mt Meru II 493
  island in Lemurian times II 264, 763 &n
  not Meru II 401n, 404, 493-4
  Sun set at foot of II 407
  where "the gods were born" II 765
  Wilford mistaken on II 401n, 402n, 404
Ātma(n) (Skt). *See also* Kshetrajña
  alone remains I 570-1n
  anātman & I 59n
  assumes illusive body I 570
  Avalokiteśvara & I 110 &n, 130n, 471
  beyond Īśvara I 573-4
  breath of life I 226n, 291
  buddhi & I xix, 119, 157, 177, 179, 193, 245, 334, 570; II 231n, 580
  central & polar suns & II 241
  Christos of Gnostics I 132n
  connection betw manas & II 579
  diagram I 157, 242; II 593, 596, 632
  highest, not spirit I 573
  neshāmāh & I 242-5
  no body or shape I 245
  not in the Tiaou I 227

not of this plane I 244
one w Paramātman I 265
passes into Non-being I 193
Pūrvaja, protologos, or II 108
ray of the One I 181, 222
relation to human ego II 79, 110
seventh (or 4th) principle I 153n, 158;
  II 403
spirit or I 153 &n, 213, 242, 571
synthesis of the 6 principles I 334
thread soul (Vedānta) I 610n
universal spirit in man I 571; II 596
Unmanifested Logos (cosmic) II 596
Ātma-bhū (Skt), kāma is II 176, 578
Ātma-buddhi (Skt)
  aupapāduka (anupadaka in tx) & I 52
  blind without manas I 242n; II 123n
  dhyāni has to be I 193
  first & 2nd races & II 254n
  guru or instructor II 113
  human monad I 178-9
  manas absorbed by I 220, 237, 243-5
  manas follows, to devachan I 334
  manas hangs fr I 238
  Parabrahman-mūlaprakriti I 68-9n
  sattva I 68-9n
  spirit-soul I 213, 216
  Uraeus of flame I 227
Ātma-buddhi-manas (Skt)
  become one II 57 &n
  eternal I 227, 570
  spirit, soul, intelligence I 18
  symbolized in *Zohar* I 339
  third order of celestial beings I 218
  three-tongued flame I 237 &n
  triple crocodile (Egy) I 220
Ātmamātra, Ātmamātrāsu (Skt)
  elements of self I 334
Ātmanah or Self I 333
Ātma-vidyā (Skt) self-knowledge
  called Rohanee by Sufis I 199
  key to 3 other vidyās I 168-9
Atmosphere
  alters matter passing thru I 142
  changes in I 554-5, 633-4; II 53, 159-60
  in early periods II 159-60
  "Father of man" impervious to II 160
  laboratory in our I 583, 625
  lungs, mouths of every globe I 144
  maruts, lower ākāśa & II 615
  of Mercury, Venus, Mars II 707
  mighty ones penetrate our I 434
  planetary, & fate of atoms I 143
  unknown substances in I 595-6

Atmu (Egy), atma or II 632
Atom(s). *See also* Aṇu, Elements, Jīva, Life-
  Atoms
  Absolute in every I 58-9; II 588
  absolutely spiritual I 543
  anu (Skt) or, is Boundless I 148, 357
  apperceptive monads inform I 632
  birth of I 453-5, 545
  born each manvantara I 545
  centers of force I 507, 630
  change in atmosphere I 142
  chemical periodicity of II 627-8
  combine differently on each planet I 142-3
  Crookes on I 546-54, 582
  Democritus, Leucippus re I 2, 64, 117, 343
  divisibility of I 519-20
  drawn together by karma II 672
  electricity & I 111n
  elementary germs I 139
  eleven-year cycle of I 290
  every, a life I 76, 248-9, 258, 454
  every, life- & death-giving I 261
  evol journey of I 183, 268, 522, 620
  fill immensity of space I 633
  Fohat hardens I 85
  force not in, but betw (Hirn) I 511
  force resides in I 511-12
  germ exists in center of every I 57
  "gods" in shape of I 568
  gods, monads & I 610-34
  heat internal, external in I 84
  inanimate, self-guiding I 569
  inseparable fr purusha I 582
  instinct w desire for life (Tyndall) I 249
  intelligent "noumenoi" of I 553
  Leibniz on I 628-31
  life-, & sleeping- II 672
  mathematical point (Mertz) I 628-9
  matter-moving nous in I 51
  metaphysical object I 485, 513
  metempsychosis of I 568n
  mineral monad & I 177
  monads, universes I 21, 107; II 672n
  mystery of, (Father Felix) I 670
  nature never leaves, unused II 170
  no, is ever created I 582
  not eternal I 545, 552
  not inorganic I 454
  not uniform I 512-13 &n
  not yet individualized I 178
  occult order of I 218n
  omniscience thrills in every I 277
  perpetual exchange of I 142
  primordial I 148, 455

progressive development of I 43
sciences differ re I 482-3
self-consciousness of every I 107
self-moving, questioned I 670
seven planes of existence I 150
smallest of the small [*VP*] II 46-7
soul, genius, angel I 567, 569
"-souls" of, (Haeckel) II 670
sound a disturbance of, (Keely) I 565
spirits of, elementals I 221, 567-9
vacuum or void & I 343
vibration, motion of I 2, 455, 633
volume unalterable I 511
vortical, (Thomson) I 117, 579
whirling souls I 568 &n
will rebecome the All I 268
worlds fr primordial II 731
Wundt on I 513
Atomic
  theory & materialism I 518
  theory borrowed fr ancients I 567-8
  theory of evolution I 625
  vibrations I 455, 562
  vortices I 117, 569
Atomic Weight(s)
  element of negative I 581, 584
  table of, & number seven II 627
Atomists, Greek & Hindu I 569, 579, 613
Atomo-Mechanical Theory I 512-13 &n
Atonement
  Christ victim of II 497
  effects of dogma of II 484, 505
  goat symbol for II 510
  original sin followed by II 699
Atri (Skt)
  Brahmā's mind-born son II 78
  sons of II 89
Attāh (Heb) thou I 78
At-tee'kah D'at-tee'keen ['Attīqā' D'Attīqīn]
  (Aram), Ancient of Ancients II 83-4
Atteekah Kaddosha ['Attīqā' Qaddīshā']
  (Aram), formed things masc & fem II 528
Attica, people of II 352
Attila I 563
Attock II 417, 418n
Attraction
  Boehme on I 494
  electricity & I 145
  gravity & I 490-1, 500-6, 529-30, 604
  kundalinī-śakti & I 293
  Le Couturier on I 492n, 494
  planetary motion not expl by I 529
  repulsion & I 12n, 102-3, 293, 489, 497, 604
  sexual polarization & I 405

Atwater, Caleb, re Aztecs I 322
Ātyantika Pralaya (Skt) I 371; II 69n, 309n
Atys (Gk), son, father, husband I 396
Atzīlatic World. *See* Aziluth
Aub, Ōb (Heb), serpent in a circle I 364n
Auction II 603. *See* Lucian
Audhumla (Norse) primeval cow
  mother, cosmic soul I 367
  nourisher I 427
Audlang [Andlang] (Norse), 2nd heaven II 100
Audubon, John James, "Birds of the South"
  yellow water lily of, doubted II 440
Augoeidēs (Gk), in final initiation I 573
Augur(s)
  more numerous now II 518
  serpent & II 209
Augustine, St
  angelic virtues of I 123 &n
  called Devil "monkey of God" II 476
  cosmogonical essays of I 441
—— *The City of God*
  Church rejected *Enoch* II 535
  Jesus called a fish II 313n
  on Venus-Earth relation II 32
—— *Sermon 160th*
  cross & circumcision II 589
Aum, Om (Skt)
  fourth world (race) lost II 408
  pranava or I 432n
Aupapāduka (Skt, Anupadaka in tx) parentless
  buddhas of compassion are all I 109
  chhāyā-loka 1st garment of I 119
  dhyāni-buddhas are I 52, 571
  Great Wheel was I 27, 47
  Kāla-chakra on I 52n
  mūlaprakriti is I 62
  point in circle I 91
  Space the eternal I 11
Aur, Aour [Ōr] (Heb) light
  En Soph [Ain-sōph] not I 354
  first primeval light I 76 &n
Aura
  dhyāni-chohans in world's II 233n
  disease &, (Paracelsus) I 538
  first race reproduction & II 117
  Kabbala re spirits in Earth's I 234n
  life copies impressions in I 261
  sound, color & I 514n
Aurgelmir. *See* Örgelmir
Auric Envelope, astral fossils in II 684
Aurṇavābha Āchārya (Vedic commentator)
  on Vishnu's 3 strides I 112
Aurora, The II 634. *See* Boehme, J.
Aurora Borealis, Australis

interstellar shoals & I 633-4
radiant matter, light & I 621n
safety valves I 205
sons of Fohat, ākāśa & I 204-5
yellow corn &, (Zuñis) II 629
Aurva (Skt), gave āgneyāstra weapon II 629
Australia II 763
  can produce no new forms II 197
  Europe &, once 1 continent II 333, 781
  formerly much closer to India II 8n
  Gardiner on II 782-3
  Lemurian remnant II 7 & 8n, 314, 324, 328,
    333, 789
  one of oldest lands II 197
"Australia and Europe formerly one Conti-
    nent." *See* Seeman, B.
Australian(s) (aborigines) II 168, 318
  archaic flora & fauna of II 196
  Atlantean offshoots II 721
  brain measurement of II 193n, 661, 682n
  descend fr late Lemurians II 195-7, 199n,
    328, 779
  dying out II 162, 195-6, 332, 779-80
  last of higher race (Gerland) II 779
  lowest race (Broca) II 195-6 &n, 725
  not descended fr anthropoids II 193
  Paleolithic hatchets II 716
  "They were not ready" II 162
  Thomas on II 729
Australoids
  fr anthropoids (Huxley) II 315n
Austria
  negroid skulls found in II 739
  old skulls in, of very tall men II 278
Auszüge aus dem Buche Sohar. See Biesenthal
Authority
  pretended, & theosophical books I xix
  scientific II 316n
Auto-generation, of the gods I 398
Automata, of Leibniz & Aristotle I 632n
Autumn, & figure six II 583
Auvergnat Man, cranial capacity of II 168n
Avabodha (Skt), knowledge II 528
Avalokiteśvara (Skt) I 471-2. *See also* Bodhisat-
    tva, Chenresi, Padmapāni
  Ādi-buddha manifests as I 110
  becomes manifest to us I xix
  incarnates in Dalai & Tashi Lamas II 178
  Kwan-shi-yin, Kwan-yin I 72, 136, 470-1
  Kwan-yin female aspect of I 72
  Logos(oi) I 71-2 &n, 74n, 108, 130n, 136,
    471; II 178, 637
  manifests periodically II 178
  mind-born sons of I 213

other names for I 110, 428; II 178-9
seven dhyāni-buddhas & I 108
seventh principle of man, cosmos I 74n
unborn, eternal energy center I 130n
Avara (Skt), inferior II 163, 183
Avasthā(s) (Skt), divine, or Trinity I 18-19
Avat (Pers), upper Earth globes II 759
Avatāra(s) (Skt). *See also* Avalokiteśvara, Kalki,
    Maitreya, Śankarāchārya
  Boar or Varāha I 368-9 &n; II 53, 321
  Buddha, of Vishnu II 578
  coming, or tenth II 420
  divine-human, of India I 349
  divine impersonality of II 478
  every, a fallen god II 483-4
  Hegel accepted periodical I 52n
  Hindu, & unseen principle II 555-6
  immaculate conception & I 399
  Kalki I 87, 268, 378; II 416n, 420
  Krishna as II 48, 225n, 359, 550
  Kūrma, of Vishnu II 549
  Kwan-shi-yin last of I 470
  Matsya first, of Vishnu I 263-4, 369, 385;
    II 69n, 139, 307, 578
  minor, & Buddhas of Confession
    II 423 &n
  Nara-Simha an II 225n
  spiritual Sun sends forth I 638
  successive, of first triad I 668
  Tsong Kha-pa, of Amitābha I 108n
  of Vishnu I 18, 653; II 33, 408n
Avayakta. *See* Avyakta
Aveling, Ed. B., transl Haeckel II 87n, 164n
Aves (Lat) birds II 656
Āveśa. *See* Amilakha
Avesta. See Zend Avesta
Avicebron. *See* Ibn Gebirol
Avidyā (Skt) ignorance I 7
Avikāra (Skt) immutability II 46
Avogadro, Count Amedeo
  atoms not uniform I 512 &n
  produced revolution in chemistry I 622
Avyakta (Skt) unmanifest I 521-2; II 46-7
Avyaktānugraheṇa (unmanifest-creation)
    Parabrahman-mūlaprakriti I 521-2
Avyaya (Skt) imperishable
  eternal life, Vishnu I 370; II 69n
  Purusha-pradhāna & I 582
  undecaying I 420
Awasthan [Arvasthān] (Skt), Arabia II 406
Axieros, Aschieros (Gk)
  Demeter is, in female aspect II 362
  derivation (Mackey) II 362n
  one of four Kabiri II 362

Sanat-Kumāra II 106
Axiokersa, Achiosersa
  derivation (Mackey) II 362n
  Persephone II 362
  Sananda II 106
Axiokersos, Achiochersus
  Pluto, Hades II 362
  Sanaka II 106
Axis, Axes. *See also* Cataclysm
  angle of, & seasons II 356
  Apollo-Diana, Sun-Moon & II 771
  changes of I 369; II 52, 292, 314, 324-5, 771
  changes of, in *Enoch* II 145, 533-4, 726
  changes of, in *Vendidad* II 356
  disturbances sank 2nd continent I 369
  inclination of Venus's II 32
  karmic disturbances of II 274, 329-30
  neutral I 148
  science & violent changes of II 314, 726
  shifting, & deluge II 145, 314, 324-5, 360, 533-4, 771
  zodiac & changes in II 431
Ayana (Skt)
  Nārāyana fr Nārā-ayana II 591n
  spirit moving over waters I 344
Ayanam (Skt) half-year
  three roodoo [ṛitu] make a II 620
Ayin (Heb) nothing I 350
  negative, female letter I 114n

Azā (Heb), to illuminate II 114
Azāēl, Uzza &, twitted God II 491
Azareksh (Zor), fire temple of II 6n
Azāzēl, Azaziel, Azazyel (Heb)
  Hebrew Prometheus II 376
  host of, taught 4th race II 376
  sacred goat in Bible I 441n; II 389n
  scapegoat of Israel II 387, 389n, 409
  serpent prototype of II 387
  wrongly associated w Satan II 376
Azburj. *See* Asburj
Azhi-Dahāka (Zend)
  war betw, & Thraētaona II 390
Aziluth, Atzilatic World [Atsīlūth] (Heb)
  first kabbalistic world II 111, 604
Azoic Age
  beginning of life (science) II 711
  hostile environment of II 159-60
  life in I 258
Azores
  remnant of Atlantis II 222-3, 791
  undersea elevation & II 792-3
Aztalan, country of Aztecs I 322
Aztec(s)
  calendar & pyramids I 322
  divine bird of II 141
  once a mighty race II 445
Azupiran(u). *See* Sippara
Azure seats II 424-5

B

Ba (Egy). *See also* Bai
  soul of breath, prāna II 632
Baal (Canaanite) Lord
  Bel, Śiva, Saturn & I 459
  Bible on I 649
  identical w Sun-Jehovah I 397n
  leaping prophets of II 460
  Mysteries (Sod) of II 212
  other names for I 353; II 540
  priests of, jumped over fires II 212n
  worship of, Hebrews hated II 471
Baal-Adonis, became Adonai I 463
Babba Battra [Bābā' Bathrā'] (Heb)
  on Samāel & angel of death II 388
Babbage, Dr Charles
—— [*Ninth Bridgewater Treatise*]
  "each particle a register" I 104, 124
Babel, Tower of
  builders of, & Atlanteans II 272, 375, 762
  legend of, before Moses II 3n
Babian, seven vases in temple near II 603
Baboon. *See also* Ape
  future human evolution & II 263
  Haeckel & catarrhine II 663n
  in Pliocene II 676
Babylon
  arrowhead inscriptions of II 793
  Aryan influence on mythology of II 130
  divinities of, & Delphi II 379
  history of, lost I xxvi
  Huschenk built II 396-7
  Moses story fr I 319-20
  "mother of harlots" II 748
  Nabatheans founded II 453
  planetary temple of II 456
  seat of Brahman learning I xxxi
  vast literature of, saved I xxxiv
Babylonia(n, ns)
  antiquity of II 690-3
  Aryan (Vedic) influence in I xxxi; II 130, 203, 566
  astrological magic of II 566
  captivity II 202, 473, 618
  Chaldees settled in II 748
  creation legends II 2, 5
  Dag-On Oannes, man-fish I 653; II 190

Ea taught writing to II 226
flying dragons of II 205-6, 206n
Gan-dunia, Ganduniyas, Gan-Aeden II 42n, 202
gods, names of II 5
gods of, & Stonehenge II 379
Hebrew initiates got wisdom fr I 352
magic in, Talmud I xliiin
Nebo, Budha, Mercury II 456, 477
Nimrod governor of II 453
Nipoor, Eridu in II 139n
Pharisees' tenets fr II 61
religion purposely confused II 691
Sargon & Moses I 319
Saros a god of I 114
serpent II 26n
seven Adams in, tablets II 4
Sin was Moon-god of I 388
sons of serpent, dragon in II 379-80
stone of, statues fr Sinai II 692
War in Heaven II 104, 383-4
were silent on the One I 425
wisdom fr India II 566
wisdom-god in the Sea of Space II 477
Xisuthrus is, Noah II 222, 309
Zu strips creative organ II 283-4n
Babylonian Legend of Creation. See Smith, G., *Chaldean Account* . . .
Bacchante, serpent in hair of II 209
Bacchic Religious Dance II 460-1
Bacchus (Gk). *See also* Dionysos
  called Fish, Savior II 313
  celestial Priapus born of II 458
  "God" of Slavonians fr I 347
  Hebrews hated worship of II 471
  lunar Jehovah I 335
  man-savior or solar- II 420
  Mysteries of II 212
  Semele, Jupiter & I 400; II 362
  son, father, husband I 396
  Sun, Adonāi, Kadush & I 463
  Sun, Jupiter, Mithras & II 419
  Venus & II 458
Bacon, Francis I 584; II 439
—— *Advancement of Learning*
  certainties & doubts II 443

curiosity in man I 165
—— *Essays*, "Of Truth"
creations of God I 481
Bacon, Roger I 611
belonged by right to the Brotherhood
I 581-2n
protyle of I 553, 582
—— *De arte chymiae* . . .
transmutation of elements I 581
Bacteria
men, animals swarming w I 260-1, 608
reproduce by spores II 167
some microbes &, need no air I 249n
visitors, disease &, (science) I 225n
Badāonī, Abdul Qādir
—— *Muntakhab ut-tawārīkh*
Akbar's interest in sects I xxiv &n
Bādhas (Skt) afflictions, 28 types of II 162
Baer, Karl Ernst von II 649n
Baetyl, Baetylos. *See also* Bethel
animated stones II 342-6
Catholics misjudge II 85
lithoi, magic stones II 346n
Baffin Bay, part of 2nd cont II 401-2
Bagavadam. See Bhāgavata-Purāṇa
Bagh-bog, Bacchus of Slavonians I 347
Bahāk-Zivo [Ziwa] (Gnos)
more philosophical than Adam II 150
ordered to create & fails I 194-5
Bai [Egy Ba?]. *See also* Ba
corr to neschāmāh (Lambert) II 633
Baibhār, Mt., Buddhist initiations at I xx
Bailly, Jean Sylvain
believed Hesiod factual II 777
believed many worlds inhabited II 706
did not know Secret Doctrine II 742 &n
on fables about Atlantis II 772
fair to Hindu astronomy I 667-8
Gk, Egy, Pers legends comp II 393-4
—— *Histoire de l'astronomie ancienne*
antiquity of zodiac I 648-9
error re biblical patriarchs I 648
Herodotus on ecliptic, equator II 534
on Sun worship orig in far north II 769n
—— *Lettres sur l'Atlantide* . . .
believed in prehistoric civ II 265-6, 742-3
disproved Rudbeck's Atlantis II 402
on 9,000 years of Egy priests II 765n
Pers legend re Huschenk II 397-9 &nn
rejected submersion of Atlantis II 265
—— *Traité de l'astronomie* . . .
antiquity of Hindu astronomy I 658-67
astronomy not carried to India I 667n
divine dynasties II 368, 371

Kioo-tche on measures of time II 621
Libra [Aquarius in Bailly] & 3102 BC
I 661, 663
proved Hindu figures II 435
sixty-day cycle among ancients II 620-1
Bain, Prof Alexander
more dangerous than Büchner I 528n
school of II 156n
—— *Logic*
ether hypothesis I 325-6
fire-lighting a mystery I 121
sees Monism as "guarded materialism"
I 124-5n
space & time as generalizations I 251n
Baissac, Jules, *Satan ou le Diable*
Satan made a real power II 509
Satan or centrifugal energy II 245
Bait-Oxly [Bait-Oualy] (Egy)
every type of cross in tomb of II 559
Bakewell, F. C., *Electric Science* . . .
on Faraday & matter I 510
Bakhan-Alenré (Egy), cross & adoration of,
[HPB, *Lucifer*] II 559
Balaam, & the "birds" II 409
Balarāma (Skt) Krishna's elder brother
divides embryo (*Rāmāyana*) II 613 &n
Bal-ilu or Mārttānda, our sun I 100
Ball [Bull in tx], Sir R. S., re Moon II 64n
Balthazar (Heb), one of three Magi I 654n
Baltic (Sea)
amber found in II 770n
level of II 751
Baltistān II 204, 416n
Balzac, H. de, [*Séraphīta*] on deity & number
I 66-7
Bamboo Books II 302
Bamian [Bāmiyān, Bāmīān]
Central Asian town II 338
Bamian Statues II 336-40
record buddhas of former cycles II 224
Bandha (Skt) bondage
moksha is freedom fr I 132
Banquet or *Symposium. See* Plato
Banyan. *See also* Wondrous Being
ever-living human- I 207-12
Tree of Life, Knowledge II 215
Baōth (Heb), chaos or I 197n
Baphomet (Heb)
astral light or, (Lévi) I 253 &n
goat-headed Satan II 389n
Baptism
Baptists' "Waters of Grace" I 458n
connected w messiah, water I 385
Council of Trent & II 209

w water, Holy Ghost, & fire II 566
Baptismal Font
Great Pyramid sarcophagus & I 317n
Baptist, John the. *See* John the Baptist
Bārā (Heb), brought forth II 134
Barahiel, Rabbi
THAT was before all numbers I 618
Barbaradeśa (Skt) II 406
Barbaras (Skt), in Purānas II 406
Barbarian(s)
Mediterranean II 753n
mlechchhas I 377; II 48n
overpowered learned cultures II 430, 742
&n
Barbary (N Africa), joined to Spain II 751
Barbelo (Gnos)
one of three "invisible" gods II 570 &n
Baresma (Zend)
twig fr Ormazd's tree II 385, 517
Bar-Hebraeus [Abu'l-Faraj]
said Enoch invented writing II 529
Barhishad(s) (Skt) II 88, 102.
See also Ancestors, Progenitors
agnishvāttas & II 77-9, 89
became first race II 94-5
devoid of mahat-mic element II 79
identified w the months II 89n
project astral models II 78-9, 89, 94-5
Barkayal, taught astrology (*Enoch*) II 376
Barnabas, called Zeus II 481
Barrows (Nagpur mounds) II 346n
Barth, Auguste, *The Religions of India*
poetry of *Rig-Veda* II 450-1
Barth & Richardson, [*Le Correspondant*]
trilithic stones in Sahara II 346n
Barthélemy Saint-Hilaire
on cradle of humanity II 204
Bartlett, A. D., *Land and Water*
on septenates in nature II 595
Bashan, tall race of II 755-6
Basht or Pasht. *See* Bast
Basilea (Gk)
"royal" island in far north II 773
Basilides, Basilidian(s). *See also* Gnostic
Abraxax supreme God I 350
serpent on, stones I 472; II 210
Basle, old map of America at II 327
Basnage de Beauval, J. (Bosuage in tx)
—— [*Histoire des Juifs*]
Isis-Osiris taught mankind II 366
Basques
American aborigines linked w II 792
Cro-Magnon, Guanches & II 740-1, 790n
language of, compared II 790

Basra, Nabatheans fr II 455
Bast (Egy)
goddess w cat's head I 305; II 552n
Bastian, H. Charlton
—— *The Beginnings of Life*
Carpenter q re lower forms II 257
on dolmen builders II 753
knowledge of extinct forms II 260
man a modified quadrumane II 258
Bāth-Kōl [Bath-Qōl] (Heb)
Kwan-yin, Verbum, etc I 137
Vāch in Hinduism I 431n; II 107
Bathybius Haeckelii I 542; II 164n, 190, 650,
656, 670 &n, 674
Batoo [Baīti, Batu] (Egy)
Noum [Khnūm] & Pandora story II 270n
Battle(s). *See* War in Heaven, Wars
Bat-winged Men II 634
Batylos [Baetylos]. *See* Baetyl
Baudry, M. F., "Les Mythes du feu . . ."
fire by friction (Hindu) II 524
re Prometheus II 526
Baumgärtner, Karl H.
—— *Anfänge zu einer physiologischen . . .*
humanity not fr single pair II 718
Beale, Prof Lionel Smith
favored vital principle I 634
on mystery of life I 540
Bear. *See also* Great Bear, Ursa Minor
Thot-Sabaoth is the II 115n
Typhon the Great II 547, 549
Beast(s). *See also* Animals
apocalyptic 666 of the great I 655n
artificially made II 427n
have no conscious ego-soul II 196n
have no devachan II 196n
w/o mind no dif betw man & II 513
mystery of woman &, (*Rev*) II 748
Beauce, Lake, Miocene man & II 749 &n
Beaumetz, Prof D., sarcode of II 153n
Beaver, instinct of II 120
Become, Becoming I 282
idea of, & the scarab I 365; II 552
nine the number of II 622
same as "to be born" in Gk I 281n
universe an eternal, (Hegel) II 449n
Bede, the Venerable I 441; II 395n
Bedouins
Sabean, invoke host of heaven II 514n
Bee(s)
Haeckel traces civilization to II 650
reproduction among II 133, 659
Beelzebub, Beelzebul [Baal-zebūb] (Heb)
monarch of hell II 389n

Beer, well of I 364n
Beethoven Sonata
  could not play itself II 348
Beetles, Moses permitted eating of I 80n
Beginnings of Life, The. See Bastian H.
Beglor [Beglar]
  discovered Fa-hien's cave I xx &n
Behemoth (Heb)
  Job & theology on II 486 &n
Behring Straits. *See* Bering Straits
Being
  Absolute I 16, 51, 54n, 193, 268
  Absolute Divine Essence is no I 629
  all-powerful, (Newton) I 498
  Be-ness rather than I 14
  conditioned I 15
  conscious & unconscious I 53-4
  endless cycle of, in eternity I 221
  ladder of II 239
  neutral center of II 731
  Non-being & I 16, 39, 45, 47, 54, 88, 193, 344
  pure, not understood I xx, 496n
  -Purusha born fr not-being I 344
  subject- & object-side of II 24
  Wondrous, or highest hierarchy I 207
Beings
  all, pass thru human stage I 275; II 322
  all, subject to karma I 221-2, 456n
  invisible I 89, 478, 608
  Kant on immaterial I 133n
  millions of, in us, we in them I 604-5
  other intellectual, in solar system I 133, 164
  on other worlds differ fr us II 700
  perceptive & apperceptive I 629
  spiritual, incarnated in man I 233
  universe real to, in it I 274
Beiträge zur Deszendenzlehre. See Weismann, A.
Beiträge zur Kenntniss. See Seyffarth, G.
Bel [or Marduk] (Bab) I xxvii, 421, 463
  Baal, Śiva, Saturn & I 459
  building of Earth & II 23
  Chaldean creator I 357; II 139nn, 144
  dragon &, among Ophites II 379
  equated w other gods II 379
  Gauls used, for Sun II 540
  Jupiter or, rules 6th world (Syr) I 435
  -Merodach &, -Belitanus II 210n
  Moon eldest son of II 386
  Nebo son of, -Merodach II 211
  Noah &, preceded Adam Kadmon II 144
  not infinite II 384n
  primeval II 139n
  -Shemesh, Moon called I 397

  slays dragon Tiamat II 477, 503
  Sun or, overpower messengers II 62
  umsimi on the seat of II 283-4n
  way to Bible thru, & Homer II 383
Bela (Heb), son of Beor II 706
Belgamer. *See* Bergelmir
Belgium, early man in II 744
Belita (Chald), Eve, Mary II 463
Bello Judaico. See Josephus, *History . . .*
Bel Merodach, Bel-Belitanus
  patron of Chaldean initiates II 210n, 211
Bel-Shemesh (Heb), Lord of the Sun
  name of Moon among Semites I 397 &n
Belt, Thomas
  axial changes & glaciations II 695, 726
Belus (Chald). *See also* Bel
  Berosus priest of I xxvi
  formed heaven & Earth II 54
  -Nimrod, de Rougemont on II 454
Be-ness. *See also* Being
  Ain or Non-being II 626
  "All," & All-Being I 55
  fr, into being is genesis II 24n
  is "non-Being" (Hegel) I 193; II 449n
  not a Being I 59
  the One I 7, 14, 143n
  Sat or I 119, 143n, 289, 556; II 310
Benfey, Theodore
  on Asura- & Ahura-Mazdhā II 92
Bengal
  mighty men of, dwarfed II 411n
  Sagara or Bay of II 572
  Tāntrikas of, & Moon I 156
Beni-Elohim. *See* Bnēi Elohīm
Beni Shamash. *See* Bnēi-Shamash
Ben-Issrael. *See* Bnēi-Iśrāēl
Benjamin (son of Jacob), & Cancer I 651
Benjamin, S. G. W., *The Atlantic Islands . . .*
  link betw Canary Isles & Amer II 790-1
Ben-Manesseh. *See* Bnēi-Menashsheh
Benoo. *See* Benu
Bentley, John
  chronology of II 76n
  ignorant of Indian zodiac II 431
  not fair to Hindu knowledge I 370, 667
  Purānic astronomy a science II 253
  —— *Historical View of Hindu Astronomy*
  dates Great War 575 BC I 369n
  hidden scientific knowledge II 499-500n
  precession of equinoxes II 550
  War in Heaven II 63, 76, 499-500 &n
Bentley, R., Newton's Third Letter to I 479, 490-1, 494
Benu (Egy) phoenix I 312

Beor, Bela son of II 706
Berē'shīth, B'rāisheeth (Heb)
  "in the beginning" I 352; Appendix
  first emanation of Logos I 375
  Gen 1:1, kab meaning of I 374, 443-4
Berēshīth Rabbah
  several creations in II 53-4, 704 &n
Bergelmir (Norse) II 774
Bergerac, Cyrano de II 702
Bering Straits
  horseshoe-like continent & II 326, 329
Berkeley, George, *A Treatise Concerning . . .*
  Human Knowledge
  on motion I 3n
Bernard, Claude
  life a process of fermentation I 249n
Bernard, St, *Sermon*
  "Sun-Christ lives in thee . . ." I 401
Bernardin de St Pierre, J. H.
  many worlds inhabited II 706
Bernouilli, Jacques II 269
  many inhabited worlds II 706
  Newton's ideas revolted I 491
Berosus, Berossus I xxvii
  account of primeval creation I 343, 345;
    II 269
  astronomical records of I xxvi, 655n
  Belus formed Earth, heavens II 54
  Chaldea had 3 keys in days of I 311
  disfigured by Eusebius I xxvi; II 53
  Ea same as Oannes of II 226
  Ilus of, or ether I 339
  obtained information fr Ea II 115
  predicted cataclysms by zodiac I 649-50
  de Rougemont on II 454
  taught evolution II 190
  ten generations of kings II 394
  on Thallath I 394; II 61, 65n, 135
  on 2-, 4-faced creatures II 504
  watery abyss of II 53, 477, 715n
—— *Antiquitates* [by "pseudo" Berosus]
  Titea-Aretia worship II 143-4
Berthollet, C. L., Comte, men of Canary
  Islands & America II 790-1
Bertrand, Abbé François-Marie
—— *Dictionnaire* [*universel historique* . . .]
  on bétyles [baetyls] II 342
Bes (Egy), stands on lotus I 385
Bestiality, & sterility II 192, 195, 689, 730
Bestla (Norse)
  Odin, Willi, & We born fr I 427
Bethel(s) [Bēīth-Ēl] (Heb). *See also* Baetyl
  oil-anointed phalli II 473
Bethlehem, Star of II 619

Bétyles (Fr). *See* Baetyl
"Be-with-us," Great Day I 129, 130-1, 134n,
  265
Bhagavad-Gītā
  all men may know Vasudeva II 48n
  Anugītā on speech I 94
  Brahm enthroned on lotus I 379
  explains *Mahābhārata* II 139
  four manus & 7 rishis II 140 &n, 318n
  Īśvara in II 114
  Kshetrajña in II 638
  lower, higher elements in I 535-6
  Pistis Sophia in light of II 569
  root or sattva is buddhi I 68n
  on Tree of Life, aśvattha I 406
  two paths at death explained I 86
  Wilson saw Buddhism in I 419n
Bhagavad Gītā Lectures. *See* Row, T. S.
Bhagavān (Skt) II 406
Bhagavat, Bhagavan (Skt) II 406
  the Eternal I 345
  hurled Brahmā to Earth (Fall) II 483
  incarnates II 48
Bhāgavata-Purāṇa
  Arjuna married Ulūpī in II 214 &n
  Chākshusha Manu of 6th period II 615n
  cross & circle in II 549-50
  curse of Vaśishtha II 247
  Hamsa caste I 79
  Kapila author of Sānkhya philos II 572
  Kapila did not slay 60,000 II 571
  mankind produced fr Vāch II 418n
  Moryas will reign over India I 378n
  nitya pralaya I 371
  opening of kali-yuga II 550
  Pañchaśikha Kumāra I 236
  rākshasas, origin of II 165n
  Vaiśvānara son of Danu II 381 &n
  vyakta in I 10n
Bhangulpore [Bhagalpur]
  round tower of II 85
Bharata, Bharateans (Skt)
  India & II 321, 369, 406n
  war w rākshasas II 776
Bhārata-Varsha (Skt) India
  divided into 9 portions II 321
  division of Jambu-dvīpa II 322, 369, 403n
  four yugas occur in II 322
  Nāga-dvīpa part of II 132, 182, 501n
  Peris counterparts of children of II 394
  Śankha-dvīpa & II 405, 408
Bhārgavas (Skt), race of II 32n
Bhāshyāchārya, Pandit N., FTS
—— *Catechism of Viśishtādvaita* . . .

evolution of matter I 522
pathway of freed soul I 132
Bhāshyas of Śankarāchārya
  on Upanishads kept secret I 271-2
Bhāskara (Skt), light-maker I 98, 103
Bhāskara Āchārya, interprets 7 dvīpas II 321
Bhautya (Skt), a manu II 309
Bhāva (Skt) I 61, 256
Bhavishya Purāṇa
  story of Sāmba & Magas in II 323
Bhons [Böns] (Tib) II 586
Bhoots. *See* Bhūtas
Bhoutya. *See* Bhautya
Bhrāntidarśana[taḥ] (Skt)
  arises in lower 5th principle I 19
  material universe as II 108
Bhṛigu (Skt)
  seven, 14 manus II 308
  Srī daughter of II 76n
  Śukra (Venus) is son of II 30, 32n
  in *Vāyu Purāṇa* I 436
Bhujam (Skt), side (of triangle) II 576
Bhūmi (Skt) Earth
  appears w 6 sisters I 250 &n; II 616
  fourth principle of, 4th round I 260
  prithivī or I 237
  sons of, & devas I 605-6
  those who watch over I 213
Bhuraṇyu (Skt)
  Phoroneus, Agni (Decharme) II 520
Bhūr-loka (Skt)
  south of equator (sidereal position) II 321
Bhūta(s) (Skt)
  defined II 102n
  evolved fr dhyānis I 183
  first & 2nd races were I 183; II 108
  flesh eaters II 163
  illusion (Bhoots in tx) I 295
  primitive man a II 91, 102 &n, 105, 108
  race w no form or mind II 91
  second or, creation I 446, 452
Bhūtādi (Skt)
  devours sound, ether I 372-3
  elements sprang fr I 452; II 108
  precedes Bhūtasarga Creation I 452
Bhūtasarga Creation (Skt)
  second or elemental I 446, 452-3
Bhūtātman (Skt), life soul II 108
Bhūteśa (Skt), Vishnu lord of elements I 452n
Bhuva[r]-loka (Skt)
  middle region at mahā-pralaya I 371
  north of equator (sidereal position) II 321
Bible (Judeo-Christian) I 212, 214. *See also*
  individual books of the Bible

allegories deal w 5th race II 252
angel & human monad in I 574n
angels few in I 632n; II 61
anthropomorphic, phallic I 382; II 472-3,
  544-5, 657-8
archaic doctrine in *Gen* 1-6 & *Job* II 537
astronomy & glyphs of I 320
based on universal traditions II 202
blinds in I 128n; II 473
borrowed fr Chald I xxxi; II 3n, 143 &n, 383
cherubim of I 126-7
chronologists & II 690-2
dead letter of I 305, 316, 318, 323n, 336;
  II 3, 95n
deals briefly w pre-cosmic period II 252
dual light of II 36-7
Eocene man &, (Fabre) II 746-7
Fall, meaning of II 283
first 6 chapters occult I 336
French translation misleading II 537
giants in II 336, 375
history in, not Jewish II 203
incongruities in Mosaic I 420
Jehovah in II 472-3
Jews, Tyrians kin in I 313n
Kabbala key to I 246, 336, 344
de Mirville sought to justify II 342
needs occult interpretation II 377-8, 747
no first man except in II 270
number 7 recurs in II 4, 35
numerical & geometric keys to I 66, 318 &n;
  II 536
pantheism behind II 472-3
plurality of worlds & I 607 &n
Purānas &, compared II 126, 624
queer chronology of I 655-6; II 395 &n
rounds, races, principles in II 747-8
Sabbath, meaning of I 240; II 747
sacred animals in I 92, 441n, 442 &n
serpents in II 206 &n, 209
six days of creation I 21, 446-7
translators knew little Hebrew I 128n
two theories re God of II 472-3
unclean birds & animals of I 355, 442n
veiled, secret, esoteric I 316, 318, 320;
  II 202, 228, 279, 473, 536
war betw black & white magic II 211
written in emblem I 306
zodiac in I 649
Bible de Vence (H. François, Abbé de Vence)
  holy usurpation of elohīm I 441-2n
Bible in India. See Jacolliot
Bibles (of humanity), all treat of Earth chain,
  planets, stars II 703

Biblical
  chronology & Noah, Titans II 390
  chronology of Adam II 71n
  esotericism II 252-3
  genealogies confusing II 42
  names numerically based II 467
Bibliotheca Historica. See Diodorus
Bibliotheca Indica, lokas in II 321
Bibliothèque Orientale. See d'Herbelot, B.
[Biesenthal, Joachim Heinrich]
—— *Auszüge aus dem Buche Sohar . . .*
  "Let there be light" I 215-16n, 356n, 450
Bimater [Bimatris] (Lat), Bacchus II 362
Bīnāh (Heb)
  Chochmah [Hokhmāh] & I 98n, 99n, 239,
    352, 355, 618; II 84, 134n, 528
  Elohīm, Tiamat, Thalatth or I 394
  female consciousness or intellect II 528
  female of sephīrōth I 230
  fem potency & male Jehovah I 99n, 355
  heart, intelligence or I 352
  Hēh letter of I 438n
  Jehovah (Demiurge) I 6n, 230, 392, 394;
    II 134n, 384n
  left side or I 239; II 269n
  Mother, Sea, Mare, Mary I 392
  Mother, understanding II 85
  Sephīrāh, Hokhmāh &, triad I 98n
  third of sephīrōth I 6n, 215n; II 384n
Binary(ies) I 237n, 239; II 592
  Pythagoreans & Gnostics re II 574-5
  symbol of sexes separated I 384
  ternary & I 384; II 575-6
  Yin the II 554
Biogenetic Law, embryo epitome of race
  II 187-9, 257, 659-60, 672
"Biographical & Critical Essay." *See* Waite
Biology
  admits separation of sexes II 184
  denies a vital principle I 603
Biot, Édouard C., Malabar tombs II 347
Bipeds II 183
  man or, before quadrupeds II 163
Bird(s). *See also* Garuḍa, Hawk, Kalahaṅsa,
    Leda, Phoenix, Swans
  black, symbol of primeval wisdom I 443
  created before Adam (*Gen*) II 181
  divination by I 362-3
  divine, in Ash tree II 520
  enemies of reptiles II 254
  First Cause symbolized by I 359
  forms fr 3rd round II 684
  Hansa, of wisdom II 293
  Hebrew symbol for angel, spirit II 292

Karshipta Mazdean, god II 292
  Kārttikeya peacock II 619
  Kaśyapa grandsire of II 181, 253-4
  Mexican symbol of ātman II 36
  oviparous II 166
  preceded mammals I 404
  fr reptiles II 55, 183, 254, 734
  reptiles preceded I 404
  Simorgh II 617-18
  steed of Tahmurath II 397-8
  symbol of aquatic I 80n, 358
  symbol of higher divinities II 771
  that lay golden eggs II 122
  use man's 3rd, 4th round relics II 290
  various sacred I 362-3
  vermilion, of Chinese I 408
  Zoroaster forbade killing I 362
Bird's Nest (*Zohar*) II 292-3
"Birds of the South." *See* Audubon, J.
Birth(s) II 622. *See also* Second Birth
  astral precedes physical II 1
  Egyptian initiation as new II 258-9
  immaculate I 398
  karma of II 161, 303
  Mars lord of II 392
  miraculous II 550
  second, for Osirified dead I 365
Bischof, Karl-Gustav Christoph
  cooling of Earth I 501n; II 694
  duration of coal formation II 695n
  stability of atmosphere II 159
Bisexual. *See also* Androgyne, Hermaph-
    rodite, Root-Races — 2nd & 3rd
  all higher gods are I 72n
  animals, before mammals II 594n
  creative deities are II 125, 130
  early humanity was II 130, 132-5
  Jehovah II 460
  mythological figures II 124, 134-5
  plants & animals II 133
  root-types of II 736
  sexless man became II 2-3, 132-4, 197
Bishop of Ayre. *See* Foix, F. de
Bishop of Caesarea. *See* Eusebius
Bishop of St Gildas II 342
Bishops of Middle Ages
  destroyed plans of Dracontia II 347
Biurasp, delegate of Dzahhak II 453
Bjerregaard, C. H. A., FTS
—— "The Elementals, . . ."
  atoms, elements, monads, I 630-4
  gods, angels, etc I 632n
  Leibniz's monads, force, matter I 623

Black. *See also* Black Magic, Kali-Yuga
  birds symb of primeval wisdom I 443-4
  brown-, 4th face on column II 178
  fourth race, w sin II 227, 250, 319
  land & White Island II 319-20
  red, yellow, brown, white &, races II 249
  storm dragons II 425
  war betw yellow &, men II 223
  waters (Kālāpāni) I xxx; II 406
  white magic & II 364
Black Age. *See* Kali-Yuga
Black Fire (*Zohar*)
  absolute Light-Wisdom II 162
Black Magic. *See also* Magic; Left-,
    Right-Hand Paths; Sorcery
  began in Atlantis I 192n
  Chaldean, at Nipoor II 139n
  Lévi's "Agent Magique" & I 254-5
  of Levites & Egypt II 212
  prayer for destruction is I 416
  Rāmāyana struggle betw white & II 495
Blake, Dr C. Carter
  coined "Pacificus" for Lemuria II 783n
—— "The Genesis of Man . . ."
  man divided into 2 species II 725
—— "Notes on Human Remains . . ."
  giant race of Palmyra II 755
—— "On the Naulette Jaw"
  early stone ornaments II 744
Blanchard, Émile
  holds atmosphere changed little II 159-60
  on Origin of Life I 253n
  rejects Pasteur's opinions II 151
Blastema
  close to occult view II 120
  Naudin's protoplasm II 119-20
Blavatsky, Helena Petrovna
  accusations against I xlv-vi, 676; II 441 &n
  claims no infallibility I 272; II 22n
  on contradictions in science I 504-5; II 649
  given proofs of teachings I xlv; II 438
  had copies of Masters' letters [to Sinnett]
    I 163n, 187
  incessantly discredited I xxxvii
  knew much of SD before 1880 I xviii
  knowledge of English I vii, xxxviii
  life of, saved thrice by sound I 555
  life study of inner meanings I 303
  limitations of European language I 272
  merely a humble recorder I 23
  owned a chimpanzee II 676n
  preferred pagan to rabbinical methods II
    545
  prepared to meet opposition I 272

  on rules of secrecy I 299
  scientific education of I 487; II 649
  takes blame for misunderstandings I 163n
  taught (in 1880) 2 Europeans portion of SD I
    xviii
  teachings difficult for I 23; II 438
  transmits what she learned I xxxvii, 318;
    II 438
  writes for the future I xxxvii; II 334, 442
—— "About the Mineral Monad"
  explains evolution of monads I 176-8
  perception in minerals & plants I 455
—— "Do the Adepts Deny the Nebular
    Theory?"
  composition of Sun I 528 &n
  matter of comets, Sun I 593-4
  validity of nebular theory I 590
—— *Isis Unveiled*
  criticized I xlv-vi, 231n
  errors in, [*See ML* p 45] II 640
  personal god not in I 579n
  Secret Doctrine & I vii, xli-ii; II 51
  quoted or referred to:
    ākāśa, ether, astral light I 338n, 341
    Amenti, Gehenna I 463n
    anthropomorphism not in I 579n
    ape a bastard human I 185n; II 262
    ark, argha symbol II 461
    astral light, anima mundi I 104, 196-7
    Atlantis II 221-2, 384, 496
    Babylonia & India II 203
    barren & fertile periods II 74
    Brewster on light I 580
    Brotherhood saves ancient works I xxiii-iv
    Cain, Seth, genealogy of II 125, 127, 391n
    chronology, Eastern II 73
    civilization & savagery II 430, 722
    Codex Nazaraeus q in I 248n
    cosmic struggle for life I 202-3
    cosmogenesis I 3-4, 340-1, 343
    cross, ancient symbol II 556-7
    cycles I 3-4, 202, 641; II 214, 330n
    decimals, antiquity of I 360-1; II 37n
    deluge, 7 meanings of II 144-5
    Eastern Ethiopians II 417
    Eden, Garden of II 202-3, 496
    electricity, various names for I 338n
    embryonic stages in II 187, 259 &n
    Enoch II 532 &n, 533
    evolution I 332; II xvi, 153, 170, 190
    Ezekiel's wheel II 128-9
    Father Felix q I 670
    Flood, Noah, Xisuthrus II 222
    Gan-duniyas or Babylonia II 202

genii of 7 planets I 198
globe chain taught in I 231-2n
Gnostics, Nazarenes I 197
Gnostic systems in II 96n
gravitation doubted in I 490
Great Breath I 43
Great Pyramid I 317n
Ialdabaōth I 449n
IAO, Iaho, Jaho II 465, 540-1
Jehovah is Adam & Eve II 125n
Jews, origin of I 115n, 313n
Jodhevah or Jehovah II 128-9
Kadeshuth dance II 460-1
Kulluka-Bhatta on Aryans, Egy II 746
Lévi's six-pointed star II 533
light I 579-80
links ancient & modern thought II 630n
memory of past lost II 430
mighty builders fr India II 417
Moses' esoteric religion crushed I 320n
Moses-Sargon story I 319-20n
Mother, Ilus, Hyle I 82
Nabatheans, Maimonides re II 455n
nought or cipher II 554
old book described I xlii
Ophiomorphos II 389
periodical births of saviors I 657
phallicism in Catholicism II 85
pitris & present man II 91n
prehistoric civilizations II 430
primordial worlds I 246n
races & elements II 220
recapitulation of embryo II 187-9
Sacred Island I 209; II 220-1
Satan discussed I 416; II 478
science must follow Hermetists I 625
sciences yet undiscovered II 130
scope of teaching in II 496-7
serpent emblem of wisdom II 214
seven planetary chambers I 568
seven principles in I 197, 231-2n
seven turns of key I xxxviii
sons of Jacob II 211-12
soulless men amongst us I 234-5n
sunken continents II 221-4
Sun's matter I 499
tetragram II 557
theology vs truth II 377
Tiphereth II 214
tree of evolution II 259n
universe created fr water I 344-5
Unseen Universe on ether I 462
the Unutterable II 190
Vamadeva Modelyar q I 376-7

Votan, Dracontia, Druids II 380
War in Heaven (*Codex Naz.*) I 194-6
war of magicians (Atlantis) II 222
yugas, etc I 655-6
zodiac in II 502n
—— "Is the Sun Merely a Cooling Mass?"
    I 530n, 541
composition of Sun I 528 &n
elements in the Sun I 583
—— "Leaflets from Esoteric History"
Egy & Atlantean knowledge II 436 &n
Greeks, Romans, Atlanteans II 743 &n
India, Americas land-connected II 327
written fr words of a Master II 327
—— *Lucifer* Magazine
Egyptian bas-reliefs II 558-9
whole cosmogony not given out I 168
—— ["Notes on 'A Land of Mystery'"]
sunken Pacific continent II 788-9
——, ed., ["Reply to an English FTS"] II 436n
cometary substance different I 142, 597
—— *The Secret Doctrine*
all that can be given I xxxviii, 306-7
belongs to no faith I viii
bulwarked against attacks I 278-9
contains translation fr Senzar I 23
described I vii-viii, xxxviii-ix, xlv; II 437
Evening Telegraph on II 441n
found in 1,000s of Sanskrit MSS I xxiii
gap of 43 Stanzas in I 478
gives only 3 or 4 of 7 keys II 797
Isis Unveiled & I vii, xxxviii, xli-ii
method of II 796-8
mistakes likely in I 272; II 640
purpose of II 449, 451, 742
purpose of Addenda I 279, 298-9, 477-81
reliability of II 437-46
student to use intuition I 278
teachings antedate Vedas I xxxvii
twentieth century will vindicate I xxxvii;
    II 442
two volumes do not complete I vii
Vol II desc 4th-round man I 22; II 68n
Vol III [never published] I xl, 11, 76
Vol III treats of Mysteries II 437
Volumes III & IV may not appear II 798
withholds more than it gives out I 278
—— "The Septenary Principle . . ."
on "thread doctrine" I 610
on various manus II 307-9
—— "Transmigration of the Life Atoms"
on the life principle II 672-3 &nn
—— "What is Matter and What is Force?"
seven stages of matter I 560

Blind(s)
  anagrammatic II 580
  conceal real mysteries II 310
  enumeration of dvīpas a II 322
  in Jewish worship II 127-8, 473, 564
  manus a II 308n
Blind Faith
  vs adepts' knowledge I 612
  vs karma-nemesis II 304-5
  theologians take all on I 669
Blind Forces
  design in the seemingly I 277
  evolution & II 648-55
  there are no I 274
Bliss. *See* Moksha, Nirvāṇa, etc
Blochmann, Dr H., translator
—— *Āin-i-Akbarī* [by Abu'l Fazl 'Allam]
  Akbar's interest in var sects I xxiv &n
Blood
  Abel's "murder" & II 273n, 388, 469
  ankh, soul, life & II 600n
  Cain's & Abel's II 43-4n, 390
  circulation of solar I 541-2
  earliest man needed no I 609
  essence of life I 538
  mankind of one II 421n
  of a pure man II 427 &n
  Richardson on I 531
  solar vitality fluid & I 541-2
  spirit & water &, (*John*) I 570-1n
  water is, of Earth II 43n, 400 &n
Bloomfield-Moore, Clara Jessup
  efforts of, in behalf of truth I 556
  Keely's commercial failure I 558n
  Keely's neutral center I 556-7
—— "Keely's Secrets" [*Theos. Siftings*]
  potential of Keely's discoveries I 560-2
—— "Psychic Force & Etheric Force"
  Keely a benefactor I 559-60
—— "The New Philosophy"
  Keely on sound, color I 564-5
Blue & Red Races, destroyed II 192
Blumenbach, J. F., on Malay race II 328
Bnēi Elohīm, Bne' Aleim, B'ne Alhim (Heb).
  See also Sons of God
  assist creator I 440
  elohīm become, including Satan II 390
  have existed & do exist II 374-6
  host of I 412, 440
  reveal mysteries to wives II 229
  zodiac & II 23
Bnēi-Iśrāēl (Heb)
  Afghans call themselves II 200n
Bnēi-Menashsheh (Heb)

  tribe of Khojar Tartars II 200n
Bnēi-Shamash (Heb) "Children of the Sun"
  Vatican's secret works & II 506
Boar. *See also* Avatāra, Varāha
  avatāra I 368 &n, 369; II 53, 75, 321
  Brahmā assumes shape of II 252
  Buddha dying of pork & I 368-9n
  Vāyu Purāna on I 368-9n
Boat(s). *See also* Solar Boat
  third race built, before houses II 399n
Boaz [2 *Chron* 3:17; 1 *Kings* 7:21]
  Jakin &, good & evil II 497
  left pillar in Solomon's temple II 461
Bode, J. E., many worlds inhabited II 706
Bodha (Skt), & Buddha, buddhi I xix
Bodhi (Skt)
  trance condition or samādhi I xix
  tree II 589
Bodhi-mur [*Bodhimör*] (Tib)
  on essence of fire & flame I 6
Bodhisattva(s) (Skt). *See also* Avalokiteśvara,
    Kwan-shai-yin
  anupadaka [aupapāduka] I 52
  brāhmanas or I 572
  buddhas in world of form I 572
  Buddhists worship human II 34n
  Chenresi a II 178-9
  chhāyās of dhyāni-buddhas I 571-2
  human dhyāni-buddhas I 42; II 34n
  initiation produces I 109
  primeval matter as seen by I 69
  sent in every round, race I 42, 571
  superhuman, emanate monads I 571-3
  Virgin Mary w lilies & I 379 &n
Body(ies) I 265. *See also* Astral Body, Rūpas,
    Sthūla-Śarīra
  astral, before physical II 1, 660 &n
  astral, in kāma-loka II 374n
  built of interstellar atoms I 632-3
  Carlyle on, as a miracle I 212
  changes every 7 years I 262-3n
  of dhyāni-chohans I 222n, 259
  fifth race first symmetrical II 294
  fleshly, numbing weight on soul I 275
  former & future human I 180-1, 609; II 195,
    610 &n
  four, of Brahmā II 58-60
  girdle of death II 235
  of the gods I 489
  healing process of II 166n
  host of lives of I 225 &n, 261
  human, not grossest principle I 260
  initiate lives in astral II 499 &n
  instrument of elementals I 294-5 &n

interrelated w all other I 511
irresponsible organ II 245, 302
man's, designed for a god II 302
no real principle II 616
not evolved fr animals I 211-12
Novalis on, as a temple I 212
one of 3 fires II 247
physical, shaped by lowest lives I 224
Śankara on nirvana & I 570
seven dhātus in human I 290
space filled w I 671
Space the, of the universe I 342
Spirit of Earth built physical II 241
spirit will animate new II 760
sunspot cycle reflected in I 541-2
swarming w bacteria I 260-3
thermal conditions & man's II 254
three principles needed to objectify I 59, 624n, 632n
tool of psychic, spiritual man II 302
Vishnu Purāna on I 420
weightless in space I 502
Winchell on different I 607-8n
Boehme, Jakob
great occultist II 595
Newton derived gravity fr I 494
nursling of nirmānakāyas I 494
—— *The Aurora*
seven fountain spirits II 630, 634
—— *Signatura Rerum*
nature's 7 properties II 595, 634
Boeotia(ns)
held Deukalion ancestor of man II 519
spelled Zeus "Deus" II 582
submerged II 270n
Boethius, A. M. S., *Ars Geometriae*
Pythagorean 1 & nought I 361
Bogaterey [Bogatiry] (Russ) giants
Russian legends of II 754-5
Bogoluboff, Professor, on cells I 249n
Böhme, Jacob. *See* Boehme
Bois-Reymond. *See* Du Bois-Reymond
Boker [boqer] (Heb)
dawn or morning II 252n
Bolivia, giant ruins in II 745, 752
Bone(s)
animals w II 105, 183
enormous human, in America II 337
Genesis & II 193
huge, of 5th race II 293
men w, & boneless men II 91-2, 105
no human, at Dauphiné II 277
paleolithic II 716, 720
phosphorus for present II 72

scarcity of human II 686
Boneless (Race)
ethereal man was II 149
gave life to men w bones II 90-1, 105
incorporeal creator II 241
mind-born were II 156
primitive race was I 583n
rib of Adam & II 193
second race called II 164-5
self-born or II 171
in Stanzas II 91-2, 105, 156, 165, 171, 183
Böns (Tibetan dugpas)
swastika on idols of II 586
Book(s) I xix
Alexandrian & Chinese, destroyed II 692
Brahmanical, made accessible I 270
of prophecies I xliii-iv
seven, stolen fr ark II 612-13
theosophical, & pretended authority I xix
very old, described in *Isis* I xlii-iii
Book of Al-Chazari [Khazarī]. *See* Ha-Levi
quoted II 40, 41, 234
Book of Ali, Turkish phoenix in II 617
Book of Changes, celestial numbers in II 35
Book of Concealed Mystery. See Siphrā' di-Tsenī'ūthā'
Book (Liber) of Drushim. See Luria, I.
Book of Dzyan II 46, 113, 220, 375, 759. *See also*
Stanzas of Dzyan
central Sun, Fohat, etc I 201
Djan, Dzan or I xx n
the eternal pilgrim I 16-17 &n
evolution of man II 241
Great Mother & numerical values I 434
language of, unknown I xxxvii
motion, spirit, matter I 258
number seven in I 674
original Senzar commentaries on I 23
Stanzas of I 27-34; II 15-21
treats of our planetary system I 13
unheard of I viii, xxii
unknown animals in II 254
why many Stanzas of, omitted I 478
Book of Enoch
agrees w archaic doctrine II 267n, 537
angels of, & gandharvas compared II 584
antiquity of II 506, 530-1
apocryphal II 454, 529, 531
book of initiation II 229, 535
John an edited version of II 497
Jude quotes fr II 230, 482, 531
Ludolph & Bruce on II 531
Pistis Sophia quotes fr II 535
plagiarisms fr II 229, 482-5, 531

rejected by church II 535
Revelation version of II 484-5, 497, 510
scientists scoffed at II 531-2
quoted:
    Adam, Cain, Abel II 124-5
    angelic Fall II 283, 529
    angels of I 523n
    Azaziel transgressing angel II 376
    cataclysms II 314, 533-4
    everlasting king II 483n
    giants II 762
    inclination of axis II 145, 533, 726
    Jacob's ladder II 281n
    Moon shall change its laws II 533
    Uriel re Sun & Moon I 609; II 533
Book of God. See Kenealy, Dr Edward
Book of Hammannunah (q in *Zohar*)
    Earth, day, & night II 28n, 773
Book(s) of Hermes II 25, 36-7, 506. *See also*
    Divine Pymander
Book of Jasher I 577
Book of Jude. See Jude
Book of Numbers (Kabbala)
    Samael (Satan) is St Michael II 378
    three races in II 397
Book of Numbers. See Chaldean *Book of Numbers*
Book of Rules
    on the element-language I 464
Book of Ruth and Schadash (in *Zohar*)
    B'ne Aleim II 376
Book of Sarparājñī [Aitareya Brāhmana V iv]
    fiery dragon in infinity I 74
Book of "The Aphorisms of *Tson-ka-pa*" I 635
Book of the Beginnings, A. See Massey, G.
Book of the Dead (Egy)
    cosmogony of Secret Doctrine in I 674
    geom figures & numbers used in I 66
    Kabbala &, on 7 principles II 633
    many interpretations of I 311
    occult chapter of I 403
    reincarnation in I 227
    rounds, on early II 634-5
    quoted:
        after-death states in I 674n
        ancestral heart I 220
        Apophis II 588 &n
        chaos ceases thru the ray I 231
        creators of man, many-shaped II 634-5
        crocodile in I 219-20; II 577, 580 &n
        "Day Come to Us" I 134n
        defunct man as crocodile I 219-20
        dragons "sons of rebellion" II 386
        egg of universe I 359, 360, 364-5
        Fohat is Toum I 673 &n

        Great Green One or Vāch, Deep I 434
        Horus fights Set II 283n
        Horus w crocodile head II 577
        "I am the Lotus," etc I 380
        "I am the mouse" explained II 635
        "I see the forms of myself" I 220
        manifestation, beginning of I 330
        monsters on Earth II 52
        number 7 in I 674; II 35
        Osiris creates own limbs I 231, 312
        Osiris double crocodile II 580n
        Osiris, Moon & conception I 228
        Ra as egg of Seb I 360, 364-5
        reaping in Field of Aanroo I 236n
        Seb lays egg-universe I 359
        serpent as hierophant II 213
        seven primeval men II 3
        Shoo & children of rebellion I 364
        Shoo as Ra II 545-6
        Thoth I 675; II 538n
        three & 4 wicked flames I 237
        Toum divider of Earth I 674
        Typhon or dragon II 385
        War in Heaven II 386
        wheat, origin & symbol of II 374 &n
        Woman-light I 403
Book of the Generations of Adam (*Gen* 5)
    Adam begat Seth II 125
    Adam is male-female II 125
    Hanoch had the II 532n
    man in image of God II 134
Book of the Keys [*Divine Pymander* ch 13]
    unity makes 10, & 10 unity I 90n
Book of the 10,000 Precepts. See Mani Kumbum
Book of the Various Names of the Nile.
    See Taifāshī
Book of [the] Wisdom [of Solomon] II 705
    Deus non fecit mortem II 422
    souls are pre-existent II 111
Books of Knowledge II 705
Books of Moses. See Mosaic Books, Pentateuch
Books of Thoth
    Pymander version of one of II 267n
    seven primeval men II 3
Boonere [Buner], Afghan tribe in II 200n
Bopaveda [Bopadeva, Vopadeva] Skt gram-
    marian, on Moon plant II 590
Bopp, Franz, laid down phonetic laws I xxxii
Bordj (Pers) Mt, myth about I 341 &n
Boreas (Gk) North Wind
    Astarte & I 468
    destroys Persian fleet I 467
    god of snows II 7, 11
    Jewish name for I 467

Jupiter, Jehovah & I 468
King of Hyperboreans son of II 771
Borlase, Dr William
   on Druids & Persian magi II 756
Borneo
   geologically of recent formation II 789
   pile villages of II 716n
   remnant of sunken continent II 222
   wild men of, Lemuro-Atlantean II 195-6n
Borsippa, Nebo worshiped at II 456
Bory de St Vincent, J. B. II 646
Boscovich, Ruggiero Giuseppe
   sees atoms as centers of force I 507
Bossuet, Jacques Bénigne
   on cosmocratores or world bearers I 331
   ideas on a star that falls II 485
—— *Élévations . . .*
   original sin cause of idolatry II 279
Bosuage. *See* Basnage
Botanists
   origin of wheat unknown to II 373-4
   searching for nerves of plants I 49
Botany
   Australian flora ancient II 196-7
   evidence for Atlantis II 322n, 739
   nodes of, & astronomy I 320
   pyramidal shape of pines II 594
   science needs occult I 262
   second race procreation & II 116
Bo-Tree, of wisdom & knowledge I 523
Bottomless Pit
   eternal fire of I 338n
   Lucifer hurled down into II 237n
Boucheporn, R. C., Baron de
   collision of Earth w comet II 330
Boucher de Crèvecoeur de Perthes, J.
   fossil man discovered by II 277, 675
   man dates fr Miocene II 714n
—— *Antiquités celtiques . . .*
   Littré's comments on II 738-9
Bouh, Sarmatian 4-letter god II 602
Bouilland [Bouillaud], Ismael (1605–1694)
   Bailly cites lunar motion of I 667n
Bouilland [Bouillaud], J. B. (1796–1881)
—— [*Astronomia philolaica*]
   derides Edison's phonograph II 784n
Boulanger, Nicolas A., *Règne des Dieux*
   kings, demigods, etc II 372-3
Boulaq [Bulaq Museum]
   mummy of Sesostris found at I xxixn
   Theban triad depicted at II 464
Boundless. *See also* All, One, Parabrahman,
      Space, That, Time
   Aditi as I 99

cannot create I 7
cannot will, think, act I 354
circle of, time I 113-14; II 488, 549
darkness I 40, 98, 327, 354; II 488
En-Soph I 109, 354
expansion, contraction in II 42-3
gave birth to Limit II 233
has no relation to conditioned I 56; II 556
Light of the Gnostics I 577
no number I 98
not a finger's breadth of void in I 289
principle I 14
ray of, penetrates Mundane Egg I 354
space & circle I 98, 113
spiritual monad is I 177
Bourbourg, de. *See* Brasseur de
Bourdin, Jules
   protested theories of Clausius I 587n
Bourgeois, Abbé, *Compte Rendu du Congrès . . .*
   flints of II 723, 752n
   man's orig in Miocene II 288, 675, 714n,
      751-2
   monkey later than man II 749n
Bourgès, A., [*Philosophie contemporaine . . .*]
   consciousness & physical nature II 654
Bourguignon d'Anville, J. B.
—— *Géographie ancienne . . .*
   one-eyed Scythian race II 769n
Bovey Tracey, extinct lake. *See also* Pengelly
   Miocene subtropical plants at II 726
Brachmans. *See* Brāhman (caste)
Brae, de. *See* Braye, de
Brahe, Tycho
   triple force in stars I 493
—— *Astronomiae inst. Progymnasmata*
   mean motion of Moon I 667n
   new star of I 590; II 486n
Brahmā (Skt). *See also* Days, Life, Nights, Years
      of; Sons of; Trimūrti
   Abhimānin eldest son of I 521
   Ādi-Sanat, Ancient of Days I 98
   Age of I 8, 206, 289, 368, 552; II 70
   āgneyāstra fiery javelin of II 629
   All-Being I 55
   androgyne (Vedic) I 427
   Anu one name of I 542
   aspect of Parabrahman I 451
   assumes form of swan I 357
   awakens I 337, 447, 454
   birth of, (Polier) I 345-6
   as boar II 53, 75, 252
   Brahma(n) (neut) & I 17-18, 61, 80
   fr *brih,* "to expand" I 8n, 83
   Burnouf on I 380n

Bythos or, periodical I 214
called forth the elements II 574
cause of potencies I 55
changes Io (cow) into deer II 418n
cosmic Logos II 247
created first man I 345
creates 4 orders of beings I 456n
creates his own limbs I 231
creates planets & zodiacal signs II 625n
creates thru daughter (Vāch) I 431
creative activities of I 8, 10, 55, 58-60;
    II 162-3, 313, 553
the Creator II 313
creatures born fr parts of II 625n
cursed Nārada II 47-8, 585
death of I 8, 54n, 373n
differentiated fr Parabrahm I 55-6
Divine Mind, Mahat I 451; II 79
does *not* create Earth I 380n
Egg of I 8, 80-1, 89, 257, 333, 335, 345, 350,
    357, 359-60, 365-7, 373, 377; II 553, 616,
    631
emanates spirit (*Manu*) I 447
evolution out of Vishnu II 31
expands to become universe I 83
Father, Mother, Son I 41
father of gods, asuras I 427
father of kumāras II 106
fifth head of II 502n, 578n
fire-god I 341
five, or Pañchāsya I 213
forms heaven, Earth I 333
four bodies of I 213; II 58-60
four-faced I 55, 110, 344; II 465
generative power II 43n, 125n
germ of Unknown Darkness I 83
Hari as, sleeps in Space I 371-2
Hiranyagarbha is I 89, 286
hurled to Earth (Fall) II 483, 515
an illusion I 333
instrumental not ideal cause I 55
issues fr lotus I 381n
Jyotis one name of II 766
Kalahansa I 20, 79-80
Kāma born fr heart of II 176
Kaśyapa son of II 382n
kriyāśakti used by II 59
Kwan-shi-yin or I 452
light of the Logos II 233
Logos & I 9, 429; II 247
lotus, enthroned on I 379
the male I 59, 78, 80
male & female, becomes I 7, 9 &n, 41, 61, 81,
    89, 137-8, 335, 355n; II 126, 128, 134n

male principle I 59, 80, 333
manifested deity I 7; II 108
manus created by II 237
Manu-Svāyambhuva II 128
many forms of II 146n
Marīchi son of II 89, 132, 253
mind-born sons of I 145, 457 &n; II 44, 78,
    86, 140n, 176n, 624-5
monsters created by II 65n
mover on the waters I 345
Nārada & II 47, 502
ninth or Kumāra Creation II 106, 579
not direct creator of man I 445
not in Vedas I xix, 426, 445
permutation of Nārāyana I 431
prajāpatis are collectively II 60
prajāpatis created by II 176n, 573
prakriti & I 542
Protologoi I 335
recoalescence of II 309n
Sanat or I 98, 459
Sarasvatī wife of II 76n, 77
Sarpa, Ahi fr hair of II 181-2n
Sephīrōthal Tree or I 352
seven & 4 principles of II 58n
Śiva hurls, into Abyss II 515
soul of the world I 365
story of Abram based on story of II 77
svar-loka abode of II 404
Theos evolving fr Chaos I 344
as tortoise II 75
universe is, & Brahma I 17-18
Vāch & I 137, 430-1; II 107, 126, 128, 147,
    418n, 472
Varāha avatāra II 53
vehicle of Brahman I 17, 80
Virāja is II 90
Vishnu Purāna on I 19, 421n
Vishnu, Śiva & I 538; II 115
weaves universe fr own substance I 83
wrathful w Vedhas, Brahmā's sons II 78
yoga power used by II 115
Brahmā, Age of. See Brahmā, Mahā-Kalpa
Brahmā, Days & Nights of. See Days of
    Brahmā, Nights of Brahmā
Brahmā, Egg of. See Brahmā, Golden Egg,
    Hiranyagarbha
Brahmachāri Bawa (Yogin V. B. Gokhale)
—— "Some Things the Aryans Knew"
    magic of ancient Aryans II 427n
Brahmacharya [or Brahmachārin] (Skt)
    pure life of II 458
Brahmadevas (Skt)
    five kumāras are 5th order of II 578

Brahmādicas (Skt), prajāpatis or seven II 142
Brahmā-Kalahaṃsa (Skt) divine swan II 122 &n
Brahma-loka (Skt)
  denizens of, at pralaya I 372
Brahman, Brahma, Brahm (neuter, Skt)
  absorption in I 134n, 636
  w/o attributes I 420
  Brahmā, Vishnu, Śiva energies of II 115
  cannot be said to be anywhere I 374
  cannot cognize I 6
  confused w Brahmā (masc) II 465
  does not create or evolve I 50n, 451
  in every atom I 17
  free fr pairs of opposites II 495
  incognizable I 50n, 61; II 108
  Kalahansa & I 20, 78, 79-80, 359; II 465
  Krishna part of supreme II 359
  Mysterium Magnum of Paracelsus I 61
  names of, in descending order II 108
  noumenon or, never rests I 374
  potencies of beings in I 450-1
  prakriti, spirit, time & I 19, 421
  -Pumis [Puṃs]-Pradhāna I 445
  radiates the gods, rests I 447
  Self or Kshetrajña II 639
  That I 451
  universe is, & Brahmā I 17-18
  universe lives in & returns to I 8-9
  Vishnu Purāna on I 256, 420, 445
Brāhman(a, as) (Skt, caste) also spelled Brah-
    man, Brahmin(s), Brachman(s)
  Abraham or A-bram & II 139n, 200
  abridged Upanishads I 271
  advised to read Purānas II 148
  Akbar & I xxiii &n
  ancient, descend fr Brahmaputras I 209
  anthropomorphized truths II 567
  Bhārata reborn as II 321
  Brihaspati (Brahmanaspati) lord of the
    II 45n
  Buddha disciple of initiated I xxi
  candidate & Golden Cow II 462
  Chaldeans pupils of I 117
  chronology of II 49, 66-74
  cross known to, before Europeans II 556
  describes initiation (*Anugītā*) II 637-8
  destroyed Buddhism in India I 368n
  distort meanings II 92-3
  do not eat eggs I 366
  Druids &, affinity between II 756
  Egyptian allegories in books of I 365-6
  fair-skinned, & dark Dravidians II 768
  forbidden to receive money II 323

four- & 3-fold upādhis of II 592-3n
gotras or caste races of II 502
greed, ambition of II 60
as grihastha II 77-8, 411n
having son religious duty of I 383
hid truth fr masses II 320
honor Agni w perpetual fire I 341
initiated, know Purānas II 320
initiated, know secret passages II 221
invaded India fr north I 270; II 768
invented Sanskrit (Stewart) II 442
Jews descend fr ex- II 200
labeled asuras demons II 487
life of traditional II 411n
Magas of Atlantis & II 322-3
misled Jones & Wilford I xxx-i &n
misrepresented suras, asuras II 93
occupation of India, effects of II 608
opposed Chandragupta II 550 &n
oppose pantheists, Advaitas I 8
oppose 7-fold division of man II 592-3n
originators of caste system I 270
origin of initiated I 209
pitris of ritual importance to II 91
primeval, initiated in Central Asia II 565
procreation not sinful w I 383
protest *Esoteric Buddhism* I xviii
proud exclusiveness of II 471
Pythagoras brought dual system of, & Iranians II 573
rabbi &, on linga symbol II 471-2
regard for monkeys explained I 185n
retires to jungle I 383
ritualism of II 567
on senses (*Anugītā*) I 87; II 637-8
seven dvīpas II 404 &n
sevenfold classification of II 29n, 641
tampered w *Vishnu-Purāna* I 423
terrestrial bodhisattvas I 572
-theosophist on cosmic pralaya II 69n
Tirvalour, Tiravalore of, & Hindu epoch
  I 661-2, 666
of Upper India (Marcellinus) II 327
Vedas once sole property of I 271
Voltaire drawn to knowledge of II 742
Brāhmana(s) (commentary on the Vedas). *See
    also Aitareya-, Śatapatha-, etc*
  Colonel Wilford & I xxxi
  Gāthās (Pers), Purānas same origin as
    II 409-10
  occult works I 68, 165
  personnel of, prehuman II 284
  require a key I xxvii, 68
  temple-Brahmans & I 271

Upanishads attached to I 269-70
Vedantin sects & I 451-2
Brahmaṇaspati (Skt) Jupiter
  Brihaspati I 120n; II 45n, 498
  materialization of divine grace II 498
  symbol of exoteric worship II 45n
Brahmāṇḍa Purāṇa
  described I 367n
  seven dvīpas in II 404
  Weber on date of I 436
Brahmāṇḍika (Skt), solar, lunar pitris I 442
Brahmanical
  Buddhist &, Logos same II 637
  cis-Himalayan secret teachings II 308n
  culture in Babylon II 203
  figures for rounds, yugas II 68-70
  genealogies confusing II 42
  sacred books & Upanishads I 270
Brahmanism
  Buddhism &, compared II 637
  kept masses ignorant II 60
  slaughtered Indian Buddhism I 368n
  Venus origin explained in II 30
Brahmā-Prajāpati (Skt) I 79-81. *See also*
    Prajāpati
  breath of, creates asuras II 500
  creates spiritually II 44
  degraded by sexual mysteries II 471
  firstborn of II 466
  Jehovah-Sephīrōth & II 126
  male-female I 89
  manifested Logos II 624
  numerological confirmation of II 466
  other names of I 436-7
  synthesis of 7 builders I 436
  Tetragrammaton II 625
Brahma Purāṇa, mind-born sons II 275
Brahmaputra(s) (Skt) II 374
  initiated Brahmans descend fr I 209
  Nārada was a I 413
Brahmarandhra (Skt)
  jīva goes fr the heart to I 132
Brahmarshi(s) (Brahma-Rishis) II 176n, 502
Brahmā-Rudra (Skt) Śiva
  kumāras mind-born sons of I 458-9
Brahmā Sāvarṇa, seed-manu, planet [globe] G,
    fifth round II 309
Brahmā's Night (Pralaya). *See* Night of
    Brahmā
Brahmā-Vāch (Skt)
  androgyne, Tetragrammaton II 601
  bisexual (*Manu* & Purānas) I 72n
  bisexual Jehovah II 125, 128, 601
  female half of Brahmā I 81, 137

manifest theogony starts w I 434
  separation of II 147
  Virāj (male symbol) fr II 472
Brahmā-Vāch-Virāj (Skt)
  bisexual creative deity II 125
  divine hermaphrodite II 126-7
Brahmā Vaivarta Purāṇa
  kalpas, life of Brahmā I 368; II 307n
Brahmā-Virāj (Skt)
  Jehovah-Adam & I 355-6; II 126
  male half of Brahmā I 81; II 128
  red II 43n
Brahmā-Vishnu (Skt) infinite space I 8n
Brahmā-Vishnu-Śiva, Trimūrti (Skt)
  Diana-Hecate-Luna & I 387
Brahmin. *See* Brāhman
Brahms & A-brahms II 130
Brain
  activity electric phenomena I 85
  animal, philosophizes (Lévi) II 74
  ape & human II 193n, 646n, 661, 676, 682
  Atlantean, & nervous centers II 761
  -change & thought I 124n
  Chochmah [Hokhmāh] or I 352
  dreamless sleep & I 266
  eyes grow fr within II 295
  gray matter of, & sexual acts II 296
  heart &, of sun I 541
  human, needed for speech II 661
  intellect & I 301
  Laing on negro II 677 &n
  mammalian II 301
  normal & abnormal states of II 296
  our, has softened II 250
  of Paleolithic man II 686n
  particles record thought I 104
  physical, forgets II 424
  reacts on pineal gland II 296, 301-2
  registers memory II 301
  size of, & intellect II 168n, 522-3
  sound & I 554, 565
  -stuff on physical plane I 291
B'rāisheeth. *See* Berēshīth
Branchiostoma, materialists & II 370n
B'rāsh. *See* Berēshīth
Brass
  feminine principle I 364
  symbolized nether world I 364n
Brasseur de Bourbourg, C. É. *See also Popol
    Vuh*
  man present when Andes formed II 745
  —— *Histoire des Nations . . . Méxique. . .*
  Nargal, Nāgal, & Nāga II 213 &n
  —— [*Lettres pour servir . . .*]

Votan son of the snakes II 379
Braun, on the Divine Breath II 649n
Braye, de, found Neolithic idols II 723
Brazen Serpent I 364 &nn
  gross symbol II 473
  healer I 414, 472; II 208, 387n
  magic agent symbol I 253n
  of Moses II 206n, 387n
  ram's horns & II 213n
Brazil, fauna of II 792
Bréal, Michel, *Hercule et Cacus*
  Kronos fr *kar*, to create II 269n
Breast-eared, Breast-eyed man II 634
Breath. *See also* Breaths, Great Breath
  of animal life I 242-3; II 56
  asura, of God II 59, 500
  becomes a stone, plant, animal, etc I 107
  cool, is Mother I 12
  creative, unrevealed deity I 2
  crystallized into Word I 79
  of Darkness moves on Waters I 64
  "dead," given back I 102
  divine I 41, 43, 289, 520; II 95, 551-2, 649n
  divine, works thru Pleiades II 551
  of elohīm I 375
  eternal, of the One, All I 11, 43, 54-6, 64, 75, 497n
  evolution of man & II 241
  Father-Mother-Son & I 41, 75, 83-5
  first II 241
  formless worlds or I 606
  God breathed, of life I 225; II 81
  heat or I 103
  hot, is Father I 12
  human monad or II 105
  knows itself not I 56
  of Life I 212, 225-6, 242-4, 342, 626 &n; II 23, 81, 162, 175, 456, 589, 604, 632
  lower Adam & II 162, 175, 456
  motion or I 2, 11-12, 14, 54-6, 97, 143, 497n; II 551
  number, deity & I 66-7
  one, & countless II 492
  pneuma or II 113
  prāna or expirational I 95
  regulation of, injurious I 95-6
  returns periodically II 43
  spirit is the fiery II 114
  Sun & planets, universe & kosmos II 23
  synthesis of senses I 96
Breathing of Earth & Universe I 541
Breaths. *See also* Prāna, Winds
  asuras highest II 92
  blow in every direction I 496

  countless, informed by one II 492
  dhyān-chohans or I 103
  fiery, & sephīrōthal triad I 213
  had life but no understanding II 109
  intellectual, or flames II 318n
  monads, of the One II 610
  rudras the 10 vital II 548
  seven, of Dragon of Wisdom I 106
Bree, C. R., *Exposition of Fallacies . . .*
  Mivart on saltations II 696
  no link betw man & monkey II 729
  no missing link in sunken lands II 727-8
Breeding
  inter-, of genus, species II 287
  of men & animals II 184-5, 191, 201, 267
Bretange. *See* Brittany
Brewster, Sir David
  other worlds inhabited II 701-2
—— *A Treatise on Optics*
  light is material I 580
Briah [Berī'āh] (Heb)
  kabbalistic Neshāmāh fr II 604
Briareus (Gk)
  giant described by Hesiod II 775-6
  Orion & II 70
  stands for polar continent II 776
Briatic World. *See also* Briah
  Metatron angel of II 111
Bride
  of Christian kabbalists I 216, 240; II 595
  Church, of Christ II 377
  marriage of lamb w, (*Rev*) II 231
Brih (Skt), to swell or expand I 8n, 83, 356
Brihadāranyaka-Upanishad
  Brihaspati father of gods I 120n
  Moon is mind, Sun understanding II 639n
  rudras, breaths, Śiva in II 548
Brihaspati (Skt). *See also* Jupiter, War in Heaven
  Brahmanaspati or I 120n; II 45n, 498
  building of Earth & II 23
  claims Budha (wisdom) as son II 499
  dead-letter worship symb II 499, 500-1
  father of gods I 120n
  second race under II 29
  Tārā wife of II 45, 138, 456, 498-9
Brimstone II 513
Brinham [Brimham in Yorkshire]
  rocking stones at II 347
Britain, legends of giants in II 754
British, regarded Indians as inferior II 287
British Association, anti-Darwinists in II 696
British Association . . . Reports
  Flower on man's antiquity II 169

Grove on ether, breath I 102
Thompson on strobic circles II 589
British Columbia
  hieroglyphs at Indian village in II 430
British Isles. *See also* England
  Atlantic ridge starts near II 333
  Egyptians reached, by land II 750 &n
  future sinking of II 266
  not white island II 402
  part of horseshoe continent II 326, 333
  rocking stones in II 342n
  submerged four times II 746n, 787n
British Linear Measures
  inch of, & esoteric system I 316
  Parker ratio base of I 313
British Museum
  Assyrian tile in, & Moses II 428
  Chaldean fragment in II 283-4n
  Coptic MSS I 132n
  Easter Island statue II 331, 337, 340, 680
  hidden Tibetan library too large for I xxiv
  Karnac monolith re Hathor I 400
  Mexican MSS II 36
  specimens of dragons II 354-5
  wealth of evidence in II 340
Brittany, Bretagne
  Carnac stones II 341, 752
  "drouk" or the devil in II 206n
  Karnak (Egy) twin to Carnac II 380
  menhirs in, & Atlanteans II 352
  rocking stone at Huelgoat II 342n
Broca, Professor Paul
  dates man to Miocene II 714n
  divides man into 2 species II 725
  on fallacies of evolutionists II 681
  Preface to *Anthropology* by II 249n
  supports Atlantis hypothesis II 790
Bronze, Race of, third root-race II 97
Bronze Age II 741. *See also* Dvāpara Yuga
  Ash tree & men of II 97, 519-20, 772
  every race, subrace has II 198
  Jupiter created, of heroes II 270
  third race (Hesiod) II 271, 520n, 772
Brotherhood. *See also* Adepts, Esoteric School,
    Initiates, Mahātmas, Masters, Teachers
  of adepts I 574; II 636-7
  concealed books I xxiii-iv
  kept 3rd race teachings II 636-7
  Nabatheans an occult II 455
  pledging oneself to the I 164
  of serpents (Gnos) II 386
  union, harmony, & I 644
Brothers of the Sun I 271n
Brown, Robert, *The Countries of the World*

Peru, Easter Island relics II 317, 336-7
Brown, Robert, Jr, *The Unicorn* II 218 &n
Bruce, James
  accused of lying II 440
  discovered *Book of Enoch* II 531
Brucker, J. J., *Historia Critica . . .*
  seed of Mot created all I 451 &n
Brunck, Richard F. P.
—— *Analecta veterum poetarum . . .*
  Mesomedes hymn *Nemesis* II 305n
Bryant, Jacob
  Christian orientation of II 364
—— *A New System . . . Mythology*
  egg symbol among ancients I 359-60
  Mt Ararat II 596-7
  Neptune greets Noah I 444n
  Sydic or Sadic was Noah II 391-2
Bubaste [Bubastis] (Egy)
  cat venerated in I 387
Buch, Christian Leopold, Baron von
  expedition to Canary Islands II 791
Büchner, Ludwig I 528n
—— *Force and Matter*
  Burmeister, Volger, Czolbe II 154
  coal formation II 695n
  vs infinite divisibility of matter I 519
  past an unfolded present I 639
  plant into animal into man I 718
  spontaneous generation II 718-19
  thought is molecular motion I 134n
Buckle, Henry Thomas
—— *History of Civilization in England*
  martyrs of human thought I 298
  q Leslie on light, heat I 515n
Buckwell. *See* Bakewell, F. C.
Buddha(s) II 222. *See also* Ādi-, Amitābha,
    Dhyāni-, Maitreya, Mānushis
  awaken (cosmic) I 337
  Bamian statues & II 224 &n, 337-40
  bodha, buddhi & I xix
  celestial, prototype of human I 108
  of contemplation I 109, 572
  earliest, of 5th race II 423
  every, meets all great adepts I 574
  four only thus far I 42
  Kwan-shi-yin will be last of I 470
  last initiation of I 574
  link betw avatāras & I 638
  manifests in 3 worlds I 572
  mānushi[ya] I 52
  Melha appears as a II 63
  race of II 415
  reincarnation & I 639
  seventh race will be of II 483

Supreme, or Vajradhara I 571
thirty-five, of Confession II 423 &n
Buddha, Gautama (Śākyamuni)
    Amitābha inner god of I 108
    Aryan Hindu, kshatriya I xxi; II 339
    austerities in time of I 47n
    avatāra of Vishnu II 578
    Brahmans & I 271
    buddhas preceded II 423
    connected w Śankarāchārya II 637
    dying of pork explained I 368-9n
    esoteric, exoteric doctrines I xxi
    four-leaved lotus flower of II 546
    gives his previous births II 359
    incarnated as Tsong-Kha-pa I 108 &n
    limited his public teaching I xx
    Māyā mother of I xxxii, 379n
    de Nadeylac on II 338 &n
    nirvāna of, on Earth II 532
    Osiris, Dionysos, Krishna or II 420
    popularized Upanishads I 270-1
    refused to eat eggs I 368-9n
    samādhi posture & drooping ears II 339
    sixth-rounder explained I 161-2
    swastikas on statues of II 586
    on tanhā in *Dhammapada* II 110
    Tashi Lama incarnation of I 471
    taught esoteric doctrine I 46-7; II 27n
    twenty-seventh buddha II 423 &n
    Yin-Sin, prohibited speculation on I 635
Buddhi (Skt). *See also* Mahā-Buddhi
    aggregate of dhyāni-buddhas I 472
    ānandamaya sheath I 570
    ātma, manas & II 57n
    ātman & (relation of) I 119, 179, 193, 471-2,
      567; II 58n, 580, 605n
    bodhi, buddha, bodha I xix
    breath first II 241
    corresponds to ruach I 242; II 633n
    cosmic monad I 177
    dhyāni-chohanic essence I 265
    diagram I 153, 242; II 593, 596, 632
    discrete & indiscrete, eternal I 453
    Diti the, of ākāśa II 613-14
    divine soul I 17, 101n, 119, 120, 216, 567;
      II 318n
    equatorial sun cements, to ātma II 241
    human soul & II 81
    intuition of, vs senses I 279, 329n
    latent consciousness II 275n
    made conscious by manas II 318n
    Mahat & I 256, 334, 373; II 614
    -manas breaks fr ātman I 193
    manas vehicle of I 101, 242-5, 334

    not the human ego II 79
    Prometheus & II 419
    Putah (Egy) II 632
    relation of, to ātman I 119, 179, 193, 265,
      471-2, 567; II 58n, 580, 605n
    sattva & I 68-9n
    second principle I 291
    sixth state of matter II 737
    spiritual soul I 119, 153n
    Sun is, of ākāśa I 527n
    tree symbol of, (*Anugītā*) II 637
    union of, w manas II 230, 231n, 247, 495
    universal ideation (cosmic) II 596
    vāhan (vehicle) II 241
Buddhism
    archaic occultism I 668
    Brahmanism &, compared II 637
    Brahmanism destroyed, in India I 368n
    budhism & I xxi
    Chinese I xxviii, 126, 408, 440; II 215
    deteriorated when transplanted I xxi
    emanation of Hinduism I 668
    esoteric I xix-xxi, 49 &n, 411; II 570, 585, 632
    exoteric, & Roman Church I 539n
    Kwan-shi-yin in I 72 &n, 431n
    moral code of II 253
    in New World discussed II 424n
    no esoteric doctrine (Williams) I 47n
    no personal god in I 635-6
    roots of, & Advaita I 636
    sevenfold man in I 157, 539n
    76,000 tracts of, lost (Burnouf) I xxviii
    upreared on Secret Doctrine I 47
Buddhism. See Rhys Davids, T. W.
Buddhism in Christendom. See Lillie, A.
Buddhism in Tibet. See Schlagintweit, E.
Buddhismus, Der. See Wassilief
Buddhist(s)
    Apollonius met, nāgas II 211
    Bamian statues not of, origin II 337
    Brahmanical &, Logos same II 637
    canon originally 80,000 tracts I xxvii
    Chinese, have no personal god I 440, 635
    Chinese, pilgrimage of II 215
    cross known to, before Europeans II 556
    doctrine kept too secret I xxi
    do not eat eggs I 366
    dragon temples II 378-9
    four truths of I 39, 42
    history of, on palm leaves II 423
    Japanese, sects I 67n, 213-14
    lost literature of I xxvii-viii
    metaphysics, "Dan," "Jan-na" I xx
    not atheists I 6

reached China 61 AD I xxviii
school of Āryāsanga I 49-50 &n
secret books of I xxxiv
seven principles of I 157-8, 539n
Sinhalese, "there is no God" I 636
svabhavat of I 46
Vedānta & I 46-7
Wilson confused Chārvākas w I 419n
Buddhist Catechism. See Olcott, H. S.
Budding, procreation by II 132, 658
  first race & II 116-17
  polyps reproduce by II 177
  second race & II 166
Budh (Skt), to know I xviii
  made phallic symbol I 472
  wisdom or I 473
Budha (Skt) Mercury, Wisdom. *See also* Thot
  author of Vedic hymn II 498
  avatāra of Vishnu [Buddha] II 578
  creator of 4th, 5th races II 456
  esoteric wisdom I xviii; II 499
  fifth race under II 29
  Hermes, Hormig, or II 366, 499
  Idā wife of II 138, 140
  men of, metaphorically immortal II 44-5
  Mercury or I 473; II 27, 366, 374, 455, 456, 499, 540
  Nebo (Chald) or II 456
  not a fiction of Brahmans II 498
  son of Soma & Tārā I 228n, 392; II 45 &n, 138, 456, 498-9
Budha-Soma
  Mercury-Moon, Thoth-Lunus I 396n
Budhism (Wisdom) I 134
  Buddhism & I xviii
  esoteric I xxi; II 100
  Esoteric Buddhism & I xvii-xviii, 539n
Buffon, Comte de II 646
  American & African fauna II 792
  believed many worlds inhabited II 706
  Earth 34 million years old II 698n
  on origin of planets I 596-7
Builder, The (illustrated weekly)
  Easter Island statues in I 322
Builders. *See also* Architects, Dhyāni-chohans, Logos, Masons
  amshaspends, pitar or I 127; II 358
  architects &, one I 579 &n
  B'raisheeth & 6 sephīrōth I 374-5
  construct kosmos on ideal plan I 104, 339
  creators of universe I 53, 88-9, 265
  cyclopean buildings & I 209n
  Cyclopes called II 345n
  Demiurge composed of I 380n

designers in nature II 732
dhyāni-chohans called I 233; II 170, 366
divine, of man II 194
Dracontia or II 380
elohīm or I 239
ether of science material of I 339
fiery lives both, & destroyers I 262n
fire, astral light & I 253
Fohat "builder of" I 139n
hosts of, First-Born I 344
initiators II 345n
men in prior cycle I 107, 277
planetary chain architects I 107n, 128
prajāpati or seven I 436
reigned over man I 265
science would not accept I 590
seven I 80, 88, 127, 213 &n, 355 &n, 480; II 514
three groups of I 127-8
various names for I 127-8, 355; II 380
Viśvakarman or II 559
work in cycles II 732
Bull, Sir R. S. *See* Ball, Sir R. S.
Bull. *See also* Cow, Taurus
  aleph or II 551, 574
  apis (Egy) I 135; II 418n
  Assyrian II 115n
  became phallic symbol II 583
  Christian sacred animal I 363
  "eye of the" I 663
  man or the, (Egy, Heb) I 390 &n
  of Mendes I 385
  Ormazd created, Ahriman slew II 93
  physical generation symbol I 67, 657
  Pleiades 7 stars beyond I 648n
  sacred I 385; II 408
  St Luke, Earth &, (diag) II 114
  symbolizes 5th race II 533
  Uriel or, of Ophites I 127n; II 115n
Bulwer-Lytton, Sir Edward
—— *The Coming Race*
  vril of I 563
—— *Zanoni*
  Zanoni faces his Augoeides I 573
Bumapa (Tib) School
  Āryāsaṅgha of, on alaya I 48
Bundahishn (Zoroastrian scripture)
  hermaphrodites described II 291n
  Karshipta & Mazdean religion II 292
  karshvars II 758 &n
  races of men II 634
Bunsen, Christian Karl J., Baron von
—— *Egypt's Place in Universal History*
  antiquity of Egypt I 435

Asian flood of, not Noah's II 141
dates Menes II 374n
Eusebius mutilated history I xxvi
Great Pyramid 20,000 yrs old II 750
original unity of Semites, Aryans I 115n
—— *God in History*
Prometheus older than Greeks II 413
Seth & Typhon II 32n, 82n
Bunsen, Robert W., achievements I 528
Burgess, Rev E., & Hindu astronomy I 667
Burham-i-Kati [Borhan Quatiu] (Pers)
Hormig or Budha in II 366-7
Buri (Norse), had 3 sons by Bestla I 427
Burma
distorting of ears in II 339
fate of Buddhism in I xx-i
nirvāna called neibban in I 38n
Burmeister, Hermann C. C.
on age of Earth II 154
Egypt 72,000 yrs old II 750n
same forces past & present I 639-40
Burnell, A. C. I 334. *See also* Hopkins
Burnes, Sir A., on Bamian statues II 337
Burning Bush (of Moses)
aspect of Archaeus I 338n
in *Exodus* I 121
Burning Valley of Fallen Angels II 535
Burnouf, Eugène
war in heaven ends on Earth II 390
—— *Commentaire sur le Yaçna*
amshaspends are archangels I 437
—— *[Introduction à l'histoire . . .]*
Brahmā as "Creator" I 380n
Buddhist canon I xxvii
Burns, Robert I 304
Bushmen

arrowheads compared II 522
fast dying out II 162, 421n
intellectuality among II 168 &n, 522
Lemuro-Atlanteans II 195-6n, 721
naturalists' opinion of II 287, 725, 779
not burdened w karma II 168
not descended fr anthropoids II 193 &n
pigmy, & future archaeology II 723
Busrah. *See* Basra
Buthon (Gnos) I 214, 349. *See* Bythos
Butler, Charles, *Horae biblicae* II 200n
Butlerof[v], Prof Aleksandr Mikhaylovich
defended spiritualism I 520
spiritualist I 251n, 581
supports 4th dimension theory I 251 &n
theosophists respect II 651
—— *Scientific Letters*
divisibility of atom I 519
force, matter, motion I 517-18
Butterfly
Greek symb of human soul I 74; II 292
humanity like grub becoming I 159
Bybline Heights II 417
[Byron, Lord, q *Childe Harold*] I xli
Bythos (Gnos)
Aeons emanate fr II 569n
angle of Gnostic square II 573
Brahmā is I 214
Ennoia of, is mind II 490
only periodical I 214
perfect Aion existed before I 349
Tiphereth issues fr II 214
unfathomable depth II 214, 569n
unknown universal soul II 574
Byzantine Painting
Bamian frescoes remind one of II 339

C

Cabala [*De Arte Cabbalistica,* Reuchlin]
  Oliver q on Heptad II 599-600
  Tetraktys, Pyramis II 601
Cab & Urim, or Kabirim (Mackey) II 362n
Cabar-Zio [Kebar-Zivo]
  produces 7 cardinal virtues I 196
"Cabbalah, The." *See* Skinner, J. R.
Cactus Plant, illustrates races II 434-5
Cadiz, Atlantis & II 371
Cadmus, Camilus (Kadmos, Kadmilos, etc in
    tx) II 267n
  alphabet of I xxiii
  Hermes or, a Kabir II 362
  Sanātana in Sanskrit II 106
  taught early man II 364
Caduceus (of Mercury) I 549-51; II 364
  cynocephalus & I 388
  double serpent I 253n
  ogdoad, cycles & II 580
  symbol of evolution of gods, atoms I 549
  wand & brazen serpent are II 208
Caelo, De. See Aristotle
Caenogenesis (Cenogenesis) II 659, 663n
Caesar, "render unto . . ." I 296
Caesar, Gaius Julius, & burning of Alexandrian
    library II 692, 763n
Caesarea, Bishop of. *See also* Eusebius
  censor of other religions I xxvi
Caesar Philippus I 311
Cagliostro, wrongly classed a charlatan II 156
Caherman, Simorgh & age of world II 617
Cain. *See also* Kain, Ka-yin
  Abel &, female & male II 43-4n, 125 &n,
    134-5, 273n
  apple, Eve & II 166
  Atlanteans prototypes of II 273
  genealogies of Seth & II 391 &n
  generated by Satan or Samael II 389
  goes to Nod to marry I 324n; II 286, 394
  Jehovah-, male part of Adam II 388
  Jehovah is, esoterically I 414, 578; II 269n,
    388
  Mars is II 390
  missionaries link, w Pulastya I 415
  murder of Abel by, explained II 43-4n, 273n,
    388, 469
  race of giants II 222

Roman Church links, w sorcery II 391
Saturn, Vulcan, or I 578
Seth son of, & Abel II 127
son of Adam Kadmon II 127
three races & II 397
Vulcain, V'elcain, or II 392-3n
Cain-Abel, primal twins I 412
Cainan, son of Enoch II 391n
Cain and His Birth [*De Cherubim* I]. *See* Philo
    Judaeus
Cainite(s) II 391n. *See also* Atlanteans,
    Root Race — 4th
  called serpent creator II 209
  cause of Noachian deluge I 415
  declared heretical II 389
  destroyed by deluge II 391
  fourth race or II 146
  races, pre-Adamite, divine II 172
Cain-Jehovah II 128, 269n, 388, 469
Cain-Jehovah-Abel
  bisexual creative deity II 125
  separation into sexes or II 469
Cairns, perfection of ancient I 208-9n
Cajetan, Cardinal, rejects *Enoch, Jude* II 531
Calcutta Review I 8n
Calendar(s)
  Accadian, (Sayce) II 693
  civil, of Aztecs I 322
  fr data of Asuramaya II 50, 67-70
  Hebrew, (Skinner) I 389-90
  of kali-yuga II 50-1 & 51n
  Ptolemy's I 663-4
  theogonies related to religious I 652
  Tirukkanda Pañchānga II 50-1
  Vedic, & Krittikā II 551
Calf
  allegory of cow & I 398 &n
  golden I 578, 675
California
  large bit of, once Lemuria II 328
  Sequoia allied to Greenland trees II 11
Callimachus, *In Delum* (*Hymn to Delos*)
  on fabricating Poseidon's trident II 390 &n
Callisthenes, Chaldean astron figures II 620
Caloric
  luminous, (Lévi) I 253n

Metcalf's I 524-7
 physical residue of ether I 524n
Calpetus, Strait of II 371
Calvary I 612; II 559
Calvin, John, lost sight of Michael II 479
Calvinists, *Catechism* of II 304n
Calypso (Gk)
 daughter of Atlas II 762
 lived on Ogygia or Atlantis II 769n
Cambodia, Nagkon-Wat of II 430
Cambrian Period
 astral fossils materialized in Laurentian
  II 684, 712
 Croll's figures for II 10n, 715n
 Darwin on II 688n
 scientists on II 10-11
Cambry, Jacques, *Monuments Celtiques*
 devil's tomb in England II 206n
 Dracontia works of nature II 347
 monoliths weighing 500,000 kg II 343
 nature made rocking stones II 344
 talking stones at Westminster II 342
Cambyses, King (Pers) I 399
 saw black & white Kabiri statues II 360
Camel
 flying, seduced Eve (*Zohar*) II 205
 llama & II 792
Camillus. See Cadmus
Campanile Column of San Marco II 85
Campbell, George J. D., Duke of Argyle
—— *Unity of Nature*
 man's early inventions greatest II 373
Canaan(ites)
 Jews married w, (Bible) I 313n
 Nebo adored by II 456
 prehistoric mysteries of II 452
 race of, taller than Jews II 755-6
 Votan descended fr Ham & II 380
Canary Islands
 Basques & Guanches of II 790n
 Cro-Magnon &, Guanches II 678n, 740, 791
 Lake Superior stones like those in II 790
 linked w Venezuela, Africa II 791
 remnants of Atlantis II 222-3
Cancer (zodiacal sign)
 Benjamin & I 651
 location of White Island II 403
 at South Pole II 431
 Tropic of II 356
Candaules [or Myrsilus]
 Lydian King II 775n
Candia, Isle of, mandrakes in II 27n
Candidate (for initiation) I 433
 attached to cross II 543, 558-9

beams of rising Sun & II 558-9
chrēstos & II 573
 entranced for three days II 558
 passions of II 380-1, 615
 personified his temple god II 466n
 sarcophagus & death of II 462, 558
Candlestick
 cross &, (Skinner) II 581n
 Jewish, symbol II 581-2
Canis [Canes] Venatici (Hunting Dogs
  Nebula) irresolvable I 598n
Cannibal(s, ism)
 earlier men not II 716n
 worse among civ man (Laing) II 723
Canon
 Jehovah does not fit into Christian II 537
 Job oldest bk in Heb I 647
 of Proportion originated w 3rd race rishis
  I 208-9n
 Pythagorean, of music II 600-1
Canstadt (la Naulette) Man II 688n, 744
Canton (China)
 aboriginal descendants near II 280 &n
Cap, The. See also Arctic, Polar Regions
 first imperishable continent II 400-1
Capella, Martianus, [*Satyra de nuptiis philo-
  logiae*] . . .
 Egyptian astronomy 40,000 yrs old I 650
Capellini, Giovanni
 humans chipped Miocene flints II 752n
 man's origin in Miocene II 288, 714n
 Pliocene man in Italy II 740n
Cape of Good Hope
 meteorite w carbon found at II 706
Cape Verde Islands
 remnant of Atlantis II 222-3, 791, 793
Capricorn(us). See also Crocodile, Makara
 crocodile or I 219, 233; II 576
 fifth hierarchy, presided over by I 233
 Makara (goat-dolphin) I 221, 376, 384;
  II 576-80
 Naphtali or I 651
 North Pole &, (Mackey) II 431
 Tropic of II 356
 twenty-eight stars of II 579
Captivity, the Babylonian II 473, 618
Caput Angelorum II 237
Carbon (element)
 early geologic eras & I 253n
 found in meteorites II 706
 oxygen, nitrogen, hydrogen & II 592
 properties of II 593
 in protoplasm I 637n; II 158
Carbonic Acid

animals supply plants w I 262n; II 290n
   early races & II 157, 160
   oceans of, in Carboniferous I 252-3n
Carboniferous Age II 257
   carbonic acid & life in I 252-3n
   giant ferns of II 276
   races 1 & 2 & II 150, 713n
Cardinal Points II 392, 591
   Christian, spirits; pagan, devils I 123
   devas, mahārājas preside over I 122-3
   four & 8, explained I 128; II 576-7
   four elements & I 462-3
   four sacred animals symbolize I 363
   in grotto of Zarathustra I 464
   Jews had no name for I 128n
   pyramid & I 617
   in var religions I 126, 346, 367, 408-9; II 556
Caresma. *See* Baresma
Carib(s) (West Indians)
   European skulls similar to II 738-40, 790
   Guanches & II 792
Caribbean Sea, Atlantis fr, to Sahara II 424
Carlyle, Thomas
   Christian & Hindu religions II 470
   —— "On Heroes, Hero-Worship . . ."
   man's body a temple (Novalis) I 212
   mystery of "I" in us I 211-12
   —— "Past and Present"
   "great antique heart" I 210-11
   —— "Sartor Resartus"
   symbols I 303
Carnac (in Brittany) II 352, 752
   Egyptian Karnac & II 380
   giants & II 341, 343
   isthmus once joined, & Britain II 750 &n
   Malabar tombs & II 347
   meant serpent mount [mound] II 380
   pre-Druidic symbolic record II 754
   relic of last Atlanteans II 343
   world history symbolized in II 754
Carnelley, Dr Thomas
   element of negative atomic wt I 584
   elements are compound I 583
Caron, Abbé II 479
Carpenter
   divine II 101 &n
   St Joseph, of Bible II 101n
   Viśvakarman, of the gods II 101, 542-3
Carpenter, Dr William
   —— *Intro. to the Study of the Foraminifera*
   Paleozoic foraminifera II 257
Carson [Nevada] (Indiana in tx)
   giant fossil footprints II 755
Cartailhac, É., man-made flints II 752n

Cartesian System. *See* Descartes, R.
Carthage
   giant skeletons at, (Tertullian) II 278
Caspian Sea
   Indian Ocean once one w II 609
   Io visits Astrakhan on II 416
Cassel, Rev Dr David I 113n; II 38, 40n
Cassini, Jacques
   secular motion of Moon I 660, 666
   tables of I 661, 667n
Cassiopeia, Brahe's new star in I 590
Cassius Hermone. *See* Hemina, L. Cassius
Caste(s) II 455
   Brahman & priestly I 270; II 130, 165n, 502-3
   Hamsa the one I 79
   of Magas II 322
   sacerdotal, & left-path adepts II 211-12, 502-3
   Upanishads before, system I 270
Castor (& Pollux)
   allegory of II 121-4
   born fr egg I 366
   Dioscuri or II 122, 361n, 362
   tomb of, in Sparta II 122n
Cat
   Egyptian symbol of Moon I 304-5
   eye of, follows lunar phases I 387
   Great, of Basin of Persia II 545-6
   as lunar symbol I 387-8
   vital fluid of, curled up II 552n
Cataclysm(s) I 273; II 138-49, 404, 751 &n.
      See also Axis, Continents, Deluges, Floods,
      Poles
   Apollo-Diana, Sun-Moon & II 771 &n
   & Aryan race II 445, 757
   Berosus figured, by zodiac I 649-50
   Bible references to II 703-4
   causes of II 314, 324-5, 329, 500n, 699,
      725-6, 771
   destroyed 4th race II 144, 314
   destroyed 2nd continent II 138
   destroy old civilizations II 311-12, 774
   at each sidereal year I 649
   every race records II 787 &n
   of fire & water II 266, 307n, 309, 311,
      725-6, 776n, 784-6
   four, already; 5th to come II 138
   fourth round, most intense II 149
   geological records of II 486
   Hindu computations re I 369
   Lyell on II 786-7
   Moon, Sun, planets cause II 500n, 699
   new forms & bodies after II 262-3, 500n
   next, & present continents II 332-3
   Orphic Hymn on II 785-6

periodical, cyclical II 145, 329, 785
pralaya also applies to II 307n
racial, not a Noah's deluge II 325
Secondary Age, destroyed 3rd race II 714
subraces subject to II 330
successive, destroy races II 307n, 309, 437, 500n, 703, 776
take thousands of years II 330
two meanings of, (in *IU*) II 144
Vendidad on II 609-10
violent & gradual II 787 &n
will destroy Europe, Amer I 646; II 445-6
wise men saved fr I 273
Catacombs
  Egyptian, Chaldean II 379
  of Ozimandyas decade I 321
  swastika, cross & II 586-7
Catarrhine. *See also* Anthropoids, Apes
  fr late Atlantean times II 193
  man & II 171, 193, 264, 328-9, 663n, 665-7, 748-9
Catechism(s) I 120
  Buddhist, quoted I 635-6
  Calvinist II 304n
  Druse II 27
  kabbalistic, esoteric I 299
  of Southern India II 31
Catechism, Esoteric or Occult
  quoted:
    Breath digs 7 holes into laya I 147
    breath exhales, inhales II 43
    flame & sparks I 120
    god-monad-atom I 619
    Great Breath, germ, space I 11-12
    head, heart, soul of Gnyana [jñāna] II 281-2
    Mother or dry waters of space I 625
    projection of forms II 57
    Space I 9, 132, 522
Catechism of the Viśishṭādvaitains . . .
  (Bhāshyāchārya)
  evolution of matter & lives I 522
  pathway of the jīvas I 132
Catherine de Médicis II 70
Catholic. *See* Roman Catholic(s)
Catholicism, Roman
  dogmas & rites originally pagan I 400-2
  later Buddhist ritual identical w I 539n
Caucasian
  Jews, Armenians, & Parsis are II 471n
  one of 3 fifth-race types II 471n
Caucasus Mt(s)
  decad in mounds of I 321
  Io travels to II 416

Koh-Kaf, Kap-Kaz or II 398, 399 &n
Prometheus chained on II 244, 414, 768-9
Cauchy, A. L., *Mémoire sur la . . . lumière*
  discontinuity of ether I 482, 486
—— *Sept leçons . . .*
  theory of atoms I 486, 489
Causality, Causation I 405
  Aeons & II 488
  avyakta or state of II 46
  cycles of I 638
  dhyān-chohanic essence is II 120
  intelligent II 738
  karma law of ethical II 302n
  latent during sandhyās II 239
  One Unknowable I 139
  physical, of forms II 736
  plane of material II 157
  science & ultimate I 465
Cause(s). *See also* First Cause, Nidānas
  Absolute, of Egyptians, Spencer I 675
  aspects of incognizable II 487
  Brahmā, of creative potencies I 55
  Causeless I 9-10n, 14-15 &n, 55, 89, 258, 280, 425, 569; II 589
  concatenation of, & effects I 171, 594
  effects of conscious I 145
  effects of suppressing bad I 644
  elementals & primary, secondary I 146
  of existence I 44-5, 55-6
  exoteric, esoteric, endexoteric II 74
  final, incomprehensible I 569
  Fohat, of cosmic electricity I 554
  infinite & eternal I 14
  instinctual I 169
  Kārana as eternal I 41, 46, 93n, 280
  karma & I 634, 644
  of light, heat, etc I 514, 554
  Mahābuddhi as the formless I 420
  Mahat, of all things I 256
  man's, awaken powers in sidereal world I 124
  One, & Primal I 618
  potency of every produced I 450
  Space & Unknown First I 9n, 342
  upādāna or material I 55, 370n
  verae, vs māyāvic I 489 &n
  Vishnu as the Ideal I 349
Cave(s). *See also* Cave-Temples, Initiations
  Bamian II 338
  of Dordogne II 522
  -dwellers I 208n, 280
  Gimil's, (Norse) II 100
  gupta, near Okhee Math I xxx
  of initiate-hermits II 381, 501
  initiation- I xx; II 181n, 237n, 541, 558

libraries I xxiv, xxxiv
Moses initiated at Hor-eb II 541
Neolithic II 352
of rishis II 381
seven, of Nahuatl II 35 &n
Zoroastrian I 126
Cave Hunting. See Dawkins, W. B.
Cave Men (European). *See also* Cro-Magnon,
    Neolithic Man, Paleolithic Man
accursed races II 319
architecture not evolved fr I 208-9n
artistry of II 741n
Atlantean descendants II 740
immigrated to Europe II 740 &n
not Haeckelian monsters II 741n
Cavernes du Périgord. See Lartet, É. A.
Cave-Temple(s)
decad in Hindu I 321
Fergusson dates, wrongly II 220n
perfection of, (Kenealy) I 208-9n
subterranean passages of II 221
Cedars of Lebanon
initiates & kings called II 494
Cedrinus, George [*Synopsis historiarum*]
on Iaō II 541 &n
Mars called *Ertosi* II 143-4n
Celaeno, daughter of Atlas II 768
Celepas Geraldinus
calls Henoch the "divine giant" II 366
Celestial "Ancestors," or śishtas I 248
Celestial Bodies
behavior of, model for Earth II 502
Brahmā creates, in 1st kalpa II 625n
genesis of I 602
"Celestial Chemistry." *See* Hunt, T. S.
Celestial Logos I 246
Celestial Men, or angels I 230
Celestial Numbers
1, 3, 5, 7 called II 35
Celestial Order of Beings I 216
Celestial Pole II 358, 785
Celestial Priapus (Gnos) II 458
Celestial Thrones, azure seats or II 424-5
Celestial Virgin I 60
ākāśa I 332, 460
of alchemists I 458n
hierarchies emanate fr I 215
Celibacy, chelaship & II 295-6
Celibate(s). *See also* Chastity, Kumāras
Adepts II 82
Eternal II 249
invisible, as creative Logos I 217
sons of Brahmā I 236
Cell(s)

arrange themselves into organs II 648
every, has its monad I 630n, 632
formation of, & crystallization II 255 &n
germinal I 223n, 224
hereditary transmission in I 219, 223n
monads inform atoms & I 632
Pasteur on I 249n, 263n
procreation of, & 1st race II 116-17, 166
reproduction II 658-9
robbing oxygen I 263n
six-ft man fr I 222-3
-souls of Haeckel II 670-4
spiritual plasm soul of I 219
"Cell-Souls & Soul-Cells." *See* Haeckel, E.
Celsus
Church Fathers destroyed books of I 445
sevenfold ladder of creation I 445-6
Celt(s)
destiny or judgment stone of II 342n
giant-legends lived late among II 754
invasion of, (Lefèvre) II 741
Sun-born god among II 44n
Cement, ancient, indestructible II 430
Cenozoic Era
third eye in animals of II 299n
Titans fought, monsters II 206, 293
Censorinus, *De Die natali*
music of the spheres I 433
Centaurs II 65n
Center(s). *See also* Laya, Monads, Point
cosmic focus I 11n
neutral, between planes I 148
seven atoms, of energy I 635
seven, of 1st root-race II 35n, 249, 732
Central America. *See also* Incas, Mayas
giants of, (Donnelly) II 276n
Le Plongeon's work in II 34-5
man in, during Andes upheaval II 745
monuments w negro heads II 790
Palenque, Uxmal II 430
Central Asia(n). *See also* Aryan
adepts led races to II 425
Chinese Garden of Eden II 203
cradleland in Gobi II 220-1
Garden of Wisdom II 204
Grotto of Zarathustra I 464
little deluge in, (Bunsen) II 141
plateau of, submerged II 609
prehistoric civilization I xxxii
primeval Brahmans initiated in II 565
rocks, inscriptions in I 229, 321-3; II 439
Russian mystics initiated in I xxxvi
Sacred Island in I 209; II 220
Senzar secret tongue in I xliii

separation of nations II 425
sixth continent will include II 404-5 &n
some dry land in 3rd race II 329
tablelands, formation of II 724
tau & swastika found in II 557
volcanism (*Vendidad*) II 356
wisdom-religion in I 376
Central Sun, Central Spiritual Sun I 231, 379.
    See also Sun, Sun-Abrasax
    causes Fohat to collect dust I 201
    central body of Milky Way II 240n
    determines motions of bodies I 673
    dhyāni-chohans have not penetrated
        beyond I 13
    electric fire of life II 114
    formless invisible fire in I 87
    our Sun emanates fr I 527n
    our Sun reflection of I 100, 639
    seven rays of I 574
    Sun-Abrasax of kabbalists II 214
    teachings re II 239-41
    uncreated beam reflection of I 275-6
Centrifugal, Centripetal Motion I 604
    both, awaken Kosmos I 282 &n
    cause of rotation I 499
    descending & ascending arcs II 261
    female-male, negative-positive I 282n
    interdependent I 416
    planets & I 593
    Satan represents II 245
    septenary evolution & I 267
Century(ies). *See also* Twentieth Century
    every, door will open wider I xxxvii-viiin
    first, & karma of Israel I xli
    Secret Doctrine sufficient for this II 742
Cephas. *See* Kēphas
Cerastes, horned viper of Philae I 363-4
Cereals
    all, except wheat traced II 373-4
    Isis gave, to man II 374
    Neolithic man used II 716
Cerebellum
    seat of animal proclivities II 297-301
Cerebral Hemispheres
    forepart of, & human intellect II 301
Cerebration, & chylification I 297
Ceremonial Magic
    in exoteric churchianity II 748
    Jewish kabbalists dealt w I 234n
Ceres (Rom). *See also* Demeter
    belongs to Kabiri class II 362-4, 390
    brought corn to Sicily II 364
    Diana daughter of, (Aeschylus) II 419n
    Poseidon becomes horse for II 399n, 775

taught man agriculture II 390
Virgin took over worship of I 400-1
worshiped at Ierna II 760
Cerinthus (early Gnostic)
    doctrine of risen Christ II 508
Cesil (Orion). *See* Kesīl
Cestrensis, Count Hugo
    Stone of Mona & II 345
Ceylon. *See also* Lankā
    astronomical allegories found in II 380
    Egyptian zodiac fr II 435
    giants (rākshasas) of II 336
    Leo vertical to II 407
    once part of Lemuria II 7, 324, 332
    remnant of Atlantis II 314
    remnant of sunken continent II 222
    Veddhas of II 196n, 421n, 723
[Chabas, F. J.], *Le Papyrus Magique Harris*
    ram-headed Ammon II 213n
Chackchuska, Chakshuba. *See* Chākshusha
Chaiah. *See* Ḥayāh
Chain. *See also* Earth Chain, Globes, Moon
        Chain, Planetary Chain
    creators act on globes of II 77
    septenary II 308n
Chaire d'Hébreu . . . *See* Renan, E.
Chaitanya (Skt), Chit & I 6
Chakna-Padma-Karpo (Tib)
    Chenresi, dhyāni & bodhisattva II 179
Chakra (Skt) wheel
    circle, disc of Vishnu I 114; II 465-6, 546
    six-pointed star, Vishnu & I 215
Chakravartin (Skt) universal ruler
    Vishnu as, in tretā age II 483
Chākshusha (Skt)
    diagram II 309
    manu 3rd round, 3rd race II 615n
Chaldea(ns). *See also* Berosus, Chaldees
    Adam fr II 42-3
    Adam was mankind II 102
    adept, Qū-tāmy II 454
    Akkadians older than I 392, 650
    allegories, legends II 282, 462-3, 477
    ancestors of II 328
    Anu of, & trinity II 62, 139n
    astrological magic & theophania I 652
    beings refusing to create in II 93
    bower of voluptuousness II 204
    catacombs II 379
    cosmogony of Berosus II 504
    creation story II 3-4, 53
    Dāgōn of, & Matsya avatāra II 139
    Damascius on oracles of I 235
    divine dynasties II 316, 429, 486

Ea a principal god of II 53, 139n
elements, angels, planets II 115n
Eusebius mutilated, records I xxxi
evil spirits emblems of chaos II 386
Fohat key to, religion I 673
four a sacred number of I 89n
fragment in British Museum II 283-4n
Garden of Eden fr II 202
Genesis of I 357; II 104
giants (Izdubar) I 266-7; II 336
initiates of, degenerated II 212
initiates' view of the Moon I 396
Java-Aleim II 215
Jews borrowed lore fr I 313, 352, 388, 655
    &n; II 240, 428
Jews sought refuge in II 200
Kabbala identical w Jewish II 461-2
Kabiri received name fr I 435n
kosmos is God (Philo) I 344
Magas, Magi, initiates of II 323, 395
measures same as Jews' I 312-13
misunderstood Jewish cherubim II 518
Moon-gods II 139n
Moses' story fr II 428
myths based on fact, truth II 236
Nabathean Agriculture & II 452-6
oracles of I 235, 348, 462
pre-Adamite Mysteries (Chwolsohn) II 452
Purānic legends understood by II 4
received lore fr Brahmans I xxxi, 117; II 226
recorded motions of planets I 660, 663
scriptures apocryphal (Renan) II 456
scriptures disfigured, destroyed I xxvi-vii,
    xxxiv, 10
scriptures fountain of Bible I xxvi
seven, 8 gods of I 575n; II 35
sevens in thought of II 97, 603, 612, 617
Sufis preserved works of I 288
swastika found among II 586
Syrians defined worlds like I 435
tablets agree w Hermes II 2
tablets are archaic records II 3, 5, 54, 202
taught 3 aspects of universe I 278
three keys in days of Berosus I 311
tree, serpent worship I 405
way to Bible thru, scriptures II 383
wisdom of Hebrew initiates fr I 352
works echo Secret Doctrine I 288
worshiped male & female Moon I 388
Xisuthrus is, Noah II 141
Chaldean Account of Genesis. See Smith, George
Chaldean *Book of Numbers* II 37, 85, 111
close to esoteric vidyā I 241
derived fr "very old book" I xliii

Ibn Gebirol used, as source II 461n
key to *Bk of Concealed Mystery* II 626n
no longer extant II 626n
oldest kab source II 461-2, 461n, 506
Zohar no longer same as I 214, 230
references:
    Ain-sōph fiery pelican I 80
    angels, 1st & secondary I 337
    Babylonia given in numbers II 202
    Blessed Ones & matter I 224
    en, ain, aiōr, self-existent I 214
    form of Crown (Kether) I 433 &n
    light is darkness to man I 337
    Ptah born fr world egg I 367
    Rishoon & 3 sons in II 397
    Samael, Michael & wisdom in II 378
    sephīrōth I 239-46
    seven principles I 197 &n
    seven worlds are 7 races II 705
    Shekhīnāh sexless in I 618
    Worker's Hammer in II 99
Chaldean Kabbala
    ancient wisdom &, identical II 461-2
    Book of Numbers or I 618
Chaldean Oracles of Zoroaster
    aether of ancients was fire I 331
    ether I 462
    mundane god of spiral form I 348
Chaldees. *See also* Chaldeans, Magi
    caste of adepts, not of a nation II 748
    gave Hindu zodiac to Greeks I 658
    governed by divine dynasties II 328
    initiates or, & space II 502
    knowledge of I 409; II 23, 35
    later, greeted morning star II 759 &n
    science has returned to I 586
    settled in Babylonia II 748
    taught succession of worlds II 756
    Taurus sacred to I 657
Chaldeo-Akkadian Accounts II 4
Chaldeo-Assyrian Accounts II 3, 477
Chalice, sacrificial, or argha (ark) II 461
"Challenger" (soundings, voyage)
    Atlantic continent II 333
    Atlantic ridges II 782, 792-3
Chambers, J. D. *See also Divine Pymander*
—— *Theol. & Philos. Works of Hermes . . .*
    seven men are Patriarchs II 2n
Chameleon, atrophied 3rd eye of II 296
Champ Dolent, menhir of II 752
Champlain Epoch
    Easter Island raised during II 327-8
Champollion, Jean-François
    amazement of, (de Rougé) I 367-8

—— *Panthéon égyptien*
Ἐιχτῶν (Eichtōn), Agathodaemon is II 210
Knouph [Chnuphis] I 472
serpent II 210
sevens in *Book of Dead* I 674
seven worlds, agents I 436
substantiates Manetho, Ptolemy II 367
Toum [Tum] or Fohat I 673 &n
Ch'an, Dan, Janna
  Chinese, Tibetan esoteric schools I xx &n
Chananea, Rabbi. *See* Joshua ben Chananea
Chance
  blind forces, in nature II 475
  Coleridge on I 653
  infinitesimal, variations II 697
  matter-force-, trinity of I 505
  no, in nature I 653
Chan-chi (Chin), demigods II 365
Chaṇḍālas (Skt)
  ancestors of Jews I 313n; II 200
  left India 8000 BC II 200
Chandrabhāgā River I 377
Chandragupta, King II 550n
  grandfather of Aśoka II 550n
  of the Morya dynasty I 378n
Chandra-Vansa [Chandravaṃśa] (Skt)
  lunar dynasties I 388, 392
Chāndrāyaṇa (Skt), lunar year I 36
Chang-ty. *See* Huang-ti
Chanina, Rabbi. *See* Ḥanina
Chantong or Chenresi II 179
Chants Cypriaques, Hyg. Tal. See Hyginus,
  Fab. Lib.
Chaos (Gk). *See also* Waters
  abode of wisdom, not evil II 503
  Abyss I 367, 427; II 503
  ākāśa I 338n, 452, 460
  ākāśa proceeds fr I 536
  in all Gk & Aryan speculation I 579
  amrita mixed w evil in I 348
  ark is spirit brooding over II 313
  bird drops egg into I 359
  ceases thru the ray I 231
  fr Χαίνω (chainō) void I 109
  cold luminous gas I 250, 599 &n
  divided into 7 oceans II 704n
  Divine Thought directed into II 704n
  dragons, serpents & II 386
  eternal feud of, (Akkadians) II 477
  evil spirits emblems of II 386
  female binary (Lévi) II 555
  female space I 90n, 431; II 84
  Flood symbolized by II 139
  Great Deep, Araṇī, Aditi II 527

Hesiod's I 336n, 425-6
Ialdabaôth & I 197 &n
infinite, boundless, endless I 336n
is Space (Aristotle) I 336n
Kon-ton I 214
macrocosm, microcosm born fr I 283
male-female I 231
manifestation starts w I 330
Mōt fr union of wind & I 340
mother, water or I 70
"nebular condition" I 579
Noun [Nūn] (Egy) or I 312
ocean is masculine aspect of I 345n
part of Orphic Triad I 451-2n, 582-3
Phanēs & Chronos (Orphism) I 583
planets evolve fr I 103
primary aspect of mūlaprakriti I 536
primitive, & nebulae (Wolf) I 598-9
primordial, is aether I 332
primordial substance I 330, 332, 338, 599
secondary, & divine dynasties II 486
to sense, cosmos to reason I 2
senseless I 340, 342
Sophia rescued fr, by Christos I 132n
Soul of the World (Plato) I 338, 343
Space &, unmanifested Deity II 269
spirit & matter latent in I 64
spirit divorced fr matter I 640
spirit in, or space II 65
Spirit of God & I 74, 461; II 505
storehouse of future worlds I 337
Tohu-bohu II 477
undifferentiated matter I 451-2n; II 505
Uranos creative powers of II 269
Vāch I 434
various names for I 283
veil betw Incognizable & Logos I 431
Virgin Mother I 65, 460
vital electricity I 338-9
Voice calls universe out of I 137
watery abyss II 503
fr wind &, sprang the seed I 340
world stuff I 579
Yliaster developed fr within I 283
Chaos-Theos-Kosmos I 342-9, 366
Chappe d'Auteroche, Abbé, *Voyage en Sibérie*
  six-month year in Kamchatka II 621
Charāchara (Skt)
  locomotive & fixed beings I 454
Charcot, J. M. II 370-1n
  Richet &, vindicate Mesmer II 156
Chariot
  heavenly form used as I 356
  vehicle or, in Kabbala I 214

Charles, Jacques A. C., Law of I 84
Charm(s) II 394. *See also* Magic
  magic incantations, etc I 468-9
  mandragora (mandrake) as a II 27n
  Sigurd became learned in I 404
Charton, Édouard T., *Magasin Pittoresque*
  bishops & Dracontia plans II 347
—— *Les voyageurs anciens et modernes*
  Irish stone fr Africa II 343
Chārvāka (Skt) Materialist school
  Wilson confused Buddhists & I 419n
Chassed. *See* Ḥesedh
Chastity, & pineal gland II 295-6
Chat. *See* Khat
Chateaubriand, François A. R. de
  on serpent as symbol I 403
Chāttam Paramba (chatam peramba in tx)
  giant bones in tombs at II 347
Chatur (Skt) four
  -mukha, four-faced Brahmā II 465
  takes on 3, becomes seven I 71
Chatvaraha [Chatvāras] (Skt) four
  term in *BG* II 140n
Chaubard, L. A., *L'Univers expliqué . . .*
  preferred Kabbala over science I 506 &n
Chauvaux, Mt, human bones at II 739
Chavah. *See* Ḥavvāh
Chayah. *See* Ḥayāh
Chebel. *See* Ḥebel
Cheiron, 7 brazen columns of II 612-13
Chela(s) (Hindi). *See also* Disciple
  called "Companions" II 504
  failure of one II 244-5n
  initiate becomes, to a higher I 206
  instructed in Upanishads I 270
  lanoo or, & third eye I 71 &n; II 295
  lay- I 163, 167
  occult figures given only to I 170
  pledged to the Brotherhood I 164
  Sagara, of Aurva & fiery weapon II 629
  schools for, & lay- I 122
  two, authored *Man [Fragments . . .]*
  II 227n
Chelaship, requires chastity II 295
Chemical. *See also* Elements
  action of terrestrial light I 597
  characteristics of comets differ I 142
  molecules & Earth's atmosphere I 625
  simple, combinations I 544n
Chemis [Chēmmis, Chēmi] (Gk)
  phantom form fr mundane egg I 367
Chemist I 144n
  Frankenstein monster & II 349
  should be psychometer I 201n

Chemistry. *See also* Physics, Science
  approaches occult I 218n, 544-54, 580-1,
  596, 620-6
  Aryan, fr Atlanteans II 426, 430
  atomic mechanics (Nazesmann) I 513
  atoms in space & I 142-3, 201 &n, 673
  cannot define fire I 121
  cannot grasp atom I 554
  compounds of, cease to combine I 478
  evolution of atoms, & I 620
  has returned to Anaxagoras I 586
  homunculi will become fact in II 349
  hydrogen & protyle II 105
  magician of future I 261
  meta elements in I 546-54, 581-6
  new alchemy or meta- I 622; II 349
  of Paracelsus I 283; II 656
  periodic table of elements II 627-8
  septenary doctrine & I 553; II 627
  some missing links of I 82 &n
  spectrum analysis & I 595-6
  theories of, re ether I 487
  Yliaster & protyle of I 283
  zero pt of, & laya-center I 138, 550-1
Chenresi, Chenrezi (Tib). *See also* Avalokiteśvara, Kwan-yin
  incarnates in Dalai, Tashi Lamas II 178
  Padmapāni, 4th race & II 173, 178
  progenitor like Daksha II 178-9
  Vanchug II 178
Cheops. *See* Great Pyramid
Cherchen, Cherchen daria [Cheerchenghe]
  (Chin), ancient ruins near I xxxiii-iv
Cherub, Cherubim (Heb). *See also* Angels,
  Śāraph
  anointed II 493
  Christian sacred symbol I 363
  copy of archaic prototype I 92
  on Egyptian & Jewish tabernacles I 125
  Ezekiel calls King of Tyre II 501
  guarded Eden I 127
  identical w devas, rishis, etc II 85
  knew well, loved more II 243
  "love most" (Jennings) II 238n
  Moses adopted, fr Egyptians II 115n
  name of celestial hosts II 501
  Ophite, & Hindu serpents I 127
  rule over 8th world (Syrian) I 435
  same as seraphim II 501
  "serpent in a circle" I 364n
  twelve wings of, & 12 signs I 651
  two, on Ark of Covenant II 460, 518
  two, on Tetragrammaton II 361n
  used to punish (Cruden) I 127

various names for I 126-7
Cherubim, De. See Philo Judaeus
Cheta, cave of Fa-hian I xx
Chevandier de Valdrôme, E.
   duration of coal formation II 695n
Cheybi II 633. *See* Khaibit
Chhandaja(s) (Skt)
   incarnate in various manvantaras II 584-5
Chhāndogya Upanishad, seven senses II 638
Chhāyā(s) (Skt) II 233n
   animal astral prototypes preceded, of men II 186-7
   became solid in 3rd race II 183
   blastema & II 120
   bodhisattvas, of dhyāni-buddhas I 572
   of the Fathers II 212
   first root-race were II 91, 102, 138, 173
   four Adams & II 503-4
   holy youths refused to enter I 192
   kabbalistic divine dynasties were II 487
   linga-śarīra or II 593
   of lunar pitris & man's body I 181
   pitris create rūpa or II 102
   -race II 90-1
   reproduced unconsciously II 116
   Sañjñā leaves, behind II 101, 174
   some Lords entered the II 161
   some waited & entered inferior II 228
   sons of self-born (pitris) II 120-1
   "third 'Seven' evolved their" II 590
Chhāyā-birth, sexless procreation II 174-5
Chhāyāloka (Skt)
   shadowy primal world I 119
Chichén Itzá, royal Kan Coh at II 34n
Chidākāśa(m) (Skt)
   plane of universal consciousness II 597n, 598
Chiim. *See* Ḥayyīm
Child
   little, term for initiates II 504
   of *Rev* 12 is universe II 384n
Child, Lydia M.
   —— *The Progress of Religious Ideas . . .*
   lofty meaning of sexual symbols I 358
Child-birth, lunar influences on I 180, 264, 387, 395; II 583
Children
   abnormal, 6th race forerunners II 445
   born w neck-clefts II 684n
   Mary mother of seven II 527
   procreating buddha-like II 415
   who die are reborn sooner II 303
   will be created, not begotten II 415
Chile, connected w Polynesia II 783 &n
Chimah, Cimah. *See* Kīmāh

Chim-nang. *See* Jen-nang
Chimpanzee. *See also* Apes
   brain measure of, (Vogt) II 682n
   evolved fr lower anthropoids II 193
   extinct in 6th race II 263
   fr 4th race man & extinct mammal II 683
   man's likeness to II 287
   owned by HPB II 676n
China
   astronomy of II 621, 766
   Buddhism declined in I xxi
   Buddhists reached, in 61 AD I xxviii
   divine dynasties of II 365, 368
   dragons of II 205-6, 209-10, 280n, 364-5
   esoteric school in I xxiii
   Kwan-yin of, equal to male gods I 136n
   Lolo aboriginal language rare MSS II 280n
   mountain tribe of, Lemurian II 195-6n
   Pa or men-serpents of II 209
   scriptures of, need key I xxv &n
   temples to Sun, dragon in II 378-9
   traditions of deluge in II 365
   true old texts of, hidden I xxxiv
China Revealed. See McClatchey
Ch'in Dynasty II 692
Chinese, Chinamen
   alphabet I 307 &n
   America known to II 424n
   antiquity of, (Gould) II 311-12
   astronomical sphere I 658
   Atlantis legend II 371-2, 425
   based Mysteries on ten II 603
   Buddhist ascetics secretive I 173-4
   Buddhists, pilgrimage of II 215
   cosmogonical symbols of II 554
   cosmogonies the most hazy I 356
   cosmogony Pythagorean I 440-1
   creation story II 54n
   cycles, solar, lunar, zodiacal II 620-1
   dragon-emperor II 364-5
   dragon legends of I 408-9; II 280n, 365, 486
   first man born fr egg I 366
   forefathers led to Central Asia II 425
   four quarters, 28 signs of I 408-9
   Garden of Eden II 203
   highest civilization of II 280n
   isolation, effects of II 425
   libraries destroyed II 692
   Mao-tse legends II 280-1
   monsters II 54n, 713
   Noah or Peirun-un II 365
   one of oldest 5th race nations II 364
   origin of II 425
   remnants of Atlantean race II 603

tabernacle, square form of I 125
taught 3 aspects of universe I 278
teachers or Brothers of the Sun I 271n
third eye legend II 301-2
toy nests & invisible worlds I 605
worshiped idols II 723
Chinese Buddhism. See Edkins, Rev J.
Chinesische Litteratur. See Schott, W.
Chin kuang ming ching (Luminous Sūtra of
    Golden Light)
  on Kwan-shi-yin I 470
Chinmātra (Skt) Parabrahman
  Vedānta term II 597n
Chior[Choir]-Gaur. *See* Côr-Cawr
Chips from a German Workshop. See Müller
Chiram. *See* Hiram, King of Tyrus
Chit (Skt)
  Parabrahman, achit I 59n
  pure thought, Brahma I 6
Chiti (Skt), Mahat or I 288n
Chitkala (Skt), Kwan-yin I 288n
Chiton (Gk) coat
  became Slavonic word II 202
Chitonuth Our [Kāthenôth 'Ôr] (Heb)
  coats of skin II 202
Chitragupta (Skt), reads out soul's life I 105
Chitra-Śikhaṇḍin (Skt)
  seven informing souls I 453
  seven rishis of Great Bear I 227n; II 631
Chittagong II 324
Chium (Egy) II 390n
Chi-Yi (Chin), 10 or 7, taught man II 365
Chnoubis, Chnumis, Chnouphis (Egy)
  Agathodaemon II 210 &n, 518
  Christos of Gnostics II 210n
  Eichtōn, Thoth-Hermes II 210-11
  Ophite serpent I 472-3
  solar, or Agathodaemon-Christos II 377
Chockmah, Chokhmah. *See* Ḥokhmāh
Chogi Dangpoi Sangye (Tib)
  Ādi-buddha or I 571
Chohan(s). *See also* Dhyāni-chohans
  fivefold, & kumāras II 578
  informing intelligences II 34
Chokrā (Hind), servant I 376
Cholula, Pyramid of (Central America)
  built by giants II 276n
Chord, odic, magnetic & sound I 555
Chou (Chin), Sun or II 372
Chow [Chou] Kung II 302. *See also* Chung Ku
Chozzar [Chorzar] (Gnos)
  dragon, Messiah of Naaseni II 356
  five androgyne ministers of II 577
  Gnostic Neptune II 356, 577, 578

Chrēsts, Chrēstos (Gk)
  Christos incarnates in II 573
  Dionysos, Prometheus or II 420
  neophytes II 562
  Ophiomorphos- I 413
  suffering man, or mankind II 420
Christ. *See also* Avatāras, Christos, Jesus,
    Logos, Messiah, Savior
  Agni suggestive of, (Jolly) II 101n
  aleph of Taurus & I 656-7
  ascending like cannonball II 708n
  Atonement II 497
  brazen serpent & I 364 &n
  buddhi not II 231n
  Catholic teachings re I 612
  Church calls itself Bride of II 377
  comes like lightning II 485
  cornerstone (1 *Peter*) II 627
  crucifixion symbol II 556, 586-7
  foretold in Joseph's dream I 649
  Gnostic value of 318 (Skinner) I 322-3
  Jehoshua, Joshua or II 539
  Jehovah II 76
  Jesus-, Angel-man II 114
  in kid gloves & Kwan-shi-yin I 473
  Logos, God in Space, Savior on Earth II 483
  Michael or, chief of aeons I 195n
  Nazarenes existed long before II 96n
  One God & Savior II 497
  one of many saviors I 653, 656-7
  Pisces does not refer to, alone I 653
  Prometheus & II 413
  Purāṇic story of Krishna & I xxxi
  race of buddhas & II 415
  St Michael Ferouer of II 478-9
  serpent, resurrection & I 472
  seven stars in hand of II 633
  -state II 604n
  -stone, -rock II 341
  Sun-, lives in thee (Bernard) I 401
  teachings of, degraded II 556
  teachings of, occult II 231n
Christian(s). *See also* Fall, Missionaries,
    Theology
  Ain-sōph ignored by I 391; II 540
  angels & devils of I 287
  angels fr Magian devs I 577
  animals & birds of I 357, 363, 384, 441-2n;
    II 210n
  anthropomorphic phallic God of I 4; II 472
  astronomical ignorance II 708
  black magic among, & pagans I 467-8
  borrowed sun, tree, serpent I 410
  called little fishes II 313n

chronology of II 73
connect Prometheus w Christ II 413
continued pagan superstitions I 466-70
couldn't destroy ancient wisdom I xl-i, xliv
creation out of nothing I 233n
cross an afterthought II 586-8
crucifixion II 560-1
deeds blackened memory of Christ II 514
deity only a creator I 439
denounced *Jupiter Fulgur* I 467
despoiled Jews of their Bible II 215
destroyed Egyptian lore I xl-i
disfigured Eastern ideas of deity II 38
disfigured Smaragdine Tablet II 113
dogmas I 196, 311-12, 400; II 103, 236n
dogmatized "evil spirits" II 386, 484
dragon, serpent I 73, 410, 657; II 354, 364, 507
early, followers of Christos I 198n
entered cycle of degradation I xxxv
exaggerated man's importance II 708
fire, cross I 384
four angels & Ophite faces I 127n
frog symbol on church lamps I 386
Genesis taken literally by II 95n, 215, 252n
God & Hindu compared II 472
God, archangels, Gnostic view of I 198
God lunar symbol I 390-1
God, Trinity I 113n; II 540
greet Morning Star II 759 &n
Hell of I 372n; II 247, 484, 507n, 774
heretical, sects II 389
hierarchy of powers I 92
Holy of Holies II 466 &n
inherited Semitic paradoxes I 383
initiates among I xxxix, 387; II 60
interpret Sabbath literally I 240
-kab disfigured *Pymander* II 114-15 &n
lotus became water lily among I 379
medieval I xli, 357
monks die to the world II 532
Moon deity I 386-7, 388, 390-1, 395
Mysteries, early compilers of II 561
mystics tampered w Kabbala II 457
nations burdened w Israel's religion II 470
Nazarenes opponents of later I 198n
new soul every birth taught by II 302-3
one divine incarnation II 555-6
personal trinity of II 236n
"plagiarized" by Hindus I xxxi &n, 654
plagiarized fr pagans II 481-2
pray for wind, rain, calm I 466-9
profane, cling to dead letter I 316
remodel earlier teachings II 61-2

Satan myth & Aryan allegories II 231-2
scriptures mistranslated II 537
spoliation of Pentateuch I 11
Svābhāvika Buddhists & I 3-4
symbols at Palenque II 557
temples are phallic symbols II 85
theology II 41, 95n, 497
Vedantic atheism & I 7 &n
War in Heaven I 68, 194, 202; II 497
Zohar altered by I 352
Christian, Paul
—— *The History of Magic . . .*
power of speech, the Word I 93-4
—— *L'Homme rouge . . .* I 93
Christian Church. *See also* Church, Missionaries, Roman Catholics
anathematized other gods II 508
basis of dogmas, rites I 310-11
carnalized Immaculate Conception I 58-60,
382n, 398-400
claims prehistoric plagiarism II 481
Councils II 279n
exalted Jewish tribal god II 507-8
invented eternal torment II 237n
karma of I xli
marriage ceremony of I 614-15n
Christianity. *See also* Church, Missionaries,
Roman Catholics
borrowed wholesale fr pagans I 410
degraded angels into demons II 93
dogmatic dualism of I 196
evil & devil of II 390, 506-9, 528
good, evil &, (de Mirville) II 515
Greek religion &, (Müller) II 764n
Hinduism & I 388
honeycombed w phallicism I 452n
made Kabiri infernal gods II 363
made paganism demoniacal II 60, 93
one-life teaching of II 304
original sin II 304
truth of, disfigured II 60
turned pagan deities into devils I 411-24;
II 231-2, 507
viewed millennia hence II 210n
won proselytes w sword I xli
Christianity and Gk Phil. See Cocker, B. F.
Christian Kabbalists I 196, 395
vs Eastern occultists II 476
mangle *Zohar* texts II 476
understood idea of Great Breath I 282
Christian Topography. See Cosmas Indicopleustes
Christology
mummified mythology (Massey) I 393

Christos
  adept becoming the full II 580
  anathematized II 377-8
  ātman w Gnostics I 132n
  Chnouphis of Gnostics II 210n, 377
  daivīprakriti light of II 38
  divine wisdom I 459; II 231n
  esoteric, is sexless I 72n
  fire or I 87
  formed of buddhi-manas II 230-1 &n
  incarnates in Chrēstos (Gnos) II 573
  incorrectly interpreted as Jesus I 132n
  Logos I 130n, 134n; II 230, 231n
  Michael is Gnostic Hermes- II 481
  names of, in various religions II 704n
  Nazarenes followers of I 198n
  "sevenfold light" II 540
  Sun is, esoterically I 134n; II 23
  tenth avatāra II 420
  universal spirit, Farvarshi or II 478
  or Word II 704n
  Zoroaster's ātman II 480
Christos-Sophia
  Kwan-shi-yin & Kwan-yin I 473
Christs & Buddhas I 639; II 415, 483
Christy, Henry
  man dates fr Miocene II 714n
  re "nallies" [tallies] & early writing II 729
Chromosphere
  hypothetical element in I 583
  not Sun's vital principle I 528
1 *Chronicles*
  Satan stood against Israel II 387n
  Satan tempts King of Israel I 414
2 *Chronicles*
  God above all gods I 421
  pillars Boaz & Jakin II 461, 497
Chronicon. See Eusebius
Chronological
  calculations II 49
  information of science II 66
  mysteries studied by occultists II 83
  order in Purānas ignored II 320
Chronology(ers, ies). *See also* Cycles, Yugas
  Babylonian (Smith) II 691-3
  biblical, dubious II 265, 336, 390, 395n
  biblical, 6,000 yrs II 71, 690
  Brahmanical II 66-74
  Chaldean, Chinese I 655; II 219, 429, 619-21
  Christian II 73
  of divine dynasties II 365-9
  esoteric among ancients II 395
  esoteric geological II 709-30, 778-9
  Hindu II 47-51, 66-74, 307n, 395, 551

  Jewish II 396, 691
  kalpas computed II 307n
  numbers keys to II 564
  occult I 340, 370-8; II 9-11, 148-9, 155, 320,
    435, 437-8
  orientalist vs Hindu II 225
  in Purānas II 225, 571-2
  scientific II 71-3, 155, 288
  secret, of *Linga Purāna* II 307n
  Smith's, of Chaldeans II 691
  Suidas & Dr Sepp II 619-20
  Western, borrowed fr India II 620
  will change greatly I 318
  world, difficult II 796-7
Chronos (Gk) Time. *See also* Kronos (Saturn)
  absolute time I 418
  derivation of term II 269n
  & Kronos I 417-18
  orders phases of evolution II 420
  Ormazd, circle or I 113-14
  Osiris & Isis children of I 381
  Phanēs, Chaos &, (Orphism) I 452n, 583
  St Michael son of I 459
  Saturn or I 417-18
  swallows his children II 269, 415-16
  will swallow Church of Rome II 341n
  Zeus born in & out of I 427
Chroub. *See* Cherub
Chrysostom, St John
——— *Commentaries on St. Paul's Epistles*
  existence of many gods I 465n
Chthonia(n) (Gk)
  chaotic Earth I 340; II 130
  Kabiri belonged to, divinities II 363
Chu. *See* Khu
Chuang [Tzŭ]
  things known & unknown II 219
Chulpas (burial places)
  giant, in Peru & Bolivia II 752
Ch'un ch'iu (Chin)
  stars (monads) fall to Earth II 486
Chung Ku. *See also* Chow Kung
  helped compile *Shan-Hai-King* II 54n
Chupunīkā (Skt) Pleiad II 551
Church. *See also* Christian Church, Chris-
    tianity, Church Fathers, Roman Church
  ancient sources of I xxvi
  angelic hosts of I 38, 88
  archangels of I 88, 235 &n
  "Bride of Christ" II 377
  built on human victims I xli
  called devil darkness I 70
  confused Jehovah w Reality II 508
  curses Satan, curses God II 235

distorted Jewish ideas I 312
filioque dogma in II 635
holds Michael Ferouer of Christ II 478-9
inhabited planets blasphemy to II 699
invented devil II 238-9, 508
lamb (*Revelation*) married to II 231
made ether abode of Satan I 331 &n
made Samael-Satan the Devil II 378
never had inner meaning of cross II 562
opposed Earth's rotundity II 708
personal god & devil of II 475
preserved legends re giants II 271-2
struggle of, w Manicheism II 238-9
unscrupulous, intolerant II 209, 377
Venus sign explained II 30
whitened sepulcher II 231
Church Council(s) II 279 &n
Church Fathers I 73, 383; II 537, 550n
blindly used cruciform couches II 559
claimed to have seen satyrs II 755
disfigured symbols I 196; II 98
failed to destroy Secret Doctrine I xl
Gnostic view of Jehovah & II 96
mutilated Gnostic systems I 350
passed keys to Nazarenes I 310-11
several, knew the old teachings I xliv
some, initiated I xxxix, xliv, 311, 386-7
woman as viewed by II 216n
Churchianity I 479; II 748
Churning of the Ocean
amrita, Rāhu & II 381
before Earth's formation I 67-8
fourteen precious things fr I 67
Lakshmī &, (Williams) I 379-80 &n
Mandara (Mt) used for I 385
nāgas, asuras employed in I 348
Soma born fr I 398
Chwolsohn, Prof Daniel Avroamovich
—— *Die Ssabier und Ssabismus*
Maimonides on Nabatheans II 455n
—— *Nabathean Agriculture*
Adam-Adami II 452-8
Moon idol instructs Qū-tāmy I 394-5
pre-Adamic Mysteries II 452-6
Schemal, Samael I 417
Chylification (modification of lymph)
cerebration &, (Dr Lewins) I 297 &n
Chyuta (Skt) II 47 &n. *See also* Achyuta
Cibola Expeditions
seven cities & II 35
Spanish met white chiefs during II 744
Cicatrization, affected by fission II 166n
Cicero, Marcus Tullius
—— [*De Natura Deorum*]

time & man's ideas II 451
—— *De Senectute*
sodalities II 212n
—— *Tusculan Disputations*
profaning the Mysteries II 419
Cichen-Itza. *See* Chichén Itzá
Cidastes (genus) II 218
Ciel et Terre [*Terre et Ciel*]. *See* Reynaud, J. E.
Cifron (Arab)
cipher derived fr, (Müller) I 360-1 &n
Cimah [Kīmāh] (Heb)
Pleiades (*Job*) I 647-8 &n
Cimmerians (Gk)
descend fr Atlantean subrace II 774
long nights & days of II 773
Cipher II 307n
hieroglyphic, the Senzar II 439
Müller on I 360-1
nought or I 94; II 554
Sephrim & I 361n; II 40, 234
Circassia, raised stones in II 346n
Circe, Ulysses & II 769n
Circle(s). *See also* Center, Diameter, Pi, Point
Aristotle omitted I 615
Boundless I 65, 99, 113-14, 239, 333, 429, 614; II 573, 589
Chinese symbols of II 554
circumference a limited symbol I 1
circumference of, or hidden deity II 536
cosmogonies begin w, or egg I 443
cross & I 5, 19; II 30, 545-53, 582
cross equivalent to, of year II 546
cube, triangle & I 612-16
darkness associated w I 443
David's, -dance around ark II 460-1
diameter of II 536, 553
dimensionless II 553
earliest form of cross & II 549
ever-eternal nature I 4
fiery, Egyptian symbol of kosmos II 357
fire, water, cross & II 550
four, & Fohat's sons I 204
God is a, (de Cusa, Pascal) I 114; II 545
golden egg & I 359, 426; II 553
Hebrew root of I 364n
how, becomes a number I 99
infinite, perfect cube fr II 465
is thought, diameter is Word II 106
nine figures, as I 99
no number I 91; II 574
nought or, symb infinite All II 553, 621
Parker's premises re I 313, 315-16; II 544
Pascal's, symbolical I 65
point, triangle, etc I 320-1, 426

Proclus on invisible II 552
seven II 80-1, 487-8
seven, of fire II 103, 232, 275n
space & eternity in pralaya I 1
spirit of life, immortality II 552
square in, potent magic I 99
squaring the I 315-16; II 450, 544
symbol of universe I 359
symbol of Unknown I 113
triad in, or Tetraktis I 99
uncrossable boundary I 134n
unmanifested I 398
zero &, as infinity I 99, 333
Circle of Necessity. *See also* Rebirth
  Egyptian after-death experiences & II 379
  monads & II 303
Circular
  dance II 460-1
  Irish, stones fr Africa II 343
  motion I 116-17
Circulation(s)
  between 2 planes I 148
  of blood I 559
  nerve-auric II 298n
  in universal ether II 74
  of vital fluid & cat symbolized II 552-3n
  of vital fluid in solar system I 541
Circulo vicioso (Lat) vicious circle I xxii
Circumcision, & the cross II 589
Circumference
  circle & I 11, 90, 426, 616; II 38
  of circle or hidden deity II 536
  diameter & II 544
  digit 9 & II 581
  relation of point to I 426
  symbol limited by human mind I 1
Cis-Himalaya(n) II 34n. *See also* Trans-
  Himalayan
  adepts, wheat, corn & II 374n
  crypts of, initiates II 588n
  Nārada or Pesh-Hun in, occultism II 48
  secret teachings of II 251, 308n, 574, 636
  sevening in, occultism II 602
  submerged in Lemurian times II 327
City(ies)
  absence of remains of II 311-12
  Atlantean II 371, 760
  built by divine kings II 366
  built on former cities II 220-1, 397
  Chaldean, of Eridu II 226
  Egyptian, before pyramids II 432
  first large, on Madagascar II 317
  founding of, symbolic (Ragon) II 795-6
  of 4th race II 20-1

holy, interpreted II 84
Lemurian, cyclopean II 317-19
"of letters," secret works in II 529
records in older Phoenician II 440 &n
seven, of Cibola II 35 &n
of 3rd race II 198
two extinct Central Asian I xxxiii-iv
City of God. See Augustine, St
Civilization(s). *See also* Atlantis, Continent,
  Nations
  ancient, preceded by others II 334
  antiquity of, (Gould) II 311-12
  Atlantean II 263
  Atlantean & Egyptian II 429-30
  Babylonian, fr India II 203
  Central Asian I xxxii-iv
  Chaldean, fr India II 226
  Christian barbarism & II 430
  earliest, date fr Eocene II 744
  Egyptian, had no Stone Age II 786n
  fate of modern II 331
  first, fr divine dynasties II 318, 364
  fourth race Chinese highest II 280n
  Haeckel traces, to ants, bees II 650
  high prehistoric II 432
  Lemurian II 317-19
  Lemuro-Atlantean I 191; II 433n
  lost II 222, 429-34
  lost arts of ancient I 208-9 &n; II 430-1
  Miocene, (Donnelly) II 266n
  most brilliant, in Tertiary II 679
  physical, at cost of spiritual II 319 &n
  physiological changes before II 317
  prehistoric Central Asian I xxxii-iv
  primeval, & Darwinists II 786n
  puzzle of autochthonous I 652
  rises & falls of II 330, 723
  savagery &, side by side II 318, 522, 717,
    722-5
  Secondary Period II 266n
  Sons of God founded I 208-9; II 198, 318,
    364
  submerged II 311-41, 393-402, 426-9
  sunken, evidence of II 742-77
Civilization of the Eastern Iranians. See
  Geiger, W.
Clacha-Brath (Celt)
  judgment stone of II 342n
Clairaudience I 470, 537
Clairvoyance(t) I 1n, 41, 470, 537; II 206, 370n,
  493
  adept's spiritual eye not I 46n
  aspect of jñānaśakti I 292
  corroborates tradition I 647

once common to mankind I 537
permeability of matter & I 251
Classical Dictionary of Hindu Mythology. See
Dowson, J.
Classics (Gk & Rom)
giants, gods, continents in II 760-77
hints in, re secret science II 795
Clausius, Rudolf J. E.
gas atoms elastic spheres I 513
theory of I 587n
Clavijero, F. X. S., 7 families of II 35
Clef des Grands Mystères. See Lévi, E.
Clement of Alexandria (Clemens Alexandrinus)
esteemed *Book of Enoch* II 535
ex-initiate I xliv; II 559
held Kabbala & Bible veiled II 536
knew Moon as Jehovah's symbol I 387
serpents, giants are demons II 279-80, 280n
understood cruciform couches II 559
—— *Stromata*
elements & pagan knowledge I 125 &n
Jewish, Egyptian temples I 462
knew astronomy of *Exodus* I 125; II 361n
Mysteries not given to all II 447
Phoroneus father of mortals II 519
sacrilege of Aeschylus II 419
Clergy
make Satan enemy of God II 377
make true saviors evil ones II 411-12
Clerk-Maxwell. *See* Maxwell, J. Clerk
Climacteric Year I 656 &n
Climate(s)
axial changes & II 314, 329-30, 356-7
changes of, & man's stature II 777n
eternal spring of early races II 135, 400, 738 &n
Fohat's 4 sons & I 204
of Greenland in Miocene II 11, 677, 726
man changes Earth's II 700
moon, sun, planets, etc cause II 699
periodical changes of II 446, 726-7, 736
polar regions once tropical II 329, 770n, 773-4, 777
secondary evolutionary causes II 262-3, 648-9
seventh II 319-20, 403, 407, 616
of third-race II 329
zones & influence II 249
Climate & Time in their Geological Relations.
See Croll, J.
Clito, Neptune marries, sires Atlas II 765
Clodd, Edward
—— "Antiquity of Man . . ."

describes Paleolithic man II 686n
European marsupials II 713n
mid-Miocene man II 710-11
no man in Tertiary Europe II 714
—— "Science and the Emotions"
on science & religion I 3n
Clymenē (Gk)
Atlas son of II 493
mother of Prometheus II 519
Coach ha-Guf. *See* Koaḥ Hagūph
Coadunation, of chain-globes I 166
Coagula, on Smaragdine Tablet II 99
Coal, formation I 253n; II 155, 695n, 712
Coasts, elevating, sinking II 787n
Coats of Skin, Matter I 189
cycles & I 642-4; II 56, 72
of early man II 154
Java-Aleim made, for Adam II 202
men, animals evolve II 299, 736
nature can produce II 56
not necessarily physical I 607
offering of, (*Leviticus*) II 748
thickened, & divine man II 281
Cobra(s)
hatched fr incense egg I 363-4
man's saliva & I 262 &n
nāgas or II 209
Coccyx, rudimentary tail & II 328-9
Cochin, China, ears distorted in II 339
Cocker, B. F.
—— *Christianity & Greek Philosophy*
Plato's "god over all" II 554 &n
Codex Nazaraeus
Adonai, Kadush, El-El I 463
arcane, arka II 463n
capital sins & cardinal virtues I 195-6 &n
Gnostic systems in II 96n
Iurbo, Adonai II 389
seven creations I 217
seven spirits & races I 248 &n
spirit female & evil in I 194n
War in Heaven I 194-6
Coecum, vermiform appendix of II 681
Coelo, De. See Aristotle (*De Caelo*)
Coelus [or Uranus]
Cyclopes sons of, & Terra II 769
Mercury son of Lux & II 541
Cogito, ergo sum (Descartes) II 242
Cognition, cognized, & cognizer are one I 56
Cohesion
Keely & I 559
Lodge on I 488
occult explanation of I 259 &n, 525

phenomena, noumenal causes I 145-6, 592
ultimate causes of I 514-17
Coincidences, re Great Pyramid I 314
Cold & Heat, progeny of electricity I 81-2
Colebrooke, H. T., *Miscellaneous Essays*
 Greeks learned fr Hindus I 47n
 manas is dual I 334
 yugas or cycles II 624n
Coleman, held Aryans ignorant of globular
 Earth II 154-5
Colenso, Bishop John William
—— *Elohistic & Jehovistic Writers*
 admits to changes in Bible II 473
Coleridge, Samuel Taylor
 on chance I 653
 Christians & heathens II 474
 on personality I 275
 time an abstraction of deity I 645
Collect. de Reb. Hibern. See Vallancey, C.
Collectio Nova Patrum. See Montfaucon, B. de
College(s)
 of astrologers, magi II 203
 sacerdotal I 168; II 215, 220, 532-3
Collingwood, J. F., editor of Büchner's *Force
 & Matter* II 154n, 719n
[Collins, Mabel, *Idyll of the White Lotus*]. *See*
 Subba Row, T.
Cologne, 3 magi in cathedral of I 654n
Color(s)
 ākāśa, sound, touch & I 205
 based on septenary law II 628
 commanding forces by, & sound I 514n
 cosmic electricity & I 554
 of early races II 97, 178, 227, 249-50, 282
 four, of sanctum curtain I 462
 Keely's occult ideas re I 564-5
 related to senses, elements II 107
 seven, fr one ray of light II 492
 "shadows" (chhāyās) of var II 90, 97
 unfading, of Luxor II 430
Colorado, monsters of II 218
[*Colossians*], day of new Moon II 76
Colossus II, 263, 294n, 369. *See also* Cyclopean
 of Rhodes & Bamian statue II 338
Coluber Tortuosus
 meaning of, distorted by Church II 230
Columbus, Christopher I 297; II 371, 788
Colure, summer tropical, & Pleiades II 407
Comet(s).
 accumulate elements by circling I 204
 all heavenly bodies become I 204
 become stars I 206
 collision w Earth theory II 330
 curds become I 206, 250

early nebular evolution & I 599
of 1811 & gravity I 504
evolution of solar system & I 599
generated in solar system (Faye) I 500
laya-center becomes I 203-4
life came via a, (Thomson) I 366n
long-haired *radicals* I 503-4
Master quoted on I 593
matter of, unknown to science I 597
origin of I 500-6
planets were, & suns I 103, 596-7
prophecy by means of I 646
same substance as planets & Sun I 602
settles down as planet, Sun I 203-4
swallowed by suns I 204
tails of, & gravity I 504-5, 606-7
unexplained by science I 593
wanderers or I 201, 206, 250
world germs I 201
Cometary Matter I 504
different fr ordinary matter I 142, 597
planets & Sun evolved fr I 101 &n
stage for all heavenly bodies I 204
visible because luminous I 606-7
"Come To Us," Egyptian Day of I 134-5
Commentaire sur le Yaçna. See Burnouf, E.
Commentarius Apocalypsis. See Cornelius à
 Lapide
Commentary(ies) (quoted by HPB)
 allegory of the 8 Ādityas I 100
 animal-human intercourse II 192, 286
 Aśvattha Tree I 549
 Atlantean man divided II 350
 breath of Father-Mother I 144
 circle, the One, the ALL II 621-2
 Darkness clothed Sons of Light I 103
 deity becomes a whirlwind I 116-17
 destruction of continents I 439n
 Dhruva & destiny of nations II 768
 dhyānis, radiations of I 259
 divine kings taught man II 201
 dragon, Serpents of Wisdom II 351
 early races, continents II 400-1
 Earth globe in var rounds I 252n, 258-60
 Earth in 2nd round I 260
 Earth's axis tilted II 329
 Earth's geological changes II 312
 Earth's rotation & Moon II 324-5
 elements & celestial beings I 216
 Eternal Bird, nest of II 293
 fate of Atlantis II 427-8
 fiery Mother-Fish & spawn I 97
 fifth race on ascending arc II 300
 fourth race black w sin II 408

fruits, grains brought to man II 373
genesis of world & numbers II 160
Heavenly Man goal of all I 183
heavenly rūpa creates man II 242
hermaphrodites & Śukra II 30
holy youths refused chhāyās I 192
humans are gods to beasts I 605-6
humans covered w hair II 287
humans look on devas as gods I 605-6
humans made complete II 255n
informing intelligences II 33-4
jīva & growth of Earth II 46
Kings of Light leave II 424-5
lives, comets, elements I 249-50
man first & highest mammal II 288
man's stature decreases II 331
Mighty Ones leave monuments I 434-5
mother, breaths, motion I 97
motion thrills sleeping atoms I 116
origin of human principles II 241
pitris & their doubles I 183-4
Poles moved (4th time) II 350
primary, secondary creation II 113
Seven & Nine II 622
seven Fathers, 49 Sons II 564
seven Lhas II 23
sevens & man as saptaparna II 590
spheres, hierarchies II 33-4
spiritual conceptions of doctrine II 81
stone & vegetation II 593-4
Sun is heart & brain I 541
Sun turns w planets I 100 &n
third eye disappears II 294
three fires II 247
time & space II 612
Trees of Knowledge & of Life II 216
white & black magic I 192n
world germs, comets, battles I 201
world of truth I 120
Commentary(ies) (referred to)
compiled by adepts II 23
compiled prior to kali-yuga II 300
as difficult as the Stanzas I 97n
Exodus story in II 426-7
expl glossaries to I 97n; II 33-4, 33n
hierarchy of creative powers I 213
on nephīlīm & bestiality II 775
new facts to profane Orientalists I xxiii
next to impossible to translate II 192n
rendered into English for first time I 23
some, intentionally veiled I xxv
Com. of Proclus on the Timaeus. See Proclus
Commentary on Purānas
re Vishnu, Śesha II 505

Com. on St Paul's Epistles. See Chrysostom
Communication. *See also* Language, Sound
between mortals & immortals I 464
between planes II 281n, 370n
between worlds I 133; II 281
Comparative Geology. See Winchell, *World Life*
Compass I 126n, 128. *See also* Cardinal Points, Mahārājas
Compensation. *See also* Karma
karmic, in next manvantara I 173
law of, stern & implacable I 639
Complexion
racial II 178, 227, 249-50
fr strata & climate II 249 &n
Compounds (chem). *See also* Crookes, W.
which cease to combine I 478
Compte Rendu du Congrès int. d'anthropologie. See Bourgeois, Abbé
Comptes Rendus. See Académie des Sciences
Comte, Auguste, pessimism of, re Sun I 528
Concarneau, balancing rocks near II 344
"Concealed Lord" (Tib) I 52
Concentration, 7 forms of II 637
Conception. *See also* Immaculate Conception, Reproductive Processes
easier for earlier women II 410
of foetus II 174
human, degradation of I 381-2 &nn; II 410-11
lunar influences on I 228-9n; II 38
Moon, gestation & I 180, 228-9n, 264, 387, 395; II 38, 76-7, 105
shedding blood & II 44n
Conception(s), (intellectual, spiritual). *See also* Anthropomorphic
of the Absolute (Cusa) II 158n
of boundless unity II 42-3
finite, & primary creation II 59
mystical, of early Aryans II 99-100
purely spiritual, few have II 81
Concepts & Theories [of Modern Physics]. See Stallo, J. B.
Concerning Protoplasm. See Stirling, J. H.
Concordance. See Cruden, Alex.
Condensation I 590-7; II 159, 253
Condillac, Étienne Bonnot de
held many worlds inhabited II 706
Confession, Buddhas of II 423
Conflagration
precedes pralaya I 371, 649; II 307n
Conflict between Religion & Science. See Draper
Confucianism(ists)
based on 5 King & 4 Shu books I xxv &n
Pythagoreanism & I 440-1

Confucius
　[*Analects*] *Lün Yü* of I xxxvi-vii
　canonized by Catholic Church I 441n
　cosmogony of I 356, 440-1
　on the dragon II 365
　fifth rounder I 162
　"great Extreme" of I 356, 440; II 554
　Lao-tzŭ predecessor of I xxv &n
　personality not immortal I 440n
　practiced magic I 441
　religion of I xxvn
　taught heliocentric system I 441
　a transmitter, not a maker I xxxvii
Congenital Idiot, has 4-fold jīva only I 224
[Congreve, Wm.], on eternal justice II 304
Coniferae in Primary era II 712
Conjunctions I 661
　began kali-yuga I 662; II 435
　foretell events I 646-7
　of Moon, Earth, Sun II 76
　planetary, & climacteric years I 650, 656 &n
　of planets & Saturn's role II 63
　of Saturn, Jupiter, Mars I 656
Connubial Life, *Laws of Manu* on II 411n
Conscience I xix
　buddhi &, in *Pistis Sophia* II 605n
　chitti, inner voice or I 288n
Conscious
　everything in universe I 49, 274
　spiritual beings I 233n
　unconscious &, not charāchara I 454
Consciousness. *See also* Self-consciousness
　absolute I 2, 15, 40, 50-1, 56, 266, 277n;
　　II 702n
　absolute, of higher self I 266
　adapts to nature (Bourges) II 654
　animal I 234; II 120, 702n
　ātma alone primeval I 570
　awakening, of plants & animals I 455
　chasm between brain &, (Tyndall) II 673
　cosmic ideation & I 329n
　deep sleep a state of II 701
　deva-, & monad I 619
　devachanic II 57n
　disintegrated by Mahat I 373
　in dreamless sleep I 266
　of 1st beings not human I 277
　of the globes II 702n
　Haeckel traces, to molecules II 650
　highest manifest, synthetic I 573
　hinders man fr foreseeing death II 525
　human & cosmic, diagram I 200
　illusion & I 329-30
　immortality & II 525

implies limitations I 56
　individualized, or personal ego II 241
　key to knowing other worlds II 701
　Logos source of individual II 24
　manifests thru matter I 328-9
　man's, linked to senses II 701
　merging individual w universal I 51
　not a brain function I 233, 296, 327n
　of the "one manifested" I 216n
　pervades everything I 49, 274; II 702n
　prajñā or II 641
　primary element I 373
　psychology rejects universal II 490n
　relation of, to 3rd eye II 306
　senseless up to 3rd round I 246-7
　seven chords of universal I 167
　seven states of I 47, 199-200; II 29n, 597n,
　　641
　on 7th globe every round I 232
　sleep & I 266; II 701
　still small voice & spiritual I 280
　time an illusion of I 37, 44
　unconditioned I 14
　universe aggregate of various states of
　　II 598-9
Conservation
　law of, of energy I 513-14, 518
　of matter & occult physics I 97
　of solar energy I 102 &n
Consolidation, of earth II 10n, 138
Consonants, & monosyllabic lang II 199
Constant, Abbé Louis. *See* Lévi, E.
Constantine, Emperor
　killed Sopatrus I 469
　turning point in West I xliv
Constantinople. *See also* Council of Constan.
　300,000 books destroyed at II 763n
Constellation(s). *See also* Draco, Great Bear,
　　Makara, Ursa Major, Ursa Minor, etc
　astrological aspects of I 105; II 179
　cycles & periodic return of I 645
　deity presides over one's I 638
　Dragon, at Pole in Flood II 352-3, 355
　four sacred animals symbolize four I 363
　Great Bear, & Seven Rishis II 549
　Harp, South Pole in, (Egy) II 360n
　influence cataclysms II 699
　occult influence of I 409, 647
　patriarchs personify the I 390
　Poseidon placed dolphin among II 578
　pyramids, deluges & II 352
　retrogression of I 389
　Scorpio or 8th, & *Job* I 648
　seven, of Plato, Hesiod II 603

sympathy between, & soul I 668
zodiacal I 652-7; II 23
"Constitution of the Microcosm." *See* Subba
    Row, T.
Consubstantiality
    globes of our chain & I 166
    of manifested spirit, matter I 614
    of rulers & ruled produces evil (Plato) II 373
Continent(s) II 313-50, 393-409, 742-77,
    778-93. *See also* Atlantis, Dvīpas, Lands,
    Lemuria, Root-Races
    African II 200, 263-4
    age of various II 606n
    American or fifth II 8, 35n, 182, 444-6
    ancient, more mts than valleys II 763
    Arctic or polar II 11-12, 138n, 398, 400-1, 727
    after Atlantis II 395
    Atlas, symbolized Atlantis-Lemuria II 762
    Australia remnant of sunken II 314
    axis change & new II 360
    born, grow old, die II 350
    civilization of lost II 222
    colossal men on submerged II 336
    destroyed by fire, water II 266, 307n, 309,
        311, 329-31, 426-8, 725-6, 776n, 784
    destruction of early I 439n
    destruction of 5th race II 445-6, 757
    destruction of "worlds" may mean II 705
    dry island a northern II 398
    Easter Island & submerged I 439; II 316n
    Europe the fifth II 8
    evidence of submerged II 324-34, 742-93
    fifth, Europe & Asia Minor II 8
    first, never perished II 6, 372n, 401, 606n
    five, of root-races II 6-9, 11
    flood connected w sinking of II 307
    four, in *Avesta* II 609-10
    four prehistoric II 6, 404
    fourth, destruction of II 314, 395n, 433n
    fourth, or Atlantis I 369; II 314, 395n
    future, & present lands II 404-5, 445
    geologists & submerged II 316
    God-inhabited II 221
    great northern, concealed II 399
    horseshoe-like II 326, 401-2
    Hyperborean or 2nd II 7, 11-12, 274, 606n
    identical, do not rise again II 333
    immense submerged, in Pacific II 788-9
    India & S America, islands &, connect II 327
    Keely's force on some new I 564
    Lemuro-Atlantean II 10
    lost, fr India to Tasmania II 221
    Magi believed in seven II 608
    man lived on now sunken, (Lyell) II 725

Mascarene II 324
    Mayas belonged to fifth II 34-5n
    northern, tropical II 326, 423-4, 727
    old, sucked under II 330
    of other lokas & globes (Purānas) II 321-2
    overlap each other II 433n
    periodical sinking, rising II 144, 266, 307,
        325-33, 400n, 703, 762n, 787n
    Persian traditions re II 393-402
    Polynesian II 222-4
    present, sunk several times II 332-3
    Purānas use, symbolically II 323
    rising & sinking of, continuous II 787n
    Romaka-pura part of lost II 50, 67-8
    Śāka & Pushkara to come II 404-5
    second I 369; II 138, 401-2
    sequence of II 8
    seven allegorical, [dvīpas] II 155, 288, 321,
        404-5, 612
    seven "creations" of new II 756-9
    seven, in *Revelation* II 748
    seven, of Bhāratavarsha II 501n
    shifting of I 273; II 333, 699
    sinking of, & planets, Moon II 699
    sixth & 7th, yet to come II 405, 445-6
    of sixth race II 757
    fr Spitzbergen to Dover II 324, 326
    Theopompus on Atlantean II 371
    third & 4th II 263-4, 606n
    third, Lemurian II 329, 371-2, 606
    third, sank 4,242,352 yrs ago I 439n
    Uranos ruled second II 765
Contra Celsum. See Origen
Contradictions, in teachings I 151-2
Contraries, attraction of I 405, 412, 416; II 111
"Contributions to the Fossil . . ." *See* Heer
Contributions to the Theory of Nat. Selection.
    See Wallace, A. R.
Cook, Captain James
    Easter Island & II 317, 331, 337
Cooke, J. P., *The New Chemistry*
    atoms not uniform I 512
    wave theory of light I 580
Cooper, Wm. R., *An Archaic Dictionary*
    Athtor [Hathor] I 346
Cope, Prof, on flying serpent II 205
Copernicus, Nicolaus
    intuitions of, re ancient ideas I 118
    lunar mean motion tables I 667n
—— *On the Revolutions of the Heavenly Spheres*
    revolution of Earth II 28n
Copt(s, ic) II 792
    adepts & Dendera zodiac II 432
    Christos of, replaced by Jesus I 132n

IOH & Moon II 464
Jewish language borrowed fr I 115n
language kin of Phoenician I 115n
Pistis Sophia, MSS II 566n
Ro, P, & Gk cross II 547
Corals
  gelatinous in Lemuro-Atlantean times II 250
  reproduce by budding II 133
  Silurian, like today's millepores II 257
Côr-Cawr (Welsh) dance of giants
  Stonehenge called II 342
Cordilleras, upheaval of II 787n
Cordovero, Moses, *Tractatus de Anima*
  Ophanim or angels of stars I 117
Corinthian Horses, Venus symbol on II 546
1 *Corinthians* (Paul)
  living soul, quickening spirit II 513 &n
  man of Earth & Heaven II 82
  man temple of God I 382n, 574n
  many gods in Heaven, on Earth I 465
  spiritual rock followed Israel II 341
  we shall judge angels II 111-12
Cor Leonis (star Regulus)
  when upon equator II 407
Corn
  -bin pyramid sarcophagus I 317n
  Isis reveals Mysteries of II 374 &n
  Kabiri first produced II 364
  seven-colored among Zuñis II 628-9
  seven cubits high (Egy) I 236n, 674n
  speckled, & priestess-mother II 629
Cornelius à Lapide. *See also* Kenealy, Dr E.
—— *Commentarius Apocalypsis*
  Bernard on Sun-Christ I 401
Cornutus, Lucius Annaeus
—— *Commentarius de natura deorum*
  Mercury a cube II 542
  three phases of Hecate I 395
Cornwall (England)
  part of early continent II 326
  traditions of giants in II 754
Coronado, Francisco II 35
Corpora Quadrigemina & Striata
  developed in mammalian brain II 297, 301
Corporeality(ies)
  incorporeal I 566
  innumerable stages of I 607-8 &n, 633
Corpuscular I 326, 484, 490, 494, 528
  theory of light I 495, 579
  theory of Pythagoras distorted I 507
"Correlation of Physical Forces." *See* Grove
Correspondences, law of I 585-6n; II 197, 301.
  See also Analogies

Cory, Isaac Preston. *See also* Berosus
—— *Ancient Fragments*
  Chaldean Oracles on ether I 462
  chaos shone w pleasure I 343
  Damascius calls Prōtogonos *Dis* I 70, 343n
  Ea & Tiamat II 477
  Elon or Elion highest god II 380
  mundane god of spiral form I 348
  Oannes-Dāgōn I 345; II 190
  Sanchoniathon on birth of univ I 340 &n
  Thallath & Belus II 54
  Thallath gave birth to monsters II 65n
  Zeus an immortal maid II 135
Corybantes, confused w Kabiri II 106, 360
Cosmas Indicopleustes, *Topographia Christiana*
  arctic continent II 399
  met learned Chaldean in India II 399
  Noah lived on Atlantis II 265
  square, flat Earth of I 522
Cosmic. *See also* Astral Light, Ideation, Matter, Planes, Principles
  activity, monads & II 311
  Darwinian principles in, life I 202-3
  deluge preceding our round II 69n
  evolution, Stanzas on I 27-34
  motion finite, periodical I 3
  solar &, pralayas I 18n
  soul II 113
  substance eternally homogeneous I 569
Cosmic Dust
  fiery wind is I 107
  some, never belonged to Earth I 609
  tail of cosmic serpent I 74
  various names for I 140
Cosmic Philosophy [*Outlines of*]. *See* Fiske, J.
Cosmic Pralaya
  concludes Brahmā's life II 69n
  Logos sleeps during II 310
Cosmocratores. *See* Kosmokratores
Cosmogenesis. *See also* Cosmogony, Cosmology, Powers
  lipika connected w I 127-8
  occult numbers symbolic of I 321
Cosmogonical Hypothesis. *See* Wolf, C.
Cosmogonie de la Révélation. See Godefroy
"Cosmogonies Aryennes." *See* Darmesteter, *Essais . . .*
Cosmogony(ies, ical). *See also* Cosmogenesis, Cosmology
  architect in every II 43
  Aryan, spiritualizes matter II 241
  beginning of, in *VP* I 545 &n, 594
  begin w egg, circle, head I 443; II 554
  Chinese, most hazy I 356

double-sexed creatures in II 130
Fohat in esoteric I 109-10, 116, 119
future, lies in Divine Thought I 1
how to master every I 424
intelligent plan in II 73
Japanese or Shinto I 213-14, 216-17
key required to old II 248
kosmocratores in all II 23
light fr darkness in all II 485-6
no evil dragon in ancient II 53
number 7 cornerstone of I 321; II 34
occult I 75, 145, 277
one universal element in all I 75
pradhāna in I 545
proof of II 251-2
recorded in scriptures II 251
secondary creation in all II 59
secrecy re, (Sinnett) I 170
of the Secret Doctrine I 272-3
Semitic, materializes nature II 241
several creations in many II 703-4
similarities in ancient II 54 &n
swastika a, sign II 99
symbolic of I 4-5, 426; II 536
uniform traditions in II 703-4
Vedānta gives a metaphysical I 269
wars in heaven in every I 418
water plays a part in all I 64
worlds destroyed, renewed in II 704
Zoroastrian II 488
Cosmogony. See Sanchoniathon
Cosmographie. See Tardy, J.
Cosmography II 564
ancients knew, well II 534-5
Aryan, based on number ten II 603
Cosmolatry
all scriptures based on II 77
looked to noumenon of forms I 461
modern science scorns I 348-9
Cosmology. *See also* Cosmogony, Powers,
Theogony
Aryan, based on number ten II 603
describes hierarchy of forces I 75
overgrown w human fancy I 424
Cosmos. *See also* Kosmos
body of Divine Thought I 3
builders fashion I 339
cycles run fr embryo to II 189
intelligent plan in II 73
manifested Word I 138
man microcosm of I 177, 181, 594
plan of, in divine thought I 339
seven rays, states of II 69n, 636
"Cosmos." *See* Humboldt, F.

Coste. *See* Acosta
Cotes, Roger [mistakenly given as Forbes]
Preface to *Principia* I 492
Coulomb's Law I 501
Council of Constantinople (692 AD) II 279n
Council of Elyrus (303 AD)
form of God not to be shaped II 279n
Council of Nicaea (787 AD)
brought idolatry back II 279n
Council of Rome (883 AD), excommunicated
enemy of idolatry II 279n
Council of Trent (1545-63)
on devil, baptism, etc II 209
Count [Comte] de Gabalis, Le. See Villars
Count de Gobelin. *See* Court de Gébelin
"Counterfeit of man . . ."
[Shakespeare, *Henry IV*] I 191
"Counterfeit of the Spirit"
buddhi or II 605n
Countries of the World, The. See Brown, R.
Cours philosophique . . . See Ragon, J. B. M.
Court de Gébelin, Antoine
—— *Allégories d'Orient*
Kabiri were allegorical I 641-2 &n
Sun & North Pole, etc II 769n
Covenants, of Bible, Kabbala, & Masonry. *See
also* Ark of the Covenant
Kabbala & Masonry II 39
Cover, Dr, debunks Audubon's bird II 440n
Cow. *See also* Argha
bull &, as symbols I 67, 398 &n
golden, & initiation II 462, 469, 470
Holy of Holies symbol II 470
-horned, Io, Isis, Moon or II 418n
horns of, Moon symbol II 31
melodious, Vāch I 137, 427n, 434; II 418n
passive generative power symbol II 418n
Scandinavian I 367, 427
-symbol & Nile River II 583
symbol of 5th race II 533
woman, & gestation I 390 &n
Cowell, Edward Byles
Upanishads reference [Elphinstone] I 270
—— *The Aphorisms of Śāndilya*
Parabrahman, etc I 7n
Cowper, William, *The Task*
knowledge & wisdom I 165
Cox, Sergeant E. W.
psychic force of, & Archaeus I 338n
Cox, George William I 304
Cracacha. *See* Krauñcha
Cradle Land(s) II 6, 171, 193n, 203-4, 220-1,
324, 424n, 679, 774n

Crânes des Races Humaines, Les.
  See Quatrefages, de, A.
Cranial Capacity
  amongst races (Davis) II 522-3
  ape & human II 193n
  French, lower than Polynesian II 522
  intelligence & II 168n
Cratylus. See Plato
Crawford, Dr J. M. (translated *Kalevala*) II 14,
  26, 122
Crawford, John, favored polygenesis II 169
Create(d)
  Absolute cannot II 158-9
  nothing, only transformed I 570
Creation(s)
  begins at 3rd stage of manifestation II 488
  Bible does not start w I 324
  Brahmā as cause of potencies I 55; II 75
  Codex Nazaraeus on I 194-6
  cosmic, profaned into sexual I 381n
  cosmogonies begin w 2nd II 59
  dark, there is no II 53
  desire (*pathos*) principle of I 110
  divine, or deva-sarga II 176n
  Divine Thought separate fr II 536-7
  Eighth I 445-6, 456
  enumerated in Purānas I 445-60
  ephemeral, described II 309-10n
  evolution is not II 42
  evolution of pre-existing matter I 233n;
    II 239n
  Fifth, I 455-6; II 580
  Fifth, & 9th, & kumāras II 579
  First Cosmic Flood II 139
  first light in I 76 &n
  fivefold II 162, 176n
  Fourth I 454-5
  Genesis mainly describes secondary II 537
  immaculate, of arhats II 173
  impossible for the Infinite I 7, 354; II 80, 159,
    239, 536-7
  intelligent beings needed in II 239
  "of Life by the Sun . . ." I 294-5
  Mahat-tattva or Primary I 450-1
  manvantara, pralaya & II 309-10n
  Mukhya or Fourth I 454-5
  Ninth or Kumāra I 445, 456; II 106, 579
  no special, or miracles II 731
  out of nothing (Christian) I 233n; II 87
  perpetual, or nitya sarga II 309-10n
  personal deities begin w 2nd I 427
  prakritis & Padma I 427
  primary or elemental II 312n
  primary, secondary I 75, 446-7, 450, 455-6;

  II 53 &n, 59, 107, 113, 312 &n
  Self-Existent called II 242
  Seven Chapters of, (Row) I 269
  Seven Days of, (Bible) I 21, 447
  seven, discussed I 445-60; II 612
  sevenfold ladder of, (Celsus) I 445-6
  seven, fr 7 Divine Spirits I 217
  seven, of Purānas & *Genesis* I 21, 446;
    II 624
  seven primary & 7 secondary I 446-7
  Seventh, is of man (Japan, Purānas) I 217,
    445, 456
  Seventh, Mystery of II 516
  Seventh, of Hindus I 445; II 233
  Six Days of II 252n, 624
  Sixth I 456
  special, (biblical) & Darwinism I 323; II 645,
    731-2
  "special," for man, apes II 678
  -story as sport (Purānas) II 53, 126
  swastika symbolizes II 98
  term not used for primary "Creation" I 446
  theological, inept II 689
  Third I 453-4
  two, animal & divine I 248
  two, in Babylonia, & in Bible II 5
  two, in Norse mythology I 427
  two or more II 53-4
  Vishnu Purāna on pre- I 445
  will acting on matter is II 173
  by will & physical procreation II 766
  work of, unbecoming to God II 159
Creation or Evolution? See Curtis, G. T.
Creative
  Architect behind, deity II 43
  barhishads possessed, fire II 94
  Brahmā as, force II 58, 126
  chief, gods androgyne I 427
  divine, fire II 283n
  faculty divine gift II 217
  fire & Prometheus II 414
  force is eternal I 374
  forces & Divine Thought II 158
  forces conscious entities I 423
  forces fr Light II 33-4
  function a religious ceremony I 209-10
  seven, angels & 7 planets II 4
  sexless, instinct II 275
  spirits as Heavenly Man II 2 &n
  swastika &, force II 99-100
  symbol profaned into sexual I 381n
  theogony of, gods I 424-45
Creative Power(s), Force(s), or Celestial
  Beings. *See also* Causality, Manifestation

abuse of, & karma II 410
of archaic philosophy II 40
Brahmā's 4 bodies & II 60
centers of, give primary impulse II 732
fail to produce man II 98
hierarchy of I 213-22
infinitude of, (Buddhists) I 4
Japanese system of I 213-14
represented as circles II 552
seven, described I 213-22
of 7 vowels II 563-4
something besides heat I 85
souls of heavenly orbs II 552
subordinate, & Semitic god II 544
of Sun-gods II 386
third stage of manifestation I 437
true nature of I 423-5
unborn Space & II 487
Creator(s). *See also* Brahmā, Elohīm, Prajāpatis
active, known to exist II 158
androgyne, of man II 388
anthropomorphic II 40, 158
Christian I 440
creates out of joy II 126
Demiurge or I 279, 347, 380n; II 5, 25
destroyers &, do battle I 199, 201
destroyers &, in body I 262-3 &n
Divine Fire is II 114
emanation *through* II 54
fallen angels & II 93-4n
finite, aspect of All II 158-9
First Logos is not a I 428
higher, fail & are punished II 98
higher, give man higher self II 95
infinite principle not a I 7-9, 355, 425
Jehovah a lower II 96
Logos, next to God (Philo) I 350
lower, gave man form II 95, 102
male, fr virgin female I 65
meaning of term I 22
no female, in exoteric religion I 136n
produces gods, germs of elements I 447
"rests" for day of Brahmā I 447
sacred name never used for I 346
seven, called elohīm I 139; II 488
spirits of Earth & heaven are II 477
subcreators & II 163
Svābhāvikas do not believe in I 4
twelve classes of II 77
"Creature of a more exalted kind" (Ovid) I 211
Creed(s), martyrs of I 298
Cremation

universal till 80,000 yrs ago II 753
Crescent I 390
became phallic symbol II 583
-form of Argha II 462
male aspect of universal spirit II 463
Satan associated w II 31n
Crest Jewel of Wisdom. See Śaṅkarāchārya
Cretaceous Period II 713
early man & II 155, 679
formation covering Atlantis II 325
globigerina of today same in II 257
Cretin, arrested man, not ape II 678
Creuzer, G. F. [*See also* Guigniaut, J. D.]
giants commanded elements II 285
intuition of II 369
wise in his generation II 285
—— *Symbolik und Mythologie . . .*
ancient view of nature II 369-70
four elements of ancients I 461
giants commanded elements II 285
oracles render fr Underworld I 463
theogonies & zodiac I 652
Tiryns, Mycenae II 345n
wisdom descends fr gods II 367
Crib. *See* Ereb
Critias. See Plato
Critias (Plato's great-grandfather)
Atlantis story fr Solon [to *his* grandfather, Critias] II 743n
Critique de la raison pure. See Kant, I.
Crocodile I 636. *See also* Dragon, Serpent
abode is Capricorn I 219, 233
air-water symbol I 358
Book of the Dead on I 219-21; II 580n, 635
dragon symbol of Lower Egypt I 409
fifth Order, 5-pointed star & I 219
five, called forth (5th Creation) II 580
hippo &, made famous steed I 397
Ibis destroys eggs of I 362
Makara flippantly called II 576-7
Makara or, 10th zodiacal sign II 354
not a, but a dragon I 219
Sebakh, Sevekh, 7th or I 219
Sun in ship on back of I 409-10
symbol (Mex, Egy) I 353; II 399n, 577, 580, 634-5
vehicle of Horus II 577
worship I 403-11
Croll, James
Eocene began 15,000,000 yrs ago II 715n
figures for beginning of Cambrian II 10n
—— *Climate & Time . . .*
cooling of Earth II 694

date of Tertiary II 9, 10, 685, 687-8n, 695, 751
glaciations & deluges II 141 &n, 144, 695
opposed axial changes II 314
—— "On the Transformation of Gravity"
the nature of gravity I 511
Cro-Magnon
American natives, Basques, & II 792
Atlantean karma crushed II 740 &n, 741
Canary Island Guanches & II 678 &n, 740
in Europe before glaciers II 740n
large-brained race II 678, 687 &n, 740
offshoots of Atlanteans II 678n, 740 &n
in South France II 790n
Cromlech(s), perfection of, (Kenealy) I 209n
Cronus. *See* Kronos
Crookes, Sir William, FTS
approached forbidden bounds I 626
approaches occult theory I 552-3, 621
believed in spiritualism I 520, 581
discovered radiant matter I 621n
introduces a new chemistry I 622
radiometer of I 514
theosophists respect II 651
—— *Address* to Chemical Section
evolution of elements I 583-6, 623
gaps in periodic table I 586n
negative atomic weight I 584
on Protyle I 283, 328n, 581-2, 598, 621
q Airy on gravitation I 584n
q Bacon, Roger I 581
q Helmholtz on electricity I 111n, 580
on the Unknown I 581
—— "Elements & *Meta*-Elements"
compound nature of elements I 140-1
limitations of spectroscopes I 143n
protyle & I 328 &n
q C. Wolf on nebulae I 597
quoted extensively I 546-53
—— "Genesis of the Elements" I 546; II 737
corroborates esoteric philosophy I 621
elements vs compounds I 624-5
generation of the elements I 623
on Hydrogen II 105 &n
Katie King experiments II 737
our elements not the primordial I 622
viśvānara or, (T. Subba Row) I 621
Crore(s) (fr karōr, Hindi) 10 million
first 20, of kalpa (Stanzas) II 312
seventy-seven, of men II 571
thirty, or 3 Occult Ages II 52 &n, 66, 68n
thirty-three, of gods in India I 71n; II 90
Cross(es). *See also* Ankh
ancient symbol II 541, 555, 557-8, 559, 582

ansated I 321, 366n; II 30, 31n, 217, 362, 546, 549, 600 &n
circle of the year II 546
cruciform couch & II 559, 586n
cube unfolded II 36 &n, 542, 561, 600 &n
decussated II 556, 561, 589
discussed II 545-53, 556-62
dissimulata II 586
Egyptians added phallus to II 542
every type of, at Bait-Oxly II 559
Fall of man, without circle I 5
false interpretation of I 405
fire, water, circle & II 550
Hermetic, known in East II 556
Hindu chakra & II 546
human passions crucified on II 549
initiation & II 558, 561-2, 586n
kabbalists misinterpret II 543
Lévi on meaning of II 562
male-female symbol II 29, 30
man not on early II 586-7
man on the I 321-2
mundane, or cross in circle I 5
now interpreted sexually II 587
origin of, beyond Bible II 545
Palenque or Mayan I 390
Paul fathomed mystery of II 556
phallic symbol I 5; II 30n, 50n, 542, 562
pre-Christ, pagan (Massey) II 587
Rose &, symbolized I 19
sevenfold, or *anima mundi* II 562
sign of recognition w adepts II 562
Smaragdine tablet & II 556
in Space, Second God (Plato) II 561
spirit & matter II 592
Sun's connection w II 559
swastika & II 556, 586
symbol of earth I 171
symbol of 4 quarters II 546
symbol of procreation II 546
symbol of Venus & II 30
tau I 657; II 30, 36, 556-8
tree, serpent & II 216, 588
Crossings (cross-breeding, human-animal) II 184-5, 192-3, 267, 286-7
anthropoid, tends to revert I 184n
anthropoids fr II 195-6
lowest humans, apes fr II 200-1
Crotch, W. Duppa
—— "Norwegian Lemming . . ."
evidence for Atlantis, Lemuria II 781-2
Crown (1st Sephīrāh) I 354; II 39
androgynous heavenly mother I 215-16 &n
Jewish trinity I 355

Kether or I 239, 352, 354, 433; II 595
   numbered one I 352
   sephīrōthal I 177
   seven splendid lights fr I 433
   Tetragrammaton & II 625n
Crucifix(ion)
   ancient American I 322
   brazen serpent & I 364 &n
   central point in II 556
   of King Ai II 558
   mystical meaning of II 560-2
   nailing to cross II 558, 561
   no Christian, before 7th century II 586-7
   Skinner on II 559-60
   three "Maries" at I 385
   on Tree of Life II 560
Cruciform
   couch & pre-Christian initiation II 586n
   couches found in Egyptian temples II 559
   lath & Vikartana I 322n
   sepulchers, pagodas, & crypts II 588 &n
Crucify(ied)
   men, before the Lord (OT) II 561
   before the Sun II 558
   Sun, by Viśvakarma I 322n
   symbol of, men universal I 323
Cruden, Alexander
—— *A Complete Concordance* . . .
   on Cherubs I 127
   temptation, 2 definitions of I 414
Crusaders
   led by goose & goat (Draper) I 357
Crustacea(n) II 712
   bisexual before mammals II 594n
   once jelly-speck II 154
   preceded man in 4th round II 594n
Crust of Earth II 10n, 11, 65
Crux Ansata. *See also* Ansated Cross, Cross,
      Tau Cross
   cube unfolded & I 321; II 600n
   on dead Egyptian mystics II 556, 586
   egg symbol & I 366n
   male-female principles in I 321; II 362
   numbers 3 & 4 in I 321
   seven fires (Gk) & II 362
   sign of Venus II 29n, 30, 31 &n
   symbol of man & generation II 600n
   unites circle & cross II 546, 549
Crux Dissimulata
   early Christian swastika II 586
Crypt(s)
   Central Asian I xxiv, xxxiv, xxxvi, 229
   cis-Himalayan, & initiates II 588n
   cross-form shape of II 588 &n

temple, or cave & initiation II 558
   of Thebes & Memphis II 379
Crypto (Gk), *Apocrypha* fr II 529
Crystal(s, -lization)
   formation of cells & II 255 &n
   life of I 49
   seven lines & II 582
   snow, shape of II 594
   of 3rd round fossils II 68n
Csoma de Körös, Alexander
   misdates Āryāsanga I 49-50n
Cube(s, ical) I 60; II 612
   allegories of I 344, 367
   base of Pythagorean triangle I 616
   circle, point & I 320-1
   circle, triangle & I 131, 612; II 111n, 626
   deity a perfect, w orthodox I 19
   dodecahedron in I 450
   Earth particles are, (Enfield) II 594
   a fertile number II 599
   Fire in triangle not in II 79
   formed fr infinite circle II 465
   four cardinal points symbolized by I 367
   four rivers of Eden I 367
   lipika & I 129-31
   manifested Logos & II 626
   Mercury as a II 542
   perfect, & angelic beings II 79
   perfect, & sacred animals I 442
   perfect, or 4-faced Brahmā II 465
   primeval perfect, in Purānas I 344
   sparks called I 93, 97
   square or, 2nd figure in nature II 594
   31415, π & I 131
   two, of good & evil I 312
   unfolded becomes seven II 600, 626
   unfolded in man II 36, 542, 561, 593, 600n,
      601
Cubit(s), Royal Egy, & Parker ratio I 313
Cudworth, Ralph, *True Intellectual System* . . .
   hylozoism of, & pantheism II 158-9
   speculations on Kabiri II 264
Cuelap (Peru)
   cyclopean structures at II 745
Cultu Egypt, De I 362. *See* Abenephius
Cumberland, Bishop Richard
   [q in Faber's *Cabiri*] II 393
—— *Origines gentium antiquissimae* . . .
   Kabiri, Noah & family II 360n, 364
   speculations on Kabiri II 264
   two races, Ham & Shem II 393
Cuneiform Text, George Smith I 357
Cunningham, Gen Sir Alexander
   on early Buddhist missions I xxviiin

Cupid
  Eros & I 109; II 65, 176
  son of Venus II 65, 418n
Cup-like Markings (on stones)
  records of oldest races II 346n
Curbati (Lat), Church made devils of I 331
Curds (primordial matter)
  become comets I 206
  cosmic matter or, & Fohat I 673
  in ocean of space I 97, 250
  origin of I 69
  radiant, in space I 66, 67, 97, 543
  Sea of, or Milky Way I 66-7; II 321
  seeds of future worlds I 69
  stage in globe evolution I 205-6n
Curetes (Gk), Faber relates, to Kabiri II 360
Curse(d, s) II 554
  belief in devil greatest II 377
  breaking the law & II 216 &n
  corruption of physical a II 283-4, 411
  Daksha, Nārada II 275n
  deluge of 3rd, 4th races not a II 410
  on Earth in Kabbala I 374-5
  Fall, dragon, gods & II 104
  gift of Prometheus a II 420-1
  God did not, Devil II 477
  incarnation a I 192-3; II 515
  of karma II 104
  of life preferred II 244-6
  on man II 216-17, 409-22
  procreation & II 282-4 &n, 410-11
  Prometheus, by Zeus II 244
  Satan, by Church II 235
  Semite God, man forever I 383
  speech a blessing or a I 93
Curtain
  hiding tabernacle I 125, 462; II 459
Curtis, George T., *Creation or Evolution?*
  lower life-forms fr man II 683
Curtius, Quintus. *See* Quintus Curtius
Cusa, Cardinal de (Nicolaus Cusanus)
—— *De docta ignorantia*
  definition of Absolute II 158 &n
  Pascal's definition of God fr II 545
Cush, given 7 stolen books by Ham II 612
Cushing, F. H., initiated by Zuñis II 629
Cutha Tablets. *See also* Smith, George
  monsters in II 2, 52-3, 55, 61, 115
  seven primal races in II 2-3
Cuttlefish
  Hugo's devil-fish II 440-1
Cuvier, Baron Georges
  aurochs a distinct species II 739
  gigantic animals & II 713

spurious human bones & II 277
—— *Discours sur les révolutions . . .*
  on "agents spirituels" I 490
  doubted nature of force I 490-1
  flying serpents (Plesiosaurus) II 205
Cuzco, cyclopean stones of I 209n
Cybele (Gk)
  lightning of, & Archaeus I 338n
  lunar goddess I 396, 400
  wife, mother, sister I 396
Cycle(s). *See also* Age, Chronology, Kalpas,
    Manvantaras, Root-Races, Rounds,
    Years, Yugas
  apses & equinoctial point II 330n
  ascending, descending I 417, 641, 642
  astronomical II 49, 70, 330
  Asuramaya, Nārada & II 47-8
  beginning of 4,320,000-year I 434-5
  of Being I 40n, 135
  celestial hierarchy evolves thru I 221
  death of races & II 780
  of decline in species II 733-4
  Dendera zodiac & II 432-3
  eleven-year, & Sun I 290, 541
  of energy I 625
  esoteric II 70, 435
  evolution endless series of I 221, 641; II 189
  figures for collapsed II 395
  5,000 yrs of kali-yuga ends I xliii-iv, 612
  Garuda stands for great I 366
  grand, of mankind I 642
  help given at close of great I 612
  history repeats itself in I 676
  human & natural I 387-90
  of incarnation or necessity I 17
  individual, of Kabbala II 188
  initiation, & sidereal year I 314
  Kabiri appear at beg of I 434-5 &n
  karma governs II 329
  known to initiates II 70
  legendary men stand for II 570-1
  long, of terrestrial existence II 246
  lunar, of 19 years II 770
  Magnus Annus II 784-5
  manvantaric I 134n, 368-78, 673; II 98, 399,
    434, 485
  mastered thru initiation I 642; II 566
  of matter & spirituality II 446
  of māyā II 146n
  of monads I 135
  multiples of seven I 36
  Nārada & II 47-9, 323
  of naros & saros I 114, 655n; II 619
  national, racial, tribal I 642; II 70, 301

new, & astronomical positions II 785
ogdoad (8) & II 580
overlap each other II 433n, 444
Pesh-Hun recorded cosmic II 49
Phoenix symbolized II 617 &n
prehistoric knowledge of I 389
racial & astronomical II 330-1, 443-6
of return of constellations I 645
sacred, of 4320 II 73
secrets of, guarded II 396
of septenary evolution I 267
Śesha is, of eternity II 49 &n, 505
sidereal II 330-1
subservient to karma I 635
swastika & II 99
table of II 69-70
teachers, world reformers & II 358-9
three thousand, of existences I 135
various, mentioned I 638
week, year & II 395
within cycles I 40n, 221, 637-8, 641-2;
 II 189, 301, 330, 620-1
"Cycle & epicycle . . ." [Milton] I 645
Cycle (Circle) of Necessity I 227; II 303
obligatory for all souls I 17
"Cycles of Matter." *See* Winchell, A.
Cyclic(al)
eternal motion is, & spiral II 80
evolution I 634-47; II 34, 199, 300
Jupiter as immutable, law II 786
languages have their, evolution II 199
law II 74, 157, 252, 298, 780
law defied by human will I 298n
law of race-evolution II 786n
law of rebirth II 232
Moon &, forms of disease I 180; II 622-3 &n
Nārada knew, intricacies II 49
nature's acts are I 640
pilgrimage II 103
precession of all life II 263
precession of equinoxes I 439n
progress of asterisms (Hindu) II 253
rise & fall II 723
septenary a, law of nature II 623n
spiral course of, law II 157

Cyclones, Moon, planets, etc & II 699
Cyclopean(s)
Atlantean source of II 745-6, 753n
civ gives way to Atlantean II 769-70
Druids heir to lore of II 754
Easter Island, remains I 322, 439; II 224,
 317, 337
monuments I 208-9n; II 344-5
oldest, buildings late Lemurian II 317
remnants II 294
stones & colossal buildings II 769
structures & giants II 341
structures in Peru II 317, 337, 745
swastika found on, buildings II 586
third or, eye II 299
Tiryns, Mycenae were II 345n
Cyclops, Cyclopes
actual giants of old II 337
Apollo killed II 770
Atlantean giant II 70, 293
Druids were not giants or II 343
initiates of Atlantis taught I 208n
initiators of true Masonry II 345n
man was a kind of II 289
may have been 3-eyed II 293-4
one eye of, was wisdom eye II 769
other races of II 769
Palaemon was a II 345n
three, last Lemurian subraces II 769
Cygnus, star in, (Schmidt) I 596
Cylinders, Babylonian, Assyrian II 4, 104, 226,
 248n, 690-1
Cyllene, Mt, Mercury born on II 541
Cynocephalus (dog-headed ape)
Egyptian glyph I 388
evolved fr lower anthropoids II 193
Cypher (nought). *See* Cipher
Cyropaedia. See Xenophon
Cyrus the Great (Pers) II 360
conquered Nabonidus II 691
instructed by signs in heaven I 652
Cytoblastema, & crystals II 255n
Cyzicus, moving stone at, (Pliny) II 345
Czolbe, H., on endless time & space II 154

D

Dābār, Debārīm (Heb)
　ten words or sephīrōth I 432; II 37, 39-40
　Word, Words, Logos I 350
Dabistan [Dādistan] (Zor)
　planetary genii & prophets I 649, 652
　twelve to 14 Zoroasters II 6n, 359
Dacca Muslin (fr India) II 226
Dactyli (Gk). *See also* Kabiri
　elect of 3rd & 4th races II 360
　Tiryns, Mycenae &, (Creuzer) II 345n
Daedalus (Gk), Zeus Triopos statue II 294n
Daemon(s) (Gk) I 461
　guardian spirits of antiquity II 478
　Nagal & Nargal both had a II 213
　Plato's elementary I 567n
　Seth an evil II 82n
　of soul of lightning I 467
Daēvas, Devs (Pers). *See also* Devas (Skt)
　Ahriman & II 517
　antediluvians of Bible II 394
　chained to planet I 577; II 538
　compelled to incarnate II 516
　devas, dhyānis became I 577
　giants or, hid jewels, metals II 396
　Peris &, located in north II 398
　pre-Adamic race II 394
　rebellious angels (Christian) I 577
　Tahmurath enemy of II 397
　war w Izeds (Peris) confused II 776
Dāg, Dāgōn (Phoen) [*Judges* 16:23]
　Chaldean man-fish I 345, 394, 653; II 54,
　　190, 495n
　corresponds to Matsya avatāra II 139
　Faber equates, w Adam I 642n
　Oannes-, demiurge II 5, 366
　Triton Greek counterpart of II 578
Daimon(es) (Gk)
　"dwell near immortals" I 288n
　genii or, rule Saturn's Age II 373
　Greeks & Hebrews believed in II 508-9
　of Socrates II 419
Dāitya (Pers), river in Airyana-Vaēgō II 356
Daitya (Skt) island II 740
　Atlantean island, sank II 141, 314n, 433, 710
　destroyed 270,000 years ago I 651
Daitya(s) (Skt) Giants or Titans
　became black w sin II 408

Daksha creates II 183
Dānavas, Titans or II 501
　defeat gods in 1st war I 419
　destroyed by Māyāmoha I 422-3
　divine dynasties & II 369 &n
　Easter Island statues & II 224
　fourth race giants II 31, 183
　giants of India II 336
　gibborīm called, in India II 273-4
　-guru II 30
　Indra & II 378
　name of Atlanteans II 227n
　parallel evolution of Vishnu w II 225n
　pious yogins I 415
　pupils of Śiva II 32
　Rāhu a II 381
　fr seventh dvīpa II 319
　Titans or II 288
　tombs of, at Malabar II 752
　turned fr the Vedas I 422
　various equivalents of I 92
　Venus preceptor of II 31
　wars between devatās & II 405-6
　were the true gods I 423
Daivīprakṛiti (Skt)
　daughter of Logos (Row) I 430n
　emanated primordial matter I 602
　Light of the Logos I 136, 216, 293, 430 &n,
　　602; II 38
　mother & daughter of Logos I 136
　seventh & sum of śaktis I 293
　universal mind I 602
　Unmanifested Logos, 7th principle I 216
Ḍākinī (Skt) female demons
　Khado, Liliths, or II 285
　offspring of 3rd, 4th races II 271
Daksha (Skt) II 89. *See also* Prajāpatis
　& Aditi I 142, 623; II 247n
　begets 3rd race females II 275
　born in every kalpa I 430; II 247n
　born of Mārishā, Brahmā II 176-7
　Chenresi is II 178-9
　chief of prajāpatis II 82, 163, 182, 247n
　column depicting II 178-9
　cursed Nārada II 47-8, 82, 275n
　disappeared II 192

early 3rd race typified by II 183
father, son, husband of Aditi I 623
forty-nine fires & I 521
giant destroyed sacrifice of II 68
Nārada & II 47-8, 140n, 171n, 502
progenitor of physical man II 176, 182
prolific creator II 78, 82
reborn as son of Mārishā II 177
sacrifice of II 68, 182-3
separated androgynes II 163
separation of sexes & II 275
son of God II 375
sons of, 3rd round, 3rd race II 78
started sexual intercourse II 182, 276, 375, 658
Vāch daughter of I 430
Vara & Avara progeny of II 163
Vaśishtha-, sons of II 78
Vāyu Purāna adds, to rishis I 436
Daksha-Sāvarna (Skt), a manu II 309
Dalai Lama(s) (Tib)
    Chenresi incarnates in II 178
    incarnation of Kwan-shi-yin I 471
    ocean symbolic name of II 502n
Damaghosha, Rajarshi (Skt)
    Śiśupāla son of II 225n
Damaru (Skt) drum
    Rudra-Śiva's, like hourglass II 502n
Damascius, *De principiis rerum*
    Protogonos called *Dis* by I 70, 343n
    seven cosmocratores I 235
    talking stones (Photius) II 342
    Unknown Darkness I 425
Damascus Blade II 430
Damavend, Mts of
    rock fr, killed Huschenk II 397
    Zohac banished to II 398
Dambhobhi, Dambholi (Skt)
    variants of Dattoli II 232n
Damnation, Damned II 237n
    personal god, salvation & I 613
Damti. *See* Tamtu
Damville, Comte de. *See* Montmorency
Dan, or Janna [Dhyāna, Skt]
    secret portion of I xx &n
Dan (son of Jacob)
    Virgo-Scorpio or I 651
    will teach black magic II 211
Dana, Prof James D.
—— ["On the Origin of Continents"]
    sunken continents II 324 &n
Dānava(s) (Skt). *See also* Giants
    born of Kaśyapa-Āditya II 382n
    Daityas & II 336, 369, 501

descendants of Danu II 381-2 &n
divine dynasties & II 369 &n
other names for I 92
pious yogins I 415
sin of mindless produced II 192
thirty million II 381
Titans, demon magicians II 183, 501
Vaiśvānara a II 381-2
Venus leader of II 498
warred against the gods II 381
Dance
    of daughters of Shiloh II 460
    David's circle-, around ark II 460-1
    Sabean, denotes planets round Sun II 460
Dangma (Tib)
    initiate & I 45
    opened eye of I 46n
    sees higher atomic principles I 218n
Daniel, great prophet & seer I 230
Daniel
    Michael "like unto a Son of Man" II 481
    Michael patron of Jews I 459
Danielo, J. F.
—— ["Le Livre de la Vision d'Enoch"]
    criticisms of de Sacy re *Enoch* II 533 &n
Danilevsky, N. Y.
—— *Darwinism: a Critical Investigation*
    book upsets Darwinism II 654
Danish Tumuli
    Atlantean survivors & II 352
Dankmoe [Denkmähler]. See Lepsius, K. R.
Danu (Skt)
    mother of Dānavas by Kaśyapa II 381 &n
Danube River
    Carib-like skulls near II 739
    Hyperborea not near II 7
Danville [Damville], Comte de. *See* Mont-morency
d'Anville, J. B. *See* Bourguignon
Daren. *See* Dārōm
Dark Ages, ancient past lost in II 430
Dark Epaphos (Gk) II 415-16, 418
Darkness
    absolute light I 41, 69, 70; II 37-8, 95, 489
    of Absolute or Parinishpanna I 53
    Ain-sōph is I 354
    Brahmā germ of unknown I 83
    breathes over waters I 63-4
    comprehends it (light) not I 70
    concealed deity (Gnos) I 74
    condition during pralaya I 69
    Deity is Nothing & I 350
    on face of deep I 70, 336-7, 374, 426; II 59
    Father-Mother or I 40-1

form of, & generation of light I 41, 110
light &, the same (Fludd) I 70
light comes fr I 40-1, 70, 110; II 485-6, 488, 492
light divided fr I 254
monad returns into I 427
Moses never explained cause of I 426
Mother Space coeval w I 99
not eternal to Zoroastrians II 488
pre-cosmic, divine All I 450n
principle of all things II 485-6
pure spirit I 70
Pymander issues as light fr II 486
self-existent Lord & I 333
Seven Fathers & II 564
Sons of Light fr absolute I 481
spirits of light & II 162
surrounds egg, circle, head I 443
svabhavat radiance of I 635
That, abstract Deity, or I 77
universal light is, to man I 337
Unknown, or Tsi-tsai I 356
voidness, non-ego & I 42
Darmesteter, James, *Essais Orientaux*
Hindu spirit in Hesiod, Orphism I 336n
—— "Introduction" to the *Vendidad*
Ahura is Asura in *Avesta* II 500
on Farvarshi II 480
seven worlds, karshvars II 607
Tree of Life, nature II 97 &n
two are born every 40 years II 291
—— *Ormazd et Ahriman* II 480, 607
Dārōm (Heb), one of the winds I 466
Darśanas (Skt)
Buddhism & Gk thought in the six I 47n
Darwin, Charles II 646. *See also* Darwinism, Evolution
on antiquity of man II 688n
—— *The Descent of Man*
Bartlett on egg-hatching II 595
effect of tides on organisms II 595
on embryo II 684-5 &n
man once androgynous II 118, 119
man's ancestors II 666, 667n, 669
reversion to ancestral types II 685
septenates in nature II 595
sterility of Tasmanians II 195-6
"those who know little" II 674
—— *On the Origin of Species*
age of Earth's crust II 10n
age of organic changes II 11
beginning of sedimentation II 694
beings have common ancestors II 190
bred animals tend to revert II 277

law of progressive development II 260
monogenetic origin of man II 169
Darwin, Sir G. H., *Scientific Papers* . . .
origin of Moon I 155 &n; II 64
Darwinism II 87-8, 185-90, 645-90. *See also* Darwin, Evolution
acquired faculties of, denied I 219
antiquity of man & II 685-9
ape origins in II 680-9
begins after astral evolution II 649
beyond, is the Unutterable II 190
Bree on fallacies of II 696, 727-8, 729
contradictory II 688
Crookes on I 585
demands great age for man II 686, 729
deserted by many II 647, 711
embryology & II 255-63
Hanoverian [Wiegand] disagrees w I 185n
inadequate but forced on us II 645
insufficient re heredity I 223n
language & II 662
Mivart's critique of II 696-7
Müller attacks II 721-2
natural selection & II 647-8
objections to II 717, 723-4n
occultism &, contrasted I 186-7, 219; II 87, 185, 190, 684
only part of evolution I 600; II 649
physicalization of root types & II 649
polygeneticists opposed II 169
principles on cosmic level I 201-3
de Quatrefages on II 56n, 87n, 315n, 645, 687-8n
Schmidt on II 667n, 734n
secondary laws partly true II 662
Spencer's view on II 730
starts at an open door II 190
theory begins at midpoint II 153
Darwinism. See Fiske, John
Darwinism: A Critical . . . See Danilevsky
Darwin's Phil. of Lang. See Müller, F. M.
Daseyn [Dasein] & Seyn [Sein] (Ger)
Fichte on I 281n
D'Assier, Paul, *Posthumous Humanity*
existence of astral body II 149
spirits, etc I 620
Dattāli, Dattobhri, Dattoi, Dattoli, Dattotri, Dattotti (Skt) II 232n
Däumling [Tom Thumb] (Ger)
principles of I 165
Davamata. *See* Devamata
David, King
biblical Jews fr II 473
danced "uncovered" I 335; II 459-61

did not recognize Moses or Laws II 541
Jewish phallicism starts w II 469
no giants in days of II 336
numbers Israel II 387n
reestablished worship of Jehovah I 320 &n;
    II 541
revelation & II 455
verses of, [*Psalms*] I 493
Davids. *See* Rhys Davids
Davikina [Davkina] (Chald)
    Ana, Belita &, female triad II 463
Davis, Dr J. B., "Contributions towards . . ."
    on Basques, Guanches II 790n
    intellect & brain size II 522-3
Davy, Sir Humphry
—— "Proteus or Immortality"
    loathed materialism I 480
Dawkins, W. Boyd, *Cave Hunting*
    Dryopithecus man's ancestor II 675-6
    modern sculptor vs Paleolithic II 716n
"Dawn of Creation, The." *See* Gladstone
Dawns & Twilights. *See also* Sandhyā,
    Sandhyāmśa
    Lucifer son of manvantaric I 53, 70-1
    Phoebe & Hilasira [Hilaeira] II 122
    seven, & 14 manvantaras II 308
Dawson, Sir John William
—— *The Origin of the World* . . .
    origin of man II 729
    unspecialized skeleton of man II 720
Day(s). *See also* Days-, Nights of Brahmā
    Brahmā creates, after Night II 59
    "of Come to Us" (Egy) I 134-5 &n
    of gods, one solar year II 620
    Great, after 7th round II 491
    Initiators & 365 II 529, 597n
    length of polar II 292
    misshapen, & our karma I 644
    & Night, Castor & Pollux II 122
    nights &, rest & activity II 545
    sevenfold night & II 756
    seventh I 240
    seventh, is sacred (Hesiod) II 603
    six, of Creation I 447; II 252n
    six, of *Genesis* (Wiseman) II 704
    twelve hours of, a blind I 450
    of week & planets I 652
Day After Death, The. See Figuier, L.
Dayānanda Sarasvatī
    on Arjuna & Ūlupī in America II 214 &n
    founder of Ārya Samāj II 68n
    greatest Sanskrit authority II 214n
    polemics w Max Müller I 360
    on primeval revelation I xxx

on secret Brahmanical works I xxx, xxxiv
Dayanisi (Heb) sun I 397n
Day "Be with Us" I 134-5 &n
    endures during mahāpralaya I 134n
    merging into One Essence I 130-1
    Ring "Pass-Not" & I 129
    spark re-becomes the flame at I 265
Day(s) of Brahmā (planetary manvantara)
        I 3, 12, 368-78, 442; II 660n. *See also*
        Nights of Brahmā
    Ananta-Śesha sleeps during II 505
    fourteen manus in I 63, 245, 375, 450; II 70,
        307, 308n
    Great Breath & II 6 &n
    Great Flood & II 146
    law governing Nights & I 62
    length of I 36, 232, 240, 340, 419n, 447, 635,
        655-6; II 69, 70, 308n, 505
    nitya pralaya closes II 69n
    1,000 mahā yugas I 63, 372; II 308n, 505
    pralaya after I 552; II 146
    Sacred Land endures for a II 6 &n
    spiritual lives māyāvic in I 635
Day of Judgment
    day "Be-with-us" I 134n
    minor pralaya II 617
Days of the Week
    characteristics of I 409
    names of planets & I 652
Dayus. *See* Dyaus
Dbrīm or Debārīm (Heb)
    ten words or sephīrōth I 432
Dead
    Hel queen of II 99
    no, or blind matter I 274, 280-1, 507;
        II 672
    Ptah Egyptian god of I 353
    something, was once living I 507-8n
Dead, Book of the. See Book of the Dead
Death. *See also* Devachan, Kāma-loka, Pralaya
    adept's, life in astral body II 531-2
    adepts solved problem of II 451
    after-, journey I 132, 227-8, 577, 673-4
    Angel of, & Satan same II 385, 388-9
    of body & Rudra-Śiva I 526n
    came w physical organism II 609n
    change of polarity at I 526n
    does not liberate fr rebirth I 39
    Egy teachings on I 227-8, 367 &n, 674 &n
    first 2 races knew no II 121, 138, 609-10
    girdle of II 235
    ignorance is II 215
    liquor vitae after rigor mortis at I 538
    of man & kosmos I 173

man prevented fr foreseeing II 523
man's, & pralayas II 309-10n
man's life-atoms after II 671-2
man's principles after I 122n, 158, 220, 242,
   526n, 538 &n
man's soul after II 364
Māra god of, & birth II 579 &n
Mars lord of, & birth II 392
no life possible without I 413, 459n
postmortem separation in II 496
resurrection (initiation) & II 462
Samael Angel of II 111, 385, 388
of secret sciences II 503
third race knew, at close II 610
time of, determines future I 86
Yama god of II 44
Debir or Kirjath-Sēpher II 529
Decad (Gk, decade in tx) II 581
   brought fr India II 573
   contains 4 unities, 3 binaries I 239
   formation of I 99
   found all over world I 321
   in interlaced triangles II 591-2
   Pythagorean I 321, 616; II 553, 573
   recorded the kosmos I 321
   twofold meaning of II 573
   unified, realm of reality I 333
Deccan (India), mighty men of II 411n
Deceiver, found in all cosmogonies I 413
December 25th
   & incarnation of solar gods I 656
Decharme, Paul
—— *Mythologie de la Grèce antique*
   ash tree & lightning II 519-20
   Bailly & Voltaire on Hesiod II 777
   Castor & Pollux II 121-2, 123-4n
   four ages, races (Hesiod) II 270-1
   kabeiron fr Gk "to burn" II 363
   Mt Atlas II 763
   Nemesis II 305-6n
   new period of creation II 269 &n
   Pandora II 270 &n
   Phoroneus II 519-21
   Prometheus II 519, 521-2, 524-5
   q Baudry on fire II 524, 526
   Rhodes birthplace of Telchines II 391
   stealing of fire II 525
   swan & golden eggs II 122
Decidua, Deciduata, Indeciduata
   Haeckel's prosimiae & II 649-50, 668
Decimal System
   antiquity of II 37n
   Great Pyramid built on I 362
   among Hindus, Pythagoreans I 360-2

Deep, Great (or Space). *See also* Abyss
   abode of Ea, wisdom II 53, 139n, 477
   Aditi, Chaos, Shekīnāh or I 460; II 527
   chaos I 65, 250, 312, 337, 344, 674; II 65, 145,
   313, 384
   energy reflected in I 337
   Flood stands for II 139, 145
   Gaia, Aditi or II 269
   Logos, Soul of World or I 353
   moist principle (*Pymander*) II 236
   Mother or I 625-6
   primordial waters I 80, 431, 460; II 65
   Thavatth, Thalassa & II 115
Definitions of Asclepios. See Kingsford, *Virgin of
   the World*
Deities. *See also* Architects, Builders, Gods
   beneficent & maleficent II 477
   cosmo-psychic powers & I 86
   creative I 127-8, 427; II 43
   female, more sacred than male I 5
   hosts of incarnated beams II 584
   lunar, solar I 229, 362, 396
   names of, change w each cycle II 90
   330 million, in India II 90
Deity I 349-58. *See also* God
   absolute, above space, time II 158
   as absolute, abstract "Ens" I xx
   absolute, in every atom I 58-9
   abstract, as That I 77
   abstract, attributes of I 438-9
   abstract, sexless I 59, 136n
   abstract triangle in occultism I 19
   Ādi-Budha or Unknown I xix
   aether as, pervades all things I 343-4
   anthropomorphic, & ether I 332
   Architect higher than creative II 43
   becomes a whirlwind I 117
   body of, 7 plus 3 limbs I 240
   boundless, infinite expansion I 120
   center of unity (Pythagoras) I 433
   chaos-theos-kosmos the triple I 347
   circle symbol of I 113-14; II 549
   concealed I 75n, 437
   creative I 332, 340-1, 346, 427; II 43
   degraded by sexual mysteries II 471
   Demiurgos no personal I 279-80
   dragon symbol of manifested II 386-7
   eternal Kārana or cause I 93n
   four-syllable symbol of I 351
   geometrizes (Plato) II 39
   given too human-like ways II 555
   hidden, or circumference of circle II 536
   highest universal, not creator I 439-40, 492-3n
   incognizable, & circle I 113

is law I 152
is One in many I 112
Jehovah & kabbalistic I 439-40n
living fire I 2
male, has mother, no father I 59
manifest, or diameter II 553
nameless, or ONE REALITY I 119
Nemesis, karma & I 645; II 304-5n
not God I 350
only Christian, a creator I 439-40
perfect cube w orthodox I 19
personal, aspects of I 280, 332, 427, 629, 638; II 518
Plato on II 554
presides over a constellation I 638
sea fr which wisdom flows I 239
shadow of, vivifies germ I 367
space, parent, etc I 8, 35
Sun original symbol of II 584
supreme, dual II 412n
theos or, expl II 545
time, space & II 382n
tribal, exalted II 507-8
unclean animals once symbols of I 355
universal, eternal in nature I 79, 295n
universal, vs anthropomorphic II 158
universe as I 92n
unknowable, breathes universe I 43
unknown I 327
unknown, passive (Justin) II 489
vacuum or latent I 343
will of, that acts II 528
"De la Croix ansée." See Raoul Rochette
Delambre, Jean Baptiste Joseph
—— *Histoire de l'astronomie* . . .
    Sun as a magnet I 499 &n
Delgarme [Dalgarno, George]
—— *Ars signorum vulgo* . . .
    universal language of I 310
Delhi, built on earlier cities II 221, 397
Δήλιος (Dēlios), or Apollo kills python II 771n
Delos
    Apollo born on Isle of II 771n
    called Basilea, Osericta II 773
    original, not in Greece II 773
Delphi(c) I 636
    gods of, & Stonehenge II 379
    Greeks consult, oracle re Xerxes I 466
    oracular vapors & I 338n
    temple & the *E Delphicum* II 580
Delta (Gk letter), Deus, Zeus & II 582
Delta (of the Nile)
    inhabited for over 100,000 yrs II 746
    Io guided to II 418

occupied fr NE II 368
once part of Europe II 8
thickness of, deposits II 750n
Deluge(s). *See also* Cataclysm, Floods, Noah
    Atlantean, an allegory (Massey) II 353
    Atlantean, buried sorcerers II 772
    Atlantean or Noah's II 69n, 142-6, 313-14, 395, 410, 423, 533-4, 751n, 774
    Book of Enoch & II 530-33
    builders of Babel after II 375
    Cain, Ham &, (Rom Church) II 391
    causes of II 144-5, 274, 699
    Chaldean & biblical, not Atlantean II 4
    changed whole Earth II 533-4
    cosmic II 69n
    Deucalion, Pyrrha escape II 270
    divine, or Tityus II 142
    early buddha of 5th race saw II 423
    Faber on Atlantean II 264-5
    fish &, in ancient symbolism I 653
    of fourth round I 444
    geological, ended 3rd race II 313
    historical events II 335
    Ilā primeval woman after I 523
    inclination of axis caused II 52
    inversion of poles & II 360
    Jewish, based on Poseidonis II 751n
    Kabirim gods of the II 360
    little, in Central Asia (Bunsen) II 141
    many, compressed into one II 141
    meanings of II 139-40, 144, 145-6
    moon, planets & II 699
    Noachian I 415, 444-5; II 3, 32, 69n, 138, 222, 265, 309, 390, 393, 466
    Noah's, not mythical II 774
    our, 850,000 yrs ago II 141, 144
    overtook 4th race II 350
    periodical, geological II 274, 410, 776 &n
    in *Popol-Vuh* II 35
    population explosion after II 453
    predicted by zodiac I 649
    pyramids, constellations & II 352
    in Samothrace & Gobi II 4-5
    satya-yuga followed I 67
    several, in 5th race II 353
    sidereal & geological II 314
    skeletons before, tall II 278
    story of, & 3rd race II 139-40 &n
    of Thessaly II 776
    third & 4th, not a curse II 410
    third, was Lemurian II 351
    Timaeus re occasional II 784
    traditions of I 322; II 141, 365, 751 &n, 774
    universal II 530

universal, watery abyss (Berosus) II 715n
Vaivasvata's I 369, 523; II 4, 69n, 139, 309,
    313
various I 67-8; II 141-6, 270-1, 313-15, 784-5
Demaimieux. *See* Maimieux, de
Dematerialization of Earth II 250
Demeter (Gk)
    feminine aspect of Axieros II 362
    sanctuary to, (Pausanias) II 363
    Zeus begot Dionysos by II 415
Demigods (Rishis, etc)
    gods, heroes, & men II 367, 368
    incarnated in man II 373n
    of 3rd race II 319
Demions [Dimyon, Heb]
    personating spirits, daimons II 508-9
Demiurge, Demiourgos(oi). *See also* Architect,
    Creator, Logos
    aggregate of dhyāni-chohans I 279-80
    angels rebelled against II 237
    anthropomorphized as Deceiver I 413
    beings refusing to create & II 93
    collective creator, architect I 279-80
    collective, or sound I 372
    compound of creative builders I 380n
    creator I 110; II 5, 25
    devoured by Bhutādi I 372
    directs Divine Thought II 704n
    Egyptian, or solar fire: Rā-Shoo I 311
    elohīm of Bible I 346
    fashions kosmos out of chaos I 346
    fiery serpents symbols of II 387n
    Horus idea in mind of I 348, 366
    Iaō called, (Fürst) II 541
    Logos or I 380n
    not perfect, not to be worshiped I 280
    not yet architect I 380
    numerological confirmation of II 466
    Second Logos, Tetraktys II 22, 478, 599
    subordinate to highest deity II 541n
    synthesis of architects I 346
    Universal Mind I 110; II 704n
    Universal Soul I 352-3
Democritus (of Abdera)
    atomic theory of I 579
    atoms & a vacuum of I 64, 343
    believed in gods I 518, 611
    gyratory atoms of I 117
    Leucippus taught I 2
    materialistic conceptions of I 50
    pupil of the Magi I 117
    skeptical but factual II 285-6
Demon(s). *See also* Adversary, Asuras, Devil
    Ahi-vritra, of drought II 384

angels of light turned into II 93
born of Kāśyapa-Āditya II 382n
Brahmā first creates II 58
Brahmans labeled asuras II 487
Christians call Boreas a I 467
dākinī, khado II 271, 285
Dānavas or, magicians II 183
fallen angels not II 516
gods by day, demons by night II 59 &n
gods made into I 202; II 232
Hindu, often pious I 415
impure, of matter II 274
"is the lining of God" I 235-6
male & female II 271
material devas are II 58 &n
more powerful by night II 59n
nine classes of II 389n
oppose clergy & ritualism I 415
pitris of the II 89
of pride, lust, hatred II 274
rākshasas as I 415; II 165n, 232n
Satan belongs to 5th class of II 389n
serpents, giants are II 280n
Seth, Typhon become II 32n, 82n
shells (kāma-rūpas) are II 111 &n
South Pole abode of II 404
"tempting" II 174
tremble at names of Hathor I 400
Venus degraded into II 45
wicked II 20
Demon est Deus inversus (Lat, Kab) I 70,
    411-24; II 274, 478, 487, 513
    astral light is I 424; II 512-13
    asuras & II 487
    light, darkness & I 70
Demonologists, Demonology
    of Roman Church re Satan II 389n, 510
Demrush, slain Persian giant II 398
Dendera Zodiac
    discovered II 431-3
    planisphere of, & Stonehenge II 344
    preserved by Coptic & Gk adepts II 432
    records over 75,000 yrs II 374n, 432
    three Virgos of II 368, 433
Denis. *See* Dionysius Periēgētēs
Denmark
    dolmens found in II 752
    shores of, have risen 200-600 ft II 787n
Denon, Baron Dominique Vivant
—— *Voyage dans la Basse . . .*
    age of Egyptian zodiac II 332, 431, 433
Denton, William & Elizabeth
—— *The Soul of Things*
    psychometrizes meteorite I 201n

Deva / 97

De placitus philosophorum. See Plutarch,
  Moralia
Depth
  Bythos, Propator or (Gnos) I 214
  seventh, & essence of things I 628
  Unfathomable, or Bythos II 214, 569n
Desātīr, The
  everything shadow of higher spheres II 268
Descartes, René
  denied soul to animals I 627
  pineal gland seat of soul II 298
  plenum of I 623
  retaught elemental vortices I 117, 206n, 492
  on rotation of planets I 206n
  Spinoza & I 628-9
—— *Principes de la philosophie*
  "Cogito ergo sum" II 242
Descending Arc. *See* Arc
Descent of Man. See Darwin, Charles
Description of Greece. See Pausanias
Desert(s). *See also* Gobi, Sahara
  destroy evidence of past II 311
  once fertile II 503
Design I 341, 643; II 261
  in action of "blindest" forces I 277
  of future in seed II 653-4, 731
Designers, builders or II 732
Desire. *See also* Kāma
  Anugītā on II 637
  Boehme on II 634
  Brahmā & I 110
  connects entity, nonentity II 176
  cosmic, becomes absolute light I 201
  Earth now body of I 260, 572
  Eros & II 65, 234
  first arose in It II 176, 578
  lower aspect of manas II 412-13
  πόθος (pothos) or, & creation I 110
  Promethean vulture & II 412-13
  for sentient life I 44-5
  sons of Vedhas without I 78, 176n
Desnoyers, J. P. F. S.
  calumnies poured on II 751
  man dates fr Miocene II 714n
Destiny I 654. *See also* Karma, Lipikas, Providence
  action of 7 agents & I 436
  cyclic, & humanity II 446
  fate & Moira II 604-5 &n
  karma-nemesis & I 642-5; II 304-6
  Pleiades connected w II 768
  written in the stars I 638-9
Destroyer(s) I 13n
  battle betw creators & I 199

creators &, in body I 261-4, 262-3nn
divine fire a II 114
fiery lives both, & builders I 262n
microbes as I 261-3 &n
Rudra as II 69n
Destruction
  constant, or nitya pralaya II 309-10n
  fifth root-race saved fr II 310
  legends of world, universal II 311
  of secret books I xxiii-iv
  of worlds, many meanings II 704-6
Deucalion (son of Prometheus)
  Adonis-Osiris worship & II 769n
  ancestor of man (Boeotians) II 519
  created men out of stones II 768-9
  escapes deluge in an ark II 270
  Greek Noah II 768-9
  name, contains story of Deluge II 335
  Vaivasvata, Xisuthrus, Noah II 309, 314
Deus (Lat)
  fr Aryan Dyaus, the day I 347
  four-letter God II 602
  Zeus, delta (Δ) & II 582
Deus enim et circulus est (Lat) II 552
Deus est demon inversus (Lat) II 478. *See also*
  Demon est Deus Inversus
Deus explicitus, Deus implicitus (Lat)
  manvantara & pralaya I 281n
Deus Lunus (Lat) I 381, 386-403
  occult potencies of Moon I 396
  same as Babylonian Sin I 388
  Soma is Hindu II 466
Deus Mundus (Lat)
  Jupiter Mundus has become I 463
Deus non fecit mortem (Lat) II 422
Deuteronomy
  eating locusts, beetles I 80n
  fiery serpents II 206
  giant King Og II 336
  God hath divided them II 477
  Jehovah as tribal god II 537
  Kadesh II 460
  Lord a consuming fire I 87, 122, 466, 626n
  Lord's portion is his people I 576
Deutsche Mythologie. See Grimm, J.
Deuxième Mémoire [de Mirville's *Des Esprits*
  vol II] I 506n
Dev(s). *See* Daēvas
Deva(s) (Skt) celestial beings. *See also* Daēvas
  act in space, time I 418
  arūpa II 585
  Aśvattha boughs are Hiranyagarbha I 406
  Brahmins rule II 111
  canon of proportion fr I 208-9n

cast no shadows II 112
classes of, given II 90
compelled to incarnate II 516
consciousness & the monad I 619
demons more material than II 58n
dhyāni-chohans I 93, 458; II 307
divine dynasties & II 369
divine men or, & primeval age II 712
each, has planet, nation, race II 538
elements stand for I 339
fire angels refuse to join II 243
gods & men II 211
gods in India I 93
Hermetic daimones, genii I 288n
hierarchies of I 92
Hindu, & devil I 73
identical w elohīm, cherubs I 92; II 85
incarnate in man II 98, 373n
Indra leads, against rebels II 382
kumāras division of I 458
lords of wisdom II 172
mānasa-, or Prometheus II 525
man cannot propitiate I 276
mānushis & I xliii
modes of motion (science) I 478
must pass thru human stage II 322
not all gods II 90
progenitors I 606
rebel, were asuras II 162
refused to create II 172
reigns of, (Bailly) II 368
seven primordial sages II 267n
solar, or agnishvātta I 181
sons of Bhūmi or I 605
war of asuras &, (Tārakā-maya) II 63
Zoroastrian devs I 577
Deva Brahmā, title of Nārada II 48
Devachan (Tib) heaven world
  analogy of, & kosmic nirvāna I 173
  animal monad has no II 196n
  divine teachers spurn II 281
  early races had no II 610
  egg as, (Egy) I 365
  Field of Aanroo or I 221
  fields of bliss I 386n
  higher principles in I 220; II 374n
  inner man spurns II 281
  manas & I 334; II 57n, 111
  man may escape rebirth & I 39
  nirmānakāyas have no II 615
  Sekhem (Egy) or I 220
  seven successive I 674n
  three witnesses & I 570-1
  winged scarabaeus symbol of I 365

Devagnanams [Devajñānis] (Skt)
  beings belonging to, listed II 90
Devakī (Skt)
  anthropomorphized Aditi II 527
  called Aranī II 524n, 527
  prayer to II 527-8
  seven children of, killed II 604n
  Vishnu & 8th child of II 48
Devaloka (Skt)
  plane of I 131
  sons of, & sons of Bhūmi I 605-6
Deva Manu (Skt), Vaivasvata was a II 715n
Devamata (Skt), dialogue w Nārada II 566-8
Devamātri (Skt) mother of gods
  Aditi or I 53, 99, 356, 527n; II 527
  ākāśa as I 527n
  cosmic space I 53n
  Sun & planets born fr I 99
Devanāgarī (Skt alphabet) I xxiii
  Kabiri-Titans invented II 364
Devāpi (Skt) I 378
Deva-putra Rishayah (Skt)
  sacrificers, sons of God II 605
Deva Rishi, Devarshi (Skt)
  title of Nārada II 48, 82-3, 502
Devasarga (Skt) divine creation I 454; II 176n
Devasenā (Skt), Vāch as, & Sarasvatī II 199n
Devatās (Skt). *See also* Śastra-devatās
  pitar (pitri)-, or gods II 148, 248
  war betw, & Daityas II 405-6
Deva Vardhika [Vardhaki] (Skt)
  name for Viśvakarma II 559
Devayāna (Skt) path of the gods
  way to immaterial worlds I 132
Dev-bend (Pers)
  name for Tahmurath II 397
Devi Bhagavata Purāna. See Bhagavata Purāna
Devī-durgā (Skt)
  Annapūrna & Kanyā I 91-2
Devil(s). *See also* Adversary, Dragon, Satan,
    Serpent, White Devil
  Azāzēl not a II 376
  belief in a personal II 377, 475
  can reunite w deity (Hindu) II 237n
  Chaldeo-Judaean myth II 477
  Church called, darkness I 70
  Church made, anthropomorphic II 508
  creative force, not a person II 510
  "doubles" are not I 235
  dragon of *Revelation* made into II 484-5
  elohīm called I 442n
  fallacy of dogma on II 209
  father of lies I 414
  forced pagans to copy Jews II 472n

"lead us not" addressed to I 414
Leviathan, Śārāph me'ōphēph & II 206n
mankind is the II 507 &n
in man's image II 228
"monkey of God" I 476
opposite of creator I 413
pagan deities became II 480-1, 507
prototype of Christian II 246
prototypes of Michael & II 478
Purānic giants called I 415
reality of, (de Mirville) II 341
Samael-Satan made into II 378
serpent made into I 344, 410, 442n; II 98, 528
Simoon, Atabutos, Diabolos II 385
Son of God (Bible) I 70, 412, 414
theology makes man a II 228
there is no II 162, 389
Titans, Kabirs linked w II 354
work of the II 472n
Zoroastrian devs or I 73

Devil-fish
Hugo ridiculed re II 440-1
Deville. *See* Ste-Claire Deville
Devon, cave of II 722
Devonian Age I 253n; II 712
Devonshire (England)
subtropical in Miocene II 726
Devotion
aspiration &, in early man I 210-12
Devourers I 258-9
differentiate fire-atoms I 259
fiery lives or I 250
Dev-sefid [Div-sefid] (Arabic) White Devil
giant killed by Krishna II 403, 407 &n
Dhairya (Skt), fortitude II 528
Dhaivata (Skt), quality of sound I 534
Dhammapada (Pāli) "Path of Dharma"
tanhā, maker of tabernacle II 110
Dharma (Skt) law, duty, religion. *See also Laws of Manu*
Kāma, son of, & Śraddhā II 176
motto of the TS & I xli; II 798
Dharma-sāvarṇi (Skt), a manu II 309
Dhātu(s) (Skt) layer, constituent element
7 substances in human body I 290
Dhīmat (Skt), all-wise deity II 176n
Dhṛiti (Skt) patience
mother of fortitude II 528
Dhruva (Skt). *See also* Pole Star
Enos & I 654
former pole star I 435; II 549
Great Pyramids & I 435
located in tail of Tortoise II 549

nine planets attached to II 488-9n
seven winds connected w II 612
tail of Ursa Minor & II 612n
year of, 9,090 years II 307n, 768
Dhruvatārā (Skt), pole stars II 401n
Dhulkarnayn, Persian conqueror II 398
Dhyan, Dan, Janna (Skt, dhyāna)
secret portions of I xx &n
Dhyan. *See* Dhyāni(s)
Dhyāna (Skt)
abstract meditation I 572; II 116
Tibetan yoga II 116
Dhyāni-bodhisattva(s) (Skt)
dhyāni-buddhas create I 109; II 116
Dhyāni-buddha(s) (Skt). *See also* Dhyāni-chohans, Dhyānis
aggregate of, as Avalokiteśvara/Kwan-shi-yin I 471-2
angel of a star I 573
anupadaka [aupapāduka] or I 52, 109, 571
ascent of soul & I 17
bodhisattvas human aspect of I 42
cannot reach Alaya's essence I 48
create w dhyāna II 116
dhyāni-bodhisattvas fr I 109; II 116
Dzyu collective wisdom of I 108
five, or pañchāsya I 213
furnished races w divine kings I 267
human monad part of a I 573
informing intelligences II 34
One becomes many or I 113
one for each round I 42
one w Alaya during life-period I 48
pi (π), circle & I 114
on primordial matter I 69
prototypes of buddhas on Earth I 108
seven I 571-2
seven, 5 have manifested I 108
sources of revelation I 10
twin-souls & I 574
two higher groups of I 267
various names for I 114, 571
Dhyāni-Chenresi, symbolism of II 178-9
Dhyāni-chohan(s). *See also* Angels, Archangels, Architects, Builders, Dhyāni-buddhas, Dhyānis, Elohīm, Planetary Spirits
Absolute beyond grasp of highest I 51
agents of cosmic law I 274-5
aggregate of, Divine Intelligence I 452, 471-2, 595, 604
Ah-hi (dhyāni-buddhic) parinishpanna I 53
Aletae, Lares, Kabiri or II 360-1, 393
Amshaspends II 358, 365-6

angels I 222n, 226, 274, 611
anupadaka [aupapāduka] & I 52
architects of visible world I 16
astral man reflection of II 170
boughs of Hiranyagarbha I 406
builders & watchers I 233
can do better than initiates I 234-5
Chenresi II 178
clothed in souls, atoms I 619
conscious, intelligent powers I 93
cosmic, cause terrestrial phenomena I 604
cosmic, dual host of beings I 604
cosmic mind & law are I 278, 579n, 595
create man & world II 242, 510
Deity's incarnated beams II 584
devas I 288n; II 307
direct causative agents of man I 229-30
do not fully remember former cosmos II 310
do not pass thru lower kingdoms I 188
dual nature of hosts of I 280
elements stand for I 339, 372-3 &n
elohīm II 37
endow man w self-consciousness II 232-3n
esoteric hierarchy of II 465
evolved 1st races II 307, 365-6
failures among I 188; II 232-3n
first group of I 197
forbidden fruit & II 267
form manifested Verbum I 278
four arms of II 179
four classes of II 60, 102
four Mahārājas kings of I 122
four primal natures of I 82
four suns of life & II 239
guide elemental forces I 277-8
Hermetic daimones, genii I 288n
hierarchy of, & 31415 I 90, 93
higher creative, or Demiurgos I 110
highest, know solar system II 700n
Host, Elohīm, Jehovah or II 510
incarnate in man I 188, 295n; II 92
invisible deity I 114
karmic agents I 274, 278
Keely under class of I 559
Kwan-shi-yin aggregate of I 471
made worlds fr primary stuff I 598n
manifest divine thought & will I 38
manifested theogony & I 434
man's 7 principles & I 226-7
manus or I 452; II 308-9, 365-6
manvantaric emanations of Logos I 429
man will merge into his I 265
man needs 2 rounds to become II 257
men fr other manvantaras I 277

minor logoi or elohīm II 37
nature's guiding intelligences I 146, 277-8
never-resting breaths I 103
in nirvāna during pralaya I 116n
not perfect or to be worshiped I 280
objective universe built on I 375
ōphanim ['ōphannīm] or I 92, 337
pass thru Circle of Necessity II 303
planetary spirits I 635
popular description of II 178-9
populations of, in other worlds I 583n
preside over constellations I 638
primordial mind or I 452
races, rounds, & I 42, 233, 442, 573 &n
reflect universal ideation I 280
refused to create II 246
rūpa, arūpa I 197; II 318n
septenary groups of I 573-4; II 361
seven primordial sages II 267n
seven rays fr Logos I 130, 573
seven rūpa classes of II 318n
sixfold, minus physical I 222n, 235
six hierarchies of, & śaktis I 292-3
sources of revelation I 10
substance of I 289-90
three lords or II 212
various names for I 42, 375; II 90, 365-6
wanted man to become a god II 246
Dhyāni-chohanic
buddhi part & parcel of, essence I 265
consciousness & manifested Logos I 573
essence & evolution II 108, 120
evolution guided by, thought II 649 &n
first men projected by 7, centers II 732
heart of the, body II 91
impulse &, Lamarck's law II 738
root of striving for perfection II 736
Dhyānipāśa (Skt) "rope of the angels"
separates phenomenal fr noumenal I 90
Dhyānis. See also Dhyāni-buddhas, Dhyāni-
chohans, Pitṛis
āngirasas, instructors II 605n
archangels II 22, 242
arhats, sages II 167
arūpa, one-third were II 93
became Zoroastrian devs I 577
Chenresī Padmapāni or II 178-9
displeased w rūpas II 57
doomed to rebirth by karma II 93-4
dragons or adepts disciples of II 210
each kalpa has its own II 179
elohīm II 2n
endowed 3rd race w mind I 457 &n; II 47n,
165, 276, 318 &n

evolved bhūtas for 1st race I 183
fire-, are agnishvāttas II 91
form nursery for future adepts I 207
give man 5 inner principles I 227
guide evolution I 181
have to be ātma-buddhi I 193
higher, not in physical creation II 80
incarnated at various times II 228
incarnated in empty shadows I 457 &n;
    II 487
kumāras I 456-7
lower order of, reigned over man I 266
lowest, or spirits of Earth I 224
lunar, 1st round globe D I 188
mānasa-, gave mind to man I 181-2
men become I 276; II 257
men in Mazdean ark are II 291
middle principles of man & I 222
monsters slain by II 115
never travel beyond visible cosmos I 13, 116n
nirmānakāyas fr other cycles II 93-4
pass thru human experience II 167
planets & II 29
projected shadows I 225; II 242-3
rays of wisdom II 191n
relation to principles II 29
of seven heavens II 273
seven orders of, & 7 elements I 259
six principled I 224
spiritual fire & II 105
spiritual plasm & I 224
various names for I 222n
watch over rounds & races I 42
Diabolos (Gk) slanderer, Devil
    Atabutos or II 385
    diable, diavolo, Teufel & I 73
Diagrams, Lists, Tables
    ankh-tie II 548
    Aryan & Semitic symb beings II 128
    astronomical I 666-7 &n
    caduceus I 550
    cosmic cycles, figures II 68-70
    cube unfolded II 600n
    Earth chain (Mazdean) II 759
    Earth chain (Kab) I 200
    elementals (*Five Years*, Blavatsky) I 177
    elements & number 7 II 627
    elements, three (alchemy) II 113
    esoteric geologic figures II 711-15
    evolution of races in 4th round II 300
    evolution of ungulates II 735, 736
    geologic ages, periods II 710
    lunar mean motions I 667n
    manus & rounds II 309

methods of procreation II 166-7
Moon chain & Earth chain I 172
principles, human, cosmic II 596
principles of man, nature II 593
races II 434, 688
senses of man & elements II 107
septenary division of man I 157
sevenfold man (Kab) I 242-6; II 633
seven globes & 7 principles I 153
seven principles, Egy & Hindu II 632
seven principles, Heb & Egy II 633
six-pointed star (Lévi, *Isis*) II 533
six-pointed star & sephīrōth I 375
ten sephīrōth II 37
triangle & quaternary II 591
variation of species II 738
vibrations of various types I 562
yugas II 69
Diameter
    androgynous Logos or pi (π) I 91
    circle & I 5, 11, 315-16; II 30, 39, 216, 536,
        544, 554
    circle &, root-race symbol II 30
    in circle or Adam Kadmon I 391
    of circle or creative power II 536
    circumference & II 544
    female deity I 5
    first symbol in cosmogony II 554-5
    gives birth to universe I 398
    god-manifested (by its works) is II 553
    immaculate mother-nature I 4
    Jehovah value is, & phallic I 6n
    nature or female principle I 91
    only during manvantara I 11
    ratio of, w circumference I 308, 313
    second-self, manifested, is I 398
    value of pi (π) & I 90-2
    the Word II 106
Diamond-Holder, -Soul, -Heart
    vajra-sattva or dorjesempa I 52, 571
Diana (Gk)
    bearded, or Artemis-Sōteira I 396
    bow & arrow of I 396
    daughter of Ceres (Aeschylus) II 419n
    destroys Niobe's children II 771-2 &n
    hides as cat in Moon I 387-8
    Isis &, parents of Earth II 23
    lunar goddess I 228-9, 395, 400; II 23, 123,
        462
    Moon transformed into I 386
    presides over childbirth I 387
Diana-Hecate-Luna
    diva triformis, 3-headed I 387
Dianoia, or Logos II 25

Diapason Harmony (Gk octave)
  planetary harmonies &, [Oliver] II 601
Diarbek, legendary Persian city II 397
Diastemes (Gk intervals), planets & music I
  433
Diatessaron (4th interval), in Gk music II 600
Dictionnaire des Religions. See Bertrand, Abbé
Dictynna, Cretan Artemis I 395
Diderot, Denis, *Encyclopédie* . . .
  many worlds inhabited II 706
Didumos [Didymos] (Gk) twin
  names Adam &, compared II 135
"Dieu est devenu . . ." (Fr) I 498
Dieu et les Dieux. See Gougenot des Mousseaux
Differentiation(s). *See also* Specialization,
  Variations
  fr ākāśa II 511
  cosmic & atomic I 152
  evolution & I 246-7, 277; II 648-9
  first I 1, 4, 138, 177, 327
  Fohat causes I 200-1, 205-6n, 328
  of monads I 178-9
  outside solar system I 673
  of primeval matter I 589, 601, 620, 633;
    II 389
  root of evil II 421n, 490, 574
  secondary causes of II 648-9, 736
  of 7 prakritis I 328
  of spirit-matter I 258, 277, 327, 421, 543
Digambara (Skt) sky-clad, naked
  Māyāmoha beguiles daityas as I 422-3
  Rudra-Śiva called II 502n
Digit. *See* Number
Dii Magni (Lat)
  Faber relates, to Kabiri II 360
Diis Syriis, De. See Seldenus
Dii Termini (Lat)
  cruciform symbol on highways II 542
Dikē (Gk)
  Nemesis daughter of II 305n
Diluvians (Titans) II 143
Dimensions (of Space) I 628
  six, of all bodies II 591
  will multiply w man's faculties I 251-2
Dinah (daughter of Jacob), Virgo or I 651
Dingir, Akkadian creative god II 365
Dinosaurians II 218
Dinotherium giganteum (tapir family)
  bones of, found in France II 277
Diocletian (Roman Emperor)
  burned Egyptian books II 763n
Diodorus Siculus II 768
—— *Bibliotheca historica*
  Atlantides cursed Sun II 407

Atlantides in Atlantis II 761
Basilea or Delos II 773
divine dynasties II 367
Egyptian year of 30 days II 620
giants II 336, 344n, 775
invention of fire II 363
Isis gave man corn, etc II 374
legend of Latona (Leto) II 770
Moses called God Iaō II 465
Osiris born fr an egg I 366
reincarnation among Druids II 760
Titea, mother of Titans II 143
Uranus 1st Atlantean king II 762, 765-6
Diogenes Laertius, *Lives of the Philosophers*
  age of Egyptian astronomy I 650
  Epicurus on soul, atoms I 568-9
  Pythagoras on numbers I 433-4
  q Zeno on nature II 159
Dionysia(c)
  egg explained in, Mysteries I 359-60
  none were licentious I 335
Dionysius. *See* Dionysos, Dionysus
Dionysius Periēgētēs (Denis in text)
—— [*Oikumenes periegesis*]
  Glacial or Saturnine Sea II 777n
Dionysos, Dionysus II 415-16
  first born, fr egg I 360
  man-savior, solar Bacchus II 420
  Osiris, Krishna, Buddha II 420
  πρωτόγονον (prōtogonon, Gk) first-born
    [*Orphic Hymns*] I 335
  son, father, husband (Dionysius in tx) I 396
Dionysos-Bacchus, "dark Epaphos" II 415-16
Dionysos-Chthonios, subterranean world &
  oracles (Dionysius in tx) I 463
Dionysos-Sabazios or Epaphos
  son of Zeus & Demeter II 415
Dionysus of Mnaseas
  Jupiter, Kabiri & II 393
Diorite, hard stone of statues II 226
Dioscuri (Dioskouroi) (Gk)
  Castor & Pollux II 122 &n, 361 &n, 362
  "heavenly measure" II 363
  Kabiri II 106, 360, 362
  the poles & II 362-3
  seven great gods, Idei II 361
  sparks on hats of I 338n
Dirghotamas [*Dīrghatamas*] (Skt)
  on pippala, fruit of Tree of Life II 97-8
Dis, "disposer of all things" I 343 &n
  Dodonean Jupiter & I 463
  Protogonos or I 70
Disc. *See* Circle
Disciple(s)

abandons illusive body I 570
accepted, & Eastern texts II 236
assumed master's names II 267n
of Buddha, worshiped by some II 34n
of Jesus had same father, star I 574
lanoo, chela or, & 3rd eye II 295
20th-century, will give proofs I xxxviii
Discipline, Mysteries, virtue & I xxxv
Disco Island (near Greenland)
Miocene subtropical flora II 726
Discours sur l'étude. See Herschel, J. F. W.
Discovery(ies)
future, of mythical cities II 236
future, re source of light I 621n
impending in science I 620, 623
will prove antiquity of civilization II 334
will prove man not apish II 744
Discus
adorning serpent's head II 213
seven-rayed, of Thoth II 529
Disease(s)
bacteria & I 225n
cosmic elements & I 347
epidemics & winds I 123
first races never died fr II 609
Keely's etheric force & I 559-60
mediumship & II 370n
Moon & cyclic forms of I 180
overpopulation & II 411 &n
serpent & II 356
sevenfold cyclic nature of II 622-3 &n
too much life force I 538n
unbelief a hereditary II 74
Disk, white I 1, 4
Disraeli, Benjamin
men associates of apes & angels II 744-5
Dissertation on the Mysteries of the Cabiri. See
Faber, G. S.
Dissolution(s). *See also* Night of Brahmā,
Pralaya
elemental I 11n, 372-3; II 309n
of heaven (2 *Peter*) II 757
manvantara, pralaya & II 307n, 309-10n
minor, & ephemeral creation II 309-10n
periods of I 12, 456n
planetary I 159
universal I 11n, 552; II 69n, 146, 310n, 579&n
Diti (Skt) limited, bounded
buddhi of ākāśa II 613-14
frustrated in dvāpara-yuga II 614
Indra, birth of maruts & II 613
770 million descendants of II 571
Diva triformis, tergemina triceps
Moon, Diana-Hecate-Luna, or I 387

Divination
by birds, egg yolk & white I 362-3
Confucius on I 441
by idol of moon & terāphīm II 455
w Nabatheans I 394-5
occult art now degraded I 362-3
by rocking stones II 342n, 346, 347
spirits of elements & I 395
by terāphīm (Seldenus) I 394
Divine
age, 7 manus as yet in II 307
beings become, thru experience I 106
bird (Aztec) precedes boat (ark) II 141
contains good & evil I 411-12
essence unmanifested I 398
eternal, boundless, absolute I 447
grace & Brahmanaspati II 498
incipient, man or element I 567
man in Purānas II 254
mind mirrored in atoms I 623
motionless, cannot be I 2
powers I 21-2; II 318n
Providence I 634
ray falls into generation II 231n
revelation I 304 &n
soul remembers all past II 424
spirit or ark II 313
spirit sustains heavens, Earth II 594n
voice or Kwan-yin I 72
wisdom, ideation & variation II 299n
Divine Breath. *See also* Manvantara
Braun's, is Fohat II 649n
in cyclic differentiation I 41
Great Breath projected called I 43
issues fr laya I 289
motion, Pleiades & II 551-2
substance informed by I 520
Divine Hermaphrodite
Brahmā-Vāch-Virāj II 126
Jehovah-Cain-Abel II 126
lotus symbol of I 379
Divine Kings, Dynasties, Instructors II 136,
365-78. *See also* Root-Race — 3rd
Agrippa MSS on II 487
Apollo most enlightened of II 774
Atlantean, & Prince of Tyrus II 492-3
Atlantean, fr Osericta, Delos II 773
Bailly on II 368
beings fr higher spheres II 328
Buddhas belonging to II 423n
built early civilizations II 318
Chaldean, 432,000 yrs of I 655 &n
destroyed red, blue races II 192
dhyāni-buddhas & I 267

each adapted to its humanity II 429
Edris-Enoch II 366
Egyptian, Chaldean II 486-7
Eratosthenes on II 367
forsook Atlanteans II 756
guru-devas, āngirasas or II 605 &n
Herodotus on II 369
Hindu version of II 369 &n
inhabit Sacred Island II 350
instructed 5th race II 353, 359, 429, 436
Kabiri II 364, 393
Kings of Light II 425
Lemuro-Atlanteans had 1st II 221-2
men will become I 309
Panodorus on II 366, 368-9
Plato describes Atlantean II 370-1
preceded Adami, "red earth" II 453-4
precede human kings I 266; II 316, 369
primitive man lived w II 349
pupils of, & genealogies II 42
rebirth of teachers & II 359
regarded as myths I 266
Rudra-Śiva king of II 502n
seven I 651; II 365-6
seven primeval gods were II 514
"the Shadow of the Shadow" II 487
taught arts, sciences I 266-7; II 29, 201, 317
third race & II 135, 194, 328, 429, 435-6
three Virgos refer to II 435-6
Tree of Life, serpent & I 407
twelve, refers to zodiac I 651
Divine Pymander. See also Hermetica
Böhme, Egyptian thought & II 630
cloaks its tenets II 455
creator not good or bad II 25
disfigured I 285; II 3, 114, 115n
echoes esoteric philosophy I 285; II 236
Manu & Thought Divine I 63
monsters generated in II 53
oldest logoi in West I 74
origin of work II 267-8n, 506
phraseology of I 674-5
St John the Baptist & II 115n
seven recurs in II 4, 109
way to Bible is thru II 383
quoted:
    animals, men bisexual II 96
    birth of pitris, men II 267
    building powers of I 601
    double fecundity of God II 134
    fallen angels I 417; II 103, 283
    God not mind, spirit, light I 285
    Heavenly Man II 236, 270, 493
    I am Thought, thy God . . . II 107

knowledge differs fr sense I 279
Latin text of Apuleius II 491n
man emanated fr 7 angels I 230
marriage of heaven w Earth I 417; II 231
mind, governors, builders I 480; II 236-7n
moyst principle of II 236, 591n
nature descends cyclically I 291n
point & circumference I 426
reality & appearances I 287
rectors, regents, supervisors II 23, 97, 488
serpent, dragon in I 74-5
seven circles of fire II 103, 232, 275n
seven hosts build world I 436; II 489
seven men, opposite sexes II 2n, 267,
    491-2
seven primal men II 2n, 97, 213
seven workmen II 97
speaking of God impossible I 286
spirit envelops universe I 286
ten is the mother of the soul I 90n
thought issues as light II 486
Word (Hermes), Word of God II 542
Divine Rebels II 79, 94. *See also* Rebel
Divine Soul
obligatory pilgrimage of I 17
spark of universal 6th principle I 17
Divine Thought I 39, 44, 325-41. *See also* Ide-
    ation, Mahat, Thought, Universal Mind
ākāśa upādhi of I 326
army of the Voice I 93
Builders & I 339
called Father by Plato I 348
cannot be defined I 327
creators moved by II 158
described I 1 &n, 61, 325-41
dhyāni-chohans & I 110-11; II 649n
Fohat & I 16, 58; II 649n
ideal kosmos & I 3
impregnates chaos, matter I 64, 340
kosmos fr I 339-40
not concerned w creation II 158, 536-7
not divine thinker I 61
plan of future cosmogony in I 1
in *Pymander* II 488-9
recorded in astral light I 104
universe temporary reflection of I 63
Divine Wisdom. *See also* Budha, Theosophy,
    Wisdom
Agathodaemon, endowed w II 210, 377
Christos or I 459; II 231n
Kwan-shai-yin, male aspect of I 473
law of Mazdā (Zor), or II 292
Mercury, Kurios, or I 353
Mētis, Minerva, symb of I 384

Nous is higher I 197n
Shekhīnāh, grace or II 293
species variation traced to II 299n, 649
Divine Year
mortal year &, explained II 619-21
War in Heaven & I 419 &n
Divisibility
of atom & matter I 519-20, 581, 628
Divo Rājah (Skt) II 622n
Div-sefid
abode of, 7th stage II 407n
killed by Krishna II 407
white devil II 403
Dixon, Charles
—— *Evolution Without Natural Selection*
evolution & natural selection II 647-8
Djin [Jinn, Jinni] (Arabic)
genii, shaitan or I 295
mech animal informed by II 427 &n
Djooljool [Gulgula(eh)] (Bamian part of)
sacked by Genghis Khan II 34
Docta Ignorantia, De. See Cusa, de
Doctor Jekyll & Mr Hyde. See Stevenson
Doctrine(s)
cannot compare w nature II 797
Eastern, kept secret II 236
Doctrine of Descent and Darwinism. See
Schmidt, E. O.
Dodecahedron. *See also* Twelve
concealed in cube (explained) I 450
first-begotten or I 340
perfect number (Philo) I 649
symbol of universe II 36
universe constructed on I 340, 344
Dodecaped, Persian myth animal II 397-9
Dodona, black doves of I 443
Dodonian Jupiter
identified w underworld I 463
Dog(s) II 54
embryo of, & human II 258
Erataōth in alchemy II 115n
Mercury as, (vigilance) II 28
wolf, fox mate w II 287
Dogma(s)
asuras of theology & II 59
Atlantean origin of II 273
born of phallic worship I 264n
Christian, fr heathen I 400-1
crude, of theology I 613
current religious II 1
curse on man II 410
effect of Christian II 484
of Egy clergy I 312, 363
every baby a new soul I 171

exoteric, often altered I 312
fallen angels a Christian II 103
historical facts become II 776
kills primeval truth II 797
Lemurians knew no II 272
Mysteries & II 124
of natural selection II 185
not-to-be-questioned II 383
Plato's paradigms & Christian II 268
Secret Doctrine not imposed as II 261
supernatural belongs to II 194
universal, in nature I 415
Zohar twisted into Christian II 476
Dogmatic
assertions of science & theology II 349
true scientists are not I 514
Dogme et Rituel. See Lévi, É.
Dog Star (Sirius), Mercury, Budha & II 374
Dolichocephalae(ic)
African races are *now* II 193n
of America & Guanches II 792
Dolmen(s)
builders of I 209n; II 750, 753-4
Cyclopean origin of I 209n
European, Pelasgic, pre-Inca II 753
not meant for tombs II 752-3
various, described II 752
Dolphin
Hindu sign Makara or II 577-8
Poseidon or Neptune became II 577, 775
Triton both man & II 578
Dolphin, soundings on Atlantic continent
II 333, 793
Dominion(s)
angel given, of outermost sphere II 233 &n
copy of ancient prototypes I 92
rule over 6th world (Syrian) I 435
Dondampai-denpa (Tib)
Paramārthasatya or I 48n
Don Juan, Zeus the Greco-Olympian II 420
Donnelly, Ignatius, *Atlantis: The Antediluvian
World*
Aryan arts & sciences Atlantean II 266n
Atlantic ridges II 333, 782 &n, 792-3
caveman not a monster II 741n
Challenger, Dolphin chart II 333, 792-3
defends Plato's Atlantis II 761n
future knowledge of Atlantis II 793
giants built Cholula pyramid II 276n
Gk, Rom, & modern institutions orig in
Miocene II 746n
modern civilization Atlantean II 782n
origin of culture in Miocene II 782n
Peru colony of Atlantis II 745

proved sunken civilizations II 786n
publication of II 221n, 791
q Renan on Egypt II 334
"Testimony of the Sea" II 782n
Dordogne, Caves of II 522
Dorjechang (Tib)
　Vajradhara, 1st Logos, or I 571
Dorjesempa (Tib)
　indestructibility in hereafter I 52n
　Vajrasattva or I 52 &n, 571
"Do the Adepts, . . ." *See* Blavatsky, H. P.
Douay Bible, followed in *SD* I 128n
Double(s). *See also* Astral Body, Chhāyās,
　Pitris, Root-Race — 1st
　agnishvāttas have no astral II 78
　astral, of Aeneas II 771
　bhūta or astral II 102n
　body &, may be miles apart I 234
　dragon or monad II 57
　-faced II 294, 575
　human, of rishis appear as kings I 442
　not devils as Church holds I 235-6
　pitris evolve astral I 174-5, 180, 183, 248;
　　II 120
Double Sexed. *See* Androgyne, Hermaph-
　rodite
Double Triangle. *See also* Six-pointed Star,
　Triangle
　Fohat central point of I 216
　six directions of space or I 118
　various equivalents of I 118
d'Ourches. *See* Ourches
Dove(s)
　Christian anima mundi I 402-3
　fiery serpent, seraph & I 441-2
　numerical expression of II 466
　sacred to Venus I 402
　sent fr Ark II 145
　symbol of Holy Ghost, Spirit I 81n, 354, 363,
　　402-3
　two black, fr Egypt to Dodona I 443
　water, fire, cross & I 384
Dover, Straits of
　once dry land II 324, 326, 746n
Dowler, Dr Bennett, found skeleton 57,000
　yrs old II 352, 753n
Downward Cycle. *See* Arc, Descending
Dowson, John
—— *A Classical Dictionary of Hindu Myth.* . . .
　Brahmā, Hansa Vāhana I 80
　Budha author of Vedic hymn II 498
　date of Parāśara I 456n
　Hiranyagarbha I 89
　Ilā, Idā II 147-8

janarloka I 116
Kaśyapa II 253
kumāras I 457n
seven worlds discussed I 115-16
Vishnu as Kalki avatāra I 87
Viśvakarma II 559, 605
Drach [Drack], "Chevalier"
　on Hebrew & pagan lightning I 467
　rabbi kabbalist, converted to Catholicism
　　II 476n
Draco (constellation)
　Lesser Bear or I 411
　once the pole star II 31-2n
　seven-headed, & serpent I 411
　symbol of Naasenian messiah II 356
Dracontia
　ancient divining rocks II 346
　not works of nature II 347
　once covered the globe II 380, 756
　plans of, destroyed by bishops II 347
　prove ancient doctrines II 756
　serpents, builders, architects & II 380
Draco Volans (Lat) flying dragon
　based on actual creature II 387
Dragg [Drac]
　meteoric fires in Languedoc II 206n
Draghedanum [Droghedanum] Sepulcrum
　devil's tomb in England II 206n
Dragon(s) II 201, 209-19, 377-90, 400. *See also*
　Adepts, Initiates, Nāgas, Serpents
　adepts, initiates I 404, 408-9; II 94n, 210,
　　212, 215, 280n, 353, 355, 501, 504
　angels w, bodies II 26
　of Apocalypse II 31-2n
　Apophis I 459
　Assyrian, "scaly one" II 354
　Bel &, w Ophites II 379, 503
　black storm- II 425
　in books of Hermes II 25
　born of fire & water I 470
　breaking heads of II 505
　Central Asia inhabited by II 203
　Chaldean, male principle II 104
　Chinese I 408; II 26-7, 203, 205-6, 209-10,
　　280n, 364-5
　Clement's cruel definition of II 280n
　constellations of the I 408, 657; II 352-3
　cosmic, of Kaśyapa-Āditya II 382n
　cosmological interpretation of II 386
　crocodile (Egy) I 219
　Dānavas, Titans, or II 381
　of Darkness, Light I 412
　of the Deep II 53, 61, 183, 477, 503-5
　devil or I 194; II 98, 506

double II 57
evil, doesn't exist II 53, 505
Fall & II 104
fallen angel, now symbol of II 506
fiery, of wisdom II 212
first disciples of dhyānis II 210
flying II 206 &n, 207n, 387, 486, 516
four hidden, of wisdom I 409
four-mouthed II 204
glyph for astral light I 73
of Gnostics, Ophites II 386-7
golden, or Kwan-shi-yin I 452
of good II 25-6
Gould on II 217-18, 280n
Great, (Draco) II 32n, 353, 355
Great or Old, is Deluge II 351-3
guard Trees of Knowledge I 128-9n
highest, lowest meanings of II 355
Hindu-Buddhist I 407
Jehovah as, tempted Eve I 73
Makara, crocodile, or II 354
mid-Atlanteans called II 756
Nidhögg (Norse) I 211
Phaëton awakened polar II 770n
polar I 407; II 274, 770n, 771n, 786
prove antiquity of man II 208
Python is Greek demon II 383, 771n
Raphael or I 127n; II 115n
red II 93-4, 379, 513, 771n
reports of seeing, killing II 207
of *Revelation* I 194, 407; II 93n, 354-5 &n,
    383-5, 484-5, 497, 506, 771n
sacred nature of, (Aelianus) II 355
St John's, & Atlantean magic II 356
St Michael mastered II 94n, 378
secret of, given to initiates II 504
septenary meaning I 407-8; II 208, 355
serpents & II 204-10, 354-6
sidereal, ever divine I 407
Sigurd ate heart of I 404
-slayers II 212, 380, 384-5
stories of II 206-7
symbolic & actual II 217-18
symb Moon's asc & desc nodes I 403
symbol of Sun II 380
symbol of wisdom I 657; II 26, 210
Tahmurath kills II 397
tail of, & Rāhu II 381
temples sacred to II 380
third race instructors, adepts II 210
Tiamat or II 384, 503
various names for II 354-6, 379-80, 485-6
Virgin or Madonna crushes I 403
waters of flood & Great I 460

winged, of Medea (Lévi) I 253n
Yellow II 365
"Dragon de Metz, Du". *See* Lenoir, M. A.
Dragon(s) of Wisdom II 22, 377
adepts & initiates II 203, 210, 353
blazing, or Logos I 71-2
crocodile is really a I 219
fallen angels are II 230
fiery serpents are not II 212
four hidden, or 4 quarters I 408-9
is the One, or Eka (Saka) I 73
Kwan-shi-yin or I 470, 472
of *Revelation* 12 II 384n
Satan has become II 234, 507
Sun-god or II 507
Dragon Seat
Chinese emperor's throne II 364
Dragon's Head, Tail
asc & desc nodes I 403; II 381
Δράϰων [Dracōn, Drakōn] (Gk). *See also*
    Draco, Dragons
Greek for dragon II 210
synonym for "evil one" II 206n
Draper, John William
—— *History of the Conflict betw. Rel. and Sci.*
permanent record of events I 104
—— *History of the Intellectual Dev. of Europe*
Crusaders led by goose, goat I 357
European man 250,000+ yrs old II 750n
Dravidians II 768, 790
Dreag, Bretagne, will-o'-the-wisps II 206n
Dream(s)
Aeschylus q on II 413
astral light &, (Lévi) I 259n
early Atlanteans had no II 761
novelists & occult II 317n
relative reality of I 566
sleep too deep for II 701
soul produces I 631
Dreamless Sleep I 47; II 701
Drogheda, devil's castle, Ireland II 206n
Drôles, les (Fr) ruffians
pagan "plagiarists" called II 482
Drop, assumes spherical shape I 98n
Dropides (Plato's 4x great-grandfather)
friend of Solon II 743n
Drought(s)
turn prehistoric lands into desert II 503
Drouk (Brittany), devil II 206n
Druid(s)
believed in rebirth II 760
believed in succession of worlds II 756
called themselves snakes II 380
circles, dolmens of I 209n

deity of, symbolized by serpent II 756
egg of I 368
fires of II 759
heirs to cyclopean lore II 754
historical men, not Cyclopes II 343
origin of, religion & priests II 756-7
say Neptune greeted Noah I 444n
seven souls, principles of II 632
understood Sun in Taurus, etc II 759
Druidical Temple
hinging stones of Salisbury Plain II 343
Druses, 7 mandragoras of II 27
Drushim, Book of. *See* Luria, Isaac
Dryden, John
—— *Cleomenes*, on virtue I 644
—— [*Religio Laici*]
"Some few whose lamps . . ." I 273
Dryopithecus
ancestor or descendant of man? II 675
brain of, & missing link II 676
gorilla, chimpanzee comp to II 676, 733
Thenay flints made by, (Gaudry) II 748
thinking man not fr II 688n
unchanged since Pliocene II 678
Duad I 355
chaos or I 433
cosmic, androgynous substance I 621n
doubled makes tetrad II 599
imperfect, detached state II 575
Jewish deity manifested II 543
monad &, re finite, infinite I 426
mother & daughter of Logos I 426
mother, evil I 614, 618
Dual(ism, ity)
every element is I 469
life a, force I 604
lotus symbol of I 57-8
manas is I 334
in Mazdean religion II 517
no radical, in Stanzas I 196
origin of I 15-16
poles of nature I 257
in Pythagorean decad I 616
Verbum of pagan Gnostics was II 515
Du Bois-Reymond, Emil Heinrich
an agnostic, not a materialist II 650n
materialism of I 518
opposed Darwinistic heredity II 711n
opposed Haeckel II 650 &n, 651, 656, 664, 673
—— *Ueber die Grenzen* . . .
Haeckel & Homer's genealogies II 656
Haeckel juggled words II 663n
on the processes of nature I 485n

psyche beyond material causes II 650n
substance eludes the senses I 670
Du Chaillu, Paul B., accused of lying II 440
Duck. *See also* Goose, Swan
in *Kalevala* lays golden eggs II 122
Dufferin, Lord
discovered hieroglyphs in Canada II 430
Dugpa(s) (Tib). *See also* Sorcerers
power of II 221n
swastika on idols of II 586
Dujardin-Beaumetz, G. O.
called protoplasm "sarcode" II 153n
Dulā (Skt), a Pleiad II 551
Dulaure, J. A., dated zodiacs 6500 BC I 652
Dumas, Jean Baptiste A., q by Winchell on
composite nature of elements I 543n
Dumbbell (nebula), resolvable I 598n
Duncan, Dr Peter Martin
—— "Address of President of Geol. Soc."
gas absorption & Sun's heat I 102n
Dunlap, S. F., *Sōd, the Mysteries of Adoni*
on Aesculapius I 353
defines Sōd as Mysteries II 212n
—— *Sōd, the Son of the Man*
Fetahil creates Earth I 194-5 &n
rebellious genii I 195-6
spirit female w Nazarenes I 194n
—— *Vestiges of the Spirit-History of Man*
older & younger Horus I 348
Duomo of Milan II 85
Dupuis, C. F.
misled by mutilated works II 620
—— *L'Origine de tous les cultes* . . .
dragon of Apocalypse II 32n
serpents as healers II 26n
on zodiacal signs I 652
Durán, Father Diego
—— *Historia de la Indias* . . .
giants built Cholula pyramid II 276n
Duration
aspect of the Absolute I 43
conditioned & unconditioned I 62
Kronos as endless I 418
matter, motion, space & I 55
nothing on Earth has real I 37
Osiris king of I 437
time & I 37, 43, 87
Durgā (Skt)
Devi-, wife of Śiva I 91
māyā, illusion or I 396
Virgin-, most ancient deity I 657-8
Durgā Kālī (Skt), goats sacrificed to II 579
Dust
Adam of I 242n, 247; II 81, 86, 112n, 457-8

animals fr cast-off II 180
clay, man's body of I 225; II 37
cosmic I 74, 107, 167, 201, 609
Fohat collects fiery I 144, 201
Duti, Dutica, sacred prostitute I 472
Duty
    moral religious II 176
    of an occultist I 589
    royal high road of I 643
Dvādaśa-kara (Skt) twelve-handed, name of
    Kārttikeya
    peacock, zodiac, etc II 619
Dvādaśāksha (Skt), twelve-eyed II 619
Dvāpara Yuga II 308n. *See also* Yugas
    differs for each race II 147n
    Diti frustrated in II 614
    length of II 69, 147
    occurs in Bhārata (varsha) II 322
    of 3rd root-race II 520n
    Vedas divided in every II 146n
    Vishnu as Veda-Vyāsa in II 483
Dvija (Skt). *See also* Twice-Born
    ancient Brahmin initiates I xxi, 209
    cycles known to II 70
    descended fr sons of God I 209
    inner sense of symbolism & II 469
    reborn 2nd time (initiation) II 462
Dvīpa(s) (Skt) island, continent
    Atala one of II 402, 408
    concentric rings of II 758-9
    continents or II 155
    dissolution of seven I 257, 373
    enumerated II 404n
    five races, islands & II 322
    Jambu-dvīpa terrestrial Earth II 326
    karshvars & II 758-9
    Meru north of all II 401n
    rākshasas, daityas on White II 288
    seven II 326, 403
    seven, of Atlantis II 350, 405-6
    seven, or planetary chain II 320
    seventh, or Pushkara II 319
    six destroyed (Wilford) II 406n, 409

surrounded by wine, curds II 320-1
Śveta-, or Lemuria II 264, 319, 366 &n, 584
two (Śāka, Pushkara) to come II 404-5
among Zoroastrians II 758-9
Dwaita (Dvaita) Vedantin sect I 79n, 451
Dwāpara Yuga. *See* Dvāpara Yuga
Dwarf(s) II 331, 425, 443
    African II 433n
    Atlantean II 433n
    forge Thor's hammer II 99
    giants &, in mythology II 754
    incarnation of Vishnu I 112
    Moola Koorumba of Nilgiri Hills II 445
Dwergar [Dvärgar] (Norse) "dwarfs"
    Turanians or, driven north II 754
Dwija. *See* Dvija
Dwipas. *See* Dvīpas
Dyaus (Skt) sky, heaven
    Brahmā merges into I 376
    Latin *Deus* fr Aryan I 347
    Sūrya son of, & Aditi I 101
Dynaspheric Force, Keely & I 560-1
Dynasties. *See also* Divine Kings
    Atlantean II 350
    of Atlantean spirit-kings II 222
    Chinese II 54n, 281, 302, 365, 368
    Egyptian II 32n, 431-2, 436
    Hindu I 378, 388; II 456
    numberless, before Adami II 453-4
    Persian II 396-8
    solar-lunar, & Budha II 456
    three divine, were 3 races II 369
Dyooknah [Dyōqnā] (Aram)
    divine phantom II 457
    shadow or, (Kabbala) II 268
Dzahhak, Nabatheans & II 453
Dzenodoo [Zen-dō] (Japanese)
    ascetics of Kioto & jewels I 173
Dzungarian, "Mani Kumbum" I 43n
Dzyan. *See Book of Dzyan, Stanzas of Dzyan*
Dzyu (Tib), becomes Fohat I 107-8
Dzyu-mi (Tib), false appearance I 108

E

Ea (Akkad) II 53, 61, 115, 139n, 226, 477, 495n, 503

Earth. *See also* Cataclysms, Continents, Gaea, Globes, Poles

age of I 206; II 68-9, 154

Aretz or II 143n, 467

Argus (Mercury) watches over II 28

Atlantean, Lemurian divisions of II 366

atmosphere of, changes atoms I 625

began as ball of fire I 191

beg of vegetation on II 10n, 112n

Bhūmi or I 213, 237, 250, 605; II 616

birth of, & foetus II 188-9

born, grows, changes, dies I 609

bottomless pit II 237n

Brahmā lifts, fr waters II 53

breathes every 24 hours I 541

building of I 257-60, 265, 267, 374-5

"calves" of, named I 398 &n

change in chemical substances on I 478 &n

changes for 3rd time II 319

churning of the Ocean & I 67-8

conjunction of, w Sun & Moon II 76

cooling of I 501n; II 154, 694

created by lower angels II 61

crust of II 10-11 &n, 252, 698 &n

curse on, (*Zohar*) I 374-5

deluge on II 52

density of, 18 million years ago II 157n

destiny of human monads 7th round I 180-1

destroyed after each round I 241

Devourers build, 1st round I 258-9

elohīm formed I 239

evolution, revolution of, (Kab) II 240

Fetahil (pitris) creates II 195 &n

fohatic forces at poles I 204-5

footstool of God [*Matt* 5:35] I 154

form of, 7th round I 260

forms fr auric envelope II 684

forty-nine fires on I 439n

fourth loka II 47

fourth round, man physical in II 310

fourth spoke of, -chain I 205

gamma (Γ) symbol of II 583, 591

gods on, in early times I 369

habitable phase of II 72

Hades II 234

heart, navel, blood of II 400-1 &n

Hvaniratha or visible, (Pers) II 607 &n

Idā goddess of II 138

inclination of axis I 369; II 52, 145, 274, 292, 314, 324-5, 329-30, 360, 533-4, 726, 771, 785

incrustation of II 65, 149n, 248

inhabited before 1st race II 315

Jupiter & II 136-7n

kliphoth [qelīppōth] in *Zohar* II 111

life cycles on I 186-7

lowest of chain II 98

Malkuth lowest world I 239-40; II 595

man born on 7 portions of II 1-4, 29, 77, 249, 400

Mania goddess of II 143

man link between heaven & II 370

man's body fr I 227

marriage of heaven & I 417

materiality of, changes II 68n

Mercury elder brother of I 155n; II 45

middle aged & little wiser II 312n

milked by rishis I 398

Moon giver of life to I 386

Moon inferior to II 45

Moon parent of II 44, 115

Moon's effect on I 156, 180; II 325

most gross in mid-4th race II 250

Nazarene teachings on I 194-5

never without life I 258

no other like our I 497n

nothing on, has duration I 37

Parāśara described II 322-3, 401n, 616-17n

periodic changes of II 266, 307n, 309, 311-12, 329, 725-7, 776n, 784-8

polar compression of I 593

poles of, & ecliptic II 332, 368, 431

predestination in history of I 641

ready for human stock II 312

rebirth of our II 703

reborn each round II 46-7

reimbodiment of, & elect of men I 309

rotation of I 117n, 569; II 155, 708

rotation of, in *Zohar* II 28n, 773

rotation of, retarded I 154n; II 324-5

rūpa of, 1st round I 259
sacred planets influence I 575 &n
Sarpa Rajñī I 74; II 47
sedimentation on II 715n
semi-astral II 250-1
seven I 53, 167, 250n; II 617-18
seven elements of I 140
sevenfold Nights, Days of II 756-60
seven, in Kabbala (Myer) I 447-8
seven logoi of II 592
seven man-bearing worlds I 167
seven planets, 12 houses & I 573 &n
seven rivers, zones, isles of II 616
seven rounds of I 159
seventh & 4th world I 240
six & 9 symbols of II 581
six earths born w our I 179
skins of I 74; II 46-7
softened since mid-4th race II 250
solidification of, (*Britannica*) II 698
Spenta Armaiti or II 385
sphericity of I 40 &n, 117n, 441; II 154-5, 708
spirit of II 241, 477
spiritual man before II 160
"Spirituous," nurse of man II 109
struggle between nous & psyche II 377
surface of, imperfectly explored II 717
symbol of, became phallic II 583
three I 250n
tripartite, septempartite II 757-9
vegetation begins on II 112n
Venus & I 155n, 593; II 31-3
Venus, & Sun's light & heat II 27-8, 29n
Venus-Lucifer alter ego of I 305
water is blood of II 43n, 400n
will return to ethereal form I 159
Earth Chain. *See also* Globes, Planetary Chain
age of I 205-6
ascending & descending arcs of I 250n
birth of, fr Moon I 171-3
creators act on globes of II 77
diagram of, w kabbalistic names I 200
Earth lowest globe of II 98
evolution of I 231-3
first appearance of humanity on II 68
globes of, in *Avesta* II 758-9
Mars, Mercury not of our I 162-70
Moon chain inferior to I 179
Myer's *Qabbalah* on I 447-8; II 503-4
next, will be superior I 173
seven globes of I 152, 158-60, 166; II 385, 607n
seven sacred planets & I 574n
small wheel I 205

three ascending globes of, (Norse) II 100
Earthquakes
cataclysms & II 787n
destroy evidence of past II 311
genii & I 294
Lemuria destroyed by II 266
Moon, planets, etc cause II 699
races twice destroyed by II 725-6
recent, & our 5th race II 307n
recent, a warning II 776n
sidereal events & I 646
Solon told of Atlantean II 786
volcanism &, destroy conts II 725, 776n
Earth's Crust. *See* Crust of Earth
Earth's Earliest Ages. See Pember, J. H.
Easam, Asam (Irish), to create II 114
Eashoor [Īśvara] (Skt), God in India II 114
East
avatars in West & II 550
frigid zone once in the II 535
God's glory fr the, (Ezekiel) I 123
Indra guards I 128
seers of the I 630
traditions of the I 303, 470
white corn depicts, (Zuñis) II 629
Easter Egg
Christian, Slavonian, etc I 367-8
Easter Island I 323
Atlanteans settled & perished on II 326
cyclopean relics on I 439; II 317, 337
decad found on I 321
legends re Lemuria II 788
part of submerged continent I 322, 439; II 316n, 337
Rapa-nui, Teapy or II 324
remnant of Lemuria II 324, 326-8, 680
rock city 30 miles west of II 317
sank & was raised II 327-8
statues, ansated cross on I 322; II 557
statues of 4th race giants II 224, 316 &n, 331, 336-7
statues record last Lemurians II 340
Eastern
occultism not gross II 85
philosophers believe in evolution II 259
Eastern Ethiopians
Egyptians called, by Herodotus II 429
lived on Indus River II 417-18
pyramids built before II 429
Ebionites (Judeo-Christian sect)
philosophy of, in *Isis Unveiled* I 197
Ecclesiastes
circuit of the spirit II 553
"the Earth abideth for ever" II 703

world destructions, etc II 704
Echod. *See* Eḥād
Eckstein, F. Baron d'
—— "De quelques légendes . . ." in *Journal Asiatique*
  Central Asia homeland of races II 204
—— "Questions relatives . . ." in *Revue arch.*
  geologic changes in Central Asia II 356
Eclipses II 693
  of Moon & kali-yuga I 662-3, 665; II 435
  rite of raising noise during II 94n
  solar, lunar, & allegories II 380
  of spiritual sun & catastrophes II 250n
  of Sun I 407; II 76
  of Sun, Moon, & Hindu epochs I 661-3
Ecliptic I 659, 662
  circuit of, (precession) II 330n, 550
  Fohat & I 204
  inclination of axis to II 292, 408, 431, 534
  Melchizedek Lord of II 392
  obliquity of II 726
  poles of, & Earth II 332, 368, 431
  when, parallel w meridian II 357, 785
Eclogae Physicae et Ethicae. See Stobaeus
Eclogues. See Virgil
Ecphantus [Ekphantos]
  taught Earth's rotation I 117 &n
Ecpyrosis, destruction by fire II 784
Ecuador, traditions of giants in II 754
Edda(s) (Norse)
  Ash is Yggdrasil of II 520
  cold "Hell" (Niflheim) of II 245
  cosmogony of I 367
  honey dew & Yggdrasil-bees of I 344-5
  Odin's ravens I 443
  serpent sacred in II 209
  twelve Aesers [Aesir] in II 27
  War in Heaven in II 386
Eddin Ahmed ben-Yahya
  on pyramids, stars II 362
Eden. *See also* Garden of Eden
  Ādi-Varsha of 1st races II 201
  cherub at gate of I 127
  derivation of word II 203-4
  elohīm sent man out of II 282
  exile fr I 397n
  Gan-Aeden or, Babylonia II 42n
  Garden of, now submerged II 494
  genetic, explained II 204
  Jewish, copied Chaldean copy II 204
  Meru & I 127
  Messiah enters, (*Zohar*) II 292
  in other cultures II 202-3

physiological Fall after II 279
  satya-yuga or II 493
  serpent of, not devil II 528
  serpent of, same as Lord God I 414
  Tree of I 114, 247; II 30-1, 97, 494
Eden Illa-ah (Genetic Eden)
  two interpretations of II 204
Edessa, Henoch built II 366
Edinburgh Medical and Surgical Journal
  Dr Stratton on human pulse II 623n
Edison, Thomas Alva
  phonograph called ventriloquism II 784n
Edkins, Joseph, *Chinese Buddhism*
  Buddhists had no personal God I 440
  Buddhists in China 61 AD I xxviii &n
  Ch'an & Dan discussed I xx &n
  Chinese had no cosmogony I 440 &n
  devas of the 4 continents I 126
  facts of, & conclusions I 72n
  Kwan-yin I 72 &n
Edom, King(s) of II 2
  allegory of, & worlds II 54; II 704-6
  Bela, son of Beor was II 706
  manus, rishis or I 376
  pre-Adamite races II 705
  produced fr divine image II 457
  refers also to rounds II 704 &n
  seven primeval races I 375; II 2, 704-5
  sexless II 55, 83-4
  shadowy pitris & II 487
  sinking of continents & I 439n
  sons of Esau II 705
  spheres of Earth chain 1st round I 375
Edris (*Koran*)
  became Thoth, Enoch, Orpheus II 529
  -Enoch or divine dynasty II 366
Effatum (Psellus). *See Chaldean Oracles*
Egg(s). *See also* Brahmā, Golden Egg, Hiraṇyagarbha
  aethereal winds impregnate I 365, 461
  Buddhists, Brahmins do not eat I 366
  Castor, Pollux born fr II 122
  cosmogonies begin w I 443
  devachan or I 365
  of Dionysiac Mysteries I 359-60
  divination by I 362-3
  divine I 69
  Easter I 367-8
  Egy symbols of I 364-6
  Eros-Phanēs evolves fr I 365, 461
  golden I 8, 65-6, 89, 91, 333, 335, 350, 359-60, 367n, 377, 426; II 122, 553
  hatching times of II 595
  Hebrews did not use, symbol I 354

Hindu allegories re I 365-6
Ialda-Baōth in I 197 &n
-like shells tampered w II 192
mundane I 81, 89, 91, 354, 357, 359, 556;
    II 616
nature a fructified I 65
prenatal, shells of 3rd race II 197
radiant, or Hiranyagarbha II 470
ray of Boundless penetrates I 354
repeats cosmic evolution I 65
sacred to Isis I 366 &n
Scandinavian I 367
serpent &, in mounds II 753n
serpent &, symbol I 65; II 756
seven, laid by duck (*Kalevala*) II 14, 122
Sibac, in Mystery language of Pueblos
    II 181n
spiritual ray fecundates I 69
sweat-born, ripening of II 131, 183
symbolizes salvation & resurrection I 367-8
symbol of eternal life I 365
symbol of solar & lunar deities I 362
universal symbol I 359-61
of viper at Philae I 363-4
virgin I 64-5
woman's ovule is II 166
world born fr I 64; II 122
Egg-born (Races). *See also* Lemurians, Root-
    Race — 3rd
androgynes, 3rd race II 116, 123, 131-2, 173,
    181, 183, 192, 197, 312, 361n, 657, 659
began separating in shells II 197
bred monsters II 192
Dioscuri & II 361n
even now man is II 131
first androgynous, then sexual II 132, 198
Genesis does not describe II 124
male, female babes born fr II 197
Mānasa would not enter II 171
perished rapidly II 312
Sons of Will & Yoga were II 181
sweat-born produced II 172, 177, 197-8
Ego(s). *See also* Higher Self, Self, Spiritual
    Egos
aroma of all births clings to II 632n
cognizes itself II 241
creation of, by ideation I 329n
divine I 309, 445; II 548
divine reaches, thru buddhi I xix
early races had no II 183, 610
effort of, to be free of senses II 587
evolved fr spiritual beings I 282
first differentiated, archangels II 242
gods are conscious spiritual I 632

hierarchies of intelligent, nature of I 629
higher self the real I 445
human, is higher manas II 79
human, latent in sleep I 429
karmic, of Gnostics II 604-5
limitations of personal I 329-30
Logos & Adversary reflected in II 162
lower, has upper hand II 109-10
Manu the non-dying I 248
monad becomes personal I 245
must experience on all planes I 329-30
not separate fr universal ego I 130-1
Plato's definition of II 88
progresses thru effort I 17
progressive awakenings of I 40
real immortal II 241
reincarnating, & sterility II 780
self-conscious, organizing principle II 654
Self parent source of I 129
shape of vehicle in other rounds II 289n
strung like beads on sūtrātman II 79, 513
Subba Row on I 428
Egoism, Egoship, Egotism I 535
absorbed by buddhi I xix
ahamkāra and/or I 197, 452; II 614
buddhi & I xix
I-am-ness or II 419-20
leads to error I 536n
Mahat & I 75; II 614
monads have no sense of I 275
mortal man moved by II 422
our globe in state of I 260
self-consciousness I 334, 335n
Egregores, energy spirits (Lévi) I 259n
Egypt. *See also* Egyptians
age of, (Bunsen [Massey]) I 435; II 32n, 374n
age of man in II 374n, 432, 746, 750 &n
alchemy had renaissance in II 763n
Atlanto-Aryan tribes settled II 746
builders, 7 great gods of I 127
catacombs of II 379-80
civilization of, always mature II 334, 786n
creation story fr II 3-4
cross on breasts of mystics in II 586
darkness principle of all things II 485-6
dated 5000 BC II 693
delta of II 746, 750n
Dendera zodiac of II 344, 368, 374n, 431-2
divine dynasties of II 316, 364-71, 486
evidence re, not understood I xxviii-ix
evil spirits emblems of chaos II 386
falling demon (Typhon) II 486
fire (Kabiri) worship in II 363
four sons of God of II 213

geologic origin of II 746
giants (heroes) of II 336
Gk & Heb ideas not fr, (Renouf) I 402
Hermes civilized, as Thoth II 367
Herodotus on II 332, 334, 368-9, 395-6, 429, 431-2, 534, 750
India &, kindred nations II 417-18
infested by winged serpents I 362
influenced Eridu II 226
Isis of, equal to male gods I 136n
Isis-Osiris brought corn to II 364
Isis-Osiris ruled, 75,000 yrs ago II 374n
Jewish kab ideas fr, & Chaldea II 240
Kabiri of II 274
land of fiery serpents II 212
lost keys at fall of Memphis I 311
lotus of, Holy of Holies I 385; II 472
once covered w sea II 368
Persia ever at war w II 393
prehistoric race of II 432
preserved Europe's history II 743
recorded 3 inversions of poles II 353
Semites in, 9000 BC (Bunsen) I 115n
Sun worship of, fr India II 379
various invasions of I 311
vast volume of inscriptions in II 793
"Egypte." *See* Creuzer, G. F.
Egyptian(s). *See also* Egypt
ākāśa, 7-fold heaven II 613
alphabet older than Chinese I 307
ancestors of II 328, 746, 750
ancient, did not eat eggs I 366
angels, planets, elements w II 115n
Aryan &, esotericism I 227 &n
astronomical records of I 650; II 620
Atlantis greater than, civ II 429-30
Atlanto-Aryan origin of II 436, 743, 750
atomic concepts fr Chaldeans I 117
Babylonians &, quarried Sinai II 692
bas-reliefs [HPB, *Lucifer*] II 558
Book of Hermes on early, tombs II 506
books burned by Diocletian II 763n
brought zodiac fr India II 435
canons of proportion I 208n
cat sacred to I 304-5; II 552-3n
civilized before Menes II 432
concealed deity I 75n
crocodile symbol I 219-21, 409-10; II 576-7
cross among I 657; II 542, 557-8, 588
dancing girls (Almeh) II 463
descend fr Saturn or Lemuria II 768
divine ancestors of man II 365
documents incomplete (Maspero) I 436
dynasties of I 266; II 436, 486

Eastern Ethiopians or, (Herodotus) II 429
egg symbol among I 359-60, 363-5
Esoteric Buddhism on II 750
Exodus story Atlantean II 426-9
fathers of, (Haggard's *She*) II 317n
fiery circle symbolic of kosmos II 357
five fingers symbol II 458
five "N's" of, & 5 races II 458
Fohat key to, religion I 673 &n
forgot much, altered nothing I 312
fourfold destruction of world II 311
gods & Jewish patriarchs I 655
gods little understood I 104-5
gods of, dual I 366-7
gods, origin of II 769
Great Bear Mother of Time I 227n
Horus, an older & younger I 348
idols in tombs of II 723
initiates, initiation II 210n, 212, 215-16n, 379, 462, 558, 588 &n, 750
Jewish language borrowed fr I 115n
Jewish tabernacle same as I 125
Jews "spoilt," of jewels, silver II 481
Karnac of, & Carnac of Bretagne II 380
keys to, lore hidden I xxxiv
knew of extinct monsters II 713
language-science [Skinner MS] I 313-14
lipikas or 40 assessors of I 104-5
literature destroyed I xl-i
lotus symbol I 379-80 &n; II 546
magi & Atlantean magicians II 428
man created 6,000 "years" ago (*IU*) I 340 &n
"man of clay" story II 291
Mars generative principle II 125n
Menes, Manu, Minos, etc II 774n
monotheism of, purely geographical I 675
Moon as a cat I 304-5
Mout, Mūt I 91n
mysteries based on number ten II 603
mystery-god a serpent II 756
Olcott taught by, initiate I xix
among oldest of 5th race II 603
pagan &, symbols in Synoptics I 384
Paleolithic &, drawing II 718
priests & Herodotus II 332
priests bound by oaths II 763
priests re Atlantis II 221, 371, 395
prophesied Jehovah (de Rougé) I 399n
Ptah divine spirit of I 353
pyramids II 351-2
reached England by land II 750 &n
recorded 3½ sidereal years II 332
records complete II 395

reincarnation taught by I 227; II 552
religion I xxviii-ix, 10, 312
remembered Poseidonis II 314
rites of the soul I 135
scarabaeus II 552
Secret Doctrine in, papyri I 674
seven & 49 fires worshiped by II 362
seven constellations of I 408
sevens in, thought I 236n, 436; II 582, 612, 617-18, 630-5
seven souls of II 630-5
seven stars of Great Bear II 631
Solon given history of Greece by II 743 &n
succession of worlds II 756
Sun called "eye of Osiris" by II 25
system of measures & Jewish I 312-13
tau-cross of I 5, 321; II 30-1, 217, 542, 557
taught masses myths, reality in Sanctuary I 366
teachings about defunct I 228-9
temples described (Clement) I 462
tree & serpent worshipers I 403-11
trinity II 462
Vulcan greatest god w later II 390n
wheat sacred to, priests II 374
who are the I 115n
year of 60, 30 days II 620
zodiac II 332, 431-3, 436
zodiacal signs of I 408
Egyptian Book of the Dead. See Book of the Dead
Egyptian Legends. See Maspero, G.
Egyptian Pantheon. See Champollion, *Panthéon Égyptien;* Jablonski, *Pantheon Aegyptiorem*
Egyptian Ritual. *See Book of the Dead*
Egyptologist(s)
    count 5 Hermes II 267n
    difficulties of I xxix, 307, 310, 385, 398, 402; II 137, 367, 374n, 506
    on Great Pyramid II 431-2
    Osiris, Menes & II 374n
    seven souls of II 630-41
Egypt's Place in Univ. Hist. See Bunsen
Eḥād [Echod] (Heb, Achad in tx)
    Ain-sōph becomes, or Eka, Ahu I 113
    elohīm called, in beginning I 112
    Jehovah in Hebrew I 73, 112-13; II 508
    masculine "one" I 129, 130n
Ehyeh (Heb), Jews used Adonai, not II 452
Ehyeh asher Ehyeh (Heb)
    "I am that I am" II 468, 539
Εἰχτων (Eichtōn), Agathodaimon II 210-11
Eighth Sphere
    forbidden ground of I 156
    mystery of I 163

Taht-Esmun (Egy) or I 227n
Eka (Skt) one I 29n
    Ain-sōph becomes, or Echod, Ahu I 113
    is 4 (chatur) I 71
    Jehovah in Hebrew is I 73
    One, Ādi, etc I 129
Ekānekarūpa (Skt) one & many II 47, 108
Ekaślokaśāstra of Nāgārjuna I 61
Ekimu, Chaldean spirits II 248n
Eku-gai-no-kami. *See* Iku-gai-no-kami
Ēl, Al (Heb, Chald) II 39
    Ajal &, or Azāzēl (Spencer) II 376
    Chaldean term for Sun II 540
    Lord God Almighty II 509
El-ar (solar deity)
    lar not contraction of II 361
Elastic, Elasticity I 513-14, 519
Eleazar, high priest of Jews II 200n
Elect, the II 314, 597n
    Buddha's esotericism for I xxi
    did not fall into sin II 319
    Dioscuri & II 361n
    of mankind I 208, 221, 267, 617
    race of dhyānis II 276, 281-2
    role of, in Atlantis II 350
    of 3rd, 4th races II 360
Electra (Gk), daughter of Atlas II 768
Electricity. *See also* Fohat
    aspect of Archaeus I 338n
    aspect of universal motion I 147
    astral fluid lower aspect of I 81
    Böhme anticipated I 494
    called a god esoterically I 672
    an effect, not a cause I 517
    an entity I 76, 111n
    first produced by friction I 517
    fluid I 508, 516
    form of atomic vibration I 562
    grossest effects alone seen I 554
    Grove defines I 469, 496
    harmony in laws of II 622
    immaterial, non-molecular I 508
    is matter & atomic I 111n, 580, 584, 671n
    Keely's views on I 560, 562
    kundalinī-śakti & I 293
    life-, aspect of Fohat I 139; II 65
    life of universe I 137, 139, 338, 541
    light & life are I 579
    light &, material I 580
    light, fire, water born of I 81-2
    matter affected by invisible power I 469
    mystery of I 79
    nature of, not understood I 493, 498
    not a property of matter I 493

noumenal, phenomenal I 145-6
noumenon of, conscious cause I 517
One Life, highest aspect of I 81-2, 139
poles of Earth & I 205
secondary effect of causes I 484
seven primary forces of I 554
springs fr upādhi of ether I 515n
Sun storehouse of I 531
Sun's vital, & matter I 602
vital, leaves body at death I 673
zero point of I 551
Electric Science. See Bakewell, F. C.
Electris or Samothrace, 7 localities II 3
Electro-Magnetic Current
circulates thru Earth II 400 &n
Ēl-Ēl (Heb), Kadush, Adonai or I 463
Ēl Elyōn (Heb), Abraham & II 380
Element(s). *See also* Aether, Ākāśa
ahamkāra secret, in *VP* I 66
ancestors met w spirits of II 356
ancient, not our chemical I 218n, 338n, 461
angels & archons rule I 604
animated by intelligence I 594-6
bhūtādi & I 372-3, 452
Brāhman allegory re birth of I 365-6
centers of force I 630
change I 253, 257, 259, 543
chemical, & number seven II 627-8
compound nature of I 583
cosmic matter forms into I 97
Crookes on I 546-54, 581, 584n, 620-6
dhyānis noumenoi of I 259; II 273
different among planets I 142-3
differentiated or abnormal I 567
differentiation of I 130, 138-44
different, in Earth periods I 142
dissolve last at pralaya I 571
dual I 347, 469
each god of, has his own language I 464
each Round develops one I 250-4, 259-60
earliest race did not need any II 160
early forms of I 253-4
Earth's, in Sun I 583
elementals inform I 146, 461
evolution of I 140-4, 330, 427, 447, 452, 583-4; II 616
evolution of man subordinate to II 107
fifth, & 5th race I 342; II 135
fifth, evolved during 5th round I 140
fivefold chohans & five II 578
four, & human principles II 593
four, called rhizomata II 599
four, evolved I 12-13, 140, 250, 342, 460-70; II 592

four Hebrew, & Jehovah I 462
four sacred animals & I 363
giants commanded, (Creuzer) II 285
gods of, celestial & infernal I 463
golden egg & seven I 65-6
homogeneous, & world soul I 203
humanities develop w II 135
invisible, spiritual I 284 &n
Isis Unveiled on I 338n
kalpic masks of I 673
known, not primordial I 542-3
magic is knowing essence of I 263
man's ruling I 294n
man's struggle w II 56n
mother substance of I 291-2
of negative atomic weight I 584
no one has ever seen, fully I 342
not as now in prior rounds I 253
occult meaning of term I 566-9
occult phenomena & I 82 &n
One, only I 13, 55, 75, 101, 110, 460, 549
origin of I 13, 284-5, 542
our, not primordial (Crookes) I 622
Paracelsus on birth of I 284 &n
Paul calls kosmic beings I 338n
periodic law of I 585-6n; II 627
personified by ancients I 141
physical forces vehicles of I 470
Plato on principles & I 491-2
primary, is conscious I 373
principles & I 334-5
propelled upward I 543
Pythagoras on 4, (Diogenes) I 433-4
St Paul's angels & demons I 373n
secondary creation & precosmic I 452
second, in 2nd round I 260
senses fr I 284-5, 534; II 106-7
seven I 12-13 &nn, 457-8n, 534; II 359, 604n
seven, & 49 subelements I 347
seven cosmic gradations of I 461
seven dhyāni-buddhas or I 572
seven Gnostic II 604-5
seventh cosmic I 135
seven, 3 secret I 65-6
seven, veil of Deity I 460
sixth & 7th, imperceptible I 12
spirits of the I 218n, 395
stand for devas, sephīrōth I 339
subdivided by ancients I 140-1
tabernacle symbol of four I 125-6, 347n
tamas or, (Hindu) I 332
third race controlled II 220
unknown, & subelements I 673
unknown, in stars & Sun I 583, 589, 673

Vishnu Purāna on I 521-2
what is the ultimate, (Crookes) I 625
worshiped when gods left II 273
Elemental(s) I 218n. *See also* Nature Spirits,
 Planetary Spirits
astral light full of I 331n
bhūtādi origin of I 372
Bjerregaard on I 630-2
chaos & II 386n
commingling of man & I 188
controlled by sound, colors I 514n
cosmic, at South Pole II 274
dhyāni-chohanic failures & I 188; II 232-3n
dhyāni-chohans work w I 278
divine workmen rule I 146
dominant in primary creation II 312n
five elements & I 294n
forces are I 146
form, build, condense body I 233
future men I 184n, 277
genii or I 294
gods of elements are not II 272-3 &n
have no form of their own II 34
higher, possess intelligence II 102
hurricanes & II 274
influence on man I 294-5 &n
inform phenomenal elements I 461
inroll at pralaya I 372-3 &n
kabbalistic teaching on I 234n
looking glass that can speak I 631
manipulate nature's forces I 277-8
mechanical animal informed by II 427n
monads or I 632
fr Mother-Substance I 291-2
seventh hierarchy or I 233
sorcerers stronger than II 427
spiritual malices of St Paul I 331n
subject to karma I 221
three degrees of I 176-7, 454-5
triple kingdom of II 616
two subphysical kingdoms of II 737
Elemental Dissolution. *See* Prākritika
 Pralaya
"Elementals, . . ." *See* Bjerregaard
Elemental vortices
of Descartes I 117, 206n
Newton gave deathblow to I 492
Elementary(ies)
devoured by Uraeus in Āanru I 674n
shade of the dead I 567
spirits possessing mediums I 233n
spooks, ghosts I 620
Element-Language
for invoking cosmic gods I 464

"Elements and Meta-Elements." *See* Crookes
Elephant II 733
pigmy, & future size of II 219
pigmy, Bushmen, etc II 723
Elephanta II 85
built on labyrinth of passages II 221
Khnoum adored at I 367
Elephas antiquas, Meridionalis II 751
Elephas primigenius
age of, & man II 687, 739, 746, 751
Eleusis, submerged II 270n
Élévations. See Bossuet, J. B.
Elihu, God-Jah or II 531
Elijah
attained nirvana II 532
died in his personality II 532
God-Jah, Jehovah II 531
heard small voice II 342n
Lord in wind & quake I 466
taken to heaven II 531
Elion. *See* Ēl Elyōn
Elivågor (Norse)
drops of, create Ymir I 367
Elixir of Life I 626n
allotropizing oxygen into I 144n
Kwan-shi-yin pours I 471
"Elixir of Life, The." *See* Mitford, G.
Ellis, William, *Polynesian Researches*
Tahitian Adam-Eve story II 193-4
Ellora
built on labyrinth of passages II 221
figures on walls of II 345n
Elmes Fire [St Elmo's Fire] I 338n
Eloha, Eloāh (Heb)
"Lord God" II 60n, 509
Elohi II 39
Elohīm (Heb). *See also* Creators, Dhyāni-
 chohans, Sephīrōth, Sons of Light
abstraction physically I 230
Adam Kadmon as host of II 112n
Adam shadow image of II 137
alhim (pl) or I 91, 114, 342, 346, 440; II 37-8,
 41
Amshaspends I 113; II 92
androgynous, feminine I 130n
angels rebelled against II 280n
asuras same as II 487-8
barhishads become creative II 78
Bīnāh, Tiamat, Thalatth or I 394
brought forth man II 134, 181, 365, 491
circumference of circle (Parker) II 544
collective, or Logos II 311
creative lower powers II 1-2n, 61, 95n
dhyāni-chohans or I 38; II 37, 510

Echod or One in beginning I 112
Ēl, Elu (Chald) II 282, 540
evolution of, downwards I 247
formed heavens & Earth I 239, 346
formed worlds six-by-six I 239
in *Genesis* I 254, 337, 346, 450; II 2n, 44, 60n, 81, 95n, 202, 452
Gnostic II 389
God-name now phallic I 316
God of Israel an inferior member of II 61-2, 75, 452
gods & also priests II 202
-Javeh, man created by II 44
jealous, invoke suffering II 95n, 104, 282
Jehovah-Bīnāh-Arelim II 608
Jehovah called I 112-13, 438-9
Jehovah one of I 197-8, 492-3n; II 75, 510
Jeremiah's curse against II 128
Jews under Saturn II 127
kabbalists' lowest designation I 619
Lord God (*Genesis*) is II 81, 509
"man is become as one of us" I 276, 493n; II 44, 202, 243, 499n
man offspring of I 224-5
manvantaric emanations of Logos I 429
men &, (Kabbala) I 230
minor logoi II 37
Noah as host of II 597
number of, & dhyāni-chohans I 90 &n
One becomes many or I 113
pitris or II 5, 137
plural noun or Chiim I 130
plural number in *Genesis* I 492-3n; II 81-2, 134
produced 1st divine ideation I 375
Prometheus & II 414
related to our soul, spirit I 230
rishis, rudras, agnis II 85, 365
St Michael one of II 379
Samael god-name for one of I 417
self-initiated higher gods II 124
sent man out of Eden II 282, 382n
sephīrōth or I 230; II 388
serpent (*Genesis*) one of II 388
seven creators I 139
seven regents of Pymander II 488
seven sublime Lords I 42
some created, some did not II 128
Sons of Light, God II 390, 489
sources of revelation I 10
synthesis of 10 sephīrōth I 98n
three groups of, in Kabbala II 388
various names for I 114
word, changed to masc sing I 129-30, 225

worshiped, yet called devils I 441-2n
zodiac & II 23
Elohistic
account of *Genesis* I 254; II 75, 252n
figures: ratio 1 to 31415 I 230
Jehovistic &, parts of Bible I 335-6
texts rewritten after Moses II 473
Elohistic and Jehovistic Writers. See Colenso
Elohite Creation II 5
Eloi or Eloai [Eloaeos] (Gnos)
Jupiter or I 577; II 538n
part of inferior hebdomad I 449
Elon or Elion (Gk)
highest Phoenician god II 380
Ēl Shaddai (Heb)
Jehovah & I 438; II 509
primal cause or I 618
Elu (Chald), elohīm or II 282
Elyrus, Church Council of
forbade limiting form of God II 279n
Emanation(s) II 80
Akkadians & Aryans taught II 54
Atzilatic or world of II 111
auric, poisoning effect of I 538
Chaldeans on II 61
Christian theology rejects II 41
first seven, or Sons of Fire I 438
gods are their own I 222
Jehovah, of Ialdabaōth II 389
Logos as first I 215
man as, both man & woman I 216n, 450
manu, fr Logos II 311
manvantaric I 18
monads pre-existent in world of II 111
nature as, of consciousness I 277n
primordial, & latent forces II 78
pure, primeval, unconscious II 80
Semites taught creation, not II 54
seventh, of matter I 291
unknowable source cause of II 43
Valentinian system of II 569n
Emanuel, Emanu-Ēl II 540
Emblem, compared w symbol I 305-6
Embryo(s). *See also* Foetus
analogy of man's, & the race I 184; II 187-9, 257, 659-60, 685
development of, fr cell described II 117
development of pineal gland in II 297
Diti's, divided into seven II 613, 614-15
eyes of, grow fr within II 295
gill-clefts in human II 684, 685n
Haeckel on II 258-9
human, contains all kingdoms II 259
is plant, reptile, animal I 184

mystery of I 219, 222-4
nourished by cosmic forces II 131
occultists trace fr, to Kosmos II 189
reversion to type & II 293n
seven month baby & 7th round man II 257
sexual development of II 172n, 659
spiritual potency in cell guides I 219
umbilicus, placenta & II 461
Embryology
    development of the eye II 295
    occult theories key to I 219, 223-4
    science of II 187n
    sex developed later II 172n, 659
    two chief difficulties of I 223-5 &n
Emepht (Egy)
    blows egg out of mouth I 367
Emerson, Ralph W., Oversoul of I 48, 140
Emims, giants of land of Moab II 336
Emotion(s), nerve molecules & I 134n
Emotional Nature, perfected men & I 275
Empedocles
    attraction, repulsion known by I 497-8
Empirical, Empiric II 664-5
En, Ain, Aiŏr (Heb), only self-existent I 214
Enchaînements du Monde . . . See Gaudry, A.
Enchantment
    Gyan's shield destroyed II 394
    Hekat (Hecate) goddess of I 387
    seven arts of II 641
Encyclopaedia Britannica
    antiquity of man II 70-1, 687
    article on astronomy II 330n
    prehistoric ages II 67
    solidification of Earth II 698
Encyclopaedia Londiniensis
    word "aspiration" in, (Mackey) II 362n
Encyclopédie, origin of rotary motion I 499
"Endexoteric" II 74
Energy(ies). *See also* Force(s)
    activities of entities I 145-6
    adepts know other forms of I 582n
    androgynous & intellectual I 137 &n
    cosmic life force I 11-12 &n
    extrinsic, of nature I 463
    Ganot on I 670
    inherent in matter I 280-2
    issues fr universal light I 337
    kinetic, potential, & atoms II 672
    known by its effects I 669
    matter & I 111n
    monadic essence as evolving I 176, 620
    One Supreme I 22
    śakti or, & trinity I 136
    spiritual & astral, more productive I 644

-substance-time a trinity I 582-3
Vibhūtayah or potencies of Vishnu II 611n
Enfield, William
    earth cubical, fire pyramidal II 594
Engelhardt, M. II 752n
Engis Skull II 744
    fair development of II 687
England I 510. *See also* British Isles
    cup-like markings on stones in II 346n
    on eve of catastrophe I 646
    King Arthur part of history of II 393
    Wilford, White Island & II 402-4 &n
Enki (Sumerian). *See* Ea
Enkidu (Sumerian). *See* Hea-bani
Ennis, Jacob, *Origin of the Stars . . .*
    origin of rotation I 500 &n
Ennoia (Gk)
    of Bythos is mind II 490
    divine mind II 214
    image of Supreme Being II 244
    Tree of Life II 214-15
Enoch(s) II 222. *See also Book of Enoch*
    accuses fallen angels II 382n
    attained nirvāna II 532
    born fr Wondrous Being I 207
    concealed books II 530
    described II 267-8n, 532-5
    died in his personality II 532
    Edris-, & divine dynasties II 366
    elect of 4th race II 597n
    fr enoïchion, inner eye II 211
    "first man" of *Genesis* II 715n
    Freemasonry speaks of II 47
    gandharva prototype of, angels I 523n
    generic name II 211, 230, 267n, 361, 532
    Hermes, Libra or II 129
    initiator, teacher, Enos II 529n
    invented writing, arts II 529
    Le Plongeon on II 229-30, 506
    lived 365 years (*Gen* 5:23) II 531
    phoenix & II 617
    pyramids & II 361-2
    seers of mankind II 134
    Seth, Cain have son named II 361, 391n
    stands between 4th & 5th races II 533
    symbol of dual man II 533
    symbology of name II 391n, 617
    taken to heaven like Xisuthrus II 141
    various spellings of II 391n, 529n
    walked w God (*Gen*) II 532
Enoch, son of Jarad II 391n
Enoïchion (Gk)
    confined to temples, colleges II 532-3
    generic name of seers II 211, 361, 529

initiator & instructor II 530
"inner spiritual eye" II 211
Enoïchion (Book of the Seer)
kept at Kirjath-Sepher II 529
Enos, Enosh (son of Seth). *See also* Enoch,
Henoch
first 2-sexed race II 125, 127, 129, 469 &n,
715n
Seth-, 4th race II 134
son of man II 126, 129, 529n, 533
stands between 4th & 5th races II 533
various names for II 361, 391n, 529, 533
Ens, absolute abstract deity I xx
En Soph. *See* Ain-sōph
Entelechies, Leibniz called monads I 632n
Entity(ies). *See also* Beings
bond connecting, w non-entity II 176, 578-9
elementals are conscious I 221
energies are I 145
every, must win divinity I 106
globes are I 154
guiding intelligences I 146
man's spiritual, drawn to parent-sun I 639
names define I 93
number is an, (Balzac) I 66
spiritual, incarnating in man I 233-4
[Entropy] I 148-51
Environment
adaptation to II 738
hostile in early period II 159-60
modifies urge to perfection II 736
plants, animals adapted to II 159-60
Eocene II 717
anthropoid fossils absent in II 679, 690n
Atlantis at height in II 433n, 710
Atlantis began to sink in I 439n; II 433n, 693
Australian race, flora of II 779
civilization fr earliest II 744
Croll's figures for II 9, 695, 715n
giants of II 340
Lemuria perished before II 313
man in II 155, 157, 675-6, 690
man's advent in, (Allen, Seeman) II 288
submerged continents & II 778-9
ungulate mammals of II 735-6
Eon. *See* Aeon
Eozoon Canadense
earliest fossil skull II 254, 712
Epaphos
Catholics make, into Christ II 414-15
Dark, Dionysos-Sabazios II 415-16
Egyptians descended fr Dark II 418
Ephesians (Paul)
prince of powers of air II 485, 515

spiritual wickedness I 331n
Ephesus, Heraclitus of. *See* Heraclitus
Ephialtēs
Orion (giant) son of II 278
Orphic Titan II 70
Ephod (Heb), high priest's robe
12 precious stones around I 649
Ephraim, elect of Jacob, & Pisces I 653
Epicurus
animated atoms of I 568-9
atomic theory of I 2, 579
believed in gods I 518, 611
gravitation & I 491
Indolentia of I 577n
material atoms of I 629
skeptical but factual II 285-6
soul of atom I 568-9
Epicycle, & cycle (Milton) I 645
Epidemics, come fr N & W (winds) I 123
Epigenēs, on Chaldean astronomy II 620
Epimetheus (Gk)
Jupiter's "fatal gift" to II 270
Prometheus has now become II 422
takes counsel after event II 521
Epiphanius, [*Panarion*] *Adv. Haeres.*
copied Aeons incorrectly II 569n
Ophites honored serpent I 404
Valentinian table of Aeons II 458
Epiphysis, & 3rd eye II 296
Epistles. See Seneca
Epistles, of Paul II 81. *See also* Paul
Epoch(s)
astronomical definition of I 658-9
Hindu I 659-68
of 3102 BC I 661-2, 665, 667
Epoch of the Mammoth. See Southall
Ἑπτα με (Hepta me, Gk)
& 7 sounding letters II 603
"E pur se muove" (Galileo) II 451
Equator
changes of II 331, 356
Cor Leonis on the II 407
ecliptic once at right angle to II 534
Fohat & I 204
retrograde motion of II 785
Equatorial
lands & polar regions II 324-5
lands of Lemuria-Atlantis II 371n
Equatorial Sun
cements buddhi to ātma, manas II 241
third group of gods II 241
Equilibrium
cosmic, must be preserved I 416
betw matter & spirit I 106

of polar forces II 84
Equinoctial
    points I 663; II 330n, 331, 785
    shadow & elevation of pole II 401n
Equinox(es) II 533, 546. *See also* Precession,
    Solstices
    Chinese divided year by II 621
    spring, & Hindu zodiac II 435-6
    symbols of living verity I 639
    vernal, & 1st point of zodiac I 665
    vernal, & origin of Greek zodiac II 436n
    vernal, Taurus & Eridu II 693
    Volney on vernal I 658
Érard-Mollien, "Recherches . . ."
    antiquity of Indian zodiac I 657-8
Erataōth (Gnos), dog symbol II 115n
Eratosthenes, on divine dynasties II 367
Erdmann [edition of Leibniz] I 630n
'Ereb (Heb) evening twilight
    sandhyā in Sanskrit II 252n
Erebos (Gk)
    & Nux (Nyx) give birth to light I 110
Erech, Chaldean necropolis II 463
Erb ya, *Er Yah* (*Rh Ya* in tx)
    man w 2 faces II 302
Ericsson, estimates Sun's heat I 484n
Eridan[us] River
    Ardan, Iardan, or Jordan I 392; II 583
    Ardhanāri-Īśvara or I 392
    Phaeton hurled into II 770n
    same as Nile (Skinner) II 583
Eridu (Bab)
    civilization of II 226
    culture fr India II 203
    seat of Sun-god worship II 139n
    6,000 years old (Sayce) II 693
Erōs (Gk)
    desire to manifest II 65, 176, 234
    Fohat & I 109, 119; II 65
    later sexual Cupid I 109; II 176, 234
    third person in Greek Trinity I 109
Erōs-Phanēs (Orphic)
    evolves fr divine egg I 365, 461
Error, runs downhill I xvii
Ertosi, Egyptian name of Mars II 143-4n
Eruptions (volcanic) II 356, 523, 699
Erythraean Sea II 202
Esar, 4-letter Turkish god II 602
Esau
    Jacob &, same as Abel & Cain II 135
    sons of, Kings of Edom II 705
    symbolizes race betw 4th & 5th II 705
Eschylus. *See* Aeschylus
Esculapius. *See* Asklēpios

Esdras, 4th book of II 454
Esikekar [Istakhr] or Persepolis
    built by Giamschid II 398
Eskimos
    carve & sketch II 718
    dying out II 780
    seventh subrace, 4th root-race II 178
Esnēh (Egypt), stones at I 311
Esoteric. *See also* Occultism, Secrecy, Secret
    Doctrine
    architectural measurements were II 465
    Catechism on secrecy I 299
    chronology II 9, 307n
    cosmogony I 116-17
    dogmas never altered I 312
    exoteric, & endexoteric II 74
    exoteric falsified copy of I 578
    fr exoteric we turn to I 443; II 497
    five, axioms re evolution II 697-8
    history buried in symbols I 307
    knowledge corroborates tradition I 647
    learning of Aryans II 34-5n
    meaning & Sanskritists II 451
    meanings of symbols I 443
    mysteries of Samothrace II 4
    order of deities II 108
    religion of Moses crushed several times
        I 320n
    scientific vs, evolution II 711-15
    Soma parent of, wisdom II 500
    teaching allegorical II 81
    teachings, corroboration of II 796-7
    Venus & Earth, connection II 32
Esoteric Buddhism. *See* Sinnett, A. P.
Esoteric Budhism (Secret Wisdom)
    I xvii-xxii; II 100
Esoteric Doctrine. *See also* Occult, Occultism,
    Secret Doctrine
    based on Stanzas I xxxvii
    comets & solar evolution I 599
    direct, inferential proof of II 410
    Non-being is Absolute in I 54n
    reconciles all religions & philos I 77, 610
    reincarnation an II 552
    taught that everything is alive I 49
    teaches rise & fall of civilization II 723
    thread doctrine or I 610
Esotericism, Esoteric Teaching, Wisdom. *See*
    also Occult, Occultism
    alpha & omega of Eastern II 449
    Aryan & Hebrew I 115n
    belongs to all races I 113
    differs fr Vedantin doctrines I 62
    doctrine of numbers chief in I 433

Eastern, never degraded I 445
of Egypt & India identical I 672
ignorance of methods of II 225
ignores both sexes I 136n
of India & *SD* II 88
of Manu & *Genesis* I 9n
opposes Darwinian evolution II 653
originated in 3rd, 4th races I 113
trans-Himalayan I 110; II 22n
Vāch goddess of I 95
Esoteric Philosophy. *See also* Occultism
acceptance of I 298
admits neither good nor evil II 162
admits no special creation II 731
admits no special gifts in man I 17
blinds conceal mysteries of II 310
of Buddhism, Brahmanism one II 637
on consciousness of 1st beings I 277
fills scientific gaps II 196
first lesson of II 487
heart & soul of Buddhism II 156n
materialism & I xx
on māyā I 11n
physical man image of deity I 445
previous mahāpralaya & I 369
reconciles all systems I xx, 55; II 3
rejects inorganic atom I 454
symbolized by female form I 351
teaches modified polygenesis II 249
teaches objective idealism I 631
teaches spontaneous generation II 150-2, 286
teaches that all is conscious I 49
three aspects of universe I 278
Esoteric School(s). *See also* Adepts,
Initiates, Masters
in China, India, Japan, etc I xxiii
have total of sacred MSS I xxiii
reject idea of "unconscious" I 453
taught 7 human principles II 603-4
two parts of, discussed I 122
"Esoteric Studies." *See* Figanière, V. de
Esoteric Treatise on the Doctrine of Gilgūl. See
Valentinus
Esprits, Des. See Mirville, de
Esprits tombés des paiens. See Mirville, de
Esquimaux. *See* Eskimos
Essais orientaux. See Darmesteter, J.
Essays. See Montaigne, M. E.
Essays on Physiology. See Spencer, H., *Principles
of Biology*
Esse (Lat)
absolute essence & I 273
genesis, logos, & II 24n, 25
manifested Logos sacrifices II 592

satya or I 48n
Essence
absolute divine mover I 56, 624, 629
degrees of monadic I 176
dhyān chohanic II 108
life-, of solar system I 541
radiant, spreads thru space I 67
spiritual, of matter I 35
svabhavat & cosmic I 3-4, 61
Essenes, believed in reincarnation II 111 &n
Estufas. *See* Artufas
Esur, God in India II 114
Eswara. *See* Īśvara
Eternal, the One, drops its reflection I 231
Eternity(ies)
amrita & I 348
egg symbol of I 65
ideas, ideal forms in I 282
Kalahansa swan in II 465
living consciously in I 459n
meaning of, in Purānas I 336n
nirvana limited in I 266
no word in Hebrew for I 336 &n, 354n
past, future & I 37
poem (last stanza) re, [John Gay] I 26
serpent symbol of I 65; II 214, 505
seven I 35-6, 53, 144 &n, 206
seventh, paradox of I 62-3
third eye embraces II 299n
time &, as Kala I 427
of universe I 16; II 490n
"White radiance of," [Shelley] I 238
Ether (element) I 527 &nn. *See also* Aether,
Astral Light
aether & I 330-2, 460, 508
agent of transmission II 105
ahamkāra surrounds II 616
air is differentiated I 534
ākāśa & I 61, 76n, 255, 296n, 326, 331, 515,
526n; II 511n
ākāśa spirit soul of I 18
all things come fr I 462
anthropomorphized & deity I 332
astral light & I 74n, 197, 326, 331n, 343, 524n
Bain on I 325-6
binds particles of matter I 526
breath of Universal Soul I 102
"caloric" agency of Metcalfe I 524 &n, 525,
526
Church made, abode of Satan I 331
continuous material medium I 487
cosmic substance I 111n, 326, 339
denizens of I 297, 331n
earth, water, fire, air & II 616

evolution of concept I 491-2
Father-, or Archaeus I 51
fifth race element II 135
fifth round & I 12, 140, 257-8
Fohat son of, or ākāśa II 400n
gross body of ākāśa I 13n, 257
interstellar I 626; II 135
in *Kalevala* II 122
Lévi's astral light lowest I 254-5
light transmitted by I 486, 595
lining of ākāśa I 97
Lodge on I 488-9
materialists rebel against I 587 &n
Moschus on I 461
Nārāyana present in I 231
Newton on I 13, 490-5
no resistance to bodies in, (Stallo) I 486
not fully manifested yet I 460
passive female principle I 57
physically unknown to us I 669
plenum, vacuum & I 495
prototypes in, (Anaxagoras) I 332
reflection of chaos I 338
resisting I 501
Richardson's nervous I 531-2, 537; II 298n
science & I 102, 296n, 297, 339, 485, 487; II 511n
seven rays bases of I 515n
seven subdivisions of I 330-2
soul of matter I 57
sound, hearing & I 255, 296n, 536, 587; II 107
spirit directs elements in I 343
Stallo on I 482, 486-7
svabhavat noumenon of I 671
synthesis of 4 elements I 97, 342, 447
vibratory, of Keely I 555-6
we will transmit, to 6th race I 342
Ethereal, Ethereality
bodies of early man II 55, 86, 149, 150, 157, 732
fluid of Leibniz I 623
nature of 1st dhyāni-chohans I 82
races evolve fr, to materiality I 188; II 68n, 298-9 &nn; 697
Ethics
Aryan codes of II 253
Buddha taught II 423
karma & universal I 637-9
national II 469
religious, of 1st races II 272-3
Ethiopians. *See also* Aethiopians
Eastern II 417, 429
Ethiopic MS, in Bodleian Library

Book of Enoch translated fr II 482
Ethiops River
Indus River &, explained II 417-18
Ethnology(ical) I xxxiii, 318; II 334, 443, 535
esoteric II 166, 710, 789-93
rebels against Bible chronology II 195
requires several Adams I 323-4
science confirms esoteric II 166
significance of Dattoli II 232n
silent re Australians II 196
of *Vishnu Purāna* II 320
"yellow hued" descendants II 425
Etruria, trilithic stones in II 346n
Etruscan(s)
Florence built on, cities II 221
Tuscan sages & 8 ages (Sulla) I 650
word *lares* fr II 361
Etudes égyptologiques. See Pierret, P.
Etudes sur le rituel . . . See Rougé, de
Etym. M. II 519. *See also* Photius
Ētz (Heb, Otz in text)
Holy of Holies I 114n
nine & 7 numbers of I 114; II 217
Tree in Garden of Eden I 114
Euclid II 522
Εὐδαιμονία (eudaimonia, Gk) II 371
Eudoxus of Cnidus
made Egyptian year 1 month I 650
Eue (Eve) or Eua (Eva)
Chaldaic verb "to be" II 129
Eugenius Philalethes. *See* Vaughan, Thomas
Eugibinus, on composite Adam II 134 &n
Euhemerization II 148, 271, 543, 658
Euler, L., gravity due to spirit I 491
Euphrates River
Gan-Eden watered by II 202, 203
Euripides, *Hercules furens*
immorality of poets II 764
—— *Hippolytus*
Kalliste I 395
—— *Orestes*
Castor & Pollux II 123 &n
—— *Troades (Trojan Women)*
three-eyed Zeus II 294n
Europe
Africa appeared before II 368
Africans crossed into II 740-1
America older than II 407n
& Australia one continent (Seeman) II 333
cyclopean towns in I 209n
Egypt older than present II 746
elevation of, & Asia II 694-5
on eve of cataclysm I 644-6
fifth continent II 8, 606n

geometric pyramids not in II 352
ice-age immigration into II 738n
Incas & Pelasgians of II 745-6
last Atlantis island preceded II 405
Mergiana & new continent of II 398
Miocene plants of, & America II 727, 781, 790
Mongolian type skulls found in II 744
Negro types found in II 744
no man in, during Tertiary (sci) II 714
north of, still rising II 787n
Paleolithic man of II 739-41
rising during Atlantean peak II 722-3
sunken during Lemurian era II 324, 327
Tertiary, Quaternary II 738-40 &n
will one day sink II 266
European(s)
age of, family [national] race II 435
ancient history of, nations II 439
Blavatsky taught 2, in 1880 I xviii
Buddhist tracts hidden fr, "pundits" I xxx
early, sought refuge in Asia II 743
fifth or, subrace II 445
fossils & proof of man's antiquity II 725
fossils linked w South America II 791
lethal influence of II 411n
Neolithic, plants African II 739
no, artifacts before late Eocene II 723
no more, in 6th race II 446
northern stocks of, originate II 743
part of Aryan race II 106, 323-4n
punishment of, nations I 644
third Aryan subrace became II 753
two, taught in 1870s I xviii-ix
Eurydice (wife of Orpheus)
bitten by polar serpent II 785
Eurymedon, children of, & 4th race II 766
Eusebius, Bishop of Caesarea
disfigured Berosus I xxvi; II 53
disfigured Manetho I xxvi; II 368, 392, 692-3
disfigured Sanchoniathon II 392, 692-3
Smith proves forgeries of I xxvi n
Tertullian known only in II 278n
—— *Chronicon*
mutilates Chaldean records I xxxi
—— *Praeparatio Evangelica*
animated stones II 342
on Egyptian zodiac II 357
Elyōn II 380
Hermes emblem of the Word II 542
Kabiri sons of Sydic II 392
mundane egg I 360
Phoenician cosmogony I 340
Sun shown in a ship (Egy) I 409

Eusebius (the physician), carried talking stones (de Mirville) II 342
Eustathius, Archbishop
Io signifies the Moon II 416n, 463
Euterpe II 334. *See also* Herodotus
Euthanasia
adepts & esoteric meaning of II 531
Euxine
Samothrace overflowed by II 4-5
search for cradle of humanity in II 203
White Island in, (Wilford) II 402n
Eva. *See* Eue
Evangel (Christian doctrine)
ancients plagiarized by anticipation II 481-2
Evangelists
symbology of four I 127n, 441-2
Evans, Sir John
—— *The Ancient Stone Implements* . . .
Neolithic, Paleolithic man II 722
no writing in Stone Age II 442
Eve, Eva. *See also* Adam, Ḥavvāh
Adam &, Fall of II 62, 95n
ansated cross symbolizes II 31n
Belita or Damti became II 463
bore Cain because of apple II 166
disobedience of, not evil II 95n
dragon that tempted I 73
fr Ha-va (chavah), life II 42n, 194n
first natural woman II 388
gave birth to Cain-Jehovah II 469
Genesis 3, 3rd race & II 410
Hebel or II 135
Houah or, (Skinner) II 467
identical w Aditi II 43
identical w Vāch II 128
Isis, Io or II 416
Jehovah male portion of II 269n
Juno a form of I 129n
made fr Adam's rib I 456n; II 193
means "to be" II 129
missionaries confuse, w Ivi II 194 &n
Norse Lifthrasir compared w II 100
not begotten but extracted II 661
placental before mammals II 166
seduced by flying camel II 205
Sephīrāh-, or Aditi-Vāch I 355-6
serpent &, like Māyāmoha-Daityas I 422
terrestrial, is Earth I 60, 240
Vāch compared w, & Adam I 137
warned not to eat forbidden fruit II 267
womb, Sarah or II 472
Zuñi Priestess-Mother & II 629
Evening Telegraph
on *The Secret Doctrine* II 441n

Even Numbers
  terrestrial, devilish (Pythagoras) II 574-5
Ever-
  becoming I 250, 268, 570; II 446, 449 &n
  existing I 278; II 545
  Present, abstract motion & I 3
  Unknowable I 280
Evestrum, or Ka II 633
Evidence
  internal, not safe beacon I xxx
  of past overwhelming II 742
  past, required I xlv
  of sunken continents II 788
"Evidence of Man's Place . . ." *See* Huxley
"Evidences of the Ice Age." *See* Woodward
Evil. *See also* Devil, Good &, Knowledge,
    Satan, Shadow
  ancient view of I 343
  antagonizing blind force I 413
  belief in personal devil & II 377
  Christians personify II 390, 478
  dominates humanity (Bible) II 515
  easy spread of II 212
  even numbers II 574-5
  fallen angels key to II 274
  God cannot be divorced fr I 413
  good &, are twins I 412-13; II 96
  keys to solution of II 303, 476, 515
  Laing on nature of II 510n
  matter or, evolution of I 73
  much of world's, could vanish I 643
  necessary in manifestation II 389
  neither, nor good per se II 96, 162
  no, dragon II 53
  no, outside mankind II 389, 512
  not an independent power I 73
  not eternal to Zoroastrians II 488
  One II 70
  origin of II 25, 274, 373, 490, 520
  polarity of spirit, matter I 416
  Prometheus & physical II 420
  punishment &, serve the good II 477
  Purānas on I 415-16
  realm of, & sublunary regions II 74
  root of, (Hindu) II 421n
  Satan personifies abstract II 478
  serpent of II 25-6
  symbols of II 386
  union & harmony palliative to I 644
  wars w powers of II 104
Evil Eye(d)
  Saturn the II 29
  of sorcerers II 427
Evil Spirits

Christians have dogmatized II 386
originally emblems of chaos II 386
seven, of Chaldea II 97
Evolution. *See also* Darwinism, Environment,
    Heredity, Natural Selection, Specializa-
    tion
  fr amoeba to man theory II 259
  analogy, law of, & II 66
  ancients knew physical & spiritual I 332
  asc & desc arcs of II 180-1
  ascending arc of, we are now on I 641
  astral merges into physical II 257, 736
  of atoms I 522
  begun by intellectual Logos I 137n
  Berosus on teaching of II 190
  of body terrestrial I 175
  changes on globe D, 4th round I 176-7
  criticism of scientific II 164-5n, 185
  cyclic I 416, 634-47; II 298, 420, 443, 732-3
  Darwinian, & reversion to type II 293n
  Darwinian, in cosmos II 202
  Darwinism not supported by occultism
    I 186-7, 191, 211; II 653
  Darwinism only part of I 600; II 153, 649
  definition of I 620; II 653
  different rates of II 256
  divine, of ideas I 280
  double, of man II 87, 167
  embryo epitomizes racial II 187, 659
  endless adaptations of I 277
  eternal cycle of becoming II 170
  of eyes II 299 &n, 302
  fallen angels & human II 274
  five esoteric axioms re II 697-8
  Fohat & cosmic I 110
  gigantic flora, fauna, men II 276
  fr gigantic to small II 153-4
  gradual, works by uniform laws II 731
  guided by intelligence (Wallace) I 107
  guided by unseen hands I 278
  Haeckel defines II 164-5n
  higher beings used in II 87-8
  human-spiritual to divine-spiritual I 224
  human, traced on walls & in heaven II 352
  & Idealists (Spencer) II 490n
  of individualization I 178-9
  infinitesimal chance variations II 697
  inherent law of development II 260
  intellectual, w physical II 411
  intelligence cause of II 649 &n
  intelligent beings adjust, control I 22
  internal laws in, (Mivart) II 697
  involution & I 416; II 294
  Isis Unveiled q on I 332; II xvi

Kabbala, only hinted at in II 241
kosmic, in geometric figures I 321
of man & ape discussed II 675-85
man masterpiece of II 475, 728
man's, difficult to trace II 152
monad & personal self compel II 109-10
natural forces working blindly (Darwin) I 139; II 652
nature's progress to higher life I 277
never-ceasing ever becoming II 545
no, for the perfect II 243
not all due to natural selection II 728
not applied to *primary* "Creation" I 446
not creation, by means of woRDs II 42
occult doctrine of II 241, 261-3, 731-4
paganism taught dual I 464
pain & suffering necessary to II 475
of perception fr apperception I 175, 179
physical evolves fr spiritual I 219
planetary life-impulses & II 697
pre-human monsters, etc & II 634-5
primary, secondary causes in II 648-9
proceeded unaided (Temple) II 645
proceeds on many levels II 87
of progenitors as gods, then men II 349
Purānas on I 451-60; II 253
of races, series of rises & falls II 721
repetitive I 232; II 256
saltations in II 696-7
scientific II 189, 347-8
second round, different I 159-60
senses, of outer vs inner I 446-7; II 294
septenary, discussed I 267-8; II 622-3n
sexual, gradual II 84
fr simple to complex II 299, 731
simultaneous, of 7 groups II 1-2
soul's influence on, (Rolleston) II 728
specialization II 720
of spirit into matter II 273
spiritual & physical I 641; II 348, 421
spiritual, of inner, real man I 175, 634; II 728
stages in, of man II 132-3, 173-4
Stanzas as formula of I 20-1
swastika symbolizes II 98
of 3rd eye II 302
three propositions re II 1, 168
triple scheme of I 181, 341; II 109
Uranos, Kronos, Jupiter & II 268-71
young subject (Wilson) II 152
Evolutionary
impulse & cyclic law II 298
journey of the Pilgrim I 268
seven Stanzas deal w 7, stages I 21

Evolution of Christianity. See Gill, C.
"Evolution of Man." *See* Wilson, A.
Evolution without Nat. Selection. See Dixon
Ewald, G. H. von, on Chwolson II 454
Examen des Principes . . . See Leibniz, G.
Exertion, personal, & higher self II 95
Existence(s)
active & passive I 281n
can cease & still Be I 54-5
causes of I 44-5
duality of I 15-17, 326
how personal, is transcended I 54
initial, & 49 fires I 290-1
matter is totality of kosmic I 514
nirvana is absolute I 266
struggle for I 277; II 648
true, only in duration I 37
Exodus
astronomy of 25th chapter II 361n
burning bush in I 121
ch 33:18-23 interpreted II 538-40
"He that sacrificeth to any God . . ." I 492n
on Hor-eb II 541
Jehovah a character of I 422
Jews marked doorposts w tau II 557
Moses hidden by the river I 319n
Moses of, an Atlantean story II 426-9
pillar of fire I 338n, 437
refabricated by Ezra I 319-20
Shaddai II 509
on Tabernacle I 125
Tetragrammaton in II 626 &n
"Thou shalt not revile the gods" I 492n; II 477
Zipporah, the well & Moses I 385 &n; II 465n
Ex Oriente Lux ("Light from the East") II 42
Exoteric(ism). *See also* Esoteric(ism)
blinds in, works II 308n
esoteric, & endexoteric II 74
of Greek writers & occultism I 507
religion & left-path II 503
religion anthropomorphic, phallic II 657-8
religion falsified copies I 578
religion, gradual spread of II 527
root ideas in, religion I 443
view of demons, angels II 93
Expansion, Contraction
change of condition, not size I 63
"from within without" explained I 62
periodical II 42-3
Exposition du système . . . See Laplace
"Extinct Lake of Bovey Tracey." *See* Pengelly

Eye(s, d). *See also* Pineal Gland, Śiva-Eye,
   Third Eye
   cat's, symbol of I 305, 387-8; II 552-3n
   central, of Śiva II 578n
   cyclopean II 293, 299
   of Dangma I 27, 45-6
   Deva-, or third II 295
   development of human II 295-9, 769
   inner spiritual I 230; II 211
   mirror of the soul II 298
   Moon as cat, of Sun I 305; II 552-3n
   one of 7 senses I 534-5
   one, or Loka Chakshuh II 22
   of Osiris, cat termed II 552n
   seven, of the Lord II 22
   statue w 3, in Argos II 294n
   Sun, of Osiris II 25
   three, & 4-armed man II 294, 744
   two, evolved fr one II 299
   two, of Ammon II 213
   two, perfected beginning 4th race II 769
   two, see neither past nor future II 298-9n
   wisdom, of Cyclopes II 769
Eye of Taurus the Bull [Aldebaran]
   equinoctial point beginning kali-yuga I 663,

   665; II 785
Ezekiel, *Book of Ezekiel*
   calls King of Tyre a cherub II 501
   chapter 1 & Chinese devas I 126
   fate of Atlanteans in II 493-4
   four animals of I 127, 363; II 533
   God's glory fr East I 123
   great prophet & seer I 230
   "I will bring forth a fire" II 494
   reports Jews worshiping Sun I 397n
   reproves King of Tyre II 492-4
   souls of heavenly bodies II 552
   stamped foreheads w tau II 557
   vision of early man II 134n
   Wheel of I 127; II 128, 552-3
Ezour Veda, Voltaire, Müller on II 442
Ezra
   adept in phallic worship I 320
   creation story fr Chaldeans II 3-4
   disfigured Mosaic books I 335-6
   Exodus refabricated by I 319-20
   ignorant of Hindu cosmogony I 655
   Moses & II 453
   remodeled Pentateuch I 319; II 4, 143, 461n,
      658

F

Faber, George S.
—— *On the Mysteries of the Cabiri*
  Aletae, Al-ait II 142n, 361
  ancient poetry based in truth II 264
  [Cumberland q] II 393
  Kaempfer q II 365
  linked mundane egg w Ark I 360
  mistake of II 142-3
  Noah, Argha, etc II 141-2, 360n, 364, 390
  Phlegyae islands were Atlantis II 144
  sinking of Atlantis II 264-5 &n
  Telchines, Kabiri, Titans II 360-1, 391
  [Vallencey q] I 641-2n
—— *The Origin of Pagan Idolatry*
  all religions fr one center II 760n
  Gentiles vs Jews II 472n
Fable(s). *See also* Allegories, Legends, Myths
  allegories foolishly called II 103
  Greek, based on facts II 769
  Satyr no II 262
Fabre, Abbé
—— *Les origines de la terre et de l'homme*
  Eocene man does not conflict w Bible
    II 747
Fabularum Liber. See Hyginus, G. J.
Face I 220; II 479, 539
  angels of the I 352n, 434n; II 479
  kabbalistic I 197
  Lesser, prototype of man I 215, 239-40
  Lords of the Dazzling II 427-8
  Microprosopus, Macroprosopus I 60, 215,
    239-40, 350
  seven spirits of the I 128, 198; II 115n
Fact(s)
  anthropology, geology & II 71-2
  cannot be destroyed I xlvi
  disfigured & revealed II 515-16
  historical, become dogmas II 776
  SD gives, & landmarks II 742
  theory can never excommunicate II 715n
Faculties
  matter & man's, increase I 252
  transmission of acquired I 219
Fafnir (Scandinavian dragon)
  Sigurd ate heart of I 404
Fa-Hien [hsien] (Chin)
  Cheta initiation cave of I xx

—— *Fo kuo Chi*
  re Garden of Wisdom II 204
Fa-hwa-king [*Fa-hua-ching*] (Chin)
  on Dragon of Wisdom I 470
Faigi Diwan. *See* Faizi's *Dīwān*
Fail, Failure(s) II 475
  of angels in creation II 239
  among dhyāni-chohans I 188; II 232-3n
  of European lang to express Law I 269
  karma of I 188
  monsters were II 192
  of nature to create beings II 312
  nature unaided will II 52, 102
  of nature vanish II 330, 446
  those who, slaves of matter II 272
Fairy Tales, embody history & religious con-
    cepts I 425
Faith
  blind, of theologians I 669
  blind, vs adepts' knowledge I 612
  blind, vs karma-nemesis II 304-5
  Lemurians had not to believe on II 272
  without will, is barren II 59n
Faizi's *Dīwān*, q by Max Müller I xli
Falconeri, E., found pigmy hippo II 219
Falconnet, E. M., on talking stones II 341-2
Fall, (the). *See also* Fallen Angels, Lucifer,
    Root-Race — 3rd, Satan, Self-conscious
  apple, tree & II 354-5
  atonement &, pagan II 505
  caused by pride (Kab) II 237
  Christian idea of I 127
  cross without circle symbolic I 5
  described, explained I 192-8; II 62-3, 92-8,
    192-3, 227-45, 283-4
  desire to learn & know caused I 416-17
  dogma of, & *Revelation* II 484-5
  Egyptian initiation &, (Lacour) II 215-16n
  first, into matter II 185, 470
  fourth Adam after II 503
  into generation or matter II 36, 104, 129,
    262, 388, 510, 515, 609
  in *Genesis* 4 II 388
  gods also undergo II 231n
  gods who incarnate in man or II 483
  human shape developed after II 227
  left no "original sin" II 261

meanings of II 139
no living soul till after II 456
occurred during early Mesozoic II 204
physiological, after Eden II 279
records of II 282-4, 486-7
result of man's knowledge II 513
Samael fell first II 112
Satan's II 484-7
scapegoat symbol of II 510
scientific when understood I 418
Semitic idea of I 383
separation of sexes & II 173, 204
Seth 1st result of II 126
seven keys to II 62
of spirit, not mortal man I 192-3
third Adam before II 503
third eye disappeared at II 301-2
third round Indra & II 615n
traceable to India I 418
two in theology II 62
various II 483-4
Fallacies of Darwinism, . . . See Bree, C. R.
Fallen Angel(s) II 60, 92-8, 475-505. *See also*
    Angels, Fall
abide in ether I 331
Achad or II 508
astral light abode of I 196
asuras same as II 500
became man's self-consciousness II 513
belong to material plane II 61
Burning Valley initiation & II 535
cast down into matter II 103-4
Christians took, fr *Book of Enoch* II 529
Church made, into Devil II 98
Church twisted meaning of I 331, 457-9;
    II 60, 94n, 228-32, 513-17
denounced by archangels II 382n
dhyānis became II 228
dogma of II 515
esoteric meanings of II 516-17
Heavenly Man or II 493
fr India via Persia, Chaldea I 198
key to human character II 274
kumāras degraded into I 458-9
man, humanity a I 450; II 274, 390
nephīlīm are II 61
New Aspects of Life (Pratt) on I 194n
overcome by Michael or Jehovah II 508
pagan in origin I 198
personified by Bel & dragon I xxvii
Prometheus a II 525 &n
rebelled against karmic law II 228
Satan, Old Dragon became II 506, 508
serpents, dragons of wisdom II 230

sons of God I 412; II 61, 229
true meaning of, in Kabbala II 228-9
truth re, cannot be given II 516-17
Fall of the Angels I 193; II 161
allegorized in *Pymander* I 417
into generation II 231n
incarnation or II 487
Kabbala &, (Ginsburg) II 284
repeated on every plane II 268
thru pride (Christian) II 171
transformed 1st-born II 283
Zohar on II 491
"False Analogies." *See* Müller, F. M., *Introduction to Science of Religion*
Families of Speech. See Farrar, F. W.
Family Race(s)
Dendera zodiac & last three II 433
duration of a II 433, 435
subdivisions of subrace II 198n, 434
subject to cleansing process II 330
Family Resemblances, explained I 261
Fane(s) II 458, 603, 756
of man designed for a god II 302
perfection of ancient I 208-9n
Faraday, Michael
atoms centers of force I 507
on force & matter I 510 &n
Faraday as a Discoverer. See Tyndall, John
Faraday Lectures. See Helmholtz, von
Faraday's Life and Letters. See Jones, H. B.
Farrar, Rev Frederic W., *Families of Speech*
Basque lang like ancient American II 790
Farses or Parses [Farsīs, Pārsīs] (Pers)
Peris remote ancestors of II 398
Farvarshi. *See* Fravashi
Fasti. See Ovid
Fatalist(s, ism)
believers in karma are not II 305
blind, result of ignorance I 643
karma is not I 639
Fate(s). *See also* Destiny, Karma, Lipikas
decrees of, in astral light II 236
Iblis agent of II 394
karma, nemesis or I 642-3; II 420-1n, 604-5
    &n
karmic, of nations II 644-6, 675-6
lead atoms back I 143-4
Μοιρα (destiny) & Moira, goddess of
    II 604-5 &n
Norns make known decree of II 520
Zeus cannot escape II 414
Father(s). *See also* Fathers
cold mist or I 82
Helios, later called II 44

"I and my, are one" I 265, 574
of Jesus & Jehovah II 509
the One II 113
parent dhyāni-buddha or I 574, 578
secret meaning of, & the Son II 231n
seven, & 49 sons II 564
seven planets or I 575
side of, 1st creation I 356n, 450
Son &, are "universal mind" II 492
Son &, as Sun & Moon I 229
vital electric principle of Sun II 105
Father-Aether or -Ether, highest principle,
   Archaeus I 51-2, 460, 465
Father-Mother. *See also* Hyle, Ilus
   breath of I 144
   cross in circle I 11
   darkness is I 40
   dhyāni fr the bright II 55
   differentiated world-soul I 140
   fire & water or I 70
   first differentiation of Kosmos I 18; II 236
   first emanation of II 43
   germ (egg) furnished by II 131
   of gods or Oeaohoo I 68
   Noun (Egy) or I 312
   one during pralaya I 41
   one w aether, ākāśa I 75-6
   primordial flame proceeds fr I 88
   ray & chaos I 70
   spins a web I 83
   spirit & substance I 41
   svabhavat or I 60, 98n
   Yliaster of Paracelsus I 283
Father-Mother-Son. *See also* Trinity
   becomes four I 58-9
   Brahmā is I 41
   Hermes on I 436
   kabbalistic I 18
   triangle & I 614; II 582
Fathers. *See also* Father(s), Pitṛis
   could not make thinking man II 102
   created bodies II 115
   failure of I 194; II 105
   human race fashioned by II 605
   lunar beings II 88, 115
   nature-spirits II 102
   pass thru all Earth forms II 115
   Pitri-Pati, lord of II 44
   progenitors of men II 45
   of wisdom called Pitar II 394n
Father Sadik
   Noah, Melchizedek & II 391-3
Fathers of Church. *See* Church Fathers
Father Tree (Koran)

phoenix myth & the II 617
Fauna
   appears cyclically II 325n, 733
   of Atlantic isles similar II 782, 791-2
   Australian II 196-7
   changes every round, race, etc I 183-4; II 262
   descends fr primordial monsters II 186, 276
   of Europe II 714
   New & Old World, very similar II 792
   West Indian & West African II 782
Faure, electric accumulators of I 580
Faye, Hervé Auguste E. A.
   astronomers & geologists I 496
   heat of nebula I 505
   nebular theory of I 588, 599
   on sun spots I 541n
—— "Sur l'hypothèse de Laplace"
   Phobos, Mars' satellite I 165
—— "Sur l'origine du système solaire"
   comets generated in solar system I 500
Félix, Father, *Le Mystère et la Science*
   science rejects life's mystery I 670
Female(s). *See also* Male, Vāch
   Adam male & II 127
   Catholic, emblem II 38
   Daksha creates II 163, 183
   earth, water, passive II 130
   form symbolic of esoteric philosophy I 351
   generative power (Arg, Arca) II 416n
   logoi male & I 246
   -male or ansated cross II 217
   Moon, generative principle I 228-9 &nn;
      II 65-6
   power in nature, 2 aspects of I 431
   seven, of *Anugītā* discussed II 639
   vertical line, male & II 30
Ferguson, James [1710-1776]
   believed many worlds inhabited II 706
Fergusson, James [1808-1886]
—— *A History of Architecture*
   cyclopean works in Peru, Greece II 745
—— *Illustrations of Rock Cut Temples* . . .
   Hindu Zodiac fr Greeks II 225
   Indian architecture, zodiac fr Greece II 225
   Indian cave temples after Egyptian II 220n
Ferho, of Nazareans I 195
Feridan [Ferīdūn] (Pers)
   vanquishes Zohac II 398
Ferment(ation)
   fiery lives, microbes, etc I 262-3 &nn
   Pasteur, Bernard I 249n
Fern(s)
   Carboniferous giants II 276
   colossal, & mosses of today II 733

forests fr 3rd round II 712
gigantic in Miocene (Pengelly) II 726
pine oldest tree after the II 594
Ferouer. *See* Fravashi
Ferrel, William II 64
Ferrier, on mind & matter I 124-5n
Fetahil [Pthahil] (Gnos)
  begat 7 races I 248
  creates our planet I 195
  identical w pitris, Prometheus I 195n
  ordered to create, failed I 194; II 239
Fétichisme II 346. *See also* de Mirville, *Des Esprits*
Fetus. *See* Foetus
Fiat Lux
  Adam Kadmon & I 246
  angels commanded to create II 239
  "Let there be Sons of Light" I 481
  Lévi on I 259n
  Rabbi Simeon explains I 215-16n
Fichte, Johann Gottlieb
  Absolute of, & Vedānta I 50
  Advaita doctrine of I 79n
  on *Seyn, Daseyn* (Ger) I 281n
  unity of man w god-spirit I 79n
  universal consciousness I 51
Ficino, Marcilio (Vicinus in tx)
  on anthropomorphic gods II 601-2
Fiend(s) I 612
  bhūtas of *Vishnu Purāna* II 102n, 163
  gods became II 237 &n, 274
Fiery
  breaths & sephīrōthal triad I 213
  gold or, masculine principle I 364
  nature of 1st dhyāni-chohans I 82
  wind, glowing cosmic dust I 107
Fiery Dragons (of Wisdom)
  comets or I 203
  dhyāni-chohans II 280n
  not fiery serpents II 212
Fiery Lives
  analogy of asc & desc arcs I 262-3n
  builders & destroyers I 262-3n
  Commentary on I 249-50
  direct the microbes I 262n
  globe, 1st round, built by I 259
  independent living beings II 117
Fiery Serpent(s) I 414, 442; II 206, 387n. *See also* Fiery Dragons, Magic, Serpents
  bite of, & brazen serpent I 364
  described I 364 &nn
  God moving on chaos I 74-5
  Levites called, black magic II 212
Fiery Wheels, Four Mahārājas or I 126

Fifth Race. *See* Root-Race–5th
Fifth Round. *See* Round–5th
Fifth Rounder(s)
  abnormally developed intellects II 167
  discussed & explained I 161-2
Figanière, Visconde de, "Esoteric Studies"
  on monadic evolution II 289n
  new types of man each round II 290
Figuier, Louis
  materialist, admits spirits I 620
—— *The Day After Death*
  traditions have scientific weight II 136-7
Figures. *See also* Numbers
  keys to esoteric system I 164
  language of the elements I 464
  occult, withheld I 170, 206; II 251
  zero & I 99, 360-1
Fiji Islands II 788
Filia Vocis. *See also* Bāth-Kōl
  Vāch, Sephīrāh, Kwan Yin I 431n
Filioque Dogma, separates Roman & Greek churches II 635
Filippi, Filippo de II 646
Fils de Dieu, Les. See Jacolliot
Finite
  cannot be perfect II 487
  cannot conceive the Infinite I 51
  infinite &, re monad & duad I 426
  infinity cannot know the I 56
Finns, 7th subrace, 4th root-race II 178
Fire (element). *See also* Agni, Elements, Fires, Heat, Pārsīs
  active, male principle II 130
  aether &, ātma-buddhi I 216
  aether in purest form I 87
  Agni (Vedic) I 101, 114, 381, 413-14n
  air, water, earth & I 284; II 114, 616
  Al-Orit god of II 361
  angels (kumāras) II 243
  born of water I 379
  burns away lower senses II 639
  circles of II 103, 232, 275n
  cold, luminous I 250
  deity presiding over time I 86
  destroyed some races II 307n, 309, 725-6
  discovered by inventors II 373
  dragon of wisdom fr water & I 470
  essence of, & flame I 6
  ethereal & terrestrial I 469
  finds refuge in water I 402
  first after the One I 216, 447
  first manifest material I 250
  flame of, endless I 85n
  by friction explained in Vedas I 523

gandharva forces of solar I 523n
genii of, are Kabiri-Titans II 363
giving knowledge of future I 339
God is a living, (*Acts*) I 121
god of II 236n
gods discussed I 340-1
higher self in *Anugītā* II 638 &n
Holy Ghost as, [*Acts*] I 402
hydrogen is "fire, air, & water" II 105
initiation trials of II 566n
is all the deities I 101; II 567
Isis & Osiris or water & II 583
kabbalistic works on I 339
Kārttikeya born fr water & II 550
least understood of elements I 120-2
life, heart, pulse of universe I 216
light, flame &, in Stanzas I 81-2 &n
living magnetic I 338 &n; II 311n
living spiritual, & man II 79, 102
lotus product of, & water I 57, 379n
male generative principle I 57
marriage of, & water I 341
Melhas or, -gods II 34
Mithra, Mithras, & II 130
never discovered II 523-4
one element or I 101
origin of, (Plato) II 373
origin of, 1st round I 259
people born of water & I 439n; II 605
pillar of, (*Exodus*) I 338n, 437
primordial, not physical I 69-70
progeny of electricity I 81-2
Prometheus & II 520, 523-4
pure ākāśa I 253
pure spirit of, in Sun I 493
purifies manas II 639
pyramid derived fr II 594
related to sight, etc II 107
Rosicrucians defined, correctly I 121
Rudra god of II 280n
sacred II 77, 80, 101n, 171, 363, 759
St Mark, lion &, (table) II 114
science does not explain I 121, 141-2, 521
sevenfold, manifested I 87
solar II 105
sons of, (agni-putra) II 363
spirit of, fructifies I 379
spiritual II 79, 105, 109
śuchi or solar II 57n, 102, 105
swallowed by air (pralaya) I 372-3
symbolizes divine spirit II 113
third race could live in II 220
thunder, Jove, Agni or I 462
triple, invisible I 87

triple, of central spiritual sun I 87
universe fr air, water & I 92 &n
Vaiśvānara is living magnetic II 311n
various names of II 114
vital II 267
water &, or Mother & Father I 70
water &, produced matter II 65
worshipers II 361
Yazatas II 400n

Fire (of Mind). *See also* Lucifer, Prometheus
-angels & divine rebels II 243, 246
black, of *Zohar* (wisdom) II 162
of the celestial gods II 210
creative II 101, 270, 414
first 2 races had no II 107, 113
higher self or II 109
holy, or Kabiri II 3
of passions II 99, 105
producer II 244
Promethean, became a curse II 412-13
Promethean, not physical II 523-4
-self or light of initiation II 570
seven circles of, (*Pymander*) II 103, 232, 275n, 448
spiritual, of middle principle II 79

Fire Atoms. *See also* Life-Atoms
become life-germs I 259

Fire Devas, divine rebels II 246

Fire Dhyānis
essence of man II 90-2
incarnate in 3rd race II 91

Fire Mist. *See also* Pāvaka
arhats of the I 207
ball of, becomes planet II 153
breath of fire I 83
after chaotic stage I 453
"Devourers" & I 259
primitive chaos luminous I 599
primordial, & elements I 201, 543
sons of the I 86, 207, 271n; II 212, 319
various names for I 140

Fires. *See also* Fire, Flames, Forty-nine Fires
alchemy & secret of II 106
Earth product of three II 247
forty-nine I 291, 439n, 520-1; II 57 &n, 85, 362, 521, 564
Nārada one of the II 83
personified in *Vāyu Purāna* I 521
represent spirit or male element II 64
sacred, or Kabiri, Kumāras II 106
seven & forty-nine I 291, 411; II 57 &n, 362-3, 564
three, 7, or forty-nine II 247, 363

Titans-Kabiri sacred divine II 363
Fire-Self
  an ever-living power II 570
  one w universal Spirit II 638 &n
First-born I 216, 399, 559
  Ahura Mazdā as II 488
  ancients had no name for I 383
  become asuras II 283
  begin each manvantara II 80
  fr chaos & primordial light I 344
  gods, protogonoi II 43, 490n
  heaven's II 224
  host of builders is I 344
  logoi or II 93
  number for I 89, 91
  Ormazd as the I 113n
  primitive or 1st man I 264
  "privations" of Aristotle II 489
  refused to create II 82, 239, 489
  various names for I 344
First Cause. *See also* Absolute, Unknowable
  Eternal Cause not I 391 &n
  gods proceed fr II 108
  Logos & I 14-15n, 426
  Naudin's theory of II 119-20
  not Parabrahman I 14 &n; II 108
  Plato's, eternal Idea I 214
  point, monad or I 426
  Pratt on, & Space I 9n, 342 &n
  Space container of unknown I 342
  Western speculation on I 327
First Logos. *See also* Avalokiteśvara, Logos,
    2nd Logos, 3rd Logos, Verbum, Word
  Ādi-buddhic monad manifests as I 571
  Aeon, Aion or I 351
  concealed deity & I 437
  heavenly man is not II 599
  Kwan-shi-yin I 452
  Microprosopus is not I 215 &n
  names of I 351-2
  One, & mūlaprakriti I 273-4
  Parabrahman unknown to I 429
  paśyantī form of Vāch I 138, 432
  ray of, uses Adam Kadmon I 214
  Second &, 2 Avalokiteśvaras I 72n
  sexless II 128
  sleeps in bosom of Parabrahman I 429
  unborn, eternal energy I 130n
  unmanifested "First Cause" I 16
  Verbum or I 137, 428
  Vishnu, Brahmā 2nd Logos I 381n
First Principles. See Spencer, H.
First Race. *See* Root-Race–1st
First Round. *See* Round–1st

Fish, Fishes. *See also* Dāg, Matsya, Oannes,
  Pisces
  amphibians evolved fr II 256-7
  androgynous forms found in II 118
  atrophied 3rd eye in some II 296
  avatāra of Vishnu I 263-4, 369, 385; II 69n,
    139, 307, 578
  Bacchus called the II 313
  bisexual before mammals II 594n
  Dāg-on was a, & messiah I 653
  divine meaning of, is savior II 313
  dogs w tails of, (Chald) II 54
  Ea (wisdom) or sublime II 495n
  forms of, fr 3rd round II 257, 712
  giant II 201
  Hea (Chald) the intelligent II 26n
  human foetus & II 684-5 &nn
  "I am the, of the great Horus" I 220
  Jesus & followers called II 313 &n
  Joshua son of the I 264
  man-, (Chald) I 264; II 54, 495n
  materialists compared to II 370
  Meenam (Mīna) zodiacal sign I 385
  men w, -bodies II 63
  Messiah connected w I 385
  most, preceded man in 4th round II 594n
  Mother-, or fiery, & spawn I 97
  septenary cycle among II 622
  sin, Moon & I 238, 263-4
  Southern, in zodiac I 663
  symbol in both Testaments I 264
  theological meaning of, phallic II 313
  Triton a man- II 578
  Vaivasvata &, avatāra I 369; II 139
  Zohar allegory of I 393-4
Fiske, John, [*Darwinism, & Other Essays*]
  defense of Darwinism II 680
—— *Myths & Myth-Makers*
  Lyell differed w, re myths II 787
  myths uncivilized, not profound II 786
—— *Outlines of Cosmic Philosophy*
  glacial epoch II 778-9n
Fission
  cell division, nucleus splits II 166 &n
Five. *See also* Pentagon, Quinary
  becomes 7 (nirvāna) II 580
  binary & ternary I 384; II 575-6
  -fold nature of kumāras II 585
  kumāras described II 577-8
  Makara & II 576-80
  strides of Fohat I 122
  symbol expl I 391; II 575-80, 583
  symb of life eternal & terrestrial II 579
  symbol of womb I 391

three, 7, &, in Masonry I 113n
Five Ministers of Chōzzar (Gnos)
  androgyne II 577
  sixth & 7th kept secret II 578
Five-pointed Star II 464. *See also* Pentacle
  microcosmic, or man I 219; II 576 &n
  reversed, symbol of kali-yuga I 5
Five Years of Theosophy I 530n; II 673n
  adepts on nebular theory I 590, 593-4
  atoms drawn back to us II 672 &n
  cometary matter different I 142, 597
  consciousness II 598
  on constitution of Sun I 528 &n
  dual meaning of Vedas I 270n
  Egyptians, Atlanteans, etc II 436
  "Elixir of Life" & initiates II 499
  Greeks vs Atlanteans II 743n
  Kalapa I 378n
  on kingdoms I 176-7
  kriyāśakti II 173 &n
  land bridges to South America II 327
  Makara II 576-80
  metempsychosis I 455
  prajñā I 139
  primary prakriti is ākāśa I 256
  septenary man I 157-8
  six primary nature forces I 292-3
  Sun has all the elements I 583
  thread doctrine I 610
Fizeau, estimates Sun's heat I 484n
F. J. B. (in *Athenaeum*)
  on meaning of term "species" II 647n
Flagae of Paracelsus, dhyānis or I 222n
Flame(s)
  agnishvāttas or II 79
  Ahriman surrounded by II 516
  assist Christian creator I 440
  battle of the I 202
  Book of Concealed Mystery re II 83
  born of Universal Mind II 232
  on descent becomes whirlwind I 97-8n
  divine or Fiery Lions I 213
  dropped spark into Australians II 318
  fr a fire, endless I 85n
  fire reflection of the One I 121
  hierarchy of spirits I 86; II 63-4
  identical w devas, rishis, etc II 85
  incarnate in 3rd race II 247-8
  Kali the black I 443
  land on Earth II 232
  light, fire &, in Stanzas I 81-2, 599n
  listed II 247-8
  lords of, refused to create II 77
  man needs 4, & 3 fires II 57 &n

Melha lord of II 63
  physical light & I 259n
  primordial I 88
  progeny of electricity I 81-2
  pure, self-conscious angels II 318n
  rays of the one dark II 234
  root that never dies I 34
  solar, are reflections I 530
  sons of the II 282
  spark is the vehicle of I 265
  spark will rebecome the I 265
  spirit of I 458n
  three-tongued, & 4 wicks I 237 &n
  in Zend Avesta II 516
Flamma [alchemy]
  -Durissima, -Virgo (chart) II 114-15
  sulphur, spiritus & II 113
Flammarion, Camille
  —— *La Pluralité des mondes habités*
  Jupiter not molten II 135-6, 707
  life on other worlds I 606n; II 45, 699, 701
  many judge other worlds by ours II 702-3
Flint
  magic properties of II 341
  psychic natures enshrined in I 608n, 609
Flints
  in Miocene II 675, 678, 688n, 723 &n, 738n,
    740n, 748n, 755
  scientists disagree re II 751-2 &n
Flood(s) I 389, 397n; II 150. *See also* Cataclysm,
  Deluge, Noah
  Atlanteans divined coming of II 429, 610
  Atlantis nearly wiped out by II 309, 350
  Babylonian & Mosaic II 222
  of Deukalion II 519
  first, at end of satya-yuga II 146
  first cosmic, was creation II 139
  first, in Aryan memory II 332
  great, allegorical & cosmic II 146, 307-10
  Great, is Old Dragon II 352-3, 786
  great, of 3rd race II 331
  great sidereal, & Vaivasvata II 310, 313
  Jupiter reanimates race after II 270
  M'bul or waters of the I 385
  Mulil caused waters of, to fall II 139n
  of the Nile II 353
  no, 3102 BC I 370
  Noah's I 370, 444n
  Noah's, not Central Asian II 141
  occult science survived great I 341
  second, of 4th race II 146
  Vaivasvata saved race fr II 309-10
  various II 141-8, 222, 353
  Zoroastrian II 356

Flora, Floral II 741
  Australian Oolitic II 196-7
  changes periodically II 53
  evidence & Atlantis II 726-7, 781, 783, 790
  men, animals &, once huge II 276, 733-4
  similarity betw Old & New Worlds II 792
Flora Tertiaria Helvetiae. See Heer, O.
Florence, built on Etruscan cities II 221
Florida, built out by corals (Agassiz) II 133
Florilegium. See Stobaeus, G.
Flower, Sir Wm. H. II 196n
—— "Classification of the Various . . ."
  three human types today II 471n
—— "The Study & Prog of Anthropology"
  monogenistic origin of man II 169
Fludd, Robert, *Tractatus apologeticus* . . .
  Light & Darkness identical I 70
Fluid
  Fohat as universal vital I 493
  primitive, of Kant I 623
  theory of electricity I 508, 516
  theory of heat discussed I 515-17
Flute of Pan, symbology of II 581
Flying
  camel II 205
  dragons II 387, 676
  fiery serpents II 206 &n
Fo-ch'ou (Chin)
  teacher, miracle maker II 215 &n
Foetus (Fetus). *See also* Embryo, Recapitula-
    tion of Embryo
  changes of, & rounds I 184; II 257, 684-5
  conception of, mystery II 174
  cycles of human I 389
  developed fr what? I 222
  digestion in II 131
  gill-clefts in human, expl II 684-5
  growth of, fr germ to man I 222-4; II 177,
    187-8
  & oviparous early 3rd root-race II 132
  tail in human, described II 685
  vegetable phases of II 685n
Fohat ("Turanian compound") II 586
  abodes of I 204
  androgynous energy I 137
  "Ares" of Paracelsus I 284
  asleep & awake I 109
  Aurora Borealis, Australis & I 205
  awakens primordial matter I 82, 110
  axial changes guided by II 329-30
  breath of I 635
  bridge betw spirit & matter I 16
  brings ray in union w soul I 119
  circular motion & I 201

  cosmic electricity I 76, 85, 111-12, 144-5,
    493, 554
  cosmic energy I 328
  desc I 16, 76, 109-12, 204-5, 328; II 400n
  differentiated light I 216
  divine love, Eros or I 119; II 65
  double triangle & I 216
  emanation of powers behind I 139
  evolution guided by II 649n
  fiery whirlwind I 108
  force accompanying ideation I 110-11
  fourth son of, & Crookes I 562
  genesis, birth of I 145, 328
  guided by univ intelligence I 493; II 330
  guides star's death, rebirth I 147
  hardens the atoms I 85
  hissing, or serpent I 76
  impresses thought on substance I 16, 85;
    II 649n
  instrument of Logos I 137n
  key to symbols, allegories I 673
  life-electricity I 137, 139; II 65
  life fr action of I 526n
  Light of the Logos I 137, 602 &n; II 400n
  lords propelled by II 86
  male-female, bipolar I 145
  manifested & unmanifested I 109-10
  as many as there are worlds I 143n
  not a personal god I 139
  objectivizes 7 centers of energy II 604n
  Pramati son of II 413-14n
  prāna, male, active I 525n
  produces 7 laya-centers I 147-8
  rich w dhyāni-chohanic thought II 649n
  runs the manus' errands I 63
  scientists not asked to accept I 590
  separates & places sparks I 116
  separates matter into atoms I 76
  sets nebulae in motion I 84
  sets world germs in motion I 672
  sevenfold I 139, 145, 554
  seven sons, brothers of I 145, 204-5, 216,
    523-4, 554
  shapes atoms fr crude material I 112
  solar energy I 111
  steed, thought the rider I 107-8
  swastika emblem of II 587
  synthesis of nature's forces I 672
  thread of, & the Spark I 238
  three & 5 strides of I 112, 122
  Toum &, identic I 674
  turns seed, curds opposite direction I 673
  vehicle of Primordial Seven I 108
Fohi (Chin) Heavenly Man

biblical patriarch (Bailly) I 648
men of II 26-7
trigrams of II 554
Foh-maeyu [Fo mai-yu] (Chin)
temple of Buddha II 215
Foh-tchou. *See* Fo-ch'ou
Foix, François de
—— *Le Pimandre de Mercure* . . .
disfigures Pymander II 114, 491 &n
man, animals double-sexed II 96 &n
man's 7 principles II 491-2
Fo-kien, sacred library in I 271n
Fo-kone-ky. See Fa-Hien
Folklore(s). *See also* Allegory, Legends,
Myths
based on fact II 393
historical lining to all I 303
similarities among II 393
Fontenelle, B. de I 304
Footprints, fossil II 10, 755
Foraminifera, Paleozoic, same today II 257
Forbes [Cotes, Roger] I 492
Force(s). *See also* Elementals, Energy, Powers
activities of entities I 146, 293
aether source & cause of I 508
ākāśa necessary to understand I 587
all bodies connected by universal I 511
atoms & molecules centers of I 507
blind, fallacy of II 298, 475-6, 648-53
breath of life, never-dying II 589
Butlerof on I 517-18
centripetal & centrifugal I 282n, 416, 593,
604; II 24, 170, 261
the coming I 554-66
commanding the I 514n
correlation of I 96, 521, 674 &n
correlations of elements & I 373n
cosmic manifestation & II 24-5
cosmic, seen by seer I 633-4
Crookes q on I 550-1
Cuvier doubted nature of I 490
danger of Keely's I 563-4
defined as body in motion I 502n, 518
design in seemingly blindest I 277
effects of the 4 elements I 342
electric & magnetic, at poles I 205
equilibrium of, (Grove) I 497 &n
ever-acting cause I 93n
first constructive, or builders I 344
generated by Powers I 520
God of religion abstract I 397
gods, called esoterically I 672
imponderable, intelligent I 587, 671n
incorporeal stuff I 508

independent of matter (Hirn) I 512
intelligence of nature's I 279, 287, 425, 499,
587, 604
intracosmic intelligent, & God I 529
Keely's "New" I 565-6
known, worshiped by ancients I 509
ladder of I 554
latent in laya I 140, 155
laya noumenon of I 148
life rules, (de Quatrefages) I 540
little understood I 424
male & female II 84
manifestation & 2 contrary I 282
manifested unknown realities I 509
matter & I 111n, 491, 511-12, 518
-matter-chance trinity of science I 505
matter-god of science I 509-10
"modes of motion" I 146-7, 671n
molecular energy or I 670
monadless spiritual I 632
motion &, not separate I 512
motion of I 517-18
motor-, Le Couturier on I 502
moving matter I 554
of nature aspects of univ motion I 147
Newton's doubts re nature of I 490
not a property of matter I 491
occult, of cardinal points I 122-3
ONE, of *Genesis* I 337
originate in solar vital principle I 591
perceivable states of matter I 143n
phlogiston & substance of I 511-12
physical, vehicles of elements I 469-70
psychic & spiritual, origin of I 515n
pure, nothing in physics I 510
a quality of *something* I 509
resides in atom I 511-12
śakti as 6-fold I 292-3
same, each manvantara I 145
secondary agents (Jaumes) I 506
semi-intelligent I 514n
septenary I 290; II 492, 612, 621n, 631, 732
space, matter &, (Pratt) I 615
spirit, matter & I 341; II 103
spirit or demon behind every I 633
spiritual entities (Pythagoras) I 492-3
spring fr upādhi of ether I 515n
Stallo on mass & I 510-11
Subba Row on I 292-3
substance of some kind I 511, 514
-substance-time a trinity I 582-3
Force and Matter. See Büchner, L.
Forces non définies, Les. See Rochas d'Aiglun
Forest, symbol of man's life II 637

Forethought, fr πρὸ μῆτις, Prometheus II 413n, 420n

[Forlong, General J. G. R.], *Rivers of Life*
  degrades tree & serpent worship I 405

Form(s) I 480. *See also* Ideas, Prototypes, Rūpas
  adept's power to change his II 705n
  all, exist in prototype I 281-2
  all primordial, spheroids I 65
  change each round, race II 262
  drop of water spheroidal I 98n
  of early races II 17-18, 102, 109, 121, 164-7
  fifth race 1st symmetrical II 294
  Heavenly Man model for all I 89, 183
  human, change least II 256
  life precedes & survives I 222
  man passes thru all, in 1st round I 159
  no, without astral prototype I 282 &n; II 660
  previous human, not lower II 260
  record of, in strata meager II 260
  rounds, races &, (Figanière) II 289n
  secondary consideration II 262
  septenary groups of II 593, 622
  spirit evolves, out of aether I 332
  thrown off fr man during 3rd, 4th rounds
    II 683, 685
  universal deity & I 492-3n

Fortnightly Review
  Grant Allen on Neanderthal skull II 687

Fortunate Islands, origin of life on II 398

Forty-nine Fires, Globes, Races, Stages
  Commentary on I 290-1
  every one of, a distinct function I 521
  explained I 520-1; II 57 &n, 564
  in *Leviticus* II 618, 747-8
  seven &, in India I 411; II 611
  seven &, worshiped II 362

Forty-nine Stations
  for Earth monad each manvantara I 238

Fossil(s). *See also* Giants, Mammals, Reptiles
  absence of transitional, (Mivart) II 697
  ancients knew of early race II 285
  astral, fr 3rd round II 68n, 684
  Atlantean II 740, 753, 791-2
  earliest known II 254
  of Eocene man predicted II 690
  Eur, cannot prove man's antiquity II 725
  few, fr earlier rounds II 730
  first 2 races left no II 289
  of flying camel or pterodactyl II 205-6
  geologic displacement of, (Winchell)
    II 325n
  geologic, record imperfect II 260
  of giants II 277, 285

of man & ape II 675-80
of monkeys in Miocene II 723n
no, missing links II 260, 660-1, 674, 681 &n
Oolitic (Jurassic), & Australia II 196-7
of Paleolithic man II 686n
Swiss cattle fr, -oxen II 287
why no giant human, in dolmens II 753

Foster, Sir Michael, *Textbook of Physiology*
  development of embryo II 131-2

Foucault, J. B. L. on heat I 502

Fou-kone-ki. See Fa-hien

Fountain of Life
  Earth's, described II 400n
  in Fortunate Islands II 398

Four. *See also* Cardinal Points, Mahārājas, Quaternary, Yugas
  becomes symbol of truth as cube II 600
  Chinese dragons, genii I 408
  female or matter I 36; II 592
  forms of Vach I 138, 432
  grades of initiation I 206
  holy, sacred I 92, 98, 99, 442
  Key-Keeper of nature II 600-1
  kumāras sacrificed themselves II 281-2
  lords full of passion II 212
  lower principles or soulless animal II 604
  Mahārājas I 122-8, 408
  man's elements & II 604
  mean betw monad & heptad II 599
  -mouthed Dragon-lake II 204
  planes of manifestation I 200
  rivers of Eden I 367
  sons of God (Egy) II 213
  soul contains number II 575
  streams of milk, etc I 367
  symbol of chaotic matter II 600n
  Tetraktys, sacred square or I 89n
  three &, male, female I 321
  three & 3 &, or ten II 564
  truths of 7 given so far I 42
  united w 3 became perfect II 601

Four, the Sacred
  allegorized in *Linga Purāna* II 282
  four-lettered ineffable name II 282n
  remain to serve mankind II 281-2
  Tetraktys, Self-Existent One or I 88

Four Circles
  equator, ecliptic, 2 tropics I 204
  Fohat's 4 sons placed in I 204-5

Fourmont, Étienne, *Réflexions . . .*
  Genesis 4 not understood II 375

Four Quarters
  each of, w 7 parts I 408

four Mahārājas preside over I 122
lipikas guardians of I 103-4 &n
Fourteen Precious Things I 67 &n
Fourth
  of any series unique I 182-3, 586n
  dimension of space discussed I 251-2 &n
  number the turning point I 586n
Fourth Gospel. *See John, Gospel of*
Fourth Race. *See* Root-Race–4th
Fourth Round. *See* Round, Fourth
Four Truths
  nidānas based on the I 39
  teachings on the, secret I 45
Four Winds, carry out karma I 123
Fox, can mate w dog II 287
Fradadhafshu (Avestic, Tradadhafshu in tx)
  globe C of Earth chain II 759
Fragment K 3454 (British Museum)
  on Chaldean god Zu II 283-4n
Fragments. See Cory, I. P., *Ancient Fragments* . . .
Fragments d'une histoire de la terre . . . *See*
  Rougemont, F. de
France
  field of giants in II 277
  land connection w Britain II 750
  nearing a catastrophe I 646
  once joined w Newfoundland II 791
  Paleolithic man in II 523, 686
  rocking stones in II 342n
Franck, Adolphe D., *La Kabbale*
  Ayin, Ain-sōph, No-Thing I 350
  Dabar or Word I 350
  modern Kabbala fragmentary II 461
  "narratives of the Doctrine" II 447
  race that was destroyed II 2
  two thaumaturgists I xliii n
Francoeur, L. B., *Philosophie naturelle*
  attraction alone not enough I 529
—— *Uranographie*
  combining attraction, repulsion I 529
François de Tours. *See* Foix, François de
Frankenstein I 594
  mechanical animal of sorcerers II 427n
  without mind man less than II 56
  Mrs Shelley's, explained II 349
  physical-chemical evolution a II 652
Fravashi (Avestan, Farvarshi in tx)
  divine impersonality of II 478
  ferouer or II 478-9
  immortal man, higher ego II 480n
  privations, ideal types II 489
  "soul" of all creations II 480

Freedom
  instinct in all creatures II 484
  intellectual, & sons of Mahat II 103
Freemasonry. *See* Masonry
Free-Will I 639; II 304n, 412
  Prometheus preferred II 420-1
French *Encyclopaedia. See Encyclopédie*
[Fréret, Nicolas], on Chinese year II 621
Fresnel, Augustin-Jean
  held ether to be discontinuous I 482
  phenomena of polarization I 486
Freund, Dr Wilhelm
—— *Latin Lexicon [Wörterbuch . . .]*
  Sodales, priest colleges II 212n
Friday, Venus day I 652
Frog(s)
  air-water symbol I 358
  church lamps shaped like I 386
  Egyptian symbol I 385-6
  in the Moon creative god symbol I 355
Frost Giants. *See* Hrimthurses
Fruit (of Tree of Knowledge)
  Adam, Eve warned against II 267
  church fathers made, forbidden II 98
  eating, brought on struggle II 272
  eating, man becomes like elohīm I 276
  soma is the II 499n
  of tree (various) II 97-8
Fruits, brought fr higher spheres II 373-4
"Fuel of the Sun." *See* Williams, M. M.
Fuerst. *See* Fürst, J.
Fuga et Inventione, De. See Philo Judaeus
Fundamental Conceptions. See Strachoff, N.
Fundamental Propositions, Three I 14-20
Fundamento Sapientiae, De. See Paracelsus
Funerary Ritual of the Egyptians. See Rougé
Fürst, Julius, *Hebrew and Chaldee Lexicon*
  Cain, Vulcain II 392-3n
  crucifixion & nailing II 558
  Yāho, IĀO II 541
Fusaiolos (terra-cotta discs)
  swastika on, at Troy II 101
Future
  adept may read I 631
  giants read, in stars (Creuzer) II 285
  of individuals & magic mirror II 179
  past &, alive in present I 105
  past, present & I 37, 43-4; II 446
  predicted on math principles I 646
Fylfot (Norse swastika)
  4-footed cross, II 546

G

Gabiri [Gabri] (Pers)
 Kabiri became II 363n
Gabirol. *See* Ibn Gebirol
Gabriel, St (archangel) II 248. *See also* Angel,
 Elohīm
 denounced fallen angels II 382n
 dhyāni-chohan or I 42
 divine rebel II 246
 eagle (Ophite) is I 127n; II 115n
 lilies of, & lotus I 379n; II 472
 Lord of Iran I 576; II 538
Gades, Wilford mistakes, as Atlantis II 406n
Gadir, Sacred Columns of
 mysterious characters on II 345n
Gadolinium, a compound I 625
Gaea, Gaia (Gk) Earth
 Aditi-, primordial matter II 65
 children by Uranos II 269 &n
 Earth & digit three II 583
 gamma (Γ) symbol of II 590-1
 great cosmic deep II 269
 Holy Ghost or I 109
 sons of, or initiates II 591 &n
 Tethys or II 65
Gaganeśvara (Skt), name for Garuda II 565
Γαιήιος (Gaiēios, Gk) Tau or initiate II 591n
Gaina [Gaṇadevas in *VP*]
 7 classes of, in orb of Sun I 290
Galen II 132
Galilean Adept (Jesus) II 231
Galilee, stone circles in II 755
Galileo II 534
 animated atoms of I 568-9
 retaught elemental vortices I 117, 623
Gall, Reverend James, *Primeval Man . . .*
 Satan & pre-Adamic races I 324-5
 science & the Bible I 323n
Gallery of Argeak. *See* Argeak
Galli, Kadeshim or II 460
Gallu, Chaldean spirits II 248n
Galukpas. *See* Gelukpas
Galvanism, aspect of Archaeus I 338n
Gamma (3rd Gk letter)
 symbol of Earth, Gaia II 583, 590-1
Gamut (scale), Hindu I 534
Gāndhāra (Skt), quality of sound I 534
Gandharvas (Skt) I 571

both psychic & physical II 585
four Mahārājas I 126
gods & men II 211
highest dhyāni-chohans II 585
inhabit astral plane II 90
instructors of men II 584
seven sons of Fohat are I 523-4
6,333 of I 523n
spirits of heaven (Purāṇas) II 369n
Vāch becomes Virāj to punish II 143
various synonyms of I 92
Gandunia(s). *See* Gan-Eden
Gan-Eden, Gan-Aeden, Gandunia(s) [Gan-
 'ēden] (Heb). *See also* Garden of Eden
 Babylonia & Mesopotamia II 42n, 202
Gaṅgā (Skt) Ganges River
 emerges thru Kapila's Pass II 571
 Mandākin or I 385
Gaṅgādvāra, door, gate (pass) of Ganges River
 II 571
Gaṅgā-putra, Kārttikeya called II 550
Ganges River II 130. *See also* Gaṅgā
 Agni, Kārttikeya & II 550
 flows fr Lake of Dragons II 204
 sources of II 571
Gånggrifter, dolmens in Sweden II 752
Ganoids, & primary oceans II 160
Ganot, Adolphe, *Éléments de Physique*
 defines matter I 670
Ganymede, cycles & Aquarius II 785-6
Gaokerena [Gaekarena] (Pahlavi)
 white Haoma II 517
Garden of Eden. *See also* Curse, Eden, Gan-
 Eden
 Adam garment of light in II 112
 Adam of, forefather of our race II 503
 Ādi-Varsha was, of 1st races II 201
 belongs to 5th race II 203
 cherub at gate of I 127
 Christian vs occult meanings of II 202
 on Euphrates River II 203
 of initiates no myth II 494
 kabbalistic, & nirvāna comp II 204
 locality of, now submerged II 494
 never property of Jews II 203
 primitive man w elohīm in II 349

Protestant, discussed I 612
serpent of I 406-7, 414, 422
[Skinner on] II 543
temptation of, invented I 383
tree in I 114, 247; II 30-1, 97, 494
true meaning of, (*IU*) II 496
Garden of Hesperides, Atlantis & II 791
Gardner, J. Starkie
—— "Subsidence & Elevation . . ."
land connections II 782-3
Garga
Nārada surpasses II 49
oldest Indian astronomer II 49n
Garuḍa (Skt)
coeternal w Vishnu I 366
descends fr reptiles II 253-4
Indian phoenix story of II 564-5
Kaśyapa father of II 253-4
king of feathered tribe II 181
manvantaric cycle or I 421
offspring of Vinatā I 366
Sāmba uses, to invite Magas II 323
son & nephews of II 570
stands for mahā-kalpa I 366; II 565, 570
vehicle of Krishna, Vishnu I 366; II 323, 564
Vishnu rides on I 421
Garuḍa Purāṇa, Wilson on II 565n
Gas(es)
atoms of, elastic spheres I 513
effect of occult, on matter I 82
solids, liquids & I 526; II 136-7n
Gassendi, Pierre
material atoms of I 629
truths of, alloyed I 622
Gastropoda Shells, in Sahara II 8-9n
Gāthā(s) [*Avestan* hymns] II 409-10, 517
Gātra (Skt) limbs
Vedhas produced fr Brahmā's II 78, 176n
Gaudapādāchārya
commentary on *Sānkhya Kārikā* I 457n
Gaudry, Jean Albert II 646, 676
—— *Les Enchaînements du monde* . . .
man dates fr Miocene II 714n
man not crown of ape-stock II 678
monkey carved Thenay flints II 748
no Miocene mammals like today's II 749
our European forefathers II 739
Gaul(s)
Bel Sun-god of II 540
isthmus once joined, & Eng II 750 &n
Gaur [Cawr] (Welsh) giant II 342
Gauramukha (Skt), a family priest II 323
Gaurī (Skt) or Śrī, bride of Śiva II 76n
Gautama Śākyamuni. *See* Buddha, Gautama

Gautier, Armand
on venoms, alkaloids I 262n
[Gay, John, *A Thought on Eternity*] q I 26
Gāyatrī (Skt), fire-sticks & syllables of I 523
Gebelin, de. *See* Court de Gébelin
Gebers, Geborim. *See* Gibborīm
Ge'boor-ah [Gebūrāh] (Heb)
globe A, Earth chain or I 200
Qai-yin (Cain) or II 315
sign of cross & II 562
Gehenna [Gē hinnōm] (Heb)
Jews immolated children at I 463n
Geiger, Dr Wilhelm
—— *Civilization of Eastern Iranians* . . .
on Amshaspends II 358
on 7- & 3-fold Earth II 757-8
Geikie, James, *Prehistoric Europe* . . .
period betw Paleo- & Neolithic man II 715n
reindeer sketch fr II 720
Geist (Ger) spirit, word gas fr I 465
Gellius, Aulus, *Noctes Atticae*
on word Maia I 396n
Gelukpas (Tib) Buddhist "Yellow Hats"
founded by Tsong Kha-pa I 108n
swastika & II 586
Gemara Sanhedrin II 473. *See Talmud*
Gemini
Castor & Pollux I 366
Simeon, Levi & I 651
Gemmation
described II 151, 177
healing, cicatrization & II 166n
Gems (Gnostic). *See* Gnostic Gems
Genealogies
Brahmanical, Biblical II 42
embrace 3½ rounds II 320-2
evolution of animals (Purānas) II 253-4
in *Genesis* II 426
fr Heavenly Man I 612-13
of humans (Haeckel) II 87n
keys necessary to understand II 248
mythical, of "Budha" II 498
of rishis I 436
of Seth & Cain II 391
symbolic nature of II 391n
Genera, intermediate, fluctuating II 256
Generation
brazen serpent related to I 364
conception, & astronomy I 312
divine function I 193
Egyptian symbols for I 365
fall into II 104, 129, 204, 230, 231n, 232, 388, 422, 515, 766
goat symbol of fall into II 510

immaculate incarnation I 398-9
Io moon goddess of II 416
Jehovah lunar or, god II 40-1, 234, 246n, 464, 466
Jewish deity symbol of II 470
lotus symbolized II 179
matter female element of cosmic II 130
Moon's influence on sexual I 228n; II 105
Pan presides over II 510
sexual union or, & Earth's symbol II 30
spontaneous II 150-2, 286, 719
Sun, Moon & I 229
tau cross symbol & fall into I 657; II 30, 36, 600n
Generatione Hominis, De. See Paracelsus
Generations of Adam (or *Gen*) II 125, 134
Generator. *See also* Generation
Ammon-Ra the I 367
Prometheus, of humanity II 519
sea goddess or Virgin as I 458n
Genesis
defined (Wilder) II 24 &n
universal, fr Commentary II 160
Genesis (1st Book of Bible) II 229, 612
Abraham & El Elion in II 380
Adam (man) before animals II 1n
Adam divides into male, female II 126, 128
Adam Kadmon in likeness of God II 46n, 467
Adam knew Eve in II 279
Adam to rule over Eve II 135
Akkad capital of Nimrod I 319n
Akkadian I 357
angels sons of God II 61
astronomical like other allegories II 143
author of II 453
begins anthropology at wrong end I 246
Bela, Son of Beor II 706
Berosus aware of source of II 143
Cain slays brother II 44n
Cain son of Lord, not Adam II 127
Cain to rule over Abel II 135
came fr Egypt II 1-2n
caricature of older original II 450
Chaldean, 2 parts II 54
in Chaldeo-Assyrian beliefs II 477
ch 1 far older than 2nd ch I 254
chs 1-5 mixed by kabbalists II 127, 128
ch 3 at beginning of 4th race II 410
ch 25:24-34 on birth of 5th race II 705
coats of skin I 607
creation begins at 2nd & 3rd stage II 488, 537
creation of Heaven & Earth I 346
creation out of nothing II 87

creation story & Purānas II 624, 625n
creations, 2 or more in II 5, 53-4, 252n, 625n
darkness on face of deep I 70; II 59
daughters of men I 412, 523n; II 265n, 284, 501, 775
dead letter, open to criticism II 252
Enoch the "Son of Man" II 529n
Enoch "walked with God" II 532
Enos 1st sexed man in II 715n
Esau red & hairy II 705
esoteric book II 203, 252n
esoteric teachings in I 335-7; II 202
Eve, creation of II 193
Fall & Egyptian initiation II 215-16n
fallen angels in II 228-9
fall into generation II 388
fiat lux I 215-16n
firmament in midst of waters I 254
first ch, meaning of I 246n, 336-7
first 4 chs philosophic fragment I 10-11
first 3½ rounds in II 181
fruit whose seed is in itself I 381
Generations of Adam (Toledoth) & 5th ch II 125, 134
giants (gibborīm) II 70, 154, 236, 273-6
Gladstone kills II 252n
God & Lord God in II 1-2n, 60n, 81, 387-8
God commands another God in I 336
"God created man in his image" II 134
God creates firmament I 254; II 75
God made woman, hence sin II 387
God's covenant w Abraham II 508
immaculate conception in I 59-60
Jacob & his sons I 651; II 211-12
Jacob's ladder II 281n
Jehovah androgynous in 1st chs of I 6n
Jehovah became tempting serpent I 422
Jehovah curses, blesses man II 410
Jehovah sexed fr ch 5 on II 125 &n
Jews have accepted, literally II 252n
Joseph dreams of zodiac I 649
Kabbala expl secret meaning of II 37
Kadeshīm in II 460
kings of Edom in II 705
light divided fr darkness I 254
light in, androgyne ray I 356n
long lapse in ch 6 betw verses 4-5 II 375
Lot & daughters I 431
lotus idea in I 380
male, female, created I 390 &n
"man . . . as one of us" I 493n; II 44, 94, 95n, 202, 243
mandrake of, Rachel, Leah II 27n
man made of clay (dust) II 291

man, plants created before animals II 112n
men called Jehovah II 127
mistranslated in ch 4:26 II 469n
nephīlīm of II 775
Noah in II 145, 392
Noah took beasts by sevens II 597-8
no date given for man's birth in II 690
numerical reading of I 264
omits Chaldean material II 104
period betw verses 1 & 2 of 1st ch II 704
picks up physical man of 3rd race II 661
plants created before 4th round I 254
pre-Adamite races in II 394
real history begins w 6th ch II 284
Rebekah's womb, 2 nations in II 705
reminiscence of Bab captivity II 202
Satan in II 244
separation of sexes I 346
serpent of II 208, 215-16, 387
Seth & Enos in II 361
Seth of, (Bunsen) II 82n
seven recurs in II 4
several Adams or races in II 46n, 457, 502-4
sons of God fallen angels I 412
sons of God not punished in II 491
Spirit of God I 346
theogony hardly outlined in II 537
third & 4th races in II 410
three races in II 124
two gods in I 336-7
wisdom in 1st 6 chapters I 336
written on the old lines II 77
"Ye shall be as gods" II 279
younger than Chaldean II 104
Genesis (Mexican), & 4 good men II 213
Genesis of Enoch II 267-8n. *See also* Enoch
"Genesis of Man." *See* Blake, C. C.
Genesis of Species, On the. See Mivart
"Genesis of the Elements." *See* Crookes
Geneto (Gk), "was generated" I 425n
Genghis Khan, sacked Djooljool II 338
Genii, Genius. *See also* Angels, Spirits
  abode of, 4 cardinal points I 347n
  agriculture & II 374
  astral man often evil I 639
  in Babylonian myth II 248n
  Bahak-Zivo "Father" of the I 194
  born to act in space & time I 418
  each star has a I 294
  fire, or Titan-Kabiri II 363
  four dragons (Chin) I 408
  Gnostic angels I 195-6
  gods &, within Plenum I 569
  guardian spirits I 288n, 453n

Hermetic daimones or gods I 288n
Jehovah, of lunar year II 539
Kwan Yin, of water I 471
lord of, or aeons I 195
Mercury as II 28
modes of motion (science) & I 478
moon lunar II 474
Origen on I 577
planetary, & Persian prophets I 649, 652
Principes, sons of light I 196
rebelled against Kronos I 418
ruled men in Saturn's Age II 373
serpent a good I 472
of 7 planets, globes I 198; II 22, 538
several kinds of Ophite I 403
soul, angel, atom or I 569
Tzyphon, of doubt II 216n
various names for I 295
watched over & guided J. Böhme I 494
work of I 294-5
Genii of Fire. See Decharme, *Mythologie . . .*
Genius Loci (Lat) local god
  5th race afterthought I 462
Gentil. *See* Le Gentil
Gentiles
  did not copy Jews (Faber) II 472n
  disciples not to go to II 231n
  every god of, related to Jehovah II 509-10
  Hebrews borrowed fr II 560
  revered the adytum II 459
  seers, Enochs & II 532-3
  Trinity & II 540
"Gently to hear . . ." (Shakespeare) I xvii
Genus, Genera, interbreeding of II 184-5,
    191-2, 201, 287
Geoffroy Saint-Hilaire, E. II 646
  astonishment of II 206n
  crown of the innovator II 651
Geognosy (Geology)
  known by ancients II 534-5
Geographical Dist. of Animals. See Wallace
Géographie ancienne. See Bourguignon
Geography
  part of ancient Mysteries II 9
  of Purānas II 320-2
Geological Evidence of the Antiquity of Man. See
    Lyell, Sir Charles
Geological Magazine, Gardner's critique of Wallace in II 782-3
Geological Periods, Ages II 709-30
  ancients calculated II 66-7
  contradictions re II 9, 10n
  diagram of II 710
  early men & past I 609

length of, unknown II 66-7, 71-2, 155, 693,
   698, 710
man in remote II 56n, 157
Pengelly on inaccuracy of II 66, 72, 696
pre-diluvian II 160
science changes lengths of II 9-11, 71, 156-7
Geological Upheavals. *See also* Axis
Atlantean remnants & II 743-4
fourth round II 149-50
last universal, 120 million yrs ago II 312
Moon, Sun, planets causes of II 500n, 699
more than physically caused I 640
betw rounds, races II 46-7, 144-7
sidereal & II 314
Geologists
astronomers should become, (Faye) I 496
French, place man in Miocene II 686
length of periods thorn in side of II 698
monoliths of natural origin II 343
Geology, Geological. *See also* Geological
   Periods
Africa before Europe II 368
ancient Aryans & II 252-3
antediluvian II 334
anthropology & II 71-2
antiquity of man in theology I 323-5
archaic science & II 314
Aryans learned, fr Atlanteans II 426
changes & root-races II 47
chronological speculations risky II 663n
dates differ w Secret Doctrine II 794
deluge of 4th race II 144
Earth's age II 698
esoteric, & science I 325
explains Moon came fr Earth II 64
figures of II 10-11, 66-7, 71-2, 156-7
monoliths brought fr overseas II 343
perceived 2nd flood II 146
proof of submerged continents II 778
records imperfect II 260, 674, 698
subsidences, elevations II 787n
supports esoteric teachings II 196
thickness of various deposits II 709
will never be exact science II 656, 663
Geology. See Winchell, A., *World Life . . .*
Geometry, Geometrical I 66. *See also* Circles,
   Skinner, Triangles
cosmogony described in, glyphs I 1-6, 272
crystal shapes & II 594
evolutionary stages & I 321
fifth divine science, 5th key II 471
figures record Mysteries I 612
Great Pyramid & I 317n
Jevons uses, figures I 430n

numbers &, relations I 639
Osiris-Isis taught, (Basnage) II 366
Parker ratio I 313, 315-16
symbolism as old as world I 320
symbols of man's evolution II 560
theogony & I 615-17
Geometry. See Boethius
George, St
Anubis compared w II 385-6
dragon &, equivalents of II 379
earthly copy of St Michael I 458
Jennings on II 238n
Kārttikeya prototype of II 382n
Michael &, kill Satan II 385
Tahmurath the, of Iran II 397
Georgics. See Virgil
Gerland, Georg Karl Cornelius
Australians last of higher race II 779
Germ(s). *See also* Cells, Germ Cell
ark contained, of life II 313, 462, 715n
cells I 219, 224, 249n; II 117, 659
creative spark II 247
in darkness I 63
differentiation of I 21-2, 455
"Elementary" I 139
ether storehouse of I 462
ever-concealed, sun or point I 379
evolution of primordial I 455
exists in every atom I 57
fecund, contains universe I 64-5
first, on meteor (Thomson) II 719, 730
Fohat set world-, in motion I 672
formation of II 718-19, 730-33
invisible, fiery I 12
life-, fr fire atoms I 259; II 139
living, & comets I 366n
manifested universe & I 73n
Pasteur on I 249n
point in mundane egg I 57
primitive II 731-2
in the root I 11
sarcophagus &, of life II 462
seed or world- I 200-1
of solar systems & worlds II 148
spiritual potency I 219
spiritual, septenary II 731-2
three trinities issued fr I 278
of the universe I 21-2, 28-9
upādhi of 7 principles I 291
whence came the 1st, of life? II 719
world, collide I 201
Germain, Count St. *See* Saint-Germain
Germany
dolmens (Hünengräben) in II 752

rocking stones in II 342n
Germ Cell(s). *See also* Cell, Heredity
  fivefold jīva must fructify I 224
  organic processes & I 249n; II 659
  ovum or, stages of II 117
  spiritual plasm of, the key I 219, 224
Geryon, giant son of Hercules II 278
Gesenius, *A Hebrew & English Lexicon* . . .
  on Iao II 465 &n
  on nephīlīm II 775
Gestation II 595
  astronomical correspondence w I 388-90
  in egg-like vehicle during 3rd race II 166
  Moon, conception & I 180, 389; II 105, 583, 595
  seven months & 7 rounds II 257
  stages of II 187-8, 258-9
  in utero II 117
Ghana (Skt) "bulk"
  Vishnu has no size, extension I 420
Gharma-ja (Skt) "Śiva's sweat"
  Kārttikeya born of II 124-5n
Ghauts [Ghats]
  Western Śringa-giri of Mysore I 272
Gholaites
  believe in "Light of Elohīm" II 514n
Ghost(s)
  lares now signify II 361
  in spaces of Space I 620
Ghoul(s)
  Maimonides on desert II 455n
  moon a I 156
Giamschid [Jamshīd] Persian king
  built Persepolis II 398
Gian-ben-Gian (Pers) Wisdom, Son of Wisdom, king of Peris II 394
Giant(s)
  allied w asuras II 500-1
  angels beget II 293
  Antaeus II 278
  antediluvian, of Bible II 70, 340, 762
  Atlanteans II 70, 236, 275, 276, 279, 286, 493
  Atlas assisted, against gods II 493
  B'ne-aleim or, (*Gen* 6) II 375
  bones of, on Mt Hermon II 409
  born of Kaśyapa-Ādityā II 382n
  both mentally & physically I 416
  Bronze Age, (Hesiod) II 772
  Cainites or II 146, 172, 222
  Chinese traditions of II 365
  Cholula pyramid built by II 276n
  colossal powers of II 346
  commanded elements (Creuzer) II 285
  Cyclopean structures & II 341

Cyclops II 70, 345n
Daksha & II 275-6
Dānavas, Daityas, or I 415; II 31, 183, 192, 336, 501
  -demon, Vaiśvānara (Dānava) II 381
  devs or, hid jewels & metals II 396
  disappeared before Moses II 755
  Druids not Cyclopes or II 343, 754
  dwarfs &, in Africa II 754
  of Eocene, Miocene II 340
  evidence of II 154, 277-88, 347, 755
  Field of, France, bones at II 277
  footprints in Carson [Nevada] II 755
  frost, in *Eddas* II 386
  Genesis on II 154, 236, 284
  Geryon or Hillus II 278
  gibborīm of Bible I 415; II 70, 279, 340
  good & evil II 70, 222
  Gould on II 218-19
  Gyges, Briareus, Kottos II 775-6
  Ham, Shem, Japhet not II 343n
  heroes or II 369
  hidden meaning of I 114
  Job refers to, (*IU*) II 496
  legends of, not baseless II 410
  man a pre-Tertiary II 9
  man mated w II 331
  man now diminutive II 348
  Medusa II 70
  modern, cited II 277, 293n
  monsters &, biblical II 194-5
  nephīlīm of Bible II 755
  Noah was a II 265
  Orion, son of Ephialtes II 278
  perished w Atlantis II 350, 753
  Philostratus on II 278
  preceded us pigmies II 194
  precosmic titanic forces II 99
  Purānic, called devils I 415
  Quinames are II 276n
  Rāhu a II 381
  rākshasas of Lankā II 70
  Rephaīm Biblical I 345; II 279, 496
  second, 3rd, 4th round I 188, 190
  serpents &, demons (Clement) II 280 &n
  Sinhalese &, of Lankā II 407-8
  skeletons at Carthage II 278
  skeletons, none found in dolmens II 753
  sorcery of, no myth II 774
  Theophrastus [Theopompus] on Atlantean II 760
  Thera, found on II 278-9
  three polar, or continents II 776
  Titans based on fact of II 154

Titan was Orphic II 70
tombs of II 752
various I 114; II 336, 749, 754-6, 774-5
Vīrabhadara the terrible II 68
written language of II 346n
yellow-faced II 425
Ymir (Norse) I 367, 427; II 97, 99
Zeus used, against gods II 776
Gibbon
Dryopithecus compared w II 733
low development of II 678, 681-2n
Gibborīm (Heb). *See also* Giants
Atlantean giants II 279
became 5th race Kabirim II 273-4
biblical giants I 415; II 70, 279, 340
mighty men of renown II 273-4
relation of, to π I 114
various equivalents of I 114
Gibbs, Josiah W.
—— [*A Manual Heb. & Eng. Lexicon*]
Jehovah pronounced Ye-hou-vih II 129
Gibraltar, Straits of
once land II 8, 740, 750, 793
Gigantes, Clement transl *serpentes* II 279-80
Gigantibus, De. See Philo Judaeus
Gildas, St, Bishop of, & Stonehenge II 342
Gilgamesh. *See* Izdubar (G. Smith's transl)
Gill, Charles, "Intro to Book of Enoch"
plagiarism fr *Bk of Enoch* II 482
Gill-clefts
in human foetus, fishes II 683-5 &nn
Gimil, Gimle (Scand) 7th globe II 100
Gin-Hoang. *See* T'ien-hoang
Ginnungagap (Scand). *See also* Chaos
All-Father dwelt in I 427
germ of universe in I 367
Ginsburg, Christian D., *The Kabbalah . . .*
on origin of Kabbala II 284
Giraldus Cambrensis, *Itinerarium . . .*
moving Stone of Mona II 345
Gizeh. *See* Great Pyramid of
Glacial Epochs, Periods I 651
Atlanteans emigrated prior to II 740 &n
axis disturbance causes II 274
black, brown races in pre- II 695
date of last II 778-9n
deluges &, numerous II 141
European man witnessed last II 750n
first, date of II 144, 147, 686, 695
Hunt, Belt, Cross, Stockwell on II 141,
778-9 &n
man existed during II 254, 677-8, 751

Paleolithic man & II 740n
"Sea of Knowledge" & last II 502-3
Tertiary, called age of pygmies II 715n
Glacial Waters
divided Asia fr *root*-continent II 401
Gladstone, Wm. E. II 254, 383, 450
disputes w Ingersoll II 767
tries to reconcile *Genesis* & science II 252n
—— "Dawn of Creation . . ." II 252n
—— "The Greater Gods . . ."
Apollo appeared 4 & 6 times II 774
misjudges Homer II 766-7
on the qualities of Apollo II 770
—— "Proem to Genesis . . ." II 252n
Gland. *See* Pineal Gland
Glass
found in extinct Asian city I xxxiii
stained & malleable, of ancients II 430
Glasses, Bacon discovered I 581-2n
Globe(s). *See also* Earth, Earth Chain, Planetary Chain
atmosphere of, maruts, ākāśa II 615
in coadunition, etc I 166
consciousness on II 701, 702n
death of, 7th round I 159, 172-3
dying & transfer of energy I 155-6, 159
each, has its own builders I 233
early stages of I 74; II 112n
elements & rounds I 252n
elohīm formed I 239
entities, "animals" I 154
every sidereal body has seven I 158-9
every sidereal, called "Dragon's head" II 505
inhabited, innumerable I 164
karshvars or II 607 &n, 758-9
Kings of Edom & seven II 705
life on, in 7 rounds I 159
lowest, only visible I 152-3, 163 &n
man-bearing, of planets II 699
Mars-Mercury confusion & I 163-7
men in next reimbodiment of I 309
mouth & lungs of I 144
phoenix symbol & 49 cycles on II 617
principles of man & I 153-4
Purānas' lokas & dvīpas II 322
rebirth of I 173; II 703
rebuilt fr old material I 199
rounds &, stages of evolution II 256
seven, & sons of Agnīdhra II 320
sevenfold nights & days of II 756-60
seven, in Hindu literature I 112, 250n
seven material transformations I 205-6n
seven, on 4 lower planes I 152-60
seven worlds of māyā or I 238

six, above Earth I 152, 163-4; II 384-5n, 607n, 608
start as a nebula I 22
stellar spirits genii of I 198
three higher, (Norse) II 100
"wheels" or I 116-17, 199
winged I 126, 365; II 552
world bibles refer to II 703
Globe A (Earth chain)
Gebūrāh (Kabbala) or I 200
man prototype on, 1st round I 175n
rebirth of monads on I 173
seventh round of, & pralaya I 172
Vaivasvata &, 1st round II 146-7
Vorubarshti (Pers) or II 759
Globe B
Arzahi (Pers) II 759
Hōdh (Kabbala) I 200
Globe C
not Mars I 163-7
Tradadhafshu (Pers) II 759
Yesōdh (Kabbala) I 200
Globe D. *See also* Earth
age of, (science) II 694-9
ape-like forms fr 3rd round I 180-1
astral humanity on II 112n
axis disturbances & II 330
born under Moon & Saturn II 29
casts off skins each round II 47
cataclysms of II 138 &n, 149, 329-31
convulsed 4 times since 1st race II 138, 776
descending arc ends on I 166; II 180
face of, changed repeatedly II 330
five continents of II 6-8
fourth in chain I 182, 192, 205; II 22, 180
Hades or hell is II 98, 234
has altered II 535
hot breath of Sun & I 205
incrusted long before man II 248
in its kāma-rūpic state I 260
Jambu-dvīpa II 320, 326
likened to woman's body II 400-1 &nn
lowest globe I 166; II 180
Malkūth (Chald Kab) I 200
man evolves pari passu w II 248, 250, 329
man on, 1st round, 1st race I 188
most gross mid-4th round II 250
no sister-globe on this plane I 182
plants in, before creation II 112n
Qaniratha (Pers) II 759
sedimentation on II 710, 715n
seven divisions, races of II 2, 35n, 77, 249
seven races evolving on II 1-4, 29, 77, 249
seven renewals of II 397n, 617-18

several "creations" on II 53
six invisible companions of II 320
spirit & guardian of II 22
Vaivasvata seed of life on II 146-7
Globe E
Netsah (Kabbala) or I 200
not Mercury I 163-70
Vidadhafshu (Pers) II 759
Globe F
Savahi (Pers) II 759
Tiphereth (Kabbala) I 200
Globe G
Chesed [Hesedh] (Kabbala) I 200
Globe Z I 163, 168
Voru-Zarshti (Pers) II 759
Globigerina, & Cretaceous species II 257
Glyph(s) I 349-58; II 356-65. *See also* Symbols
ancient use of I 66
degeneration of Sun- II 584
dog-headed ape I 388
esoteric cosmogony in I 272
identical in Egypt, America I 323
lotus, egg, etc I 362-5
misinterpreted I 406
tree & serpent I 406
Gñana. *See* Jñāna
Gñana-Devas. *See* Jñānadevas
Gnatha. *See* Jñātā
Gnomes
earthly, money, wealth I 294n
fire elementals & II 427
influence on some people I 294n
sylphs, etc derided today I 606
Gnosis (Gk) knowledge, wisdom I 72n
echo of archaic doctrine I 449
Gnostic, rested on square II 573
of John & Jesus II 566
Mahat 1st-born of jñāna or I 62
serpent mystery the highest I 405
seventh principle of, hidden I 278
Gnostic(s). *See also* Aeons, Gnostic Gems, Marcus, Pistis Sophia, Valentinus
Abraxas of II 474, 565
Aeons of, & *Anugītā* II 569n
aim of, schools & Buddhism I 668
Alexandrian, & initiation I 416
Catholic &, astrolatry I 402
Chnouphis is Christos of II 210n
Christian, edited *Zohar* I 214
Christos of I 132n; II 540
Church mutilated, systems I 350
creators were lower gods II 61, 96
dragon was Son w II 355
five sacred words of II 580

genii of 7 planets II 538 &n
gnosis of, rested on square II 573
Horus the, Christ II 587
iconography of, fr India II 565
identified Jehovah w evil I 197
knew mystery language II 574
light-shadow, good-evil II 214
mystery gods of II 539-42
Nazarenes were II 96n
numerical value of Christ I 322
Ophios-Christos as Logos of I 364
Ophites were Egyptian II 386
opinion of Jewish God II 95n, 96, 235
Peratae- II 356, 577-8
philosophy of I 197
phoenix, man-lion of II 564 &n
planetary origin of monad I 577
rounds, races, figures II 618
Satan angel of matter II 235
savior, Agathodaemon II 458
sects founded by initiates II 389
serpent I 73, 404, 410, 472; II 208, 210, 280n, 386-7
seven angels of II 611
seven arts of enchantment II 641
seven heavens II 563
seven vowels of I 73, 410-11; II 280n, 458, 563, 565
Sophia of, Holy Ghost I 72n
tau or procrustean bed of II 573
teachings faithful to SD II 96n
tetrad, etc I 351, 448
various Adams of II 458
Verbum or Son dual II 515
view of God, archangels I 198
wisdom of Hindu origin II 570
Gnostic Gems II 604
allegorical monsters on II 565
Horus depicted on II 474
pre-Christian II 564n
serpent symbol I 472-3; II 210
seven-rayed Iao I 227n; II 541
symbols fr India II 565, 570
symbols of 5 races II 458
Gnosticism, Sects, Schools
based on correct symbolism II 389
Christian, & Neo-Platonism I xliv
influence of Buddhistic theosophy I 668
Jehovah personated Christ in II 508
Gnostics and Their Remains. See King, C. W.
Gnyana. *See* Jñāna
Goat(s)
androgyne, of Mendes I 253
in army of crusaders I 357

Azāzēl or I 441-2n; II 389n
Capricornus & II 578-9
-men II 54, 63
of Mendes or astral light I 253
sacrificed to Durgā Kālī II 579
scape-, of Israel II 389n, 510
symbol of, among Gnostics II 386
witches' sabbath, Pan & II 510
Gobelin, De. *See* Court de Gebelin
Gobi Desert II 324. *See also* Shamo
deluge changed, into a sea II 5
extension of ancient continent II 327
formed in last glacial period II 502-3
future continents & II 404n
immortal man found refuge in II 372
island in, now an oasis II 220, 503
Kalki avatāra & region of II 416n
Sahara & II 405
Śambhala island in II 319
"Sea of Knowledge" once in II 502-3
statues discovered in II 331
God. *See also* Anthropomorphic, Deity, Personal Gods, Unknowable
Advaitis view of I 636; II 598
altar to the Unknown I 327
anthropomorphic, denied I 499n
anthro, w 4-letter names II 601-2
author of nature I 412
Buddhists have no personal I 635
Buddhist, Vedantin on I 636
came to West fr phallic source I 346-7
cause of mind, spirit, light (*Pymander*) I 285
Christian & Hindu II 472
Christian, & Sun, Jupiter II 540
Christian, not the Unknowable I 391
collective being II 239
commands another god (*Gen*) I 336-7
consuming fire I 121-2; II 114
covenant w Abraham II 508
"created in man's image" rejected I xx
creative, of Jews II 543-4
Devil & I 235-6, 412-18, 421
"dwelleth not in temples" I 327
elohīm or I 139; II 488
evolution of the, -idea I 326
extracosmic, & intelligent forces I 529
extracosmic, fatal I 529, 569; II 41
Father in *Pymander* I 74n
finite, imperfect, rejected I 533
form of, shall not be limited II 279n
geometrizes (Plato) II 39, 41
Gnostic view of, & archangels I 198
God of Jews is not, (Basilides) I 350
good & evil fr I 412

gravity is, matter its prophet I 492
heavenly bodies temples of I 578
fr Hebrew yōdh, yod I 347
of human dogma rejected I 9
a hypothesis (Laplace) I 498, 576n
inner II 272
is a circle (Pascal, Cusa) II 545
is light, Satan shadow of II 510
is man in Heaven (Lévi) II 584
is number w motion (Balzac) I 67
Israelite's, a tribal god II 507-8
Jesus rebelled against commandments of
    I 576-7
Jewish-Christian, lunar symbol I 391
Jewish, genius of Moon & Saturn II 540
Jupiter &, hurled thunderbolts I 467
"Lead us not . . ." addressed to I 414
life & motion of universe I 3n
Logos is the, of *Genesis* II 1-2n
Lord, agent provocateur II 387
Lord, of *Genesis* 2 is elohīm II 1-2n
manifested, in nature I 292
man is, on Earth (Lévi) II 584
Maqōm rabbinical symbol of II 612
of Moses a temporary substitute I 374
-names key to Bible II 536-45
names of, & Michael II 480
names of, in India II 114
in nature acceptable I xx
never used for 1st Principle II 555
Newton's I 492, 498
no being, no thing I 352
not fr word good I 347
one w nature I 412
orthodox, shaped by man I 9
passive, becomes active I 281n
predestination of, (Calvinism) II 304n
St Michael & II 478-9
Satan &, anthropomorphized I 412; II 507
Satan, Devil, son of, [*Job*] I 412, 414; II 376,
    378, 477, 489
Satan, in manifested world II 235, 515
Satan scapegoat for Christian I 412
Semite, tempts, curses man I 383
seven-lettered, & Jehovah I 410
shadow of man's imagination I 635
should not be given form (Lévi) II 536
in space, Christ, Logos II 483
spirit of, aspired II 576
"such is the will of" II 304
Sun the highest II 361
two hypotheses re, of Bible II 472-3
of the Unknown Darkness I 425
weaving garment of, (Goethe) I 83

who curses not infinite II 384n
Zeus a jealous II 419-20
God and His Book. See Ross, W. S.
Goddess(es). *See also* Mother, Virgins
connected w "M" & water II 65
demiurgical I 399
Diana-Luna I 395
lunar gods & I 387-8, 396, 399-400, 403;
    II 23, 31-2
Moon & I 228-9 &nn, 264; II 76
nemesis made into a II 305n
of the 7 stars II 547
Godefroy, N. P., *La Cosmogonie de la révélation*
prefers Kabbala over science I 506
rotation & centrifugal force I 499
Godh (Sax), Gott, & God I 347
Godhead
Central Sun & the II 240n
union of 3 persons in I 381, 668-9
God-Idea
cannot be divorced fr evil I 413
evolution of I 326-7
God in History. See Bunsen, C. C. J.
God of Wine II 363
Gods. *See also* Angels, Chohans, Deities,
    Devas, Dhyāni-Chohans, Divine Kings,
    Fall, Kumāras, Pantheism, Polytheism,
    Rectors, Suras, War in Heaven
addressed in own language I 464
agents of universal harmony II 99
ancient, fr Lemuria II 769
ancients called planets I 2n
Aristotle rejected I 493
arūpa II 318n
asuras opposing II 78
autogeneration of I 398
avatāras are fallen II 483-4
become no-gods or asuras II 237, 248
believers & non-believers in I 611
beneficent, maleficent II 477
bodies of I 489
bore, nursed, instructed man II 358
Brahma radiates I 447
bright shadow of, (3rd race) II 268
circle of necessity of II 303
confusion in genealogies of II 42
conscious spiritual egos I 632
cosmic, cannot reach Alaya I 48
cosmic, fr 4 higher principles I 292
"created the Heavens & the Earth" I 374
created, would be unjust I 221-2
creative, often degraded II 471-2
creators were the lowest II 96
defeat daityas by ruse I 422-3

defeated by daityas I 419
demigods, mortals & II 368
departed (became invisible) II 273
descend, ascend (zodiac) II 357
die — hence māyāvic I 54n
disappear in mahā-pralaya I 373n
dragons or II 355
dynasties of, recorded II 367-72
on Earth I 369
elements, elementals, & I 461; II 273
enlighten 3rd race adepts II 211
evolved protoplasmic human forms I 282
fall into generation II 231n, 232
fire II 34, 381, 578
first, androgynous II 130
Fohat objectivized thought of I 111
forsake Earth II 358, 785-6
four-armed Hindu II 294-5
four classes of II 240-1
"fr, to men, fr worlds to atoms" I 604
genii &, within the Plenum I 569
genii fulfill will of I 294-5
God vs, discussed I 492-3n
Hebrew tribal, worship of II 274
Hermetic, genii, daimones, theoi I 288n
heroes &, of antiquity II 172
human once I 106; II 322
husbands of their mothers I 91 &n
incarnated in early men II 373n, 483
incarnate in new manvantara II 232
incarnation of solar I 656
inmetalization & I 188
intelligent architects I 632
interference of I 498
jealousy of II 283
Lords (pl) in *Genesis* II 81
lotus symbol & Egyptian solar I 385
male, became Sun-gods II 43
"man has become as one of us" I 493n
manifested theogony starts w I 434
man-like, of Hindus II 377
man will be freed fr false II 420
many, (St Chrysostom) I 465n
many, (St Paul) I 465
men &, fr one source II 24
minor, & God-principle I 465n
minor, carry symbols of higher II 545-6
minor, regents of zodiacal signs II 358
-monads-atoms discussed I 610-34
names of, change each age II 90
national, tribal I 421-2
no speculation beyond manifested II 42
noumena of phenomena II 517-18
numbers & II 575 &n

orders of I 438-9, 672
of our fathers, our devils II 32n
patriarchs & I 349
perish not, but are reabsorbed I 36n
planetary, source & head of II 608
plurality of worlds & many II 538
prayer to, re elements I 465-6
primitive names connected w fire- II 114
principles of, are monads & atoms I 633
proceed fr First Cause II 108
produced in Primary Creation I 446-7
reborn in various kalpas II 248
refused to create I 192; II 92-3
regents of worlds, rishis or I 99
river-, sons of the ocean I 345n
sacrificing to, (*Exodus*) I 402n
Satan eldest of II 234
secondary, are nature forces II 78-9n
septiform pantheon of II 765
seven Babylonian II 5
seven, descend each new cycle I 434-5
seven great, of Egypt I 127
seven great, or Dioscuri II 361
seven, of Chald Genesis II 2, 35, 61-2
seven primeval II 514
sidereal, & initiates I 653
solar & lunar II 427
strife betw, & the Raumas II 182
Sun-, discussed II 379, 381-3
Syrian, 14 classes of I 435-6
temples of God I 578
theogony of creative I 363, 424-45
theos, theoi or, (Plato) I 2n; II 545
"Thou shalt not revile the" I 492-3n; II 477
330 million, in India I 71n; II 90
three classes of, & 4th II 241
Titans &, rebelled against Zeus II 776
twelve great, Apostles, zodiac I 400
walked the Earth II 273
war betw asuras & II 63, 384n
were once men II 255 &n
"ye shall be as" II 279
Goethe, Johann Wolfgang von
    archetype of, discussed II 737
    believed many worlds inhabited II 706
—— *Faust*
    weaving the garment of God I 83
Gogard (Avestan Tree of Life) II 97
Golādhyāya of the *Siddhānta-śiromaṇi*
    dvīpas, lokas, etc II 321
Golcar, rocking stones of II 344
Gold I 364, 409; II 271, 520
Golden Age. *See also* Satya-Yuga
    Astraea descends to renew II 785

dawn of new root-race II 785
early man started in a II 722
every race, sub-race has II 198
first root-race & II 121, 270, 271
Plato's II 264, 372-3
of Saturn (Kronos) II 372-3, 421, 777
of 6th sub-race II 147n
of 3rd race II 520n
when gods walked the Earth II 273
Yggdrasil lasts till end of II 520
Golden Apples
　Apollodorus on legend of II 770n
Golden Calf
　higher classes worship I 578
　of our age I 675
Golden Cow (India). *See* Cow
Golden Egg(s). *See also* Brahmā, Eggs,
　Hiraṇyagarbha, Mundane Egg
　Absolute All could not evolve I 8
　Aryan birds that lay II 122
　Kalahansa or Brahm lays I 359
　seed becomes I 333, 350
　surrounded by elements I 65-6
　symbol of manifest kosmos I 556
Golden-Winged Cup (the Sun)
　Phoibos-Apollo arises out of II 383
Goldstücker, Theodor, *Sanskrit Dictionary*
　on arani II 524 &n
Golgotha, of life I 268
Goliath [I *Sam* 17:4] II 336
Gonpa (Tib) lamasery
　cave libraries in I xxiv
Good, J. M., on monad I 570
Good, the Supreme, (Plato) II 554. *See also*
　Agathon
Good & Evil I 343; II 25-6, 60, 303. *See also* Evil
　Adam, Eve ignorant of II 95n
　in all manifested worlds II 214
　aspects of the same Unity I 235-6
　cannot exist alone I 73, 413-14; II 96, 162,
　　214, 477
　Christ & Satan as forces of II 497
　Church's extreme views of I 235-6
　discussed I 413-14; II 162, 303-5, 488
　Divine contains both I 411-12
　karma & II 477, 510n
　knowledge of II 81, 124, 210, 214-15, 279,
　　292-3
　light & darkness as I 412
　man is both II 515
　mankind determines, (karma) II 512
　no such thing as, per se II 162
　one completes the other II 214
　origins of concept of II 412

Rāmāyaṇa struggle betw II 495
seven gradations of II 212
Tree of Knowledge of I 247; II 4, 124,
　214-15, 293, 626n
twin brothers I 412; II 96
Goose. *See also* Duck, Kalahaṅsa, Swan
　Egyptian sacred bird I 353
　lays golden eggs II 122
　symbol of I 79-81, 355, 357-8
Gordon-Cumming, accused of lying II 440
[Gore, Nīlakaṇṭha], *Rational Refutation . . .*
　on ākāśa I 296n
Gorgon, sparks on head of I 338n
Gorilla. *See also* Anthropoid, Ape
　brain capacity of II 682n
　Dryopithecus compared w II 733
　every bone of, varies fr human II 315n, 681,
　　687
　evolved fr lower anthropoids II 193
　fr 4th round man & extinct mammal II 683
　man's likeness to II 287, 677-8
　not missing link II 676
　will become extinct II 263
Gorresio, Abbé G., Pulastya & Cain I 415
Gospels I 570n
　borrow fr *Book of Enoch* II 531
　four angels, elements & I 127n; II 114 &n
　four, only (Irenaeus) I 42
　little ones (initiates) in II 504
　meanings perverted in I 226
　production of Church II 230
Gosse, P. H., *The Romance of Natural History*
　charges against Madame Merian II 440 &n
Gothic Deities (7) II 603
Gotras, caste-races of Brahmans II 502
Gott (Ger) God
　four-letter German God II 602
　fr Hebrew yōdh I 347
Gougenot des Mousseaux, H. R.
　makes Epaphos into Christ II 414-15
—— *Dieu et les Dieux*
　prophetic or mad stones II 345-6
—— *Les Hauts Phénomènes . . .*
　on Eastern phallicism (*IU* q) II 85
　q Father Felix I 670
Gould, Charles, *Mythical Monsters*
　antiquity of civilization II 311-12
　Chinese dragon explained II 280n
　Croll on geologic eras II 9, 695, 715n
　Darwin on Cambrian period II 688n
　Darwin on Earth's crust II 10n
　dragon & unicorn factual II 217-19
　man on submerged Atlantis II 219, 429
　men w 2 faces II 302

monsters & men II 55, 218, 293n
more geologic time needed II 688n
new discoveries suspect II 440-1
period betw Paleo- & Neolithic man II 715n
on Shan-Hai-King II 54n
tropical vegetation in Greenland II 11
Wallace on Lemuria II 7-8
Governors, 7, of Hermetics I 440, 480, 601;
     II 2n, 97, 103, 236n, 267
Grace, materialization of Divine II 498
Grain(s), brought fr other spheres II 373-4
Grāmaṇīs, yakshas or minor gods II 211
Grandezze del Archangelo . . . *See* Marangoni
Grandidier, Ludwig II 668
Grass, & animals interdependent II 290n, 373
Grasshoppers
     Greeks called, winged serpents II 205
     Jews were as, to giants II 336, 340
     Moses permitted eating of I 80n
Gratiolet, Pierre
     on brain of apes, men II 682
     fallacies of, re man & ape II 681
Gravity, Gravitation. *See also* Attraction
     attraction & repulsion I 513, 604
     bodies not under, (Airy) I 584n
     cause of rotation, revolutions I 501
     causes of I 513, 529-30
     dual force, cosmic magnetism I 497
     as force in open space I 511
     hydrodynamical theories of I 486
     is God, matter its prophet I 492
     Kepler on I 497-9
     merely a word (de Maistre) I 604
     Newton on I 478-9, 490-1
     rotary motion &, theories I 504-6
     secondary effect of other causes I 484, 490
     tails of comets & I 504
Gray, Dr Asa, on Asian land bridge II 783
Great Age I 36, 63, 372; II 308n. *See also* Mahā-
     yuga
Great Bear (constellation). *See also* Ursa Major
     called Rikshā, Chitra-Śikhandinas I 227n,
         453; II 631
     circle of, & ankh-cross II 547
     Mother of Time (Egy) I 227n
     seven builders, rishis of I 213 &n, 357n
     seven stars of, (Massey) I 227n, 407; II 631
     seven stars (rishis) of I 198, 227n, 453; II 89n,
         318n, 488-9, 549, 550, 768
Great Beast, & number 666 I 655n
Great Book of the Mysteries
     seven lords create 7 men II 212
Great Breath I 2, 11, 12n, 147, 496. *See also*
     Breath, Divine Breath, Manvantara

aspect of the One Reality I 14
becomes Divine Breath I 43
Christos anointed by II 23
Day of Brahmā II 6 &n
differentiates in 1st atom I 455
digs 7 holes in laya I 147
eternal ceaseless motion I 2, 43, 282, 455
Father, Mother, Son & I 41
is, yet is not I 43
as the One Life I 226n
outbreathing, inbreathing I 4, 43
precosmic ideation I 15
reentering, is paranirvāna I 266
root of individual consciousness I 15
smaller breaths & I 496
Great Britain, will sink II 266
Great Day, end of 7th round II 491
Great Deep. *See also* Abyss, Chaos, Mother,
     Waters
     Āditi, Chaos, Shekhīnāh or I 460; II 527
     chaos or female power in nature I 431
     water is I 460; II 65
Great Dragon or Deluge
     respects serpents of wisdom II 351, 355
     waters of the flood or I 460
"Greater Gods of Olympos." *See* Gladstone
Great Extreme (of Confucius)
     Boundless Age or I 356
     Parabrahman or II 553
     short & suggestive cosmogony I 440
     symbol used by Taoists, others II 554
Great Four (karmic gods)
     Four Mahārājas or II 427 &n
Great Mother I 43, 81, 291, 434; II 83, 384n,
     416, 462, 503
Great Pyramid (Cheops, Gizeh). *See also*
     Pyramids
     built at beginning of sidereal year I 435
     built by Atlanteans II 429
     built on decimal system I 362
     "coincidences" in I 314-15
     date of I 435; II 429, 431-2, 435-6, 750
     Holy of Holies & I 264; II 462
     initiation & I 314, 317-18n; II 462, 558
     measurements of I 115n, 313-15; II 465-6
     sarcophagus called corn bin I 317n
     sound could raise the I 555
Great Pyramid. See Wake, C. S.
Great Range II 34. *See also* Himālaya
"Great Sacrifice" I 207-12
     Wondrous Being or I 207-8
Great Serpent Mound (Ohio)
     not a tomb II 752-3 &n
     symbol of eternal time II 756

Great War [*Mahābhārata*]
　date of I 369n
　historical I 397
Great Year. *See* Sidereal Year
Greece
　devas class symb as Prometheus in II 95
　giants of II 336, 344n
　Hyperborean & S Apollo of II 769
　Peruvians & Pelasgians of II 745
　poetry of, & India II 450
　Python, falling demon in II 486
Greek(s)
　Achaean, & tetrad II 601
　adepts preserved Dendera zodiac II 432
　Adonis of the II 44, 769n
　ancient, fr Atlanto-Aryans II 436, 743
　anthropomorphism of I 326
　architecture & Vitruvius I 209n
　ash tree of II 519-20
　Atala, Atlantis & II 408
　Atlantean civ greater than II 429-30
　atomic concepts fr Egypt I 117
　before becoming Hellenes II 367
　butterfly symbol of mind-soul w II 292
　canons of proportion I 208n
　Christian &, religions (Müller) II 764n
　chronology of, fr India II 620
　claimed descent fr Saturn II 768
　confused Thessaly w Atlantis II 776
　could not have devised zodiac I 648
　cross described II 547
　daimons II 508
　divine dynasties of II 316
　Eden (hēdonē) in, is voluptuousness II 203
　egg symbol among I 359-60
　Egy sages gave Solon hist of II 743 &n
　Enoch called Enoichion by II 529
　forefathers of, destroyed II 749
　in fourth century BC were moderns II 286
　gibborīm became Titans w II 273-4
　greeted morning star II 759
　Helios Sun-god of II 540
　Hermes of, Egypt & II 137, 367
　Hindu zodiac fr, (Weber) I 647-8; II 225, 332
　Indian arts & sciences not fr II 225
　initiated, view of moon I 396
　knew mystery language II 574
　knew of polar day & night II 773
　knew of 2nd continent II 7, 11-12
　Michael same as Mercury of II 481
　millennium, length of II 395
　myths based on truth II 236, 271, 410, 769
　naturalized their gods II 770n
　no, ideas came fr Egy (Renouf) I 402
　northern origin of, gods II 769
　number 7 of, fr Hindus II 408, 612
　"Old Time" of, w scythe I 459
　origins in Miocene (Donnelly) II 746n
　Poseidon-Neptune of, & dolphin II 577
　rites became phallic II 362
　sacrifice to the winds I 466
　Sanskrit once called, dialect I xxxviii
　seven vowels of, & 7 races II 458
　spirituality & intuition of II 158
　system of sacred measures & Jewish I 312-13
　taught succession of worlds II 756
　taught 3 aspects of universe I 278
　tragedy, Aeschylus father of II 419
　world destruction & renewal II 784
　worshiped stones (Pausanias) II 341
　zodiac, age of, (Volney) II 436 &n
　zodiac fr India via Chaldea I 658
Greek Church
　filioque dogma & II 635
　inner meaning of cross in II 562
　Latin Church &, idolatrous II 279
　powers of darkness & angels in I 295
　symbol of marriage ceremony I 614-15n
　wind translated *spirit* in *John* of I 226
"Greek Kabbala," of Valentinus I 310
Greek Lexicon. See Parkhurst, J.
Greek Poet (untraced)
　seven letters of deity II 603
Greeley, Horace
　amiable infidels of society I xxii
Greenland
　coast sinking II 787n
　part of horseshoe continent II 326, 402
　part of northern continent II 423-4, 775
　part of Śveta-dvīpa II 327
　remnant of 2nd cont II 11-12, 138, 402
　subtropical in Miocene II 11-12, 677, 726
Gregor, Dr H., denies giants II 277
Gregorie [John Gregory], *Notes & Observations*
　Adam's body kept above ground II 467
Gregory, Pope II 587
Gregory Nazianzen, Saint, "visible things are
　　but the shadow" II 268
Griechische Götterlehr. See Welcker, F. G.
Griffin(s) (Persian), same as cherubim I 364n
Gṛihastha (Skt) householder
　laws of, & married life I 210
　priest of exoteric ritual II 499
　those failing to attend home fires II 77-8
　until begetting a son II 411n
Grimm, Jacob, *Deutsche Mythologie*
　Flood, reanimation of race II 270
Grimm's Law, Odin & Buddha I xxix

Grip, Master Mason's, & decad II 581
Gross, J. B., *Heathen Religion*
  preformation of lotus I 57 &n
Grote, George, *A History of Greece*
  Atlantis a myth, mirage II 760
  Hesiod & Homer illiterate II 440
Grotto of Zarathustra I 464
Grove, Sir William
  ideas of, now accepted I 499
  put to death the imponderables I 486
  truth should be aim of science I 509
—— *Address to British Association*
  solar system gradually changing I 102
—— *On the Correlation . . .*
  ancients saw spirit in phenomena I 465
  defines light I 483-4
  ether as a fluid criticized by I 491
  physical phenomena & motion I 496-7 &n
  speaks of nature's forces I 492
  storing up light I 508-9
  Sun's gaseous matter & heat I 102
  ultimate generating power I 469
  we are ignorant of causes I 465
Grypes, & Arimaspi fr Aeschylus II 417
Guanches (Canary Islanders)
  American tribes & II 740, 792
  Atlantean descent of II 791
  Cro-Magnon & II 678 &n, 740, 790n, 791
Guardian(s)
  & spirit(s), angel(s) I 104, 128n, 220, 222n,
    288n, 575-6, 644, 663; II 31, 477, 478
Gubernatis, A. de I 304
Guebra, Kabiri, fire worshipers II 363n
Guf [Gūph] (Heb), physical body II 633
  united w lower nephesh II 457
Guha (Skt) the mysterious one
  Kārttikeya is the II 549
  Kumāra, or Kārttikeya II 382
Guhya (Skt), parama, sarvātman or I 90
Guhya-Vidyā (Skt) secret knowledge
  knowledge of mantras, etc I 169
Guide . . . Musée de Boulaq. See Maspero
Guide for the Perplexed. See Maimonides
Guigniaut, J. D. (transl Creuzer's *Symbolik*)
—— *Religions de l'antiquité . . .*
  Dionysus Chthonios & oracles I 463
  doctrine of the spirits II 369-70

psychic paganism I 461
Rig-Veda the most sublime II 484
  theogonies, zodiac I 652
  wisdom descends II 367
Guinness, H. Grattan
—— *The Approaching End of the Age . . .*
  q Laycock on periodicity II 622-3n
  on sevens & forms, colors, sound II 623-4
Gujerāt, flight of Parsis to II 323
Gulf of Mexico
  once linked to Sahara II 424
Gulf of Tartary II 327
Gull, Dr, attacks vitality theory I 540
Gultweig [Gullveig] (Norse)
  thrice purified gold or manas II 520
Guna(m,s) (Skt)
  agents of action & I 535
  seven, composed of trigunas I 348
  three, aspects of prakriti II 635
  triple aspect of ahamkāra I 335n
Gupta Cave
  storehouse of Brahmanical works I xxx
Gupta-Vidyā (Skt). *See also* Secret Doctrine
  diagram of planes & worlds of I 200
  Tārā & initiate's powers of II 498
  20th-century disciple will prove I xxxviii
Gupta-Vidyā Sūtra
  fructifying of Universal Mother I 356
Guru(s) (Skt) II 32n, 45n, 109, 626n
  above sex II 458
  ātma-buddhi is man's II 113
  Brihaspati, of gods II 498-9
  of the daityas II 31
  Nārada surpasses Garga's II 49
  teach under banyan tree II 215
Gurudeva(s) (Skt)
  Catechism & I 120
  dhyānis, āngirasas or II 605n
Gyalugpas. *See* Gelukpas
Gyan, Gnan [Jñāna] (Skt)
  King of the Peris II 394
Gyges
  giant described by Hesiod II 775-6 &n
  stands for polar continent II 776
Gyi (knowledge) I 279
Gyu(t) (Tib), division of the *Kanjur* I 52n

H

Hā (Skt), to abandon II 182n
Habel. *See* Ḥebel
Ḥabir-on, or Kabir town II 541
Haches (Fr) rude stone hatchets
  Neolithic, Paleolithic II 722
  prehistoric, resemble modern II 716-17
Hachoser. *See* Ha-ḥozer
H'adam-[h] II 467
Hades II 415, 523. *See also* Hell, Tartarus
  Axiokersos, Pluto or II 362
  cave of initiation II 237n
  cold realm of shades & II 774
  Hyperborean II 138
  Jesus guides souls to II 542
  limbo, kāma-loka or I 244; II 374n
  Mercury guides souls to II 364, 542
  our globe is, (Hinduism) II 234
  Prometheus sent to II 412
  Satan angel of, (Havas in tx) II 235
  spiritual ego descends into II 558
  Zeus wished to send Titans to II 776
Haeckel, Ernst
  crass materialism of II 651
  father of mythical Sozura II 656, 745n
  man-ape of Miocene a dream II 745n
  mixes theories w facts II 662-3
  monera of, criticized II 151
  moneron II 164-5n, 658-9, 685n
  occult science & II 348
  stupendous pretension of II 649-50
  terms coined by, spurious II 663n
  theosophists do not respect views of II 651
—— *Anthropogenie . . . [Evolution of Man]*
  fr Amphioxus to man II 663
  development of embryo II 659
  man fr Catarrhine apes II 665
  man's evolution II 190
—— "Cell Souls & Soul Cells." *See Pedigree of Man* (below)
—— *History of Creation [Natürliche . . .]*
  ape-like man absolutely unknown II 729
  ape-man, gorilla, orang II 317n
  development of embryo II 258-9
  five divisions of global history II 711
  human ancestral races II 656
—— *The Pedigree of Man*

ape-man or homo primigenius II 193n, 317n
atoms have sensation II 673
atrophied eyes in animals II 296n
Australian aborigines II 328, 779
Bathybius I 542; II 164n, 190, 650, 656, 670 &n, 674
"Cell-Souls & Soul-Cells" II 649, 650, 671n
civilization traced to ants, bees II 650
consciousness molecular II 650
critics of, ignorant men II 664
evolution of the eye II 295, 299n
geology & paleontology not exact sciences II 656
giant Pacific continent II 328
Lemuria & orig of man II 171, 327-8, 789
limits of knowledge II 673-4
man & ape II 87n, 164-5n, 264, 665, 668, 679-80
man & ape have common ancestor II 189
man fr Catarrhine ape II 264, 327, 663n
moneron II 164-5n, 658-9, 685n
natural forces working blindly II 652
origin of life II 164-5n
prosimiae II 668
q du Bois-Reymond II 656
soul organs & functions II 671n
S Asia not cradle of human race II 789
speech fr animal sounds II 661
vegetable phase of foetus II 685n
—— *Perigenesis of the Plastidule*
wave motion of particles II 671-2
—— "Present Position of Evolution" II 650, 670
—— "The Proofs of Evolution"
  embryo mirrors the race II 187 &n
—— *Quarterly Journal of Microscopical Science*
  q Haeckel re monera II 153n
Hāgār (Heb), the bond-woman II 76
Haggard, Sir H. Rider
—— *She*, quoted II 317n, 319
Ha-Ḥoser (Heb), reflected lights I 506
Ha Idra Zuta Kadisha. See Idrā Zūṭā
Haima (Skt) golden
  Hiranya or, egg (*VP*) I 360
Hajaschar. *See* Hayyāshār
Ha-Levi, Jehudah [Judah Halevi]

—— [*Kitab al-Khazarī*]
  calculation & weighing II 41, 234
  Kabbalistic number values II 40
Halévy, Joseph
—— [*Mélanges d'épigraphie* . . .]
  fallacy of Turanian mania II 203
Haliaetus Washingtonii
  Audubon's, doubted II 440
Haliburton, Thomas Chandler
  on listening to both sides II 794
Hall, A. W., *Scientific Arena* I 146n
Hall, FitzEdward (editor, *Vishṇu Purāṇa*)
  ādibhūta in *VP* I xix
  Brahmā caused creative potencies I 55
  defends Wilson I 453n
  heliocentricism in *VP* II 155
  Jagad-Yoni defined by I 46
  more able than Wilson II 89
  preferred *Orig. Skt. Texts* (Muir) I 453n
  q Vans Kennedy I 419n
—— *Rational Refutation* . . . (transl)
  on ākāśa I 296n
Hallam, Henry
—— *Intro. to the Literature of Europe* . . .
  man image of God & ape II 728
Halley, Dr Edmund
—— "An Account of several . . . Meteors . . ."
  recognized self-luminous matter I 590
Halliwell, James O.
—— [*Rambles in Western Cornwall* . . .]
  giant bones in Malabar tombs II 347
  megalithic remains II 342-3
Hall of Misery (Scand), or human life I 407
Hall of the Ancestors (Totmes [Thut-
  mose] III), fragment (cross) fr II 559
Ḥām (Heb)
  Arkite Titan (Faber) or myth II 343n
  Cainites & sons of II 146
  chaotic principle II 597n
  Jupiter as Adam & II 270
  Mizraim &, Kabiri II 393
  Nabatheans descend fr II 453
  parallels Chaldean story II 283-4n
  Roman Church links, w sorcery II 391
  seven brazen columns of II 612-13
  some Titans descend fr I 417
  stole 7 books fr ark II 612
  symbol of race that sinned II 397
  Votan descended fr II 380
Hamilton, Sir William
—— [*Lectures on Metaphysics*]
  definition of Absolute (Cusa) II 158n
  on the word "theory" II 665
Hamite(s), Hamitic

African sorcerer called II 343
Atlanteans prototypes of II 272
  "family race" II 147n
Hamlet II 306
Hammannunah. See Book of
Hammer of Creation. *See also* Swastika
  continual motion II 99
Haṃsa, Haṅsa (Skt). *See also* Kalahaṅsa
  bird of wisdom II 293
  interpretation of I 78-81
  Man-Swan, of later 3rd race II 131
  mountain range north of Meru I 79
  one caste [Dowson] I 79
  Swan of Life I 549
  term for Brahma I 20
Haṃsa-vāhana (Skt)
  Brahma (neuter) or I 20, 78, 80
Hamy, Jules T. E. II 744
  Cro-Magnon & Guanches II 678 &n, 790n
  flints human handiwork II 752n
  man dates fr Miocene II 714n
Handbook of Hist. of Philosophy. See
  Schwegler, A.
Ḥanina, Rabbi, thaumaturgist I xliii n
Hanneberg [Haneberg, Dr D. B. von]
  on *Bk of Enoch* II 532
Ḥanoch, Hanokh, Henoch II 361, 391n, 529.
  See also Enoch
  exploits of I 366
  gave astronomy to Noah II 532
  initiator, teacher, Enos II 529n
  male, female beings & II 469
  son of Seth II 469
Hansa. *See* Haṃsa
Hanumān (Skt)
  advisor to Rāma I 388
  genealogy of I 190
  monkey-god of *Rāmāyaṇa* II 680
  reconnoitered Lankā II 163
Haōma (Avestan). *See also* Soma
  beautiful, golden II 517
  church made, forbidden II 98
  fruit of Tree of Life II 97
  white, or gaokerena II 517
Hapsburgs, Habsburgs, motto of II 458
Hardenberg, F. von. *See* Novalis
Hardvār II 324
  Pass of, or Kapila's Pass II 571-2
Hardy, R. Spence, *The Legends and Theories* . . .
  on Buddhist Canon I xxvii &n
Hare, Robert
  phenomena of spiritualism I 520
Hari (Skt)
  Ādikrit or, sleeps I 371-2

born of Sambhūti II 89
destroyer, flame of time I 370
incidental or ideal cause I 372
male principle II 76n
one of the hypostases I 18, 286
Vishnu or I 286, 421
Harikeśa (Skt)
one of 7 mystic solar rays I 515n
Haris (Skt), class of gods II 90
Harivaṃśa
Agni & Lakshmī II 578
asuras doomed to incarnate II 93
Brahmā as a boar II 75
Daksha curses Nārada II 82
Kāma son of Lakshmī II 176
Kapila as son of Vitatha II 572
maruts II 613, 615
seven sons of Vasishta [II 146n]
Śukra imbibing smoke II 32
untrustworthy Fr transl of I 457-8n
Virājas & elder agnishvattas II 89
Harmony
absolute, only karmic decree I 643
contraries produce I 416
evils of life & I 644
gods agents of universal II 99
law of, depends on altruism II 302n
Logos source of I 433
music of the spheres & II 601
in nature & disturbances II 74
Naya or II 528
of numbers in nature II 622
Pan-pipe emblem of septenary II 581
betw 2 natures of man II 268
union, brotherhood & I 644
universal, & karmic law II 305, 420
Haroiri [Haroeris] (Egy). See Heru-Ur
Harp
constellation of, & South Pole II 360n
[Harpe or sickle] of Kronos II 390
Harpasa (Asian city)
balancing rock at, (Pliny) II 346-7
Harpocrates (Gk)
god of silence II 396
Isis suckling, (Gnos) I 410
Harris. See *Papyrus Magique Harris*
Har-Ru-Bah (Egy), Apophis & II 588
Hartmann, Franz, *The Life of Paracelsus*
all matter living I 281
animal man & elements I 294n
birth of elements I 283-4 &n
liquor vitae, etc I 532, 538-9
Mysteria Specialia I 283 &n
Paracelsus anticipated science I 283

transcendental reality I 281-2
Tritheim on magic, astral light II 512n
—— *Magic, White & Black*
mistakes made in II 640
Hartmann, Karl Robert Eduard von
"Absoluter Geist" of I 50
agnostic I 19n
evol guided by the Unconscious I 1n; II 649
evolutionary plan & Unconscious I 1-2n
pessimism of II 156n, 304n
reflects Plato's ideas I 281
Spencer, Schopenhauer & I 19n, 615n
Unconscious of, Western Logos II 670
—— [*Philosophie des Unbewussten*]
evol guided by the Unconscious II 649
insufficiency of Darwinism II 648
transcendental reality I 282
the Unconscious of, & language II 662
—— *Der Spiritismus*
immaterial beings of Kant I 133n
Harvey, William
circulation of blood I 559
stood alone for years II 156
Haryaśvas (Skt), sons of Daksha II 275n
Hasōth. See Yesōdōth
Hatchets (*haches*, Fr)
of early man II 219, 439, 716-18, 722, 724, 738
Haṭha-yoga(i) II 640
acquiring prāṇāyāma of II 568
dangerous without higher senses I 95-6
lower form of yoga I 47n; II 568
Hatho, on Ararat fr Arath (Earth) II 596-7
Hathor (Egy)
infernal Isis I 400n
as Moon, suckling Horus I 399-400
Mout (Mut) aspect of II 464
Night or, as primeval substance I 346
Hati (Egy), animal soul II 633
Hatteria Punctata (NZ lizard)
atrophied third eye of II 296, 298
Haug, Martin
Aitareya Brāhmana translated by I 101
conflicting views of Vedic chronicle I xxx
on heliocentrism II 155
Haughton, Professor Samuel
age of Earth II 695
Cambrian age II 11
elevation of Europe II 694-5
Haute Garonne, skeletons at II 739
Hauvah. See Havvāh
Havas. See Hades
Havvāh (Heb). *See also* Eve, Hēbē
Abel &, feminine serpent II 125n

Adam-Kadmon fecundates I 240
Eve, Eden (Aeden) or II 42n
inquisitive wife of Ad-am II 220
life or, made into Eve II 194n
Mother Earth II 31n
part of name Jehovah II 125, 388n, 467
Havyavāhana (Skt), fire of gods I 521
Hawaiians, decimated by Europeans II 780
Hawk(s)
Egyptian use of I 359, 365, 366n; II 356n, 357, 360n, 558, 634-5
killer of golden, risked death I 362
Hay, Mr, on colors & forms II 622
Hayo Bischat. *See* Ḥayyāh Bishah
Ḥayyāh (Heb, chaiah, chayah in tx) life
Gnostics got, fr Aziluth II 604
kabbalistic human principle II 633
nephesh-, or living soul I 226n
Ḥayyāh Bishah [Rā‘āh?] (Heb) evil beast
apes descend fr II 262
Hayyāshār (Heb), light forces I 506
Hayyīm (Heb), elohim identical w I 130
Hē, Hēh (Heb) letter H II 85. *See also* Hoa, Hū
borrowed fr pagans II 473-4
Eve & I 394
letter for Bīnāh I 438n
symbol of womb I 391; II 460, 473-4
YHVH, Tetragrammaton & I 438n
Hea, Hoa [Ea] (Chald). *See also* Ea
Chaldean god of wisdom II 26n, 531
Oannes-Dāgōn or II 5
Silik-Muludag [Merodach] son of II 477
universal soul I 357
would deny man knowledge II 282
Hea-bani (Chald) or Enkidu (Sumerian)
raised to heaven by Hea II 531
Head(s) II 282
cosmogonies begin w egg, circle & I 443
multiple, stand for races II 775-6
three, of Kabbala or Trimūrti I 381; II 25
white, or 5th race II 706
Healer(s)
adept-, (or Idei) by metals II 361
gods are all II 26n
how to become a II 517
Mercury, of the blind II 542
Rudra, & destroyer II 548
Healing
effected by fission, gemmation II 166n
Hearing
developed at beginning of 5th race I 535n
related to ether, sound II 107
Heart II 282
ancestral, is permanent ego (Egy) I 220

concealed Sun is I 290
of dhyāni-chohanic body II 91
diamond-, or vajrasattva I 571
great, beats in every atom II 588
human, compared w solar I 541-2
sevenfold human II 92
solar, & sunspots I 541-2
Heart of Africa. See Schweinfurth, G. A.
Heart of the Hydra [Alphard] I 664
Heart of the Lion [Regulus in Leo]
solstitial pt at beg of kali-yuga I 663
Heart of the Scorpion [Antares in Scorpio]
equinoctial pt at beg of kali-yuga I 663
Heat II 15. *See also* Fire
affections of matter I 484, 493
fr air, (Upanishads) I 330
aspect of anima mundi II 562
aspect of universal motion I 147
atomic, internal & external I 84-5
breaks up compound elements I 83-4
breath or I 103
called a god esoterically I 672
cold &, expl I 82
conversion of, into mechanical force I 522
correlation of electricity I 81-2
creative fire or I 201
fire, motion & I 69, 81-2, 97-8n
fluid theory of I 515-17
Fohat cause of I 139
Hunt on Sun & I 530-1
light &, aspects of fire I 2-3; II 130
light &, compared (Leslie) I 515n
Mercury's, 7 times Earth's II 27-8
Metcalfe's calorie & I 524-5
mode of motion I 516, 525
nebular, pure theory (Faye) I 505
not matter (science) I 515
not property of matter I 493
noumenal & phenomenal I 145-6
paraśakti, light & I 292
pertains to manifested worlds I 82
de Quatrefages on I 540
springs fr upādhi of ether I 515n
stage in cosmogony I 250
of Sun & ether (science) I 102
Sun not cause of I 580, 591
thru contraction I 84-5
ultimate causes of I 514-17
Venus', twice Earth's II 28
water fr, (Upanishads) I 330
Heathen(s). *See also* Pagans
do not eat sacred symbols II 210n
Jewish monotheism & II 472 &n
public scoffs at, sources I 279

Heathen Religion, The. See Gross, J. B.
Heaven(s). *See also* Hell, Lokas, Mt Meru,
    Wars in Heaven
  Chinese I 356
  creation of, & flood story II 139
  Egyptian I 674
  Elijah taken up alive to II 531
  elohīm shaped the I 239
  fiery serpents of I 126
  Gnostic angels or I 448; II 563 &n
  higher globes or, (Norse) II 100
  hosts of, will-less II 484
  initiates taught revolution of I 569
  man link betw, & Earth II 370
  marriage of, & Earth I 417
  the "Mountain," North Pole, or II 357
  primary, 7-fold II 631
  sabbath & I 240
  seven I 447-8, 450n; II 403, 563, 612
  seven, in Parsi mythology II 607
  solid & revolving, (*Zend Avesta*) II 516
  spirit of, & Earth creators II 477
  struggle in II 377
  superior & inferior hebdomad in I 448
  Taka mi onosubi no Kami (Jap) & I 214
  three, are ascending globes I 250n
  two, of Jews I 254, 354
Heaven & Earth. See Reynaud, J. E.
Heavenly Bodies
  every one the temple of a god I 578
  genesis of I 203-4
  suggested early geometry I 320
Heavenly Man. *See also* Macroprosopus
  Adam Kadmon I 137; II 596, 704 &n
  Ain-sōph's chariot I 214
  as celestial Logos I 246
  creative subordinate powers II 544
  dhyāni-chohans or II 683
  Divine Man & II 194
  evolutionary model I 183
  first born II 25
  Fohi or, (China) II 26
  four emanations (Adams) fr II 457
  Hermes calls Jupiter the II 270
  host of angels II 236
  incarnated in man (Prometheus) II 413
  Kwan-yin, Verbum, etc & I 137
  as light II 37
  Logos is II 234, 236 &n
  manifested Logos II 626
  marriage of, (*Pymander*) II 231
  Microprosopus I 240; II 626
  monad & II 186
  π (pi), circle & I 114

  Purusha or II 606
  in *Pymander* I 291n; II 97, 103, 267 &n, 493
  quaternary symbol of II 595
  śaktis of I 356
  Sephīrāh wife & mother of I 430
  synthesis of sephīrōth II 704n
  ten sephīrōth or I 215, 337
  terrestrial man reflection of I 619
  Tetragrammaton I 240; II 25, 599, 625n
  took form of Crown (Kether) I 433
  unmanifested spirit I 215
  various names for I 110, 114
Hebdomad(ic) (septenary)
  Gnostics had three I 448-9
  mysteries of II 590-1
  structure of men, gods II 91-2, 590-8
  tetrad unfolded becomes II 599
  of Valentinus I 446
Hebdomas, name of Iaō I 448
Hēbē (Gk)
  Heve or Eve, bride of Heracles II 130
Ḥebel (Heb). *See also* Abel, Cain
  Abel or, female II 125n, 127, 135, 469
  Adam-Rishōn & II 315, 397
Hebrew(s). *See also* Israelites, Jewish, Jews
  adopted Phoenician system II 560
  alphabet has occult meaning I 94
  angelology & Hindu gods I 92
  ank taken fr Egyptians II 31
  death for betraying, secrets II 396
  dragon symbol fr Chaldea II 354
  esoteric *Genesis* taken literally II 95n
  followed oriental philosophy I 618
  God same as Horus II 474
  hated Bal, Bacchus worship II 471
  Hecate & jealous God of I 395
  Hindu &, language comp I 115n
  Holy of Holies of, not orig II 468-9
  Job oldest in, canon I 647
  kabbalists & I 393
  language a science I 313-14
  language divine (Skinner) I 308-9, 316-17
  letters phallic symbols I 114n
  Leviticus fr Chaldees II 748
  man created in 6th millennium I 340
  never had higher keys I 311
  no, ideas came fr Egypt (Renouf) I 402
  number value of, letters I 78, 90n, 91
  phallic worship & sexual theog I 115n
  rabbinical value of, letters I 316
  secret god of I 391
  sexual religions of II 274
  temples described by Clement I 462
  ten perfect number in II 416n

theogonic key to, symbolism II 595
time regulated by Moon II 75
traditions imply pre-Adamites II 394
twelve hours of kabbalists I 450
used bull & cow for man & woman I 390
week & year of II 395
wisdom of early, initiates I 352
word for week is "seven" II 623-4 &n
worshiped Moon I 390
worship of tribal god II 274
Hebrew and Chaldee Lexicon. See Fürst, J.
Hebrew & English Lexicon. See Gesenius, H.
Hebrew-Egyptian Mystery. See Skinner, J. R.
Hebrew Lexicon. See Parkhurst, J.
"Hebrew Metrology." *See* Skinner, J. R.
Hebrews (Paul)
    creation of worlds II 704
    eternal sabbath I 240
    God made worlds by the Son II 703
    Melchizedek II 392
    "that he should not see death" II 531
Hebron [Hebrōn] (Heb)
    David first ruled at II 541
    Hebir-on or Kabeir-town II 541
    Smaragdine tablet at II 556
Hecatē (Gk)
    Diana-, -Luna & Trinity I 387
    infernal goddess I 400
    triple, & god of the Rabbins I 395
    wife, mother, sister explained I 396
Hēdonē (Gk) voluptuousness
    country of delight & Eden comp II 204-5
Heer, Professor Oswald
—— "Contributions to the Fossil Flora . . ."
    European Neolithic plants African II 739
    facts of botany suggest Atlantis II 739
    Miocene magnolias at 70th parallel II 726
—— *Flora tertiaria Helvetiae*
    supported Atlantis theory II 783
Hegel, Georg Wilhelm F. I 96n
    Absolute Being & Non-being I 16; II 449n
    Supreme Spirit of I 50
    things exist by their opposites II 490
    unconscious & self-conscious I 51, 106
—— *The Philosophy of History*
    accepted periodical avatāras I 52n
    aim of world history I 640-1
    Christ-man, Vedantins, etc I 52n
    nature perpetually becoming I 257n; II 449n
ἡγεμών (Hēgemōn, Gk) leader, guide
    Metatron II 480n
Heh [Heb letter "H"]. *See* Hē
Hekat [Heket], Egy frog goddess I 385, 387
Hel (Norse)

Ases no longer bound by II 99
    frigid region, kāma-loka I 463n
    goddess-queen of the dead II 774
Helanos [Helenos]
    foretold ruin of Troy II 342
Helen(s)
    Hindu, is Tārā II 498
    Menelauses &, before 5th race II 276
    symbol of 4th principle II 796
Helheim (Norse) II 774
Heliocentric Theory
    ancient initiates taught I 117n, 569
    Confucius taught I 441
    denied by Aristotle II 153
    popes burned heretics over I 441
    taught in *VP* II 155
    Zohar taught II 28n
Heliolatry
    came to Egypt fr India II 379
    not idolatry I 392
    once universal II 378
    in Roman Church I 395
Heliopolis I 674
    lying priests of II 367
    planets, elements, zodiac & I 395
    Ra the One God at I 675
    schools of I 311
Helios, Helion, Helius (Gk) II 540
    Aesculapius was II 106
    birth of Apollo as II 383
    "Father" became, later II 44
    Jehovah appeared as II 509
    "Sun in the highest" (Mackey) II 357
Helium (element) I 218n
    abundant in Sun I 583
    primitive matter & I 596
Hell(s) II 507n. *See also* Hades, Heaven,
        Pātālas, Pit
    angels' fall into II 103, 230, 244
    Atala is a II 402n, 405n, 408
    Beelzebub monarch of II 389n
    cold, or Niflheim (Eddas) II 245
    devils of Christian II 507n
    Earth is II 98, 234, 246
    effects of dogma of II 247, 484, 774
    eternal, of Christians I 372n
    lokas of Brahmans I 204, 372
    or matter II 103-4, 516
    pātālas or I 372
    Pit, South Pole or II 274, 357, 404, 785-6
    Satan burning in his own II 244-5
    seven II 403
Hellenbach von Paczolay, Lazar B.
—— *Individuality . . . [Individualismus]*

consciousness & matter II 654
—— *Die Magie der Zahlen* . . .
  number 7 & color, sound, elements II 627-8
Hellenes, Hellenic. *See also* Greek(s)
  age of, zodiac II 436n
  alone had altar to the Unknown God I 327
  brought zodiac to Greece I 647
  pre-Homeric I 304n
  Prometheus older than, (Bunsen) II 413
  sensed oneness w nature I 466
Helmholtz, Hermann Ludwig F. von
  cooling of Earth I 501n; II 154
  fr nebula to Sun in 20 million yrs II 694
  tidal retardation II 64
—— *Faraday Lecture*
  electricity as matter I 111n, 508, 580, 584,
    671n
Helmont, Jan Baptista van I 611
  Archaeus of, not new I 51-2
  correlation of sound, color I 514 &n
  pupil of Paracelsus I 51
Hēmera, aether & I 110
Hemina, L. Cassius
  q by Macrobius, on Kabiri II 363
Hemp, bisexuality in II 133
Henoch, or Idris II 366
Hephaestos, Hēphaistos (Gk)
  Kabir, instructor of metal arts II 390
  molded first woman (Pandora) II 519
  thunderbolt & II 521
  -Vulcan presided over fire I 464
Heptachord, lyre of Apollo I 167
Heptad (seven)
  four is the mean betw monad & II 599
  number of a virgin II 602
  sacred to Mars, Osiris, etc II 602
Heptagon. *See also* Seven
  religious & perfect number II 602
  Tetraktys &, explained II 598-605
Heptakis [Heptaktys] (Gk)
  Iaō or, seven-rayed Chaldean I 227n
Ἑπτα με (Hepta me, Gk)
  & 7 sounding letters II 603
Heqet (Egy). *See* Hē
Herabkunft des Feuers. See Kühn, A.
Heraclides or Herakleides (Plato's pupil)
  taught Earth's rotation I 117 &n
Heraclitus, Hērakleitos
  condemned Homer's immorality II 764n
  fire underlies all nature I 77
Heraclius
  could pick out animate stones II 342
Herakles. *See* Hercules
d'Herbelot de Molainville, B.

—— *Bibliothèque Orientale*
  Fortunate Islands II 398
  Huschenk's 12-legged horse II 397
  Légendes Persanes in II 394n
  seventy-two Solomons II 396
Herbert, Lord Edward
  man's body a miracle II 653
Herculaneum II 793
  once thought fanciful II 236, 441
Hercule et Cacus. See Bréal, M.
Hercules, Heracles, Hēraklēs
  Aesculapius or I 353
  carries away golden apples II 770n
  descends into Hades II 237n
  Geryon or Hillus son of II 278
  Hebe wife of II 130
  Hiram built temple to, & Venus II 541
  not a solar myth II 769n
  Palaemonius was the Tyrian II 345n
  priests of, or Mel-karth II 202
  savior of Prometheus II 413
  as Sun-god II 44, 237n
  two serpents & I 403
  various names for I 353
Hercules furens. See Euripides
Hereditary Transmission I 223 &n
Heredity I 457; II 738
  of acquired characteristics I 219; II 711n
  of anthropoids II 688n
  biogenetic law of II 659
  cause of, unknown to science I 223
  karma overrides II 178
  opposed by German scientists II 711n
  servant of karma II 178
  transmission of atoms & II 671-2
  Weismann's views on I 223n
Hermaphrodite(s, ism) II 125, 172n, 291.
  See also Androgynes
  all species were, once II 119, 299, 657
  animals & men were, (Schmidt) II 184
  Darwin on II 118-19
  divine, in mythologies II 124-30
  double, rod I 114
  early man was II 2 &n, 118-19, 125
  four-armed, w 3 eyes II 294
  intermediate, 2nd & early 3rd races II 167
  Jah-Eve as II 126
  lotus symbol of divine & human I 379, 392
  majority of plants are II 659
  Plato's "winged" &, races II 264
  in *Pymander* II 2n
  races in Bible I 325
  separating, 3rd race II 134
  symbol for 3rd race II 30, 104, 132-3

Zeus separates, (Plato) II 134, 177
Hermas, Hermeas, Hermeias, Hermias (Gk)
   fragment of, on Chaos & Protogonos I 70,
   343
Hermes. *See also Divine Pymander*, Hermes
   Trismegistos, Hermetica, Mercury, Thoth
   -Anubis II 28
   Books of II 25, 268n, 454, 455
   born fr Wondrous Being I 207
   Budha, wisdom II 45 &n, 234, 455, 499, 540
   caduceus & II 364
   Chaldean tablets agree w II 3
   civilized Egypt, Greece II 367
   cynocephalus glyph of I 388
   on daimones I 288n
   disciple of Agathodaemon II 366
   emblem of the Word II 542
   Enoch, Libra same as II 129, 361
   -fire I 338n
   Freemasonry speaks of II 47
   generic name given to great initiates II 210n,
   267n, 364
   Hindu astronomy & I 664-6
   Idris or II 361, 366
   interpreter, word, Logos II 541
   invented initiation of men into magic I 473
   ithyphallic, of Herodotus II 362
   Kadmos, Kadmilos or II 362
   kosmocratores & II 23
   magic not invented by II 211
   Mercury planet of II 542
   Michael, -Christos of Gnostics II 481
   moist principle of II 542, 591n
   nom-de-plume of mystics I 286
   on number ten I 90n
   Parāśara the Aryan I 286
   Pesh-Hun compared to II 48
   product of Greeks in Egypt II 137
   -Sarameyas II 28
   secretary, advisor of Isis I 388
   on sense & knowledge I 279
   serpent & I 73, 472-3; II 26n
   Seth Jewish travesty of II 380
   seven agents & circles I 436
   "sevenfold light" II 540
   seven governors, builders I 480, 601
   Smaragdine Tablet of II 99, 109, 556
   son of Seth (Sabean) II 361-2
   symbols along highways II 542
   taught occult sciences I 362
   Thot-, & fire of gods II 210-11 &n
   Thoth or II 267n, 462, 538n
   Universal Soul septenary II 562
   various names of II 380, 529-30

   way to Bible thru II 383
Hermes. See Divine Pymander
Hermes, Tablets of. *See* Smaragdine
Hermesians (followers of Hermes)
   four becomes truth as a cube II 600
Hermes Trismegistos. *See also* Thoth
   all matter living, becoming I 281
   founder of Mysteries II 267n
   on Hermes & initiation into magic I 473
   linked to Enoch II 532
   Ophites adopted rites fr II 379
   says Thoth-Hermes "invented" magic
   II 210-11
Hermes Trismegistus. See Divine Pymander
Hermetic(a, ism, ists). *See also Divine
   Pymander*, Hermes
   books agree w esoteric doctrine I 288
   elements of I 461
   fragment q by Stobaeus II 137-8
   monotheism not in Egypt I 674-5
   narratives explained II 103
   nature [*Divine Pymander*] I 291n
   one of oldest religions I 285
   scientists will have to follow I 625
   seven zones of postmortem ascent I 411
   two secret, operations I 76
   Vedanta doctrine in, philosophy I 281n
   works disfigured I 285, 674-5
Hermone, L. Cassius. *See* Hemina
Hermoutis [Hermonthis] (Egy) I 657
Hero(es)
   dynasties of, universal tradition I 266-7
   giants of Egypt II 336, 369
   gods &, deified men of 3rd race II 172
   gods, demigods & II 367, 369, 372, 436
   Hesiod's, of Thebes or Troy II 271
   Hindu rishis & I 94, 114-15, 436
   listed II 364
   male, of 4th race II 135
   national, tribal gods & I 655
   prehistoric (Creuzer) II 285
   reign after "Watchers" I 266
   rishis' human doubles or I 442
   seven, & primal races II 35 &n
Herod, King
   Krishna & the Indian II 48
   source of Bible story of II 504n
Herodotus, *History*
   on Aeschylus II 419n
   Atlantes cursed Sun II 761-2, 771n
   Boreas destroys Persian fleet I 467
   Cambyses in Kabiri temple II 360, 363
   Cyclops & Assyrian Perseus II 345n
   divine dynasties II 367, 369

"Eastern Aetheopians" of II 429
Egyptian civ before Menes II 431-2
Egy kings date back 17,000 yrs II 750
Egyptians record 12,000 yrs II 334
Egyptians re Earth's poles II 332, 431
Egyptians re equator & ecliptic II 534
Egypt once a sea II 368
Euxine II 4-5 &n
giants II 336
Hyperboreans II 769n
Ibis, two types of I 362
IU q on Great Pyramid I 317n
ithyphallic Hermes II 362
Jews & Phoenicians I 313n
Mt Atlas "pillar of heaven" II 763
Mysteries in Egypt II 395-6
Nemesis II 305n
people who sleep 6 months II 772-3
Rawlinson's notes on Menes II 432
statues of 345 Egyptian rulers II 369
Sun twice rose where it now sets I 435
Ural or golden region II 416-17
Zeus-Belus II 210n
Heroica [Heroicus]. *See* Philostratus
Hero-Worship II 281
Herschel, Sir F. William
    believed in intelligent forces I 499
    believed in spiritual world I 589
    believed many worlds inhabited II 701, 706
    colleagues derided theories of I 590-1
    estimated stars in Milky Way I 576n
    on Nasmyth's willow leaf theory I 541, 590-1
    photosphere like mother of pearl I 530
    Uranus discovered by I 99n
    vital organisms in Sun I 529, 530-1, 541
—— "Astronomical Observations . . ."
    nebular theory of I 590, 595
Herschel, Sir John F. W.
—— Article in *Musée des Sciences*
    disguised causes under a veil I 492n
—— *Discours sur l'étude* . . .
    on gravitation I 604
    on light I 580
    will to impart or end motion I 503
Ḥeru-amen (Egy). *See also* Horus
    Mout-Isis suckles II 464
Ḥeru-sa-Āst (Egy, Horsusi in tx)
    confused w Haroiri I 366n
    son of Osiris & Isis I 366n
Ḥeru-Ur (Egy, Haroiri in tx)
    the older Horus or Khnoum I 366n
Ḥesedh (Heb)
    globe G, Earth chain I 200

Habel or, son of Adam II 315
    sign of the cross & II 562
Hesiod
    an adept II 530
    condemned for immorality II 764n
    dated 8th century BC I 648
    historical, factual II 765, 777
    Jupiter as disrespectful son II 270
    poetized history II 775
    Prometheus story of II 413, 525
    writing unknown to, (Grote) II 440
—— *Theogony*
    appeared after Vedas II 450
    Calypso daughter of Atlas II 762
    Chaos, Space I 336n, 425
    Hindu spirit in I 336n
    mutilation of Uranos II 268
    Night before Day in creation II 59
    Prometheus story II 525
    three Cyclopes named II 769, 775-6
    Titans I 418; II 777n
    war of Titans I 202; II 63
    winds fr sons of Tiphoeus I 466
—— *Works & Days*
    bronze race fr Ash tree II 97, 181n, 519-20,
        772
    four ages & races II 270-1
    giants of bronze age II 772
    gods, mortals of common origin II 270
    seventh is sacred day II 603
    third race or bronze II 271, 520 &n
Hesperides, Garden of II 791
    golden apple tree of I 129n
Hesperornis, link betw reptile & bird II 183
Hesperos (Gk) Venus as evening star
    Moon's light overshadows I 386
ἑτερήμεροι (heterēmeroi, Gk)
    alternate days for Castor & Pollux II 122
Heterogeneity(ous)
    elements & I 141, 595
    homogeneity & I 130, 411, 595
Heterogenesis II 177
Heva(h). *See* Ḥavvāh
Heve (Eva, Eve or). *See* Hēbē
Hexagon I 320. *See also* Six-pointed Star
    Fohat center of I 216
    represents macrocosm I 224
    six limbs of Microprosopus I 216
    snow crystals & II 594
Hexagram, pentagram, male & female I 78
Hezekiah
    altered faith of Israelites I 320 &n
    breaks brazen serpent I 364n; II 387n
Hgrasena. *See* Ugrasena

Hia Dynasty. *See* Hsia Dynasty
Hibbert Lectures. See Sayce, A. H.
Hicetas [Hiketas] (Gk) a Pythagorean
 taught Earth's rotation I 117 &n
Hierarchy(ies). *See also* Cosmogony, Hosts
 all, emanate fr Sephīrāh I 215-16 &n
 of angels I 129, 218-19, 331; II 60, 273
 of archangels I 42
 Christian, of Powers, Kab & Hindu I 92
 of creative forces I 213-18; II 33-4
 of dhyāni-chohans & humans I 90, 93, 189n,
  293, 586n
 divine, has spirit united w soul I 193
 each, has a mission to perform I 274-6
 elect of men will be celestial I 220-1
 fifth, makes man rational being I 233
 of Flames I 86
 individuality resides in I 275
 invisible Logos w seven II 23
 kosmos animated by endless I 274-6
 Lha & heavenly II 22
 of lunar ancestors I 160
 mystery of universe built on I 89
 perceptive & apperceptive beings in I 629
 present celestial, replaced I 221
 of purely divine spirits I 133
 septenary, of divine powers I 22
 seven great rūpa II 318n
 seven, of monads I 171-6
 seven, of pitris I 189n
 seven planetary, (Gnos) I 73, 171
 seven powers of nature & II 273
 seventh, or elementals I 233
 six lower, of spirits I 133
 sixth, gave man shadow-body I 233
 sixth, of dhyāni-chohans I 293
 symbols orig fr, of wise men II 630-1n
 third race, never died II 281
 twelve, of Tien-Huang II 26-7
 Universal Mind comes into action thru I 38
 in various cosmogonies I 424, 436, 449-56
 Wondrous Being root-base of our I 207
Hieratic
 Mayan & Egyptian, alphabets I 267n
 records of Egypt I 310; II 130
 sciences & symbols I 307
Hieroglyph(s, ic) II 130, 464, 633
 cake unites cross, circle II 546
 Christian cross Egyptian, Tat II 557
 early, named Senzar II 439
 Egyptian, for 5 races II 458
 Fohat & I 674
 method in ancient texts II 335
 on pillars of Seth (Josephus) II 530

prehistoric Egyptians used II 432
Hierogram, within circle I 426, 613-14
Hierophant(s)
 Atlantean, Bab, & Egy name of II 530
 in *Book of the Dead* II 213
 called serpents II 379
 Chaldean, taught Hebrews I 352
 early, "Sons of God" II 470
 Egyptian, headdress & tau II 557
 guard temple libraries II 529-32
 had keys to symbols, dogmas I 363
 Indian (Lévi) I 255
 -initiators during ceremony II 559
 Java-Aleim were chief II 202, 532
 language of I 310-11
 Mercury as II 28, 558
 sons of the dragon II 379
 sudden death of I 312
 twelve, at Abyss of Learning II 502
 two categories of II 221 &n
 Viśvakarma was, -initiate II 559
Higgins, Godfrey, [*Anacalypsis*]
 on hydrogen II 105-6
Higher Self, Ego. *See also* Ātma, Self
 absolute consciousness of I 266
 alone is divine I 445
 buddhi & self-consciousness II 231n
 divorcing, fr senses I 329-30
 Farvarshi or II 480 &n
 higher creators (pitris) II 95
 informing principle or monad II 102-3
 kārana-śarīra & II 79
 must gravitate towards monad II 110
 non-separateness of, fr the One I 276
 Plato on ego as II 88
 reigns after 3½ races II 110
 speech & mind consult, (*Anugītā*) I 94-6
 spiritual ego II 230
 spiritual fire is man's II 109
Hilaire, G. St., crown of thorns II 651
Hilasira [Hilaeira] (Gk)
 & Phoebe, twilight & dawn II 122
Hilkiah (Heb)
 found the "Book of God" II 473
 high priest I 649
Hillus [Hyllos] (Gk)
 giant son of Hercules II 278
Hillwell. *See* Halliwell, J. O.
Himālaya(n, s) (Skt) I 271; II 145
 Brahmans fled to II 608
 cavern in, w giant bones II 293n
 "Garden of Wisdom" in II 204
 Hamsa a range of the I 79
 ocean once washed base of II 571-2

part of belt around globe II 401 &n
peaks of, holy II 494
"Preservers" beyond the II 165n
result of upheaval II 787n
seat of esoteric schools beyond I xxiii, 122
separated Lemuria fr Gobi Sea II 323-4
Sivatherium in II 218
war of Titans in, heaven II 500
Himavān, Himavat (Skt). *See also* Himālaya
belt around globe II 401 &n
as a calf I 398n
Vaivasvata lands on II 146
Hīnayāna Buddhism
Mahāyāna &, re nidānas, etc I 39-40
Hindu(s). *See also* Aryans
Ādityas the 8 & 12 gods of I 100
on age of humanity I 150n
apes descended fr humans I 185n
asexual reproduction known to II 658
astronomers were initiates II 500n
astronomy I 658, 666-7; II 253, 332, 551
astronomy, exactness of I 661; II 499n
astronomy not borrowed I 659, 667n
Atlantis & II 406-7, 425, 742-3
avatāras of II 555
branch of Aryan race II 106
brought civilization to Babylon II 203
Buddha an Aryan II 339
calendar of II 620
Carlyle on II 470
chronological table of II 68-70
chronology labeled fiction II 73
chronology 33 sidereal years II 332
creations of I 427
cross understood & used by II 556
decade in, system I 321
destruction of world II 144, 311
devotion of I 212n
divine dynasties of II 316
division of world II 403
four-armed gods of II 294n
fourteen upper & nether worlds I 115-16
Great Bear or 7, Rishis I 227n
Greek 7 fr II 408
have zodiac of Asura Maya II 436
hid true dates fr foreigners II 225
hymns & mantras of I 623
idol worship among modern II 723
initiated, & chronology II 395
kali-yuga II 435
knew of Plato's island II 407
knew of 7 planets I 99-101 &n
lotus symbol of 4 quarters II 546
lunar tables of I 667 &n

man on cross II 542-3
mind most spiritual, (Müller) II 521
mysteries based on ten II 603
mythology of I 304 &n
myths & Sun, Moon worship I 388
myths based on facts II 236
Noah or, Vaivasvata II 35, 140, 222
Olcott taught by, initiate I xix
among oldest races I 326; II 470-1, 603
orientalists dwarf dates of II 76n, 225
origin of Gnostic wisdom II 570
pagodas & nautch girls of II 460
pantheon reshuffled II 61
philosophy older than Egyptian I 387; II 432
Phoenician &, astronomy II 551
Pleiades &, esoteric philosophy I 648n
record 8 million years II 436
record sinking of Atlantis II 332
religion is unity in diversity II 310
sacred books symbolic II 326
sages did not anthropomorphize I 326
septenary system of I 114-15, 126n
Smārtava Brahmans I 271-2
solar & lunar dynasties of I 388
on sound & senses I 534
succession of worlds II 756
33 crores of, gods I 71n
worship rishis as regents II 361
yuga-kalpa II 307n
zodiac not fr Gks I 647; II 50, 225, 332, 395
Hindu Classical Dict. See Dowson, J.
Hinduism II 68n, 622n. *See also* Hindus
Brahmā, Prajāpati, & creation I 346
child of Lemuro-Atlantean wisdom I 668
egg symbology in I 365-6
gods of II 107n
Holy of Holies in II 472
one of most ancient religions I 285
pantheism of I 545
refers to cosmic & terr events I 369
rejects inorganic atom I 454
Hindu-Kush, Central Asian mt chain II 338
Hindu Pantheon. See Moor, E.
Hindustan II 222. *See also* India
Arab figures fr I 361
Aryan Brahmans descend into II 609
decad found in caves of I 321
Hiouen Thsang. *See* Hiuen-Tsang
Hipparchus I 658, 660
& records of the Assyrians I 409, 650
Hipparion (early horse)
anchitherium &, evolution II 716, 735
found in America II 792
Hippocentaurs II 54

Hippocrates II 132, 688
    embryology of, (Weismann, etc) I 223n
    embryonic stages known to II 259
    occult virtues of number seven II 312n
Hippolytus, *Philosophumena*
    Aeons & Radicals of Simon II 569n
    Chozzar of Gnostics II 577, 578
    Kabir Adamas II 3
    Marcus on 7 heavens II 563
    Marcus on the Logos I 351-2
Hippolytus. See Euripides
Hippopotamus(i) II 735
    crocodile & II 397, 399
    divine symbol in Mexico, Egypt II 399n
    pigmy, pioneer of future II 219
Hiquet. *See* Hekat
Hiram, King (of Tyre)
    secret work of Chiram or II 113
    temples to Hercules, Venus II 541
Hiram Abif I 314
Hiraṇya (Skt) shining
    Dayanand Sarasvatī on I 360
Hiraṇyagarbha (Skt) radiant egg. *See also*
        Brahmā (Egg of), Eggs, Golden Egg
    Brahmā is I 89
    highest aspect of Brahman, Brahmā I 406
    luminous golden egg or I 66, 89, 333,
        359-60, 406, 556
    one of 3 hypostases I 18, 286
    prajāpati I 90
    Rig-Veda begins w, & prajāpati I 426
    temple II 470
    Vishnu is, Hari & Śankara I 286
Hiraṇyakaśipu (Skt) king of daityas
    Purāṇic Satan I 420n
    reborn as Rāvana II 225n
    slain by avatar Nara Simha II 225n
Hiraṇyāksha (Skt) golden-eyed, son of
        Kaśyapa
    ruler of 5th region II 382n
    770 million descendants II 571
Hiraṇyapura (Skt) golden city
    Dānavas live in II 381-2
    is Greek Asteria II 383
Hirn, Dr G. A., *Théorie mécanique . . .*
    force in space betw atoms I 511
—— "Recherches expérimentales . . ."
    no agreement in, re atom I 482-3, 487
Hisi (Finn), principle of evil II 26
Hissast'han. *See* Misrasthān
Histoire de la magie. See Lévi, É.
Histoire de l'astronomie ancienne. See Bailly
Histoire de la terre. See Rougemont, F. de

Histoire des nations civilisées du Mexique. See
    Brasseur de Bourbourg
Histoire des Vierges . . . See Jacolliot, L.
Historia ante-Islamitica. See Abul Feda
Historia antigua de la Nueva España. See
    Durán
Historians, dwarf ancient dates II 437n
Historia Religionis . . . See Hyde, Thomas
Historia Religio Veterum. See Hyde, T.
Historical Facts
    become theological dogmas II 776
Historical View of Hindu Astronomy. See
    Bentley, J.
History
    adept will impart symbolic I 306
    in allegories & myths I 304n; II 335
    "annalists" will wreck, (Michelet) I 676
    Constantine turning point in I xliv
    covers but tiny field I 406
    historians have dwarfed II 437n
    our, is of 5th subrace only I 406; II 351, 444
    primitive, human not divine I 229
    profane, hardly begins 2000 BC II 796
    reliability of II 437-46
    religious, buried in symbols I 307
    repeats itself in cycles I 676
    tradition &, are proofs II 336
    world, realization of spirit I 640-1
    written & oral traditions II 424
    zodiac contains, of world II 438
History of Ancient Skt. Lit. See Müller, F. M.
History of Civilization . . . See Buckle, H. T.
History of Creation. See Haeckel, E.
History of English Literature. See Taine, H.
History of Herodotus. See Herodotus
History of Indian Lit. See Weber, A. F.
History of Japan. See Kaempfer, E.
History of Magic. See Christian, P.
History of Magic. See Lévi, E.
History of Paganism in Caledonia. See Wise, T.
History of Persia. See Malcolm, Sir J.
History of Sanskrit [Indian] Literature. See
    Weber, A. F.
History of the Conflict betw Rel. & Sci. See Draper
History of the Intel. Dev. of Europe. See
    Draper
Hiuen-Tsang (Chin)
    on worship of disciples II 34n
—— *Si-yu-ki*
    on Bamian statues II 338
Hivim
    of the race of the dragon (Mex) II 380
Hoa, Hū (Heb). *See also* Hē, Hēh
    -Attāh-Ani explained I 78

concealed, masculine I 618
fr, is Ab, the Father II 83
Hoang-Ty. *See* Huang-Ti
Hod [Hōdh] (Heb)
   globe B, Earth chain I 200
Hodgson, Adam
—— *Letters from North America . . .*
   on moving stones II 342n
Hodgson, Brian Houghton
—— "Notice on Buddhist Symbols"
   on swastica cross II 546-7
Ḥokhmāh (Heb, often Chochmah in tx)
   Bīnāh (intelligence) & I 355; II 134 &n, 528,
      626
   brain or, numbered two I 352
   diffused in Bīnāh (nature) II 84
   divine name is Jah [Yah] I 355
   is Father, Bīnāh Mother II 85
   left shoulder of Macroprosopus I 239
   male wisdom I 99n; II 528
   masculine, active potency I 355
   names of, in various religions II 704 &n
   right side or II 269n
   Sephīrāh, & Bīnāh higher triad I 98n, 99n,
      438
   Vau letter of I 438n
   YHVH is Bīnāh & I 618
Holiaetus [Haliaetus] Washingtonii
   Audubon doubted concerning II 440 &n
Holmboe, C. A., *Traces de Bouddhisme . . .*
   Buddhism in USA & Norway II 424n
Holy City, or human womb (Kab) II 84
Holy Fires, generic name of Kabiri II 3
Holy Ghost
   Ancient of Days or I 109
   appeared as a dove I 80-1n, 354, 363
   astral light body of, (Lévi) I 253
   baptism w, explained II 566
   female principle I 72n, 136, 197, 353, 618
   fire symbolized, [*Acts*] I 402
   first of sephīrōth or I 337
   Lucifer is, & Satan II 513
   Ptah is, of Christians I 353
   seven gifts of II 604n
   Sophia or, (Gnos) I 72n, 197; II 512
   Swan & goose symbols of I 357
   tongues of fire I 379n
   universal soul I 353
   Venus or, & Trinity II 540
Holy of Holies. *See also* Ark
   adytum, sanctum sanctorum II 234, 459
   argha or II 468
   Babylon had its II 456
   cherubim & II 518

discussed II 459-74
four elements & I 462
Heb, Egy, Hindu, compared II 469, 472-3
Jewish symb of womb I 264, 382-3, 391-2
King's Chamber I 264; II 462, 466n
Ma-qom, womb & II 457 &n
number symbol of I 114n, 264
phallus in ark II 467
Pope & Christian II 466n
pyramid & II 466-71
tent of, described I 462
tree of Garden of Eden or I 114 &n
universal abstraction II 472
Holy One (in the *Midrash*)
   created several worlds II 53-4
   desired to create man II 490-1
   Logos or II 490
Homer, Homeric II 404
   Castor & Pollux II 121-3
   Cyclopes, Titans II 293
   date of, & *Job* I 648
   esoteric meaning of, & *Rev* II 383
   giants II 336
   Gladstone misunderstood II 766-7
   heroes had huge weapons II 755
   Plato dates, much earlier I 648
   Poseidon god of the horse II 399n
   scientists deny existence of II 429
   seven constellations II 603
   silent re 1st 3 principles I 426
   songs of, & patriarchs II 391
   Veda &, compared II 450
   way to Bible thru Hermes & II 383
   works of, condemned II 764n
   writing unknown to, (science) II 439, 440
   zodiacal signs I 648
—— *The Iliad*
   Apollo appears to seers II 771
   Artemis-Lochia & childbirth I 395
   divine kings, Apollo, etc II 774
   Helen as 4th principle II 796
   Laomedon building a city II 796
   λίμνη (limnē, "sea") II 766
   Ocean & Tethys II 65
   Tartaros II 776
   "terrible are the gods" II 355
   uses astral double of Aeneas II 771
   Zeus reverences Night, the One I 425
—— *The Odyssey*
   Atlantis II 761
   Calypso daughter of Atlas II 762, 769 &n
   Hyperborean day & night II 7, 11
   Moira II 604n
   Tityos II 591n

Homeric Hymns, Leda allegory II 122 &n, 391
L'Homme Rouge des Tuileries. See Christian, P.
Homo Afer II 725
Homo Diluvii, giant II 352
Homogeneity
 absolute, is unconscious I 247
 absolute, of prakriti I 522
 basis of heterogeneity I 46, 328
 elements & I 143n
 essence of good & evil in I 411-12
 of matter & natural law I 640
 of matter outside solar system I 601
 "One Form of Existence" I 46
 relative, of prakritis I 328
 of solar nebula I 589
 universal unity or I 58, 130
Homoiomerē. See Anaxagoras
Homo Primigenius
 antiquity of II 288, 317n, 690, 734
 descended fr apes (Haeckel) II 189, 193n
Homo Sapiens II 675, 690
Homunculi
 fact of alchemy II 349
 inferior men are II 376
 Ischin help to produce II 376
 Paracelsus made, fr alkahest I 345
 similar to self-born II 120-1
Honey-Dew, or astral light I 344-5
Hönir (Norse)
 gives man intellect & senses II 97
Hooke, Dr Robert
 axial changes & glaciation II 726
Hopkins, E. W. (editor, *Ordinances of Manu*)
 ātman, elements, etc I 334-5
 more intuitive than Burnell I 334
Hoppo & Stadlein (sorcerers)
 killed for charming harvest I 469
Hor, Horsusi. *See* Ḥeru-sa-Āst
[Horace, *Satires*]
 Credat Judaeus Apella II 451
Horae Biblicae. See Butler, C.
Horae Hebraicae. See Schöttgen, C.
Horaios, Horaeus (Gnos, Osraios & Orai in tx)
 genius of Venus I 577; II 538n
 stellar spirit, inferior hebdomad I 449
Hor-Ammon. *See* Ḥeru-amen
Horchia, title of Vesta (Earth) II 144
Horeb (cave near Sinai)
 Moses initiated at II 541
Hor-Jared [Yared], Ararat, Areth II 596-7
Hormig (Mercury, Budha) II 366
Horn(s)
 Greek, Hindu, & Jewish symb II 418 &n
 hoofs & II 510

Lucifer's II 31 &n
 of Satan II 507
Horne, Reverend Thomas Hartwell
—— *Introduction to the . . . Holy Scriptures*
 admits changes in Bible II 473
Horoscope(s), Horoscopy. *See also* Astrology
 rationale of I 105
 thirty-six, & Pantomorphos I 672
 zodiacal records I 647
Horse(s)
 ass &, produce (sterile) mule II 287
 evolution of, (Mivart) II 697
 evolution traced fr Tertiary II 735
 fossils of II 773n
 gradual evolution of, (Laing) II 716
 ogdoad of earth-born II 31
 originated in America (science) II 792
 seven, of Sun I 101, 290
 symbolic meaning II 399n
 twelve-legged, of Huschenk II 397-9
 white, symbol I 87
Horseshoe-like Continent
 Professor Seeman confirms II 333
 rose as Lemuria sank II 326
 of 2nd race II 401-2
Horsusi. *See* Ḥeru-sa-Āst
Horus (Egy)
 Abraxas Iao, Jehovah, & II 474
 Ammon becomes, or Hor-Ammon II 464
 -Apollo I 367
 bisexual I 72n
 born fr Osiris-Isis II 472
 "crocodile" the fish of I 220; II 577
 defunct resurrected as I 228
 divine king II 368
 elder, demiurgic Idea I 366 &n
 Gnostic Christ or II 587, 635
 on Gnostic gems II 474
 Hathor & Isis suckled I 400
 immaculate birth of I 59
 Isis daughter & mother of I 430
 Isis virgin mother of II 43
 light of the Logos II 233
 Logos, Christos or I 134n
 lotus symbol w, & Osiris I 379
 Older, Younger, & Osiris I 348, 366n
 -Osiris, father & son I 220
 raised the dead II 557
 second, Idea in matter I 366
 servants of, glean wheat II 374
 Seth, Thoth & II 283n, 380
 slays Typhon (dragon) II 385
Hosea
 Kadeshīm in II 460

verb "he will be" II 129 &n
Hoshang (Huschenk in tx)
  Persian king II 396-9
Host(s). *See also* Hierarchy
  cherubim general name of II 501
  of creative powers II 487
  elohīm, dhyāni-chohans or II 510
  guide regions during manvantara I 119
  heavenly, or Prometheus II 421
  Jehovah collectively II 75
  of Logos I 94
  seven, build world II 489
  seven creative, in Vedas II 605
  seven, will-born lords II 86
  superior, inferior explained II 421-2
  will-less spiritual II 484
Hotris (Skt) priests
  seven, & 7 senses (*Anugītā*) I 87, 96
Hottentots
  mixed Atlanto-Lemurians II 779
Houah. *See* Ḥavvāh
Houghton, Professor J. *See* Haughton
Houris (Pers), Paradise of, & Eden II 203
Hours, 12, of day explained I 450
House(s) (zodiacal)
  Earth said "my, is empty" II 15
  Mars held, of Venus II 392
  planet, of a dhyāni II 29
  seven planets, races & I 573 &n; II 602n
Hovah. *See* Ḥavvāh
Hovelacque, Abel, *The Science of Language*
  polygenetic origin of man II 169
Howard, L., on aerolites II 784n
Hrāda (Skt), daityas &, defeat gods I 419
Hrimthurses [Hrimthursar] (Norse)
  war of Ases w II 386
Hrishīkeśa (Skt)
  spiritual or intellectual soul II 108
Hrossharsgrani (Norse), Starkad & II 346n
Hsia Dynasty (Chin, Hia in tx) II 54n
Hsiang of Wei (Seang of Wai in tx) II 302
Hsien-Chan (Chin) I 136
  filled w elementary germs I 139
  fr Tien Sien, Heaven of Mind I 139
  Vāch, voice calls forth I 137
Hsi-Tsang (Tib), great teachers of I 271n
Hū I 618. *See also* Hē, Hoa
Huang-Ho River (Chin, Khuan-Khé in tx)
  civilization in upper course of I xxxii
Huang-Ti, Lord (Chin)
  king of divine dynasty II 281
  sees his sons fall II 516
Huc, Abbé R. E., [*Recollections of a Journey*]
  Dalai or "ocean" Lama II 502n

Hudson Bay, was part of former land bridge to
  Norway II 423-4
Huelgoat (Brittany), stones at II 342n, 344
Huggins, Sir William
  on spectra of nebulae I 598n
Hugo, Victor, [*Travailleurs de la mer*]
  description of cuttle fish II 440-1
Hugo Cestrensis
  & moving stone of Mona II 345
Huien-Tsang. *See* Hiuen-Tsang
Human(s). *See also* Humanity, Man, Mankinds, Races, Root-Races
  brain needed for speech II 661
  character & fallen angels II 274
  development of, embryo II 187-8
  differences in sevenfold, nature II 212-13
  door into, kingdom closed I 173, 182; II 303
  early, created, not begotten II 415
  ego is higher manas II 79
  enormous, bones II 337, 347
  evolution traced in stars II 352
  in 1st round I 173-4, 182, 188
  god-informed, & lower II 421n
  key 1 of seven II 291n
  mind-soul & Karshipta II 292
  monad or higher self II 103
  monads & lower kingdoms, 1st round II 635
  monads clothed by barhishads II 94-5
  monads fr cosmic monads II 311
  monads phase of immetalization II 150
  monsters fr animals & II 689
  no new, monads since mid-Atlantis I 173,
    182; II 303
  origin of 1st, stock II 86-7
  pre-, periods II 315, 322
  primitive, groups II 605-7
  progress, ebb & flow of I 641
  races, 1st & Manu II 307
  rudimentary organs explained II 683
  shape after the Fall II 227
  simultaneous evol, groups II 1-2, 29, 35, 77
  soul is of earth, water II 43n
  species can breed together II 195
  stage, all must pass thru I 106; II 322
  super-, intelligences II 194
  type repertory of organic forms II 683-4
  union of semi-, w, sterile II 195-6
  var of, & previous world's karma II 249n
  will never incarnate as animals I 185n
Humanity(ies). *See also* Human, Man, Mankinds, Races, Vaivasvata Manu
  age of I 150n
  appeared in numerous races II 718
  asexual, bisexual, oviparous II 132

astral, condensed into physical I 188; II 151
astral light & karma of II 513
astral, on Earth globe II 112n
brown-white & yellow races form II 250
builders are progenitors of I 128
cradle of II 204
descended fr ape-man (Haeckel) II 317n
descended fr 3 couples (Bible) II 453
develops in 4th round I 159
dhyāni-chohans & I 93, 193, 226, 229-30,
    267, 458, 619; II 232-3n
differences in II 249
divided into 2 sexes II 147-9
each Manu creates his own II 311
elect of, will replace Watchers I 267
elements & development of II 135
fallen angels are II 274
fifth, & *Mahābhārata* II 139
finite number of I 171
first, pale copy of progenitors II 95
Flammarion on, of other worlds II 707
four-armed, 3-eyed II 294-5
guides of early I 208
higher beings watched over I 273
India cradle of II 203-4
innate powers of early II 319
lipikas concerned w I 126, 128-30
lowest specimens of II 168
manu of 4th round II 308
oneness of origin of II 249
other, in other worlds I 611
other, in solar system I 133; II 700-1, 708
physical, 18 million yrs old II 149, 308n
planetary regents & monads of I 575
polar regions & earliest II 324, 400-1
primeval form of I 159
Prometheus incarnated in II 413-14
relics of former I 609
same monads reincarnate in each root-race
    II 146n
saviors of I 470; II 173, 179
seed, or śishtas I 182
seven cradles of II 220, 324
of 7, only 3 remain II 471n
spiritual, within physical I 106
stars &, bound together II 352, 431
taught arts & sciences II 267n
terrestrial Eve becomes I 60
third, fr androgyne to male & female II 24
Titans-Kabirim brought mind to II 363
wide variety of II 444
world-adepts in records of I xlv
Human Kingdom. *See* Humanity, Humans,
    Man, Mankinds, Races

Human Soul. *See also* Soul
    ancestry of II 81, 88, 113, 241-2
    has beg, but no end (Christian) I 570
    irrational animal soul & I 247
    Leibniz on I 630 &n
    lower 5th principle I 19
    mind-principle I 101n, 153n, 291; II 513, 596
Human Species, The. See Quatrefages, de
Humboldt, F. H. A. von
    Aztecs originally at 42nd parallel I 322
    describes pyramid of Papantla I 322
    Mexican version of flood, ark II 141
    monad of, & hornblende atom I 178
    never gave authoritative opinions II 753n
    —— *Kosmos* II 674
    on auroras (Trumboldt in tx) I 205
    —— "Lettres . . ." in *Revue Germanique*
    other solar systems like ours I 497n
Hume, David, denied phenomena II 156n
Humility (Samnati) II 528
Hünengräben
    giant tombs in Germany II 752
Hungarian(s)
    giant II 277
    Olcott taught by, initiate I xix
    seventh subrace, 4th root-race II 178
Hunt, E. B., *Silliman's Journal* [*Amer. Journal of
    Science and Arts*]
    upset theories of Cauchy, Fresnel I 486
Hunt, James
    dates man 9 million years old II 739
    favored polygenesis II 169
Hunt, Robert
    dated glacial epoch II 695
    —— *Researches on Light* I 580
    —— "The Source of Heat in the Sun"
    curdy appearance of Sun I 530
    man's vital force & Sun-force I 538n
    solar magnetism, etc I 498
    vital force resides in Sun I 530-1
Hunt, T. S., "Celestial Chemistry . . ."
    Newton, ether & void I 495
Hurricane(s)
    force behind I 291
    Moon, planets, cause II 699
Huschenk [Hoshang, Haoshyanha in Zend]
    Persian king II 396-9
Huxley, Thomas Henry I 528n, 625
    age of solar system I 501
    avoids man-ape theory (Dawson) II 729
    beginning of organisms, sedimentation
        II 11, 72, 694
    British Isles 4 times depressed II 787n
    coal formation II 155

defense of Darwinism II 680
derides vitalists I 540
discovers moneron II 164n
does not believe in vital force I 634
favors monogenetic origin of man II 169
on Haeckel's origin of life II 190
man & apes II 87n
on Miocene man II 288
molecularist I 637n
Paleolithic man not pithecoid II 716n
replies to Gladstone II 252n
science as common sense I 477
theos do not respect opinions of II 651
—— ["First Volume . . . Challenger"]
Atlantic continent possible II 780-1, 784
—— *Man's Place in Nature*
antiquity of man II 686, 687 &n, 719
five races fr anthropoids II 315n
gap betw man & ape II 665n, 677n, 681 &n, 698 &n
gap betw man & troglodite II 668
homo sapiens, Pliocene, Miocene II 675
Neanderthal not missing link II 686 &n
no final answers II 152
"question of questions" II 656
"Time will show" II 718
—— ["On the Persistent Types . . ."]
certain forms persist II 256
—— ["On the Physical Basis . . ."]
matter not directly known I 669
—— ["Review of Kölliker's . . ."]
nature makes "jumps" II 696
—— "Yeast"
Stirling's reply to Huxley I 637n
Huygens, Christiaan
—— *Théorie du Monde*
inhabitants of other worlds II 33n
Hvaniratha, Qaniratha [Khvaniratha] (Pers)
globe D, Earth or II 607 &n
Jambu-dvīpa in Sanskrit II 758
Hwergelmir [Hvergälmer] (Norse)
roaring caldron I 407
Hyades, deluge constellation II 785
Hybrid(s) II 714, 723
anthropoids are II 200
of Atlanteans & semi-humans II 195
Jews a, people after Moses I 313n
not always sterile II 287
Hyde, Thomas
—— *Historia religionis . . . Persarum*
Kabiri & Zoroastrians II 363n
Hydra (Gk), water-serpent II 205
Dendera lion stands on II 432-3
heart of constellation I 664-5

Hydrargyrum, Natura, Aqua & II 113
Hydrogen II 593
ceases to exist in water? I 54-5
constituent of protoplasm I 637n
corresponds to kāma-rūpa in man II 593
element lower than, (Crookes) I 583
found in stars, nebula I 143n, 595
on Jupiter II 137n
man's 3 highest principles & II 113
nearest to protyle (Crookes) I 626
noumenon(oi) of II 112-13, 592
oxygen, nitrogen & I 623
in pregenetic ages I 626
properties of II 105-6, 593
relation of, to air II 114-15n
spiritual fire in alchemy II 105
threefold nature of II 112-14
Hyg. Tal. See Hyginus, C. Julius
Hygeia (Gk) II 132
Hyginus, C. Julius, [*Fabularum Liber*]
Atlas assisted giants against gods II 493
Dawn & Twilight II 122
—— *Poetical Astronomy*
Apollo legend of killing Cyclopes II 770
Hyksos (Shepherd Kings of Egypt)
Jews descend fr, (Josephus) I 115n, 313
Hyle (Gk, material). *See also* Father-Mother, Ilus
latent & active I 82
one of intellectual quaternary II 599
primordial flame proceeds fr I 88
Roger Bacon on, (Crookes) I 581-2
Hylo-idealism(ists) I 297, 479
annihilationists II 156n
copyists I 96n
Hylozoism (Cudworth's term)
God cannot set hand to Creation II 159
highest aspect of pantheism II 158
Hymns to Minerva. See also Pindar
Minerva at Jupiter's right hand I 401
Hyperborean Arimaspian Cyclopes
last race w wisdom eye II 770
Hyperborean Atlantis II 770n
Hyperborean Continent. *See also* Polar, Root-Race–2nd
birthplace of 1st giants II 775
first continent to disappear II 606n
golden apples in, Atlantis II 770n
Greeks had, & S Apollo II 769
Greenland remnant II 11
home of 2nd race II 7, 11-12
Lemurians gravitated towards II 274
North Pole or II 274
Pausanius, Herodotus on II 769n

Persian account of II 398-9
portions of Lemuria-Atlantis II 371n
tropical climate of II 7, 11-12
Hyperboreans
  descend fr Atlantean subrace II 774
  king of, high priest of Apollo II 771
  servants of Apollo II 769n
  sow, reap, harvest in 1 day II 773
  Titans of, descended fr giants II 775
Hyperion (Gk), 1 of 7 Arkite Titans II 143
Hypnotism. *See also* Mesmer
  Kandu in state of II 175
  magnetism, mesmerism & I 297; II 156

of serpents I 409
will become satanism II 641
Hypostasis(es). *See also* Logos, Trinity
  divine, & church I 434
  first triadic I 428-9
  of human 5th principle II 275
  man's, by divine beings II 275
  never personal I 574n
  three of I 18-19
  triple, (Hindu) I 286, 571
"Hypoth, 1675." *See* Newton, Sir I.
Hypothèses cosmogoniques, Les. See Wolf, C. J. E.

I

I (letter) I 78, 453. *See also* Aham, Ego, Self
  symbol of body erect II 574
"I," Carlyle on I 211-12
Iacchus (Gk), as Iaō or Jehovah II 460
Iah (Heb) II 129, 541
Ialdabaōth (Gnos)
  chief of astral gods I 449
  child born in egg of chaos I 197 &n, 449
  Demiurgos or, filled w rage II 243
  described I 197 &n, 198; II 389
  described (King) II 243-4
  father of Ophiomorphos II 244, 481
  first couple & II 215
  -Jehovah genius of Saturn I 449n, 577; II 538
    &n
  produces 7 or 6 stellar spirits I 198, 449
  Sophia Achamoth mother of I 197, 449
Iamblichus (often Jamblichus in tx)
  on Agathodaemon II 210-11
  on Assyrian records I 409, 650
  serpent symbol 1st of gods I 472-3
—— *De mysteriis* . . .
  archangels & archons I 235
"I am I"
  Kalaham-sa or I 78
  manifest consciousness produces I 15
I-am-ness. *See also* Ahaṃkāra
  egotism or I 197, 452; II 419, 614
"I am that I am" (Ehyeh Asher Ehyeh)
  chaotic matter & II 601
  explained kabbalistically II 468, 539
  Kalahansa & I 78
  man as attribute of II 243
  Moses, Jehovah numbers are II 539
"I and my Father are One" [*John*] I 574
Iaō (Gnos) II 536
  androgyne creator II 388
  chief of superior 7 heavens I 448
  Demiurgos called, (Fürst) II 541
  distinct fr Jehovah II 474
  genius of the Moon I 448, 577; II 538 &n
  Iacchus, Jehovah or II 460
  Jāho or, mystery name II 541
  Moses termed God II 465
  serpent (in *Genesis*) is II 388

seven rays (souls) of I 227n
triune, called 4-fold II 603
wrongly confused w Jevo II 541
Iaō-Jehovah, Jao-Jehovah II 389
Iaō-Sabaoth [Tsebāōth] II 603
Iapetus(os) (Gk) a Titan
  Atlas son of, & Clymene II 493
  brother of Atlas II 762
  one of 7 Arkite Titans II 143
  Prometheus son of II 525
Ibis (Egy) I 353
  air-water symbol I 358
  -headed god, Thoth, Mercury II 558
  killing of, a crime I 362
  kills serpents, destroys eggs I 362
  Thot-Lunus crowned w II 464
  two kinds of I 362-3
Iblis or Eblis (Moslem)
  fate's agent, defeats devs II 394
Ibn Gebirol, Solomon (*Kether Malkuth*) I 347,
    376
  basis of his sources II 461n
  on Jehovah I 393-4
  poem on the One I 439-40n
  seven heavens, earths of I 450n
  voiced esoteric philosophy II 461n
Ibn Wahohijah [Ibn al-Waḥshīya]
  transl *Nabathean Agriculture* II 455n
Ibrahim, Abraham (Renan) II 454
Ice
  ether allows water to become I 527
  polar II 326, 329
Ice Age II 71, 726, 738n. *See also* Glacial Epochs
"Ice-Age Climate and Time." *See* Pengelly
Iceland, part of northern cont II 423-4, 781
I-Ching, Yi King, Y-King
  celestial numbers in II 35
  discovery of agriculture & II 374
  fails to give cosmogony (Edkins) I 440
  falling stars, Satan (Ti) in II 486
  Great Extreme in I [356], 440
  Pyth numerals like those in I 440-1
Ichthyosauri II 258

law of dwarfing & II 733
Ἰχθῦς (Ichthys, Gk)
    fish, Pisces, as messiah & Vishnu I 653-4
    symbol of Bacchus II 313
Iconography I 384
    Christian, of catacombs II 586-7
    Gnostic II 565
    pre-Christian, perverted I 403
Icshu. *See* Ikshu
Ida (Norse), field of II 99, 100
Idā (Skt). *See* Ilā
Idaean Mysteries of Mighty Mother II 212n
Idam (Skt) this
    6 worlds above Earth II 384-5n
Idas (Gk) son of Aphareus
    wounds Castor, killed by Zeus II 122
Idaspati (Skt) or Vishnu
    Hindu Neptune, Poseidon II 765 &n
Idea(s). *See also* Ideation
    Absolute Thought & II 490
    active, passive thought & II 492
    all that was, is, & will be exists as I 282
    divine evolution of I 280
    First Cause as eternal I 214
    manifests by kriyāśakti I 293; II 173
    moves the aether (Plato) I 365
    older Horus, in demiurgic mind I 348
    Plato's innate, (von Hartmann) I 281
    Plutarch defines I 622
    Propator is abstract I 214
    the Word, speech, & names I 93-4
    Younger Horus is, in matter I 348
Ideal
    forms & archetypal ideas I 281n
    matter built on, forms I 281
    noblest, caricatured later I 326
    as opposed to real discussed I 55-6, 614
    plan held within Parabrahman I 281
    Vishnu as the, Cause I 349
Idealism
    in Eastern philosophy I 556n
    objective, of esoteric philosophy I 631
    occultism vs materialism & I 479
    Vedantic, Kantian I 603n
Idealist(s)
    pseudo-, & II 451, 651
    Spencer on II 490n
Ideality, plane of II 335
Ideation(s). *See also* Divine Thought, Mahat,
        Thought, Universal Mind
    ākāśa is cosmic I 326
    astral, reflects terrestrial things II 596
    ceases during pralaya I 328-9; II 598
    ceases in deep sleep I 38

cosmic, & substance one I 337n
cosmic, or Logos I 329 &n; II 24
cosmic, reflection of Univ Mind I 110
cross & cosmic II 561
dhyāni-chohans reflect I 280
divine wisdom in its II 299n
elohīm & 1st divine I 375
Fohat energy of cosmic I 16
lipikas amanuenses of eternal I 104
logoi perceive, & build I 380
lotus symb, passing into form I 380
man created by spiritual II 241-2
mysterious circuit of II 636
precosmic, or Great Breath I 15
reflected thru matter II 299n
spiritual, & 1st race II 242
spiritual, of divine monad I 266
univ, gives plan to Architect I 279-80
variation (evol) originates w II 299n
Vedantic view of universe I 596, 597n
Idei or Idaei (Gk). *See also* Dactyli
    Faber relates, to Kabiri II 360
    finger or adept-healer II 361
Ideograph(s, ic) II 582, 587
    hieroglyphs I xxiii
    records of the East II 438
    seven keys to symbolical II 584
    symbolism & I 303-9
    symbols of symbols used in II 547n
    writing of early man II 439, 530
Ideos, chaos or, of Paracelsus I 283-4
Idiot II 242
    an arrested man, not an ape II 678
    congenital I 224
Idol(s) I 397
    examples of I 392, 578, 675; II 560n, 586
    Jewish worship of II 588
    masses worship I 578
    of moon & Qū-tāmy I 394, 401; II 455
    personal god & I 414
    satanism of II 341
    worship died out in 4th race II 723
Idolatry(ous)
    astrolatry, heliolatry & I 392
    Church councils re II 279n
    Egyptian II 137
    exotericism same as II 281
    of gentile world (Faber) II 264
    Jewish I 649
    Mysteries degenerate into II 281
    fr "original sin" (Bossuet) II 279
    paganism & I 464
    prophets sought to stem II 492
    rapid progress of, in 5th race II 503

Idolatry [*Theologia Gentili*]. *See* Vossius
Idrā Rabbā Qaddishā (Heb) *Greater Holy*
    Assembly
    companions or eyes II 626
    Macroprosopus & Microprosopus II 625-6
    number 7 used in II 312n
    obscuration of worlds II 705 &n
    six & 7 lights II 625, 628
    tetrad & 2nd, 3rd of sephīrōth II 626
    White Head [II 705-6]
    white hidden fire [I 339]
Idrā Zūtā Qaddishā (Heb) *Lesser Holy Assembly*
    "all things become one body" I 240
    creating the forms of man II 83-4
    destruction (obscuration) II 704-5
    hammer, sparks, worlds I 246n; II 704
    "from Hoa is AB, Rūach . . ." II 83
    "I am that I am" I 78
    phallic, cruder than Purānas II 625n
    three Heads of Kabbala II 25
Idris or Idrus, Hermes, Enoch or II 361, 366-7
"Idyll of The White Lotus" [Mabel Collins]
    I 574
Ieov [or Jeu] (Gnos), primal or 1st man I 449
Ierna, sacred isle & worship on II 760
Ieve, Ieva (or Eve), pronounced Ya-va II 129
Ievo or Jevo. *See also* Jave
    genii antagonistic to Abraxas II 541
    Philo Biblius spelled, Jehovah II 129, 465
Igaga [Igigi], angels of heaven II 248n
Ignis (Lat) fire
    all is II 114
    fr Skt Agni II 101
Ignorance I 7, 198, 643
    is death II 215
    Īśvara as personal deity is I 330
    superstition & II 797
Iguanodon (giant reptile)
    early man & II 676
    genesis of, described II 151
    now small iguana II 154n, 348
I Hi Wei (fr *Tao-teh-ching*)
    means Jehovah (Rémusat) I 472
IHΣ, symbol of savior Bacchus III 313
IHVH. *See* YHVH
Ikshu (Skt) sugar cane
    Black Sea, Euxine or (Wilford) II 402n
Ikshvāku (Skt)
    Moru [Maru] of the family of I 378
    Nimi, Janaka & II 524n
Iku-gai-no-kami (Jap)
    fem part of duality I 217
Ilā or Idā (Skt)
    becomes Sudyumna (male) II 135, 143, 148

daughter, wife of Vaivasvata II 138, 140, 143,
    147-8
    primeval woman after deluge I 523
    same as Rhea, Titea II 144
    Vāch or I 523; II 143
    wife of Budha (Purānas) II 138, 140
Ildabaoth. *See* Ialdabaōth
Iliad. See Homer
Iliados, chaos of Paracelsus I 283
Ilios. See Schliemann, H.
Illusion(s, ory). *See also* Mahāmāyā, Māyā,
    Samvriti
    all save Parabrahman is I 522
    bhūtas, devas are I 295
    described I 329-30
    earth life desert of I 208
    everything, but the Absolute I 295
    great, or mahāmāyā I 278; II 88, 384n
    grossest matter acme of I 63
    man dominated by I 603n; II 458
    māyā, maria, maïa, Durgā I 396
    nirmānakāyas (maruts) beyond II 615
    phenomenal universe an I 145-6, 329
    physical nature bundle of II 475
    reality & I 295-6
    real to egos involved in it I 631
    in stanzas I 71
    time, of consciousness I 37
Illustrations . . . *See* Fergusson, J.
Ilmatar, virgin daughter of air II 26
Ilus (of Berosus). *See also* Ether, Father-
    Mother, Hyle
    elements latent in I 140
    ether of science I 339
    mud, mōt or I 58, 340
    primordial flame proceeds fr I 88
    prolific slime I 82
    rests in laya I 140
Ilythia [Ilithyia, Eileithyia] (Gk)
    Moon-goddess I 395
Image(s). *See also* Idolatry
    astral body, of man (Lévi) I 242
    cult & adoration of II 279
Imagination. *See also* Thoughts, Visions
    all forms of, fr prototype I 282n
    based on reminiscence II 293
    cosmos & I 309
    materialistic II 451
    scientific I 670-1; II 137n
Imat (Pers), "this" or globe D, Earth II 759
Imhot-pou [Imhotep] (Egy)
    Logos, creator or I 353
Immaculate Conception I 58-60. *See also*
    Kriyāśakti

church carnalized I 59
disfigured mystery teaching I xliv
Latin Church teaches two I 382n
manifested quaternary & I 88
de Mirville I 393
pagan & Christian, compared I 398-400
root fructified by ray I 65
Immetalization, Immetalized
    on globe A II 180
    gods pass thru state of I 188
    human monads & II 150, 169, 180, 185
    minerals are light II 169
Immortal(s), Immortality
    amrita or I 69 &n
    ātman imparts, to ego II 110
    bird of II 36
    circle symbolized II 552
    consciously, & 3rd race II 164
    cross in circle & II 556-7
    emblem of I 253n
    four, or lipikas I 104n
    of inner principle I 276
    Lucifer & II 388, 511
    for man alone I 225
    mantras & I 464
    plant of II 93
    serpent symbol of I 73, 404; II 283
    static & spiritual II 243
    true meaning of I 36n
    water of, stolen, story of II 381
Imperishable Sacred Land II 6. *See also* Conti-
    nent, Hyperborean Continent
Impersonality
    divine, of avatāras & Logos II 478
    of omnipresent reality I 273
In (Jap). *See also* Shinto
    Earth or I 241
    seven divine spirits born fr I 217-18
Inachos(us) (Gk)
    Io daughter of II 414
    Phoroneus son of II 519
Inca(s). *See also* Peru
    built like Pelasgians II 745
    seven, repeopled Earth II 141
Incantation(s) I 169, 354
    mantras or, & sound I 464
    stop hailstorm I 469
Incarnate(ion, s). *See also* Reincarnations
    causes of I 193
    "curse" of, & the Rebels II 246
    cycle of I 17
    of the dhyānis II 228
    divine, & avatāras II 555-6
    of Eastern heroes II 225n

of the 4 & the three I 222
gods must pass thru I 188
of highest seven I 638
immaculate I 399
in inferior & higher intellectual races II 162
karma overrides heredity in II 178
kumāra, of Śiva II 249
of monad in lower kingdoms II 180, 186
monad's cycle of I 16n, 175, 182-3
never-ceasing cycles of human II 515
of 1 of the seven II 358-9
personality cannot remember past II 306
premature, of the host II 421
same atoms in every II 671-2
same star for all I 572
777, problem of I 168
successive, & absorption I 636
those who no longer I 86
Varāha or boar avatāra I 368
Inch
    British, & esoteric system I 316
    Egyptian cubit & I 313
    "Jehovah is Noah" or British II 467-8
    Parker ratio origin of British I 313
Inclination of Axis. *See* Axis
Incognizable
    Ain-sōph, deity II 472
    Brahman is II 108
    cause does not put forth evolution II 487
    circle &, deity I 113
    deity & time & space I 432-3; II 382n
    deity, Ea is II 53
    exhibits aspects of itself II 487
    light, sound & I 432
    Principle I 330
    veil betw, & Logos I 431
Incorporeal Corporealities I 566, 632
Incorruptible, fr corruptible II 95
Incrusted Age. *See* Sedimentation
India. *See also* Bhārata-Varsha
    Akkad tribes fr I 392; II 202-3
    ape sacred in I 190
    Babylonia got wisdom fr II 566
    cave temples in II 220n
    claims desc fr kingdom of Saturn II 768
    cradle of humanity II 203
    deity is the universe in I 92n
    doubly connected w Americas II 327
    dragon story in II 384
    Egypt &, kindred nations II 417
    Egyptian zodiac fr southern II 435
    esoteric schools in I xxiii
    giants 56 ft tall in, (Mandeville) II 755
    giants of II 336

invasion of, by twice-born I 270
Jewish measurements fr I 316, 320-1
Jews fr I 313n; II 200, 471n
kali-yuga reigns supreme in I 377
language of mantras in I 464
lotus symbolism of I 379-86; II 472
memory of sorcery in II 503
occultism of, fr Central Asia II 565
occupied by Brahmans after flood II 608
poetry of, & Greece compared II 450
Pythagoras' knowledge fr I 361, 433
rishis, manus no longer in II 178
savages live in trees in II 676
secret MSS hidden in I xxxiv
seven seas, rivers, mts of II 603
small-brained aboriginals of II 686n
southern, part of Lemuria II 324
still has adepts w 7 keys I 311
subterranean cities in II 220-1, 397
Sun worship given to Egypt by II 379
taught 3 aspects of universe I 278
temples of I 209n
war in heaven fr I 418
writing in II 225-6
zodiac of II 50, 432-3
India House, Śiva statue at II 591
Indian(s) (American)
  languages of II 199
  many kinds of, writing II 439
  petition to U.S. president II 439
  fr red-yellow Atlanteans II 249-50
  Retzius links, w Guanches II 740
  Zuñi, traditions II 628
Indian(s) (Asian)
  ate serpents' hearts I 404
  British opinion of dark II 287
  concealed deity in, theology I 75n
  knew of extinct monsters II 713
  legends re buried libraries I xxxiv
  religion among oldest I 10
  schools of philosophy I 269, 278
  sevens in, thought II 612-14
  of smaller stature II 332
Indian Antiquities. See Maurice, T.
Indian Ocean
  islands in, part of Atlantis II 405
  Lemuria buried under, (Haeckel) II 327
  once reached Central Asia II 609
India: What Can It Teach Us? See Müller
Indische Altherthumskunde. See Lassen, C.
Individual(s, ity)
  accidental death of II 303
  acquired thru effort I 17

atoms possess no I 630
atyantika pralaya & I 371
condition of man's II 241
constant rebirth of same II 303, 306
cycle of evolution (Kab) II 188
distinct, behind every noumenon I 493
each man's true star deals w I 572-3
hierarchies, their units & I 38, 275-6
immortal II 422
impersonal, of celestial yogis II 246
of Kapilas of satya- & kali-yugas II 572
man's higher I 158
memory generates notion of I 292
monads as atomic souls I 619
nirvāna & I 266
nonhumans & I 275
personality &, explained II 306
spiritual, of monad I 265
Individuality . . . See Hellenbach, L. B.
Indo-Chinese, stature of II 332
Indo-European, 5th subrace I 319
Indolentia, Epicurean, & nirvāna I 577n
Indovansas. *See* Induvamśas
Indra (Skt)
  Apollo & II 383
  Asura name applied to II 92, 500
  beguiles yogis II 614
  called Manojava, 3rd round, race II 615n
  as Earth's calf I 398n
  Fohat scientific aspect of I 673
  god of air I 462
  god of visible heaven II 501
  guards the East I 128
  heaven of, & Eden II 203
  kumāra in early life II 383
  located in tail of Tortoise II 549
  loka of, & gandharvas I 523n
  Lord of the maruts (Marutvān) II 615n
  maruts allies of II 613
  Michael & II 378, 384, 498, 549 &n, 614
  now degraded in kali-yuga II 614
  potency of space I 9-10 &n
  punishes those who break laws II 606
  Rig-Veda, Purānas re II 378
  Śakra or secondary divinity I 376
  supports Brihaspati in war II 498
  tempts Kandu II 174-6
  various names of II 382
  Vul (Assyria) same as II 386
  War in Heaven & I 202; II 384, 501
Indrāni or Aindrī (Skt)
  personified the senses II 614
  Śrī, Lakshmī are II 76n

Indriya or Aindriyaka Creation (Skt)
  described I 446, 453-4
  modified ahamkāra in I 453
Indriyātman (Skt)
  spiritual or intellectual soul II 108
Indu (Skt), physical Moon, not Soma II 45
Indus River
  flows fr Lake of Dragons II 204
  Nile, Ethiops or II 417-18
Induvaṃśas (Skt)
  lunar kings I 392
  war of, w Sūrya Vanśas I 397
Inertia
  blind & intelligent powers I 520
  coma of minerals or I 626n
  greatest occult force I 511
  solar evolution & I 501
  spiritual II 62
  static, & Brahmā resting II 244, 507
Infallibility
  HPB claims no personal II 22n
  false, & science I 520
  no theosophist ought to claim II 640
  of pope II 316n
  scientific, theological II 349
Infinite(y, ies). *See also* Boundless
  cannot know finiteness I 56
  circle symbolizes I 65, 113, 134n
  discussed I 8
  Eternal Cause I 14-16
  existence spreads throughout I 289
  finite cannot conceive the I 51, 132
  finite into, & physical body I 181
  the One I 130
  Plato's finite &, re monad, duad I 426
  principle cannot create I 7-8
  serpent symbolizes I 74, 253n, 371, 379;
    II 552
  two, cannot exist I 7
Infinitude. *See also* Parabrahman
  deific, circle of II 541
  within ourselves II 703
Inflectional Speech, discussed II 200
Infusoria
  bacteria like elephants to I 225n
  classed among algae I 177
  in drop of water I 146-7
  filamentoid, & giant animals II 151
Ingersoll, Colonel Robert G. II 767
Inhabitants. *See also* Beings
  adepts know only, of our solar system
    II 700 &n
  on other planets I 602
  of other spheres I 605-8; II 33 &n

Initiate(s, ed). *See also* Adepts, Brotherhood,
    Dragons, Mahātmas, Masters, Seers, Ser-
    pents of Wisdom, Twice-Born
  Aeschylus an II 419 &n, 524
  āngirasas instructors of II 605n
  ape's origin known to I 190
  arhan not highest I 206
  Aristotle not an I 493
  arts & sciences preserved by II 572
  Aryan, built menhirs, zodiacs II 750, 754
  Aryan, knew whole cosmogony II 500
  ashes of, kept 7 lunar years II 588n
  Atlantean, taught Cyclopes I 208n
  called little ones II 504 &n
  cannot divulge all he knows II 760
  can trace soul's history I 381 &n
  Christian II 60
  chronology of Brahmin II 49
  -commentator would not explain II 637n
  connected w Sun, wisdom II 210n
  crucified on Tree of Life II 560
  cycles known to II 70
  darkness is absolute light to I 41
  decipher myths II 138-9, 764-5
  descent into Hades, etc II 558
  dhyāni-chohans more powerful I 234-5
  "dragons," "serpents," refer to I 408; II 94n,
    203, 210n, 213, 280n, 501, 572
  early Greek sages were I 117
  Egyptian, went to England by land II 750
  Enoch an II 506
  Father & Son, knew meaning of II 231n
  feud betw, of left- & right-path II 494, 501
  few, master all 7 keys II 584
  five becomes 7 at death of II 580
  fourth race, in Central Asia II 339
  of Garden of Eden II 494
  Gnostic sects founded by II 389
  great, fr Advaita School I 522
  -hermits lived in caves II 501
  Hesiod's *Theogony* history to II 765
  highest, known to few adepts I 611-12
  history of races known to II 133, 437-8
  Hungarian, taught Olcott I xix
  idolatry, sought to stem II 492
  inflectional speech language of II 200
  Jesus an I 577-8, 653; II 504, 566
  Julian an II 587n
  Kapila, of kali-yuga II 572
  knowledge gained by generations of II 700
  know racial figures II 312
  language of, plain II 786-7
  live in every age I xlv
  lives in his astral body II 499

magi of Persia, Chaldea were II 395
Marcus an II 563
meaning of Vedas, Purāṇas, know I 520
Moses an I 73, 314, 316, 352; II 212, 456, 465n, 541n
Mysteries inherited by II 125
nāgas or I 408; II 572
names given to II 210n, 215
Nazarenes, among II 96n
not influenced by genii I 295 &n
Paul an I 8-9, 240; II 268, 504, 513n, 704
perfected faultless system II 133
Plato an II 88, 266, 395, 554
popes, some early, were I 311
priest-, knew the noumena II 517-18
priests read Dracontia II 346
produced rarely fr age to age I 211
profane &, will remain I 207
prophets or II 492
Purāṇas, hold key to I 423
pyramids & II 353, 558
Pythagoreans were II 153
Ragon a European I xxxvi
rākshasas are II 165n
reborn after crucifixion II 560
records of, fr beginning of 4th race I 646
ring pass not & I 131
rising Sun & II 558, 559
ruled early 5th races II 364
rule the gods (devas) II 111
Russian mystics, in Central Asia I xxxvi
Śankarāchārya greatest I 271-2
saved w secret teachings II 230
secret records of I xxxiv
see beneath māyā I 45
Senzar once known to all I xliii
serpents & II 26n
seven number of II 35
soma given only to II 498
spiritual overcomes physical w II 499
swastika over hearts of II 586
symbolism, knowledge of II 439, 796
taught evolution of atoms I 522
three-day trance of II 580
tomb of an, at Saïs II 396
trials of, symbol for II 505
twice-born II 70, 111
veil information re early races II 715n
war betw, & sorcerers I 419
will judge angels II 112
wisdom of early Hebrew I 352
withhold knowledge II 518
Initiation(s)
  Aryan & Jewish II 469-70

astrology one of secrets of II 500n
awakens inner sight II 294n
Book of Enoch record of II 229, 535
Buddha overshadows highest I 109
buddhas meet adepts in I 574
candidate & dragon fight in II 381
Christians eliminated memory of I xl
circle squared at supreme II 450
cycle of, & sidereal year I 314
discussed [*Lucifer*] II 558-9
Egyptian, & Fall (Lacour) II 215-16n
facing one's Augoeides in final I 573
fourth race temples of II 211
fourth race wisdom only thru II 134
Greek writers gave truths of I 507
Julian re II 35
light of, & Fire Self II 570
manus, śishtas & 3rd degree of II 308
mastery of cycles thru I 642
performed in Great Pyramid I 314, 317-18n; II 461-2, 558
Phenoch or Enoch symbol of II 617
into pre-Adamic Mysteries II 452-3
precede secret teachings I 164
psychic, spiritual elements & I 229
religious history related in I 307
sacred numbers known thru I 66-7
SD taught to Egyptians at II 137
secret II 378-80
secrets of higher II 51
septenary division taught in I 168
serpent & tree symbolize II 354-5
sevenfold mystery of, & lyre II 529
seven forms of, (*Anugītā*) II 638
seven grades of I 206
tau cross, crucifix & II 542-3, 557, 586n
truth preserved thru I xxxvi
Upanishads prepared chelas for I 270
wand of candidate for II 518
water, fire in II 566n
Initiator(s)
  Builders or II 345n
  first, into Mysteries II 267n
  "Great Sacrifice" called the I 208
  Hanoch, Enoch, Enos & II 529n
  high, creates bodhisattva I 109
  Wondrous Being or I 207-12
Injustice(s)
  apparent, of life II 303-5
  humanity & causes of I 644
Inland Sea of Central Asia II 5, 220, 502-3, 637
Inman, Thomas
  degrades tau cross I 405

—— *Ancient Faiths . . . Ancient Names*
  derivation of Jehovah II 129
  engraving of Mary II 38
  symbol of fish II 313
In Matrem (Deorem). See Julian, Emperor
Inmetalization. *See* Immetalization
Inner Eye. *See* Eye, Pineal Gland, Senses,
  Third Eye
Inner God
  animal-self vs II 272
  man links, w matter II 274
Inner Man, drawn into Parent-Sun I 638-9
Inner Voice, conscience, chiti, or I 288n
Innocents, slaughtered by Herod II 504n
Inorganic
  every, particle living I 261
  Leibniz endowed, matter w life I 628
  nothing in nature is I 280-1, 507, 626n;
    II 672
  occultism does not accept I 248-9, 340
Inquisition II 38
  alchemists & II 238
Insanity
  reality of delusions of I 295
  soul free of body during I 234
Inscription(s)
  at ancient Troy II 440
  cuneiform & other II 4-5
  in Egypt & Babylon II 793
  on Egy tombs I 436-7
  of lunar mother goddess I 400
  at Saïs of Neith I 393
  on speaking stone II 342
Insects (sarīsripa) II 52, 185
  compared to materialists II 370
  cycles in life of II 622
  eyes of, part of skin II 295
  gigantic II 198
  man created II 290
  fr man's relics 3rd, 4th rounds II 290
Instinct(ual) I 640
  animal I 234, 291
  animal, & homunculi II 349
  of animal monad II 103
  of lemmings discussed II 782
  monad & I 175
  primordial blastema had blind II 120
  sexless creative, of early man II 275
Institutes of Justinian, on sorcery, etc I 469
Institutes of Manu. See Laws of Manu
Instructors. *See* Divine Kings
Intellect (Human). *See* Manas, Mind (Human)
  of Atlanteans I 192n
  brain size &, (Davis) II 522-3

  can deal only w emanations II 41
  development of, in 4th round I 188-9
  dhyānis gave, to man II 47n
  divine, veiled in man II 74
  gauging human II 301
  great 2-edged weapon II 163
  gulf betw, of man & ape II 677n
  power of, & śaktis I 292-3
  soul made room for physical I 225
Intellectual(ity)
  "breaths" or angels II 318n
  capacities different II 103
  developed in 4th race II 167
  egotism of, vs spiritual insight II 158
  evolution goes w physical II 411
  faculties develop later II 728
  faculties influence evolution II 728
  part of triple evolution I 181-91
  replaced spiritual in 5th race II 300
  rudras, kumāras developed II 585
  over spiritual in civilization II 319
Intellectual Development . . . See Draper
Intellectual System. See Cudworth, R.
Intellectual World, 2nd plane I 200
Intelligence. *See also* Consciousness, Wisdom
  absolute, & heat I 85
  all beings must acquire human I 277
  buddhi & universal I 256
  chaos impregnated by I 64
  corporeality &, unrelated I 608n
  cosmic, active II 596, 597n
  esoteric meaning of, (*Anugītā*) II 567
  Fohat is guiding I 493
  Mahat or, in Purānas I 330
  mundane, or nous I 50
  one indivisible, in universe I 277
  subconscious, pervades matter II 649
  time & universal I 62
  waters of wisdom flow into I 239
Intelligences
  animate centers of being II 34
  animate manifestation I 634
  behind rotation I 502-3, 505-6, 594
  condemned to reincarnate II 248
  within the Cosmic Soul I 530
  elements ruled by I 146, 535n, 594
  evolution guided by, (Wallace) I 107, 339
  Fohat guided by universal II 330
  formless, inhabit planets I 103
  free, rebellious II 79
  guiding, generate elementals I 146
  invisible I 133
  De Maistre on, & forces I 484
  not supernatural II 194

Jupiter created II 270
  several Aryan races in I 644-5
Irruentes, fallen ones II 279
Īśa (Skt), & Īśvara II 114
Isaguri or Issachar (now Ashnagor)
  Afghan tribe II 200n
Isaiah
  angel saved Israelites II 480
  Assyrian armies called trees II 496
  denounces Jewish phallicism II 588
  evils come fr north & west I 123
  fiery serpents II 206n, 212
  Lucifer & morning star I 70; II 501
  new moon & feasts II 462
  reproofs of, to King Ahaz II 492
  seraphim in II 63, 387n, 501
Isanagi, Isanami [Izanagi, Izanami] (Jap)
  two kinds of ancestors (pitris) I 217, 241
Isarim (an Essenian initiate)
  found Smaragdine tablet II 556
Iscariotes (Judas), not understood II 389
Ischin [Ishīn] (Heb) II 375-6
Isdubar. *See* Izdubar
Ishtar (Assyrian Venus)
  Ashtōreth or II 145
  eldest of heaven & Earth II 248n
  helped Sin overcome Messengers II 62
  identical w Aditi & Vāch II 43
Iside, De. See Plutarch
Isidorus (of Seville)
  on talking stones (Photius) II 342
Isis (Egy) I 388, 399; II 462
  Aditi is II 43
  ansated cross symbolic aspect of II 31n
  cat sacred to I 387
  corner of veil of, lifted I 299
  crown of, an asp II 26n
  daughter, mother of Osiris I 430
  daughter, wife, sister of Osiris I 137
  Diana &, parents of Earth II 23
  egg sacred to I 366 &n
  equal to Egyptian male gods I 136n
  has horns, hence Vāch I 434
  Horus born fr Osiris & II 472
  ibis sacred to I 362
  Io, Eve or II 416, 418n
  Kabiri or, taught agriculture II 390
  lunar goddess I 228-9, 390, 396; II 23
  Mout (Mut) aspect of II 464
  Osiris interchangeable w I 72n
  revealed mysteries of wheat & corn II 374
  Saïs inscription about I 393
  shown suckling Horus I 400
  suckling Harpocrates (Gnos) I 410

symb of Nile riverbed & lunar year I 390;
  II 583
  Venus &, w horns II 31
  Venus or II 30
  virgin mother of Horus II 43
  wife, mother, sister I 396
Isis and Osiris. See Plutarch
Isis-Latona (Egy)
  earth & water I 340; II 130
  wives of Osiris I 340
Isis-Osiris (Egy)
  ansated cross or II 217
  cosmic allegory of II 143
  Kabiri or, brought corn II 364
  reigned over 75,000 years ago II 374n
  taught arts, sciences (Basnage) II 366
  Thoth &, man's ancestors II 365
Isis Unveiled. See Blavatsky, H. P.
Islam. *See also* Koran, Mohammed, Sūfis
  minarets of II 85
  won converts w sword I xli
Island(s). *See also* Daitya, Dvīpas, Rhodes,
    Ruta, Sacred Island
  Atlanteans inhabited surviving II 326
  Atlantic, continental remnants II 790
  classics on, & continents II 760
  dry, of Tahmurath II 398, 399
  of good spirits II 371
  holy, became black w sin II 67, 372 &n
  India, South America joined by II 327
  Lemurian II 7, 327
  Ma-li-ga-si-ma legendary Chinese II 365
  Plato's II 8, 9, 141, 250n, 314, 322, 352, 395,
    693, 765
  Polynesian, once large continent II 222-4
  Purānas use, as symbols II 322
  Samothrace II 3, 4-5
  seven allegorical, of Purānas II 320-2, 326,
    758
  seven, belonged to Atlantis II 350
  sidereal, Delos or Asteria II 383, 773 &n
  twelve, centers & zodiac II 502-3
  White II 67, 147, 288, 319, 322, 402-4, 407,
    408n, 584
Islanders, South Sea II 168, 421n
Island Life. See Wallace, A. R.
Isle of Mona, moving stone at II 345
Isolation
  effects of, on races II 425
  factor in variation II 738
  secondary evolutionary cause II 648-9
Ispahan [Isfahan]
  Persian city built by Huschenk II 397

Israel. *See also* Jews, Prophets, Semites
  children of, & Jehovah II 537-8
  David numbers II 387n
  goat &, as symbol II 510
  God of, lower angel II 61
  Jehovah & Michael guide II 480
  karma of, glowed over 1st century I xli
  kings of, called cedars II 494
  no phallic Jehovah for 1,000 yrs II 469
  race of, under Saturn I 576-7
  Satan stood up against II 387n
  seventy Elders of, & planets I 576
  spiritual rock that followed II 341
  tribes of I 651; II 130, 200n
Israelite(s). *See also* Hebrews, Jews
  Baal of, is Sun-Jehovah I 397n
  beliefs once pure as Aryan II 471
  Carlyle on II 470
  God of, tribal god II 508
  may have worshiped Nebo II 456
  mystery gods of II 3
  primeval faith of, different I 320 &n
  repeated Vaivasvata story (Noah) II 265
  sacrificed often to wind, fire I 466
  Sadducees refined sect of II 472-3
  tribal god of II 420
Issa, woman, Earth, & Israelites II 200n
Issachar (son of Jacob)
  Isaguri or II 200n
  Taurus or I 651
Istakhr, or Persepolis II 398
Ister. *See* Ishtar
"Is the Sun Merely . . ." *See* Blavatsky
Isu [Tse]-no-gai-no-kami (Jap)
  male portion of duality I 217
Īśvara (Eswara, Iswara) (Skt). *See also* Logos
  ātma is beyond I 573-4
  in *Bhagavad-Gītā* II 114
  cannot see Parabrahman I 351n

creative potency or I 296n, 451
daivīprakriti & I 136
Hari or II 76n
ignorance &, as personal deity I 330
Logos or I 130 &n, 137, 434, 573; II 637
Lord or I 428; II 473
Mahat or I 256
male aspect of māyā I 332
as manifested deity II 108
mūlaprakriti known only to I 349n, 351n
Parabrahman & I 55, 130n, 451
plus māyā is manifested world I 7
śuddhisattva essence of body of I 132
unchanged in pralaya & manvantara I 573-4
various names for I 110
Wilford "saw Assur in" I 654
Iswur. *See* Īśvara
It. *See also* Absolute, All, Parabrahman
  Brahman the noumenon I 374
  breath of Absoluteness I 290
  causeless cause I 258
  desire first arose in II 176
  invisible Deity I 114
  Supreme as cause I 6
I't, King, fr the waves II 406
Italy
  crosses along highways in II 542
  Peruvians built like Pelasgians in II 745
  rocking stones in II 342n
Itchāsakti [Ichchhāśakti] (Skt)
  described I 292-3
  will power used by yogis I 293; II 173
Iurbo (Gnos), name of Jao-Jehovah II 389
Ivi (Tahitian) bone, woman made fr II 194
Izdubar [Gilgamesh] (Chald) II 336, 531
Izeds or Peris (Pers)
  Aryan race II 394
  war of, w devs [daevas] II 776

J

Jabal, Kabir instructor II 390
Jablonski, P. E., *Pantheon aegyptiorum* . . .
    Io signified Moon II 463
    sons of rebellion II 386
Jachīn (Heb) [1 *Kings* 7:21 & 2 *Chron* 3:17]
    Boaz &, Christianity rests on II 497
Jack the Ripper II 507n
Jacob
    covenant of, w tribal deity II 470
    Ephraim elect of I 653
    Esau &, like Cain & Abel II 135
    God of, not Father of Jesus II 509
    ladder of II 281n, 357
    "lot of Jehovah's inheritance" II 537-8
    pillar of, phallic II 471-2, 473
    sons of, allegory of black, white II 211-12
    sons of, & Arabs II 200n
    twelve sons of, & zodiac I 649, 651; II 200n
Jacob, Major G. A., *The Vedāntasāra*
    Parabrahman, etc I 7 &n
Jacolliot, Louis I 636
    much truth in *Bible in India* II 442
—— *Les Fils de Dieu*
    q Vamadeva Mudaliyar I 376-7
—— *Histoire des Vierges*
    evidence of Pacific cataclysms II 788n
    Pacific continent & submergence II 222-4
    prehistoric civilization existed II 786n
Jadoo [Jādū] (Hindu & Pers), sorcery II 232n
Jagaddhātrī (Skt)
    conveyed 6 embryos to Devaki II 527
Jagadyoni (Skt) womb of the world
    gods & men proceed fr II 108
    ideal kārana or cause I 46
    material womb of world I 582
    not Parabrahman II 108
Jagannātha (Skt) Lord of the World
    bigotry & materialism cars of I xli
    Rawlinson on II 130
Jagat (Skt) the universe
    "This" refers to I 7
Jāh [Yāh] (Heb), Lord II 39, 467. *See also* Yāh,
    Yāho
    divine name of Chochmāh [Ḥokhmāh] I 355
    Hebrew, discussed II 129
    same as Yāh II 126

Jahāngīr (Akbar's son)
    published Badā'ūnī's book I xxivn
Jahé, Yahra II 465
Ja-Heva. *See* Yāh-Ḥavvāh
Jah-, Jod-Hovah. *See* Yāh-Ḥavvāh
Jāh(navī) (Skt) Ganges II 130
Jah-Noah [Yāh-Noah]
    Jehovah of Bible II 596
    śishta identical w II 596
    Tetragrammaton, quaternary or II 595-6
Jāho-Jāh [Yāho-Yāh] II 129, 465
    Mystery name II 541
Jah-Veh. *See* Yāhweh
Jain(as)
    settlement in southern India II 224n
    Tīrthankaras of II 423n
Jaina Cross (Jain, Masonic)
    swastika called II 98
    tau, Christian, &, same meaning I 657
    Thor's hammer or I 5
Jakin. *See* Jachīn
Jalālābād II 338
Jala-rūpa (Skt) water form
    name of sign Makara II 577
Jamaica, Voodoos of II 209
Jamblichus. *See* Iamblichus
Jambu-Dvīpa (Skt) rose-apple tree island
    Bhārata-Varsha best part of II 369
    at center of dvīpas II 758
    described II 320-2, 403-4 &n
    divided among 9 sons II 320
    North & South America & II 182, 403
    only terrestrial dvīpa II 326
James (Epistle)
    God does not tempt man I 414
    wisdom, earthly, sensual I 194, 197n; II 134n;
    275n
James, Sir Henry
    cataclysms due to axis changes II 314
Jamshīd, built Persepolis II 398
Janaka (Skt), birth of, (*Vāyu-Purāna*) II 524n
Janārdana (Skt) Vishnu or Krishna
    Rudra becomes, breathes rain I 370
Janarloka (Skt)
    beings in, at mahā-pralaya I 371

fifth division (or world) I 116
one of 7 lokas II 321
Jaṅgama (Skt), locomotive or fixed I 454
Janna, or Dan [Dhyāna, Skt]
  reform by meditation & knowledge I xxn
  secret portions of, & wisdom religion I xx
Jannaeus, Alexander (of Lyda) II 504n
Jao-Jehovah. *See* Iaō-Jehovah
Japan, Japanese I xxxiv; II 727
  birth of 7 spirits I 216-18
  Buddhism declined in I xx-i
  Buddhist ascetics secretive I 67n, 173-4
  can read Chinese writing I 307n
  cosmogony of I 213-14
  cyclopaedia, chart fr II 204
  esoteric school in I xxiii
  figures for cycles II 566
  hierarchy of creative powers I 213-14, 215-18
  most learned Taoists among I xxv
Japan. See Kaempfer, E.
Japhet, listed among "Arkite" Titans II 143,
  343n
Jared, Jarad [Yārād, Yered] (Heb) II 391n, 597n
Jāta (Skt), a kumāra II 319
Jaṭāyu (Skt), son of Garuḍa
  cycle of 60,000 yrs II 565, 570
  king of feathered tribe II 570
Jāti (Skt), birth I 373
Jaumes, Prof A., "De la distinction . . ."
  forces as secondary agents I 506
Java
  geologically recent II 789
  remnant of sunken continent II 222
Java-Aleim. *See* Yāhweh Elohīm
Jave, Javo, Jevo. *See also* Ievo, Jehovah, Yava,
  YHVH
  Jehovah, Jupiter (numbers) II 466
  Sanchoniathon on II 129
Jayas (Skt) 12 creative gods
  Adityas or II 182
  born each manvantara II 90, 585
  identical w mānasa, rājasas II 90
Jealousy of the gods II 174, 283
Jebel Djudi [Judi], Arab deluge mt II 145
Jeho, Jah, Iah (Heb), Jehovah II 129
Jehoshua, Joshua, Christ or I 264; II 539
Jehoshua ben Chananea [Joshua ben-
  Ḥananyah], performed miracles I xliii n
Jehovah [Yāhweh, Jah-Heva]. *See also* Tetra-
  grammaton, YHVH
  abstract sephīrōth not I 438-9
  Adonai of later Rabbins II 452, 465
  androgynous first, then sexed I 60, 72n;
    II 125-30, 134, 601

Azāzēl & I 441-2n; II 376, 387
Bīnāh or I 6n, 99n, 215n, 230, 355, 392, 394;
  II 134n, 384n, 595
Cain, esoterically I 414, 578; II 269n, 388
  chosen people II 538
  connected w child-giving I 264
  copy of Osiris I 316
  curses, then blesses II 410
  dark aspects of, will vanish II 420
  David brought name to Israel II 541
  Deity of *Genesis* falsely called II 388
  demon & deus I 394
  descended in pillar of fire I 341
  diameter of circle (Parker) I 6n; II 544
  double-sexed II 62, 125, 130, 463
  Elijah, Elihu & II 531
  elohīm, host & I 73, 112-13, 129, 197-8,
    492-3n; II 509-10
  an emanation & one of sephīrōth I 230
  etymology of name II 129-30
  exoteric national faith II 472-3
  fiery serpents & I 414; II 387n
  a fighting god II 43-4n
  forbids reviling the gods II 477
  -Frankenstein & devil II 508
  Gnostic view of I 197-8; II 389
  god among other gods (*Psalms*) II 508
  God not II 388
  God of *Genesis* 1-4 is not II 388
  Iacchus, Iaō or II 460
  Ilda-Baoth [Ialdabaōth] or I 197; II 244
  incognizable deity behind II 472
  Jah or, is Noah II 467-8
  jealous, tribal god II 420, 508, 537-8, 597n
  Jesus rebelled against I 576-7
  Jve, Jave, Jupiter or, (Skinner) II 466
  kingdom of II 245
  light of, refers to man II 38
  Lord of the Moon II 75
  lower, material class II 95n, 96
  Lucifer higher & older than I 70-1
  lunar, god of generation I 387-94; II 40-1,
    139n, 234, 397, 464, 466
  lunar, or Dionysos, Bacchus I 335
  male aspect Moon, Venus II 462
  male-female I 18, 60; II 126, 537
  Michael angelic form of II 383
  Moon linked w I 198n, 387; II 62, 77, 462,
    464, 474, 540
  Moses &, permutations II 539
  mystic letters of, on "Ark" II 460
  name became ineffable II 509
  name of, a screen I 438-9
  Nārada compared w II 48

Noah, Adam &, numerically same I 444
not perfection II 413
not phallic for 1,000 yrs II 469
not superior to Vishnu I 423
number of, thrice seven II 40
one of the sephīrōth I 197-8, 438
the One, yet personal god I 426
Ophites called, Son of Saturn I 577
"personating spirit" II 243, 508-9
phallic symbol I 6n, 316; II 472-3
Prajāpati same numbers as I 90 &n
procreative organ & II 574
produces 7 stellar spirits I 197-8
resurrection as brazen serpent I 472
St Michael as II 379, 479, 508
Samael &, are identical I 417
Satan adversary of II 243
Satan &, identical II 387n
Satan is, upside down II 510
Saturn &, glyphically same I 417, 578; II 235, 540
sends Satan to tempt Job I 422
sent Sarah to tempt Pharaoh II 174
seraphim symbols of II 387n
serpent in Garden of Eden I 422
as serpent tempted Eve I 73
seven letters of name I 335
Source of Measures explains II 125
spiteful, vengeful god I 439-40n
substitute god, explained II 472-3
tempter, known as II 215-16n, 269n
tempts David to number people I 414
ten the number of II 416n
third rate potency I 349
three sons of, 3 races II 397
took Israel as his portion I 576
traces of androgyne, in Bible I 6n, 397n
trickery, deceit of, & Vishnu I 421-2
true & perfect serpent I 410
various Jupiters & I 463
various names of I 438, 578
war against the theological I 619n
working forces of I 440
Jehovah-Adam, Brahmā-Virāj & II 126
Jehovah-Bīnāh-Arēlīm, head of the elohīm II 608
Jehovah-Cain-Abel
divine hermaphrodite II 126
explained II 388
Jehovah-Eve, Adam-Kadmon becomes II 128
Jehovah-Sabbaoth [Tsebāōth] (Heb)
Baal, Bel, Śiva, Saturn & I 459
Jehovah-Satan, man in the moon I 393
Jehovah-Sephīrōth (Heb)

Brahmā-Prajāpati & II 126
Jehovistic
account of Genesis II 252n
texts 800 years after Moses II 473
Jehovite Creation II 5
Jekyll, Dr & Mr Hyde. *See* Stevenson, R. L.
Jellalābād [Jalālābād] rock cut temples II 338
Jen-nang, Chinese divine man II 365
Jennings, Hargrave, *Phallicism . . .*
evilly inspired author of II 544
q Gregorie on Adam's body II 467
q McClatchey on Kwan or Yin I 471
q O'Brien on round towers I 472
St George, St Michael, Lucifer II 238n
stone in Ark phallic YHVH II 473
Swan of Leda priapic I 358
yoginī a prostitute I 472
—— [*The Rosicrucians . . . Rites & Mysteries*]
astro-theosophic chart II 461
Jeremiah II 425
children immolated to Moloch I 463n
curse against elohīm II 128
evils fr north & west I 123
Jeremiah ben Eliazar, Rabbi
on 139th psalm of David II 134n
Jeruskoven [Jernskoven, Norway]
frigid zone in East II 535
Jeshida. *See* Yehīdāh
Jesuits(ism)
assisted de Mirville II 481-2
deceit, craft among I 423
turned knowledge into sorcery I 311
Jesu-Maria, story of statue of I 72n
Jesus. *See also* Avatāra, Christ, Messiah
believed in reincarnation II 111n
"Be ye wise as serpents" (*Matt*) I 74
birth time unknown I 653
called great fish II 313 &n
called "Tree of Life" II 496
clairvoyant powers of II 231n
communed w Father I 578
contempt of, for Sabbath I 240
crucifixion of II 560-2, 586-7
disciples of, of same star I 574
Father of, explained I 574 &nn
Father of, not Jehovah II 509
five words on garment of II 580
Galilean adept II 231
an initiate I 578, 653; II 504, 566
Joshua &, man-fish I 264
Joshua was, kabbalistically II 359
mother of, & Buddha I xxxii
"mysteries" for disciples only II 231n
mystically, man-woman II 134

not to be painted as a lamb II 279n
number of, is 888 II 518
Pharisees cursed II 378
in *Pistis Sophia* I 132n; II 563-4, 566, 569
on prayer I 280n
rebelled against Christian god I 576-7
rebuked the wind I 468
recognized no Jehovah I 577-8
serpents, wisdom & II 386
in women's clothes I 72n
Jethro (Midian priest)
initiated Moses II 465n, 541
Jetzira. *See* Yetsīrāh
Jevo. *See* Ievo
Jevons, William Stanley
use of numbers, figures I 430n
—— *Investigations in Currency . . .*
on sunspots I 541n
—— *The Principles of Science*
matter registers all events I 104, 124
Jew(s). *See also* Hebrews, Holy of Holies,
Israel, Jewish, Judaism, Semites
Abraham of, fr A-Bram II 139n, 200
acquainted w sorcery, etc I 230
Adam of, fr Chaldea II 42
Ain-sōph now lost to II 540
an Aryan race born in India I 313n; II 200,
471n
Basilides on God of I 350
Bible history of, not Jewish II 203
borrowed fr Chaldea I xxxi, 313, 655; II 3-4
characteristics of II 470
Christian religion fr II 588
chronology of, not their own II 691
creation ideas of, fr Moses II 3-4
creation out of nihil I 233n
cursed by their own prophets I 230
distorted Egyptian wisdom I 312
esoteric worship & Vedānta II 472-3
evolved under Saturn I 576; II 127
exalted their deity over all II 470
four modes of interpretation of I 374
four winds of I 466
Garden of Eden not property of II 203
gilgūlīm, believed doctrine of I 568 &n
God of I 381; II 412n, 536-8, 543. *See also*
Adonāi, Ain-sōph, Elohīm, Jehovah
horns of shittim wood II 418n
ignored higher hierarchies I 390-1
initiated, & Aryan dvijas II 469
Jah-oudi regarded by, as insult II 127
modern, fr David not Moses II 473
monotheism of II 252, 588
monsters, knew of extinct II 713

Moon-god of, Jehovah I 390; II 139n
mystery language known by II 574
N, E, S, W, no names for I 128n
number for elohīm fr Chaldea I 90n
occultism, knew little of I 230
origin of I 313n; II 200, 471n, 473
patriarchs of, made of old gods I 655
pre-existence, believed in I 568n; II 618
profane, cling to dead letter I 316
rebels called "deprived" by II 246
reincarnation & I 568 &n
rounds, races borrowed & lost by II 618
St Michael patron angel of I 459
secret books of I 349
seven-headed serpent of space w I 342
seven prominent in religion of I 392
"spoilt" Egyptians of jewels II 481
Talmudic, profaned symbols II 471
Taylor on speculations of I 426
theogony of, pagan II 465
told to hate heathen II 472
twelve tribes of II 130, 200n
zodiac of I 668
Jewish. *See also* Hebrews, Jews
Aryan &, symbols compared II 469-74
-Christians in *IU* I 197
chronology confusing II 691
cosmogony I 381; II 657
fire god is "consuming fire" II 114
glyphs & language, origin of I 115n
measurements fr Egypt, India I 316
myths based on truth II 236
religion & Satan, devil II 232, 477
religion follows Bab magism I 10
scriptures & Purānas II 251-2
sevens in, thought II 612
system of measures I 312-13
tree & cross worship phallic II 588
Jhāna-bhaskara. *See* Jñāna-bhāskara
JHVH. *See* YHVH
Jigten-gonpo (Tib). *See also* Chenresi
Chenresi called II 179
Jinn, Jinni. *See* Djin
Jishnu (Skt)
Indian prototype of Michael II 498
Indra, Kārttikeya called II 382 &n
leader of celestial host II 382, 498, 614
Jīva(s) (Skt) life, living being
complete in man alone I 224
of Earth & man compared II 46
elemental atom or I 567-8
in every particle of matter I 522
functions of, on Earth 5-fold I 224
Haeckel's moneron ignores II 185

hangs fr flame I 238
human, animal, same II 81
"Imperishable" I 218-19
is, a myth? I 603n
Lords of the Moon & II 75
monads or I 629-30
Parabrahman pervades every I 522
passes thru all forms I 246-7
personal consciousness of II 241
ray of the Absolute I 247
some, were not ready II 161, 162
souls of atoms I 619
sunspots & ascent of, in death I 132
vijñānamaya &, blood, water I 570n
Jīvanmukta (Skt). *See also* Jīvātma
can double his nirvāna I 371
freed fr 7 principles II 604n
high adept, mahātma or I 46n
Jīvātma(n) (Skt). *See also* Ākāśa
ākāśa or I 140
Logos of Greeks II 33
Nous, motion or I 50
prāna & I 226n
Jīvātmas (Skt) I 132. *See also* Jīvanmukta
Jñāna (Skt) wisdom
head, heart, soul, seed of II 282
king of the peris II 394 &n
Mahat first born of I 62
Jñāna-bhāskara, re Asuramaya II 67
Jñānadevas (Skt), class of gods II 90
Jñānaśakti (Skt), 2 aspects of I 292
Jñātā (Skt), center of energy I 428
Job I 330
antiquity of I 648
Bailly used astronomical refs in I 648-9
behemoth & ways of God II 486
"dead things are formed" I 345
he shall have no name (Haeckel) II 651-2
IU ref to Atlanteans in II 496
leviathan in II 206
precedes Moses, Homer, Hesiod I 647-8
Satan a son of God in I 70, 412, 414, 422n;
  II 375-6, 378
true archaic doctrine in II 537
zodiacal refs I 647-8
Jod. *See* Yod
Jod-Heva. *See* Jehovah, Yāh-Havvāh, YHVH
John
"before me were thieves, robbers" II 229,
  482
Devil father of lies I 414
Egyptian & pagan symbols in I 384
God was light II 39
"I & my Father are one" I 265, 574

"I ascend to my Father" I 574
Jesus disputed Pharisees I 578
life was the light of men I 470, 626n
light shineth in darkness I 70
my doctrine is not mine II xv
"my Father is greater than I" I 574n
ophanīm of, & dhyān-chohans I 337
plagiarizes *Book of Enoch* II 229, 482, 531
"wind" should be "spirit" in I 226
1 *John* [5:6-8], spirit bears witness I 570n
John, St. *See also* *John, Revelation*
dragon in *Rev* of II 93n, 355-6, 383
eagle, air &, (table) II 114
gnosis of, exoteric II 566
"I am the true vine" I 195n
non-initiated ascetic II 566
seven Gnostic vowels of II 565
John Chrysostom. *See* Chrysostom, St John
John, Patriarch of Constantinople
excommunicated II 279n
John the Baptist, St
axe laid to root of trees II 496
Bacon & II 443
baptism by water, fire II 566
mystic Christians of I 194
Pymander & II 115n
Joly, Prof Nicolas, *Man Before Metals*
age of man, Egypt, Europe II 750n
agni as akta (anointed) II 101n
on Basques II 790n
isthmus joined Gaul & Eng II 750-1 &nn
man has evolved fr original stock II 747n
man never an ape II 661-2
reindeer hunters II 749n
Jonas, the sign fr heaven I 653-4
[Jones, H. B.], *The Life & Letters of Faraday*
q Airy on gravitation I 584n
Jones, Sir William II 442. *See also* *Asiatic
  Researches*
on Divine Mind mirrored in atoms I 623
misled by Brahman forgeries I xxx-i &n
—— "On the Gods of Greece . . ."
called Nārada a messenger II 48
on lotus & water lily I 57, 379, 380
Joonagad. *See* Junāgadh
Jordan Valley & River
Neolithic flints of II 755
same mythical use as Nile II 583
source of descent or I 392
Jordon, C.
"most adopt, not beget opinions" I 647
Joseph (son of Jacob) I 653
dream of zodiac [*Genesis*] I 649

Sagittarius or I 651
Joseph, St, same as Tvashṭri II 101n
Josephus, Flavius, *Against Apion*
  Jews descend fr the Hyksos I 115n, 313n
  law forbids cursing Adversary II 477
—— *Antiquities of the Jews*
  bones of giants on Mt Hermon II 409
  Elijah & Enoch disappeared II 532
  Enoch hides books II 530
  Holy of Holies I 462
  tabernacle pillars I 125-6, 347n
  transfer of law books II 200n
—— *History of the Jewish War*
  souls descend into bodies II 111
Joshua, *Joshua*
  anakim of II 340
  crucified King of Ai on a tree II 558
  Enoïchion kept at Debir II 529
  giants of, Israelite fancy II 336, 340
  Jesus was, kabbalistically II 359, 539
  son of Nūn or the Fish I 264
  stopped course of Sun II 535
Joshua ben-Ḥananiah, miracles of I xliiin
Josiah, King, puts down idolatry I 649
Jotun(s) (Scand)
  Mimir as thrice-wise I 402
  war of, w Asathor II 386
Journal asiatique. See Eckstein, "De
  quelques . . ."
Journal Chemical Soc of London. *See*
  Crookes, Wm., "Elements & . . ."
Journal des colonies, Lavoisier on conscious ele-
  ments I 468
Journal des savants, q Indicopleustes II 399
Journal of Asiatic Researches. See Asiatic . . .
*Journal of Microscopical Science. See Quarterly
  Journal* . . .
Journal of Science. See Quarterly Journal . . .
Journal of the Anthropological Inst. See Blake, C.,
  "Notes . . ."
Journal of the Royal Asiatic Soc. . . . See Hodgson,
  B., Muir, J.
Journal of the Royal Microscopical Soc. See Ro-
  manes, G. J.
Jovah Rabbah II 54. *See also Idrā Rabbā
  Qaddishā*
Jove. *See also* Jupiter
  aerial, or aether I 464
  fire, thunder & I 462
  Jehovah, or 2nd hebdomad I 449
  North Pole throne of II 357
  son of Ialdabaōth I 449
Jove-Juno, Tetragrammaton II 601
Jovians, perceive our world I 166

Jowett, Prof, doubted Atlantis II 761n
Jubal, fashioned harp, trident II 390
Judah
  kings of, worshiped zodiac I 649
  Leo or I 651
  lion's paw of tribe of II 581
  men of, & signum tau II 557
  one of two tribes II 130
Judaism. *See also* Jewish, Jews
  basis of Christianity I 264, 384
  built on phallic worship II 471-2
  contains 2 of the 7 keys I 318
  creator in, anthropomorphic II 40
  exoteric, is astrolatry II 41
  Hinduism & II 472
  religion of hate II 471
Judas Iscariot
  true character of II 389
  twelfth absent apostle I 649
Jude
  angels in chains II 491
  q fr *Bk of Enoch* II 230, 482, 531
  Roman Catholics reject II 531
  speaking not evil of gods II 477-8
Judges, on dance of Shiloh II 460
Judgment, Day of I 134n; II 617
Jukes, Joseph B., *Manual of Geology*
  Australian flora, fauna II 196-7
  flying dragons were real II 219
Julian, Emperor (the Apostate)
  initiate II 587n
  prayed to occult sun II 28
  waged war w the cross II 587
—— *Oration to the Mother of the Gods*
  seven-rayed god II 35
Julien, S., transl of *Tao-teh-Ching* I xxv
Junāgadh (India), Mitford's tomb II 245n
Juno (Roman goddess). *See also* Jove
  gave Jupiter tree w gold fruit I 128-9n
  Latona pursued by II 771n
  Moon-goddess I 228-9
  mother of Mars, no father II 550
  numerical equivalents of II 466
Jupiter (god). *See also* Bṛihaspati, Jove, Zeus
  -Aerios (or Pan), -Amon, & -Bel-Moloch,
    cosmic nature or I 463
  aether & I 331, 423, 464
  androgynous originally I 72n
  assumes form of swan I 357
  Atlantean island sacred to II 408
  Bacchus &, symbol of II 362-3
  Barnabas confused w II 481
  Castor, Pollux & II 121-2
  deceived by Prometheus II 525

dethrones his father II 269
Dionysus of Mnaseas & II 393
Dodonean, & Aidoneus I 463
Eloi or, (Gnostic) II 538n
fought w Neptune for Atlantis II 765
fourfold, master of 4 elements I 464
had female breasts II 135
hurled to Earth by Kronos II 483, 515
hurls Phaeton into Eridan River II 770n
immutable cyclic law II 786
Jve, Jave, Jehovah or, [Skinner] II 466
Mercury son of Maia & II 541
Merodach (Chald) became II 456
Minerva as right hand of I 401
Minerva sprang fr brain of II 660
myth of, & Leda II 197n
pursues Io (the cow) II 418n
re-animates human race II 270
Semele wife of I 400
Sun, Mithras, Bacchus & II 419
war w Lucifer-Venus I 202
world re-enters, is reborn (Seneca) II 757
Zeus & II 269-70
Jupiter (planet)
belongs to human Atlantean cycle II 270
Brahmanaspati or II 45n
building of Earth & II 23
conditions on, (Williams) II 136n
conj w Mercury beg kali-yuga I 662
Eloi genius of I 577; II 538n
eternal Spring of II 135-6
is a planetary chain I 164
on molten state of II 135-6, 707
Moon, Saturn &, high triad II 462
polar compression of, & Earth I 593
rare conj of Mars, Saturn & I 656

satellites of, more dense I 593
seasons due to orbit of II 706-7
second race under II 29
Seven Sons of Light & I 575
Sun guardian of, (Pythagoras) I 493
superior globes of, invisible I 153
tonans, the thunderer II 498
Jupiter, or Bel (6th world of Syrians) I 435
Jupiter Fulgur or Fulgurans
soul of lightning I 467
Jupiter-Jehovah, ritualistic worship II 45n
Jupiter Lapis
swallowed by father, Saturn II 341
Jupiter Mundus, four elements I 463
Jupiter Pluvius I 467, 554
Jupiter-Titan, & Father-Aether I 423
Jurassic (Period)
beds of Rocky Mts II 218
fossils of Afr, Amer & Europe II 791-2
fossils of, & Australia II 196-7
man physicalized in II 737
middle of Reptilian Age II 156
third root-race appeared in II 156, 713
Jurbo-Adonai. *See* Yurbo-Adonāi
Justice, Nemesis or immutable II 305-6n
Justin Martyr, *Dialogue w Trypho*
rejected by Pythagorean School I 433n
unknown passive deity of II 489
—— *Second Apology*
spirit female w Nazarenes I 194n
"Just, though mysterious . . ." I 644
Jyotis (Skt), teacher of astronomy II 766
Jyotisha (Skt) astronomy
weeks, sevens in, of Vedas II 624 &n
Jyotsnā (Skt), morning twilight II 58, 527

K

Ka (Egy), astral body corresponds to nephesh (Heb) II 633

Kabala. See Lévi, É.

Kabbala, Kabala, Cabala, Qabbālāh
referred to:
    adjusted for Christian tenets II 37-8, 128, 457, 476
    fr Aryan SD I 376; II 239
    Chaldean, & ancient wisdom I 200, 241, 439; II 461-2
    Cis-Himalayan teachings & II 308n
    deity is the universe I 92n
    early, metaphysical II 457
    edited & re-edited II 469, 536
    esoteric & exoteric II 41
    Jews got, fr Chaldea & Egypt II 240
    key to Bible I 336, 344; II 624, 625n, 691
    key to, Parker on II 544
    Masonry, Bible & II 39
    Midrash before, of ben-Iochai II 704
    modern, but fragments (Franck) II 461
    modern, disfigured I 241, 391; II 461
    monotheists & I 129, 391
    phallic element taints II 457-8, 469, 544, 625n
    reveals occult facts of Bible I 336, 344, 443-4
    seven meanings in II 538
    synonyms of Hindu gods in I 92
    Temūrāh I 90n
    Vatican MS of II 239
    veiled, secret, now re-edited II 536
quoted:
    Adam Kadmon I 99n, 433n; II 37, 467
    on Blessed Ones & matter I 224
    central Sun (Pratt) II 240
    creations, more than one II 54, 704
    curse on man came w woman II 216
    death for giving secrets of II 396
    deity, one & triple I 59
    diagram of 7 principles II 633
    early races II 315
    esoteric meaning of *Genesis* II 37
    Fall caused by pride II 237
    fallen angels II 228-9, 487
    five Adams & 5 races II 503-4

    four & monad & heptad II 599-600
    four-lettered Ineffable Name II 282n
    four worlds of II 111
    Genesis 1:1 & 2 reversed II 128
    Immaculate Conception & I 59
    is esoteric vidyā I 241
    Jehovah & Moses interpreted II 465-8
    Jehovah replaces Adam Kadmon I 433n
    King Hiram of II 113
    light in, (*Zohar*) I 357; II 37-8, 39
    light, sound, number, creation I 432; II 41
    Lucifer, Venus, Sun's 3rd palace II 31
    Moon linked w Jehovah II 62
    numerical values II 37-40
    only true etymology of Jehovah II 129
    relation betw elohīm & men I 230
    Satan is adversary II 235
    seven creations I 447
    seven kings (races) II 2-3
    seven number of divine mysteries I 36
    seven preeminent I 241
    seventh, all things depend on II 312n
    Shekīnāh, Bath-Kōl II 107
    sparks are worlds I 199
    system of weeks fr India II 623-4
    ten sephīrōth I 432; II 37
    tetrad esteemed II 599
    Tetragrammaton I 99n; II 624-5
    Trinity II 38
    two creations II 54
    Western, ignores circle w point I 19
    worlds, destruction of II 704-5

Kabbala denudata. See Knorr von Rosenroth

Kabbalah, The. See Ginsberg, C. D.

Kabbalah [Qabbalah]. See Myer, I.

Kabbalah Unveiled. See Mathers, S. L. M.

Kabbale, La. See Franck, Adolph

Kabbalist(s)
    Adam's earth of I 543n
    Bible popular blind to II 473
    ceremonial magic & I 234n
    Christian, gross explanations of II 247
    Christian, interpret *Genesis* II 234
    cross, circle & modern II 543
    deity is one & triple I 59

dodecahedron in cube I 450
earth, water make living being II 188
embryonic stages known to II 259
esotericism unknown to modern II 603
evil force essential to good I 413
evolution of embryo discussed II 188-9
expound ancient traditions I 287
Father-Mother & ether one I 75-6
fiery serpents II 212
four distinct Adams, taught II 457
Genesis, shifted order of II 127-8
gnostic I 351-2
grasp wisdom of Bible I 316
Hecate predecessor of God I 395
immutable deity of I 374
individual cycles of II 188
interprets man & God I 444-5
Jewish, dwarf cosmic cycles II 564
Levi & I 243, 245, 259n
Levites &, Holy of Holies II 459
made 2 lives of body & soul I 234
"Man becomes stone, plant . . ." II 186
medieval, man microcosm in I 283 &n
name of Jehovah screen among I 438
number basis of biblical names II 467
"Pymander" remodeled by II 267n
on ruach & nephesh I 193; II 633 &n
sectarian, distort *Zohar* II 476 &n
serpent spiritual sun of II 214
Son or cosmic electricity I 75-6
Space unknowable & living I 615
Tetraktys became Tetragrammaton II 463n
theists I 317
thought orig metaphysical I 619n
Tritheim greatest, of his day II 512n
Western I 255; II 86
Kabbalistic
    axiom stone, plant, beast . . . I 107, 197,
        246; II 186, 258
    elemental spirits I 234n
    esoteric &, pneumatics compared I 243-5
    esotericism, curse in II 411
    faces in *IU* I 197
    Garden of Eden II 204
    Hindu &, systems compared I 355-6
    Jehovah &, deity compared I 355-6
    a modern, MS on ansated cross II 31n
    numerals based on 7 & 3 I 239
    planes & worlds I 199-200
    system does not contain all I 318
    terms discussed I 114
    Trinity discussed I 337
    view of astral light I 195-6

Kabir(i, im), Kabeiri(m). *See also* Dhyāni-
    chohans, Divine Kings, Fires, Kumāras,
    Manus, Rudras, Titans
    appear at beginning of cycles I 435n, 641
    archetypal man II 3
    build everlasting monuments I 434-5 &n
    cherubs of Jews & II 115n
    derivation of word II 362n, 363
    described II 362-4
    dhyāni-chohans II 360, 390-3
    divine Titans or II 141
    ethereal fire emanation of I 469
    generic name II 363
    gibborīm in 5th race II 273-4
    incarnated in 3rd, 4th races II 360
    instructors in agriculture I 642n; II 364-5,
        390
    kumāras, rudras II 106
    Manes also called II 143, 360
    mysterious ancient gods II 264
    Noah & family II 360n, 390-3
    occult powers of nature II 106
    pi (π), circle, & I 114
    regents of seasons, cycles I 641, 642n
    seventh II 365n
    sons of Sydic or Zedek II 392
    Telchines or II 391
    temples of, at Thebes, Memphis II 363
    theology links, w devil II 354
    3, 4, & 7 II 106, 115n, 142, 143, 362
    Titans &, same as 7 rishis II 142
    two races of, (Cumberland) II 393
    var named I 114; II 360, 362, 365-6 &n, 393
    Vulcan greatest II 390n
Kabiri-Titans II 360-1, 363-4
Kabolitae, Kabul tribes, Ptolemy on II 200n
Kabul, Arabs fr II 200
Kadesh-Kadeshim. *See* Qādēsh Qedēshīm
Kadeshuth. *See* Qedēshōth
Kadim [Qādīm] (Heb) I 466
Kadmos, Kadmilos. *See* Cadmus
Kadra, Kadrū (Skt)
    Kapila son of II 572
    Kaśyapa's wife II 132
Kadushu. *See* Qādēsh Qedēshīm
Kaempfer, E., *History of Japan & Siam*
    Chinese Atlantis, Noah II 365
Kāf, Koh-Kāf, Kaph Mts
    or Caucasus, continent beyond II 399
    described II 362, 398
    devs (giants) dwelt in II 397
    gallery of statues in, (Herbelot) II 396
Kaffirs II 725
Kai-caus, fights the white devil II 403

Kaikobad (Pers), starts new dynasty II 398
Kailas Range I xxviii n
  Indus River springs fr II 417-18
  part of Arghya Varsha II 416n
  real war in Himalayan II 500
Kaimurath (Pers)
  Siamek son of II 396
  Simorgh (Phoenix) older than II 397
  tenth Persian king II 394
Kain. *See also* Cain, Ka-yin, Kin
  fr *Kanithi*, "I have gotten" II 127
Καιω (kaiō, Gk) "to burn"
  Kabeiron (Kabiri) fr II 363
Kakodaimon (Gk) evil spirit
  Agathodaemon &, same roots I 412
  bad Logos, serpent I 344, 410
Kāla (Skt) time
  Brahmā emanation of I 427
  circle of boundless time II 142n, 233, 549, 756
  evolution of I 407
  fire deity presides over I 86
  Khandakāla & I 62
  Kronos-Saturn or I 72n, 452n
  purusha-pradhāna-, & creation I 451-2n
  St Michael, son of time or I 459
  "Sarvaga" & I 582
  serpent deity II 756
  Vishnu is I 427; II 549, 564
Kala-bagh (Kalabagh), Indus River called Nīl (blue) near II 417-18
Kalabhana (Skt). *See* Kālanābha
Kāla-chakra, on anupadaka [aupapāduka] I 52n
Kālāgni (Skt), consumes Earth I 370
Kal-aham-sa (Skt), "I am I" I 78
Kalahaṅsa [-Haṃsa] (Skt). *See also* Haṃsa, Man-Swan, Swan
  Brahma(n) or I 20, 79-80
  described, explained I 77-81
  Kwan-shi-yin floating on I 471
  lays golden egg I 359
  "Swan in Eternity" I 359, 362; II 122, 465
Kālakā (Skt), wife of Kaśyapa II 381-2
Kālanābha (Skt), name of Tāraka II 382n
Kalāpa (village of)
  Devapi, Moru [Maru] reside at I 378 &n
Kālapāni (Skt) black waters
  early Arabs did not cross II 406
  few sacred books crossed I xxx
Kalevala (Finnish epic)
  dragon, serpent in II 26
  duck lays golden eggs in II 14, 122
Kālī (Skt) black
  seventh tongue of Agni I 443

Śiva's consort & cord symbol II 548
  waters of, agitated II 406
Kali-Hansa (Skt). *See* Haṃsa, Kalahaṅsa
Kali-Kāraka (Skt) strife-maker
  Nārada called II 48
Kāliya (Skt) serpent slain by Krishna
  various equivalents of II 379
Kali-Yuga (Skt), dark, iron age II 308n. *See also* Dvāpara-, Satya-, & Tretā-Yuga, Yugas
  age "black w horrors" I 645
  began 5,000 yrs ago I 650; II 147, 300
  began 3102 BC I 662, 663; II 435
  began w death of Krishna I xliii; II 140, 527, 550
  calculations re I 662, 664-5
  calendar of II 50-1 &n, 69-70
  discussed in *Vishnu Purāna* I 377-8
  5,000 years of, ended I xliii-iv, 612
  Indra degraded in II 614
  Kalki avatāra ends I 378; II 483
  Kapila great sage of II 572
  length of I 369; II 69, 147
  lunar eclipse & II 435
  no world savior in our I 470
  now reigns in India I 377
  occurs in Bhārata (Varsha) II 322
  our Aryan race now in II 147n
  reversed 7-pointed star I 5
  St Yves d'Alveydre on II 549 &n
  seven rishis in Maghā began II 550
  some West Aryans now in I 645
  war in *Mahābhārata* preceded II 395
  Yudhishthira at opening of I 369
Kalki [white horse] Avatāra (Skt)
  expected fr Arghya Varsha II 416n
  Io symbolizes race of II 416n
  last messiah of great cycle I 384
  Maitreya or 5th buddha & I 384
  paranirvāna, 2nd Advent & I 268
  Sosiosh or II 420
  Vishnu will return as I 87; II 483
  will close kali-yuga I 378; II 483
Καλλίστη (Kallistē, Gk) most beautiful
  name given Luna-Artemis I 395
Kalpa(s) (Skt) II 147. *See also* Age, Cycle, Day/Life of Brahmā, Rounds
  applied variously II 307n, 320
  bearing on human life I 637-47
  catastrophes at close of II 325
  changes during II 312, 325
  Chenresi, Padmapāni & II 179
  Daksha lives in all I 430
  defined I 368; II 307n
  dhyānis live as long as Brahmā I 442, 457

each, has its dhyāni II 179
eternity & I 336n
former, & Daksha II 176-7
fourteen manus for every II 307
gods, demigods reborn in II 248
infinite in number I 368; II 179
karma unites creative forces I 635, 637
law of sevens & II 611, 616
of life I 116
local, or round II 46
mahā I 36, 206; II 70
major & minor I 369
"Mirror of Futurity" records all II 49
motion of bodies varies w I 530
Nārada regulates II 48, 82-3
Pesh-Hun guides II 48-9
previous, & nirvānīs II 232
seven creations in each II 53n
seven in present manvantara II 711
several distinct I 454
sons of Brahmā reborn in every II 82-3, 90,
    232, 247n
table of manvantaras in II 68-70
twenty-ninth (mid-Atlantean) II 249
various colors of Śiva in I 324; II 249
Vishnu relates story of seven II 611
Kalpic Masks
    temporary appearance of elements I 673
Kāma (Skt) desire II 161. *See also* Desire, Kośa
    Aja or the unborn II 176, 578
    animal soul II 671
    cosmic aspect of II 175-6
    first god of Vedas II 579
    god in oldest Purāna, not Indra II 174n
    intensity of, varies in animals II 255
    kumāras sprang fr II 579
    later became sexual II 176
    Makara-ketu or II 578
    manas &, completes man II 79
    manas, & root-races II 254n
    manas drawn down by I 244-5; II 254n, 614
    Prometheus left, unchanged II 412-13
    wedded to manas (Zeus) II 419-20
Kāmadeva (Skt)
    Makara on banner of, explained II 578
    not Indra sends Pramlochā II 175-6
Kāma-loka (Skt)
    Aanru is Egyptian I 674n
    early races had no, or ego II 610
    Hades or I 244
    limbus on Earth I 334, 463
    no worse abode than I 463 &n
    region of the Manes or II 374n
    shells disintegrate in I 122n

Kāma-rūpa(s) (Skt) II 105. *See also* Rūpas
    animal-human soul II 241, 596, 632
    correspondence w globes & I 153
    disintegrates in kāma-loka I 122n
    dregs of manas remain w I 334
    Earth in its, state I 260
    first race had no II 116
    grossest principle in man I 260
    kabbalists call, shells II 111n
    kabbalists' confusion re II 633n, 634
    Karabtanos & I 195 &n
    seat of false personality II 241
    Sons of Wisdom intensify II 161
    suns are, of ākāśa I 527n
    third race 1st to have II 116
    vehicle of desire I 153n; II 105, 593
    vehicle of manas II 241
Kamchatka
    part of 2nd race continent II 402
    six-month year of aborigines of II 621
Kamsa (Skt)
    killed Devakī's sons II 504n, 604n
    Nārada & II 48
Kamu-mi-musubi-no-kami (Jap)
    one of the arūpa triad I 214
Kanāda (Hindu atomist) I 579
    believed in gods I 518
    gods of, & Pythagoras I 495
Kandu (Hindu) holy sage
    age of ethereal man II 411
    Mārishā daughter of II 177
    Merlin & Vivien parallel II 175 &n
    Pharaoh & Sarah parallel II 174
    Pramlochā & II 171n, 174-6
    stands for 1st race II 175
Kānithi (Heb), Kain (Cain) fr II 127
Kanjur, The (Tib Buddhist canon)
    Gyu(t) division of I 52n
    108 volumes of I xxvii
Kansa. *See* Kamsa
Kant, Immanuel I 79n, 103
    believed in spiritual worlds I 589
    believed many worlds inhabited II 706
    on inhabitants of other planets I 602
    primeval matter of, or ākāśa I 598n, 601-2
    primitive fluid of I 623
—— [*Allgemeine Naturgeschichte . . .*]
    nebular theory I 149-50n, 597, 601-2
—— *Critique de la raison pure*
    hidden & revealed Logos, monad I 614
—— *Träume eines Geistersehers*
    immaterial natures I 133n
Kanyā (Skt) Virgo, Virgin
    Anaitia, Devī-durgā or I 91-2

represents śakti or mahāmāyā I 292
Kanyā-durgā (Skt)
 virgin goddess, Hindu zodiac I 657
Kaph. *See* Kāf
Kapila (Skt) I 207, 284 &n; II 522
 Bhagavata-Purāna re II 571
 chides Brahman yogis I 426n
 conscious guiding power II 652
 esoteric name of a kumāra I 457 &n
 founded Sānkhya philos II 42, 571-2
 Keely's force & Eye of I 563
 Manu & I 585n, 600
 reduces 60,000 to ashes I 563; II 570-1
 rishi, born fr Wondrous Being I 207
 of satya- & kali-yugas II 572
 taught evolution I 186; II 259
 Vishnu as, imparts wisdom II 483, 572
Kapilāksha (Skt) Kapila's Eye
 destroyed 60,000 men I 563
Kapilasthān (Skt)
 where Kapila meditated II 571
Kapilavastu, Prince of (Gautama) I 271
Kapivaktra (Skt) monkey-faced
 Nārada called II 48
Kara(m) (Skt) hand, & pentagon II 576-8
Kāra-bhāra (Skt), load of taxes I 377
Karabtanos (Gnos)
 begets 7 races I 248
 kāma-rūpa minus mind I 195n
 seven spirits born fr I 217
 united w spirit creates planets I 195
Karakorum (mts, NW Tibet)
 ancient civ fr, to Khuan-Khé I xxxii
 collapse of mountains near II 356
 hidden libraries in I xxiv &n
Karamania [Karaman, Turkey]
 mandrakes in II 27n
Kārana (Skt) cause II 46. *See also* Cause,
  Upādāna
 "alone" during pralaya I 41
 eternal, of ceaseless motion I 93n
 ideal spirit of Cause I 46
 shrine of incognizable, in heart I 280
Kārana Śarīra (Skt) causal body
 ego image of Logos in I 592-3n
 human ego, & sūtrātman II 79
Kāranopādhi (Skt). *See also* Upādhis
 spiritual soul or I 157
Karens of India II 632
Kārikā. See Sānkhya-Kārikā
Karli (in India), labyrinth, passages of II 221
Karma(n) (Skt). *See also* Destiny, Fate, Lipikas,
  Providence
 absolute harmony only decree of I 643

for abuse of creative power II 410-11
adjusts effects of man's plans II 305
of ape egos II 262-3
apparent injustices & II 303-4
Atlantean II 302-3, 740-1
Book of Life belongs to I 535n
both action & effect II 302n
cannot be called Providence I 634
creates & designs nothing II 305
cycles & I 641
defined & discussed I 643-7; II 302-6
dhyāni-chohanic failures & I 188
divine souls checked by I 17
does not reward & punish I 643
dying out of races & II 779-80
Earth's changes & II 372
Europe's racial, & catastrophe I 646
evil & punishment agents of II 477
extinction of races & II 780
fate, nemesis I 639; II 420-1n, 604-5n
forced gods to incarnate in man II 373n
four Mahārājahs & I 123-4, 126, 294n
fundamental universal law II 510n
genii fulfill will of I 294
God & II 554-5n
"the great ADJUSTER" II 329
heredity servant of II 178
Iblis agent of II 394
individual liberty & II 305
inner god cannot arrest II 554-5n
Israel's, glowed over 1st century I xli
Jewish religion & Christianity I 10-11
law of ethical causation II 302n
law of retardation & II 260
limited number of monads & I 171, 182
lipikas record I 104-5, 128
man & angel alike under I 194
man weaves, thread by thread I 639
moral effects of I 634
muktas not subject to I 132
Nārada executor of universal II 48
nations cannot escape I 675
Nemesis &, compared II 305-6n
nidānas & I 39
no creature exempt fr I 221, 636
no respecter of persons II 679
numberless entities guide I 111n
Örlog (Norse) or II 520
peregrination of life-atoms & II 671-2
physical & moral effects I 280
fr previous worlds II 249n
reincarnation interwoven w II 303, 306
of retarded monads I 173, 175
Satan magistrate of II 234, 478

savage races & II 317-18
sexual relation as II 458
silent influence of unerring II 475
sin & II 302n, 412-13
sixth race & II 445-6
sons of wisdom & II 185, 191-2, 228
svabhavat & I 635
term God used for II 492
third eye & II 302
triform fates & II 414
Vishnu Purāna on I 456n
Karma-Nemesis. *See also* Providence
adjusts everything harmoniously II 304-5
vs blind faith II 304-5
creator of nations & mortals I 642
Deity is I 645
described I 642-4
is eternity, action itself II 304-5
Karmic
axial changes by, law II 329-30
law "great ADJUSTER" II 329
law preordains spiritual cycles I 642
mysterious workings of, will II 232
national & tribal cycles are I 642
Karna [Kirana(?)] (Skt) ray or beam of light
origin of Greek Karneios II 44n
Karnak II 70
Egyptian, & Carnac of Bretagne II 380
& other ruins II 430
statue of Hathor, Isis fr I 400
Karneios (Gk) Sun-born
Apollo or, fr Karna [Kirana(?)] II 44n
Karshipta (Pers), human mind-soul II 292
Karshvar(es). *See* Keshvars
Kārttikeya (Skt). *See also* Mars, Michael
Apollo & II 383
born of sweat & earth II 43n, 124-5n
born to kill Tāraka II 383
born without woman II 43n, 125n, 550, 619
desc & expl II 381-2, 549-50, 619
head of rudras II 106
a kumāra II 383, 549, 619
Mars identical w II 43n, 124n, 382, 549, 619
Michael &, compared II 382n, 549
Pleiades nurses of II 549, 551, 619
six-faced Mars II 382
six heads of II 551
war god II 124n
Kashmir, Kaśmīra I 377
Apollonius meets Nāgas in II 211
& cradle of mankind II 203
extension of ancient continent & II 327
Kashyapa. *See* Kaśyapa

Kāśi-Khanda (part of *Skanda-Purāna*)
describes decapitation of Daksha II 182
Kasmera. *See* Kashmir
Kaśyapa (Skt)
cycle of time II 253-4
described II 132, 253-4, 382 &n
& Diti's offspring II 613
father of dānavas (giants) II 381, 382 &n
father of Kapila II 572
father of Nārada II 47-8
father of reptiles & demons II 259n
grandsire of birds & Garuda II 181
Indra son of II 382
star in Ursa Minor & II 612n
symb of animal evolution II 253-4
taught Buddhism to Ming-ti I xxviii
Ursa Minor & II 612n
Vinatā wife of I 366
Kaśyapa-Āditya (Skt)
Agni, Apollo, etc & II 382-3 &n
*Katakopanishad, Kathaka Upanishad. See
Katha Upanishad*
Katāpa or Kalāpa
village in Tibet (R. R. Rao) I 378n
Katha Upanishad [also *Kathopanishad, Kāthaka
Upanishad*]
Prajāpati-Vāch produces I 431
sattva called buddhi in I 68n
soul born fr spirit & matter I 365, 461
"Katie King," physicalization of II 737
Kaumāra[ī] (Skt) or Senā
female aspect of Kārttikeya II 619
Kauravya (Skt)
king of Nāgas in Pātāla II 214
Kavkaz or Caucasus II 399 &n
Kavya(s) (Skt), identified w cyclic yrs II 89n
Kavyavāhana (Skt) oblation-vehicle
fire of the pitris, fathers I 521; II 102
Ka-yin [Qayin] II 397. *See also* Cain
Keb [or Qeb] (Egy, Seb in tx)
carries goose on his head I 357
deceased as egg or I 365
god of time I 357, 359
inhabits devachan II 374n
kāma corresponds w II 632
king of Egypt II 368
lays egg or universe I 359
Osiris elder son of I 437
soul that procreates (Massey) II 632
Kebar-Zivo of Nazarenes I 195-6
Kedara, Pulastya dwelt in, (Gorresio) I 415
Keely, John Ernst Worrell
causes behind phenomena of I 566
danger of discovery of I 563-4

discovered cosmic force I xxxv, 253-4n, 563
etheric force of I 555-66
motor of I 148n, 555, 558n, 561-2
natural born magician I 558
on neutral center I 557
only one able to use force I 253-4n, 558-9,
  561-2
on subdivisions of matter I 564-5
table of vibrations I 562
termed laya "etheric centers" I 148n
unconscious occultist I 557, 565
under class of dhyānis I 559
"Keely's Secrets." *See* Bloomfield-Moore
Kelvin, Lord. *See* Thomson, Wm.
Kem-our [Kemur, Qem-ur] (Egy)
  Horus of II 577. *See also* Khem
Kenealy, Dr Edward
—— *Bk of God: Apocalypse of Adam-Oannes*
  Agnus Dei & Agni II 383
  cow, bull & Holy Spirit II 418n
  cycles fr Chaldea II 565-6
  dissolution of world II 757
  Eustathius on Io II 463
  Kārttikeya symbol of naros II 619
  Nārada II 48
  navis fructified by male god II 463 &n
  perfection of ancient bldg I 208-9n
  q Vallancey on Morning Star II 759n
  rabbins on cycles II 397n
  on the serpent I 364n
  Simorgh, cycles & II 617-18
  various names of God & fire II 114
  wall [well] of Syene I 209n
—— *Enoch: [The Second Messenger of God]*
  antiquity of *Bk of Enoch* II 506
Kenite. *See* Cainite
Kennedy, Colonel Vans
—— *Researches into . . . Ancient & Hindu Myth.*
  Babylon seat of Brahman learning I xxxi
  Chaldea borrowed fr India II 226
  unity in diversity II 310
—— ["On Professor Wilson's Theory . . ."]
  refutes Wilson re Buddhism in Purānas
    I 419n
Kent's Cavern
  flints in, & Bushman's flints II 522
  Neolithic & Paleolithic finds in II 724
Kep, Kepti (Egy)
  septenary kronotype (Massey) I 408
Kēphas, symbol of Peter II 341n
Kephren or Chephren (Egy)
  builder of 2nd pyramid II 226
Kepler, Johannes I 103
  angelus rector of I 479

believed in spiritual world I 589
climacteric year of I 656 &n
Hindus borrowed fr Christians I 655n
hypothesized Sun as magnet I 497
importance of conjunctions I 656
lunar tables of I 667n
mystical astronomy of I 653
occult ideas of I 498-9
on planets conjunct at Jesus' birth I 654
on ring around Moon I 590
solar magnetism of I 498
solar vortex & vortices of I 623
truths of, alloyed I 622
—— *De motibus . . .*
  species immateriata I 479
  spirit of fire in Sun I 493
—— *De stella nova . . .*
  "new" stars of I 590; II 486n
Kerkes, Turkish Phoenix II 617
Kerya [Keriya oasis]
  tradition of buried cities at I xxxiv
Keśarī (Skt), father of Hanumān I 190
Keshvar(s) (Pers) [Karshvar, Avestan]
  diagram of II 759
  parts of Earth II 758-9
  seven, spheres of Earth chain II 384-5 &n,
    607 &nn, 757-9
Kesīl (Heb) constellation Orion
  mentioned in *Job* I 647-8
Kesim [Keśin] (Skt)
  monster Krishna slays II 48
Kether (Heb)
  brow of Macroprosopus I 239
  Chochmāh, Bīnāh &, triad I 99n
  Crown of Sephīrōthal Tree II 595
  Crown or I 177, 239, 352, 354, 355, 433
  female of Adam-Kadmon I 215n
  head of upper triad I 90, 438
  numbered as one I 352
  seven splendid lights fr I 433
  yōd (10) symbolic letter of I 394, 438n
Kether Malkhuth. See Ibn Gebirol
Ketu (Skt), descending node II 381
Key(s)
  allegories & symbols have seven II 291n
  geometry the 5th II 471
  Hebrew physiological I 311
  human, one of seven II 291n
  IU gave, one turn I xxxviii
  Massey used two or three II 632
  Mysteries unlocked by seven II 632
  new, needed for mysteries II 795
  occult science a I 341
  Rabbis lost II 537

Ragon on the, to symbols I 363
required for old theogony II 248
seven, must not be mixed II 517
seven, open past & future I 325
seven, taught in occultism I 155n; II 523
seven, to man's genesis I 323
seven, to meaning of swastika II 99
seven, to universal symbology I xxxviii,
310-11, 363
in Skinner's *Source of Measures* I 318 &n
to theogonies & *SD* II 23, 767
three of 7, only given II 517
three or 4 used in *SD* II 797
of wisdom found in nature II 797
to *Zohar* & Bible II 536-45, 590-8
Key-keeper of Nature
Pythagoreans called "4" II 600-1
Keynotes, seven in nature II 492, 601
Key of Urania. See Mackey, S. A.
Key to the Hebrew . . . See Skinner, J. R.
Kha (Egy). *See* Khat
Kha (Skt) ether, ākāśa I 372
Khaba (Egy), the shade, astral body II 632
Khado (Tib) female demons
Lilith, Dākinī or II 285
w little minds II 271
offspring of 3rd & 4th races II 271
Khaibit (Egy) spiritual soul
Chayah [Ḥayyāh] in Kabbala II 633
Khaldii I 396. *See* Chaldeans
Khamism, or old Coptic I 115n
Khan, or Yang
phallic symbol [Jennings] I 471
Khaṇḍa(s) (Skt) I 367n
Khaṇḍakāla (Skt), conditioned time I 62-3
Khāndogya Upanishad. See Chhāndogya Upan.
Khanoch. *See* Ḥanoch
Khanoom (Iranian city), 10 kings of II 394
Khara Bhara. *See* Kāra-bhāra
Khat, Kha (Egy) body
gûf (Heb) or II 633
soul of blood, the formative II 632
al-Khazarī, Book of. See Ha-Levi
Khem (Egy) or Horus
abode of (Sekhem), is devachan I 220
defunct "Osirified" becomes I 220-1
Khepera or Khepri (Egy)
scarabaeus or, & rebirth I 365; II 552
Khih Yu or Chih Yu (Chin)
beguiled Mao-tse II 280-1
Khīyūn (Egy), time, Cain, Saturn & II 390n
Khnoom, Khnoum, Khnumu (Egy). *See also*
Asklēpios, Kneph
Batoo &, Pandora story II 270n

confused w Ammon I 366-7
Haroiri is I 366n
healer, enlightener II 26n
moist power I 385
mundane egg placed in I 365
Sati, Anouki & I 367 &n
Khnūm. *See* Khnoom
Khoda (Pers), God I 347
Khojar Tartars
sons of Manasseh among II 200n
Khonsoo [Khons(u)] (Egy)
Thot-Lunus, Ptah & II 464
Khonsoo Iri-sokru (Egy)
who executes destiny II 464
Khoorassan [Khūrāsān]
tribe fr Afghanistan I xxxiii
Khopirron, Khopri, Khoprod, Khopron. *See*
Khepera
Khu (Egy) divine spirit
Jeshida [Yeḥīdāh] in Kabbala II 633
Khuan-khé [Huang-ho River]
ancient civ fr, to Karakorum I xxxii
Khunrath, Henry I 611; II 120
Khūrāssān. *See* Khoorassan
Kiddusheem [Qedōshīm]. See Talmud
Kīmāh (Cimah in tx, Heb)
Pleiades I 647-8 &n
Kimmerian Bosporus
Io journeys past II 416
Kimnaras (Skt)
four Mahārājas & I 126
inhabit astral plane II 90
men w heads of horses II 65n
Kimpurushas (Skt)
divine dynasties & II 369
spirits of heaven (Purānas) II 369 &n
Kin (Cain), son of Eve by Samael II 388
Kinaras. *See* Kimnaras
Kinetic & Potential Energy
life atoms, sleeping atoms & II 672, 673n
King, Charles W.
intuition of II 570
modern Gnostic authority I 577
—— *Gnostics & Their Remains*
Barbelo II 570n
boundless light & nirvāna I 577 &n
cherubim over Ark II 518
Chnumis II 518
fifteen pairs of Aeons II 569n
Gnostic gems pre-Christian II 564n
Gnostic iconography fr India II 565
Ialdabaōth (Demiurge) I 449n; II 243-4
IAO in Ophite gems II 541
IAO same as Mithra II 474

influence of Buddhist theosophy I 668
Jesus' garment of glory II 580
Kabbala fr Aryan sources I 376
lion-headed Gnostic gem II 481
Marcus on 7 heavens II 563
Origen's 7 Orphic gods II 538n
phallic nature of Ark II 518
Pistis Sophia re man's elements II 604-5
Pythagorean numerals I 361 &n
q *Pistis Sophia* II 563-4
sarcophagus of Porta Pia I 410
stellar spirits listed I 449
wisdom symbol female form I 351

King Arthur
giants said to live in time of II 754
legends of, based on fact II 393
Morgana fairy-sister of II 398n

King (or Ching) Books
Five, & Confucianism I xxvn

King Chia. *See* Kung Chia

Kingdom(s). *See also* Animals, Elementals,
     Humans, Mineral, Vegetable
all, began as ethereal models II 594
anima mundi & II 562
astral of lower II 68n
bodies of lower, fr human II 169-70
consolidated (2nd period) II 594
door into human, closed I 173, 182
filmy prototypes in 3rd round II 186-7
lower, & monad's evolution I 178
lower, "created" by man II 290
man a distinct II 56n
man macrocosm for, below him II 169
man passed thru all lower I 159; II 185-7,
     254, 260, 635
man worshiped, when gods left II 273
mineral, turning point I 176
seven, ten I 176
sparks animate all I 246
three elemental, preceded man II 312n, 616
three lower, & higher powers II 242
time taken for 2 lower, to evolve II 308n
transmigrations thru I 159, 173-4, 176-9,
     183-4, 267-8

Kingdom of God, enter, as a little child II 504
Kingdom of Heaven
is within man I 280n
taking, by violence II 244, 516n

King I't
brings peace to Śankha-dvīpa II 406

King James Bible
cautious translation I 336
only 3 translators knew Hebrew I 128n

King of Assyria, armies of, called trees II 496

King(s) of Edom. *See* Edom, Kings of
King of Tyrus (Tyre)
Atlantean sorcerer II 492-3
Ezekiel calls, a cherub II 501
reproofs of Ezekiel to II 492-3

Kings. *See also* Divine Kings
arūpa pitris appear as II 93-4
of divine dynasties II 487
everlasting in *Bk of Enoch* II 483 &n
five fallen, or 5 races II 618
pre-Adamite II 83-4
ruled by Grace of God II 233n
of 7, 5 have gone II 565n
seven, or root-races I 241; II 618, 748
taught 3rd race II 194
ten Persian, given by Berosus II 394
of varshas, dvīpas II 320-2

1 *Kings*
Elijah heard small voice II 342n
leaping prophets of Baal II 460
Lord, wind, earthquake I 466

2 *Kings*
brazen serpent I 364n; II 387 &n
day of new moon II 76
Elijah taken up to heaven II 531
Kadeshim II 460
zodiac worshiped I 649

King's Chamber (Pyramid of Cheops)
circle w diameter used in I 391
Egyptian Holy of Holies II 462, 466n
initiation in II 462, 558
symbol of regeneration II 470
symbology of II 466

King Seang of Wai
Bamboo Books in tomb of II 302

Kingsford, Dr Anna Bonus. *See also Divine
     Pymander*
—— *The Perfect Way* II 229n
Satan [in *Appendix* xv] II 233-5
—— *The Virgin of the World, Definitions of
     Asklepios*
creation of world by Titans I 285
extract fr, on All, God I 286
God fr passive becomes active I 281n
"incorporeal corporealities" I 566
innumerable choirs of genii I 294-5
matter is living, becoming I 281
nothing on Earth is real I 287
orders of the gods I 672
void a fullness of beings I 671

Kings of Light. *See also* Divine Kings
name for divine dynasties II 424-5

Kin-kwang-ming-King I 470. *See Chin kuang
     ming ching*

Kinnaras. *See* Kiṃnaras
Kin-yu [*K'ung-tzu chia yü* — "Discourses of the Confucian School"] I 441
Kioo-tche [*Kieou-tche*] (Chin)
Chinese astronomical measures II 621
Kioto, monks of, & 7 jewels I 173
Kippūr (Heb), prayers of I 439n
Kircher, Athanasius, *Oedipus Aegyptiacus*
believed in divine dynasties II 371
egg floating above mummy I 365
Mor Isaac on Syrian gods I 435
saw a dragon II 207n
Kirchhoff, Gustav Robert
achievements of, & Bunsen I 528
Kirjath [Kiryath]-Sēpher (Heb) city of letters
Enoïchion kept at II 529
Kiu-ti or *Khiu-ti* [Tib works of which the *Book of Dzyan* is one]
compiled fr "very old book" I xliii
Ki-y. *See* Chi-Yi
Klaproth, Heinrich Julius
Garden of Wisdom in Himalayas II 203-4
Klée, Frederick, *Le déluge*
Earth's axial changes II 534
Klippoth [Qelīppōth] world of action
contains 6 other spheres II 111
our world, Earth II 111
shells or, of various colors (Myer) II 504
Kneph (Egy). *See also* Asklēpios, Khnoom
concealed breath of I 353
god hatches fr egg in mouth of I 364
healer, enlightener II 26n
snake-water emblems of I 344, 353
Knight, Richard Payne, degrades tau I 405
Knights of the Round Table II 393
Morgana (of Orient) among II 398n
Knorr von Rosenroth, Christian
——— *Kabbala denudata* . . .
Latin of, distorted I 391
lights & reflected lights in I 506
Ophanim, Angels of Spheres in I 117
a puzzle, not a guide I 215
——— *Liber mysterii*
fallacy re Microprosopus I 215
Knoum. *See* Khnoom
Knouph. *See* Chnoubis
Knowledge. *See also* Tree of Knowledge
absolute, only in paranirvāna I 48
adepts' I 605; II 216, 716
avabodha or II 528
curiosity &, (Bacon) I 165
fire of I 87; II 567
generations of seers acquired II 700
gives immortality II 215

of good & evil II 4, 81, 124, 214-15, 279, 292-3, 382n
hidden under symbols II 452
innate, of Lemuro-Atlantean II 285
intellectual, of 4th race I 189
pagans had divine I 125
records of occult, preserved I xlv
relativity of human, & time I 44
science offers guesses, not II 316n
serpent symbol of occult II 26n
seven branches of I 168-9
space realm of divine II 502
sword of I 536
of things in themselves I 330
too much, 2-edged weapon II 163
Tree of I 128-9n, 375; II 216-17
fr Tree of Good & Evil I 247
unlawful, & Atlanteans II 331
Knowledge (periodical, London), articles:
Burke, E. ["Descent of Man"] II 655
Clodd, F. II 686n, 710-11, 713n, 714
Proctor, R. A. I 314; II 352-3, 431, 435
Williams, W. M. I 102, 585; II 136n
Wilson, A. II 152
"knowledge dwells . . ." [Cowper] I 165
Koaḥ Hagūph (Heb), life force II 633
Kobhibaba [Koh-i-Baba], near Bamian II 338
Koeus [Koios] (Gk), Arkite Titan II 143
Koh-kāf, Keph or Kāf, mts of II 398
Koloē, Artemis-Anaitis inscription at I 395
Kon-ton (Jap), chaos (Shinto) I 214, 241
Koorgan [Kurgan]
giant tombs in Russia II 752
Kōr, city in Haggard's *She* II 317n
Koran, Kurān [*Qur'ān*] II 454
Ababel or Father-Tree in II 617
Alm or virgin in II 463
Edris (Enoch, Thoth) in II 529
Korē (Core or Persephone) (Gk)
sanctuary to, (Pausanias) II 363
Koros. *See* Kurios
Korscheldt, E., on 3rd eye II 299n
Koshas [Kośas] (Skt), sheaths I 610n
man composed of five I 157-8; II 603
Śankarāchārya on I 570-1n
Κοσμοκράτορες, Kosmocratores (Gk)
Ases, Pitris, etc, or II 97
assist Christian creator I 440
build solar system II 23
Church made devils of I 331
Damascius on dual 7 of I 235
Roman Catholics misjudged I 124
world bearers (Bossuet) I 331

Kosmos(oi). *See also* Cosmos, Universes
  birth of I 43, 64-6, 340
  chaos-theos & I 342-9
  chaos to sense, to reason I 2
  death of, analogous to man's I 173
  divine thought becomes I 43
  egg of I 65, 359
  egg-shaped zero or I 91
  elements of, & man's same I 58
  emanated fr triple One I 337, 447
  emerging in boundless space I 65
  endless hierarchies animate I 274-6
  eternal collectively I 151
  in Eternity I 1
  evolution & reinvolution I 148-9
  finite, called space I 277
  finite in manifestation I 151
  Fohat in I 109-12
  full of invisible existences I 611
  geometry 1st record of I 321
  heptachord of Apollo & I 167
  intracosmic soul or ideal I 3
  is the Son I 60, 348
  Law for everything in, is One I 145
  manifest, & golden egg I 556
  manifested & ideal I 282, 614
  manifested, is Verbum I 138
  may refer to our solar system I 199n
  nothing inorganic in I 248
  noumenal & phenomenal world I 3
  pralaya of I 373
  pregenetic, symbol of I 19
  progressive evolution of I 440
  pyramid, pregenesis & genesis of I 616-17
  real, casts phenomenal shadows I 278
  "rope" of, noumenal & "Pass not" I 90
  secret teachings re I 13
  seven esoteric kingdoms of I 455
  sevenfold I 598
  seven planes of I 199-200
  seventh principle in man & I 74n; II 616
  spirit & matter two states of the One I 258
  unity & mutual relations of I 480
  Vāch or, in 4 aspects I 138
  visible, creatures of karma I 635
  visible, the sthūla-śarīra I 598
Kottos
  giant described by Hesiod II 775-6
  stands for polar continent II 776
Kouin-long-sang. *See* Kunlun Mts
Kouyunjik, Kuyunjik
  Layard's excavations at II 5
  Moses story on tablets at I 319-20 &n

Kratidvishas [Kratudvishas] (Skt), enemies of
  exoteric shams II 501
Kratu (Skt), mind-born son II 78
Krauñcha (Skt) (Wilford gives Cracacha)
  king of Krauñcha II 405
Krauñcha-dvīpa, 1 of seven II 320-1, 404n
Krause, K. C. F., on inhabited worlds II 706
Krisāśwa [Krisāśva] (Skt)
  sons of, & legendary weapons II 629
Krishna (Skt)
  allegedly plagiarized fr Bible I xxxi
  Bala-Rāma elder brother of II 613n
  belongs to 5th race II 140
  birthplace of, & cross II 588
  born without father or mother II 550
  Christos & Vishnu II 580
  or Christ-state & 7 principles II 604n
  crucified II 561
  embryo of, conveyed to Rohinī II 527
  identified w Rishi Nārāyana II 359
  incarnation of Vishnu II 225n
  kali-yuga began at death of I xliii; II 140,
    527, 550
  Kansa & II 504n
  -karna & Apollo Karneios II 44n
  on Kshetrajña in *Gītā* II 638
  Logos incarnate II 318n, 527
  lower, higher forms of I 535-6
  manus, rishis born fr II 140, 318n
  Nārada lauds II 48
  Osiris, Dionysos, Buddha or II 420
  part of a part of supreme [*VP*] II 359
  Sāmba reputed son of II 323
  "saves" w the teachings II 230
  secret wisdom of I 539n
  slays Śankhāsura II 405
  slays Śiśupāla II 225n
  a solar god II 407
  union w I 406
  Vallabāchāryas distort symbols of I 335
  various equivalents of II 379
Krita-Yuga. *See* Satya-Yuga
Krittikās (Skt) the Pleiades
  Āgneya synonym of II 550
  month of I 664
  nurses of Kārttikeya II 549, 550, 618-19
  Poussinière, Pillāloo-codi or I 663-4
  six, then 7, & 7 rishis II 551
  Virgo & II 435
  when pyramids were built I 435
Kriyāśakti (Skt). *See also* Sons of Will & Yoga
  Brahmā creates w II 59-60
  Brahman zodiac fr those born by II 436n
  creation on plane of II 283

described I 293; II 172-3
Divine Ones of 3rd race born by II 636
mānushyas created woman by II 140
mind-born sons fruit of I 211
nirmānakāyas & II 652
power of sages II 181
regarded as magic II 174
seed of adepts created by II 228
Sons of Will & Yoga fr I 207-9; II 172, 181
yogi's miracles fr I 293
Kroenig, A. K., gas atoms elastic I 513
Kroeus [Kreios] (Gk), an Arkite Titan II 143
Kronan, is probably karma II 269n
Kronid Brothers (Gk)
   Neptune, Poseidon, Nereus II 766
Kronos (Gk) Saturn. *See also* Chronos, Saturn,
   Time
   Adam alleged to be I 642n
   Agruerus, Saturn or II 142n
   confused w Chronos I 418
   endless duration I 418
   generated god in Orphism I 19
   imprisons 3 polar giants II 775-6
   Jubal fashioned harp [harpē] of II 390
   Jupiter hurled to Earth by II 483, 515
   Jupiter Lapis & II 341n
   mutilated Uranus I 418; II 268, 283n, 766
   one of 7 Arkite Titans II 142-3
   Ormazd identical w I 113-14
   in *Prometheus Bound* II 414, 415-16, 420-1
   ruled over Lemurians II 765
   St Michael son of I 459
   serpent swallowing tail I 253n
   Sevekh-, (Massey) I 408
   symbology of II 268-71, 421-2
   Titans sons of, & Rhea II 142, 269
   Uranus &, insufficient II 270
Kronos-Saturn
   Jupiter son of I 72n
   personified 3rd race Lemurians II 766
   Rudra-Śiva or II 502n
   sydyk or II 142, 391-2
Kroszharsgrani [Krossharsgrani] (Norse)
   magician-teacher of Starkad II 346n
Krūra-lochana (Skt) evil-eyed
   Saturn called II 29
Krüss, G., elemental bodies of I 547
Kshatriya (Skt) warrior caste
   Buddha born a I xxi
   kings & Brāhmanas I 270
   Moru [Maru] will restore I 378 &n
Kshetrajña (Skt)
   ātma or I 570
   embodied soul II 108

as the One Witness I 570-1
presides over pradhāna I 284
soul's spiritual sun II 639-40
Supreme SELF (*BG*) II 638 &n
Kshīra (Skt), ocean of milk II 403
Kuan-Shih-Yin. *See* Kwan-shai-yin
Kuan-Yin. *See* Kwan-Yin
Kuen-lun-shan Mts. *See* Kunlun Mts
Kühn, Franz F. A.
—— *Die Herabkunft des Feuers* . . .
   derivation of word Prometheus II 413n
   gave Prometheus phallic slant II 526
   identifies swastika w Arani II 101n
Κυκλοσ (Kuklos, Gk) ring or cycle I 637
Kuklos Anagkes [Anankē] (Gk) "Unavoidable
   cycle" after death II 379
Kullūka Bhaṭṭa
   Aryan immigration to Egypt II 746
   Hopkins & Commentary of I 334 &n
   Nārā, Spirit of God II 495n
   sons of Marīchi, pitris II 89
Kumāra(s) (Skt). *See also* Dhyāni-chohans,
   Pitris
   agnishvātta are II 78, 89
   aquatic & fiery II 578
   Brahmā father of I 457; II 106, 249
   celibate I 236; II 82, 199n, 249
   chaste youths II 78
   class of devas II 90
   connection w zodiac II 93, 576
   degraded into Satan, demons I 458-9
   dhyānis or I 456-7
   every, has prefix Sana(t) I 459
   five, exempt fr passion II 577
   fivefold II 578-9
   flames or, incarnate in 3rd race II 247-8
   fourfold, 7-fold I 89
   four mentioned, 3 secret I 457
   four preceding manus & II 318n
   four, sacrificed themselves II 281-2
   highest dhyāni-chohans II 585
   incarnate in 1st 2 races I 457n; II 165
   incarnate in men II 176n, 199n
   Indra a, in early life II 383
   Kapila 1 of 3 secret II 572
   Kārttikeya a II 106, 619
   married Devasenā (Vāch) II 199n
   maruts, rudras & II 613 &n
   ma used as anagram of II 577-9
   Michael, Kārttikeya, Virgin & II 383, 549,
   619
   Nārada virtually a II 82
   one of 7 div of dhyāni-chohans I 458
   patrons of yogins II 576

rebellious & fallen gods II 232, 246
rebels, called by Hindus II 243
refused to create I 191-2, 236, 457-8; II 243, 584
rudras or II 192n, 576, 613
Sanat Sujāta chief of I 459-60
seven names, of II 319
seven, visited White Island I 236; II 584
Śiva, as Śvetalohita or root- II 249
solar deities, angels I 87-8
tempting demons II 174-5
Vāmadeva a I 324
various numbers of, (Purānas) II 577-8
Kumāra [Kaumāra] Creation (Skt) I 75
  both primary & secondary I 456
  Ninth or, [*VP*] II 106
Kumāra Guha (Skt), virgin youth II 382
Kumbhakarna (Skt), brother of Rāvana II 224
Kumuda-Pati (Skt), Earth's parent II 44
Kundalinī-Śakti (Skt) I 293
Kundzobchi-denpa (Tib)
  illusion-creating appearance I 48n
Kung Chia (Chin)
  compiled *Shan-Hai-King* II 54n, 302
Kuni-toko tachi-no-mikoto (Jap)
  first man (Shinto) I 241
Kunlun Mts
  betw China & Tibet II 215 &n
  libraries hidden in I xxiv
Kunte, Prof Mahadeo, defines rishi I 346
Kuntī (Skt), called Pānavārani II 527
Kun-ttag, Kun-tag (Tib)
  belief in something not existing I 48
Kurān. See Koran
Kurgan Mounds, in Russia II 752
Kurile (islands) II 327
Kurios, Koros (Gk), Logos, god-mind I 353
Kūrma (Skt). *See also* Śiśumāra, Tortoise

avatāra of Vishnu II 549
Kaśyapa & II 253
Kūrma-Purāna
  kumāras exempt fr passion I 458; II 577
  lists 7 winds or principles II 612
Kuru (Skt), Devāpi of race of I 378
Kuśa Dvīpa (Skt) II 404 &n. *See also* Dvīpas
  globe of planetary chain II 320-1
  king of, & 7 sons II 369n
Kuvera (Skt), guards the North I 128
Kwan-shai-yin [Kuan-shih-yin] (Chin) I 71. *See also* Kwan-yin
  Avalokiteśvara or, androgynous I 72 &n, 471
  Dalai Lama incarnation of I 471
  described I 72 &n, 470-3
  "first to appear . . . last to come" I 470
  Kwan-yin called the triple of I 136
  Logos or Verbum I 431n
  male aspect of divine wisdom I 473
  phallicism &, (McClatchey) I 471
  Primordial Logos, Brahmā or I 452
  will appear as Maitreya Buddha I 470
Kwan-yin [Kuan-yin] (Chin) divine voice
  Chitti or, explained I 288n
  female Avalokiteśvara I 72
  female Padmapāni II 179
  Hindu Vāch similar to I 136n, 137, 431n
  informing spirit of water I 471
  mother, wife, daughter of Logos I 136
  patron deity of Tibet I 72
  various equivalents of I 137, 473
Kwan-yin-Tien [Kuan-yin-T'ien] (Chin)
  abode of Kwan-yin I 136, 137
Kwoh-P'oh or Kuo P'o
  comments on monsters II 54n
Kyriel of Gods II 22
Kyrillitza (Russian alphabet)
  "R" of, is the Latin "P" II 547n

L

Laboratory, in our atmosphere I 583
Labyrinth I xxviii; II 220-1, 436
Labyrinthodon(ts) (Saurian)
    third eye developed in II 299n, 697
Lacaille, Abbé N. L. de
    astronomical tables of I 661
Lacertilia (lizards) II 205, 296
Lachelier, Henri
    & monads of Leibniz I 629, 630 &n
Lacour, P., *Les Aeloïm*
    on the Fall II 215-16n
Lactantius Firmianus, *Divine Institutions*
    Logos brother of Satan II 162
Ladder. *See also* Jacob
    of being II 239
    gods ascend, descend II 357
Lady of Urka, Omoroca or II 135
Laertius. *See* Diogenes
Lahgash [Laḥash] (Heb)
    secret speech, incantation I 354
Laing, Samuel
—— *Modern Science & Modern Thought*
    cannibalism & civilized races II 723
    crossbreeding among animals II 287
    data on early man lacking II 717
    Dryopithecus man's ancestor II 675
    embryo of man II 259
    evolution described II 731
    First Cause & good & evil II 510n
    geology & astronomy compared II 71-2
    Jews had merit of monotheism II 252
    length of periods uncertain II 155
    man in the Miocene II 677
    on meteors I 503-4
    methods of reproduction II 116
    Moon thrown off fr Earth I 154
    oldest fossil man still man II 716
    review of, quoted I 669
    sequence of life II 254-5
—— *A Modern Zoroastrian*
    African, British flints similar II 522
    Eve not begotten II 661
    methods of reproduction II 166, 658-9,
        661-2
    our atoms those of ancestors II 671-2
    religious evolution sexual II 657

sex appears late in embryo II 172n
Lajard, J.-B.-F., ["Recherches sur le Culte...,"
    in *Mémoires de l'Académie Royale . . .*]
    on the elements I 125n
Lake Dwellers II 722
    flora of, of African origin (Heer) II 739
    Neolithic, of Europe II 716, 722
Lake Superior, stone symbols II 790
Lakshmī (Skt)
    Agni son of II 578
    black side of II 579
    called padma or lotus I 380
    female aspect of Vishnu I 379-80; II 31, 76n
    later Kāma son of II 176
    Moon, water & II 77
    Śrī, Venus are I 380; II 76n, 77
Lalande, J. J. L. de
    believed many worlds inhabited II 706
Lalita-Vistara, self-maceration, etc in I 47n
Lama(s, ism)
    confused w Buddhism I 539n
    Dalai & Teschu (Tashi) I 471; II 178, 502n
    little known of I xxvii
    uninitiated, I xxi
Lamarck, J. de Monet
    Crookes on evolution of I 585 &n
    evolutionists & II 646
    "inherent & necessary" law of II 738
Lamaseries, cave-libraries in I xxiv
Lamb I 384
    Christianity & the I 441-2; II 210n
    tortoise &, as symbols I 441
Lambert, Franz
—— "Die Altägyptische Seelenlehre"
    diagram of 7 principles I 227n; II 633
Lamech (Heb)
    perished in Deluge II 265n
    son of Methusael, Methuselah II 391n
Lamps, Church, & frog symbol I 386
"lamps shone brighter" [Dryden] I 273
La Naulette (Belgium). *See* Canstadt Man
    jaw & ornaments at II 744
Lancet, The
    disease & cycles (Laycock) II 622-3 &n
Lanci, M. A., *Sacra scrittura . . .*
    Azāzēl has become a devil II 376

Land(s) II 6, 399-401 &nn. *See also* Continents
　of eternal Sun, Hyperborean II 11-12
　of fire & metal (E & N) II 428
　need rest, renovation II 726
　periodic redistribution of II 725-7
Land and Water, Bartlett article in II 595
Lane, Homer, heat, contraction I 84-5
Lang [Lung] (Chin), dragon II 210
Lange, on atomic theory I 518
Language(s). *See also* Sounds, Speech, Writing
　Darwinism & II 662
　dependent upon reasoning faculties II 199
　development of I 189; II 199-201
　divine origin of I 307-9
　of gods & magic I 464
　of initiates I 568
　isolated, of Basques II 790 &n
　Kabiri invented devanāgarī II 364
　within a language I 308-10
　mankind once of one I 229, 341; II 198, 452,
　　760n
　monosyllabic II 198-9
　Mystery I 310-25; II 574-89
　number is basis of I 320-3; II 560
　of occultism is varied II 616
　Plato, Magi used veiled II 395
　religion & I xxix
　Sanskrit, of the gods I 269
　secret sacerdotal I xliii, 362
　seven keys of II 334-5
　Skinner on symbolic I 308
　thought &, identical (Müller) II 199n
　a universal I 310
Laṅkā (Skt) Atlantis-Ceylon
　Ceylon northern portion of II 332
　Egyptian zodiac fr II 435
　giants of II 70, 236, 408
　Hanumān reconnoitered II 163
　Hindus now on, not Atlanteans II 323-4n
　men-demons of II 752
　rākshasas or giants of II 276, 776
　Rāvana giant king of II 224, 225n, 232n, 495
Lankester, Professor Edwin
　on development of eye II 295
Lanoo(s) (disciple, chela) I 11, 71, 77, 120;
　II 300
　deva-eye will not help impure II 295
　inner, taught 7 principles I 122
　studies practical esotericism I 71n
Laomedōn (Gk)
　symbolic meaning of II 796
Lao-tzŭ. *See also* Confucius
　Japanese sect of I 173
　many works of, disappeared I xxv

spirit emanates ethereal life II 36-7
—— *Tao-teh-ching*
　brevity of I xxv
　I Hi Wei is Jehovah (Rémusat) I 472
Lapides igniti caelorum (Lat)
　incandescent celestial stones I 440
Lapis Philosophorum (Lat) philos stone
　one in essence, 3 in aspect II 113
Laplace, Pierre-Simon de
　answers Napoleon on God I 498, 576n
　believed worlds inhabited II 701, 706
　Crookes refers to I 585
　derided Pictet re aerolites II 784n
　fusion of nebular matter I 505
　Indian & European day names I 652
　near occult theory I 588
　on Phobos, Mars satellite I 165
　solar atmospheric fluid of I 502
　solar system fr nebular rings I 149-50n
　theory not hypothetical (Mill) I 588
—— *Exposition du système du monde*
　comets are strangers I 500
　deals w Buffon's comet I 597
　motion a blind law I 498
　nebular theory of I 591-3
Laplander(s), call corpses "manee" II 774n
La Pluche, Abbé, on mathematical pt I 613
Lars, Lares (Etruscan)
　esoteric definition of II 361
　Faber relates, to Kabiri II 360
Lartet, Édouard A. I. H.
　man dates fr Miocene II 714n
　man lived in Tertiary II 751
　races larger before Deluge II 278
　on "tallies" & early writing II 729
—— *Cavernes du Périgord*
　man lived w extinct species II 746
—— "Nouvelles Recherches . . ."
　Christian datings pushed back II 690-1
　no date of man in *Genesis* II 690
Lassen, Christian, *Indische Alterthumskunde*
　Chinese visited New World (Neuman)
　　II 424n
　early Buddhist monastery I xxviii n
Last Judgment Day
　or "Day-be-with-us" I 134n
Latency
　Parabrahmic II 24
　pre-cosmic I 58
"Latent Dynamical Theory . . ." *See* Thomson
Lateres Coctiles I 357
Latham, R. G., q by Retzius II 792
Lathe, cruciform II 322n, 543, 559
Latin Church. *See* Roman Catholic

Latin Lexicon [Wörterbuch]. *See* Freund
Latitude, place of no (*Sūrya Siddhānta*)
  II 401-2n
Latona (Rom, Leto in Gk)
  born fr Leda's egg I 366
  brought forth Sun II 771n
  Diana, Ceres & II 419n
  Hyperborean continent or II 770
  Isis or II 130
  story of II 771-2 &n
Laurence, Archbishop Richard. *See also Book of Enoch*
—— Introduction to *Book of Enoch*
  on age of *Bk of Enoch* II 230, 506
  plagiarism fr *Bk of Enoch* II 482
  translated *Bk of Enoch* II 531
Laurentian Period (Pyrolithic age) II 151
  age of, rocks II 709
  astral forms physicalized in II 684, 712
  first condensation of oceans in II 159
  Gladstone on II 254
Lava, Lemurian cities of stone & II 317
Lavaṇa (Skt) salt water
  surrounds Jambu (dvīpa) II 320
Lavater, Johann K., many worlds inhabited
  II 706
Lavoisier, Antoine L., *Journal des Colonies*
  living elements I 468
Law(s). *See also* Karma, Lipika
  absolute will & II 164
  of analogy I 150-1, 173, 177, 586n, 604
  of birth, growth, decay I 144-5
  Deity is I 152
  dhyāni-chohans enact nature's I 38, 278
  eternal cyclic, of rebirth II 232
  evolution guided by II 731
  Fohat & I 109-11, 139
  of harmony depends on altruism II 302n
  immutability of natural I 640; II 731
  impressed on plastic minds I 269
  intelligences started, (Newton) I 594
  intelligent I 22, 38, 139, 277-8
  internal, in evolution II 697
  Kabiri-Titans laid down II 364
  karma, of ethical causation II 302n
  karma or fundamental II 510n
  manvantaric, immutable I 529-30; II 489
  mechanical, alone insufficient I 594, 601
  no blind or unconscious I 274, 278
  of offering II 747-8
  one eternal, produces harmony II 420
  of periodicity (2nd Fund Prop) I 16-17
  of probabilities I xlvi-vii
  of retardation, many still under II 172n, 197

  of retribution I 634; II 304-5
  rules smaller creators I 199
  science ignorant re origin of I 498; II 655
  scientific, often variable I 501-2
  working w occult, of nature I 489n
Laws, The (De Legibus). See Plato
Laws of Manu (Mānava-dharma-śāstra)
  all matter living I 280-1
  Brahmā as creator II 58
  Brahmā awakes, emanates spirit I 447
  Brahmā divides into male, female I 9n,
    137-8; II 126, 134n
  Brahmā-Vāch bisexual in I 72n
  Chandālas (Jews) in I 313n
  on connubial life II 411n
  Deluge not in I 67-8
  evolution of universe I 333-5
  exaggerations in II 67
  fourteen manus in kalpa II 307, 308 &n
  grihasta & laws of marriage I 210; II 411n
  Hiranyagarbha, Brahmā I 89, 360
  Kapila esoterically explained I 600
  Nārāyana resting on waters I 457-8n
  fr not-being is born being I 344
  Om, Bhūr, Bhuva, Swar I 432n
  pitris lunar ancestors II 91 &n
  pradhāna I 256 &n
  Rudras paternal grandfathers II 164n
  sarīsripa II 185
  six (7, 5) elements II 574
  sons of Atri, Marīchi II 89
  Svāyambhuva Manu & man I 248
  teaches evolution II 259
  ten prajāpatis, 7 manus I 449; II 573
  true Brahman a trisuparna I 210; II 590
  Vasus, Rudras, Ādityas, etc II 248n
  Virāj creator of world II 311 &n
Laws of Moses
  enacted against nations II 456
  Sadducees held to I 320-1n
Laya (Skt)
  absolute homogeneity I 522, 589
  awakens, becomes a comet I 203-4
  -centers a condition, not points I 145
  condition, "central sun" in II 240n
  described I 147-8
  divine breath issues fr I 289
  dying globes transfer energy to I 155-6
  evolution of atoms fr I 522
  Ilus rests in I 140
  Keely terms "Etheric Centers" I 148n,
    556-7
  life even in I 258-9
  nirvāna of 7th principle I 289 &n

nirvāna or, & elements I 140
points visible to adepts I 489
primitive, state of atoms 568n
protyle & I 522; II 105
seven, centers I 138-9, 147-8
state normal condition I 567
transfer of principles & I 172
univ Virgin-Mother emerges fr I 88
fr, to vortex of motion I 258
zero point or I 130, 147-8, 545, 551, 620
Layard I 125n, 126. *See* Lajard, J.-B.-F.
Layard, Austin H., excavations of II 5
Laycock, Dr Thomas
—— "Periodicity of Vital Phenomena"
cyclic nature of disease II 622-3 &n
man's 3 septenary cycles II 623n
"Lead us not . . ." II 517
addressed to God, not Devil I 414
"Leaflets from Esoteric History." *See*
Blavatsky, H. P.
Leah, mandrakes, magic &, [*Gen*] II 27n
Lebanon
initiates called cedars of II 494-5
Nabatheans of Mt II 455n
Le Clerc, Jean
oulām [ōlām] not eternity I 336n, 354n
Le Couturier, Charles H.
—— *Panorama des mondes*
attraction just an idea I 492n
combated Newton's vacuum idea I 494 &n,
495
Earth 350 million years old II 698n
force & mass I 502
gravitation merely a word I 604
rotation on Sun I 500
"Lecture on Protoplasm." *See* Huxley, T. H.
"On the Physical . . ."
Lectures on Mr. Darwin's . . . *See* Müller
Lectures on the Bhagavad-Gītā. See Subba Row
"Notes . . ."
Lectures on the Origin . . . *See* Sayce, A. H.
Lectures on the Philosophy of History. See Hegel
Lectures on the Sci. of Language. See Müller
Lectures on the Sci. of Rel. See Müller, F. M.
Introduction . . .
Leda (Gk)
Apollo, Latona fr egg of I 366
fable of Jupiter & II 197n
legends of, various II 121-4
mother of Castor & Pollux II 121-2
swan, Kalahansa, etc I 358-9; II 122
Ledrenus. *See* Cedrinus, George
Lefèvre, Professor André
—— *La Philosophie*

chronological info uncertain II 66 &n
on death of old races II 780
geological time imperfect II 685 &n
last glaciation 100,000 yrs ago II 779n
man dates fr Miocene II 714n
man last of mammals II 714n
monogenism vs polygenism II 169 &n
recapitulation of embryo II 187n
relative figures of Periods II 709-10
Tertiary man on sunken lands II 782n
traces pre-Aryan Europe II 741
vegetable phase of human foetus II 685n
Left-Hand Path I 417-18
adepts of, called trees II 494-5
adepts of, or Levites II 211
Atlanteans followed I 192n; II 331
persecution of right by prophets of II 503
right &, began in Atlantis I 192n
South Pole & II 400n
started sacerdotal castes II 503
Legend(s). *See also* Allegories, Myths
based on facts in nature II 293, 393
of deluges II 314
of 4 previous races universal II 311
Gould on actuality of II 217-19
more true than history II 182
of reclaiming buried libraries I xxxiv
of 3rd race propagation II 132
transformed by popular fancy II 777
worldwide community of II 311
Légendes Persanes. See d'Herbelot
Legends & Theories . . . *See* Hardy, R. S.
Le Gentil de la Galaisière, G.-J.-H.
on Hindu zodiac I 663
Legge, James
—— *The Life & Teachings of Confucius*
Confucius transmitter, not maker I xxxvii
Legibus, De. See Plato, *Laws*
Legum Allegoriae. See Philo Judaeus
Lehm, gravel deposit in Belgium II 744
Leibniz (Leibnitz), Gottfried W.
all matter connected I 615, 627
believed many worlds inhabited II 706
Couchy's points are monads of I 630-1n
ethereal fluid of I 623, 626
Haeckel's theories & monads of II 671, 673
metaphysical intuition of I 627
monadic evolution of I 619-20
monad reflects itself in root forms II 186
monads of, & early atomists I 579
monads of, or elementary germs I 139, 489
on Newton's agent of gravity I 491
not initiate or mystic I 619
objective pantheist I 629

science should weigh theories of I 625
sought univ philos tongue [Merz] I 310
theories of, dealt w lower planes I 626
truths of, alloyed I 622
—— *Examen des Principes* . . .
God made nothing but monads I 631
—— *Letter to Father Des Bosses*
distinguishing betw monads, atoms I 631
—— *The Monadology* (*Monadologie*)
atoms as mathematical points I 628
brushes esoteric secrets I 626
endowed nature w life I 627, 630
monads as entelechies I 632n
monads indestructible I 179
monad universe in itself I 107
universe reflected in monad I 632
—— *Système nouveau* . . .
on atoms I 630n, 631n
Leibniz. See Merz, J. T.
Lemaître, Jules, on Renan II 455
Lemmings, migration of, & Atlantis II 782
Lemminkainen (Finn), good magician II 26
Lemniscate, symbol of, & caduceus I 550-1
Lemnos, Island of
   fire (Kabiri) worship in II 363
   giant skeleton at II 278
   sacred to Vulcan II 3
   volcanic isle (Decharme) II 391
Lemprière, Dr John, on Sanskrit I xxxviii
Lemur, & modern pithecoids II 717
Lemuria. *See also* Lemuro-Atlanteans, Root-Race–3rd
   Africa never part of II 263, 368
   archaic names of, secret II 263-4
   "Atlantis" &, may rise again II 333
   Atlas personified II 762
   Australia remnant of II 314, 779
   HPB on, (*Theosophist*) II 788-9
   broke into smaller continents II 324, 327-8
   climate of II 777 &n
   colossi & cyclopean ruins fr II 263, 346n
   combustion & submersion of I 439n
   complete records of II 334
   continents of II 220, 326, 781n
   cradle of ape-man (Haeckel) II 171, 193n
   cradle of physical man II 46, 679-80, 715n, 737, 789
   described II 7-8 &n, 221, 264, 323-4, 326-8, 333-4, 405, 781n
   destroyed by fire II 266, 316, 331, 762
   destruction of I 439n; II 197, 221, 313-14, 332, 371-2, 776
   Dioscuri, 7 dhyāni-chohans of II 361n
   Easter Island remnant of II 326-8

elect of, in Śambhala II 319
evidence for II 781-2, 788-9
extended up the Atlantic II 337
giant peaks of II 763
Latona-Niobe story & II 771-2 &n
Madagascar remnant of II 177
man originated in, (Haeckel) II 679-80
New Zealand part of II 296
no sharp line betw, & Atlantis II 333
origin of name (Sclater) II 7, 171, 323-4n
perished before Eocene II 313, 779
pre-Tertiary II 8n, 433n
risings, sinkings of II 320-31
sank in Indian Ocean (Haeckel) II 679-80
Sons of Light & of Darkness in II 772-3
southern Hyperborean continent II 770n
stretched to polar regions II 769n
submerged continent of, (Crotch) II 782
Sweden, Norway part of II 402
tilting of axis & II 329
volcanism destroyed II 141n, 266
Wallace admits, a reality II 193n
written language of II 346n
Lemurian(s). *See also* Lemuro-Atlanteans, Root-Race–3rd
   accursed races of II 319
   adepts II 351
   ancient nations descend fr II 768-9
   Andaman Islanders fr late II 195-6
   androgynous then bisexual II 777
   animals, mated w II 286-7, 775
   bred monsters II 285-6
   built huge cities II 316-17
   continent broke apart II 324-8
   continent submerged II 606n
   cyclopean ruins of II 263
   divine dynasties of II 366, 774
   early, androgynous II 777
   early, were astral II 737
   elect of, on Sacred Island II 319
   failures among II 272
   first physical man II 46
   gravitated toward North Pole II 274
   hermaphrodite then sexual II 178
   holy race of giants II 171-2
   later, highly intellectual II 263
   looked upon as mythical II 761
   male, forefather of apes II 201n
   mindless wives of II 283, 286
   no outward worship among II 272-3
   physicalization of II 736-7
   pineal a gland after fall of II 301
   polar regions tomb of II 324
   records of II 334-5

Saturn governed II 765
seven, divisions of Earth II 366
seven kumāras, White Island & II 584
sin of the mindless of II 683
size of II 171-2, 316, 340, 344, 446
sorcerer & circular stones II 343-4
sorcery of II 286
Tasmanians fr late II 195
third deluge destroyed II 351
two classes of II 772
ungodly Atlanteans comp w II 350
Wealdon remnant of, river II 333
worshiped their own statues II 316
Lemuridae
Haeckel's, & Prosimiae II 649-50, 668
Lemuro-Atlantean(s). *See also* Lemuria
age of II 751
bred monsters I 184n; II 285, 775
civilization of, drowned II 426
continents II 10
descendants of II 195, 199n, 779
dynasty of spirit-kings II 221-2
fell victim to animal natures II 285
first physical races II 772
had no dogmas II 272
highly civilized, speaking race I 191
innate knowledge of II 285
kings of, not always good II 222
overlapping of Atlantis & Lemuria II 433n
"Sons of Night, Sons of Sun" II 772
took wives of lower race II 195, 283, 284-5
Lenoir, Marie-Alexandre
—— "Du Dragon de Metz" II 386
Lenormant, François
—— [*Manuel d'Histoire ancienne de l'Orient*]
prehistoric Egyptians II 432
Leo (Constellation)
fiery lions or divine flames & I 213
heart of, & beginning of kali-yuga I 663
Hydra & Dendera II 432-3
Judah & I 651
vanquished II 785
vertical to Ceylon II 407
Virgo inseparable fr II 785
Leo [III] Isaurus
burned Constantinople library II 763n
Le Plongeon, Augustus
discovered Kan Coh sepulcher II 34n
—— *Sacred Mysteries* . . .
on *Book of Enoch* II 229-30, 506
Mayan & Egy alphabets alike I 267n
Mexican Sephīrōthal Tree II 36 &n
number 7 in antiquity II 34-5
Leporine (hare-rabbit), fertile hybrid II 287

Lepsius, Karl Richard
—— *Denkmäler aus Aegyptien* . . .
Osiris-Lunus I 228
Leslie, Sir John
—— *An Experimental Inquiry* . . .
light & heat related I 515n
Lesser Bear. See Ursa Minor
Lesser Holy Assembly. See Idrā Zūṭā Qaddīshā
Lethe (Gk), river of forgetfulness II 690
Leto (Gk). *See* Latona
Letter(s)
M & its symbolism I 384-5
P & R evolve fr one II 574
seven, of Jehovah's name I 335, 351-2
Letters from North America. See Hodgson, A.
"Letter to a Theosophist"
race of buddhas, christs II 415
"Letter to Father Des Bosses." *See* Leibniz
"Let there be Light" (*Gen*) I 215-16n
"Lettres et conversations." *See* Humboldt
Lettres Persanes. See Montesquieu, Baron de
Lettres pour servir . . . *See* Brasseur de Bourbourg
Lettres sur L'Atlantide. See Bailly, J. S.
Leucippus (of Abdera)
atomic theory of I 2, 117, 579
atoms in a vacuum I 64, 343
believed in gods I 518
Leucomaines
men, animals swarming w I 260-1, 262n
Leverrier, U. J. J., predictions of II 441
Levi (son of Jacob) II 211-12. *See also* Levites
Simeon &, or Gemini I 651
Lévi, Éliphas I xliii n; II 268n
astral light of I 196, 253-5, 338n, 421; II 74, 409, 485
re concept of God II 545, 555
confuses rūah & nephesh II 633n
full of contradictions I 259n
God should not be given form II 536
hesitated re Fall of Angels II 238n
incarnated paradox II 584
kabbalist II 238n, 506
miracles he claimed I xliii n
pandered to Rome II 507, 510-11, 562
paradoxes of II 510, 589
phallic interpretations of II 555
terminology of I 242
universal agent of I 76
veiled references of II 511
—— *La Clef des Grands Mystères*
angels aspire to become men II 377
sevenfold man (Kabbala) I 241-2, 243-5
—— *Dogme et Rituel* . . .

Enoch & 6-pointed star II 533
    sign of cross II 562
    yang, yin explained II 554
—— *Histoire de la Magie*
    astral light I 259n
    Fall of Angels II 238n
    grand kabbalistic symbol II 359-60
    Lucifer or astral light II 511
    Satan described II 506-7
    Sēpher Yetsīrāh, Zohar, etc II 536
—— *The Mysteries of Magic* [A. E. Waite]
    on astral light I 253-4n, 255
    [Waite] q re *Book of Enoch* II 506
—— [*Paradoxes of the Highest Science*]
    [Master KH] II 415
Leviathan (flying serpent) II 577
    in *Job* II 206
    Neptune riding on II 268n
    saraph mehophep & II 206n
Levites. *See also* Jews, Levi
    Ark in Holy of Holies of II 459
    degraded Holy of Holies II 468-9
    "fiery serpents" name given to II 212
    of left-hand path II 211, 212
    priestly caste, disappeared II 130
Leviticus
    disfigured *Laws of Manu* II 748
    offering of "coats of skin" II 748
    seven rounds, 49 races II 618, 747-8
    seven Sabbaths II 565n
    twelve cakes I 649
    unclean foods I 80n
Lewes, George Henry
    "guarded materialism" of I 124-5n
    more dangerous than Büchner I 528n
Lewins, Dr
    effects of Newton's discoveries I 484n
—— "Phreno-Kosmo-Biology"
    on cerebration I 297 &n
Lewis. *See* Lewes, G. H.
Lewis, G. C.
    Capella on Egyptian astronomy I 650
Lexicon Pentaglotton. See Schindler, V.
Lha(s) (Tib) spirits, pitris
    create the world II 23
    defined II 22
    fivefold I 238
    incarnate in men II 191
    inferior, & man's body II 57
    Melha a revered II 63
    of Moon gave man form II 102
    solar II 17, 105, 109, 110
Lhakhang (Tib) I xxiv
Lhamayin (Tib), of below & Lhas II 63

Lhasa (capital of Tibet)
    word derived fr Lhas II 63
L'Homme rouge des Tuileries. See Christian, P.
Lhy [Li] (Chin), cuts communication betw
    heaven & Earth II 281
Liafail (Celt)
    speaking stone at Westminster II 342
Liberation. *See also* Nirvāṇa
    creators who have reached II 77
    marut-jīvas attained final II 615
    way to final II 322
Liber de Culture . . . See Abenephius
Liber mysterii. See Knorr von Rosenroth
Libra
    Aries, & Greek zodiac II 436n
    Asher or I 651
    Enoch, & Hermes are one II 129
    Hindu zodiac & I 661, 663
    invention by Greeks explained II 502n
    three Virgos betw Leo & II 368
    Volney on Aries & I 658
Library(ies)
    Alexandrian I xxiii, xxxiv; II 692, 763n
    Atlantean, Babylonian, & Chinese II 692
    Central Asian underground I xxxii
    destruction of II 692, 763n
    Mazarine II 531
    Russian I xxxvi
    sacred, of Fo-Kien I 271n
    Sargon's, at Akkad II 691
    subterranean cave- I xxiv-v &nn
    teachings of all adepts in I xxxiv
    temple II 529
Libya (Lybia in tx)
    golden apples not in II 770n
Libzu (Bab), "wise among the gods" II 5
Lice, aphides or plant- II 133
Lichen(s), emergence of I 246, 608n
Liddell & Scott, *A Greek-English Lexicon*
    re Deus II 582 &n
Liechan [Liuhan] (Norse) enlighten
    Loki, Lux &, same origin II 283n
Liège, old skulls at II 278
Lif, Lifthrasir (Norse)
    coming Adam & Eve II 100
Life I 157n. *See also* Fohat, Jīvas, Lives, Neph-
    esh, Prāṇas
    animated by atomic vibration I 633
    atoms instinct w desire for I 249
    battle of mortal, w immortal II 272
    bundle of, (*Zohar*) II 315
    came fr molecular action II 730
    cosmic, an electric ocean I 604
    death necessary for evolution of II 389

desire to live, tanhā II 109-10
earth never without I 258
egg symbol of eternal I 365
germs of II 719
light is, & electricity I 579
light of men was I 70
"like a dome" [Shelley, *Adonais*] I 238
mahā-buddhi becomes universal I 572
march towards a higher I 277
mechanical origin of II 652
meteor brought, to earth (Thomson)
    I 366n, 488; II 158, 719, 730
"molecular arrangements" I 502n
nature of, not understood I 493, 540
non-separateness of I 68-9
now an empty word II 730
no, without death I 413
Odin gives man, & soul II 97
"the one form of existence" I 49
origin of II 164-5n
orthodox & esoteric science on II 711-15
on our planets II 706-8
pervades spirit, soul, body I 49
primordial germ of I 455
radiates fr the Unreachable I 59
respect for, in ovum & egg I 366
science ignorant of origin of II 655
secret of, series of lives I 238
spirit & I 284
spontaneous generation (*Gen*) II 151
Sun origin of, -essence I 540-1
terrestrial & stellar II 703, 707
too much, may kill I 539
traced back to Silurian II 72
union of circle & diameter II 106-7
universality of I 49, 225 &n, 248-9, 258;
    II 702n, 703
Vaiśvārana aspect of the One II 311n
water of II 400 &n
what is, (Felix) I 670
Life, the One I 110, 291, 539, 591. *See also*
    Boundless, That
as electricity I 81, 137, 139; II 65
eternal motion attribute of I 2
highest aspect of electricity I 81-2
jīvātman or I 50
law &, ever unknown II 732
lives & I 250, 268
related to one law — karma I 634
"secondless" I 120
THAT or I 258
the Unmanifestable I 10
wrongly identified w God I 225
Life and Letters of Faraday. See Jones, H. B.

Life-Atoms. *See also* Atoms
anima mundi & II 672 &n
of prāna & heredity II 671-2
sleeping atoms & II 672
Life-Cycle. *See also* Cycle
end of this, 7th race II 49
men of this, & next I 267, 309
Vaivasvata Manu & this II 321
Life Germs
aggregate, produce other lives I 259
via a meteorite I 488; II 158
fr Moon II 139
Life of Brahmā
length of I 206; II 70
mahā-kalpa or I 368; II 179
100 years of 360 days I 36
universal pralaya after I 552
we have passed ½ of the I 368
Life of Confucius [*Life & Teachings* . . .].
    See Legge, J.
Life of Jesus. See Renan, J. Ernest
Life of Moses. See Philo Judaeus
Life of Paracelsus. See Hartmann, F.
Life Principle. *See also* Liquor Vitae, Nervous
    Ether, Vital
anima mundi source of II 562
Archaeus or II 654
astral form instinct w II 117
astral light, of every creature I 196
daivīprakriti or I 602
force as noumenon of II 672-3
kinetic & potential energy aspects of
    II 673n
meaningless to science II 730
omnipresent, indestructible II 672-3 &n
Sun source of I 593-4
too much, too little, may kill I 539
Life Winds, *Anugītā* on I 96; II 496 &n, 566-9
Light
absolute, is darkness I 69-70, 201, 337;
    II 95, 489
Adam Kadmon, Sephīrāh or I 337
adepts know every phase of I 516
Aditi or primordial II 107
aspect of universal motion I 147
"Boundless," of Gnostics I 577
called a god esoterically I 672
can be stored (Grove) I 508-9
chemical action of terrestrial I 597
comes fr darkness I 40-1; II 485-6, 488, 492
cosmic desire becomes absolute I 201
cosmic principle of II 41
creative II 233, 239
darkness & I 70, 450; II 162, 412-14

darkness &, eternal ways (*Gītā*) I 86
differentiated, becomes Fohat I 216
disc I 41, 70, 481-9, 579-80; II 37-40
drops ray into Mother I 64
electricity & I 508-9, 579-80
eternal, or Ptah II 553
fatal, of Lévi II 512
Fire, Flame &, (Stanzas) I 81-2 &n
force, vibration I 483
generated in darkness II 492
in *Genesis* I 337, 356n, 450
God not, but cause of I 285
heat & I 2-3, 515n; II 130
infinite ocean of I 481
is cold flame I 82
of Logos, Christos I 216; II 38
Lords of Being & condensed II 33
minerals are, crystallized & immetallized
    II 169
mysteries focus of II 281
nature of, not understood I 493
not matter (Grove) I 484
noumenal, phenomenal I 145-6
Occult Catechism on I 120
physical, reflects divine I 259n
Pleroma vehicle of II 511
primeval, Amun as source of II 130
primordial, dual II 36-7
primordial, is 7th principle I 216
primordial, Mithras as II 130
primordial, or central sun I 344
produces no evil II 490
purely phenomenal effect I 146
science re I 530-1, 554, 591, 595, 597
secondary effect of other causes I 484
shadow &, exist eternally II 214
shineth in darkness I 70
sidereal, of Paracelsus I 255
Sons of I 31, 106, 138-9, 196, 239, 481, 572,
    575
spirit & matter I 481
spiritual, how men put out II 413
springs fr upādhi of ether I 515n
Sun not cause of I 580
svara &, (Subba Row) I 270n
swan symbol of I 357
three kinds of II 37-8
three sacred number of II 590
true source of I 621n
ultimate causes of, discussed I 514-17
unknown, & Logos II 703 &n
Light-Bringer. *See* Lucifer
[Lightfoot, J. B., q by Oliver]
    on 7 sounding letters II 603

Lightning
    ash tree & II 520
    Baudry's speculations on II 526
    Christ comes like II 485
    of Cybele I 338n
    fury, evil spirit (Heb) I 467
    globular, derided II 784n
    Jupiter Fulgar or I 467
    Karshipta incarnation of II 292
    Prometheus, aranī & II 526-7
    Satan falls like II 230-1 &n, 485
Light of Asia. See Arnold, Sir Edwin
Light of the Logos. *See also* Daivīprakṛti
    awakens in animal man II 42
    creative, generative II 233
    daivīprakriti I 136-7, 293, 430 &n; II 38
    everything created thru I 430
    link betw matter & thought I 137n
    Madhyamā form of Vāch I 432
    seven sons of Sophia or I 430 &n
    three kinds of, (Kabbala) I 432
Lights
    Light of, or fire self II 570
    physical light & I 259n
    seven, & monads I 120
    seven, fr one I 122
    seven splendid I 433
    six, fr a 7th II 625
    three, in Kabbala I 432; II 37-8
    "of thy Father" II 564
    uncreated, created (Mazdean) II 291
Light-waves, hypothetical agent of I 528
Light-Wisdom, Black Fire is absolute II 162
Līlā (Skt) amusement
    universe created as in II 53, 126
Lilalohita. *See* Nīlalohita
Lilatu. *See* Lilīth
Lilīth
    Adam, & chhāyā-birth II 174
    degenerate, of 3rd race Adam II 679
    described II 174, 285 &n
    Pramlochā is Hindū II 175
    Samael-, ape descended fr II 262
Lillie, Arthur, *Buddhism in Christendom*
    errors in I 539n
Lilliputians, future men, in size & giants in
    mind II 289n
Lily(ies). *See also* Water Lily
    archangel Gabriel & I 379 &n; II 472
Limbus (Lat) border, fringe
    astral light or I 353
    kāma-loka or I 334, 463
Limbus Major, chaos, primordial matter I 283
Limbus Minor, terrestrial seed, sperm I 283

"Limestone as an Index of Geological Time."
    See Reade, T. M.
λίμνη (limnē, Gk) sea (*Iliad*) II 766
Line
    has length only II 553
    point fructifies the I 91
Liṅga (Skt) sign, symbol. *See also* Phallus
    Catholic writers on II 85
    Hindu, & Jacob's pillar II 471-2
    Hindu, & rabbinical Holy of Holies II 469
    Jehovah on par w yoni & II 474
    pāśa can be viewed as II 548
    sacr, yoni & II 465 &n, 467 &n, 588
    stone in Ark, yoni & II 473
    symbol of jōd in Kabbala II 126n, 473-4
    -worshipers of India I 347; II 472
Liṅga Purāṇa
    complexion of early races II 249-50
    "First was Mahat" I 451, 454n
    lists 7 winds or principles II 612
    names for Mahat I 256
    names of Dattoli II 232n
    Nārāyana, waters I 457-8n
    Rudra was first rebel II 613n
    Sanat-Kumāra I 458
    Śiva reborn in each kalpa II 282
    Vāmadeva reborn in many colors I 324
    year of 7 rishis, year of dhruva II 307n
Liṅga-Śarīra (Skt) II 242. *See also* Astral Body
    action of stars & I 532
    astral body or I 157 &n, 242; II 596
    chhāyā or II 593
    corresponds to globe five I 153 &n
    spirit of Earth builds man's II 241
    vehicle of prāna I 157 &n
Lingha(m). *See* Liṅga
Linghayic, Śiva becomes, & yonic II 548
Linnaean Classification
    lists most plants as bisexual II 133
Linnaeus, Carl von, remark of II 287
Linus (legendary Gk poet), poems of I 648
Lion (Leo, Simha) I 663
    Christian sacred animal I 363, 441-2
    in Dendera & Indian zodiacs II 368, 432-3
    on Gnostic gems II 481, 564, 565
    grip of, paw & decad II 581
    inverted (Dendera) II 433
    Mikael, Michael I 127n; II 115n
    Mother of God sitting on a I 400
    Ophite, or Christian Michael I 127n
    Paleolithic man lived w II 722 &n
    puma or, in New World II 792
    St Mark, Fire &, (table) II 114
    Satan &, devour men I 442n

symbolizes 4th race II 533
tribe of Judah I 651
two, & Toum or Fohat I 673n
Virgin &, [Leo] II 431
Lip, or language (*See Genesis* 11:1)
    mankind once of one I 229; II 198, 452,
        760n, 774n
Lipika(s) (Skt)
    agents of karma I 294 &n
    barrier betw EGO & SELF I 129
    concerned w man's hereafter I 126
    exist as entities I 106
    Fohat, Sons of I 107
    meaning of word I 128-9n
    mysteries to highest adepts I 128
    not linked w death, but life I 105
    objectivize plan of universe I 104
    only, cross line betw finite & infinite I 132
    recorders of karma I 103-5, 128, 129
    Ring "Pass-Not," pi (π) & I 131
    separate world of spirit fr matter I 130
    Sons (gods) come under eye of I 192
    stand in middle wheel I 31-2, 118
    three groups of I 127-8
    various equivalents of I 105
Liquid(s)
    gases, solids & I 526; II 136-7n
    spherical form of drop of I 97-8n
Liquid Fire II 106
    water is II 114
Liquor Amniae
    foetus amidst, in womb II 188
Liquor Vitae (of Paracelsus)
    life fluid I 538-9
    nervous ether of Richardson I 532 &n
Lithos(oi). *See also* Baetyl, Bethels
    decad &, of Egypt & America I 321
    magic stones, betyles or II 346n
    phallus, lingham or II 85
Lithuanian Legend
    of man's regeneration after Flood II 270
"Little Ones," initiates (*Zohar*) II 504
Little Tibet
    Baltistān & II 204, 416n
    part of home of physical man II 416n
Littré, Maximilien P. E.
——— *Revue des deux Mondes*
    potentialities of matter I 502n
——— "*Y a-t-il eu des hommes sur la terre . . .*" [in
        Revue]
    man before last geological epoch II 738-9
Lives
    countless, build man, nature I 260-1
    fiery I 249-50, 259, 262-3n; II 117

infinitesimal, bacteria I 225n
life collectively I 268
myriads of unknown I 607-8
spiritual, śishtas, seeds II 164
Lives of Alchemystical Philosophers (anon)
destructions of Earth II 762n
Lives, Past, personality ignorant of II 306
Livia Augusta, transmuted bronze E to gold
facsimile II 580
Livre des morts, Le. See Pierret, Paul
Lizards
atrophied eye in II 296 &n
w bird's wings II 55
flying II 218-19, 258, 387
Iguanodon of Mesozoic & II 154n
Lizeray, Henri
—— *La Trinité Chrétienne dévoilée*
dragon as the Verbum II 355n
Llama, copy of camel II 792
Lob-nor (lake in Central Asia)
tradition of buried cities at I xxxiv
Loch-Maria-ker [Locmariaquer, Fr]
conical menhir of 2 x 20 yds II 752
Locke, John, *An Essay Concerning Human
Understanding*
space has no resistance, motion I 8, 615
Locusts, Moses permitted eating of I 80n
Lodge, Sir Oliver
—— "The Ether & Its Functions"
properties of ether I 488-9
Lodur (Norse)
gives man blood, bones II 97
Logan, or rocking stones II 342n
Logic. See Bain, A.
Logograms, or symbol-letters I 307; II 335
Logography
ancient names tell history II 335
Logos(oi). *See also* First, Second, Third Logos;
Brahmā, Heavenly Man, Īśvara, Manu,
Verbum, Viśvakarma, Word
Adam Kadmon I 99n, 214, 246, 436; II 234
Ahura Mazdā or II 358
Aja in *Rig-Veda* II 578
ākāśa mother-father of II 400n
androgynous I 72 &n
apex of Pythagorean triangle II 24
asuras, rebels & II 162
Avalokiteśvara I 136, 429
awake, asleep II 310
became first leader of men II 373
born fr mind I 350
born only metaphorically II 69n
Brahmā or I 9, 137, 436; II 128, 247
Breath crystallized in the Word I 79

buddhas & I 571-3
bull symbolized II 418n
cannot see Parabrahman I 351n
celestial I 246
Christos II 230-1 &n
collective elohīm II 311
creative I 109-10; II 237
creative, or Demiurgos I 110, 279-80
-creator or Imhotep I 353
daivīprakriti & I 136, 293; II 38
Demiurge or 2nd, role of II 478
"Dragon" or "Son" I 71-2; II 355
Ennoia & Ophis II 214
every philosophy has II 36
explained I 428-30; II 24-5
female I 72n, 431
firstborn, First Cause I 14-15n; II 489
first unmanifested I 9, 14-15n, 16, 72n, 73n,
214-16, 278, 333, 349-51, 381n, 426, 448,
571, 573; II 2n, 24-5, 37, 128, 310, 596
Fohat & I 109-10, 137n; II 400n, 649
God of *Genesis* II 1-2n
of God, revealer of man II 589
great unseen, evolves other II 310
Greek, equivalent of Vāch II 199n
of Greek philosophers II 33
heptad, Aja & II 602
Hermes II 541
Holy One (*Zohar*) II 490
of India given 1,008 names I 349
invisible, hierarchies of II 23
is spirit I 573
Īśvara as I 130 &n, 136-7, 573; II 637
Krishna is, incarnate II 318n, 527
Kwan-yin & I 136-7, 473
light & II 37-8, 42
light in darkness I 439-40
light of one's own I 574
Lucifer is, in highest aspect II 162
manifested I 214; II 310, 592
man septenary symbol of I 79
manus, rishis of same II 310
Manu-Svāyambhuva, Brahmā II 128
Mēmrāh or I 346
mirror of Divine Mind II 25
motion begets Word or I 67n
mūlaprakriti & I 130n, 273-4
Nārada ever-incarnating II 48
Nārāyana & I 7
non-Christian, satanic II 236n
one, & mūlaprakriti I 273-4
of Ormazd, Amshaspends are II 488
passive wisdom in heaven II 231
Plato's I 214

point symbol of I 426, 429
Prometheus symbol of II 413
ray or, contains 7 rays I 80
reason & speech II 199n
reflection of the One I 130
reflects universe in Divine Mind II 186
Satan one w II 234, 515
"saves" II 230
see Ideal World & build it I 380
self-active wisdom on Earth II 231
self-born, egg-born I 363
seven, & 7 principles II 636
seven, & 7 solar elements I 138-9
seven, or creative potencies II 563
seventh principle in man, cosmos I 74n
soul of the world or I 353
-soul or Ptah I 353
symbolized by Sun I 134n; II 43
Tetragrammaton is 2nd I 72 &n, 99n; II 599
universal monad or II 311
universal, not a personality II 318n
unknown light or II 703-4n
Unmanifested. *See* first unmanifested
Vāch daughter & mother of I 430
various equivalents of I 110, 134n
Verbum I 72, 136
Vishnu 1st, Brahmā 2nd I 381n
visible, Sun & planets II 23
wisdom falling like lightning II 230
word made flesh I 349
world reformers emanation of II 358-9
Lohita (Skt) red
　Adam, Brahmā, Mars are II 125n
　Kārttikeya called II 43n
Lohitānga [Mars] (Venus in tx)
　third race under II 29
Loka(s) (Skt) world
　called rings, circles I 204
　dvīpas & II 321, 402
　Fohat's 7 sons & hot, cold I 204
　fourth, Earth II 47
　Indra's, & the gandharvas I 523n
　Purānas use, symbolically II 322
　seven devachans & I 674n
　seven dvīpas & II 321
Loka-Chaksuh (Skt) eye of the world
　our Sun I 100-1; II 22
Loka-Pālas (Skt)
　eight points of compass I 128; II 577
　guardian deities I 128
Lokapati, Lokanātha (Skt)
　names of Chenresi II 179
Loki (Norse)
　brother of Odin II 283n

falling demon of Scandinavia II 486
hid in waters & the Moon I 402
identical w Lucifer II 283n
Lolo, language of Chin aborigines II 280n
Longman's Magazine
　Professor Owen exposes Allen II 687n
Longomontanus [or Christian Séverin]
　lunar tables of I 667n
Lord(s) I 371, 420
　calling upon the, (*Gen* 4:26) II 469n
　God of Eden same as Satan I 414
　of Hosts, Jehovah II 43-4n
　Jehovah or II 537-8
　one of 7 planets II 538
　"rebuke thee, Satan" II 478
　Self-existent I 85, 333-4
　seven eyes of the, (Christian) II 22
　term for first II 452
Lord God II 267, 269n
　of *Genesis* 2 is elohīm II 2n, 81
　original mischief-maker II 387
　phallic character of II 467
　possible mistake of II 557
　serpent of *Genesis* II 215
Lord of Ghosts (Akkadian)
　Moon-god II 139n
Lord(s) of the Flame
　Chinese had their II 486
　did not create II 77
Lord of the Lotus (Kumuda-Pati, Skt)
　Moon, Earth's parent II 44
Lord of the Prajāpati (Skt)
　creates on Earth II 163
Lord of the Shining Face II 44
Lord of the World, Chenresi called II 179
Lord of Wisdom II 27, 44
Lords of Being
　killed off 1st race II 411-12n
　light & forms of II 33
　prajāpati are II 60, 163
　some, incarnated in man II 103
Lords of Light I 479
Lords (*Nath*) of Pranidhāna (Skt)
　solar angels II 88
Lords of the Dark Eye, Face II 427-8
Lords of the Dazzling Face
　white magician II 427
Lords of the Fires
　gnomes, fire elementals II 427
Lords of the Genii I 195-6
Lords of the Moon (pitris, lunar ancestors)
　II 75
Lords of the Zodiac & Spheres
　rebellious angels & I 577

Lords of Wisdom
  brought man fruit, grain II 373
  did not incarnate in monsters II 201
  identical w Hindu devas II 172
  incarnated in man (Prometheus) II 413
  kumāras as II 172-3
  quickened mental evolution II 411
  third race vehicle of II 172
Lost Arts II 430
Lot (Old Testament) I 452n
  had incest w daughters I 431
  wife of, & pinch of salt II 674
Lotus. *See also* Padma
  air-water symbol I 358
  Aryan in origin I 384
  bearer of its own seed II 472
  Chenresi holds a II 179
  Egyptian aquatic symbol I 353, 385
  flower of power or II 424-5
  four-leafed, & cross II 546
  golden, & wisdom II 578
  Horus, Vishnu & II 472
  man like I 184
  seed of, pictures the plant I 57, 379, 380
  Skinner on I 381-2
  symbology of I 57-8, 379-81, 384-6; II 179,
    472
  womb, symbol of I 385
Loubère, S. de la
  Siamese lunar tables I 666-7
Love. *See also* Eros
  Fohat & I 109, 119
  gravitation, hate & I 497
  Kāma-deva Hindu god of II 578-9
  material, physiological II 234
Lower Dauphiné (France)
  Field of Giants at II 277
Lubbock, Sir John (anthropologist)
  —— [*Origin of Civilization . . .*]
  Indians' petition to president II 439
  —— [*Prehistoric Times*]
  monogenetic origin of man II 169
  Neolithic giant skeleton II 749
  Neolithic, Paleolithic man II 722
Lubbock, Sir John W. (astronomer)
  cataclysms due to axis changes II 314
Lucae (or Lucä), vs ape-theory II 646
Lucan [Lucanus] (M. A., Lucian in tx)
  —— [*Pharsalia*]
  Druid belief in reimbodiment II 760
Lucian. *See* Lucan
Lucian, showed discrimination II 285-6
  —— *Auction . . .*
  Pythagorean reckoning II 603

  —— *De Dea Syria*
  Deucalion a northern Scythian II 768-9
Lucianists (2nd century sect)
  teachings about soul II 239n
Lucifer. *See also* Agnishvāttas, Angels, Asuras,
    Fall, Prometheus, Satan, Venus
  Adversary in lowest aspect II 162
  aether, astral light II 511-13
  both Holy Ghost & Satan II 513
  conferred spiritual immortality II 243, 388
  crescent-like horns of II 31-2n
  essence of Mahat II 513
  fallen cherub II 501
  first archangel fr chaos I 70
  "Harbinger of Light" II 243
  higher, older than Jehovah I 70-1
  Hindu, can reunite w deity II 237n
  Lévi on II 511
  "light-bringer" II 238n
  Logos in highest aspect II 162
  Loki, Prometheus were II 283n
  Mahāsura, Prometheus II 237n
  messenger, seraphim, cherubim II 243
  Morning Star I 70-1; II 45n, 238n, 239, 501, 540
  origin of II 490-2
  pontiff name II 33
  presides over light of truth II 512
  Satan & I 70-1; II 31-2 &nn, 45n, 111, 230,
    283n
  serpent of *Genesis* II 243
  spirit of intellect II 162
  Uśanas-Śukra is our II 45n
  Venus called, by Christians II 30-2, 45n,
    501, 512
  Verbum &, are one II 515
Lucifer (magazine)
  Egyptian initiation scenes II 558-9
  revelation of cosmogony I 168
Luciferians, Gnostic sect II 239n
Lucifer-Venus
  Michael & I 202
  Pistis Sophia on II 512
  St Augustine's ideas & II 32
  Titans & II 31
Lucina (Lat)
  Moon goddess I 395
  in Virgil's quote I 401
Lucretius, *De rerum natura*
  animated atoms I 568
  atomic theory I 2, 579
  fortuitous atoms I 594
  miserable state of humanity II 521
  modern theories refinement of I 486
  nothing can come fr nothing I 569

q on nature of divinity (Latin) I 7n
Ludolph, H., rejected *Bk of Enoch* II 531
Luke
  devils subject to us II 231n
  "I fast twice in the Sabbath" I 240
  Jesus rebuked the wind I 468
  lilies in hand of Gabriel II 472
  no one knows Father but Son II 231n
  render unto Caesar I 296
  Satan falling like lightning II 231, 485
  serpent fallen fr on high II 230
  tree is known by its fruit I 421
Lü-lan (Chin)
  q Confucius on dragon II 365
Lumbaka [Lambaka] (Skt) II 401-2n
Luna (Lat) goddess of Moon
  Artemis was, in heaven I 387
Luna-Artemis, surnamed Kallistē I 395
Lunar. *See also* Monads, Moon, Pitris, Soma
  ancestors I 155-7, 160, 180-1, 198, 263-4;
    II 44-5, 77-8, 102, 142n
  asterism II 550
  chain & transfer of globes I 171-5, 179-82
  cycle governs menstruation I 389
  cycles discussed II 620-1
  gods, goddesses I 396; II 23, 31, 427, 464
  Jehovah a, generation god II 40-1
  lower mind is II 495
  magnetism I 394, 398
  men produced Earth men II 45
  month 4 cycles of seven I 387
  months II 464, 624
  mysteries & occult knowledge I 228n
  phases & sex I 229n
  running astray into, path I 265
  Sepp on, year I 654-6; II 619
  solar &, deities mixed up I 362
  solar &, years in Bible II 391n
  solar gods, devas, struggle of II 495
  week, occult nature of I 409
  wind (ether) II 105
  worship I 387-8, 392-3, 396-8
  year I 36; II 466, 539, 561, 583, 619
  year & Isis, Nile, Earth II 583
  year & Kabbala II 38, 464
  years (4,320) explained I 655-6
Lunar Dhyānis, Fathers, Monads, Pitris,
    Spirits. *See* Pitris (Lunar)
Lundy, Reverend J. P.
—— *Monumental Christianity*
  cross in space, 2nd god II 561
  other saviors satanic II 482
Lung (Chin). *See* Lang

Lungs, globe's lower atmosphere I 144
Lung-shu (Chin) I 61
Luniolatry Ancient & Modern. See Massey, G.
Lunus (Lat) Moon
  Khonsoo as the god of II 464
  Osiris- I 228
[Luria, Isaac], *Book of Drushim*
  three groups of sephīrōth I 438
—— *M'bo Sha-arim* [*Sēpher M'vo Sheārīm*]
  emanation & meditation II 116
Lutaud, Dr L. A. J.
  rejects Pasteur's opinions II 151
Luther, Martin, transl of *Genesis* 4:1 II 127
Lux (Lat) light
  liechen (enlighten, Norse) & II 283n
  Lucifer or I 70
  Mercury son of Coelus & II 541
Lux Maris (Lat) light of the sea
  on statue of Hathor I 400
Luxor, unfading colors of II 430
Luz [Susa?], ancient Pers city built by Hus-
    chenk II 396-7
Lybia. *See* Libya
Lydus, Joannes Laurentius
—— *De mensibus*
  Iao, Mercury II 541-2 &nn
Lyell, Sir Charles
  differed w Fiske re myths II 787
  erroneous ideas re Atlantis II 787
  geological nomenclature II 10n, 11, 693
—— *Geol. Evidences of the Antiq. of Man*
  fossil records meager II 686
  Hallam on man & ape II 728
  inferior man not oldest II 721
  mammals extinct since man II 725
  Oliver on Asian land bridge II 783
  reconciling scriptures w I 323, 325
  Unger & Heer believe in Atlantis II 783
—— *Principles of Geology*
  Alps elevated since Eocene II 727, 778
  cataclysmal changes II 787
  Jupiter & moral depravity II 786
  sedimentation in Europe II 694
  world destruction, renovation II 784-5
Lynceús, killed by Pollux II 122
Lyra
  brilliant star in I 664
  certain star in, [La Caire in Bailly's tx]
    I 665
  nebula resolvable I 598n
Lyre, phorminx or 7-stringed II 529
Lystra (town in Lycaonia)
  Paul, Barnabas mistaken in II 481

M

M(s) [letter]
  androgyne I 384
  five, or Makaras II 579
  sacred names begin w I 384-5
  water hieroglyph I 384; II 65
Ma, Egyptian goddess (de Rougé) II 368
Ma (letter), equiv to "5" I 384; II 576-8
Ma, Greek root meaning nurse I 396
Mabbūl, waters of the flood I 385
Macben or Mac-benah (Heb)
  symb of animal kingdom II 575
Maccabees, Third Bk of, & *Bk of Enoch* II 532
Macedonian Greek(s), Indian art, science fr,
  cock & bull hypothesis I 647-8; II 225
McClatchey, Rev, *China Revealed*
  phallicism of Kwan or Yin I 471
[McFarland, R. W.]
  —— *American Journal of Science*
  glacial periods, floods II 141 &n
McGaldus, Albus (King of Scotland)
  alleged skeleton of II 749
Machinery, ancients knew of I 209n
MacKenzie, Kenneth R. H.
  learned Mason, theosophist I 305
  —— *The Royal Masonic Cyclopaedia*
  antiquity of swastika II 556n
  compares emblem & symbol I 305-6
  Elihu, Elijah taken to heaven [II 531]
  magical sigillae I 306
  three, 5, 7 in Masonry I 113n
  on translators of Bible I 128n
  whirling souls, gilgūlīm I 568 &n
Mackey, Sampson Arnold
  astronomer-shoemaker I 654
  self-made adept of Norwich II 362n, 431n
  time periods recorded by Pyramid II 436
  —— *"Mythological" Astronomy* . . .
  adept re Atlantic island [II 406]
  date of Purānic Atlantis [II 407-8]
  derivation of Kabiri, Axieros II 362n
  Earth's pole & ecliptic II 357, 431
  Egyptians re poles II 360 &n
  gods descend, ascend II 357
  Helion, Acheron II 357
  Hindu astronomy II 332
  inversion of poles II 360, 432-3

Lion on Dendera zodiac II 432-3
Mt Asburj II 407
mutilating Hindu chronology I 654
Sinhalese heirs of Lankā II 407-8
Virgo in Denon's zodiac II 433
Macmillan's Magazine (1860)
  new discoveries always suspect II 441
Maçonnerie occulte. See Ragon, J. B. M.
Macrobius, Ambrosius T., *Saturnalia*
  q Hemina on Kabiri II 363
Macrocosm. *See also* Microcosm
  came out of Ideos (Hartmann) I 283
  decad applied to, & man II 573
  hexagon star symbol of I 224
  Makara represents, & microcosm II 577
  meaning of swastika & II 99
  microcosm (man) & I 168, 181, 268, 274,
    334, 594; II 177, 580n, 685
  our planetary II 639n
Macroprosopus (Kab) Great Face
  abstraction in Chaldean Kabbala I 350
  Ain or Non-being II 626
  hairs on head of II 625
  Microprosopus & I 60, 78, 239; II 625
  perfect square, Tetraktys, etc II 626
  three higher planes I 239
Madagascar, Madagascans
  area betw Atlas &, was ocean II 264
  first large cities on II 317
  legend of woman fr man II 177
  Lemuria, part of II 7, 177, 222, 317, 324,
    327, 333
  Maki of, originally in sunken land II 789
Maddena Nag (Chald), Venus II 759n
Maddin Nag (Irish), morning star II 759n
Madeira
  Atlantis theory & II 791
  Europe-America land bridge & II 781
Mādhava, Mādhavī (Skt) Spring
  gods & goddesses called I 384
Madhusūdana (Skt), on the Aśvattha I 406
Madhya (Skt) middle
  beginning & end unknown I 138n
Madhyama (Skt) intermediate
  Light of Logos is, form of Vāch I 138, 432
  quality of sound I 534

Mādhyamika School, Yogāchāras &, re
    paramārtha I 44n, 48
Mādim [Ma'adīm] (Heb) Mars
    Adam same as II 144n
Madonna. *See also* Virgin Mary
    in crinolines & Kwan-yin I 473
    Devakī antetype of II 527
    Gnostic, nursing Jesus I 410
    Qū-tāmy's idol & I 401
    "Mad Stones" II 345-6
Madurese [Malay of Madura, Java] II 523
Maedler, Johann Heinrich
    on the Pleiades II 551
    Sun revolves around Alcyone I 501
Magadha (Skt)
    Andhra dynasty of II 220n
    Rājagriha ancient capital of I xx
Magas (priests of the Sun)
    first Zarathushtra fr II 322-3
    inhabited early Atlantis II 322
Magendie, F., *Précis élémentaire* . . .
    digestion in foetus II 131
Maghā (Skt) a lunar asterism
    kali-yuga beg w 7 rishis in II 550
Māghada. *See* Magadha
Maghāyanti [Meghayantī] (Skt)
    one of the Pleiades II 551
Magi (fr *mag*, Old Pers) I 410; II 393-5
    affinity betw Druids & II 756
    Aryan, emigrate to Sagdiani II 356
    astronomical observations of I xxvi
    believed in 7 globes, continents II 608
    college of, on Euphrates II 203
    Democritus pupil of I 117
    Egyptian, & Atlantean sorcerers II 428
    greeted morning star II 759
    Magas of Atlantis became II 323
    Nargal Chaldean chief II 213
    Orsi 4-letter god of II 602
    Persian, not fr Persia II 756n
    requirements to become a I 409
    Rosicrucians drew fr I 81n
    seven devs of I 577
    sevenfold doctrine of II 608-9, 756, 759
    star of the I 654 &n
    Three (NT), sepulchres at Cologne I 654n
    used stone to elect a king II 346
    used veiled language II 395
    of Xerxes sacrifice to Tethys I 467
    Yima was "man" to II 609
Magian Religion II 610. *See also* Mazdean
    asuras (ahuras) in II 92-3
    occult, magical, symbolic II 517
    origin of evil in II 490

works of, destroyed by Alexander II 6n
Magic. *See also* Black Magic, Sorcerer
    art of divine, (Tritheim) II 512n
    astral light &, (Lévi) I 253n, 254-5
    astrological, in Chaldea I 652
    astrology, kalpas & II 179
    Bacon, Roger & I 581 &n
    beings of lower spheres & I 605-6
    black, of Egy, Chald, Jews II 139n, 211-12
    black, white, struggle betw II 211, 364
    ceremonial I 234n; II 748
    Christian & pagan black I 416, 467-9
    Confucius believed in I 441
    Dracontia used for II 346-7
    early, meant science of wisdom II 319
    followed beginning of Christianity I xl
    head is astral light (*Zohar*) I 424
    Hermes initiated men into I 473
    initiation & II 380
    Kabiri-Titans demonstrated II 364
    knowledge of primary causes is I 263
    left-path, & castes, ritual I 503
    mandrake used in black II 27n
    Moon rules over I 387, 397
    nehhashīm (serpents) or, (*Zohar*) II 409
    Neptune symbol of Atlantean II 356
    North & South Poles & II 274, 400n
    number 5 symbol in II 579
    Paracelsus versed in I 263
    powers I 427
    reverse of, is sorcery II 179
    right- & left-hand II 25-6
    seven, number II 629-30
    sorcery often I xl, 467-9
    speaking stones & II 341-2
    speaking to gods in their language I 464
    swastika a, sign II 99
    "There is no," (*She*, Haggard) II 319
    white, black, in Atlantis I 192n; II 427-8,
        495, 762
Magician(s)
    Atlantean, perished II 350
    good & bad, North & South Poles II 274
    ishīn help, produce homunculi II 376
    Keely a natural-born I 558
    mighty builders, good & bad II 754
    of Ruta & Daitya II 428
    seventh son of 7th son II 213
    wicked, of Atlantis II 222, 223
Magic Papyrus. See Papyrus Magique Harris
Magic: White & Black. See Hartmann, F.
Magie der Zahlen, Die. See Hellenbach
Magism, Babylonian I 10
Magna Graecia (Lat), Hermes & II 367

Magna Mater (Lat)
  Greek & Syrian Virgin Mary, Moon I 392
  old world, a plagiarism (de Mirville) I 400
  spouse of son she conceives I 393
Magnes (of Paracelsus)
  aether, living fire or I 343-4
  magus &, 2 branches I 339
  "Spirit of Light" & I 338-9
Magnetism
  aspect of universal motion I 147
  atmospheric, of naturalists I 338n
  cosmic, & gravitation I 497-9
  Fohat & 7 forms of I 145
  iron &, occult properties of II 371 &n
  kundalinī śakti & I 293
  lunar I 394, 398
  mesmerism & I 297
  molecular expl of, inadequate II 719
  nature of, not understood I 498
  not a mode of motion I 484, 496, 516
  noumenal, phenomenal I 145-6
  secondary effect I 484
  solar system revolutions & I 501
  terrestrial, & anima mundi II 562
  ultimate causes of I 514-17
Magnetizer, fluid radiating fr I 338
Magnolia, in polar regions II 326, 726
Magnus, Johannes
—— [*Historia de omnibus . . . regibus*]
  Starkad carrying rune stones II 346n
Magnus, Olaus, [*Historia de gentibus . . .*]
  kings elected by divination II 346
Magnus Annus. *See* Annus Magnus
Magnus Limbus. *See* Limbus Major
Magus & Magnes, 2 branches I 339
Mahā-Ātma (Skt)
  "great soul" of world I 365, 461
Mahābhārata (Skt)
  āgneyāstra weapons II 629
  Anugītā part of I 94n
  Arjuna married Ulūpī II 214 &n
  Atlantean War in II 395
  cataclysm ending 4th race II 146
  Daksha creates II 275
  destruction of rākshasas II 232n
  explained by *Bhagavad-Gītā* II 139
  history as much as *Iliad* II 183
  Karttikeya's birth II 43n
  Mayāsura's gift to Pāndavas II 426
  Nārada II 47
  Nārāyana II 591n
  Pāndavārani or Kuntī II 527
  prajāpati are 21, 10, 6, 5 in I 90; II 40
  prologue to 5th race drama II 139

seven mind-born sons II 78
seven rishis I 436
sweat-born II 68, 183
War in Heaven II 390
war in, real, not fabulous I 397
Mahā-Buddhi
  Ādi-Buddhic monad manifests as I 572
  cosmic ideation, Mahat or I 16
  difference betw, & water I 257n
  Mahat or I 335, 572
  manas in man springs fr I 334
  Universal Soul I 420
  Vaishnavas' idea of I 451
  vehicle of spirit I 420
Mahā-Chohan(s)
  called Arghyanāth II 416n
  Egyptian, born without woman II 369
  Java Aleim or II 220
Mahādeva (Skt)
  destroying Tripurāsura II 591
  lingam symbol of II 85
  parent of rudras, maruts II 548
  pāśa or ankh-tie of II 548-9
  symbol of generative powers I 358
Mahā-Guru (Skt). *See also* Wondrous Being
  guides teachers of man I 208
Mahā-Kalpa (Skt). *See also* Mahā-Manvantara
  beginning of, & asuras II 500
  Brahmā's Age I 36, 53, 368; II 70
  Garuda emblem of I 366; II 565, 570
  Great Round & rounds, races II 615n
  Great Wheel or I 40n
  length of I 36, 40n, 53, 144n, 206, 368; II 70,
    615n
  mahatmic state & II 309n
  pralaya of I 53
  present, (Varāha) or Padma II 179
  role of Satan & I 198
Mahaleel [Mahalaleēl] (Heb)
  or Mehujael II 391n
Mahā-loka. *See* Maharloka
Mahā-Manvantara (Skt). *See also* Mahā-Kalpa,
    Manvantara
  Ādi-śakti, lasts for I 10
  beginnings of I 289
  Brahm lays Golden Egg each I 359
  dawn of I 11 &n
  heptad perfect number of our II 602
  nirvānīs fr preceding II 79
  paranishpanna at end of I 42
Mahāmāyā (Skt)
  of the ABSOLUTE IS II 446
  conscious egos & I 631
  dragon of absolute wisdom & II 384n

as Gautama's mother, & lotus I 379n
manifested universe is II 88, 384n
snares of, & real kosmos I 278
swastika & II 100
Virgo, Kanyā or I 292
Mahā-Pralaya (Skt) I 140, 368-72
all born in space & time die at II 549
all returns to one element at I 373 &n
Brahmā pralaya or I 172n
after Brahmā's Age I 552
dissolution of universe II 146
gods die in I 373n
initial existence after I 289
knowledge previous to I 369
length of I 134n, 371
Microprosopus destroyed in I 215
paranirvāna during entire I 134n
sweeps out gods, atoms I 151
Mahāpurusha (Skt), Supreme Spirit II 108
Maharajah of Benares, motto of, & TS I xli
Mahārājas, Four
Christian, Jewish equivalent of I 125-7
described I 122-8
do not punish or reward I 124
each of the, enthroned on a lotus I 379
four Genii, Dragons or I 408
Great Four or II 427 &n
protectors of mankind I 126, 294n
regents of elements, quarters I 126
Maharloka (Skt)
beings go to, at Mahā-pralaya I 371
one of seven dvīpas II 321
progenitors go to, return fr II 92
Mahāsura (Skt), Hindu Lucifer II 237n
Mahat (Skt) I 88. *See also* Mind (cosmic), Universal Mind
ahamkāra, 5 tanmātras & I 256n, 335; II 639
all wisdom reflection of II 81
appears 1st as Vishnu I 75; II 639n
awakened, & self-consciousness I 51
Brahmā & I 350; II 79, 163
buddhi characteristic of I 256, 373
cosmic ideation or I 16
egg symbol & I 360
egoism of matter II 639n
first aspect of Parabrahm I 451
first creation of Brahmā I 216n, 454n
first manifest intellect I 385
first product of pradhāna I 216n, 256, 284
flames of, landed on Earth II 232
God, Logos I 256, 602
incarnating spirits of II 230
Indra personifies II 614
intellectual understanding II 378

Kantian mind & I 602
later called egotism (*Anugītā*) I 75
Lucifer essence of II 513
mahā-buddhi or I 335, 572
manas & ahamkāra I 334
manas & chitti I 288n
mānasaputras & II 167
manifested wisdom or I 110
mati synonym of II 414n
Mōt (Phoen) & Mut (Egy) I 451
Nous (Gk) I 350
occult & Vedānta views of I 62
our globe progeny of I 260
phantasm fr absolute wisdom I 62
Second Logos 1st emanation fr II 478
sons of, quickened man II 103, 230
subtile elements originate fr I 284-5
Thought w Gnostics I 74
transformed into human manas I 75
universal intelligent soul I 16, 420, 450; II 58-9, 639 &n
Mahātma(s) (Skt) *See also* Adepts, Arhans, Brotherhood (The), Initiates, Masters, Occultists
buddhas &, historical II 423
personality of I 52
Sons of Will & Yoga ancestors of II 173
spiritual intuition of I 46n
Mahatma Letters [all refs in *ML*]
Avalokiteśvara I 471
Divine Essence fr Adam [error in *IU*, q in *ML* p 45] I xlii
failures among dhyāni-chohans I 188; II 232-3n
fifth round men I 161
fourth race civilizations II 429-30
giant bones in Himalayan caves II 293n
impossible to give details I 164n
man in 2nd round I 159-60
man's evolution thru 4th round I 188-9
many inhabited globe chains I 164
concerning Mars & Mercury I 163-6
metaphysics, East & West I 169
nomenclature needed I 167-8
777 incarnations I 168
seven man-bearing worlds I 167
time I 44
unable to give whole truth I 168
Māhātmya(s) (Skt), local legends I 367n
Mahatorvavat [Mahatomahīyān] (Skt) "greater than the great" I 357
Katha-Upanishad I, 2, 20
Mahat-tattva (Skt), First Creation I 446, 450-2
Mahāvansa [Mahāvaṃśa] (Skt)

Morya (Maurya) name I 378n
Sattapanni cave I xx
Mahā-vidyā (Skt), magic, now tāntrika I 169
Mahāyāna Buddhism(ists)
  adepts of, & Tāraka division I 158
  Alaya in I 48-9
  Hīnayāna &, re nidānas, etc I 39-40
  originated after Buddha's death I 39
  "Vedāntins in disguise" II 637
  worship of bodhisattvas II 34n
Mahāyogin(s) (Skt) II 613
  inhabited White Island II 584
  pāśa or ankh-tie of II 548-9
  Śiva called I 459
Mahā-yuga(s) (Skt) I 641
  aggregate of 4 ages I 63
  Chaldeans also used I 655n
  equals total of 4 ages I 450; II 308n
  length of II 69 &n, 70, 321, 624n
  no figures more meddled w II 73
  1,000, in Day of Brahmā I 63, 372; II 308n, 505
  rebels tied to Earth during II 246
  71 in a manvantara II 307n, 321
Mahendra (Skt)
  star in Ursa Minor & II 612 &n
Mahody [Mahādeva], of Elephanta II 85
Mahomet. *See* Mohammed
Maia (Gk)
  daughter of Atlas II 768
  Māyā, Mary, Mare & I xxxii, 396
  mother of Hermes, Mercury I xxxii; II 540, 542
Maier, J. *See* Mayer
Maillet, B. de II 646
Maimieux, J. de, *Pasigraphie*
  universal & philosophic tongue I 310
Maimonides, Rabbi Moses
—— *Moreh Nebuchim*
  Adam male & female II 134n
  Adam "prophet of Moon" II 466-7
  Azāzēl a mystery II 376
  divination I 394
  esotericism & II 456-7
  flying camel II 205 &n
  Nabatheans II 455 &n
Maistre, Joseph-Marie de, Comte
—— *Soirées de Saint Pétersbourg*
  gravitation merely a word I 604
  Newton's celestial intelligences I 484
  planets made to rotate I 502-3
Maitland, Dr M. Samuel Roffey II 441
Maitreya (Skt) II 155
  body of Brahmā II 58

elemental dissolution I 372-3
Hindu Asclepios I 286
kali-yuga described to I 377
last of buddhas in 7th race I 470
Parāśara desc 7 creations I 445, 456 &n
  in *Vishnu Purāna* II 155, 322
Maitreya Buddha
  last messiah of great cycle I 384
  secret name of 5th buddha I 384
Majority, seldom right II 156 &n
Makara (Skt)
  Assyrian "scaly one" or II 354
  connected w birth, death of univ II 579
  crocodile-headed god (Egy) II 580
  crocodile, water symbol I 384
  discussed I 219-21; II 576-80
  fifth hierarchy presided over by I 233
  kumāras & II 93, 576, 577-9
  leviathan or II 268n
  once 8th instead of 10th sign II 576
  Sun passes away behind I 376; II 579n
  Varuna & I 220; II 268n, 577
Makhbena' (Heb, Maoben in tx)
  symbol of animal kingdom II 575
Maki (of Madagascar), sunken land of II 789
Malabar (India)
  giant bones in tombs at II 347, 752
Malacca (Indonesia), traditions of II 223, 788
Malachim [Mal'ākhīm] (Heb)
  B'nē-aleim & II 375-6
  descended to eat w men I 441-2n
  elements &, now Jehovah I 462
  messengers II 514n
  theoi, of the manvantaric law I 346
Malay(ans). *See also* Jacolliot
  beliefs common to, & Polynesia II 328
  legends of sunken continent II 222-3, 788
  mixed Atlanto-Lemurian stock II 779
  Pacific continent &, (Haeckel) II 328
  seventh subrace, 4th root-race II 178, 332
  Sunda island cataclysm II 787n
Malayak. *See* Malachim
Malayalam-speaking People of S India I 658
Malay Archipelago. See Wallace, A. R.
Malcolm, Sir John
—— *History of Persia*
  Persian tradition of zodiac I 649
Male
  deities born immaculately I 59
  figure or unveiled mysteries I 351
  Moon as I 228n, 397; II 65-6
Male & Female
  Adam in *Genesis* [1:27] II 127
  diameter of circle II 536

hexagram & pentagram are I 78
Jah-veh II 388
lines in cross II 557
man (*Genesis*), host of sephīrōth II 1n
prepared astrally II 84
Seven Men all, (*Pymander*) II 2
Mal Feu (Fr), evil fire II 526
Malices, or elementals I 331n
Maligasima, Chinese sunken island II 365
Malkuth [Malkhūth] (Heb)
   bride of Heavenly Man I 216; II 595
   Earth Chain, globe D (Kab) I 200, 216, 239
   Earth's lowest principle II 595, 626
   seventh & fourth world I 240
   sign of cross &, (Lévi) II 562
   thrice destroyed I 241
   various names for I 240
Mallet
   swastika survives in Masonic II 100, 556n
Malta, pygmy elephants at II 219, 723
Malthusians, questionable lit of I 228n
Maluk. *See* Malachim
Mammal(s), Mammalia(n). *See also* Animals,
   Anthropoids, Apes, Man
   antediluvian, found w humans II 739
   anthropoids & present apes II 193
   astral prototypes of II 684, 688-9, 736
   Atlantean, not perfected II 286
   Darwin on II 118-19
   diagrams of II 688, 735
   evolution of II 180-5, 734-7
   evolved fr man in 4th round I 455; II 186-7,
      635, 688
   evolved fr man's cast-off tissues II 736n
   first forms of II 181
   first, marsupials II 594n, 684, 713 &n
   hermaphrodite, then 2-sexed II 184
   lower animals bisexual before II 594n
   man arose fr, (Haeckel) II 165n
   man 1st & highest II 288-9, 594
   man 1st not last II 155, 168, 714 &n
   man most perfect of I 248
   fr man, not reverse II 118, 170, 186, 635
   man preceded II 1, 56n, 170, 180, 274, 684
   many, extinct since man (Lyell) II 725
   no Miocene, like today's II 749
   origin of, described II 169-70, 736
   ovoviviparous II 166
   placental I 190n; II 667-8, 736n
   procreation parallels man's II 713-14
   seven root types of II 736
   sexually separated before man II 736 &n
   third race, w bones II 183-4
   three, orders & 3 root-races II 713-14

Mammoth(s) II 352, 733, 773n
   exhumed w hatchets II 738
   frozen in avalanche II 660n
   paleolithic man & II 721, 724
Man (Men). *See also* Adams, Androgyne, Embryos, Giants, Humanity, Humans, Mankinds, Pitṛis (Lunar, Solar), Prototypes,
   Purusha, Races, Root-Races, Savages,
   Yāh-Ḥavvāh
   adapted to early thermal conditions II 254
   age of, this round II 250-1
   agnishvāttas & spiritual II 78-83
   all beings are, were, or will be I 275
   anatomy of, & apes II 680-5
   ancient, knew of extinct monsters II 206,
      218-19
   androgyne or male-female, & deities I 113,
      231; II 458, 467, 626
   angel & ape (Hallam) II 728
   angels, can transcend II 111
   animal &, compared II 81
   animals fr 3rd round II 186-7
   animal up to 3rd race II 161
   anthropoids fr II 185-7, 193, 677 &n
   fr ape (science) II 87, 164-5 &nn, 171, 187
      &n, 189, 729
   ape &, common ancestor II 443, 674, 677
      &n
   ape &, discussed II 665n
   ape-like, but not an ape I 187
   ape-like in 3rd round I 188-9, 234; II 57n,
      185, 261-2
   apes imitate, not the reverse II 676 &n
   appears 1st on globe D, 4th round II 180
   Arvāksrotas or II 162-3
   becomes stone, plant . . . I 246; II 186
   bisexual astrally first II 84
   bisexual later (embryology) II 659
   blind to other worlds II 701
   body of, changes every 7 years I 262-3n
   body of, divine harmony I 212
   body of, merely developed animal II 733-4
   body of, ready at beg of 4th round II 660
   body of, stable II 256
   born fr lowest angels II 25
   born fr superior being II 274-5
   born under a star I 572-3
   born without sin, will be II 420
   Brahmā creates, last II 60
   breathes "Mother's" refuse I 144 &n
   breath of life in I 212
   builders are progenitors of I 128
   building of complete, explained I 247-8
   came fr Moon, will return I 227-8

can break w the monad I 265
cannot propitiate angels I 276
casts off skin periodically I 74
changes Earth's climate II 700
compared to Amphioxus II 370n
complete in 3rd & 4th races II 255n
composite being II 87
consciousness of, & senses II 650, 701
"created" insects, birds, etc II 290
created in 6th millennium I 340
created not as he is now II 87
created on 6th, 8th day I 448, 449
creation of, (*Zohar*) II 490-1
crossing w animals II 195-6, 262
crucified in space II 561
cube unfolded II 36
curse on, explained II 216-17
cycles in life of, (Laycock) II 623n
Cyclops in former days II 289
Daksha progenitor of physical II 176
death of, & of cosmos I 173
declined in Atlantis II 411
destiny of, traced in astral light I 105
determined shape of lower lives II 290
devotion & aspiration in early I 210
dhyāni-chohans creators & cause of
    I 229-30, 232-3 &n, 450, 559; II 34, 242,
    683
differences among II 103, 318 &n
discovered way to immortality II 283
divine, dwells in animal man I 210, 339
divine, in primeval age II 712
divine intellect veiled in II 74
divine, older than Earth II 721
does not know himself II 702n
dragon proves antiquity of II 208
dual & triple nature of II 27, 37, 274
dwarfed in mid-3rd race I 329
early divine, dwelt in his animal form I 210
early hostile environment & II 159-60
early, not the same all over world II 443
earns way thru lifetimes I 17
on Earth beginning of 4th round II 254
elements important in life of I 284 &n
& elements, in occultism I 567
elohīm sent, out of Eden II 282
emanated as both man & woman I 450
emanates fr septenary group I 230
emanations of Mother Substance I 291
embryos of, & dog compared II 258-9
Enos of *Genesis* is 1st sexual II 715n
in eternal sunlight would die I 413
ethereal, projected on 7 zones II 732
European fossils no test of age of II 725

every, latent anupadaka [aupapāduka] I 52
evolution of, & elements II 107-8
evolved fr divine men II 747n
evolved on many levels II 87
existed in Tertiary II 155, 751
fallen angel, god in exile I 450
Fall of, was no fall II 228, 261-2
false personality of II 254
fiend in his heart allowed by II 274
first & highest mammalian II 288-9, 594
first mammal II 155, 274
first, red like Adam II 43n
first, was breathed out II 86-7
fivefold jīva in I 224
flints of, in Pliocene II 688n
form of, evolved fr inner model I 184
forty-nine fires in I 291
fossil of modern, will look like small ape
    I 184n
four-armed, 3-eyed II 294, 744
giant ancestors of II 352
globe &, reawaken for new period II 730
god in animal form II 81
"god on earth" (Lévi) II 584
gods &, fr one source II 24
gods fell to complete divine II 232
Heavenly I 110; II 103, 458, 626
height of, less in Aryan race II 753
higher, goaded by lower II 109-10
image of dhyāni-chohan II 728
imprisoned spirit II 733
indirect ancestor of apes II 289
inferior, not always older II 721
influenced by genii-elementals I 294-5
inner, real, outer false personality II 306
"is become as one of us" I 493n; II 44, 202,
    243, 499n
Jupiter, Bacchus symbolic of II 362
karma adjusts plans of II 305
Lévi & theosophy on 7-fold I 242-5
lhas of Moon gave, form II 57, 102
life of, & his constellation I 638
link betw heaven & Earth II 370
lived in Miocene II 12
lived w extinct species II 746
lunar ancestors of II 45-6
lunar pitris become I 180
mammals fr, in 4th round II 170, 186
manas, mind principle, human soul I 101 &n,
    334
manifested deity, good, evil II 515
Massey mistaken re II 632-3
mating w animals II 189

microcosm & macrocosm I 101, 177, 181, 274; II 97-9, 169, 177
Microprosopus prototype of I 215
middle principle of, grossest I 260
in mid-Miocene (Fr geologists) II 686
mindless I 185n, 188-91; II 80, 102, 161-2, 186-8, 189-90, 191-2, 198
mind of, awakened II 89
monads of I 119, 174-5 &n, 177-82, 184-5 &n, 265; II 88, 105, 109-10, 150, 161, 167, 180, 185-6, 256-7, 635
more than life & body II 56
mortal, born fr Viraj II 606
most material in mid-4th round II 250
Nārada leads, to become god II 584
nirmānakāyas sacrificed for II 94
no date for, in *Genesis* II 690
no first II 270, 610
no pithecoid blood in II 193
not fr ape II 185, 646, 674, 682-3
not fr apes (Quatrefages) II 666-7
not material alone II 81
numerical equivalent of II 560
nursed by wind (air) II 113
older than higher mammals II 714
old remains of, in high places II 723-4
only since Miocene (science) II 745
organism without organs once II 154
origin of, (Haeckel) II 165n
origin of, each round I 232-3
outward, an animal I 234
paleolithic & neolithic II 686-9 &nn, 715-21
passed animal stage in 3rd round II 299
passed thru all kingdoms & stages I 282; II 185-7, 254, 260, 659, 660
past & future of, in zodiac II 431-3
pentagon symbol of II 576 &n
perfect, above the angels II 377
perfected w spiritual fire II 113
perfect, quaternary & ternary II 576
perfect septenary, 7th round II 167
physical & spiritual II 281-3, 362-3
physical, before Cretaceous II 679
physical, 1st appearance of II 57, 72, 157, 170, 251, 310, 312, 679, 736-7
physical, image of minor god I 445
physically, product of evolutionary forces I 636
physical, product of nature's forces I 636
physiological, out of astral II 737
pineal gland of, active, inactive II 298
pitris create I 86-7
polygenetic origin of II 168
preceded animals I 159-60; II 197n, 255-6

preceded huge reptiles II 274
preceded mammals II 1, 56n, 168-70, 180, 274, 684
pre-Tertiary giant II 9
primary, could fly II 55
primeval, huge, filamentoid II 151
primeval, not all savage II 722
primitive, a phantom II 102
primitive form of, (Haeckel) II 193n
primitive, had fire II 524
primitive, lived w elohīm II 349
principles of, (diagram) II 593
problem of man's origin & destiny I 636
procreation of, various methods II 166-70
product of matter (Thomson) II 719
Prometheus as a II 244
prototype of all forms II 289-90, 659, 683, 705
a quinary (5 principles) when bad II 575
realized "sin" too late II 267
reflection of reality I 278
reflects dhyāni-chohans II 108, 170
religion & science re age of II 796
responsible in 5th race II 255n
rudimentary organs of II 681
Satan set, free of ignorance I 198
savage & civilized, in all ages II 716
science on antiquity of II 70-1
in Secondary Age II 10, 157, 266n, 288, 686, 687n
seek remains of, in high places II 723-4
senses of I 96, 534; II 106-7, 294-5, 298, 637-40
sephīrōth created II 44
septenary cycles of II 312n, 622-3
septenary symbol of Logos I 79
septenary when virtuous II 575
seven planes & consciousness of I 199
seven primeval, born II 2 &n, 606-7, 607n
seven principles of I xxxv; II 29, 79
Seventh Creation I 217
sexual & physical 18 million yrs ago I 150n; II 157
should be co-worker w nature I 280
skeleton of, unspecialized II 720-3
speech & II 198
spirit & matter equilibrized in II 180
spirits animate, of clay II 273
spiritual ancestors of II 165-6n
spiritual beings incarnate in I 233-4
spiritual, existed before Earth II 160
spontaneous generation of II 150-1
stature of, decreased II 329, 331, 352, 753
storehouse of life seeds II 289-90

storehouse of types II 187 &n, 683-4
structure of, unchanged (Lyell) II 725
swarming w lives I 260-1
tabernacle of spirit(s) I 185n, 224-5
tallest, in northern countries II 777 &n
tends to become a god I 159
thinker in, a masterpiece of evol II 728
as Third Logos II 25
three higher principles of II 113, 267
three streams in I 181
tradition of early civilized II 722
transparent creature once II 295
Trees of Life & II 97
two million years ago II 287
upādhi of 7 principles I 291
vegetation different before II 290n
venomous alkaloids in saliva of I 262n
when women knew no II 415
will merge w his dhyāni-chohan I 265
will never incarnate as animal I 185n
in world of desire I 572
worship higher beings I 280; II 34
Zeus divides, in two (Plato) II 133-4
Man and Apes. See Mivart, St G.
Manas (Skt) mind. *See also* Intellect, Mahat,
      Mind, Principles
   abuse of II 411-13
   aroma of, jīva I 238
   ātma-buddhi-, become one I 220; II 57 &n
   ātma-buddhi blind without II 123n
   body follows whims of I 245
   -buddhi or chitti explained I 288n
   chief soul is mind or II 496
   Christos union of buddhi & II 230-1 &n
   conscious principle of monad II 110
   corresponds to globe six I 153 &n
   cosmic ideation working thru I 329n
   after death I 334
   desire primal germ of II 578-9
   dhyāni-chohans develop, in man II 232-3n
   dhyānis gave, to 3rd race II 47n
   diagram I 153; II 593, 596
   dual, buddhi- & kāma- I 334; II 614
   dual, lunar & solar II 495, 639n
   effort of, to be free of senses II 587
   eleventh breath II 548
   fallen angel becomes our II 513
   fifth round development of I 162; II 301
   fifth state of matter II 737
   first on plane of personality II 58n
   Gultweig [Gullveig] (Norse) or II 520
   higher, absorbed in devachan I 220
   higher, is human ego II 79
   Hindu, Egyptian, (Massey) II 632

human soul, mind I 153 &n; II 596
impersonal, above senses I 96
Indra personifies II 614
language impossible without II 199n
Laws of Manu on I 334-5
link betw spirit & matter II 98, 164
Lords of Wisdom quickened II 411
Mahat transformed into I 75
mānasaputras endowed man w II 608
middle principle, pivot II 241
missing in 1st race II 164
Prachetases solar portion of II 496
primeval man lacked II 80
proceeds fr ākāśa I 13n
seat of intellect II 378
Seb (Egyptian) or II 632n
serpent stands for II 98
solar angels are of II 88
third race, succumbs to kāma II 254n
twofold II 175, 639n
union of buddhi & II 247
upādhi of buddhi I 101
vehicle of personal consciousness II 241
wedded to kāma, Zeus as II 419-20
without, there can be no man II 241-2
Mānasa(s,ic) (Skt) II 98
   -deva, Prometheus was II 525
   discussed II 89-90
   fifth race in, period II 300
   -pitris awakened man II 525n
   refuse to incarnate II 171
Mānasa-Dhyānis (Skt). *See also* Agnish-
      vāttas, Mānasaputra(s), Pitṛis (Solar)
   brought mind to man I 181-2; II 89-90
Mānasaputra(s) (Skt)
   anupadaka, dhyāni-buddhas or I 571
   connected w Ahura Mazdā II 608
   dhyānis were II 167
   informed mindless man I 180-1; II 608
   mind-born men I 543
   seven rishis or II 625
   "Sons of God" II 374
   Vishnu a, to Krishna II 48
   would not people Earth II 375
Mānasarovara [or Mānasarovara], Lake
   seven swans, rishis & I 357n
Manasseh ben Israel, Rabbi
   Adam 2 faces, 1 person II 134n
Manasvin (Skt) full of mind
   intelligent, high celestial beings II 90
Mānava-Dharma-Śāstra. See Laws of Manu
Manavaha & Chatvāraha [chatvāno manavas]
   (Skt) 4 manus
   (*BG* 10:6) II 140n

Man-bearing
  worlds, globes I 167, 635; II 77, 153, 699
Man Before Metals. See Joly, Professor N.
Manchuria II 327
Manco Capac, Peruvian Noah II 365
Mandākinī (Skt) heavenly Ganges I 385
Maṇḍala (Skt) circle II 524
  orb or 10 divisions of *Rig-Veda* I 384-5
Mandara (Skt)
  mountain used to churn Ocean I 385
Mandeville, Sir John, *The Voyage & Travels of . . .*
  giants 56 ft tall in India II 755
Mand or Manth [math] (Skt)
  & Prometheus II 413n
Mandrake, Mandragora
  magic properties of II 27n
Māṇḍukya Upanishad I 6, 83. *See also Muṇḍaka Upanishad*
  First Principle unthinkable I 14
Manee
  Laplanders call their corpses II 774n
Manes (Gk) II 367
  annihilated after death I 227
  Faber relates, to Kabiri II 360
  ghosts or II 222, 774n
  glean the Field of Aanroo I 236n
  region of, or kāma-loka II 374n
  ruled Egypt after "Watchers" I 266
  semi-divine astrals II 436
  sons of Mania (Arnobius) II 143
  Titans, Kabiri, Manus or II 143-4
Manes. *See* Mani
Manetho, Synchronistic Tables of
  on Athothis son of Menes II 334
  confirmed by Champollion II 367-8
  divine dynasties of II 367-8
  Egyptian tables of I xxvi
  figures of, disfigured by Eusebius I xxvi;
    II 53, 368, 392, 692-3
Man-Fish. *See* Dāg, Oannes
Man: Fragments of Forgotten History
  asuras, rākshasas, Atlanteans II 227n
  HPB's estimate of I 160-1
  mistakes in I 151 &n, 168; II 640
Maṅgala (Skt), Hindu Mars II 124n
Mani [Manes in tx)
  exoteric dualism of II 509n
Mania (Gk), mother of Kabiri II 143
Manichaeans(ism) (Pers gnostic religion)
  Christians haven't improved on II 509n
  Church struggled against II 238-9
Manifestation(s). *See also* Creation, Logos, Manvantara

dual II 24-5
first, primordial I 16
infinite cannot be limited to single II 556
infinite horizon of I 287
monads of II 150
purpose of periodic I 268
septenary I 139
unbroken series of I 238
in various religions I 437
Mani Kumbum, Book of 10,000 Precepts
  [Schlagintweit] I 43n
Maṇipūra, King of, & Ulūpī II 214n
Mañjuśrī, worship of II 34n
Mankind(s). *See also* Humanity, Man, Races
  advanced, taught mystery language I 309
  appeared as many races II 718
  born on 7 parts of globe II 1-2, 29, 35, 77, 86, 249
  cataclysms mark changes in II 500n
  contemporary w extinct animals II 206, 218-19
  cradle of II 203-4, 220
  declined in Atlantis II 411
  descent of, fr 3 couples illogical II 453
  determines good, evil II 512
  different fr present II 96
  divided psychically I 559
  elect of, raised I 221
  emanates fr cosmic agents II 108
  fell into sin II 319
  future, of adepts II 446
  gods gave birth to, nursed, taught II 358
  guides of, next manvantara I 267
  hermaphrodite formerly (Schmidt) II 184
  Mercury, Budha, instructor of II 374
  monads of II 150
  most of, 7th subrace, 4th root-race II 178
  multiple origin of, (Agassiz) II 607n
  never more selfish & vicious II 110
  offspring of elohīm I 224
  of one blood, but not same essence II 421n
  of one lang, one rel once I 229, 341; II 198
  only humans in cosmos absurd II 149
  portion of, hypostasized II 275
  Satan father of spiritual II 243
  serpent as Ophis taught II 215
  taught by divine rulers II 366
  third eye inactive in most of II 295
  three propositions & evolution of II 1
  will become self-redeemed II 420
Man-Lion ([Nara-]Singha)
  & Indian phoenix II 564
Mannus, ancestor of German race II 774n

Mano (Nazarean)
    resembles Hindu Manu I 195 &n
Manojava (Skt) speed of thought (Indra)
    II 615n
Manomaya Kośa (Skt). *See also* Kāma
    lower mind & desire I 157, 158
Manoushis. *See* Manushis
Mansarovara Lake. *See* Mānasarovara
Man-Savior, Zeus, Dionysos II 419-20
Man's Place in Nature. See Huxley, T. H.
Man-Swan or Haṃsa, & 3rd race II 122, 131
Manthāmi [Manthanī] (Skt)
    process of fire-kindling II 413n, 524
Manthanō (Gk), to learn II 413n
Mantra(s) (Skt). *See also* Invocation
    books of, kept secret I 471
    chanting, rationale of I 94
    force, power of letters & I 293
    guhya-vidyā, science of I 169
    hidden voice of I 345n, 354
    key to element language I 464
Mantradruma (Skt) mantra-tree (Indra)
    II 615n
Mantra Śāstra I 293
Mantrikā-Śakti (Skt)
    power of letters, speech, music I 293
Manu. See Laws of Manu
Manu(s) (Skt). *See also Laws of Manu*, Root- &
    Seed-Manus, Svāyambhuva, Vaivasvata
    all things come fr II 148
    birth of II 308 &n, 624
    Brahmā created II 237
    conscious guiding power II 652
    created by Virāj II 308n, 311
    creates 10 prajāpatis I 449; II 308n
    on Days & Nights of Brahmā II 3
    descend into generation II 322
    dhyāni-chohan or I 375, 452; II 308-9
    diagram II 309
    discussed I 63; II 307-13
    divine thought personified I 63, 74
    each race under a II 140n
    emanate universe II 310
    first human races & II 307, 365
    first thinking man or I 449
    flames of, incarnate in 3rd race II 247-8
    forbade Brahmins to receive money II 323
    four preceding, explained II 140n, 318n
    fourteen, in every kalpa I 63, 245, 370, 375,
        442, 450; II 70, 307, 308n, 309, 321, 614n
    heavenly man & II 704n
    Hindu Noah II 139-47
    informing intelligences II 34
    Kabiri same as II 360

Kaśyapa father of II 253
    length of reign of II 69, 308-9
    Mahat connected w I 452
    Manes same as II 143-4
    fr *man* (Skt) to think I 63, 452; II 91, 774n
    minor, preside over 7 races II 309
    Nazarean Mano resembles I 195n
    Noah root- & seed- II 597
    no longer appear in India II 178
    Phoenix symbol of forty-nine II 617
    pre-Adamic men are II 311
    primeval, is unseen Logos II 310
    rishis & I 442; II 129, 248n, 310, 359, 425
    -rishis & races II 615
    root- & seed- I 8 &n, 235n; II 146-7, 164,
        308-9, 321, 597
    root-races, subraces & II 614-15
    second hierarchy of I 453
    seven I 433; II 307
    seven, & 7 races I 248
    seven, 14, 21 of, expl I 235n, 442; II 308n
    seventh, & 4th-round man II 308, 321
    śishtas & II 164, 307n, 308
    Svāyambhuva II 307, 310-11, 704n
    symbol of cycles I 641
    ten or 7, sired man II 365
    thinking entities I 174n
    used as mankind II 102
    Vaivasvata II 138-48, 307-10, 313-14, 321,
        715n
    Vaivasvata, & human period II 69, 250-1
Manual of Geology. See Jukes, J. B.
Manual of Mythology. See Murray, A. S.
Manubhāshya. See Medhātithi
Manūn, or Munīn (Skt) II 573
Manuscript(s), MS, MSS
    Agrippa II 487
    ancient, re initiation couches II 559
    archaic I 1; II 36
    Christians destroyed millions of I xl
    Coptic II 464
    47 in Nicoll's catalogue II 366
    giving history of subraces II 423
    Pistis Sophia in a Coptic II 566n
    785 in Uri's catalog II 366
    vast numbers of, have disappeared I xxv
MSS, St Germain
    location of Garden described in II 202
    on number 365 II 583
    on various numbers II 582
MSS, Unpublished. *See* Skinner, J. R.
Mānushi-Buddhas (Skt)
    anupadaka [aupapāduka] & I 52 &n
    dhyāni-buddhas & I 52, 109, 571

govern Earth in this round I 109
Manushis, Manushyas (Skt). *See also* Pitṛis
Adam or, discussed II 102
created woman by kriyāśakti II 140
first of, on Earth II 91
place of, in hierarchy I 436
sages of 3rd race I xliii
second race & II 103, 165-6
Manu Svāyambhuva. *See* Svāyambhuva
Manu Vina, led Aryans to Egypt II 746
Manvantara(s) (Skt). *See also* Days of Brahmā,
Pralaya, Vaivasvata
atoms born at each new I 545
celestial hierarchy in next I 221
days & nights (pralayas) I 373-4
described I 63, 368-78
"Deus explicitus" or I 281n
each man has star for entire I 572-3
Earth's true form at end of I 260
elements change during I 673
equals 71 mahā-yugas II 307n
forty-nine stations in each I 238
four, in *Gītā* explained (Row) II 140n
fourteen, each Day of Brahmā I 63
fourteen, or 7 dawns & twilights II 308
gods who start, described II 232
ideation before every I 375
law fr one, to another II 87-8
length of II 69, 308-9
Logos appears at every new II 33
mahā- I 42, 118n, 289, 359; II 79, 602
mahāmāyā of I 278
major & minor I 369; II 309
manus & II 140n, 308-11
meanings of, several II 320
men of this, teach men of next I 267
millions of worlds in each I 143n
minor, & initiates I 207
minor, cycle & mid-Atlantean I 189
monads become human I 173, 182, 187
monads betw, state of I 570; II 57n
names of gods change in each II 90
new sun at new I 655-6
numbers, cycles & II 73-4
our, repeats 1st 3 creations I 454
pralayas &, described I 11n; II 309-10n
pralayas &, equal in duration I 240
pregenetic period & I 398
renovation of forms & II 730
rotary motion to end of I 505
same humanity throughout II 146n
seven new suns in next I 290
seven rounds in a I 36; II 180, 307, 434
seventh (Vaivasvata), we are now in II 146-7

shadow of ideal prototype I 63
Simorgh (winged) symbol of II 399
succession of I 3
Svārochisa or 2nd II 765-6
Svāyambhuva presided over 1st II 321-2
third, & 7 rishis II 78
third, may mean 3rd race II 94
various, named II 309
Vishnu-Purāna on pre- I 445-6
wheels or I 41
worlds built like preceding I 144
Maoben. *See* Macben
Maoris, decimated, spared II 780
Mao-Tse. *See* Miāotse
Map(s) of America, Basle (1522) II 327
Ma-Qom [Māqōm] (Heb) shrine
human womb II 84, 457 &n
symbol for God, space II 612
Mar. *See* Mare
Mar (Skt), Mars fr, (Müller) II 392 &n
Māra (Skt) Death
kumāra, kāma & II 579
quickener of spiritual birth II 579n
Marangoni, Giovanni
—— *Grandezze dell' Arcangelo . . .*
St Michael II 478-9 &n
Marcelinus Vicinus. *See* Ficino, M.
Marcellinus. *See* Ammianus M.
Marcellus, on Atlantis II 408-9
Marco Polo, travels of, called absurd II 441
Marcosians (followers of Marcus, Gnos)
tetrad of I 448
Marcus
chief of 2nd-century Marcosians I 350-1
more Pythagorean than Gnos I 449; II 563
—— *Revelation*
deity is 30 in 4 syllables I 351-2
good & evil serpent, dual Logos of I 410
seven heavens of I 449; II 563
truth shown as a woman I 352
Marduk. *See* Merodach
Mare (Lat) sea
Jehovah-Bīnāh-Venus or I 392
Maia, Māyā, Mary & I xxxii
three "Maries" at crucifixion I 385
waters, the sea I 402
Maria, Mara, Maia, Māyā or I 396
Marīchi (Skt)
father of agnishvāttas II 89
Kaśyapa son of II 253, 382n
mind-born son II 78, 132
Mariette (Bey), A. F. F.
Maspero succeeded I 311

—— *Abydos*
Osiris renews himself as Lunus I 228
Osiris whose name is unknown I 75 &n, 437
Marine Life, present fr beginning II 712
Mario. See Plutarch, *Lives, Caius Marius*
Mariolatry (worship of Virgin Mary)
based on lunar goddesses I 388
Mārishā (Skt)
mother of Daksha II 177
offered to adepts as a bride II 495
sweat-born child, 2nd race II 175-7
Marius, slew Tautobochus II 277
Mark II 114, 231n
faith will move mountains II 59n
Kingdom of God, little children II 504
Lion, Fire & Saint (table) II 114
Mysteries for disciples only II 231n
"Render unto Caesar . . ." I 296
Mārkaṇḍeya Purāṇa
Nārāyana on the waters I 457-8n
Marriage Ceremony I 614-15n; II 467n
Mārrtānda. *See* Mārtānda
Mars (the god). *See also* Kārttikeya
Artes, Aretia or II 143n
born fr Juno, w no father II 550
born fr no woman II 125n
Cain personifies II 390-2
Ertosi, Earth & II 143-4n
generative powers symb II 43n, 390, 467
heptad sacred to II 602
is Kārttikeya II 619
names, functions of II 382, 390-3, 392n
Pistis Sophia on II 462
Sabao (Gnostic) II 538n
Mars (the planet). *See also* Kārttikeya
adept knowledge of II 699
conj of, w Saturn & Jupiter I 656, 662
day of, almost same as on Earth II 707
density of inhabitants (Kant) I 602-3
does not belong to our chain I 164
error concerning, & Mercury I 163-70
genius of I 577; II 538n
Hindu Mangala is II 124n
judicial astrology & I 575n
men of, ethereal I 602
Mercury, Venus &, lower triad II 462
in obscuration I 165
planetary chain I 164-5
red in color II 43n, 124-5n
satellites of I 165
secret relation of, to Earth I 163-4
Semelē presides betw, & Venus I 400
six-faced planet II 382
Sun, ether, & I 102-3

superior globes of, invisible I 153
"tone" of II 601
Virtues rule I 435
water on, solid (Williams) II 136n
Marsh [Mudge], Professor II 218
Marsupial(s) II 166
astral progenitors of II 684
both living & fossilized II 196
Lemurian types of II 7
origin of, (Haeckel) II 165n, 667-8, 713n
reptile monsters contemporary w II 594n
Rütimeyer on II 789
sac of, (Darwin) II 118
Mārtāṇḍa (Skt). *See also* Sun, Sūrya
ākāśa as Aditi, mother of I 527n
allegory of, & 7 Ādityas I 100
eighth son of Aditi I 99, 448, 527n, 529, 625;
II 210n
feeds on sweat of Mother I 100, 102
first-begotten ogdoad I 448
gives back "dead breath" I 102
placed in center by Aditi I 529
pursues 7 brother planets I 100, 529
Martians, perceive our world I 166
Martin, Sir Theodore
—— ["Mémoire sur la Cosmographie . . ."]
interprets Atlas myth II 762-3
Martinists, astral light term of I 348; II 409,
511. *See also* Astral Light
Martyrs, of human thought (Buckle) I 298
Maru (Skt)
restorer of Kshattriya race I 378 &n
Maruts (Skt). *See also* Kumāras, Nirmāṇakāyas,
Rudras
beings of cosmic & psychic nature II 615
born in every manvantara II 613, 615
desert Rudra (Śankara) II 498
Diti mother of II 571
half of, gentle, half ferocious II 548
fr Mars, Ares (Müller) II 392n
sons of Rudra II 280n, 548, 613
Maruts-Jīvas (Skt)
refuse liberation, serve mankind II 615
Marutvān (Skt) lord of the maruts II 615n
Mary. *See also* Virgin Mary
clothed w Sun & w Moon underfoot I 401
"conceived without sin" I 91
Eve, Sea, Virgin, nave II 463
mare or I 392, 458n
Māyā, Maia, mare I xxxii, 384, 396; II 101n
Queen of Heaven, Moon I 403
seven children of II 527
Maryādāḥ (Skt), lines, paths II 191n
Mascarene Continent, described II 324

Mash-Mak, sidereal force of Atlanteans I 563
Mason(s). *See also* Architects, Builders
  architect leaves building to I 279
  decad & grip of Master– II 581
  Hiram Abif, etc I 314-15
  hosts of intelligent powers I 279
  identify Enoch w Thoth & Hermes II 529
  monad throne of deity w I 613
  mystic numbers of I 113n
  no chronology for creation II 696
  Ragon founded society of II 575
Masonic Cyclopedia. See MacKenzie, K. R. H.
Masonic Review
  "The Cabbalah" (Skinner) I 429; II 37 &n,
    38-40, 41, 76-7
  "Hebrew Metrology" (Skinner) I 90n
Masonry, Freemasonry
  archives I xxxvi, xliv
  degrees in II 575
  foundation of true II 345n
  Kabbalah, Bible &, ratios of II 39
  mallet in II 100, 556n
  persecuted by Roman Church I xliv
  Ragon on true meaning of II 795-6
  Russian, initiation & Tibet I xxxvi
  serpent & Templar degree of I 472
  speaks of Hermes, Enoch II 47
  swastika, Jaina cross & II 98, 100
  use emblems, symbols I 306
  white stone of II 530
Māsorāh (Heb) I 463-4
Masoretic Points II 388n, 464-5
Masoudi [al-Mas'ūdī] (Arab)
—— [*Les Prairies d'Or*, q by de Mirville]
  Nabatheans II 453
Maspero, Gaston
  on prehistoric Egyptian race II 432
  successor to Mariette Bey I 311
—— *Egyptian Legends* [*Popular Stories* . . .]
  Pandora story II 270n
—— *Guide du visiteur . . . Boulaq*
  Egyptian documents incomplete I 436
  Egyptian religion & *Book of the Dead*
    I 311-12
  frog goddesses I 386n
  Khonsu & Theban triad II 464
  Mout mother, wife of Ammon I 91n
  neter, nut I 675
  Osiris King of Duration I 436-7
  Ptah I 353
Massey, Charles Carleton
—— Preface to *Der Spiritismus*
  quoting Kant I 133n

Massey, Gerald
—— *A Book of the Beginnings* II 631
—— "Luniolatry: Ancient & Modern"
  cat symbol I 303-5, 387; II 552-3
  man in Moon, Trinity I 393
  Renouf q I 402 &n
  true value of myths I 303-5
—— *The Natural Genesis*
  Ankh, Ru, etc II 547
  antiquity of Egypt I 435
  Atlantis only an allegory II 353
  cat as Egyptian symbol I 387
  cross, various usages of II 588
  crucifixion on cross came later II 586-7
  Egy & other astronomical records I 650-1
  iconography I 403
  limited to psycho-theistic I 405
  oath-taking, meaning of II 603
  q Böhme re 7 principles II 634
  q Raoul Rochette on Venus II 546
  de Rossi on swastika II 586
  serpent worship I 404-5
  seven Fountain Spirits of Böhme
    II 630-1
  seven stars, cardinal points I 407-8, 408-9
  swastika, cross II 546-7
  tau cross I 405
—— "The Seven Souls of Man . . ."
  critique of 7 races II 634
  heaven 7-fold II 631
  Sebekh I 219, 220
  seven forces of nature II 631-2
  seven principles (Hindu, Egy) I 227n;
    II 632
  seven stars of Great Bear I 227n; II 631
  various 7-rayed Moon-gods I 227n
Massireddin [Nāṣir al-Dīn al-Ṭūsī] (Arab)
  astronomical tables of, (1269 AD) I 658
Massorah. *See* Māsorāh
Master(s) II 445. *See also* Adepts, Brotherhood,
    Initiates, Mahatma Letters, Serpents
  referred to:
    HPB had copies, letters to Sinnett I 163n
    disciple coming in 20th cent I xxxviii
    examines initiation symbols I 307
    Rider Haggard & letters of II 317n
    teach lesson to Western minds I 161
    twelve hierophants & II 502
    unable to give whole truth I 168
  quoted: I 163-70, 187-90
    Australian aborigines II 328
    on confusion of teachings I 190
    elevation of Alps II 751n
    on 5th & 6th rounders I 161-2

fourth race civilizations II 429-30
on globes, etc I 159-60, 166
[K.H.] on future procreation II 415
land bridge across Pacific II 327
light, heat, sound, vibrations I 514 &n
man present w antediluvians II 773n
names for I 271n
nebular theory of I 593-4, 597
on past, present, & future I 44
path to wisdom I 167
possess history of man II 437-8
present mankind & 4th race II 178
on Senzar, Stanzas, Skt, Tibetan I 23
sinking of Atlantis II 433n
sinking, rising of continents II 332
Master Builder, Paul an initiate II 704
Master Mason
builders, designers work under II 732
ONE LIFE & LAW II 732
third side of triangle, (Ragon) II 575
Mastodon II 219, 258, 352
Mātariśvan (Skt) Vedic fire god
Agni &, in Vedas II 413-14n
Mater (Lat) mother
"M" of, water glyph II 65
Pro-, divine fire II 114
Sal, Sanguis & II 113
Terra or 8th planet II 393
Materialism
agnosticism veiled I 327
anthropomorphism produces I 382
ape-ancestor myth causes II 680
atomic theory kills I 518
bigotry & I xli
created by religion I 183
Davy on I 480
a disease II 719
disfigures ancient wisdom II 451
Gladstone, Ingersoll & II 767
killing, of present age II 520
man's gross body & I 480
modern, & of Middle Ages II 708n
more frank than agnosticism I 528n
natural sciences & I 518
negative psychology, monism & I 124-5
nothing exists outside matter I 587
occult sciences & I 298
often miscalled science I 279
priesthood causes I 323
theology or I 323
vicious circle I 519
Materialist(s,ic)
believers in karma cannot be II 305
branchiostoma & II 370n

deny all but matter I 676
German, the worst II 101
metaphysicians & II 665
monists worse than I 528n
real science not I 518
rebel against ether I 587 &n
space a boundless void to I 587, 615
symbologists misjudge Aryans II 526
Materiality
acme of I 610
of early & present rounds II 68n
of Earth changes w races II 68n
Materialization
began in 4th round II 68n
parallels physicalization II 737
spiritualistic, & early races II 86, 737
Materializing
Kabbala on II 41
left-path adepts, religion II 503
Materiaux pour l'histoire. See Mortillet, G. de
Mathams, Maths [Maṭhas] (Skt) monasteries
bhāshyas hidden in I 271
Śringa-giri a, in Mysore I 272
Mathematics(cal)
atoms, points (Leibniz) I 628-9
divine rulers cultivated II 317
four Pythagorean divisions of I 433
law of probabilities I xlvi-vii
Parker on I 313, 315-16
point or monad, Pluche on I 613
fr point to solid figures I 616
present, line betw past & future I 37
racial, astronomical cycles & II 330-1
Mathers, S. Liddell McGregor
——— *The Kabbalah Unveiled* II 543n
Ain or non-being II 626 &n
Be-resheeth, Be-raishath I 352
Bird's Nest II 292-3
diagram of 7-fold man in I 241-2
fires, sparks, flames II 83 &n
Jehovistic deity I 619n
phallicism in *Zohar* II 625n
——— Unpublished MS
kabbalistic personal pronouns I 78
Māthra Spenta (Zor), Holy Word II 480
Mathurā (India)
Gauramukha priest to king of II 323
pagoda of II 588
Mati (Skt), understanding II 413-14n
Mātrā-Chit [Ātma-mātrābhiḥ] (Skt)
by elements of Self I 334
Mātripadma (Skt) Mother Lotus I 57-8
Matrix. *See also* Womb
Aditi the, of sura gods II 527

ākāśa, of the universe II 511
Earth re-emerges fr, of space II 46
the Eternal I 40-1
heavenly II 84
human body as a I 226n
of nature & resurrection II 460, 470
second round Earth a foetus in I 260
sun's 7 self-born fr I 290
universal I 62, 80, 283; II 511
Virgin, of kosmos I 91, 99
Matrōnāh (Heb), name for Malkuth [Mal-
    khūth] Earth I 240
Matronethah [Matrōnīthā'] (Heb)
    way to Tree of Life II 216
Matsya (or Fish) Avatāra (Skt)
    avatāra of Vishnu I 263-4, 369, 385;
    II 139, 307
    Triton connected w II 578
    Vaivasvata Manu & I 369; II 69n, 139, 307
Matsya Purāṇa
    gives Katāpa for Kalāpa I 378 &n
    Jyotis one of 7 prajāpatis II 766 &n
    Krittikās II 550
    Nārada, son of Brahmā- II 47
    on the pitris II 89n
    rishis appear 7 by seven II 611
    Rudra is 1st rebel II 613n
    Seven Rishis conjunction II 550
    sons of Marīchi II 89
    ten Maurya kings I 378n
    Vishnu speaks of 7 kalpas II 611
Matter. *See also* Earth, Elements, Māyā, Mūla-
    prakriti, Pradhāna, Prakritis
    abstract I 328
    active & passive states of I 281n
    Atlanteans sacrificed to god of II 273
    basis for agents on this plane I 493
    becomes atomic periodically I 552
    beings of invisible I 607-8
    blending of spirit & I 118
    body of, & linga-śarīra II 593
    called mother by Plato I 348
    centers of force I 519
    child of fire & water I 341
    co-eternal w reality I 340
    cometary I 101 &n
    corresponds w carbon II 593
    cosmic heat actuates I 82
    cosmic, scatters & forms elements I 97
    creation out of pre-existent II 239n
    Crookes discoveries I 581-6; II 211
    dead, does not exist I 274, 280-1, 507, 626n;
    II 672
    densest, permeable in next round I 258

descent into & ascent out of II 732
descent of spirit into I 176-7
differentiated or abnormal I 567
diffused cosmic, stages of I 22
dissociates at high temperatures I 543n
divine thought impregnates I 340
dregs of light I 481
dual in metaphysics I 10n
duration, motion, space & I 55
electricity is, & atomic I 111n
electricity is no known I 517
essence of, eternal I 147, 281n
eternal I 280-1 &n, 340, 545, 552; II 239n
evil or, evolution of I 73
evolution of, into spirit I 550-1
expanse of cosmic, or veil I 428
fire, pure ākāśa or 1st I 253
first differentiation of spirit I 258
Fohat, mind & I 16
force & I 111n, 491
-force-chance trinity I 505
force not property of matter I 491
fourth dimension & I 251-2
grossest, acme of illusion I 63, 628
has everything in it (Littré) I 502n
homogeneous, beyond perception I 601
homogeneous in pralaya I 624, 290n
impure demon of II 274
inseparability of spirit & I 614, 640
intelligent powers behind I 520
life immanent in I 139
light, electricity, heat & I 493, 579
lipika separate, & spirit I 130
lowest point of activity I 633
manas link betw spirit & II 98
man product of, (Thomson) II 719
meaning of, (Faraday) I 510 &n
mid-4th race lowest point of II 308n
mind ordered primordial I 595
mode of motion (science) I 147
"Mother" or prima materia I 291
motion &, (Spencer) I 12n
motion not property of passive I 502
mukta not subject to quality of I 132
mūlaprakriti abstract, ideal I 75, 136
nebular hypothesis & I 599-600
nervous ether refined form of I 532
no objective reality to I 519
nothing directly known of I 669
not outside our perceptions I 603n
noumenon of, fr svabhavat I 84
nous & psyche, spirit & II 134n
now beginning to spiritualize I 185-6
obtuseness of II 285

occultism based on illusion of I 520
occultists study septenary II 592
occult science knows true nature of I 516
particles of, a register I 104, 124
permeability of I 251, 258
ponderable & imponderable I 524-7 &n
potency of, (Paracelsus) I 283
pradhāna primordial I 176
prakriti or I 62
primal impress of, (Temple) II 645
primordial I 55, 67, 82, 589; II 256
science on mind & I 124 &n
science studies only fourfold II 592
in 2nd round I 251
self-luminous, of Halley I 590
septenary I 10n, 139, 289; II 592
seven states of I 289, 291, 560, 564;
    II 29n, 597n
six consolidation stages of I 116
sixth characteristic of I 251
slaves of, those who fell II 272
soul of, 1st principle in I 481
source of laws of II 24
space, force &, (Pratt) I 615
spectrum analysis of I 595
spirit &, aspects of Parabrahman I 15
spirit &, māyā I 633
spirit &, reconciled I 623
spirit &, struggle II 64, 134 &n
spirit &, 2 poles same subst I 247, 542-3
spirit, force & I 341
spirit is, & vice versa I 179, 416
spirit latent in II 42
substance & I 329
substance not, in metaphysics I 508
substance-, same each cycle I 145
supersensuous & earthly I 200-1 &n, 515
swastika, spirit & II 99
terrestrial & subjective I 514
three noumenoi of, unknown II 592
totality of cosmic existences I 514
ultimate structure I 670-1
undifferentiated I 35, 567; II 505
universal, reduces to 4 elements II 592
vāhan of spirit II 58n
of various worlds differs I 143 &n, 589
vehicle of the soul I 49
world soul born of purusha & I 365
world stuff, chaos or I 579
Matter, Jacques, [*Histoire critique* . . .]
    Horus carved on Gnostic gem II 474
Matthew
    angel-man, water (table) II 114
    baptism w water & fire II 566

"Be ye wise as serpents . . ." I 74
calling brother "fool" (*raca*) I 578
Christos as lightning II 485 &n
eagle as carrion-eater I 442n
Earth as footstool of God (Watts) I 154
faith can move mountains II 59n
"Father who is in heaven . . ." I 574n
Gentiles & Samaritans II 231n
John the Baptist axed trees II 496
Jonas was the sign to heaven I 653
"Lead us not . . ." I 414
"narrow, strait gate" I 317-18n
praying in secret I 280n
"Render unto Caesar . . ." I 296
seven children of Mary II 527
take kingdom by violence II 244
tree known by its fruit I 421, 467
Mau (Egy), term for cat & seer I 305
Maurice, Thomas, *Indian Antiquities*
    affinity betw Druids, Brahmans II 756
Maurigosima [Maligasima]
    sunken Chinese island (Faber) II 365
Maury, Louis Ferdinand A.
—— [*La Magie et l'Astrologie* . . .]
    kabeiron fr Greek "to burn" II 363
    pagan virgins transferred to Mary I 400-1
—— ["Des Divinités et des Génies . . ."]
    strife betw good & evil II 497
Maurya, Morya (Dynasty)
    will restore kshatriya caste I 378n
Mauvaises Terres (Colorado), fossils II 218
Maximus, Emperor, 7½ ft tall II 277
Maximus of Tyre, [*The Dissertations*]
    on Persians & fire II 114
Maxwell, A., *Plurality of Worlds*
    calumniated Newton I 607
Maxwell, J. Clerk
    Crookes on objections of I 552
    pressure of sunlight I 514
—— ["On the Motions . . ."]
    gas atoms elastic spheres I 513
—— *Treatise on Electricity & Magnetism*
    electricity is matter I 111n
    elements not homogeneous I 143n
    ether as a gas I 486
Māyā (Skt). *See also* Illusion, Mahāmāyā
    Ādi-śakti & I 10
    all things relatively real I 39
    bhrāntidarśanatah, false perception or II 108
    cycles of II 146n
    desire to exist & I 44-5
    Durgā I 396
    every finite thing is I 11n, 39
    Ginnungagap & I 367

good, evil under sway of II 96
grossest matter acme of I 63
illusion or, discussed I 39-40
includes Ādi-budha & gods I 54n
initiate can penetrate I 45
Īśvara plus, & avidyā I 7
light is matter or I 70
lower astral light becomes I 74n
Mare, Mary, water, etc I xxxii, 384-5, 396
moonbeams dancing on water or I 237
mother of Tvashtri (Jolly) II 101n
nirvana freedom fr I xix
objective universe as I 631, 638
Parabrahman alone above I 54n
personality on waves of I 237
phenomenal univ a I 18, 145-6, 274, 367;
    II 108
plane of, & dreams I 566
reality removed fr world of I 145-6
samvritti illusion creating I 48n
sensation is I 2n
seven worlds of I 238
spirit & matter both I 633
spiritual lives also I 635
was not I 38
we are victims of I 525n
Māyā (Skt). *See also* Maia
mother of Buddha I xxxii, 379n, 384
Māyāmoha (Skt) illusory form
ruse of, won war for gods I 419-23
Wilson felt, implied Buddhism I 419n
Mayas (Mayans), of Central America
antiquity of, zodiac II 50n
belong to 5th continent II 34-5n
coeval w Plato's Atlantis II 34-5n
Egyptians & I 267n, 888n
Mayasabhā & Sabhā (Skt). *See also* Aryans
Aryans given, by Atlanteans II 426
Mayāsura (Skt), gift of, to Pāndavas II 426
Māyāvi (Skt), or astral body II 241
Mayer, Johann T.
lunar tables of I 660, 661, 666, 667
Mazarine Library, MSS of *Bk of Enoch* II 531
Mazdā (Zor) II 92, 517
law of, or divine wisdom II 292
Mazdean(s, ism). *See also* Ahura Mazdā, Magi,
    Zoroastrians
compared w other religions II 60-1, 270,
    290-2, 358, 409-10
dualism of II 517
flood & cataclysm II 610
religion among oldest I 10
religion re asuras (ahuras) II 92-3
Roman Catholics & II 476, 480

scriptures, universal myths in II 97
septenates in, religion II 617-18
on 7 spheres of Earth II 607 &n
seven worlds, continents II 608, 758-9
six aspects of Logos in II 358
succession of worlds II 756
Unknowable in, religion I 113
Mazzārōth (Heb) 12 zodiacal signs
mentioned in *Job* I 648
M'bo Sha-arim. See Sepher M'bo Sha-arim
M'bul [Mabbūl] (Heb), flood waters I 385
Mc. *See* Mac for names beginning w Mc
Measurement(s)
of cross & circle II 582
esoteric foundation of II 465
Jewish, fr Egypt, India I 316
sarcophagus unit of, (Smyth) I 317n
three dimensional I 252
Measures. *See also* Skinner, *Key to . . .*
    Source of Measures
kabbalistic II 38-41
origin of, & Parker ratio I 313
Meborākh (Heb), name of God I 385
Mechanics, Mechanical
ancient knowledge of I 209n
animal of Atlantean sorcerers II 427 &n
chemistry is atomic, (Naumann) I 513
forces of science I 604, 669-70
laws & primeval matter I 601
origin of universe I 594-6
Medea
magi of Persia fr II 756n
winged dragon of, & astral light I 253n
Medha (Skt)
ascetic son of Priyavrata II 369n
Medhātithi (Skt) son of Vīrasvāmin
Wilford confuses, w Priyavrata II 406n
—— *Manubhāshya*
atomic destructible elements II 574
commentary on *Laws of Manu* I 333
consciousness of the "I" I 334
origin of mind I 334
Mediator, man's spirit the sole I 280
Medical Review
q on harmony of numbers in nature II 622
Medicis, Catherine de II 70
Medicine
applies occult laws to disease II 623n
Meditation I 48; II 613
dhyānis & abstract II 116
knowledge thru I 434
Mediterranean
age of, race (Winchell) II 695
once an inland sea II 740

region disappears & reappears II 776
Medium(s), Mediumship
  communication w other planes II 370n
  elementary or nirmānakāya possesses I 233n
  exuberance of nervous fluid II 370n
  form oozing out of II 174
  materializations of II 86, 174
  spirits of, not monads I 233n
Medulla Oblongata
  inductive action of, on pineal gland II 296
Medusa (Gk), Atlantean giant II 70
Medusa(e) (jelly fish)
  Naudin on II 119
  stauriolium becomes II 177-8
Meenam. *See* Mīna (Pisces)
μεγάλοι δυνατοί (megaloi dunatoi, Gk)
  or Kabiri II 363
Megalonyx, sloth dwarfed remnant of II 733
Megalosaurus(i) II 151, 195, 713
Meganthropos (giant man)
  man was, in each round II 733-4
Megatherium II 218, 258
  sloth dwarfed remnant of II 733
Mehujael (Heb), son of Irad (Jared) II 391n
Melanochroics, fr anthropoids II 315n
Melchior, one of Three Magi I 654n
Melchizedek (Heb) II 391-2
Melek, Moloch, Maluk, etc. *See* Malachim
Melelva Nahil, on Hermes, disciple of Agatho-
  daemon II 366
Melha(s) (fire gods)
  Buddhist St Michael II 63
  informing intelligences II 34
Melia (Gk), a nymph II 519-20
Melita, Melytta. *See* Mylitta
Mel-Karth, Lord of Eden, Hercules II 202
*Mem. Acad. Ins. See Mémoires de l'Académie
  Royale des Inscriptions*
Membrum Virile
  Jod (Yōd) or II 125, 460, 467
Memnon, or King Amenophes I 398
Mémoire. See de Mirville's *Des Esprits*
Mémoire sur la dispersion. See Cauchy, A. L.
Mémoires . . . (Damville). *See* Montmorency
Mémoires à l'Académie. See also Mirville, de
  paintings of extinct reptiles II 206 &n
  second Jehovah & ferouers II 479
  the serpent II 209 &n
  talking, moving stones II 341
*Mémoires de l'Académie des Sciences de Mont-
  pellier*, A. Jaumes on forces I 506
Mémoires de l'Académie Royale de Belgique
  Hirn on views of the atom I 482-3
Mémoires de l'Académie Royale des Inscriptions

Érard-Molien on antiq of zodiac I 657-8
Falconnet on Ophites, etc II 341-2
[Fouchet] on Persian religion II 516
[Fréret] on Chinese year II 621
Lajard on the elements I 125n
Martin on Atlas myth II 762
Raoul-Rochette on the cross II 546
Mémoires de la Société de la Linguistique
  II 524n. *See* Baudry, M. F.
Mémoires de la Société des Antiquaires . . .
  Biot on Malabar tombs II 347
Memory
  in abeyance in deep sleep I 38
  aspect of jñānaśakti I 292
  cognition & I 56
  divine soul & past, future II 424
  in every atom II 672 &n
  Haeckel's plastidular soul has II 671-2
  independent of brain II 301
  of mankind II 271-2, 293, 364, 443, 503
  nirvana & I 266
Memphis
  catacombs of II 379
  Egypt lost keys w fall of I 311
  first tomb of, 3rd dynasty I 311
  palace, temple of II 334, 363
  Phtah national god of I 367n, 675
Memrab. *See* Mimra
Men-animals, breeding of II 201
Ménard, Louis, *Hermès Trismégiste*
  Greek *to be born* same as *become* I 281n
Mendeleyeff, Dimitry Ivanovich
  eighth family of atoms I 553
  Periodic Table of I 585-6n
Mendēs (Egy)
  androgyne goat of I 253
  sacred bull of, a form of Thoth I 385
Menelaus & Helen II 796
Menelauses & Helens, before 5th race II 276
Menes (Egyptian King)
  date of II 374n, 431-2
  dynasties before I 266-7; II 368-9
  Egypt civilized before II 334
  Egyptian, fr Skt *man* II 91, 774n
  first human king II 369, 436
  Osiris not II 374n
Menhirs (Breton) men-stones
  Atlantean survivors built II 352, 753
  discussed II 750, 752-4
Mens (Lat) mind, fr Skt *man* II 91
Men-serpents of China (Pa) II 209
Mensibus, De. See Lydus
Men-Spirits or Ischin II 376
Menstruation, lunar cycle governs I 389

Mental Capabilities
  carried over fr other worlds II 249 &n
Mentality, plane of, has widest range I 175
Mentone Man, European fossil giant II 749
Meracha'peth [Meraḥepheth] (Heb)
  spirit of God breathing on chaos II 505
Mercabah (Heb). *See* Merkābāh
Mercury (god). *See also* Budha, Caduceus,
    Hermes, Mithras, Thoth
  Asklepios &, are one II 208, 211
  aspects of, described II 28
  Budha, Hermes or II 366, 499
  budh, wisdom, etc I 473
  caduceus & I 549; II 208, 364
  called Tricephalos II 542
  cynocephalus glyph of I 388
  elder brother of Earth II 45
  guides souls of the dead II 364, 542
  Hermes II 45n, 499, 541
  Ibis sacred to Thoth or I 362
  intercedes for Julian II 28
  kurios, divine wisdom or the Sun I 353
  "Lord of Wisdom" II 27
  Maia mother of, on Earth I xxxii; II 540-1
  Masons identify Enoch w II 529
  Messiah of the Sun II 541
  Michael is, of pagans II 480-1
  Roman Church makes, a devil II 208
  St Thomas calls, a devil II 478
  Seth or, pillars of II 530
  Sirius star of II 374
  as the Son II 540
  son of Soma & Tārā II 45 &n, 499
  sparks on staff of I 338n
  Sun &, one II 28
  Thoth-Hermes or I xxxii
  Thoth-Lunus, Budha-Soma I 396n
Mercury (planet)
  Astaphai genius of, (King) I 577; II 538n
  coming out of obscuration I 165
  cynocephalus glyph of I 388
  day on, almost same as Earth II 707
  fifth race under II 29
  Hormig, Budha or II 366
  kali-yuga beginning & I 662
  Mars-Mercury errors I 163-70
  Mars, Venus &, lower triad II 462
  men of, immortal II 44-5
  moon & I 396n
  more occult than Venus II 28
  Nebo deity of II 455
  no satellites I 165
  parent Moon of, dissolved I 155-6n
  polar compression of I 593

  secret relation of, to Earth I 163-4, 575
  sevenfold chain of I 164-5
  Sun's light, heat on II 27-8, 540, 707
  superior globes of, invisible I 153
  times lunar & solar events I 389n
  water on, gaseous (Williams) II 136n
Mercury, 2nd world of Syrians I 435
Mercury-Thoth
  assessor of Osiris-Sun II 558
  as the Son II 462, 540
Mercury Trismegistus. *See also* Hermes Tris-
    megistos
  God is a circle II 545
"Mercy is the might of the righteous" I 416
Mergain [or Morgana]
  fairy sister of King Arthur II 398n
Mergiana (Pers), the good Peri II 398
Merian, Madame, accused of lying II 440
Merkābāh (Heb). *See also* Vāhana
  Ain-sōph uses, as 1st Cause I 214, 356
  animals of Ezekiel's I 363
  lahgash & I 354
Merlin, tempted by Vivien II 175n
Merodach [Marduk] (Bab). *See also* Bel
  archangel Michael or II 384
  became Jupiter II 456
  Nebo son of II 210n, 456
  slays sea dragon Tiamat II 53, 503
Meropē, daughter of Atlas II 768
Meropis. See Theopompus
Meru. *See* Mt Meru
Merz, John T., *Leibniz*
  brushed esoteric theogony I 626
  endowed all creation w life I 627-8
  inertia more than geometrical I 627
  mathematical points I 628, 629
  perception, apperception I 629-30
  sought to create univ & philos tongue I 310
Meshia & Meshiane (Pers)
  were single individual II 134
Mesmer, F. Anton
  vindicated by Charcot, Richet II 156
Mesmerism, Mesmerize(d)
  experience a blank when awake I 47
  science terms, hypnotism I 297; II 156
  white magicians "send sleep" II 427
Mesomēdēs, *Hymn to Nemesis* II 305n
Mesozoic Era. *See also* Secondary Age
  animals bisexual at end of II 594n
  duration of, & later ages II 155
  Fall occurred during early II 204
  gigantic monsters of II 293, 733
  mammals lived in II 713n
  supposing man lived in II 676

Messecrates [Menecratēs] of Stire
  on giant skeleton II 278
Messenger(s). *See also* Angels, Malachim
  angels, angelos II 48, 243, 514n
  of Anu II 62
  descend to eat w men I 441-2n
  of Jewish God II 61
  of Life (Nazarean) I 196
  Maluk, Muluk, Maloch, etc II 514n
  metatron or II 111
  theoi, of manvantaric law I 346
Messiah
  born in lunar year 4320 I 654, 656
  Brahman's, Vishnu as a fish I 653
  connected w water, baptism I 385
  "Good and Perfect Serpent" II 356
  Jupiter, of the Sun II 541
  Kalki avatāra as last I 384
  Kenealy saw Nārada as II 48
  perfect, enters Eden II 292
  Pisces constellation of I 653, 654
  Sun is, esoterically II 23
Metachemistry I 622
Meta-Elements, Crookes on I 546-9
Meta-Geometry, -Mathematics I 616
Metals, formed by condensation I 595-6
Metamorphoses. See Ovid
Metaphor(s)
  conceal real meaning I 520
  in every religion II 98
Metaphysica. See Aristotle
Metaphysics(al), Metaphysicians
  abstractions became the universe I 45
  antagonism betw science & I 485n
  apparent contradictions & II 62
  atoms belong to domain of I 513
  conversion of, into physics I 45
  Eastern, anticipated Western I 79n
  Eastern, not grasped in West I 496n
  endless cosmic rebirths in II 80
  essential for globes, monads I 169-70
  modern, pale copies of ancients I 96n
  more important than statistics I 169
  occult, & 3rd race androgynes II 116
  ontological, & physics I 544
  physics & I 45, 544, 610
  real science & I 588
  science honeycombed w I 485, 544
  science rushes into, & derides it II 664
  seven elements & II 359 &n
  sound, speech, ether & II 107 &n
  Tyndall called, "fiction" I 584n, 669
  Western, & triune man I 225-6
  Western, materializing of I 161-2, 327

Metator [Meṭāṭōr] (Aram), Hēgemōn
  (ἡγεμών, Gk) guide II 480 &n
Metatron [Meṭaṭrōn, Mīṭaṭrōn] (Aram)
  angel of 2nd (Briatic) world II 111
  beyond, not "near," throne II 479
  God & Michael both called II 479-80
  perfect man I 339
  united w Shekīnāh II 215n, 216
Metcalfe, Samuel
  caloric of I 524-8
  ether of I 580
  solar magnetism & I 498
  Sun-force of I 538n, 582
Metempsychosis(es)
  development of embryo & II 187-8
  ego wins way thru many I 17, 185
  scarabaeus symbol of II 552
  thru lower kingdoms I 568n
Meteor(ites, ic)
  Denton psychometrizes a I 201n
  four, found w carbon II 706
  gravity & I 503-4
  life came via, (Thomson) I 366n, 488;
    II 158, 719, 730
  origin of planets & I 500n
  retrograde orbit of, & Fohat I 673
  showers I 646, 672-3
  substance of, laws governing I 504
  system unexplained I 593
Meteorology(ical)
  Aryans learned, fr Atlanteans II 426
  changes & Moon, planets, etc II 699
Meter, of Vedas I 270n, 290
Methusael (Heb), son of Mehujael II 391n
Methuselah (Heb)
  age of, literal, symbolic II 194-5
  son of Enoch, grandson of Jared II 391n
Mētis (Gk)
  Divine Wisdom I 384
  wife of Zeus-Zēn I 340; II 130
Metrology(ical)
  Hebrew, & term Jared II 597n
  key to Hebrew symbology I 308; II 595
  occult Heb & Christian Mysteries II 561
  Pythagorean numbers & I 460
Metronethah. *See* Matronethah
Meunier, Stanislaus
  atmosphere changed little II 159
Mexican Genesis. See Popol Vuh
Mexico(an)
  antiquity of man in, tradition II 745, 793
  Atlantis, Sahara & II 424
  civilizations of II 793
  legends I 345; II 97, 160, 182, 486

MSS, symbolic drawing in II 36
myths of divine rulers I 266-7
nagals [naguals] of II 182, 209
sculptures, pictures, symbols II 36
snake god, crypts II 379-80
tradition of world destruction II 311
Mexico, Gulf of, lands at bottom of II 424
Miãotse (Chin)
  beguiled by Tchy-Yeoo II 280-1
  giants II 337
  grottos of, turned into vihāras II 339
Michael. *See also* Archangels, Mikael
  angel guardian of Christ II 478
  Anubis & II 385-6
  Apollo & II 383
  archangel I 42; II 229n, 479
  called God in *Talmud* II 478
  Christ or I 195n; II 114, 115n
  conquered dragon (Satan) II 94n, 378, 382n, 384-5, 479, 505
  dared not speak against Satan II 478
  denounced fallen angels II 382n
  discussed I 458-60; II 478-81
  divine rebel II 246
  divine Titan (de Mirville) I 418
  elohīm, one of I 42; II 379
  Fall & II 62-3, 238n, 246, 248, 382n, 508
  Hermes Christos (Gnostics) II 481
  Indra the Hindu II 378, 384, 498, 614
  influenced by neshāmāh II 378
  -Jehovah Lord of Hebrews II 538
  Kārttikeya compared to II 382n, 549
  kumāra I 458-60; II 549
  Ophite lion or I 127n
  praying to I 611
  presides over Saturn I 459
  refused to create I 88, 458-9; II 94n
  represents Jehovah II 62-3, 379, 508
  Revelation on I 194
  St George earthly copy of I 458
  Samael, Satan or II 378
  Sanaka prototype of I 372 &n
  Seraphim (de Mirville) II 479
  slayer of Apophis I 459
  slayer of dragon's angels II 498
  terrestrial wisdom or II 378
  unmanifested, free, virginal II 235, 238n
  various names for I 459-60; II 379, 480-1
  war of, w dragon I 202
  watched over promontories I 42; II 505
  went before Jews (*Exodus*) I 437
Michelangelo, Moses statue w horns II 213n
Michelet, Jules, history in 20th cent I 676

Mico
  Egy egg, supported by tau cross I 364n
Microbes
  bacteria & I 608
  evolutionary process & I 636-7 &n
  "fiery lives" &, in human body I 262-3n
  lowest subdivision of prāna I 262-3n
  men, animals swarming w I 260-1
  some, & bacteria need no air I 249n
Microcosm. *See also* Macrocosm
  ancients applied, to Earth I 283n
  birth of spiritual, death of physical II 579
  decad applied to, & universe II 573
  humanity the, of 3rd group of builders I 128
  kabbalists applied, to man I 283n
  macrocosm &, man I 177, 181, 274; II 290, 580n
  man as, & swastika II 99
  manas in, fr Mahat I 334
  manas, of buddhi I 101
  Paracelsus q on I 532
  pentagon within hexagon I 224
  represented by human body II 577
  septenary, formerly esoteric I 168
  solar system is, of macrocosm I 594
Microcosmos(ic)
  is man II 98
  tree II 97, 98
Microprosopus (Kab) Small Face
  brain of, & 32 paths II 625
  destroyed during pralaya I 215
  heavenly man or manifested Logos I 215 &n; II 626
  later kabbalists link, w Jehovah I 215n
  Macroprosopus & I 60, 78, 239-41, 350
  prototype of man I 215
  Second Logos or I 240
  sevenfold cube II 626
  six limbs of I 215-16; II 705
  term for firstborn II 43-4
  Tetragrammaton or I 240; II 601
  totality of 4 lower planes I 239-40
Midas the Phrygian
  dialogue w, w Silenus on Atlantis II 760
Midgard-Snake I 407
Midian (Sinai region)
  giant race in II 755-6
  Revel [Reuel]-Jethro, priest of II 465n
  seven daughters of I 385n
Midrash(ism,im) (Heb scriptures)
  Ibn Gebirol used, as source II 461n
  oldest, q *Book of Enoch* II 535
  some, no longer extant II 461n
  Talmudists &, differ re Enoch II 532

written before Kabbala II 704
—— *Berēshīth Rabbah*
several creations in II 53-4, 704-5
—— *Pirke de-Rabbi Eli'ezer*
on Hanoch II 532
Migration
of European fauna II 793
of lemmings II 782
of Miocene flora II 783, 790
of plants II 727
Migratione Abraham, De. See Philo Judaeus
Mihr. *See* Mithras
Mikael [Mīkhāēl] (Heb). *See also* Michael
first of Aeons, the Savior II 381
Jesus Christ, angel-man II 114-15
the Lion II 115n
Michael or, Prince of Water I 459
Sun principle I 242
"who is as God" I 459
Milieux (Fr)
environment or, (de Quatrefages) II 736
Milk. *See also* Churning of Ocean
four streams of, (Norse) I 367
Sea of, or Milky Way II 321
symbol of spirit I 79
Milky Ocean (Atlantic)
belongs to 3rd war I 419 &n
defeated gods retired to I 419
Milky Way
adepts call, serpent II 356
celestial bridge (Jap) I 217
central body in II 240n
cosmic matter & I 69
ethereal substance (Brahe) I 590
Herschel estimated stars in I 576n
Kircher on I 435-6
Pleiades central group of II 551
Sea of Milk, curds or II 321
tenth world of Syrians I 435-6
world stuff, primordial matter I 67, 69, 217, 435-6
Mill, John Stuart, *System of Logic*
Laplace's theory not hypothetical I 588
limits of man's understanding I 636
Millennium, Millennia
of anthropogenesis I 376
first 5, of kali-yuga I xliv
first 6 words of *Genesis* cover six I 375
Hindu Jyotisha describe II 624 &n
for 100s of, 6th race will overlap 5th II 445
hoped-for, of Christians I 612
initiated Greek view of II 395
man created in 6th, expl I 340
betw pre- & post-Christian eras I xl

Pymander describes ten I 417
Millepores, like Silurian corals II 257
Milne-Edwards, Henri
on pigmy bushmen, elephants II 723
on prosimiae II 668
—— *Recherches . . .*
pygmy hippopotamus II 219
Milton, John
Eastern traditions & II 506
Moon favorite theme of I 386
poetical fictions of, now dogmas II 355
—— "Il Penseroso"
fire, air, water, earth I 252n
—— *Paradise Lost*
battle of angels II 506
"better to reign in Hell . . ." II 484
"with centric and eccentric . . ." I 645
"Fair foundations laid" I 148
light "Offspring of Heaven" I 481
Lucifer and the Fall II 62
"one first matter, all" I 622
Mimir (Scand)
drew his wisdom fr water I 402
Mimra [Mēymrā'] (Aram)
Voice of the Will, the Word I 346, 384
Mīna, Meenam (Skt) Pisces
messiah, water, baptism & I 385
Night of Brahmā, Sun & I 376; II 579n
Minarets of Islam II 85
Mind (cosmic). *See also* Mahat, Universal Mind
Abraxas created I 350
Adam-Kadmon is, (Philo) II 490
collective or universal II 487
dhyāni-chohans as I 278, 595
Divine, & architects I 632
Divine, does not create I 214
Divine, mirrored in atoms I 623
Eternal, actuates universe II 594n
Fohat link betw, & matter I 16
"is & is not" (*Laws of Manu*) I 333-4
Kantian, & Mahat I 602
Logos mirrors Divine II 25
manifesting, dual I 604
Manu same as II 88
ordered primordial matter I 595
universal, or Father & Son II 492
Mind (human). *See also* Intellect, Manas
Anugītā on I 94-5
builders & 1st, -born I 127
chasm betw, & animal II 189
circumference of circle & I 1
defiled by sin & science II 651
developed in 5th round II 162, 167

dhyāni-chohans or primordial I 452
dominates after 3½ races II 110
dual nature of II 495-6
dual, under Sun & Moon II 639n
higher, drawn to buddhi I 158; II 495
human soul or I 219
incognizable cause & finite II 487
"is not" I 38
jñānaśakti & power of I 292
Lilith had instinct, not II 285
limitations of I xvii, 56
link betw spirit & matter I 182
lower, drawn to desire I 158; II 495-6
manas & I 334
monad, ego & II 110
nous (νοῦς) or, (Plato) II 554
portion of a higher being II 81
rests on sensation I 2n
science on matter & I 124 &n
sensations & power of I 292
seven stages of sleep & I 47
-soul is Karshipta, bird god II 292
spiritual, above senses I 96
spiritual, & 6th sense I 95
stones moved by II 342n
sum of thought, will, feeling I 38
tempter & redeemer II 513
third race endowed w II 89
Western, degenerated II 158n
Mind (London), article on Aristotle II 286
Mind-born Sons I 106. *See also* Agnishvāttas,
    Kumāras, Mānasaputras
awakened 3rd race I 180-1, 539n; II 525 &n
become kumāras II 579
born fr parts of Brahmā II 625 &n
four & seven I 457; II 140 &n
hurled down to Earth II 93
refuse to create, born as men II 93
rishis, of Brahmā II 44, 78, 176n, 284, 624-5
of 3rd race II 156
watch over man & Earth I 213-22
were once men I 107
will be produced in 7th race II 275
Mindless. *See also* Amānasa
first root-race was II 84, 315
fourth race took wives fr II 271, 283, 286, 689
gods incarnate in, men II 198
humans, origin of II 286
man & anthropoid II 187, 189, 191-3, 195-6
    &n
primeval man was II 80, 189
Prometheus drama II 411-12 &n
sin of the II 180, 184-5, 189, 191, 271, 689
Sons of Wisdom informed II 608

symbolized by Ham II 397
Mineral (Kingdom)
apperception latent in I 455
builds upper kingdom bodies II 169-70
"cast-off dust" for lower kingdoms II 169-70
crystallized light II 169
development of, before human II 68n, 149
first line of triangle (Ragon) II 575
has consciousness of its own I 277n
human monad passed through II 185-6
luminous in early stages II 312
mid-journey of atomic soul I 619
-monad is one I 177-8
organic but in coma I 626n
processes precede, kingdom I 176
prototypes of 4th round II 186
received opacity in 4th round II 730
seventh emanation of Mother & I 291
soft, & vegetation II 730
transformation (crystallization) II 255
Tubal-Cain symbolized II 575
Mineral Monad," "About the. *See* Blavatsky
Mineralogy
Aryans learned, fr Atlanteans II 426
Minerva (Lat)
divine wisdom I 384
heptad sacred to II 602
lunar goddess I 396, 400
more powerful than other gods I 401
sprang fr father's body II 247n
sprang fr Jupiter's brain II 660
temple of, in Saïs II 396
Ming Dynasty II 54n
Ming-ti, Emperor
Kaśyapa taught Buddhism to I xxviii
Minos (King of Crete) I 105
derivation of name II 774n
Miocene II 745 &n
apes & men in I 184n; II 676
apes fr semihuman mammal of II 683, 689
Atlantis destroyed in II 8n, 314n, 395n, 433,
    693, 710, 740, 778
Atlantis in, (Crotch) II 782
civilization in, (Donnelly) II 266n, 786n
Devonshire subtropical in II 726
duration of II 690, 710, 714-15 &n
eternal spring of II 738-9 &n
Europe & America joined in II 781
European man of, Atlantean II 790
few geologists put man in II 155
first anthropoid in II 688n, 690 &n
flora of Europe & America II 727, 790
fourth race submerged in II 156, 314n, 395n,
    433 &n

giants of II 340
Greenland subtropical II 11-12, 677, 726
man immigrated to Europe in II 740n
man in mid-, (de Mortillet) II 710-11
man saw the, (de Quatrefages) II 746 &n
man's origin in, (Bourgeois) II 288, 675
man's origin in, (Haeckel) II 680
man taller & stronger in II 749 &n
monkey not before II 749
no mammals of, like today's II 749
origin of culture before II 782n
Sahara sea in, (Crotch) II 781-2
Miölnir. *See* Mjölnir
Miracles
  esoteric philosophy rejects II 731
  by means of *Sepher Yetzirah* I xliii n
  natural to primitive man I 210n
Miriam (Heb) I 384
Mirku, Babylonian god II 5
Mirror(s)
  magic, & Azāzēl II 376
  magic, & sorcery II 179
  Sun as a I 290n
Mirror of Futurity (secret book)
  records all kalpas, cycles II 49
Mirville, J. E. Marquis de
  Age of Saturn [II 372-3]
  enemy of occultism I 506n
  helped by converted rabbi II 476n
  de Mousseaux &, fanatics II 414-15
  official defender of the Church II 481-2
  sought to justify Bible II 342
  sought to prove reality of Devil II 341
  wrote great truths I 506n
—— *Des Esprits . . .*
  ancients & extinct animals [II 206n]
  ante-historical Catholicism I 401
  Atlantis legend [II 371]
  Azaziel [II 376]
  Book of Enoch [II 531, 533-4]
  Christian dogma fr heathens I 400-1
  Chrysostom on many gods I 465n
  Le Couturier, Tardy q [I 502]
  devil's power over man II 209
  divination by moving stones II 346
  divine kings, reality of II 367
  dragons II 207 &n
  Earth's axis of rotation II 534
  elohīm & divine names I 442n
  Farvarshi or Ferouer II 480
  giants II 278-9, 375
  god-king (Plato) II 373
  Henoch II 366
  Hymn to Jupiter II 552

intelligent planetary motions [I 503, 505-6]
Jehovah's names in Bible I 441-2n
Jupiter-lapis II 341
Klee on Earth's axis [II 534]
lightning an evil spirit I 467
lower, higher angels [II 375]
manes [II 222]
many names for creative powers [I 440]
Masoudi on Nabatheans [II 453]
oracular stones II 341-9
Panodorus q II 368-9
Pausanias re altar of Mercury [II 28]
plagiarism by anticipation I 401-2; II 481-2
de Sacy & Danielo q II 533 &n
Sepp on star, nativity [I 654-5 &n]
serpent of *Genesis* II 208
serpent worship [II 209]
seventy planets, etc [I 654 &n]
sons of God [II 374-5]
spirit kings, manes, ghosts [II 222]
Taurus, symbolism of I 657
Titans, giants, works of II 347
two pillars of Christianity [II 515, 530]
Verbum, Michael, Metatron II 479
Virgin Mary, Magna Mater I 393, 400
wonders of antiquity II 347
zodiacal signs, etc I 651, 652
Zohar on Sun II 553
Miscellaneous Essays. See Colebrooke, H. T.
Mishnāh, on 12 hours of day I 450
Misorte, human bones at II 337
Misrasthān, W African Arab land II 406
Missing Link(s)
  betw ape & man I 190; II 189
  brain size of Dryopithecus & II 676
  great number of, needed II 661
  located in man's astral body II 720
  man not descended fr pithecoid II 717
  meaning of term II 184n
  Neanderthal man not, (Huxley) II 686n
  not found II 87, 189-90, 260, 263, 287, 317n,
    660, 674, 678, 727, 744
  not on objective plane II 190
  prosimiae of Haeckel not II 668
  betw reptile & bird II 183
  third race man created I 190
  useless to search for I 184n
Missionaries. *See also* Christianity, Church,
    Roman Catholic
  call Nagalism "devil worship" II 182
  call swastika devil's sign II 98
  confuse Eve w Ivi II 194n
  Hindu trad a reflection of Bible I 415
  link Pulastya w Cain, etc I 415

misled by Brahmans re Trinity I xxxi &n
slur Brahmā-Vāch liaison I 431
Mission des Juifs. See St Yves d'Alveydre
Mistakes, in theosophical books I 152, 160;
    II 640
Mitāksharā [by Vijñāneśvara]
    Commentary on *Yājñavalkyasmriti* I 432n
Mitford, Godolphin (Murad Ali Bey)
    extraordinary mystic II 514n
    a warning to chelas II 244-5n
—— "The 'Elixir of Life'"
    initiate lives in astral body II 499
—— "The War in Heaven"
    nature of Satan II 245-6
    worship of scattered sects II 514n
Mithra (Pers)
    mother-wife of Mithras I 340; II 130
Mithraic Mysteries
    Sabasia a variant on II 419n
Mithras, Mithra (Pers god). *See also* Mercury
    Abraxas, Iaō or II 474
    male, mundane fire I 340; II 130
    Mercury identical w II 28
    Mihr or I 384
    rock-born god I 340 &n; II 130
    seven fires on altars of II 603
    sevenfold mysteries of, (Celsus) I 446
    son of Bordj, fire mountain I 341 &n
    Sun, Jupiter, Bacchus & II 419
Mitra (Skt)
    secrets not to be revealed II 269n
    Vaivasvata sacrifices to II 147-8
Mivart, St George J.
    staggered by theory of man fr ape II 729
—— *On the Genesis of Species*
    saltations in evolution II 696-7
—— *Man & Apes*
    nothing new in II 680
μιξαρχαγέτας (mixarchagetas, Gk) demihero
    Castor called, at Argos II 122n
Mizpeh (Heb)
    land of giants on Mt Hermon in II 409
Mizraim (Heb), & Ham Kabiri II 393
Mjölnir (Norse). *See also* Thor's Hammer
    in Norse prophecy II 100
    swastika is II 99
Mlechchhas (Skt) foreigners
    even, may know Vasudeva II 48n
    in kali-yuga I 377
    must wait for revelation I xxx, xxxiv-v
    Śankha-dvīpa peopled w II 405
    Upanishads now accessible to I 270-1
Mnaseas (of Patera) II 362, 393
Moab, Ēmīms (giants) of land of II 336

Moabites
    Nebo adored by II 456
    Shemesh of, was Sun-Jehovah I 397n
Mobed (Zend) II 517
Mochus, *Theogony*
    deity born fr mundane egg I 365
    visible universe fr ether, air I 461
Mode(s) of Motion
    believed & opposed I 668
    devas, genii have become I 478
    forces are I 604, 671n; II 719
    heat became, (science) I 516
    matter is, (science) I 147
    nature's 7 powers & II 273
    sound more than a I 565-6
    theosophical critique of I 296-9
Moderatus, Pythag numbers symbolic I 361
Modern Chemistry. See Cooke, J. P.
Modern Genesis, The. See Slaughter, Wm. B.
Modern Materialism. See Wilkinson, Wm. F.
Modern Science & Modern Thought. See Laing
Modern Thought (magazine). *See* Blake, C.,
    "The Genesis of Man"
Modern Zoroastrian, A. See Laing, S.
Mogadha. *See* Magadha
Mohammed, Prophet II 463
    coffin of, in midair I 544
    paradise of, & Eden II 203
Mohammedan(s). *See also* Mussulman
    brought seclusion of women to Hindus I 382
    burned ancient books II 763n
    religion perverts old allegories II 232
Moira (Gk), fate, destiny, & II 604-5 &n
Moist Principle. *See* Moyst Principle
Moisture, light, heat, Deity & I 2-3
Moksha (Skt) I 132. *See also* Jīvanmukta,
    Jīvātman, Mukta, Mukti
    kundalinī-śakti & I 293
    seven paths to I 38-9
    various names for I 38n
Molech (Heb). *See* Malachim
Molecular
    consciousness a, by-product (sci) I 327n
    life is protoplasmic, action (sci) II 720
    vibrations (Keely) I 562
Molecularist(s) I 637n
Molecule(s). *See also* Atoms, Protyle, Sub-
    stances
    centers of force I 103, 261, 507, 670
    compound nature of, (Crookes) I 141n
    contraction & heat expl I 84-5
    difference in weights I 512 &n
    differ on other planes I 150
    higher principles of I 218n

informed atoms inform the I 632
life force, "nervous ether" I 531-3
life in every I 225n, 248, 258, 261
motion of, & mind II 650n
produced in Earth's atmosphere I 625
protyle, elements (Crookes) I 621-5
science on I 513-15, 547-8, 583; II 655
thicker than sand in space I 150
Moles, atrophied eyes in, (Haeckel) II 296n
Moleschott, Jacob
nerve fibrils of brain I 297
without phosphorus no thought II 244
thought a movement of matter I 124n
Moloch (Heb). *See also* Malachim
Baal, Sun-Jehovah or I 397n
Jews immolated children to I 463n
messengers, angels II 514n
Mon (Egy), Ammon I 366
Monad(s) I 170-86, 384. *See also* Leibniz
all-potent on arūpa plane II 110
angel-, & human- I 574n
animal, lives animal life II 525n
animal, reincarnated in higher species II 196n
apex of manifest triangle I 614
aroma of manas I 238
ātma-buddhi I 178
ātma, buddhi, higher manas I 570
breath of Absolute I 247
cannot be desc by chemical symbol I 177
circling globes, planets I 171-8, 577
cosmic, manus & creation II 311
cosmic, or buddhi I 177
cycles of, in matter, spirit I 175
descent & reascent of I 668
divine regardless of kingdom I 175; II 185-6
divine, transform animal man II 377
does not progress or develop I 174n
door to human kingdom closed to I 173
duad &, re finite & infinite I 426
dual I 69n
during first 3 rounds I 174, 184
each, a world to itself I 630
elementals or I 632
elementary germs I 139
entered 1st race shells II 303
every cell is a I 630n
evolves triad & retires (Pythag) I 427
finite number of I 171
force & matter I 623
four the mean betw heptad & II 599
free of matter end of 7th round II 180-1
Gnostics on planetary origin of I 577
gods-, -atoms I 610-34
gods-, -atoms compound unit I 613

gradual individualization of I 178-9
gradual return of, to source I 171
Haeckel on human II 673
highest human, hypostasized II 275
homogeneous spark I 571
how, attains paranirvāna I 135
human & animal II 81, 102-3, 185-6
humanity's, & planetary rectors I 575
human, never becomes animal I 185n
human, passed thru kingdoms I 174, 246-7, 267; II 42, 150, 180, 185-6, 256-7
impersonal god II 123n
individual dhyāni-chohan I 265
indivisible (Good) I 570
indivisible mathematical points I 631
infinitude of I 632
intelligent noumenoi of I 553
jīvātmas or I 132
laggard I 175
Leibniz', & Cauchy's points I 489
Leibniz', & early atomists I 579, 629-31 &nn
looking glass that can speak I 631
lunar I 179-80
may refer to atom, solar system I 21
mineral, I 176-9
needs manas for devachan II 57n
newly arrived human, fate of II 168
no new human, since mid-Atlantis I 182; II 303
not discrete principles II 167
number of human, limited I 182-3; II 303
pass thru Circle of Necessity II 303
past karma of II 318n
personal self &, urge evolution II 109-10
pilgrim I 16-17n
point or I 426
Porphyry on I 618
preexistent in world of emanations II 111
progression of, & forms II 289n
Pythagorean I 64, 426-7, 433, 440-1, 619; II 575
rays fr absolute II 167
ray united w soul is I 119
rebirth of, on globe A I 173
reemergence of, (Stanza 3) I 21
reflection of 7 lights I 120
remain on higher plane I 174-5n; II 199
same, emerge after paranirvāna I 266
second, of Greeks androgyne I 427
semi-conscious in animals I 267
seven classes of I 171
slumber betw manvantaras II 57 &n
spiritual I 177; II 79, 242
spontaneously self-active I 631

three hosts of I 174-5, 632-3
unconscious on this plane I 247; II 123n
universal, & first triad II 80
universal mirrors I 632
universal, or Logos II 311
universe in itself I 107
used progenitors' astral body II 660
waiting human, & nirmānakāyas II 94
will enter human kingdom I 173
zodiacal signs linked w I 668
Monadic
    essence I 176, 178-9, 619
    host I 174-5, 632-3
    no, inflow till next manvantara I 187
    part of triple evolution I 181
Monadless, explained I 632
Monadologie. See Leibniz, G. W.
Monas (Gk)
    conscious, thinking unit II 91
    of Peripatetics signifies unity I 177-8, 614,
        619
    Pythagorean monad I 619
    & Sanskrit *man*, to think II 91
Mona Stone II 345
Moneron(a). *See also* Protoplasm
    defined by Haeckel II 165n
    "discovered" by Huxley II 164-5n
    evolution of, to man II 189
    genesis unknown II 99
    Haeckel's, critique of II 151, 185, 713n
    man once like II 154
    Newton, Shakespeare & II 674
    no jīva in II 185
    not homogeneous matter II 653
    origin of, discussed II 158-60
    protistic I 455 &n; II 153n
    reproduced by division II 166, 658
    sarcode of Haeckel's I 542
    spiritual man existed before II 160
Mongolia(ns, n)
    Amilakha of II 34n
    Aryans, Negroes &, have same ancestors
        II 607n
    denominated Scyths II 203
    distorted Buddhist schools I xxi-ii
    distort their ears II 339
    forefathers of, led to Central Asia II 425
    legends re, buried libraries I xxxiii
    one of three 5th-race types II 471n
    fr red-yellow Atlanteans II 250, 425
    sea in Lemurian times II 323-4
    seventh subrace, 4th root-race II 178
    swastikas on hearts of buddhas in II 586
    type skulls found in Europe II 744

"wan" (swastika) of II 556
Mongolo-Turanian (4th Race)
    commingled w Indo-European I 319
Monier-Williams, Sir Monier
    contempt for "Esoteric Buddhists" II 570
—— *Indian Wisdom*
    Lakshmī, verses on I 380
—— "Mystical Buddhism . . ."
    no Buddhist esoteric doctrine I 47n
Monism I 581
    double-faced Pecksniff I 528n
    materialism &, negative I 124 &n
    pretended, of psychologists I 620n
Monkey(s). *See also* Anthropoid, Ape, Dryo-
        pithecus
    Brahmin's regard for I 185n
    came ages after man II 749
    developed fr 3rd-race man II 729n
    earliest, & modern pithecoid II 717
    evolution & II 258
    man common origin w, (sci) II 686
    no link betw man & II 729
    of *Rāmāyana* (Figanière) II 289n
    skeletons in Miocene strata II 723-4n
Monkey God. *See* Hanumān
"Monkey of God," Devil called II 476
Monochord, made by Tetraktys II 600
Monogenesis II 195-6
    polygenesis & II 169, 610
    will have to be abandoned II 118
Μονογενής Θεοῦ, (Monogenēs Theou, Gk)
    one Mother of God I 400
Monoliths, forests of immense II 343
Monosyllabic Speech
    developed at close of 3rd race II 198
    languages of yellow races II 199
Monotheism(ists)
    astrolatry & II 41
    blasphemies of, upon God II 304, 305
    creator of, clashes w logic II 158
    deity of, called architect II 101n
    God of, & karma II 304-5
    "Jehovah is Elohīm" led to I 112-13
    Jewish & Christian II 41, 459, 588
    of Jews II 252, 471-2
    mistakenly apply One to Jehovah I 129-30
    not in Egy Hermetic works I 674-5
    Plato not a II 554
    polytheism vs I 466, 492-3n, 499n, 575
    purely geographical in Egypt I 675
    seven gods & II 607n
    some, hate Buddhism I xix-xx
Monsoon
    a few drops . . . do not make I 161-2

Monster(s)
  ancestors of anthropoids II 201
  ancients knew of extinct II 206, 713
  Atlantean records on skins of II 692
  Australians begotten of II 197
  Chaldean II 54, 65n
  destruction of last of II 316
  evolutionary possibility II 55
  Frankenstein- II 349
  giant men coexisted w II 218-19
  giants &, biblical II 194-5
  Gould re II 217-19
  half-human, -animal II 52, 55-6, 192
  fr human-animal parents today II 689
  Lemuro-Atlanteans bred II 285, 679
  mindless men bred II 286-7
  pre-human II 115, 634-5
  second race gigantic semihuman II 138
  slain by dhyānis II 115
  fr tampered 3rd race eggs II 192
  Titans fought Mesozoic II 293
Montaigne, Michel E. de, *Essays*
  folly of measuring truth II 340
  "nosegay of culled flowers" I xlvi
Montanists, Bossuet links, w *Rev* II 485
Montenegrin Giant, Danilo II 277
Montesquieu, Baron de, *Lettres Persanes*
  asylums for supposed madmen I 676
Montfaucon, Bernard de
—— *L'Antiquité expliquée . . .*
  cruciform symbol of Hermes II 542 &n
  on Greek inscription I 400
—— *Collectio nova Patrum . . .*
  on Indicopleustes II 399
Month(s)
  ancient lunar, solar II 620-1
  each day of lunar, influential I 409
  lunar, & number seven I 387
  lunar, & yugas II 624
  synodic, & saroses I 655n
  year &, of Chinese, Arabs II 621
Montlosier, F. D. de Reynaud, Comte de
—— *Des Mystères de la vie humaine*
  grand divinity of Plato II 554-5n
Montmorency, Henri II, Duc de (Comte de
    Damville), *Mémoires . . .*
  on Persian traditions II 394n
Monument(s)
  Dracontian, grandeur of II 380
  mighty ones leave lasting I 434-5
Monumental Christianity. See Lundy, J. P.
Monuments Celtiques. See Cambry, J.
Moola Koorumba [Mūla Kurumba]
  once great race, now dying II 445

Moon (Earth's). *See also* Artemis, Diana, Iō,
    Juno, Lunar, Satellite, Soma
  Adam prophet of II 466-7
  argha or II 462, 468
  Ark, woman, navel II 461
  Ashtōreth, Jehovah & II 462
  -beams dancing on water I 237
  Budha son of II 45, 138, 456
  calculating mean revolution of I 392
  catastrophes caused by planets & II 699
  cat Egyptian symbol of I 304-5; II 552n
  conception & I 179-80, 228-9n, 264, 395;
    II 76-7, 105
  conjunction of, & Sun II 76, 435
  connected w Earth's mysteries I 305
  creation of, (Chald) II 145
  crescent, female & male II 463
  daily motion of, (Hindu) I 664-5
  dead yet living I 149n, 156
  Diana or I 228, 386-7; II 23, 123, 462
  dissolves before 7th round I 155n
  dragon eternal enemy of I 403
  Earth satellite of, explained I 180
  Earth's parent I 155-6; II 44, 64, 115, 474
  eclipse of, at beginning of kali-yuga I 663
  eclipses of, & allegories II 380
  eldest son of Bel (Assyria) II 386
  eye of Horus, Osiris I 388
  eye of Odin I 402
  eye of the Sun I 304-5
  feminine I 228-9, 396; II 123
  forces represented by many images I 396
  formed & peopled Earth I 180
  fourth globe of Moon chain I 172
  fourth race, globe under II 29
  gave Earth all but her corpse I 155n
  generation, Jehovah & II 464, 466
  giver of life & death I 386-7
  -goddess I 228-9, 386-403; II 418n
  -god worshiped at Ur II 139n
  guides occult side of nature II 595
  Hindu ½-month cycle of II 620
  Iaō genius of I 448, 577; II 538
  inferior to Earth, planets II 45
  influence of, on Earth I 156, 180; II 325
  "insane mother, sidereal lunatic" I 149n
  Jehovah linked w I 198n; II 62, 77, 139n, 462,
    464
  Jupiter, Saturn &, higher triad II 462
  Kepler's rings around I 590
  keys to, symbol I 390-1
  king & queen I 386
  Kumuda-Pati II 44
  Lakshmī-Venus, Śrī & II 77

linked w Anu, Jehovah II 62, 139n
Lord of Śrī II 76n
luminous ring around I 590
masc & fem I 396-7; II 65-6, 139 &n
Massey on I 393
mean motion of, (tables) I 667n
Melita [Mylitta] queen of II 135
menstruation governed by I 389
mind or II 639n
more evil than good I 396
Moses' face in the II 468
"Mother" containing life-germs II 139
mother of physical man II 105, 109
mother of pneuma, human soul II 113
Mother or Isis II 462
Nebo son of II 456
Night Sun, path of (Tiaou) & I 227
node of, & Hindu epoch I 663
not Earth's calf I 398
Osiris inhabits I 228
phantom of II 115
physically semi-paralyzed I 149n
Queen of Heaven, Mary I 403
Rāhu & legend of II 381
regent of secret planet I 394
secular motion of I 660
Semites called, Lord of Sun I 397
septenary influence of I 389; II 595
seven phases of I 396-7
seventh day & the new II 76
shell of former world II 115
sorcerers calling down the II 762
sorcerer's friend, foe of unwary I 156
substitute for sacred planet I 575; II 23
Sun &, affect man's body I 229
Sun &, cycles discussed II 620-1
Sun &, Father & Son I 229
Sun &, saluted by Gnostics II 474
sushumna ray lights I 515n, 516, 537
sweat-born egg & II 131
symbol of divine soul II 113
symbol of reincarnations I 228
Thoth-Hermes has retreat in I 403
thrown off fr Earth I 154-5 &nn; II 64
twofold, threefold I 393
various cycles of, (Hindu) I 666-7
womb, ark & II 139
Moon(s) (of other planets). *See also* Satellites
Mars' two satellites I 165
mystery of planets having many I 155-6n
of Venus & Mercury, dissolved I 155n, 165
Moon Chain, Lunar Chain
formed Earth chain I 155-6 &n, 171-3
inferior to Earth chain I 179

Moon-colored II 178, 227, 249, 351, 425.
   See also Root-Race–1st
Moon-God(s), -Goddess(es). *See also* Lunar,
   Moon
conception, childbirth & I 264
cursed by Christians II 507
Moons, beyond our solar system I 497n
Moor, Edward, *Hindoo Pantheon*
Man crucified in Space II 561
nail mark in Wittoba's foot II 560n
Śiva's pāśa II 548 &n
Mor, Isaac, q on Syrians I 435
Moral, Morality. *See also* Ethics
effects subserve karma I 280
faculties influence evolution II 728
far-reaching, effects of karma I 634
pagan & Christian I 468
Morals. See Plutarch, *Moralia, De fraterno amore*
Morbihan (Brittany). *See also* Carnac
initiates traveled to II 750
menhirs in II 352, 752
Mōrēh Nevochim. See Maimonides
Morgana, Mergain, Mergiana
fairy sister of King Arthur II 398 &n
Mori, Rajput tribe I 378n
Morning Star I 400, 604, 632n; II 45n, 61,
   238n, 540, 759 &n. *See also* Lucifer-Venus
Morocco, ancient battles south of II 405
Morse Code, Ahgam writing & II 346n
Mortillet, Gabriel de
man orig in mid-Miocene II 686, 714n
Miocene flints splintered by fire II 678
—— *Matériaux pour l'histoire . . .*
man in mid-Miocene II 710-11 &n
—— *La Préhistorique*
allows man 230,000 years II 710n
prehistory a new science II 721
—— *Promenades au Musée . . .*
flints of Thenay made by man II 748n
Morya, Mauryas, [Maru] II 550n
will restore kshatriya race I 378 &n
"Moryas and Koothoomi, The." *See* Rao, D. B.
   R. R.
Mosaic Books. *See also Genesis*, Pentateuch
Ezra debased, disfigured I 319, 335-6;
   II 143, 658
first, & archaic records II 426
full of occult knowledge I 336
"Genesis of Enoch" anterior to II 267-8n
Skinner's theory re I 313
spurned by Sadducees I 320-1n
Mosasaurus II 205
Moschus. *See* Mochus

Moses II 222. *See also* Mosaic Books, Pentateuch
  ansated cross introduced by II 31
  ark of rushes & I 319-20n
  asks Lord to show his glory II 538-40
  author of *Genesis* II 453
  brazen serpent I 364n; II 206n, 208, 387
  burning bush (*Exodus*) I 121, 338n
  called God Iaō II 465
  chief of Sodales, hierophant II 212
  creation story of, fr Egypt II 3-4
  w Deity on Sinai I 374
  did not write *Exodus* I 320
  died on mount sacred to Nebo II 456
  drawn fr water & so named I 385
  earth & water & living soul I 254, 345, 354;
    II 43n, 124n, 188
  Egyptian II 465n
  esoteric religion of, crushed I 320-1n
  exodus of, Atlantean story II 426-9
  face of, in the Moon II 468
  & fire (true gnosis) on Mt Sinai II 566
  forbids eating of pelican I 80n
  God of, temporary I 374
  Holy of Holies, & elements I 462
  initiated I 73, 312, 314, 316, 352; II 212, 456,
    465n, 541
  Jehovah, Shaddai, Helion & II 509
  Jews distorted Egy wisdom of I 312
  Job prior to I 647
  learned in Egy wisdom I 115n, 352; II 560
  life of, that of Sargon I 319; II 428, 691
  Masoudi [Mas'ūdī] agrees w II 453
  mentions Noah's 15 grandsons II 141
  modern Jews not fr, but fr David II 473
  never married II 465n
  numbers of II 539
  ram's horns in II 213n
  Sadducees guardians of law of II 61
  speaks of giant King Og II 336
  story of, fr Chaldea II 428
  tabernacle of, & Egy I 125, 314, 347n
  tables of stone of, & pillars II 530
  & tau cross on Jews' lintels II 557
  Zipporah wife of I 319n, 385n
Moses de Leon [Moses ben Shemtov de Leon]
  Christian Gnostics infl I 214; II 461n
  re-edited *Zohar* in 13th cent I 214; II 28n
  Talmudic Christian sectarian II 461n
  Zohar much older than II 461n
Mosses, spore reproduction of II 167
Most High II 537, 538, 541n
Mōt, Mut (ilus, mud). *See also* Mahat
  Mahat & I 451
  sprang fr chaos & wind I 340

Mother. *See also* Father-Mother, Virgin
    Mother
  ākāśa, pradhāna I 256, 332
  in all religions I 215-16
  ansated cross & II 31n
  awakened hyle called I 82
  breathes out protean products I 143
  chaos or I 70
  expands into objectivity I 62
  Father &, or fire & water I 70
  -Father, space called I 9, 18
  fifth principle I 293
  goddesses I 91n; II 43, 464
  gods are born in I 674
  Great I 43, 81, 291, 434; II 83, 384n, 416,
    462, 503
  immaculate I 59, 88, 91, 256
  Kwan-yin, daivīprakriti or I 136-7
  man breathes refuse of I 144
  mūlaprakriti or I 136
  number 10 & I 94
  Occult Catechism on I 11-12, 625
  overshadowed by universal mystery I 88
  pi & I 434 &n
  prima materia I 291-2, 625
  side of, is 2nd Creation I 450
  -space or Aditi I 99, 625
  spawn of, & kosmos I 199
  universal, or Nuah, Ashtōreth II 462-3
  var names for I 136-7, 384-5, 434, 460
  water & I 70, 384-5, 460, 625-6
Mother-Nature
  diameter in circle symbol of I 4
Mother of God
  now idolatrous in Latin Church I 382n
  sitting on a lion I 400
Mother-Substance I 289-92
Motibus planetarum harmonicis, De. See Kepler
Motion. *See also* Breath, Perpetual Motion,
    Rotary Motion
  absolute, immovable I 56
  abstract I 3 &n, 14
  alchemical solvent of life I 258
  all, is perpetual (Grove) I 497
  aspect of absolute I 43
  becomes circular in kalpas I 116-17
  begets the Logos I 67n
  of bodies alters each minor age I 530
  breath or I 14, 55-6; II 551
  cosmic, finite, periodical I 3, 97n
  divine breath or, & Pleiades II 551
  duration, matter, space & I 55
  "esse" of, unknown I 518
  eternal, ceaseless I 2, 3, 43

eternal, cyclic, & spiral II 80
eternal even in pralaya I 497n
external, produced fr within I 274
Fohat & circular I 201
force & I 509, 512, 517-18
Hammer of Creation is continuous II 99
heat, attraction, repulsion & I 103
idol of science I 509n
intelligence needed to sustain I 502
jīvātman, Nous or I 50
laws of manvantaric I 529-30
Law stops, to make 7 laya holes I 147
fr laya into vortex of I 258
matter &, (Spencer) I 12n
modes of I 604; II 273, 719
nature of, unexplained I 498
never ceases in nature I 97
not property of passive matter I 502
periodical in manifestation I 97n
perpetual, of great breath I 2-4, 43, 55-6,
　93n, 147-8, 455
perpetual, of sat & asat II 450
perpetual, or the ever-becoming II 545
physical phenomena & I 496
primordial, not physical I 69-70
real, in space, vacuum I 496n
regulated by cosmic movers I 530
senseless (science) I 139
Spencer's great breath & I 496
spiral, of cycles & ogdoad II 580
thrills thru every sleeping atom I 116
unconditioned consciousness or I 14
vortical, in phenomenal world I 118n
will to impart & to restrain, (Herschel)
　I 503
Motionless, nothing is I 2
Motto of Theosophical Society I xli
Mounds
menhirs, dolmens & II 752-4
in Norway & USA II 424n
tall skeletons in American II 293
Mountain(s)
Atlanteans fled to high II 724
chains of, uplifted II 330
of the gods II 493
heaven or, described II 357
holy, of many nations II 494
Sinai or, of Moon II 234
Tree of Life hidden among three II 216
Mt Aetna, "celestial pillar" (Pindar) II 763
Mt Armon (Hermon) II 409
angels descend upon, (*Enoch*) II 376
Mt Atlas. *See* Atlas, Mount
Mt Caucasus. *See* Caucasus

Mt Kajbee, Prometheus crucified on II 44
Mt Lebanon, Nabatheans of II 455n
Mt Meru
Airyana-vaēgō or II 204
called Mountain of God II 493
celestial pole or II 785
described I 126-7; II 401 &n, 404
Eden & I 127
guarded by serpent I 129n
Indra's heaven on II 203
lotus symbolized I 379
middle of Jambu-dvīpa II 403-4
milks the Earth I 398n
N pole I 204; II 326, 357, 401n, 403
Olympus, Kaph, or II 362
Pātāla & II 357
roots of, in Earth's navel II 401n
seventh division, ātma or II 403
Śiva personates I 341
Śveta-dvīpa or II 6, 366n
symbolism of II 546-7
various equivalents of II 767
Mt Pelion, Xerxes' fleet wrecked at I 467
Mt Riphaeus II 7
Mt Sinai II 494
Deity descended on I 444
Moses & fire (gnosis) on II 566
Moses' vigil on I 374
mountain of the Moon II 76-7, 234
numerology of word II 466
quarries at, Egy & Bab II 692
symbol of 19 tropical years II 76
word fr Bab *Sin* (Moon-god) II 692
Mousseau. *See* Gougenot des Mousseau
Mout, Mouth I 91n, 384; II 464. *See also* Mut
Mouth, globe's higher atmosphere I 144
Movers, Dr F. K., *Die Phönizier*
Assyrian priest bore name of his god II 380
Deity born fr mundane egg I 365
demiurgic & manifested Idea I 366
Horus, Logos I 348
visible universe fr ether & air I 461
Votan son of the snakes II 379
Moving Stones II 342n. *See also* Stones
Moyst (Moist) Principle, in alchemy, her-
　metica II 236, 542, 591 &n
Mozart's *Requiem*
blind forces, organ & II 348
M'rira [Mriḍa, form of Rudra] (Skt)
King I't a subordinate incarnation of,
　(Wilford) II 406
"Mr. Sinnett's *Esoteric Buddhism*" [Some In-
　quiries suggested by] II 436n. *See also* Bla-
　vatsky, H. P. "Reply to an English FTS"

Mudge (Marsh in tx), Professor B. F. II 218
Muir, John (1810–1882)
  Hall prefers, to Wilson I 453n
  —— *Original Sanskrit Texts*
  Atharva-Veda on time II 611-12
  Varuna II 268-9n
  Vishnu I 349
  —— "Verses . . ."
  transl fr Vedas I 422-3
Mukhya (Skt) Primary Creation
  evolution of vegetable kingdom I 454
  fourth, or inanimate bodies I 446
  betw 3 lower, higher kingdoms I 455
Mukta (Skt) freed. *See also* Jīvātman, Moksha
  may choose to return to world I 132
  unconditioned, or Parabrahman I 7
Mukti (Skt) liberation, nirvāṇa
  Enoch, Elijah attained II 532
  freedom fr māyā I xix
Mūlaprakṛiti (Skt). *See also* Pradhāna, Prakṛiti,
    Primorial Matter, Svabhavat
  Aditi or I 430
  ākāśa radiates fr I 35
  asat or II 597n
  chaos primary aspect of I 536
  conceals absolute point I 346
  described I 10n, 75, 428-32
  duad, veil, mother, daughter I 426
  eternal root of That, All I 10, 147, 340
  inert without force II 24-5
  Īśvara or Logos & I 351n
  Kwan-yin, daivīprakriti or I 136
  Light of the Logos & I 430
  manifestation of II 24-5
  one Logos appears as I 273-4
  Parabrahman & I 46, 273, 337n, 346, 629
  potentialities within I 137n
  precosmic root-substance I 15, 35, 62, 147;
    II 24-5
  protyle next neighbor of I 582
  root of prakriti I 62; II 65
  root principle I 256, 522
  seven kingdoms & I 176
  Shekīnāh or I 629
  soul of one infinite spirit I 35
  super astral light 1st radiation fr I 75
  svabhavat & I 61
  three principles born fr I 620-1
  unevolved prakriti I 19
  veil of Parabrahman I 10n, 130n, 179, 274,
    428-9
Mule
  sterile, fr horse & ass II 287
  Uriel or Thartharaoth II 115n

Mulil, Mul-lil
  Akkadian creative god II 365
  caused the flood II 139n
Müller, Friedrich Max II 73
  cited I xxv, xxvii-ix, xxx-xxxi, xxxvii-viii, xli,
    xlvi
  darśanas show Greek infl I 47n
  Dayānand Sarasvatī I xxx
  Dayānand Sarasvatī's polemics w I 360
  derivation of Mars, Ares II 392n
  devotion of Hindus I 212n
  Hindu mind most spiritual II 521
  Indian arts, science fr Greeks II 225
  Massey on solar myths I 303-5
  missed meaning of Nārada II 567
  on phonetic laws I xxxi-ii
  placed opinions before facts I xxix-xxx
  War of Giants II 754
  writing unknown in early India II 225
  wrong about Aryan origins II 425
  —— *Chips from a German Workshop*
  Arab figures fr Hindustan I 360-1
  Greek & Christian religions II 764n
  Jones, Wilford &, forged MSS I xxx-i &n
  Rémusat on Jehovah I 472
  review of *Popol Vuh* II 97 &n
  Tahitian traditions II 193-4
  Vedas, Avesta, etc I xxxviii
  Vedas, Hesiod, etc II 450
  —— *A History of Ancient Sanskrit Literature*
  gives Morya for Moru [Maru] I 378n
  q *Rig-Veda* I 26
  —— *India: What can it teach us?*
  attacks Darwinism II 721-2
  —— *Introduction to the Science of Religion*
  Badáoní I xxivn
  Confucian, Taoist compared I xxv &n
  Confucius I xxxviin
  Egy religion not understood I xxviii-ix
  missionaries confuse Eve w Ivi II 194n
  Mother, Māyā, Mary I xxxiin
  Odin came before Homer, Vedas I xxix
  only one true religion I xli
  Rémusat on I Hi Wei I 472
  Saddharmālaṅkāra I xxvii
  vanity of religious doctrines I xli
  Wilford misled by forgery I xxx-i &n
  —— *Lectures on Mr. Darwin's Phil. of Lang.*
  Darwinian theory vulnerable II 662
  speech needs human brain II 661
  —— *Lectures on the Science of Language*
  D. Stewart on Sanskrit, etc II 442
  —— *The Science of Thought*
  thought & language II 199n

Müller, Karl Otfried
—— A History of the Lit. of Ancient Greece
  "Spirit of God" I 365, 461
Muluk-Taoos (Yezidi) lord peacock
  emblem of initiation II 514n
Mummy(ies)
  w crocodile head I 220 &n; II 577
  egg floating above, (Kircher) I 365
  frog goddesses found on I 386
  god II 464, 577
  marks on, tell sex of I xxixn
  Ptah unveils face of I 353
  of Sesostris at Cairo I xxixn
  tall male, at Tchertchen I xxxiii
  tau cross placed on II 557
  wheat placed w II 374 &n
Münchhausen, Baron [K. F. H. von] II 441
Mundaka Upanishad
  lower & higher Krishna I 535
  Parabrahman I 6
  universe as spider & web I 83
Mundane Egg. See also Egg, Golden Egg
  carried in Ptah's hand I 365
  Christians adopted I 367-8
  described I 65-6, 88-9, 359-68
  Dionysius [Dionysos] sprang fr I 360
  germ in the I 57
  Keely near secret of I 556
  Khnoum fashioned man fr I 366
  Nārāyana penetrates I 80-1
  point in, becomes universe I 1
  Scandinavian I 367
  swan symbol & I 357
Mundane Tree. See also Tree of Life,
  Yggdrasil
  Nidhögg gnawed roots of I 211
  Son of Kriyāśakti compared to I 211
  tree of evolution II 259n
Mundi Domini (Lat) world dominators
  Church made devils of I 331
Mundi Tenentes (Lat) world holders
  Church made devils of I 331
Mundo, De. See Aristotle
Muni(s), Munin (Skt) sage(s) II 175
  fathers of various beings II 259n
  great, or first man I 345
  fr previous manvantara I 207
  rebellious & fallen gods II 232
  ten prajāpatis create seven II 573-4
Munk, Salomon, [Palestine]
  Gnostic influence on Zohar II 461n
Muntakhab-ut-Tawārikh. See Badāonī
Murad Ali Bey. See Mitford, G.

Murray, A. S., Manual of Mythology
  prowess of Atlanteans II 753n
Mūrtimat (Skt), embodied I 372
Musée des Sciences
  disguised causes (Herschel) I 492n
  gravitation (Herschel) I 604
  Le Couturier & motor force I 502
Mushrooms, cobra venom & I 262
Music
  division of mathematics (Pythag) I 433
  Māntrika-śakti, speech & I 293
  Osiris-Isis invented, (Basnage) II 366
  Thoth inventor of II 529
  world called out of chaos by I 433
Musical
  notation & Greek diatessaron II 600
  scale & sacred planets II 602
  scale & septenary laws II 628
Music of the Spheres
  Celsus on I 445-6
  Censorinus on I 433
  chords of universal consciousness I 167
  Pythagorean II 602
  Vāch or Pythagorean I 432
Muslin, fr India known in Chaldea II 226
Muspell (Norse)
  war of sons (flames) of I 202
Mussulman(men). See also Mohammedans
  crescent & II 31-2n
  lethal influence of II 411n
Mut (Egy)
  daughter, wife, mother of Ammon I 91n,
    384, 430
  Isis, Hathor or I 91n; II 464
  mother, Moon, etc II 464
Mut (Phoen), Mahat (Skt) & I 451
Mut(h)-Isis (Egy)
  suckling Hor-Ammon II 464
Mycenae, cyclopean structures at II 345n
Myer, Isaac
  antiquity of Zohar II 461 &n
  studied Kabbala well I 374
—— Qabbalah
  Adamic race II 315
  Ain-Sōph creates in delight II 126
  allegory of man w heavy load I 393-4
  all things made male & female II 528
  astral first race (Zohar) II 137
  B'raisheeth bārā elohīm I 352
  continued creation II 457
  Earth chain II 503-4
  four Adams II 457
  God lowest designation I 619
  Jews used Adonai, not YHVH II 452

Kabbala fr Aryan sources I 376
Logos brother of Satan II 162
Moses & Lord's glory (*Exodus*) II 538-9
mystical interpretation of *Genesis* I 374-5
One Cause, Primal Cause I 618
Pre-Adamite Kings II 83-4
on rebuking Satan II 478
rotation of Earth II 28n
seven Earths, seas, days I 347-8, 447-8
six-month night, day (*Zohar*) II 773
spirit, chaos, universe II 84-5
Superior emanates into all beings II 116
two creations in *Zohar* II 54
various worlds, shells, etc II 111, 504
wisdom-religion in Central Asia I 376
YHVH, Tetragrammaton I 438 &n
Zohar on bird of wisdom II 292-3
Mylitta (Babylonian Moon-goddess)
  identical w Aditi II 43
  same as Thalatth, Omoroca II 135
  wife, mother, sister I 396
Myorica, swans of II 772n
Myrrha (Gk) I 384
Mysore, Śringa-giri mathams near I 272
Mystère et la science, Le. See Félix, Father
Mystères de la vie humaine. See Montlosier
Mystères de l'horoscope. See Star, E.
Mysteria Specialia of Paracelsus
  seeds fr which all develops I 283 &n
Mysteries, The (Mystery Schools). *See also*
  Initiations, Mystery
  Aeschylus initiated into II 419
  Alexandrian, texts destroyed I xxiii-iv
  astrology secret of II 500n
  blinds conceal real II 310
  Book of Enoch & II 229, 535
  bull, dragon (Lat saying) fr II 133
  church fathers initiated in I xxxix, xliv, 311
  circle-dance prescribed for II 460
  compilers of Christian II 561
  crucifixion & II 560-2
  custodians of II 281-2
  desecration of II 503
  Dionysiac, & egg I 359-60
  a discipline & stimulus to virtue I xxxv
  Egyptian I 312
  founders of II 267n
  gave rise to religions I xxxvi
  geography part of II 9
  great, & candidate's death II 462
  Greek sages initiated in I 117
  Hermes in Samothracian II 362
  Herodotus on II 395-6
  ideal & practical I 363

ineffable name & I 346
initiation into I xxxvi; II 795-6
lunar, & occult knowledge I 228n
Masonry once based on II 795-6
medieval, 7 natural properties in II 630
of Mithras I 446; II 419n
Nazarene II 96n
origin of II 281, 560
philosophers initiated into I 326-7
pre-Adamic, (Chwolsohn) II 452-3
psychic & spiritual element belong to I 229
pyramids symbolize I 314-15, 317-18n
reestablished in 5th race II 124
rounds & races taught in II 435
Sabazian II 415-16, 419
at Saïs II 396
Samothracian, & Deluge II 4
secrecy re II 124-5, 451, 518, 535
SD vol III records downfall of I xxxix-xl
secret of the fires in II 106
serpent taught men, (Gnos) I 404
Sods, Sodalian I 463; II 212n, 633
  unlocked w 7 keys II 632
War in Heaven taught in II 386
Mysteries of Adonis. See Dunlap, S. F.
Mysteries of Magic. See Lévi, E.
"Mysteries of Ro-stan" I 237
Mysteriis, De. See Iamblichus
Mysterium Magnum of Paracelsus
  astral light of Alchemists II 511
  Brahma (neuter) or I 61
  chaos or I 283
  elements born fr I 284
  homogeneous matter I 584
Mystery(ies). *See also* Mysteries, The
  cosmic, & Nārada II 83
  fatality of science I 670
  geometrical figures &, of being I 430 &n
  initiation & I 229
  male figure symbol of unveiled I 351
  "negation of common sense" I 669
  of postmortem separation II 496
  psychological, key to II 225n
  seventh, of creation II 516-17
  universal, & Mother I 88
  veil of, over zodiacal signs II 580
"Mystery about Buddha, A" I 118
Mystery God, or 7th planet (Uranus) I 99-100
Mystery-Gods (Planetary Regents)
  chief of, is Sun II 22-3
  seven, of ancients II 22
  various, given II 3
Mystery Language
  described I 308-25; II 574-89

every theology sprang fr I 310
Hebrew scrolls read numerically in II 208
imparted by advanced beings I 309
now called symbolism I 309
numerical & geometrical keys to I 318
pictorial & symbolical II 574
seven dialects of, & nature I 310
seven keys of I 310-11
Mystery of the Ages [by Marie, Countess of Caithness] II 229n
Mystery Schools. *See* Mysteries
Mystery-Tongue, of initiates II 200
Mystic(s)
 planetary conjunction important to I 656
 Russian, traveled to Tibet I xxxvi
Mysticism
 Hindu I 212n
 persecuted by Roman Church I xliv
Myth(s), Mythology(ies). *See also* Allegories, Legends
 antiquity of, (Gould) II 219
 Aryan influence on Babylonian II 130
 astronomy & astrology part of I 389n
 of Atlas II 762-5
 based on ancient history II 235-6, 754-5, 769, 777
 based on facts in nature II 197n, 293, 443
 came fr the north II 774n
 cosmos fr Divine Thought in I 339-40
 crude, coarse, dangerous II 764-5 &n
 described I 425
 double-sexed creatures in II 130
 evolution & Hindu I 22
 of fallen angel II 475-505
 four races in Greek II 270-1

giants important in ancient II 754-5
gods of I 668
historical lining to all I 303, 304n, 339
intelligent nature-forces basis of I 424
kernel of tradition in II 235
keys to II 517
Massey on value of I 303-5
meanings of persons in II 775
monsters of, actuality II 217-19, 293, 443
moon goddesses in I 264
Norse II 97, 100, 283n, 535, 754
oldest Greek, echoes primeval teaching I 109-10
origin of Satanic II 378-90
orthodox symbolism of modern II 335
Pococke on I 339
primitive disease (Renouf) I 303-4, 398
sevenfold interpretation of II 517, 765
Sun II 381-3, 386
various classical, interpreted II 769-77
of Vedic Aryans II 498, 520
wars in I 202
zodiac basis of I 652, 667-8
"Mythes du feu . . ." *See* Baudry, F.
Mythical, ancient texts not purely II 335
Mythical Monsters. See Gould, Charles
Mythological Geography [*Mythische Geographie* . . .]. *See* Völcker, Karl H. W.
Mythologie de la Grèce antique. See Decharme
Mythologie des Indous, La. See Polier, de
Mythology. See Murray, A. S.
Mythopoeic Age, not a fairy tale I 266-7
Myths and Marvels of Astronomy. See Proctor
Myths and Myth-Makers. See Fiske, John

N

N's, five, & 5 races (Egy) II 458
Naasenians(i), Naassenes (Gnos sect)
  dragon was Son w II 355
  messiah of, a serpent II 356
Nabathean(s)
  Chaldean star-worshipers II 452-3
  giants of Midian II 755-6
  Masoudi on II 453
  of Mt Lebanon, doctrines of II 455n
  occult brotherhood II 455
Nabathean Agriculture, transl by D. A.
  Chwolsohn I 401
  Adam-Adami II 452-8
  copy of Hamitic treatise II 453
  Maimonides on II 455n
  moon idol instructs Qū-tāmy in I 394-5;
    II 453, 455
  not apocryphal I 395; II 454-5
  pre-Adamic mysteries II 452
  Schemal, Samael I 417
  Secret Doctrine in II 455
  transl fr Chaldean, Arabic I 394; II 453
Nabhas-tala (Skt), all space I 371
Nābhi (Skt) son of Agnīdhra
  hundred sons of II 320
Nabin (Chald) seer, prophet
  Nebo personifies secret wisdom II 456
Nabō (Gk for Nebo)
  word Nabathean fr II 455
Nabonidus
  dates founding of Babylonia II 691
Nach. *See* Nahash
Nachan, or Palenque II 35
Nāchnīs (Hind). *See* Nautch-girls.
Nadaillac, Marquis de
  termed Bamian statue Buddhist II 338 &n
Nadir-Shah [Nādir-Qulī-Shāh]
  warriors of, & Bamian II 338
Nāga(s) (Skt). *See also* Initiate, Serpents
  allies of asuras in war II 500-1
  in America 5,000 yrs ago II 214n
  Apollonius met, in Kashmir II 211
  Arjuna married daughter of II 628
  asuras &, used in creation I 348
  Brahmā, Vishnu, Śiva crowned w I 437n
  brazen, fiery serpents & I 364n

celestial, or 4 cardinal points I 408-9
  cobras II 209
  cosmic, born of Kaśyapa-Āditya II 382n
  do not creep, but walk, run II 181-2n
  first, "Sons of Will & Yoga" II 181
  four Mahārājahs & I 126, 408-9
  Hindu "King-Snakes" II 381
  Indra & II 378
  initiates or I 408
  Jewish seraphīm were II 501
  Kapila, of kali-yuga II 572
  Kaśyapa father of II 132
  lived in Nāga-dvīpa II 501n
  Nāgals [Naguals], Nargals [Nergals] &
    II 213
  nirmānakāya of the II 201
  race of, in India, America II 132
  sarpa &, defined II 181-2n
  septenary meaning II 208
  symbolize immortality, time I 404
  wise men II 26-7n, 211
Nāga-Dvīpa (Skt)
  division of India II 132
  nāgas dwelt in II 501n
Nagal(s), Nargal (of Mexico).
  See Nagual
Nāgārjuna
  Ekaślokaśāstra of, in China I 61
  rival of Āryāsanga I 49
Nägeli, Karl W. von
  principle of perfectibility II 649n
Nagkon (Angkor)-Wat (in Cambodia) II 430
Nagpur (City of Snakes, India)
  markings on stones near II 346n
  one of India's oldest cities II 501n
Nagual (of Mexico)
  Arjuna married daughter of II 628
  chief sorcerer of Mexican Indians II 213
  Nargals & II 182
  revered serpent II 209
Nahash [Nāhāsh] (Heb)
  Jews called rebels II 246-7
  symbolized by serpent II 246n
  tempter or, (Nach) II 215-16n
  word means brass & serpent I 364n

Nahbkoon [Neheb-Kau] (Egy)
astral light or I 472
Nahuatls, 7 caves & II 35
Nail
to, to in Heb means crucify II 558, 561
Wittoba, mark on foot of II 560n
Naimittika ("occasional") Pralaya
contingent re-coalescence II 309n
described I 370; II 69n
Naja (Egy)
Uraeus, serpent, nāga or I 437 &n
Nakash. *See* Nahash
Nakshatras (Skt), 27 lunar asterisms II 551
Nallies. *See* Tallies
Nāman (Skt) name I 373
Name(s). *See also* Word
Atlantean, transl by Solon II 767
four-letter ineffable I 351; II 282n, 557
ineffable, not a creator I 346 &n
Jehovah a mystery II 508-10
key to mystical Bible II 536
māntrikā-śakti & I 293
mystery II 536-45
occult meaning of ancient II 335
our words &, influence our future I 93-4
power of, great II 767
power of the ineffable I 293
sacred, of 7 letters universal I 438-9
secret, & Prometheus I 195n
seven vowels & II 569-70 &n
tetragram contains ineffable II 557
to, something limits it I 330
"Nameless One." *See* Wondrous Being
Nanda (Skt) or Chandragupta
first Buddhist sovereign II 550 &n
Nandi (Skt) sacred bull
remained on White Island II 408
Nannak, Nannar [Sumerian Nanna]
Moon-god (Chaldean) II 139n
Nan-Schayn (Nan Shan Mts)
ancient civilization in eastern I xxxii
Naphtali (Heb) son of Jacob
Capricorn or I 651
Napoleon, reply of Laplace to I 498
Nara (Skt) man, & Nārā [nārāḥ, Skt] water.
See also Nārāyaṇa
Brahmā's universe evolves out of central
point II 31
Nārāyana moves on I 457-8n; II 591 &n
water as body of II 495n
Nārada (Skt)
appears in each root-race II 83, 323
Asuramaya's work based on records of
II 49

Brahmaputra & I 413
calculations of II 70
cursed to incarnate II 585
dialogue w Devamata II 566-8
executor of universal karma II 48
feuded w Brahmā, Daksha II 502
first Adversary I 413
Gītā reference to II 48n
leader of the gandharvas II 584
leads men to become gods II 584
"Mirror of Futurity" work of II 49
reborn as a man II 82
reborn constantly II 275n
refuses to procreate II 82, 140n, 275n, 584
son of Brahmā II 47-8, 82
"strife-maker" I 413; II 171n
Vedic rishi II 47-9, 82-3, 275n, 502
virgin ascetic of every age II 323
Nārada-pañcha-rātra II 82
Nāradīya-Purāṇa
laws of celibate adepts II 82
Naraka (Skt), Hindu hell II 98
Naraksha. *See* Niraksha
Naram-Sin (son of Sargon)
built original Babylonian temple II 691
Naras (Skt), centaurs II 65n
Narasiṃha (Skt) man-lion
avatar, slew Hiranyakaśipu II 225n
Vishnu relates story of II 611
Nārāyaṇa (Skt). *See also* Nara, Trimūrti,
Vishnu
birth of, (universe) I 333-5, 345
Brahmā permutation of I 431
dwelt over (on) waters I 457-8n; II 578
he who abides in deep II 495n, 591 &n
invisible flame sets all afire I 626
Krishna identified w Rishi- II 359
Mover on the Waters I 64, 336, 345;
II 591 &n, 765n
personifies breath of Parabrahman I 64
ray of Logos appears as I 80-1
Śrī wife of II 76n
transformed into substance I 7
Universal Soul, Rā or I 231
worshiped by Prachetases II 578
Nargal(s). *See* Nergals
Naros, Neros(es), Chald cycle I 655n; II 619
Narrow-brained II 168 &n
bred w she-animals II 184-5
Narrow-headed II 161, 271
Narthēx (Gk)
candidate's initiation wand II 518
Prometheus hid stolen fire in II 525

Nasmyth, J. H., observed objects like willow
    leaves on Sun I 530, 541, 590
Nāstika (Skt), rejection of idols I 279
Nath [Nātha(s)] (Skt), "Lords" II 88
Nation(s). *See also* Civilizations
    in all ages II 716
    American II 444
    ancient, knew of extinct monsters II 206
    astronomical cycles & fate of II 330-1
    cataclysms recorded by all II 787n
    clothe truth w local symbols I xxxvi
    deluge sweeps, out of existence II 351
    descended fr Lemuria II 768
    disappear w no trace II 743
    each, receives its own truth I xxxvi
    every, has its deva or spirit I 576; II 538
    extinct, near Tchertchen I xxxiii-iv
    karma maps progress of I 326
    many new, in 6th race II 446
    overlap each other II 433n
    predestination in history of I 641
    prehistoric, versed in science I 673
    rise & fall of, & writing II 442
    survival of fittest among II 330
Nation, New York (*Nature* in tx)
    criticism of Stallo I 483 &n
National Cycles
    called karmic in East I 642
    within subrace II 301
National Library of Paris
    Egyptian fragment in II 559
National Reformer
    Dr Lewins on cerebration I 297 &n
Natura Animalium, De. See Aelianus
Natural Genesis. See Massey, G.
Natural History. See Pliny
Natural History Review, Oliver on floral evi-
    dence for Atlantis II 322n, 727
Naturalist [*American Naturalist*], man, cross,
    carvings, South American I 322
Natural Philosophy [*Treatise on*]. *See* Thomson
    & Tait
Natural Selection II 348, 426
    cannot originate variations II 299n, 648
    criticisms of II 185, 647-9, 654, 657, 696
    does not affect basic type II 737
    evolution not entirely due to II 728
    future prospects of I 600
    law of retardation & II 260 &n
    not an entity II 648
    only partially true II 734 &n
    de Quatrefages accepted II 662
    & Romanes' alternate theory II 647
    secondary cause only II 648-9

super- II 260
    Wallace felt, inadequate I 107, 339; II 696
Natura naturans I 412
Natura non facit saltum, corroborated by
    esoteric science II 287, 696
    Darwin believed II 696
Nature (cosmic, terrestrial)
    "abhors a vacuum" I 64, 343, 495
    aggregate of nature spirits II 732
    all, is consecrated I 578
    ancient & modern concept of II 369-70
    aspect of absolute consciousness I 277n
    author of, is nature herself I 489n
    behaves esoterically I 610
    belief in powers of II 592
    blind, unintelligent (science) I 587
    cannot be unconscious I 277n
    cause of phenomena I 2-3
    corporeal & spiritual I 464
    creative potency of, infinite II 153
    creative principle of, & pyramid I 317n
    creeps onward to perfection I 185n
    deceitful on physical plane I 610
    deceptive appearance of II 475
    dhyāni-chohans enact laws of I 38
    dies only to be reborn I 149
    ether-matter-energy or I 668
    ever-becoming I 250, 257n
    everything organic in I 281, 626n
    feminine I 5
    forces of I 145-7, 506-23
    geometrizes I 97
    good, evil, suffering in II 475-6
    ground plan of II 737
    higher, in bondage to lower II 109-10
    humanities &, altered (*Enoch*) II 533-4
    inseparable fr the Deity I 489n
    invisible worlds behind veil of I 284n
    is an egg fructified I 65
    Jews profaned symbols of II 471
    makes certain unions sterile II 195-6
    makes "jumps" (Huxley) II 696
    man should be co-worker w I 280
    mechanical forces of, a fallacy II 298
    monads & I 619, 633
    motion never ceases in I 97, 257
    moves in cycles II 443, 261
    mysteries of, & "4320" II 73
    mysteries of, recorded fr beg I 612
    never creates without purpose II 298
    never leaves an atom unused II 170
    never proceeds by jumps II 195, 445
    never repeats herself I 184n; II 700
    no inorganic or dead matter in I 507

nothing is outside of II 194
Pan (god) is II 389n, 510
Pascal on God & I 412
physical, correlation of forces I 185n
physical, illusory II 475
powers of, are entities I 106, 554
prakriti & I 256; II 65
principles of physical, diagram II 593
progressive march of I 277
religion is silent worship of I 381n
rent in veil of, by 1897 I 612
running down of, refuted I 149-51
secrets of, public in 3rd race II 319
septenary division of II 574
seven forces of I 139; II 631-2
seven mysteries of I 310
Space &, are one I 555n
spirit &, form our illusory universe II 36
time confirms judgment of II 451
triple evolutionary scheme in I 181
unaided, & prehuman monsters II 634-5
unaided fails I 181-2; II 55-6, 102-3, 269
under sway of karmic law II 446
unity of I 276
unseen principle throughout all II 555
utilizes everything II 700
Zeno on, as a habit II 159
Nature (human)
  psychic & rational II 275
  spiritual, overcomes physical II 499
Nature (magazine)
  Ball, Sir A., on Moon II 64 &n
  Crookes' *Address* I 111n, 581-6
  Huxley on Atlantis II 780-1, 784
  Lodge on metaphysical arguments I 488
  Siemens on Sun's heat, etc I 102n
  Stallo, criticism of I 483 &n
  Thomas, Professor, on Australians II 729
Nature Spirits. *See also* Elementals
  countless kinds, varieties I 221
  fathers or lower angels are II 102
  intervene in all phenomena I 147
  materialism prevents belief in I 276
  nature an aggregate of II 732
  psychic, or elementals I 146-7, 221
  work on model of dhyānis I 225
Natürliche Schopf. See Haeckel, *History of Creation*
Naudin, Charles Victor
  on Adam as asexual II 119-20
  critique of sleep of Adam II 181
  critique of theory of blastema II 120
  scientific hypotheses & II 646
Naulette Jaw. *See* Canstadt Man

Naumann, Dr Alexander
—— *Grundriss der Thermochemie*
  chemistry is atomic mechanics I 513
Nautch-girls [Nāchnīs of India]
  called Almeh in Egypt I 463
  same as Hebrew Kadeshuth II 460, 463
Nautchnis. *See* Nautch-girls
Nave. *See* Navis
Navel (of Earth) II 401n
  Ark corresponds to II 461
  currents stored in II 400n
  lotus in, of Vishnu I 379; II 31, 472
Navigation
  aereal I 560; II 426-7
  Hindu, older than Phoenician II 406
Navis (Lat) ship
  initiation & II 462
  yoni & Ark of Covenant II 463
Naya (Skt), harmony, conduct II 528
Nazar, Nazarite (Heb) ascetic
  Moses was II 465n
Nazarenes [also Naṣoraeans] (Gnostic)
  echo the SD II 96n, 150
  followers of true Christos I 198n
  had keys to mystery-language I 310-11
  Ialdabaōth or Demiurge II 243
  many of, initiates II 96n
  mystic Christians, initiates I 194
  opponents of later Christians I 198n
  philosophy of I 197
  religion of I xxxv
  re spirit as fem & evil I 194-6
Nazesmann. *See* Naumann, Dr A.
N'cabvah [Neqēbāh] (Heb)
  tau cross became, in 5th race I 5
  yoni or II 467
Neanderthal Man
  of earliest Paleolithic age II 724
  not missing link (Huxley) II 686n
  skull of, not apelike II 193n, 729
  skull of, of average capacity II 686n, 687
Nebat-Iavar bar Iufin Ifafin (Nazarean) I 195
Nebelheim (Ger). *See* Niflheim
Nebo [or Nabu] (Chald) god of wisdom
  creator of 4th, 5th races II 456
  Nabō in Greek II 455
  name given initiates II 210n, 211
  overseer of 7 planets II 456
  son of (Bel-) Merodach II 210n, 211
  Son of Hea or Ea II 477
Nebonidus, Babylonian king II 691
Nebuchadnezzar the Second II 453
Nebula(ae) I 102-3, 131, 205n
  collision of, & rotation I 500

condensation of, (Hindu) II 253
in elemental dissociation I 588
fiery whirlwind 1st stage of I 22
Fohat sets, in motion I 84, 673
fusion of matter of I 505
gaseous, self-luminous I 588
Laplace, Kant on I 149-50n
matter of, unknown I 505, 595
milk, curds & congeries of II 321
occult cause of rotation of I 97-8n
resolvable, irresolvable I 250, 543, 595, 598
    &n
star is condensation of I 595-6
suns, planets start as I 22
Wolf on, & primitive chaos I 598-9
Nebular Theory I 500, 505
adepts on I 590-7
Alexander confirms I 588
beginnings of rotation & I 97n
discussed I 588-600
Herschel's I 590
Humboldt on I 497n
Kant's, close to esoteric doctrine I 601-2
Laplace, Faye on I 588, 591-3
modern, variation of Laplace's I 597
of planets fr Sun denied I 101
Spencer criticizes I 600
what, is not (Winchell) I 599-600
Necessity. *See also* Cycles
all universes sons of I 43
Egyptian cycle of I 227; II 379
gods pass thru Circle of II 303
universe of, & accidents II 648
Neck (of Earth), land emerged fr II 401 &n
Necromancer, serpent & II 209
Negritos, descent of II 195-6n
Negro(es) II 780. *See also* African
"anthropoids" & II 717n
Aryans, Mongols &, fr same ancestors
    II 607n
Blake on II 725
Central American monuments & II 790
race apart (Broca, Vivey) II 725
skulls like those of, in Austria II 739
survivors of hybrid 4th race II 723
types found in ancient Europe II 744
wide gulf betw, & apes II 677-8
Negroids, fr anthropoids (Huxley) II 315n
Nehhaschim [Neḥāshīm] (Heb), Serpents'
    "Works" or magic (*Zohar*) II 409
Neḥushtān (Heb)
Hezekiah calls brazen serpent II 387n
Neibbān (Burmese), nirvāna I 38 &n

Neilos, Nīl, Nīla (Indus R). *See also* Nīla
numerical value of I 390; II 583
true meaning of II 417-18
Neith (Egy) Queen of Heaven
brought forth, not begotten I 399
Christ-Sun clothed in I 393
as the Moon radiates the Sun I 393
other half of Ammon II 135
wife, mother, sister I 396
Nemean Odes. See Pindar
Nemesis (Gk)
cycles, karma & I 641
karma &, compared II 305-6n, 421
karma-, discussed I 642-3
karma-, law of retribution II 304
Nemesis, Hymn to, by Mesomedes II 305n
Nemi. *See* Nimi
Neolithic Man, Men II 675, 739. *See also* Cave
    Men
cannibal II 715, 716n, 723
caves of, & Atlantean survivors II 352
forerunner of Aryan invasion II 716n
lake-dwellers II 716
Paleolithic man & II 686 &n, 715-16 &nn,
    722-3
in Palestine, were nephīlīm (giants) II 775
remains of, in Kent's Cavern II 724
Neophytes, Chrēsts or II 562
Neoplatonism
Christian Gnosticism added to I xliv
Neoplatonist(s) I 611
archetypal ideas of I 281n
bound by oaths of secrecy II 763
bright period ended w I xliv-v
Chaldean religion & II 541
Clement defected fr II 279-80 &n
divided man into 4 parts II 602-3
Hermetic books edited by I 675
infl of Buddhistic theosophy on, (King) I 668
Jewish, used microcosm as man I 283n
Mysteries, discipline, virtue I xxxv
seven rectors of world I 409
Neopythagoreans
decimals known before the I 361
Nephesh (Heb). *See also* Astral Body
breath of life I 212
-chaiah [hayyāh], living soul I 226n
garment of II 315
Gnostics get, fr Asia ['Aśiyyāh] II 604
Ka (Egy) or, (Lambert) II 633
lower or 1st Adam had only II 162, 456
lower, united w gūf II 457
Michael, Samael proceed fr II 378
mind, manas or I 242-5

rūah must unite w I 193
vital soul, not spirit I 225, 633n
Nephīlīm (Heb) giants
  angels beget II 293
  in *Genesis* II 61, 775
  satyrs &, descend fr man & animal II 755
  term refers to 3rd race II 279
  theosophy fr the, (Pember) II 229n
  transl "hairy giants" (Bible) II 755
Nephtys, Nephthys (Egy) Moon-goddess
  as wife, mother, sister I 396
Neptune (planet)
  not one of 7 sacred planets I 575
  relation to solar system I 102n, 575
  satellites of I 101-2, 149-50n, 575, 593
Neptune (Roman god). *See also* Poseidon
  Atlantean island sacred to II 408
  called Chozzar II 356, 577, 578
  congratulates Noah I 444n
  divided Atlantis II 406n, 765
  god of reasoning (Ragon) II 796
  Hindu Idaspati, Nārāyana, etc II 765n
  Nereus aspect of II 578, 766
  Poseidon- & Aether I 464
  Poseidon-, dolphin vehicle of II 577
  saves Latona II 771n
  symbol of Atlantean magic II 356
  titanic strength of 4th race II 766
  Varuna like, riding leviathan II 268n
  Varuna reigns as II 65
  water, Varuna or I 462
Neqēbāh (Heb) I 5; II 467
Neras. *See* Naras
Nereids (Gk) nymphs of the sea
  goats sacrificed to II 579
  Nereus & II 766
Nereus (Gk)
  one aspect of Neptune II 578
  Poseidon, 4th race & II 766
Nergal(s) (Nargal in tx, Bab)
  Chaldean, Assyrian chief of magi II 213
  nagals & II 182
  nāgas & II 213, 628
Nergal-Serezer [Sharezer] (Bab), Nagal
  [Nagual] & Nargal [Nergal] fr II 213
Nergas II 2. *See also* Nergal
Neriosengh, transl of the *Yasna* II 758
Neroses. *See* Naros
Nerve(s). *See also* Vibration
  -cells II 670-3
  -centers of Sun I 540-1
  -centers of Sun I 540-1
  currents I 293
  -force I 454, 508, 531, 566n, 633

in lower kingdoms I 49
Nerve-Aura (of occultism) II 298n. *See also*
  Nervous Ether
  aspect of all-pervading Archaeus I 338n
Nervous Ether I 531-2, 537-40. *See also*
  Archaeus, Nerve-Aura
  animal spirits of Descartes II 298
  descends via sushumnā ray I 537
  energy behind matter I 603
  of one may poison that of another I 538
  Richardson's I 508; II 298n, 654
  too much, leads to disease I 538n
  vital principle or I 634
Nervous Fluid
  exuberance of, & mediums II 370n
  liquor vitae of Paracelsus I 532 &n
Nescience, or avidyā I 7
Neshāmāh (Heb)
  clothed in bundle of life II 315
  Egyptian intellectual soul & II 633
  Gnostics get, fr Brīah [Berīāh] II 604
  highest soul or spirit II 457
  inspirations of I 245
  Michael, Samael proceed fr II 378
  spirit, ātman or I 242, 243, 244
Nether World
  brass symbolizes I 364n
  Hathor another aspect of I 400n
  Hindus call America the II 446
  lords of, & white vs black magic II 427
  our Earth or II 98
  poem on I 475; II 643
  womb of life I 364n
Netzah (Heb), globe E of Earth I 200
Neumann, K. E., Chinese visited New World
  [Lassen] II 424n
Neutral Center II 261, 731
  center between planes I 148
  Keely's center I 556-7
  laya-center or I 155-6, 557
New Aspects of Life and Religion. See Pratt, H.
New Chemistry, The. See Cooke, J. P.
Newcomb, Professor Simon
—— *Popular Astronomy*
  Earth's heat II 149n, 694
  irresolvable nebulae I 543
  Sun's heat loss, contraction I 84
New Encyclopaedia. See Rees, A.
Newfoundland
  continent once joined France & II 791
  large cuttle fish found off II 440-1
New Guinea II 7, 328
Newman, Professor
  Arismaspi inhabited the Ural II 416-17

New Orleans, skeleton 57,000 yrs old II 352
"New Philosophy." *See* Bloomfield-Moore
New Testament I 442n
  abyss betw OT & I 382n
  borrowed fr *Book of Enoch* II 482
  esotericism of writers of I 384
  light created God II 37
  not borrowed fr Hindus I xxxi
  OT &, fr same source I 115n
  phallicism in I 318
  plurality of worlds in I 607 &n
  reincarnation in II 111 &n
Newton, Sir Isaac
  advocated corpuscular theory I 494-5
  gravitation & I 490-2, 494-5, 496n, 497-8
  ideas of, perverted I 484 &n, 491
  intelligences behind laws I 594
  Kant's views solve problems of I 601
  personal working god of I 479
  profoundly religious I 492, 496n
  Pythagorean corpuscular theory I 484
  resisting ether & motion I 501
  space as a vacuum I 491, 494
  speculated on *Revelation* II 484-5
  Sun's heat estimated by I 484n
  traces zodiac to Argonauts I 652
  world often needs repairing I 503
  would be idiot without manas II 242
  would have eaten his apple I 484
—— "An Hypothesis explaining . . ."
  all things originate in ether I 13
—— *Opticks*
  hesitated re gravitation I 496n
  plurality of inhabited worlds II 706
  thin vapors in space I 494-5
—— *Principia* II 674
  all-powerful Being of I 498
  Forbes' [Cotes] Preface I 492
  gravity won't explain everything I 490
  inertia a force I 511
—— "Third Letter to Bentley"
  agent causing gravity I 479, 490-1, 494
  subtle spirit moves matter I 490, 491
New World
  already old when discovered II 213-14
  never connected w Atlantic island
    (Oliver) II 322n
  pātāla, nether world or II 446
  SD in, before Buddhism II 424n
  seeds of grander race in II 446
  senior to the Old World II 446
  settled by Scandinavians I 297
New York *Nation* (*Nature* in tx)
  criticism of Stallo in I 483 &n

New York Sun, World
  attack HPB's pyramid views I 317n
New Zealand, part of ancient Lemuria
    II 223, 296, 788
Nicaea, Council of II 279n
Nidānas (Skt)
  desire to exist & I 44
  eternal, Oi-Ha-Hou I 93
  four truths & I 39
  series of, or causes, effects I 509
  teachings on, secret I 45
  twelve causes of existence I 38-9 &n
  various names of I 38n
Nidhögg (Norse)
  gnawed World Tree I 211, 407
Niflheim (Norse; Nebelheim, Ger)
  cold hell of Eddas II 245
  Helheim & II 774
  world matrix, astral light I 367
Night(s). *See also* Pralaya(s)
  before Day in Creation II 59
  Day &, Castor & Pollux II 122
  Day &, 2nd Fundamental Prop I 17
  Days &, activity & rest II 545
  Homer on I 425
  sevenfold Days & II 756-60
Night(s) of Brahmā I 3, 55; II 244. *See also* Days
    of Brahmā, Manvantara, Pralaya
  coming of I 371, 376-7; II 579n
  Days of Brahmā & I 17, 368-78
  duration of I 36, 240, 655-6; II 70, 505
  Father-Mother one during I 41
  Kārana alone during I 41
  Makara, Mīna (Pisces) & II 579n
  naimittika pralaya II 309n
  1,000 great ages in I 372
  pralaya applies to II 307n
  primary state of matter in I 103
  SD about our kosmos after I 13
  That & II 80
  Vamadeva Modelyar [Mudaliyar] on
    I 376-7
Nihil (Lat) nothing, creation out of I 233n
Nihilism, atheism, idealism II 651
Nīla, Nīl, Neilos. *See also* Neilos
  blue mountain II 403n
  Indus R, explained II 417-18 &n
  Sun sets at foot of II 407
  Wilford mistakes, for Nile R II 405 &n
Nīlakaṇṭha (Skt)
  commentary on *Anugītā* II 496n, 567-8
  dead letter commentary of II 637n
  on sons of Virāja & Mānasa II 89-90
  on speech, mind & higher self I 94

Nīlalohita (Skt) blue, red complexioned
    form of Śiva I 457
    Ninth or Kumāra Creation & II 106
    Rudra as a kumāra II 192n
Nile River. See also Neilos
    delta II 8, 368, 746
    Ethiops, Nīl, Nīla & II 417-18
    five crocodiles in celestial, expl II 580
    Great Deep, water or I 319
    Horus fr lotus of celestial II 472
    Indus confused w II 417-18 &n
    kabbalistic I 381
    Moses rescued fr I 319 &n; II 428
    number of, is solar year II 583
    Osiris-Isis stopped flooding of II 366
    Osiris symbol of I 390
    periodical rising of II 429
    soundings in valley of II 750n
    Wilford mistakes, for Nīla Mts II 405 &n
Nilghiri Hills [Nīlgiri] (Skt)
    Moola Koorumba of II 445
Nilson, elemental bodies of I 547
Nilsson II 749
Nimi (Skt) son of Ikshvāku
    rishis create his successor II 524n
Nimitta (Skt), the efficient cause I 55, 370n
Nimrod(s) (Heb)
    Akkad capital of I 319n
    Atlanteans prototypes of II 272, 279
    Chaldean giant Izdubar [Gilgamesh] II 336
    epic of Assyrian tablets II 353
    governor of Babylonia (Mas'ūdī) II 453
    not wicked giant II 375
Nine
    Aryan Hindu explanation of I 114-15 &n
    decimal system of I 361
    in Egy cat symbolism II 552 &n
    figures & zero form universe I 99
    kabbalistic symbolism II 217
    number of male generative energy I 114;
        II 217
    occult value of I 76
    sacred number of being II 622 &n
    svabhavat is 1 & nine I 98
    various symbols of II 580-1
Nineteenth Century Magazine, The
    on the Deluge II 353-4
    Gladstone in II 252n, 766-7, 770
Nineveh
    library at II 692
    Oan or fishman of I 653
    Tahmurath founded II 397
Ninth or Kumāra creation I 75, 456
Niobe (Gk), story of II 771-2 &n

Nipoor [Nippur] or Niffer (N Bab)
    center of black magic II 139n
Nippang (Chin), liberation I 38n. See also
    Moksha
Niraksha (Skt), place of no latitude II 401-2n
Nirguna (Skt) without attributes
    Parabrahman or I 62
    perfection II 95
Nirmāṇakāya(s) (Skt)
    beyond illusion, no devachan II 615
    Boehme nursling of I 494
    human forms created for II 652
    maruts one name given to II 615
    may possess mediums I 233n
    muktas who help world I 132 &n
    fr other manvantaras II 93-4
    sacrificed selves for 3rd race II 94, 201
    siddhas or II 636n
    spiritual-astral remains of II 255n
Nirmathya (Skt), & fire by friction I 521
Nirukta
    sushumnā ray lights up Moon I 515n
Nirupādhi (Skt) without attributes. See also
    Nirguna
    Purusha-prakriti in pralaya I 582
Nirvāṇa (Skt) II 204. See also Devachan, Para-
    nirvāṇa
    ākāśa &, objectively eternal I 635
    aspired to by kumāras II 243
    devachan & I 173
    dreamless sleep & I 266
    Enoch, Elijah attained II 532
    Epicurean Indolentia & I 577n
    five becomes 7 in II 580
    four paths to I 206
    individual pralaya I 371
    laya a synonym for I 140, 289 &n
    man loses self in I 570
    maruts renounce II 615
    men can reach II 246
    merging w Alaya is not I 48
    monads not reaching, fate of II 57 &n
    nirmānakāyas, elect, renounce II 281-2, 615
    no, for men without personal egos II 610
    passage of spirit to Be-ness I 193
    post-manvantaric I 373; II 491
    promised land or I 568 &n
    qualifications to enter I xix; II 81
    reached by Buddha II 532
    reached by suffering II 81
    Sabbath or I 240; II 491
    scholars misunderstand I xxi, 266
    seven paths to I 38-9
    thread of radiance dissolves in II 80

turīya samādhi or I 570
vanishing point of matter I 177
various names of I 38 &n
Nirvāṇī(s) (Skt)
    highest, start manvantara II 232
    returning II 79-80, 232
    spirits of men becoming I 240
Nishāda (Skt), element of sound I 534
Nissi, Babylonian god II 5
Nitatui [Nitatni] (Skt), a Pleiad II 551
Nīti (Skt), parent of harmony II 528
Nitrogen II 158-9, 592-3
    air element & I 253-4
    correlated w linga-śarīra II 593
    discovered by "quack" Paracelsus I 297
    Earth-born cement I 626
    noumena of II 592
    oxygen, hydrogen & I 623; II 592
    properties of II 593
    in protoplasm I 637n
Nitya (Skt) eternal, continuous I 69
Nitya Pralaya (Skt) perpetual dissolution
        II 69n
    applies to all beings II 309-10n
    in *Bhagavata-Purāna* I 371
Nitya Sarga (Skt) constant creation
        II 309-10n
Niza, Marcos de, describes 7 cities II 35
Nizir, Chaldean mountain II 145
Noachidae, Hindus perverted, II 142
Noah (Heb). *See also* Ark, Deluges, Floods,
        Manus, Vaivasvata, Xisuthrus, Yima
    Adam, Jehovah & I 444
    American, Humboldt on II 141
    Atlantean Titan II 265 &n, 390
    Bel &, preceded Adam II 144
    black raven of, symbol of pralaya I 443
    Chaldean Nuah is II 145, 463
    Chinese, or Peiru-un II 365
    Cosmas Indicopleustes on II 399
    creative law forming Earth II 595
    deluge of, late Atlantean II 69n, 774
    deluge of, not univ deluge II 4
    feared coming catastrophe II 534
    female, or Nuah, Ashtōreth II 462-3
    flood of, not Central Asian II 141
    flood of, zodiacal allegory II 353
    Hanokh gave astronomy to II 532
    heir to Enoch's wisdom II 532n
    Jah- II 595-6
    a just man II 392
    Kabir or Titan II 390
    Melchizedek or II 391
    name contains story of II 335

new man of new race I 444
offspring of, saviors & magicians II 222
one w Saturn II 142n
pithecoid, of science & 3 sons II 655
prayed before Adam's body II 467
Root- & Seed-Manu II 597
śishta, the human seed II 596
sons of, & population II 453
spirit falling into matter II 145
story explained I 444n; II 468
symbol of fifth race II 532, 597n
theogonic key to II 595
three sons &, are quaternary II 597n
three sons of, last 3 races II 397
took creatures by sevens II 35
Vaivasvata, Xisuthrus as II 222, 265, 306-7,
        309, 314, 597, 610
version of Samothracian mystery II 360n
war of gods, giants & II 222
-Xisuthrus is 3rd race separated II 397
Yima same as II 610
Nobeleth' Hokhmah [*Novelēth Hokhmāh*] (Heb)
    worlds created by delight II 126
Nod [Nōdh] (Heb) Land of (*Gen* 4:16)
    Cain goes to, & marries I 324n; II 286, 394
Node(s)
    aspects & I 320
    dragon, serpent symbol of I 403
    Moon's, in Hindu astronomy I 7, 661-3; II 76
    term used now in botany I 320
Noητός (Noētos, Gk)
    intelligible (deity) I 365, 461
Nofir-Hotpu (Egy)
    or Khonsoo, Lord of Thebes II 464
Nome, Egy city [district], gods of I 675
Nominalist(s)
    arguments re motion & God I 3n
    medieval, & occult philosophy I 274
Non-Being
    Absolute Being & I 16, 53, 54n, 88, 193
    dark mystery of I 2
    eternal, & the One Being I 45
    pure spirit lost in Absolute I 481
    state of universe when asleep I 54-5 &n
"The Non-Defined Forces." *See* Rochas
        d'Aiglun
"None has ever lifted my veil"
    Isis inscription at Saïs I 393
Nonentity
    bond connecting entity w II 176, 579
Nonnus (Gk poet), *Dionysiaca*
    Phlegyae (Atlantis), sinking of II 144
    Semelē carried to heaven I 400

Nonseparateness
　of all things, active, passive I 68
　of divine & human II 568n
　of everything fr Absolute All II 384n
　of higher self fr One Self I 276
　of man's ego fr universal ego I 130-1
Noo. *See* Nu
Noor Illahee, light of the elohīm II 514n
Noot. *See* Nūt
"Nor Aught nor Nought . . ." *See Rig-Veda*
Norberg, M. *See Codex Nazaraeus*
Nordenskiöld, Nils Adolf Erik
　on islands w fossil sheep II 773 &n
Nork, F. N. [pseud of Selig Korn]
　Ararat for Arath ['erets] Earth II 597
Norns, Norse goddesses II 520
　ravens of Odin whisper to II 100
Norse. *See also* Scandinavia
　cosmogony I 427
　giants, dwarfs in, myths II 754
　gods of the II 283n, 754
　legends II 97, 100, 283n
　mundane tree I 211
　mythology on axial changes II 535
　mythology on man II 97, 754
　prophecy about 7th root-race II 100
　three, goddesses II 100
North (direction)
　ankh cross & II 547
　evil comes fr, & West I 123
　gods, myths fr II 774n
　Kuvera (Kubera) guards the I 128
　Sabean worship & II 362
　Toum is, wind & spirit of West I 673
　we curse the, wind (Ambrose) I 123
　yellow corn depicts, (Zuñis) II 629
North America
　colossal ruins in II 337-8
　egg symbol in I 366
　mystery language of I 308
　rocking stones in II 342n
North Pole. *See also* Aurora Borealis
　cap of, will never perish II 372n, 401, 403
　Capricorn once at II 431
　ever green continent at II 12
　fohatic forces at I 204-5
　fountain of life at II 400n
　heaven, mountain or II 357
　heaven of Lemurians' progenitors II 274
　Hyperborean continent & II 7, 274
　legends re, continent II 138n, 398-9, 400n,
　　401
　passing of, to South Pole II 360
　pole of ecliptic & II 431

　region of, & Meru II 326-9, 357, 403, 785
　separated fr continents II 138n
　serpent in *Vendidad* II 356
　source of good influences II 400n
　Sun dies for 6 months at II 769n
　upper station of gods II 404
Norway, Norwegians
　ancient records of, (runes) II 346n
　discovered America I 297; II 424n
　& Greeks on Hyperborean continent
　　II 11-12
　has risen 200-600 ft II 787n
　lemmings of II 782
　part of early northern continent II 423-4
　part of Lemuria, Atlantis II 402, 775
　severed part of Arctic land II 399n
　sinking of Lemuria began in II 332-3
"Norwegian Lemming . . ." *See* Crotch, W.
Norwich, Mackey adept of II 362n
Notes, 7 of the scale I 534; II 492, 602. *See also*
　Keynotes
Notes and Observations . . . See Gregorie, J.
"Notes on Aristotle's Psychology . . ." *See* Rigg
Notes on the Bhagavad Gītā. See Subba Row
No-Thing
　Ain-Sōph or Absolute, endless I 214
　Dābār & I 350
　God is I 352
　symbol of circle & II 553
"Nothing can come from nothing." *See*
　Lucretius
"Nothing is created, only transformed" I 570
Nothingness, Abyss of, is divine Plenum I 148
"Notice on Buddhist Symbols." *See* Hodgson
"Not Ready," expl II 161, 167, 168, 171
Notre Dame de Paris
　dragon on portal of II 207 &n
　planets, elements, zodiac & I 395
Nott, J. C., & Gliddon, G. R.
—— *Types of Mankind*
　Agassiz' Intro re polygenism II 610-11
Nought (zero). *See also* Circle, Zero
　or circle, plane above number II 574
　no-thing or infinite & all II 553
Noum. *See* Khnoom
Noumenon(a, oi, al)
　ākāśa the, of ether I 255
　consciousness is pure, of thought I 14-15
　of electricity I 531
　of the elements I 218n, 522; II 273
　of every force intelligent I 493
　First world realm of I 119
　Fohat as, of cosmic substance I 148
　of the four elements II 592

of hydrogen II 105, 112
invisible powers as II 517-18
known to initiates I 535n
of matter, atoms I 57
mūlaprakriti, of prakriti II 65
nature's imponderable forces II 273
phenomenon & I 38, 45
Self, of personal ego I 129
spiritual fire & II 113
substance the, of matter I 329
tanmātras, of elements I 572n
of the "Three in One" II 113
unmanifested or II 24
Noun (Egy). *See* Nūt
Nous (Gk, Gnos) spiritual mind
angle of Gnostic square II 573
in close affinity w Good II 25
created by Abraxas I 350
dominates after 3½ races II 110
enters matter & agitates it I 451 &n
higher, divine wisdom I 197n
matter-moving, pervades all I 51-2
mundane intelligence (Anaxagoras) I 50, 451
Plato on II 554
Propator & I 349
Psyche & I 197n; II 134n, 377
Pymander as I 74
quaternary & II 599
Nouter, Nouti [Nutar, Neter] (Egy) a god
generic name never personal I 675
Nouvelle Recherches . . . See Lartet, É.
Novalis [pseud for F. von Hardenberg]
on man's body as a temple I 212
Novaya Zemlya, & glacial sea II 398
Nu (Egy) I 353, 437. *See also* Nūt
Nuah
Chaldean Noah II 145
female Noah or Ashtōreth II 462-3
Nubia, Aryans reached Egypt thru II 746
Nucleole(s)
part of Absolute II 33
of superior world I 213
Nucleus, Nuclei
astral form &, of cell II 117
central, of snow crystals II 594
of cosmic matter in space I 203-4, 609
of future man II 188
periodical & finite II 33
spheroidal, & 3rd race egg II 166
Sun, of Mother Substance I 290, 540
Nuctemeron. See Apollonius of Tyana
Nuctemeron of the Hebrews, 12 hours in I 450
Numa. See Plutarch, *Lives*

Numa Pompilius (2nd Roman king)
circular religious prostration & II 552
Number(s). *See also* Decad, Duad, Four, One,
Sacred Numbers, Seven, Three
Arab, fr Hindustan I 361
basis of Pythagoreanism I 433-4
celestial, of China II 35
of creation II 39
five II 575-6
four a sacred number I 88-9 &n
432 & 4320 disc I 655-6; II 73-4, 624
geometrical symbols of II 36
geometric relations & I 639
God is a, endowed w motion I 67
harmony of, in nature II 622
of the hierarchies I 119, 213, 221
how circle becomes a I 99
identical, in Egypt, America, etc I 323
IO first decimal II 463
is an entity (Balzac) I 66-7
Jevons explains thru I 430n
Jewish Deity II 539, 543
Kabbala & II 39-41, 539, 560
key to esoteric system I 164
language older than Egyptian I 322
limited, of monads I 171
mystical, & Masonry I 113n
no, a circle II 574
odd & even, discussed II 574-6, 602
One, & No-Number I 86, 87-8, 94, 98
1065 explained I 89-90
phallic w Jews II 463, 467-8
Proclus & self-moving II 552
Pythagorean, symbolic I 361, 433-4, 460
relation betw gods & II 575
reveal intelligent plan in cosmos II 73-4
sacred, in scriptures I 66-7, 89-91; II 551-3,
580
secrecy re I 170
seven a compound of II 582-4, 598
significance of II 574-6
the 10, in double triangle II 592
31415 discussed I 88-92
unequal, please gods (Virgil) II 602
universe built on I 88-92, 98-9
Word, Logos begets I 67n
Number of Creation, in Book of Al-Chazari
II 40. *See also* Ha-Levi
Numbers (Bible)
Anakīm (giants) II 336
brazen, fiery serpents I 364 &nn, 414;
II 206n, 387n
crucifying against the Sun II 558
seventy elders or planets I 576

Numerals. *See also* Numbers
 Chinese cosmogony & occult I 440-1
 Hebrew I 320
 origin of decimal I 361, 427
 science of I 89-92
 two kinds of I 66
Numerical
 ancient, mysteries II 564
 Book of Dzyan, values in I 434
 cosmogony &, facts I 170, 206
 Hebrew, system fr Phoenicia II 560
 interpretation of *Genesis* I 264
 Patriarchs as, symbols II 391
 sexual separation &, values I 114n
 system of universe I 119
 values of biblical names II 536
 values of var beings I 89-91, 90n, 114, 131, 213
Nun (Chaldee)
 Joshua son of, or Fish I 264
 'nun-ah Sabah or I 394
Nuntis [Nuntium] (Lat), or Mercury II 28
Nuraghi[e], prehistoric Sardinian buildings of
  Atlantean origin II 352
Nursery

of conscious, spiritual souls I 218, 573
 for future human adepts I 207
Nursling of Nirmānakāyas (Boehme) I 494
Nūt, Noot, Noun, Nout, Nu (Egy)
 celestial river, Deep, chaos I 312
 defunct crosses, to Tiaou I 228
 expanse of heaven I 229
 Nu &, cosmic duad I 353, 437
 Tum or Fohat born of I 673 &n
Nutation (oscillation of axis)
 climate &, (Croll) II 314
Nutrition, of foetus II 131
Nux. *See* Nyx
Nyam-Nyam (African pigmies)
 once a mighty race II 445
 side by side w "giants" II 754
Nyāya (Skt) school of philosophy
 atoms of the I 335
 nimitta & upādāna defined in I 55, 370n
Nying-po (Tib), Alaya or I 48
Nympaea Lutea (yellow water-lily) II 440
Nymphs II 175, 519, 614. *See also* Apsarasas
Nyx (Gk, Nox in Lat)
 Erebos &, give birth to light I 110

O

Oannes (Chald) biblical Dāgōn II 139n
  described by Sayce II 226
  Ea (wisdom) prototype of II 503
  leaves waters to teach wisdom II 495n
  man-fish I 264, 345, 394, 654; II 54, 139n
  taught Babylonian writing II 226
  taught early man I 345; II 190
  Triton much like II 578
  world created out of water I 345
Oannes-Dāgōn (Chald)
  Demiurge II 5
  seven divine dynasties & II 366
Oasis I xxxii
  Gobi, remnant of inland sea II 220, 502-3
Ob (Heb), evil fluid of sorcerers I 76n
Ob, or Aub (Heb), serpent or circle I 364n
Obelisk(s)
  in America II 430
  Christians destroyed I xli
  Herodotus on, at Saïs II 395-6
  symbolize 4 cardinal pts I 125
Object, subject, sense, etc I 329-30
Objectivization of Forms I 282
Obliquity, of ecliptic II 408, 726
[O'Brien, H.], *The Round Towers of Ireland*
  "Budh" signifies male organ I 472
Obscuration II 703. *See also* Pralaya
  absolute, or ātyantika pralaya II 309-10n
  described I 172n; II 660n
  Mars, Mercury & I 165
  one hemisphere awoke fr II 309
  pralaya also applies to II 307n
  betw rounds I 159, 161; II 47, 704-5, 713n
  of spirit in evolutionary cycles II 732
  temporary II 705n
  betw 3rd & 4th rounds I 182
Observations of Bel, The (Chald astron work)
  dates Babylonia 4700 BC II 693
Observatory, The
  star changing into a nebula I 596
Occult. *See also* Esoteric
  anthropology & human eye II 295
  arts & sorcery I xl
  chemistry approaching the I 544
  cosmogenesis, number symbol of I 321
  doctrine based on 7 sciences II 335

doctrine on races guarded II 693
  doctrine synthesis of 6 Indian schools I 269
  forces in nature I 672
  inertia greatest, force I 511
  interpretation II 112n
  Keely's, ideas on color & sound I 564-5
  knowledge & lunar mysteries I 228n
  law concerning silence I 95
  law of dynamics I 644
  laws & phenomena I 488n
  metaphysics II 116
  mysteries seldom divulged I 558; II 124
  mysticism II 33
  philosophy & modern science I 586
  powers in nature II 74
  scientific imagination approaching II 137n
  symbolism II 335
  teachings confirmed by science I 624
  theories key to embryology I 223
  training & spiritual perception II 288
  treatises on 7 manus II 308
  version of *Vishnu Purāna* II 58-9
  virtues of number seven II 312n
Occult Ages, 30 crores or three 300 million-
  year cycles II 52n
Occult Catechism. *See* Catechism
Occult Fraternity. *See also* Adepts, Brotherhood (The), Esoteric School, Initiates,
  Masters, Occultism, Teachers
  secret libraries of I xxxiv
Occultism II 68n, 77, 117, 119. *See also* Esoteric,
  Esotericism, Secret Doctrine
  on ākāśa I 487, 536-7
  all matter is living I 280-1
  astral shadows teaching of II 46
  atoms called vibrations in I 633
  atoms not uniform I 512-13
  attraction, repulsion & I 497, 504, 604
  believes in divine dynasties II 194
  Cis-Himalayan II 48, 602
  condemns phallicism II 85
  contains all 7 keys I 318
  Darwinist theories not held by I 186
  differs fr materialism & theology II 449
  discerns life in every atom I 225n, 248-9,
    258, 260-1

divulged every century I xxxvii-viiin
does not accept "inorganic" I 248-9
does not deny mech orig of univ I 594
Eastern II 85
Eastern student of II 47
egg symbol in I 65
electricity an entity in Eastern I 76
on evolution I 186; II 259, 261-3, 657
Father-Mother one w ākāśa in I 75-6
force & motion I 512-13
infinite divisibility of atoms I 519-20, 605
on invisible worlds & beings I 604-8
jars nerves of some people II 650
Jews knew little about divine I 230
many substances, names in I 510
matter in I 487, 489, 514
mechanicians behind elements I 594
more logical than science I 154
motion law of I 97
Nārada deva-rishi of II 48, 82-3
natural selection not enough II 696
never separates force & matter I 512, 633-4
no above or below in I 605, 671-2
nothing is created I 570
nothing is outside nature II 194
on the one element I 549
origin of life-essence in Sun I 540-1
orthodoxy views, as work of devil II 795
our, is of Central Asia II 565
pantheistic I 317, 569
persecuted by Roman Church I xliv
practical, & geometric figures I 430
practical, & phenomena I 82 &n
pre-Christian mystics practiced I xl
public views, as superstition II 795
repudiates special creation II 157
Rig-Veda corroborates II 606
science &, discussed I 477-81
science drawn into maelstrom of I 124
science must compromise w I 496
SD written for students of I 23
secret books of II 51
self-defense of II 649
senses develop fr within outward II 295
seven is scale of nature I 656n
sorcery, Christianity & I xl
soul of science I 634
space oldest dogma of I 9-10n
spontaneous generation II 718-19
substantial nature of light I 483-4 &n
on the Sun I 530-2, 540-1
supported by universal tradition II 194
three "First-born" & hydrogen, oxygen,
 nitrogen I 623

three kinds of light in II 37-8
three standpoints of II 335
time will vindicate II 718
unity of ultimate essence I 120
universal unity 1st dogma of I 58
why secrets of, are guarded I 558
Occultist(s) II 11, 38, 46, 92
accused of devil worship II 370n
agree w Vedāntins on pantheism I 8
arraigned by public opinion I 298
astral light & II 409
author of nature is nature I 489n
believe in cosmic entities I 106
Bible wisdom grasped by I 316
Brahman & II 72
Christian theology & II 70
deals w cosmic soul, spirit I 589
defend ancient gods fr slander II 354
disregard scorn of science II 725
dugpaship & II 221n
Eastern, & kabbalists I 230, 234n, 243-5, 374
Eastern, objective idealist I 615
endow creation w mental life I 627
on esoteric philosophy II 3
in every age I 484
on evolution & involution II 294
expound ancient traditions I 287
feel & see spirits II 370
force resides in the atom I 511-13
God no-being, no-thing I 352
have no quarrel w facts of science I 636-7
have right to present views I 600
Indo-Aryan II 8
inorganic strange word to I 340; II 672
intelligent law pointed to by I 139
Keely an unconscious I 557
light of spirit & matter to I 481
magic feats of II 179
matter of I 515
medieval I xliiin
myths have meaning for II 138-9
opposes dead-letter interpretation II 202
Paracelsus an I 263
perceive "creators" II 158
physical nature illusory to II 475
properties of Moon known to I 156
prophecies of I 646-7
recap of embryo known to II 187
reject gravity of science I 604
revelation is fr finite beings I 9-10
scientists & I 483
sees in every force its noumenon I 493
seven modes of interpretation I 374
spirit & ātman I 226n

study septenate of matter II 592
Sun vehicle of a god I 479
take nothing on trust I 669
theologists vs, re fallen angels II 228
trace cycles merging into cycles II 189
trace man thru vegetable II 187n
on transcendental reality I 281-2
two European, & AIR I 260
unity of life basic law of I 120
Vedāntins differ fr I 17n, 62
verified causes & effects I 509
war in *Mahābhārata* real to I 397
will be thought ignoramuses I 479
Occult Philosophy. *See also* Esoteric Philosophy
 could learn fr science I 586
 divulges but few mysteries I 558
 noumenal essences more real in I 274
 science & I 586
 & word creation I 446
Occult Science(s) II 322n, 335
 adepts masters of II 280n
 blending of, w modern science I 520-1
 brought fr higher planes I 516
 claim less, give more II 9
 consistent, logical II 348
 forgotten, perverted II 124
 key to world problems I 341
 knows true nature of matter I 516
 monads & I 632
 ridiculed at present I 298
 source of all religion & philos II 794-5
Occult Solvent, union of 3 elements II 113
Occult World. See Sinnett, A. P.
Ocean(s). *See also* Chaos
 aether the celestial I 75
 of carbonic acid I 253n
 cede place to continents II 703
 chaos in its masculine aspect I 345n
 churning of, & amrita I 348; II 381
 condensation of, in Laurentian II 159
 displacement of, & pole change II 360
 floors, breaking asunder of II 314
 gaped wide to swallow Atlantis II 494
 giants buried under II 277
 gods fashion chaos into seven II 704n
 of the infinite I 436
 of life I 66-8
 of matter I 84, 97, 178
 periodic shifting of II 325-6
 primitive, or chaos I 348
 seven, or samudras I 348
 of space & Nārāyana I 458n
 of space & pralaya I 371-3

spirit in chaos or, as SPACE II 65
universal, geology records II 715n
violently displaced II 703
washed base of Himalayas once II 572
Wisdom-, Dalai Lama's name II 502n
Oceanic Tribes
 some, "were not ready" II 162
"Ocean of Milk,"
 churning of, in satya-yuga I 67-8; II 403
Oceanus(os)
 daughters of II 413
 father of the gods II 65
 one of seven Arkite Titans II 143
[Ochorowicz, Julian]
—— *De la Suggestion mentale . . .*
 G. Richet on science I 640 &n
Octaves, in music, color, elements II 628
Od(ic)
 aspect of all-pervading Archaeus I 338n
 light, brightness (Tib) I 76n
 magnetic or, chord I 555
 of Reichenbach I 338n
 vital fluid I 76n
Odd Eye II 299, 301. *See also* Pineal Gland,
 Third Eye
Odd Numbers, divine (Pythagoras) II 574
Odin, Woden (Norse)
 before Homer, Veda (Müller) I xxix-xxx
 black ravens of I 443; II 100
 endows man w life, soul II 97
 father of gods, Ases I 427
 Loki brother of II 283n
 one of the 35 buddhas II 423-4
 pledged eye to Mimir for knowledge I 402
 spirit or, son of Bestla I 427
Odor I 565, 566n
 sound &, real substance I 564
Odyssey. See Homer
Oeaohoo I 71-2
 equated w Gnostic Ophis I 73n
 Hebrew 9th letter teth or I 76
 Oi-Ha-Hou permutation of I 93
 pictured as serpent (Fohat) I 76
 septenary root of all things I 68
Oedipus, legend & Christian God II 540
Oedipus Aegyptiacus. See Kircher, A.
Oelicius (Lat)
 Elicius or Jupiter Fulgur I 467
Oeloim, Les. See Lacour, P.
Oeon. *See* Aeon
Oersted [Ørsted], Hans Christian
 believed in spiritual world I 589
 force "Spirit in Nature" I 484
Og, King, biblical giant II 336

Ogdoad II 580
  eight sons of Aditi are I 72n
  Gnostic Sophia mother of I 72n
  seven (stars) later became II 358n
  Śukra's car drawn by, of horses II 31
Ogdoas (Gnos), mother of Iaō I 448
Ogygia, Calypso's Isle, Atlantis II 769n
Ohio, serpent mound in II 752-3
Oi-Ha-Hou (whirlwind)
  force behind eternal motion I 93 &n
Oitzoé. See Atizoë
Oken, L., urschleim of II 158
Okhee Math, cave near I xxx
Ōlām, Oulom (Heb), Ulom (Phoen)
  born fr ether, air I 461
  born fr mundane egg I 365
  highest Aeon or time II 490
  meaning of term I 336n, 354 &n
  visible, material universe I 365, 461
Olaus Magnus. See Magnus, Olaus
Olcott, Henry Steel
  held electricity is matter I 111n
  taught by 3 teachers I xix
  transl Posthumous Humanity II 149n
  —— A Buddhist Catechism
  on personal God I 635-6
Old Testament. See also Bible, Exodus,
    Genesis, New Testament
  abyss betw New & I 382n
  allegory in II 426
  borrowed fr Chaldeans I xxxi
  chronology of, altered (Whiston) II 395n
  connects each event w birth II 544
  contradictions in I 414
  crucifixion in II 561
  dates fr Babylonian captivity II 473
  eternity not infinite in I 336n
  full of references to zodiacal signs I 649
  God creates light in II 37
  Ieve (Ya-Va) in II 129
  names of God in II 129
  not borrowed fr Hindus I xxxi
  numerous changes in II 473
  old Chaldean & Hindu records & I xxxi
  Pentateuch of II 544
  phallicism in, & NT I 318
  Satan of I 416, 442n
  teaches plurality of worlds I 607n
Old World
  New World man senior to II 446
Oliphant, Laurence
  on churchianity I 479
  —— Scientific Religion
  q by Moore on future I 560-1

Olive Branch (Noah's) I 444
Oliver, Professor
  —— "The Atlantis Hypothesis . . ."
  q by Prof Pengelly II 322n, 727
  —— Lecture at the Royal Institution
  q by Lyell II 783
Oliver, Reverend George
  —— The Pythagorean Triangle
  anthropomorphic 4-letter gods II 601-2
  diapason II 601
  heptad regarded as virgin II 602
  hierogram I 613-14
  monochord, tetrachord II 600
  Pythagorean numbers, geometry I 616-17;
    II 599-602
  q Greek poet II 603
  seven principles of man II 640-1
  tetrad II 599, 601
  T.G.A.O.T.U. I 613
  three, 5, 7 in Masonry I 113n
Olla (Indian, palm leaf for writing) I 305
Olympus
  Castor, Pollux share in II 123
  Eden & II 203
  gods of, septiform II 765-72
  Hindu II 45n
  Mt Meru, Kaph or II 362, 404
Om, Am, deity in many languages II 43
Om, Aum
  fourth world (race) lost II 408
  pranava or, mystic term in yoga I 432n
Omar, Kaliph, general of, destroyed Alexan-
    drian Library II 692
Omens, & "mirror of futurity" II 49 &n
O-mi-to-fo [A-mi-ta-fo, Amita Fo] (Chin)
  name of Amitābha II 179
"Omnis enim . . ." I 7n. See also Lucretius
Omoie [Tetszunotszuke or Capt Pfoundes]
  —— ["Cultus of the Far East" in Theos.]
  Shinto cosmogony I 214, 216-17, 241
Omorka, Omoroca (Chald)
  Moon-goddess II 115, 135
Oɴ, Tò oɴ (Gk) the One II 105, 113
On Amos. See Ambrose
On Rosenkranz. See Fludd, Robert
On the Cherubim. See Philo Judaeus
"On the Conservation of Solar Energy." See
  Siemens, C. W.
"On the Naulette Jaw." See Blake, Dr C. C.
"On the Philosophy of Mythology." See
  Müller, F. M., Chips . . .
"On the Physical Basis of Life." See Huxley,
  T. H.

"On the Transformation of Gravity." *See*
  Croll, J.
"On Yeast." *See* Huxley, T. H.
One, the. *See also* All, Boundless, Space, That
  the All or I 20, 21
  becomes the many (elohīm) I 113
  becomes 2, then three I 109, 206, 231
  "circle of Heaven" I 426
  does not create I 425
  eka, saka, or I 73
  endless, boundless circle I 239
  everything originates in I 568
  first differentiation of I 277
  Great Breath or II 23
  Greek Tò oΝ or II 105, 113
  higher than the Four II 282
  man's divine ray & I 222
  the many & I 113, 129, 349, 429; II 732
  mistakenly applied to Jehovah I 129-30
  not eternal save in essence I 94
  not spirit or matter I 258; II 598
  occult catechism on I 11
  one-, 3- & 7-voweled terms for I 20
  Parabrahman-mūlaprakriti I 18, 69
  point in circle, triangle I 426
  reflection of, differentiates I 277
  sexless I 18
  triangle the 1st, cube the 2nd I 131
  unbroken circle or I 11
  Unity or Universal Life II 672
  unknowable causality I 139
  various authors on I 425-6
  various equivalents of I 129
One (number)
  aleph, bull, ox or II 574
  becomes 2, 3, 4 II 621
  born fr spirit I 90n
  circle becomes II 621
  first manifested principle II 599
  monad or, (Pythagoras) I 440-1
  nine &, discussed I 98 &n
  Spirit of Life I 94
  triad, Tetraktys, decad fr I 440-1
Onech (Heb) Phoenix
  fr Phenoch or Enoch II 617
Oneness, One
  Ain-sōph becomes I 113
  alhim-ness or II 40
  alone is Good (Pythagoras) II 575
  sense of, of early races I 210
Onkalos [Onkelos]. *See Targum of Onkelos*
Ono-koro [Onogoro]
  Shinto island world I 217
Ontogeny, development of embryo II 659

Ontology(ical)
  metaphysics & modern physics I 544
  science & speculative I 150
Oolite, Oolitic
  Araucaria of, almost unchanged II 257
  Australian plants & Eng, fossils II 196
  variety of, fossils II 258
Operations . . . at the Pyramids . . . See Vyse
Op et D (*Works & Days*). *See* Hesiod
Ophanim [Ōphannīm] (Heb)
  assist Creator I 440
  forces, dhyāni-chohans I 337
  informing souls of spheres I 117
  wheels or world spheres I 92
Ophidia (order of snakes) II 205
Ophio-Christos (Gnos)
  Alexandrian wisdom-serpent I 364
  so named before Fall I 413
Ophiomorphos (Gnos)
  created by Jehovah II 389
  Demiurge's reflection created II 243
  Ialdabaōth & II 244, 481
  Michael identified w I 459; II 481
  Ophis & I 413-14, 459
  rebellious opposing spirit I 459
  Satan or, (King) II 244
  serpent, Satan, evil II 389
  waters of the Flood or I 460
Ophiomorphos Chrēstos (Gnos)
  so named after Fall I 413
Ophis (Gnos)
  divine wisdom or Christos I 459
  Ennoia &, are Logos II 214
  forbidden fruit & II 215
  Ophiomorphos & I 413-14, 459
  serpent as, taught mankind II 215
  shadow of the light II 214
  Tree of Knowledge II 215
  triple symbolism of I 73n
  waters of the Flood or I 460
Ophite(s) (Gnos sect)
  Adamas, primeval man II 458
  Agathodaemon, Ophis, logoi of II 214
  angels, planets, elements II 115n
  called serpent Creator II 209
  cherubim & Hindu serpents I 127
  Chnouphis serpent of II 210
  Christian &, four faces I 127n
  Christ, serpent, resurrection w I 472
  dual Logos, serpent of I 410
  honored serpent I 404
  IAO on gems of II 541
  Jehovah son of Saturn w I 577
  Michael Ophiomorphos of I 459; II 481

precursors of Roman Church I 459
religion, Bel & dragon in II 379
reverenced serpent as wisdom II 386-7
rites fr Hermes Trismegistus II 379
several kinds of genii of I 403-4
true & perfect serpent of I 410
Ophites (serpent stones), described II 341-2
Opifex (Lat), Maker I 465
Opificio Mundi, De. See Philo Judaeus
Opticks. See Newton, Isaac
Optic Thalami, developed in mammalian
brain II 297-8, 301
Ŏr, Aior, Aour, Aur (Heb) light I 76 &n, 214,
354
Oracle(s)
Chaldean I 235, 462
at Delphi I 466
of Mercury II 542
Sibylline II 454
Simorgh & Persian II 617-18
stone II 342n, 346-7
teráphím & I 394
Oracles of Zoroaster. See Chaldean Oracles
Orai. *See* Horaeus
Orang-outang, Orangutan
"creation" of II 678
evolved fr lower anthropoids II 193
fr 4th race man & extinct mammal II 683
has human spark II 193, 260, 263, 666n
Orbit(s)
eccentricity of Earth's, caused deluge
II 144-5
planetary I 498, 503, 593, 602
retrograde, of satellites I 149n
Orcus (Lat) Pluto or nether worlds
Bahak-Zivo & I 194
living fire of, & elements I 543
souls evoked fr, by Mercury II 28
Orders. *See also* Hierarchies
of angelic hierarchy I 129
degrees or, of spiritual beings I 233-5
four, gods, demons, pitris, men I 457-8n
seven, of celestial beings I 213-22
Ordinances of Manu. See Laws of Manu
Orestes. *See* Euripides
Organ (instrument)
blind forces never built II 348
Organ(s)
atrophied II 119
cells blindly form, (Haeckel) II 648
rudimentary human II 681, 683
sense-, originate fr elements I 284-5
Organ, Mrs Margaret Stephenson
every force & subst correlated I 566 &n

Organic
all matter is, or alive I 280-1
inorganic & I 249n, 626n
Organisms
adapt to reigning elements I 257
Herschel saw, on Sun I 530
multiply beyond subsistence II 648
Örgelmir (Norse)
giant Ymir or, fr 1st creation I 427
primordial matter fr chaos I 427
Orgueil (town in S France)
meteorite w turf & water II 706
Oriental(s), effects of isolation upon II 425
Oriental Collection
bird-steed Simorgh-Anke II 397-8
Simorgh & Earth cycles II 617
Orientalist(s)
Aryan wisdom dead letter to II 449
believe Yima was 1st man in *Vendidad* II 270n
call invocations superstition I 521
call the Brotherhood "mythical" II 636-7
caught in theological groove II 60
Christian, & Vedantic atheism I 6-7 &n
complete Veda text of, doubtful I xxiiin
confused II 320-1, 451, 528, 570, 577
cycles in Purānas unknown to II 70
deny what does not dovetail I xxxii
differ on Vedas I xxx
disfigured Purānas I 115n
disfigure mystic sense of Skt tx I 453n
dwarf Hindu dates II 76n
Hindu chronology fiction to II 73, 551
Hindu chronology vs II 225
Hindu zodiac fr Greece I 647; II 332
ignorant of esotericism I xxi-ii; II 225
ignorant of Indian origin of Gnos II 570
re immorality of ancient pantheons II 764
lack of intuition among II 565n
like white ants I 676
misinterpret allegories I 310
misinterpret *Avesta* II 757-9
misinterpret pāśa or ankh-tie II 548
misled re anupadaka [aupapāduka] I 52n
mistake cycles for persons I 570
misunderstood *Anugītā* passage II 638
no Hindu cycle ever unriddled by I 370
not one, sees beyond contradictions II 147
no, understand genealogies II 248
prejudice great in hearts of I 420, 647
Purānas Brahmanical fancy to II 585
Purānic creations confuse I 55, 453n
Purānic story, Bible & I xxxi &n, 80
on Purānic symbols II 322
read sex into ancient rel I xxii; II 588

reject what they cannot verify I xxxvii
sevenfold divisions led, astray II 608
take everything literally II 322
think they know more II 569
translation of, untrustworthy I 162, 457-8
&nn
Vedic world divisions & II 622
why, misunderstood Purānas II 320, 585
Origen
ex-initiate I xliv; II 559
held *Book of Enoch* in high esteem II 535
knew Moon was Jehovah's symbol I 387
understood cruciform couches II 559
—— *Contra Celsum*
Gnostic chart I 448, 577
septenary theogony of Celsus I 445-6
seven rectors (*Gnos*) I 577; II 538 &n
—— *De principiis*
Bible & Kabbala veiled, secret II 536
Original Sanskrit Texts. See Muir, J.
Original Sin. *See also* Sin
Adam, Eve, serpent & II 699
animals & II 513-14
Congreve re II 304
Fall left no, on humanity II 261
God tempts, curses man w I 383; II 387
idolatry fr, (Bossuet) II 279
origin of dogma of II 215-16
problematical consolation of II 484
there never was an II 413
Orig. & Sig. of Gt. Pyramid. See Wake, C. S.
Origine des cultes. See Dupuis, C. F.
Origines de la terre, . . . See Fabre, Abbé
Origines gentium antiq. See Cumberland, R.
Origin of Nations. See Rawlinson, G.
Origin of Species, On The. See Darwin, C.
Origin of the Stars. See Ennis, J.
Origins of Christianity. See Renan, J. E.
Orion (Gk) hunter slain by Artemis
Atlas or, supports world II 277
Briareus & II 70
giant, son of Ephialtes II 278
Orion (constellation)
mentioned in *Job* I 647-8
nebula in, resolvable I 598n
Orissa, Nīla Mt range in II 403n
Örlog (Norse) karma or fate
Norns make known decrees of II 520
Ormazd, or Ahura Mazdā (Zor). *See also* Ahura
Mazdā, Zoroastrian
Ahriman destroys bull created by II 93
Ahriman twin of evil I 412; II 283n, 420
birth of II 488
commands Yima to build ark II 291

Desatir on II 268
father of our Earth II 385
firstborn Logos I 113n, 429
head of 7 Amesha Spentas I 127-8; II 608
instructs Yima to make man II 291
issues fr circle of time I 113-14
Logos, "King of Life" II 488
mystical tree of II 385, 517
Osiris as chief Amshaspend I 436-7
as Sun-god II 44
synthesis of Amshaspends II 358, 365n
synthesis of builders I 436-7
uncreated & created lights II 291
Ormazd et Ahriman. See Darmesteter, J.
Ornithology
realm of, & septenary cycle II 623n
Ornithorhynchus of Australia II 206n
Ornithoscelidae, betw reptile & bird II 183
Orpheus II 777n
aether & chaos of I 426
born fr Wondrous Being I 207
chaos of I 426
generic name II 267-8n, 364
Grecian Enoch II 529
never lived (critics) I 648
Noah linked by Faber, etc w II 364
seven-stringed lyre of II 529
sources of wisdom of II 530-1
on talking stones II 341-2
taught man zoömancy I 362-3
theogony of I 19, 343, 359, 395, 426, 452n,
582-3; II 70, 143, 658
Orphic(s)
Druid &, priests II 756
Egg described by Aristophanes I 359-60
poems & zodiacal signs I 648
Protologos II 107
theogony Hindu in spirit I 336n; II 658
Titan Ephialtes II 70
triad & Creation I 452n, 582-3
Trimorphos of I 395
Orphic Hymns II 143
Arkite Titans in II 143
authenticity of II 506
destruction, renovation of Earth II 784-5
Dionysos as creator (Gk tx) I 335
Eros-Phanēs & divine egg I 365, 461
esotericism in II 785
Saturnine Sea II 777n
Zeus male, female II 134-5
zodiacal signs in I 648
Orsi, four-letter Magian god II 602
Orthodoxie Maçonnique. See Ragon, J. B. M.
Osch. *See* Ush

Osericta, "island of divine kings" II 773
Oshoi [Oshaiah or Hoshiah] Rabbah,
    thaumaturgist I xliiin
Osirified, Osirification
    of the defunct I 228, 365
    defunct, in *Bk of Dead* I 219-20
    Khem & I 220-1
    soul becomes, after 3,000 cycles I 135
Osiris (Egy)
    Aanru domain of I 674n
    as aether I 340; II 130
    fr aish, asr, fire-enchanter II 114
    born fr an egg I 366
    cat termed "eye" of II 552n
    confers justice in Amenti I 312
    cosmic war betw Typhon & I 202
    degraded by sexual mysteries II 471
    Dionysos, Krishna, Buddha or II 420
    double crocodile II 580n
    elder son of Sib [Keb] I 437
    Fohat corresponds to I 673
    Garuda pictured as II 565
    god of life, reproduction I 228
    god "whose name is unknown" I 75n
    hawk symbol of I 362
    head of 7 Egyptian builders I 127
    heptad sacred to II 602
    Horus born fr Isis & II 472
    Horus brother, son of I 348
    Horus is I 430
    inhabits the Moon I 228
    interchangeable w Isis I 72n
    Isis daughter, mother of I 430
    Isis daughter, wife & sister of I 137
    Isis-Latona wife of I 340-1
    judgment before, after death I 228
    lotus symbol w Horus & I 379n
    Michael counselor of II 481
    Moon eye of Horus & I 388
    not Menes II 374n
    reappears as Thoth-Hermes II 359
    Set or Typhon murders II 385-6
    seven rays, solar boat, ark & II 141
    son, father, husband I 396
    soul accused before, & Lipika I 104-5
    Sun as eye of II 25
    as Sun-god I 387, 390; II 44
    Sun personifies, in trinity II 462
    symb fire, solar year, Nile I 390; II 583
    synthesis of builders I 436-7
    Taurus connected w I 656
    Thoth &, initiate candidate II 558-9
    Typhon & II 379-80
    Typhon brother of II 283n

Typhon cuts, into pieces II 93
    various names of I 105, 110, 429, 436-7;
        II 379, 704n
Osiris-Isis, Tetragrammaton II 601
Osiris-Lunus
    occult potencies of Moon I 396
    various refs describing I 228
Osiris-Ptah, creates own limbs I 231
Osiris-Sun, hawk dual symbol of I 365
Osiris-Sut, man in the Moon I 393
Osiris-Typhon, twins of good & evil I 412
Osraios. *See* Horaios
Ossa, Mt (in Greece), giants & II 754
Os sacrum (Lat), holy bone II 329
Ostervald, Jean Frédéric
    misleading Bible transl II 537
Otizoé. *See* Atizoe
Otz. *See* Ētz
Oulom. *See* Ōlām
Ouranos, Uranos. *See also* Uranus (planet)
    creative powers of chaos II 269
    fell into generation II 268-9 &n
    first king of Atlanteans II 762
    Kronos & II 270
    mutilation of I 418; II 268, 283n, 766
    ruled over 2nd Race II 765
    Sun used as symbol of I 99-100n
    symbology of II 268-71
    taught astronomy II 765-6
    Varuna or II 65, 268n
D'Ourches, Count
    persecuted by de Mirville II 476n
Outlines of Cosmic Philosophy. See Fiske, J.
Oversoul
    brooding over the Earth I 375
    Emerson's, not world soul I 140
    Emerson's, or Alaya I 48
    identity of all souls w I 17
    universal 6th principle I 17
Ovid, *Fasti*
    Castor & Pollux II 122 &n
    Mars born of mother alone II 550
—— *Metamorphoses*
    "creature of a more exalted kind" I 211
    Deucalion, Pyrrha escape deluge II 270
    Diana escapes Typhon I 387-8
    Niobe granddaughter of Atlas II 772
    Prometheus, Athena & new race II 519
Oviparous (egg-laying) II 735
    corroborations of, races II 132-3
    humanity was II 131, 181, 659
    third race was II 132, 165-6
Ovoviviparous, hatch eggs in body II 166
Ovule, of women is an egg II 166

Ovum
  analogy of, & 2nd race II 117
  assumes carrot, onion shape II 188
  epitomizes evolution II 684-5
  future man in II 188
  mystery of II 131-2
  respect for the life in I 366
  septenary law in II 622n
  six-foot man fr I 222
Owen, Professor Richard II 646
  Egypt civilized before Menes II 334
  fallacies of, re man & ape II 681
  hoofed mammal in Secondary II 713
  man's ear muscles formerly used II 681n
  tendency to perfectibility II 649n
—— "Our Origin as a Species" (*Longman's
     Magazine*)
  exposes Allen's exaggerations II 687n
Ox, Oxen II 574. *See also* Bull
  driven out of temple I 442n
  fossil II 287
  one of Holy Four (Christian) I 441-2
  Ophite, or Christian Uriel I 127n
Oxfordshire, stone-field slates II 196

Oxus River I 462
  Arabs along banks of II 200
  flows fr Lake of Dragons II 204
Oxygen
  corresponds w prāna or life II 593
  Crookes on I 546, 551, 584
  elixir of life allotropized fr I 144n
  Huxley on, in protoplasm I 637n
  hydrogen &, as water, non-being I 54-5
  hydrogen, nitrogen & I 623
  instills fire into the "Mother" I 626
  lack of, & fermenting, decay I 262-3 &nn
  noumenon of II 592
  Pasteur on, & vital potency I 249n
  Winchell on I 608n
Oxyhydrogenic, dhyāni- & chohans I 82
Ozimandyas, decad found in catacombs I 321
Ozone
  elixir of life I 144n
  missing link in chemistry I 82n
  sound can produce an I 555
  two European occultists & I 260
Ozonic (or nitr-ozonic)
  dhyāni- & chohans I 82

P

P, signifies paternity II 574
Pa, men-serpents of China II 209
Paccham, 15 solar day cycle II 620
Pachacamac, Temple of (Peru)
  cyclopean in style II 317, 337
Pacific Ocean
  Atlantis in portions of N & S II 405
  evidence of, continent II 788-9
  huge Lemurian islands in II 327
  Lemuria disappeared beneath II 7
  Lemuria extended far into II 324, 333
  Wallace on, continent II 789
Pacificus
  Blake's term for Pacific Lemuria II 783n
Padma (Skt) lotus. See also Lotus, Mātṛipadma
  golden, & wisdom II 578
  Lakshmī, Śrī or I 380
  prakriti &, creations I 427
  Primary Creation II 53 &n
  symbol of I 57-8
Padma Kalpa (Skt) lotus age
  Brahmā awakes fr I 454, 457
  last kalpa was I 368; II 179
  Matsya avatāra in I 369
Padmapāṇi (Skt). See also Bodhisattva
  Avalokiteśvara or II 178, 637
  fourth race & II 173, 178
Padma Purāṇa
  description of White Island II 319
  Pañchaśikha worships Vishnu (Bhagavata
    Purāṇa in tx) I 236
  Piśāchā mother of piśachas I 415
  770 million descendants of Diti II 571
  sons of Marīchi II 89
  spirit (male) entered prakriti I 451-2n
Padmayoni (Skt)
  Abjayoni or lotus-born I 372
Pagan(s), Paganism
  Christians &, re superstitions I 466-70
  Christians borrow fr I 198, 312-13, 399-403,
    410
  Christians claimed, demoniacal II 60
  converted, not morally advanced I 468
  Devil forced, to imitate Jews II 472n
  Egy symbols &, dogmas in Synoptics I 384
  giant skeletons mentioned by II 336

good & evil twin brothers among I 412
  idol worship, Catholic & II 341
  Pentateuch &, birth stories II 544-5
  philosophers sought causes II 589
  plagiarized II 481-2
  taught dual evolution I 464
  wisdom repudiated by West I 642
Paganini du Néant, le [The Paganini of Noth-
    ingness], Lemaître called Renan II 455
Pagoda of Mathurā, built in form of cross
    (Massey) II 588
Pain, value of suffering & II 475
Palace(s)
  of Śankhāsura II 405
  of seven creative angels II 4
  seven, of Sun II 31
  seventh, in Zohar I 356
  of Solomon II 396n
  sun window in solar I 541
Palaemonius, the Tyrian Hercules II 345n
Palenque II 430, 751
  cross I 321, 390
  decad in ruins of I 321
  initiation scene bas-reliefs II 557
  Nachan or II 35
Paleolithic Man. See also Cro-Magnon
  Africo-Atlantean stock II 740
  age of II 206
  Atlantean karma & II 741
  Atlantean offshoot, remnant II 721
  canon of proportion & I 208-9n
  civilized man lived beside II 522, 717
  Cro-Magnon was II 791
  disappeared II 741
  European, Atlantean II 790
  moved to Europe II 740-1 &n
  Neolithic & II 722-3
  non-cannibal II 715, 716n, 723
  not fr "missing link" II 717
  not small-brained II 686n
  in Palestine before nephīlīm II 775
  period betw, & Neolithic man II 715n
  remains of, at Kent's cavern II 724
  remarkable artist II 715-21
  savage & civilized II 317
  skeleton of, superior II 257-8

Paleontologist(s)
   think 3rd eye once functioned II 297
Paleontology II 205, 736
   & pre-physical types II 684
   on stature of animals II 733
   on 3rd eye in Cenozoic animals II 299n
Paleotheridae, roots of explained II 736
Paleozoic Age
   animals bisexual near II 594n
   fishes of II 170
   high tides of, [G. H. Darwin] II 64
   rocks of II 251
   today's foraminifera & II 257
Palestine I 656; II 472n
   dolmens found in II 752
   Nebo adored throughout II 456
   Paleolithic man in II 775
   Seth primitive god of II 82n
   symbol of nirvāna I 568
Palgrave, William Gifford
—— *Narrative of a Year's Journey . . .*
   Sabeans and pyramids II 361-2
Palingenesis II 659
Pāli Shepherds (India)
   origin of Jews & I 313n
Pallas (Gk) or Athena
   Moon-goddess of Athenians I 400
   sparks on helm of I 338n
Palmyra, giant race of, (Blake) II 755
Palus Maeotis, Cimmerians at II 773
Pamir (mts, Central Asia)
   Garden of Wisdom on plateau of II 204
Pamphos (Gk)
   first called Artemis Kallistē I 395
Pan (Gk) nature god
   flame on altar of, & Archaeus I 338n
   had goat's feet II 579
   Jupiter-Aerios or I 463
   later became merely a rural god II 581
   linked w water birds, geese I 358
   nature is the god II 389n
   presides at physical generation II 510
   symbology of pipes of II 581
Πάν, Tὸ Πάν (To Pan, Gk) the All I 353-4
Panadores. *See* Panodorus
Παν Βασιλέια (pan basileia, Gk)
   Semele, Queen of the World I 400
Panca [Pañcha] Krishtayah (Skt)
   five races in *Rig-Veda* II 606
Panca Pradica [Pañcha pradiśāḥ] (Skt). *See also*
      Continents
   five regions in *Rig-Veda* II 606
   three submerged, 1 & 5 existing II 606n
Pañchadaśa (Skt) fifteen

   became Gnostics' "Five Words" II 580
   five words became the, (Vedas) II 579
   Greeks had their II 580
Pañchakaram (Skt) five-sided
   Makara or pentagon II 576
Pañchama (Skt) the 5th (note) I 534
Pañchānana (Skt) five-faced
   Śiva called II 502n, 578n
Pañcha Pāṇḍava (Skt) five Pāṇḍus
   stone circles & II 347
Pañchaśikha (Skt) five-crested
   one of 7 kumāras I 236, 457n
   visited Śveta-dvīpa II 319
Pañchāsyam (Skt) five-headed
   five Brahmās or dhyāni-buddhas I 213
Panchen Lama. *See* Tashi Lama
Pāṇḍavas (Skt)
   gift of Mayāsur(a) to II 426
   Kuntī mother of II 527
   stone circles & II 347
Pandora (Gk)
   Egyptian story of II 270n
   & "fatal gift" to Epimetheus II 270
   Hephaestus molded II 519
   saviors blamed for gift of II 411-12
Pāṇḍu (Skt). *See* Pāṇḍavas
Pāṇini (Skt grammarian)
   grammar of II 253, 439-40
   writing in time of II 225, 439
Panjkora, Afghan tribe in II 200n
Panodorus, on divine dynasties II 366, 368-9
Panorama des Mondes . . . See Le Couturier
Panoramic Visions, of the soul I 266
Pansophia (Gk) universal wisdom
   initiates perfect knowledge of II 133
Panspermic, occult teachings are II 133
Pantheism, Pantheist(s) I 533-4
   ancient I 382-3
   animating spirit-soul is I 51-2
   Atlantean, described II 273-6
   atomists were spiritual I 569
   cross in circle is pure I 5
   of German school I 51, 79n, 124
   Hindu, q *VP* I 545
   Hindu, reveals profound knowledge II 107n
   hylozoism highest aspect of II 158
   of India I xxviii
   Jewish, became monotheism I 112
   karma of abandoning I 412
   Leibniz on objective I 629
   may be physically rediscovered I 533
   polymorphic, of Gnostics II 509n
   righteous Atlanteans were II 273
   SD corrects ideas of I 6, 349, 412

Spinoza a subjective I 629
true I 6-8, 533
of Vedānta & Judaism II 472-3
venerated sarcophagus II 459
Western I 16, 641; II 24
Pantheon(s)
   four Adams (races) & II 503
   heathen, distorted II 475-6
   of human fancy will vanish II 420
   origin of II 769
   universal, nationalized I 655
Pantheon Aegyptiorum. See Jablonski, P. E.
Panthéon égyptien. See Champollion, J. F.
Pantomorphos (Gk) having all forms
   prince of fixed stars I 672
Papantla, Pyramid of
   described by von Humboldt I 322
Papua(n)
   brain larger than French II 168n, 522
   descends fr ape-man (Haeckel) II 193n
   dying out II 780
   mixed Atlanto-Lemurian stock II 779
   Pacific continent &, (Haeckel) II 328
Papyrus Magique Harris [F. J. Chabas]
   ram-headed Ammon in II 213n
Para (Skt) beyond, supreme
   highest form of Vāch I 434
   latent light & sound I 432
   Parabrahman is, form of Vāch I 138 &n
Parable(s) II 94, 335
   a spoken symbol I 307
   of the *Testaments* unveiled I 315
Parabrahm, Parabrahman (Skt) I 15. *See also*
   Ain-Sōph, All, Boundless, Sat, That
   alone above māyā I 54n
   can have no attributes I 7, 130n
   cannot will or create I 451
   central point turned inward I 340
   chimmātra in Vedānta II 597n
   circle, naught or II 553
   creative gods illusive aspect of I 451
   ever unmanifested principle II 233
   First Cause not II 108
   hidden nameless deity I 6
   ideal & Īśvara the real I 55-6, 130n
   ideal plan held within I 281
   indivisible, unknown II 99
   known only thru point I 432
   Logos, Īśvara cannot see I 351n
   Mahat first aspect of II 58
   manifestation of II 24-5
   mūlaprakriti & I 46, 69, 273, 337n, 340
   -mūlaprakriti & avyaktānugrahena I 521-2
   mūlaprakriti vehicle, veil of I 10n, 130n, 179

Nārāyana personification of I 64
   as nirguna I 62
   not God, not a god I 6
   Oeaohoo or I 68
   One Life, Great Breath or I 226n
   one-, 3-, 7-voweled terms & I 20
   para aspect of Vāch I 138
   passive because absolute I 7
   pradhāna & I 256
   purusha & I 582
   Śabda Brahman latent in I 428
   spirit & nature merge into II 36
   spirit moving on waters II 128
   Subba Row on II 310n, 598
   Tree of Life springs fr I 536
   ultimate unconsciousness II 598
   Unconscious of pantheists & I 51
   unknowable, Ain-sōph II 128, 553
   unknown darkness or I 134n
   unspeakable mystery I 330
   various names for I 15, 113; II 553
   Viśishtādvaita on I 59n
Paracelsus I 611
   Archaeus of I 51-2, 532 &n, 538-9
   called a quack I 297
   criminal hand ended life of I 263
   dhyānis called Flagae by I 222n
   discovered nitrogen I 297
   European most versed in magic I 263
   father of modern chemistry II 656
   on force behind all phenomena I 281-2
   Haeckel vs II 656
   homunculi of I 345; II 120-1, 349
   limbus major & minor of I 283-4
   mysterium magnum of I 61, 584; II 511
   phenomena, noumena of I 492
   potency of matter I 283
   vibrations, sound, color & I 514
   wanted to agree w Bible I 294n
   Yliaster of I 283
   —— *De fundamento sapientiae*
   animal elements in man I 294n
   —— *De generatione hominis*
   on liquor vitae I 532 &n, 538
   —— *De viribus membrorum*
   Archaeus or liquor vitae I 532
   —— *Paragranum*
   vital force of I 532n, 538-9
   —— *Philosophia ad Atheniensis*
   everything fr the elements I 284
   everything is living I 281
Paracelsus, Life of. See Hartmann, F.
Paradeśa (Skt) remote country

highland of 1st Skt-speaking race II 204
Paradigms of Plato II 268
Paradise(s)
 garden of II 559
 lokas are the various II 321
 of man's heart II 587
 theosophic school in II 284
Paradise Lost. See Milton, John
Paragranum. See Paracelsus
Parahydrogenic
 ākāśic or, & dhyāni-chohans I 82
Parama (Skt) remotest, highest
 supreme, guhya, or sarvātma I 90
Paramapada (Skt) final beatitude
 jīva goes to, via sun-spot I 132
Paramapadātmavat (Skt) supreme essence
  I 420
Paramarshi (Skt) great rishi I 420
Paramārtha (Skt) highest or whole truth
 Alaya & I 48-50
 illusion, time & I 44 &n
 Mādhyamikas vs Yogāchāras re I 48
 parinishpanna without I 53-4
Paramārthasatya (Skt) the real truth I 48 &n
Paramārthika (Skt)
 one true existence, Brahman I 6, 356
Paramātman (Skt) supreme self II 108
 ātman one w I 265
 jīvātma, Logos issue fr II 33
 nara, Nārāyana & II 495n
Paranirvāṇa. *See* Parinirvāṇa
Paraoxygenic
 "ethereal" or, & dhyāni-chohans I 82
Parārdha (Skt) half life of Brahmā I 368
Paraśakti (Skt) supreme force I 292
Parāśara (Skt) Vedic rishi. *See also VP*
 account by, of great pralaya II 757
 Aryan Hermes I 286
 date of I 456n
 describes the Earth II 322-3, 401n
 on elemental dissolution I 372-3
 instructs Maitreya I 286, 456n
 in *Matsya Purāna* II 550
 placed gods betw dawn & twilight II 163
 rākshasa devoured father of I 415
 on rebellious, fallen gods II 232 &n
 received *VP* fr Pulastya I 456n
 on rudras having 100 names II 182
 on seven creations I 445
 on Śri & the Moon II 76n
 titled Nārada a divine rishi II 47-8
 on various pralayas II 309-10n
 Vaśishtha advises I 415-16
 in *Vishnu Purāna* II 76n, 163, 309-10n, 321,

  326, 401n, 611n
 on War in Heaven I 419
Paraśu-Rāma (Skt) Rāma w an ax
 & race of Bhārgavas II 32n
Paratantra (Skt), defined I 48-9
Parāvara (Skt) supreme & not supreme I 6
Paravey, De, on extinct animals II 206n
Parcha, Rabbi [Parḥa Rabba]
 on Malachim, Ischin II 375
 wheel of II 397n
Parent, Eternal, or Space I 35
Parent Doctrine, evidence of, remains I xliv
Parent Planet, triads born under I 574
Parent Star II 33. *See also* Stars
Parent Sun, inner man drawn into I 638-9
"Pāreshu guhyeshu vrateshu" (Skt, *Rig-Veda*)
 Vishnu's 3 strides II 622n
Parguphim [Partzūphīn] (Aram) I 375-6
Parikalpita (Skt) contrived I 48
Pariṇāmin (Skt), purusha-pradhāna & I 582
Parinirvāṇa (Skt). *See also* Parinishpanna
 absolute existence I 266
 becoming one w I 48
 begins, ends, not eternal I 42-3, 266
 "Day of Be-With-Us" or I 134n, 265
 duration of I 134n
 how monad attains I 135
 Kalki avatāra, 2nd Advent & I 268
 past, present, future blend in I 265-6
 same monads will emerge fr I 266
 squaring the circle & II 450
Parinishpanna (Skt) utter consummation
 paramārtha & I 48, 53-4
 paranirvāna [parinirvāna] or I 53
 perfection at end of mahā-manvantara I 42
Parker, John A.
 —— *Quadrature of the Circle*
 geometrical key to Kabbala II 544
 propositions of I 315-16
 ratio of π (*pi*) I 313, 315-16
Parkhurst, John, *Greek & English Lexicon . . .*
 ark, arkē discussed II 313, 460
 —— *Hebrew & English Lexicon . . .*
 defines *eue* or Eva, etc II 129-30
Parmenides. See Plato
Parnassus, Greek holy mountain II 494
Paropamisan (Hindu-Kush)
 Central Asian mountain range II 338
Pārsī(s)
 Atash-Behram of, & Gk Archaeus I 338n
 ceremony of, described II 517
 fire worshipers I 121
 flight to Gujerāt (India) II 323
 Jews, Armenians &, Caucasians II 471n

Kabiri & ancient II 363n
Māgas forefathers of II 323
numbers honored by I 113n
Peris remote ancestors of II 398
scriptures, do not grasp own II 607, 757
Sun-worshipers I 388, 479
Parthenogenesis II 177. *See also* Sweat-Born
    origin of species & II 657, 659
Particle(s)
    act fr internal principle I 630
    distance between I 507-8n
    each, is a life I 261
    noumenon of every I 218n
    occult phenomena & I 489
    world germ is spiritual I 200
"Part of a part" (amśāmśāvatāra, Skt)
    explained re rebirth of teachers II 359
Parturient Energy, & ansated cross II 31n
Parturition (birth time)
    nine calendar months or I 389
    periods worldwide I 390
Pāśa (Skt) noose, snare, cord II 548-9
    Hindu equiv of Egy ankh-tie II 548
Pascal, Blaise, *Pensées*
    on God & nature I 412
    God is a circle . . . I 65; II 545
Pasht or Basht. *See* Bast
Pashut (Heb) literal interpretation I 374
Pasigraphie. See Maimieux, J. de
Passion(s)
    candidate's war in heaven w II 380
    every evil, will be subdued II 420
    hot, & South Pole elementals II 274
    human, & Sagara II 571
    lower, chain higher aspirations II 422
    maruts represent II 615
    senses &, obstacles I 459
    titanic, insatiable, in man II 412
"Pass Not" I 90, 129-35
Past
    Earth forces same as now I 639-40
    future &, alive in present I 105
    helps realize present I xlvi
    is present unfolded I 639
    mystery of the, in symbols II 588
    present, future & I 37, 43-4; II 446
    present helps to appreciate the I xlvi
Pasteur, Louis
    best friend of "destroyers" I 262-3 &n
    organic cells without oxygen I 249n
    spontaneous generation & II 150
Pastrana Species
    breeding "anthropoid ape" fr II 717n

Paśus (Skt) sacrificial animal
    Brahmā creates in 1st kalpa II 625n
Paśyantī (Skt) she looks on
    latent light, ideation I 432
    Logos is, form of Vāch I 138, 432
Pātāla(s) (Skt) nether regions
    America, Antipodes II 132, 182, 214 &n, 446,
        628
    Arjuna visited, 5,000 yrs ago II 214 &n, 628
    Atala one of 7 regions II 402-3
    fifth region of II 382n
    Hindu naraka (Hell) II 98
    infernal & antipodal regions II 407n
    Meru &, described II 357
    Nārada visits II 49
    race of nāgas for peopling II 132
    Śiva hurled Mahāsura down to II 237n
    South Pole associated w II 357
    spiritual ego descends into II 558
    wither up at pralaya I 372
Patañjali, [Yoga] School of
    adepts of, & Tāraka division I 158
Pater Aether, Pater Omnipotens Aether (Lat)
    ākāśa or I 488n
    deified by Greeks & Latins I 331
    unknown cause of Greek, Roman I 9-10n
Pater Deus, Pater Zeus
    no phallic meaning (Ragon) II 574
Paternoster (Lord's Prayer)
    occult verse of, (Lévi) II 562
Path, Paths
    Atlantis & right-, left- I 192n; II 495
    beams of light or II 191n
    Bible re right-, left- II 211
    four, to nirvāna I 206
    initiates of right- & left- II 494
    left-, followed by many II 331
    one of the seven II 191
    prophets of left- & right- II 503-5
    thirty-two in Kabbala II 625
    two, eternal I 86
    two, lie before man I 639
Path, The (magazine), Bjerregaard in, on
    monads I 623, 630-1, 632n
Patience, or Dhṛiti II 528
Patriarch(s)
    borrowed fr Bab, Egy I 655
    Chaldeo-Judaic gods I 349
    convertible w rishis II 129
    Enoch the seventh II 529
    higher gods made into I 390-1
    Homeric songs & II 391
    Jehovah came to, as Shaddai II 509
    -names key to Bible II 536

Noah explained by Faber II 360n
prajāpatis & I 355
ruled Egypt after Watchers I 266
Seth, made one of 7, w Arabs II 366
signs of zodiac & I 651
symbols of solar & lunar yrs II 391n
years of, are periods, cycles II 426
Paul, St
  Adams of II 81-2, 513
  Church colored esoteric hints of II 515
  compared to Mercury II 481
  "elements" of I 373n
  fathoms mystery of cross II 556
  initiate I 240; II 268, 504, 513n, 704
  on man of Earth & of Heaven II 82
  "Master Builder" II 704
  on observing the 7th day II 76
  Prince of the Air of II 485, 515
  Principalities & Powers of I 632n
  on sabbath or eternal rest I 240
  Saul or II 504
  on soul & spirit bodies II 513 &n
  "stars" known as "worlds" to II 704
  taught of cosmic gods I 235, 464-5
  unknown God of I 327
  "we shall judge angels" II 111-12
  world the "mirror of pure truth" II 268
Pausanias, *Description of Greece*
  Aeschylus II 419n
  altar to Mercury, Jupiter II 28
  Castor's tomb in Sparta II 122n
  Euxine a lake II 5 &n
  giants Asterius & Geryon II 278
  Hyperboreans now mythical II 769n
  Kabirim had a sanctuary II 363
  Pamphos & Artemis-Kallistē I 395
  Phlegyae & Atlantis destroyed II 144
  Phoroneus II 519
  prayers stopped a hail-storm I 469
  slime formed into new race II 519
  worshiping stones II 341
  Zeus Cataibates I 338n
Pāvaka (Skt) fire, god of fire
  creative spark, germ II 247
  electric or Vaidyuta fire I 521; II 57n
  fire of pitris II 57n, 247
  Śuchi &, made animal man II 102
Pavamāna (Skt)
  father of Saharaksha I 521
  fire of Asuras & II 57n, 247
  son of Abhīmānin I 521
  union of buddhi & manas II 247
Pavana (Skt), Hanuman son of I 190

Peacock II 514n
  bird of wisdom II 619
  Hindu phoenix II 619
Pedigree of Man. See Haeckel, E.
Pègues, Abbé, *The Volcanoes of Greece*
  giant skeletons found on Thera II 278-9
Peiru-un, Chinese Noah II 365, 774
Peking [Beijing] Imperial Library II 206
Pelagus (Gk), great sea II 774
Pélasges et Cyclopes. See Creuzer, G. F.
Pelasgian(s)
  Atlantean structures of II 745-6
  came fr East II 3
  colonized Samothrace II 3
  Cyclopes initiated, in Masonry II 345n
  descend fr Atlantean subrace II 774
  dolmen builders were II 753
  Peruvian works like those of II 745
Pelenque Cross. *See* Palenque
Pelican
  air-water symbol I 358
  fiery soul of, or Ain-sōph I 80
  Moses forbade eating swans & I 80n
  Rosicrucian symbol I 19-20
Pelion, Mt, Persian fleet & I 467
Pember, G. H., *Earth's Earliest Ages*
  Satan & theosophists II 229 &n
Penates, related to Kabiri (Faber) II 360
Penetralia, wife's dwelling-place I 382
Pengelly, Professor William
  Asia, America once joined II 322n
  on geologic ages I 567n; II 66, 72
  submerged Atlantis possible II 778
  —— "Extinct Lake of Bovey Tracey"
    possibility of Atlantis II 726-7
  —— "The Ice-Age Climate & Time"
    geological time II 695-6
Pentacle I 114, 131. *See also* Five-pointed Star
  circle, point & I 320-1
  curtain hid 5 pillars of I 125
  line, triangle & I 91
  symbology of, described, explained I 125
  triangle, cube, & *pi* (π) I 131
Pentaglott. See Schindler, V.
Pentagon
  fifth order of celestial beings I 219
  Makara, pañchakara or II 576 &n
  represents microcosm I 224
  symbolism of, explained I 384; II 576-7
  triangle becomes, on Earth II 79n
Pentagram I 78, 219
Pentateuch. *See also* Mosaic Books, Moses
  collection of allegories I 10
  compiled fr "very old book" I xliii

crudest origin of birth in II 544-5
Ezra remodeled, disfigured I 319, 335-6;
 II 143, 658
four elements & I 462
Gladstone, Homer & II 383
mechanical construction, not theogony in
 II 537
NT &, symbols fr same source I 115n
no revelation II 3n
numerous changes in II 473
spurned by Sadducees I 320-1n
"thou shalt not revile the gods" II 477
time fr Eden to Flood missing in I 397n
wisdom in Purānas & I 336
Zohar & II 461n, 487
Pentecost, Jewish liturgy for I 618
Pentecostal Fire-tongues
 aspects of Archaeus I 121, 338n
Πέρας (peras, Gk) finite, & apeiron I 426
Peratae Gnostics
 Chozzar (Neptune) & II 356
 five androgyne ministers of II 577-8
Perception(s) II 597n
 apperception & I 175, 179, 630
 mental, physical, & light II 41
 nature a bundle of deceptive II 475
 seven aspects of I 139; II 599
 thraldom of sensuous II 587
Perdition, effect of dogma of II 484
Peregrinations, Scarabaeus symb & II 552
Pereisc [Peiresc, N. C. F. de]
 gave Enochian MSS II 531
Perfection, Perfected
 absolute, & unknown deity II 413
 born out of imperfection II 95
 can never make imperfection II 555
 human, described I 275
 no ultimate I 42-3
 striving towards II 736
Perfect Way, The. See Kingsford, A.
Περὶ ἀρχῶν (Peri archōn, Gk). *See* Damascius,
 De principiis rerum
"Perigenesis of the Plastidule." *See* Haeckel
Périgord, giant skeletons of II 749n
Period(s) (geological). *See also* Eocene, Glacial,
 Miocene, Tertiary
 diagram of esoteric II 710
 every, a mystery in its duration II 698
 possible to calculate approximately II 709
Period(s). *See also* Cycles
 longest astronomical, observed I 667
 primary & secondary, of evolution I 455
 various, of Hindu astronomy I 666
 years of Patriarchs are II 426

Periodicity
 law of, 2nd Fundamental Prop I 16-17
 in laws of nature II 621
 septenary law of II 627-8
 in universal manifestation I 268, 552
 in vital phenomena II 622-3 &n
"Periodicity of Vital Phenomena." *See* Laycock, Dr T.
Periodic Table
 of elements I 547, 553, 583-6
 illustrates occult law I 585
Peripatetics
 materialists in their way I 343
 monas of I 177-8
 "nature abhors a vacuum" I 64, 343
 pantheistical, & monas I 619
Peris (Pers) or Izods, "angels"
 Aryan race symbolized by II 394
 derivation of word II 394n
 devs &, in the North II 398
 devs (giants) made raids on II 397
 postdiluvians of Bible II 394
 reigns of, (Bailly) II 368
 war w devs later confused II 776
Périsprit, fluidic, or astral soul I 196
Permeability
 next characteristic of matter I 251
 sixth sense &, this round I 258
Peronne [Perrone], Father Giovanni
—— *Praelectiones theologicae . . .*
 b'ne-aleim or sons of God II 375
Perpetual or Eternal Motion. *See also* Breath,
 Motion
 all motion is, (Grove) I 497
 coexistent w space I 55
 ever-becoming of II 545
 of Great Breath I 2-4, 55-6, 93n, 97, 147-8,
 282-3, 455, 599n
 Keely on I 556
 laya-centers & I 147
 never ceases in nature I 97
 of Sat & Asat II 450
 sound & I 525n
 unmanifested is I 97n
Perry, Charles, *A View of The Levant*
 S Pole in constellation Harp II 360n
Persea, Basin of II 545
Persephone. *See also* Proserpine
 Axiokersa or II 362
Persepolis (or Esikekar)
 built by Giamshid II 398
Perseus, an Assyrian (Herodotus) II 345n
Persia. *See also* Iran
 Atlantean traditions in II 393-9

conquered Egypt I 311
fleet of I 467
folklore of II 393-401
Greece, Egypt ever at war w II 393
legendary history of II 398-9
legendary kings of II 368, 394, 396
magi of II 608-10, 756 &n
magi of, used veiled language II 395
scriptures of II 607-8
War in Heaven fr India thru I 198
Persian(s). *See also* Iranians
  ancestors of ancient II 328
  astronomy of I 658-9, 663
  egg symbol among I 359
  Kabiri of II 363n
  legends & Greek comp II 393-401
  Meshia & Meshiane among II 134
  phoenix or Simorgh II 397, 617
  planetary genii, prophets I 649, 652
  seven earths, races II 617-18
  stone oracles of II 346
  treatment of fire among II 114
  two extinct nations of II 396
Persian Gulf, man-fish rose out of II 139n
"Personal and Impersonal God." *See* Subba
  Row, T.
Personal God(s)
  Christians degraded God into I 426-7
  of Church I 492n, 499n, 635-6; II 475, 555-6
  discussion of I 2n, 6n, 139, 193; II 475, 544,
    598
  gods vs, discussed I 492-3n
  not Blavatsky's idea I 579n
  not Buddhist belief I 635
  occultists reject I 492n, 545
  Plato could not believe in II 554-5
  salvation, damnation & I 613
  Satan & I 412, 612
  source of idea of I 332
  third-rate emanation, Logos I 437-8, 614
  unphilosophical I 2n, 6n, 139, 193, 280n;
    II 475, 544, 598
Personality(ies)
  of advanced beings II 276
  almost interminable series of II 306
  aroma of, hangs fr flame I 238
  astrological star of I 572
  body of egotistical desires II 241
  earthly characteristic I 275
  essence of, not lost I 266
  false II 254, 306
  human, & Logos II 478
  individuality & I 572-3; II 306
  lethal virus of II 110

Logos is no II 318n
manas & kāma-rūpa duality of II 241
merging of, w ātma-buddhi I 52
monad & I 174-5n, 238, 245
moonbeams dancing on water I 237
no immortality for I 440n
none till end of 3rd race II 610
personal will part of II 241
portion of, remains I 238
reality devoid of I 629
real man concealed under false I 220
selfishness of II 110
Personal Self
  monad &, urge evolution II 109-10
Personating Spirits
  demions (dimyon, Heb; daimons, Gk) or
    II 508-9
Perspiration. *See also* Sweat-Born
  primeval mode of procreation II 174-7
Perturbations, of planets by Sun I 503
Peru, Peruvian(s)
  Acosta on, buildings I 209n
  built like Pelasgians II 745
  Egyptian &, myths same I 266-7 &n
  European skulls like II 739, 740, 790
  giant tombs in II 752
  Manco Capac &, races II 365
  marvelous civilizations of II 793
  structures of, Atlantean II 745-6
  swastika found among II 586
  Tiahuanaco II 317, 337
  traditions of, re flood, ark II 141
Pesh-Hun (messenger)
  Nārada called II 48
  regulates cycles II 48-9
Pessimism
  & doctrine of karma II 304n
  Schopenhauer's & von Hartmann's II 156n,
    304n, 648
Peter, St
  Church of Rome built on II 341n
  Church trustee of II 377
  Kronos (Saturn) will swallow II 341n
  personified by pope II 466n
—— *Peter, 1st Epistle of*
  Christ cornerstone, etc II 627
  circumambulating of Earth II 485, 515
  lion compared w Satan I 442n
—— *Peter, 2nd Epistle of*
  destruction of 5th race II 757, 762n
Petermann, J. H., published Latin transl of
  Pistis Sophia II 566n
Peter's Lexicon II 605n. *See also* Roth, R. von
Peter the Hermit, led crusade I 357

Petrarch, killed a dragon II 207 &n
Petrie, Sir W. M. Flinders
   Eridu used Egyptian measures II 226
   —— *The Academy* (letter in)
   pyramid figures I 314
   —— *Pyramids & Temples . . .*
   differs fr Smyth's figures I 315
   —— *Stonehenge*
   stones of, fr afar II 344
Petronius Arbiter (*Petronii Satyrica* in tx)
   —— *The Satyricon*
   degradation of goose symbol I 358
Peuple Primitif. See Rougemont, F. de
Peuret [Peuvret], on cube unfolded II 601
Peyrère, theory of II 725
Pfaff, Dr F., *Alter und der Ursprung . . .*
   brain size of human, ape II 193n, 661
   fossil skulls w larger capacity II 523
   gibbon & man since Tertiary II 681-2n
   gulf between man & ape II 87n, 687n
   skull capacity of various races II 522-3
Pflüger, Dr Edward
   opposed Darwinian heredity II 711n
Pfoundes, Captain C. *See* Omoie
Phaedo. See Plato
Phaedrus. See Plato
Phaeton [Phaethon] (Gk)
   made Sun deviate fr its course II 535
   myth of, explained II 770n
Phallic(ism)
   ancient theology & I 312
   anthropomorphism led to I 451-2n
   Ark of Covenant became II 459
   body-worship, 4th race II 279, 285
   of brazen serpent I 364 &n
   Christianity honeycombed w I 451-2n
   develops w loss of keys I 264n; II 471
   fatal turning away fr truth I 264n
   Greek rites became II 362
   Holy of Holies degraded to II 459-60
   Isis Unveiled on II 85
   Jewish I 438n, 444; II 85, 125, 459
   later Kabbala suffocated by II 457-8
   man in image of, god II 472
   no divine II 544
   no, Jehovah for 1,000 yrs II 469
   none in earlier nations II 44
   number 10 later became II 463
   in old religions II 657-8
   of Pramantha story II 101 &n, 524-5
   Prometheus myth & II 521, 524-5, 561-2
   ram's head & II 182
   sacr', sacred, etc are I 5n; II 465 &n, 467
   Semites introduced II 54

starts w King David II 469
swastika degraded into II 101n
symbols I 318-21; II 30n, 62, 104, 182, 471-3,
   542-3, 583, 588
Phallicism . . . See Jennings, H.
Phallus(i). *See also* Liṅga
   batylos, lingam, lithos II 85, 467
   carrier of the germ II 467n
   Christian architecture & II 85
   dragon symbol of II 104
   Egyptians added, to cross II 542
   oil-anointed in Bible II 473
Phanerogamous Plants, lotus I 57
Phanēs (Gk) or Eros
   part of Orphic triad I 451-2n, 582-3
Phantom(s)
   Earth's early protoplasmic I 191
   lunar pitris & II 89, 91 &n, 102 &n
   vortex-atom a metaphysical I 489
Pharaoh
   Atlantis legend & Bible story of II 426-8,
      494 &n
   daughter & Moses story I 319 &n, 385 &n
   "fairest tree of Eden" (*Ezekiel*) II 494
   God tempts & then plagues I 383n
   seven souls of, in Egyptian texts II 632
   Sinaitic peninsula ruled by II 226
   tempted by Sarah I 422; II 174
Pharisees
   fanaticism of, cursed Jesus II 378
   Jehovah, Saturn father of I 578
   Jesus & the I 653
   tenets of, fr Babylonia II 61
Phenoch. See Enoch
Phenomenal Universe
   shadow of the pre-existing I 278
Phenomenon(a). *See also* Keely, Noumenon
   all potencies have their I 470
   causes of nature's I 2-3
   creation of perceiving ego I 329
   Dhruva & cosmic II 612 &n
   geological & sidereal II 314
   invisible powers noumena of II 517-18
   kriyāśakti & I 293; II 173
   manifested, illusory I 18
   noumenon & I 38, 481, 522, 535n
   occult I 82 &n, 489
   produced by elementals & matter I 146
   will, thought & II 173, 652
Pherecydes (Gk)
   God is a circle II 552
   good & evil, light & darkness I 196 &n
   on Hyperboreans [Pherenicus?] II 775
Phidias (Gk sculptor) II 660n

Philae (Egy temple)
  egg of incense hatched at I 363-4
  Horus shown raising dead at II 557
  initiation scene at II 558-9
  Khnoum adored at I 367
Philalethes, E. *See* Vaughan, Thomas
Φιλάνθρωπος (philanthrōpos, Gk)
  Prometheus was II 526
Philebus. See Plato
Philip the Apostle
  authored *Pistis Sophia* II 566n
Philistines
  David brought name Jehovah fr II 541
Phillips, Sir R
  axial changes & glaciations II 726
Philo Judaeus
  forbade cursing Satan II 477
  on hating the heathen II 471
—— *De cherubim* . . .
  Adam as Mind II 490 &n
—— [*De fuga et inventione*]
  twelve signs of the zodiac I 649
  wisdom II 489
—— *De gigantibus*
  souls descend to bodies II 111
—— *De migratione Abrahami*
  kosmos is God w Chaldeans I 344
—— *De mundi opificio*
  man a divine idea I 71
  numbers 6 & 7 I 407
  seven (heptagon) II 602
—— *De somniis*
  souls descend to bodies II 111
—— [*Allegories of the Sacred Laws*]
  Adam Kadmon as Mind II 490
—— [*On the Life of Moses*]
  Heb law transl into Greek II 200n
—— *Quaestiones* . . .
  Logos next to God I 350, 352
Philology, Philologist(s)
  claim writing unknown to Homer II 439
  give out conclusions as facts I xxix
  scientific, questioned I xxix-xxx
Philo of Byblus (Herennius Bibylius)
  animated stones of II 342
  Sanchoniathon on Javo II 129, 465
  Sanchoniathon on univ birth I 340 &n
Philosopher(s)
  can look beneath coarse myths II 764-5
  defined by Plato II 554-5
  modern, content w effects II 589
  pagan, sought causes II 589
Philosophia ad Athenienses. See Paracelsus
Philosophiae Naturale . . . *See* Newton, I.

Philosophical Magazine . . .
  article by Dr Babbage I 104, 124
  article by James Croll I 511
  article by Sir I. Newton I 13
  articles by Kroenig, Clausius, Maxwell I 513
  articles by Sir Wm. Thomson I 117, 513-14
Philosophical Transactions
  arctic magnolias (Heer) II 726
  botany suggests Atlantis (Heer) II 739
  intellect & skull size (Davis) II 522, 790n
  self-luminous matter (Halley) I 590
  stars of Milky Way (Herschel) I 590
Philosophie naturelle. See Francoeur, L. B.
Philosophie religieuse. See Reynaud, J.
Philosoph. Plant. II 526. *See* Plutarch (*De placitus*)
Philosophy(ies)
  Advaita & Buddhist, identical I 636
  analogy is key in occult I 150-1
  of blind faith vs knowledge I 612
  Bright Space in esoteric I 71-2 &n
  common belief of ancient I 341
  Egyptian same as cis-Himalayan II 374n
  esoteric, reconciles many systems I 55, 77
  an essential truth of occult I 77
  immortality & Vedic I 36n
  incorporeal entities in I 218n
  Indian, six schools of I 269; II 42
  occult, in Spinoza & Leibniz I 629
  our, compared w ancient I 507
Philosophy Historical and Critical. See Lefèvre
Philosophy of History. See Hegel, G. W. F.
Philosophy of the Inductive Sciences. See Whewell
Philosophy of the Unconscious. See Hartmann
Philostratus, *De vita Apollonii*
  feeding on serpents I 404
—— *Heroica*
  giant skeletons II 278, 336
Philo-Theo-Sophia, pantheism & I 533
Phineata[e], Hermes worshiped at II 367
Phlegyae, Phlegyan (Gk) Atlantis isle
  destruction of II 144, 265, 365
Phlogiston. *See also* Caloric
  substance of force I 511
Phobos (inner moon of Mars)
  not a satellite I 165
Phocea [Phōcis] (Gk), Prometheus fashioned
  man fr slime at II 519
Phoebe (Gk)
  Moon transformed into I 386
  wife of Castor as the dawn II 122
Phoebe & Hilaeira (Gk) Dawn & Twilight
  wives of Castor & Pollux II 122

Phoebus (Gk)
-Apollo, delight of senses II 383 &n
Apollo or II 770
light of wisdom II 235
Phoenicia(ns)
ancestors of II 328
astronomy fr, (Orientalists) II 551
Baal sun god of II 540
circumnavigated globe II 430
claimed descent fr Saturn II 768
colonized Samothrace II 3
cosmogony of I 110, 451-28n
did not invent writing II 439
earlier navigators than II 406
Elon or Elion highest god of II 380
fire (Kabiri) worship in II 363
Hebrew numbers fr II 560
Hindu Aryans older than II 406-7
Iαω (Iaō) supreme god of II 541
invented writing (Grote, etc) II 440
Jews &, (Herodotus) I 313n
Kabiri of Egyptians & II 274
moving or animated stone of II 342 &n
origin of, Atlanto-Aryan II 743
origin of gods of II 769n
sailors pray to Astarte I 468
Sanchoniathon wrote in II 440n
secretive re navigation II 764
seven Earths of II 617
Venus sign & Ram on coin of II 546
Phoenix
Bennoo, bird of resurrection or I 312
Garuda the Hindu II 564
peacock as Hindu II 619
self-consumed & reborn 7x7 times II 617
Simorgh the Persian II 397-8, 617-18
solar cycle 600 yrs II 617n
Phonetic Laws I xxxi-ii
Phönizier, Die. See Movers, F. K.
Phonograph, called ventriloquism II 784n
Phorcys (Gk), Arkite Titan II 143
Phoreg, one of Hesiod's 7 Titans I 418
Phorminx (Gk), 7-stringed lyre II 529
Phoroneus (Gk), first man II 519-21
Phorōnidae (Gk), poem on Phoroneus II 519
Phōsphorus I 553
Satan "Lord of" II 513
"without, no thought" II 244
Photius, [*Bibliotheca* or *Myriobiblion*]
Ophites, talking stones II 342
on Prometheus II 519
Photograph(s, y)
ākāśic or astral, & pralaya I 18n
astrological influences & I 105

mystery of I 508-9
Photosphere, R. Hunt on I 530-1
"Phreno-Kosmo-Biology." *See* Lewins, Dr
Phrygia
fire (Kabiri) worship in II 363
priests of, described Atlantis II 371
Phta. *See* Ptah
Phylogen(esis,y) (Haeckel's term)
development of race, species II 659
laughed at by some scientists II 656
will never be exact science II 663
Physica. See Aristotle
Physical I 176n
astral before, body II 1
astral merges into II 257
bodies belong to Earth II 199
body built by Spirit of Earth II 241
body, death of, & adepts II 531
body shaped by lowest lives I 224
Earth's astral &, now grosser II 157n
every, form has astral prototype II 660n
form fr protoplasmic model II 150
improvement at expense of spiritual I 225
links between many classes II 257
man apart fr divine & spiritual II 254
man became, thru reabsorption II 170
man, birthplace of II 416n
man 18 million yrs old II 157, 251, 310
moral, political &, blended II 369-70
nature, diagram of II 593
no, iniquity II 302
part of triple evolution I 181
plane has no contact w astral II 157
power of psychic over II 192
psychic man uses, body II 302
races 1st & 2nd not II 289
spiritual &, evolution II 348
"Physical Basis of Life." *See* Huxley, T. H.
Physical Eclogues. See Florilegium of Stobaeus
Physicalization
of root-types II 649, 736
same as spirit materialization II 737
Physician's Hymn of *Rig-Veda* [X, 97]
plants came 3 ages before gods II 52n
Physics, Physicists. *See also* Science
analogy key to cosmic I 150
Aryans learned, fr Atlanteans II 426
borrowed ancient atomic theory I 567-8
deals w lowest forces I 554
fifth element & II 135
has returned to Anaxagoras I 586
Hindu knowledge of II 107n
initiates' knowledge of I 516
occult I 97, 200-1, 262

scorn of modern, for ancient I 495
space-force-matter in I 615
unity in the sphere of II 24
Physiological(ly)
  Adam's sleep not II 181
  age of, mankind II 156
  Aryan religion higher than II 526
  Atlantean mammals not perfect II 286
  civilization &, transformation II 317
  conjectures on foetus vague II 131
  cross-breeding &, law II 196
  differentiations II 120
  Fall after Eden II 279
  key to Moon symbol I 390, 398
  key to symbolism I 363
  man evolved fr astral II 737
  psychic element develops the II 176
  purity of 3rd race II 172
  refusal to incarnate was II 171
  selection II 738
  separation of sexes II 275
  symbol & Prometheus II 100-1
  Titans a, fact II 154
  transformation of sexes II 147-8
  transformations symbolized II 178-9
"Physiological Selection." *See* Romanes
Physiology
  denies a vital principle I 603
  ignorant of Moon's influence I 264
  magician of the future I 261
  of man & animals II 187-90
  occult facts of II 295-8
  of organisms II 116-17
  psychic knowledge would widen II 370n
  septenate in II 623 &n
Physiology, Text Book of. See Foster, M.
Physique, Éléments de. See Ganot, A.
Pi (π)
  Angel of Face, synthesis or I 434 &n
  kabbalistic II 38-40, 465-6, 544, 560
  number of circle, swastika I 90-1
  numerical value of I 90-1, 114, 131, 230, 313
  Ring "Pass-Not" of lipikas & I 131
Picardy II 738, 750n
Pickering, on diversity of Malays II 332
Pictet, Raoul
  derided by Laplace re aerolites II 784n
Picture Writing II 130. *See also* Glyphs, Symbols
Pierius
  on Numa's circular religious posture II 552
Pierres Branlantes (Fr) rocking stones
  of Huelgoat, Brittany II 342n
Pierret, Paul, *Etudes égyptologiques*

Osiris-Lunus I 228
—— *Le Livre des Morts*
  "Day come to us" (Egy) I 134 &n
Pierron, P. A., transl of ἔχει (echei) II 763
Pigeon I 81n; II 595
Pigmies. *See* Pygmy(ies)
Pikermi, fossil monkeys near II 723n
Pilgrim(s)
  comets or I 250
  eternal, masterpiece of evolution II 728
  monad during its embodiments or I 16n
  suffers thru every form of life I 268
Pilgrimage
  obligatory, for each soul I 17, 40, 570
Pillaloo-codi [Pillālu-Kodi] (Tamil)
  Pleiades, Hindus observed rising of I 663-4
Pillar(s)
  Abraham's, of unhewn stones II 472n
  in ancient temples I 125-6, 462
  Ases (Scand) or, of world II 97
  of fire I 338n, 341, 437
  four, of Tyre I 125-6
  of Jacob, oil-anointed phallus II 473
  Mercury, Seth, Josephus & II 530
  pyramids became, at Tyre I 347n
  of salt & Lot's wife II 674
  seven I 356, 408
  world- I 235
  of Zarathustra I 464
Pillars of Hercules
  Atlantis beyond II 147, 323-4n, 394
  Greeks did not sail beyond II 223
Pimandre .... *See* Foix, F. de
Pindar
  held pantheons to be immoral II 764
—— *Hymn to Jupiter*
  Kabir Adamas first man II 3
—— *Hymn to Minerva*
  Minerva on Jupiter's right hand I 401
—— *Nemean Odes*
  Castor & Pollux II 122, 123
  Gods & men of common origin II 270
—— *Olympian Odes*
  Pherecydes [Pherenicus?] on Hyperboreans II 775
—— *Pythian Odes*
  Aetna a celestial pillar II 763
Pine(s), oldest after ferns II 594
Pineal Gland. *See also* Third Eye
  atrophied II 119, 294n, 296n, 298
  discussed II 294-301
  highest development of II 299
  once physiological organ II 295
  witness of third eye II 294-5

Pino, Don Bautista
—— [*Three New Mexico Chronicles*]
 secret meetings of Pueblos II 181n
Pipe(s) of Pan, symbology of II 581
Pippala (Ficus Religiosa)
 fruit of Tree of Life II 97-8
Pirōmis, Pontiffs-, of Egypt II 369
Piśāchā (daughter of Daksha)
 mother of the Piśāchas I 415
Piśāchas (Skt) I 415, 571
Pisces II 656. *See also* Fish, Mīna
 constellation of Messiah I 385, 654
 does not refer to Christ alone I 653
 Night of Brahmā & I 376; II 579n
 planets conjunct in, at Jesus' birth I 654
 runs throughout 2 *Testaments* I 264
 southern, & beg of kali-yuga I 663
 Zabulon [Zebulun], son of Jacob, or I 651
Pisciculi (Lat) little fishes
 Christians called themselves II 313n
Pistis Sophia
 Barbelo invisible god II 570 &n
 discovery & publishing of II 566n
 earlier work than *Revelation* I 410
 echoes archaic belief I 577
 Ieov in I 449
 King's transl conforms to Church II 569n
 oldest Gnostic gospel II 604
 original, probably pre-Christian II 566n
 quotes *Book of Enoch* II 535
 read in light of *Gītā, Anugītā* II 569
 rescue fr Chaos by Christos I 132n
 seven elements of man II 604-5
 seven great gods, triads II 462, 512
 sevens, forty-nine II 618
 seven vowels, 49 powers I 410-11; II 564
 sound, speech, voices II 563
 vowels, lights, powers II 569-70
Piśuna (Skt) spy, Nārada called II 48
Pit. *See also* South Pole
 in *Ezekiel* II 492
 South Pole, Hell or II 274, 357, 785
 Virgo or Astraea descends into II 786
Pitar, Pitara [Pitaras] (Skt) fathers. *See also*
 Pitṛi(s)
 Brahmā (esoterically) II 60
 -devatās created lower man II 94-5
 divine, of 1st race II 394n
 divine sacrificers, pitris or II 605
 first race evolved fr II 329
 Peris of Persia fr II 394n
 progenitors of 5th race II 394n
 progenitors of man II 88
 Zeus, primeval progenitors of II 421

Pitar-devatās (Skt). *See also* Pitṛis
 first gods before "no-gods" II 248
 modes of procreation & II 148
 progenitors of physical man II 94-5, 171
 solar month is one day of II 620
Pithecanthropos alalus
 caveman was not II 741n
 fossils of, absent in Eocene II 679
 man never was, (Joly) II 661
 speechless savage of Haeckel II 677n
Pithecoid(s). *See also* Anthropoids, Apes
 accidental, unnatural creation II 261
 ancestors in Tertiary I 190
 breeding of, explained I 190; II 286
 fr 4th race man & extinct mammal II 683
 Haeckel's theoretical, man II 667
 Huxley tries to prove II 687
 -man a fiction II 669
 modern, & lemur compared II 717
 -Noah & his 3 sons II 655
 skull not under Atlantic II 727
 stocks & Eocene II 676
 third round, -like ancestor of man I 234
Pitṛi(s), Lunar I 179-91. *See also* Barhishads
 ancestors of man, become man I 180-1;
   II 102
 astral shadows of first Adams II 45-6 &n,
   91n, 137
 Brahmā as II 60
 cannot progress alone I 181-2
 ethereal doubles of II 5
 ethereal humans of 3rd round I 182
 evolve primordial man II 269
 evolve shadows of 4th round man I 174, 180,
   248
 first root-race progeny of I 160
 formed physical, animal man I 248
 four lower, corporeal, create man II 91-2
 have to become men I 180-1
 Lords of the Moon I 448; II 75
 lunar beings I 264; II 88
 mankind offspring of I 224
 most developed monads I 174
 Pitar Devatās or II 171
 progenitors of men II 45, 88, 91, 110
 progenitors of physical man I 86-7; II 171
 reach human stage in 1st round I 174
 shadows of, dominate 3½ races II 110
 shadowy, in Agrippa MSS II 487
 various names for I 227n
Pitṛi(s), Solar. *See also* Agnishvāttas, Asuras,
   Kumāras, Self-conscious
 adepts of past manvantara II 94
 discussed II 88-94

doomed to rebirth by karma II 93-4
endowed man w mind II 89
fashioned the inner man I 87
higher, no physical creation II 80
incarnated in 3rd race II 89, 92-3, 247-8
informing intelligences II 34
our race sprang fr rishis or II 365
prajāpatis &, are seed manus II 164
pranidhāna & II 88
Prometheus was II 95
three higher classes (arūpa) II 91-4
various names for II 92
Pitṛis (Skt) fathers. *See also* Ancestors, Asuras,
    Creators, Dhyānis, Fathers, Kumāras,
    Lhas, Pitar, Progenitors
endowed man w mind I 539n
forefathers of man I 445; II 683
Kabiri same as II 393
kumāras confounded w II 106
lunar & solar, described I 86-7
material classes of, create man II 91
men &, on Earth & God, demons I 457-8n
not ancestors of present man II 91n
one third of, arūpa pitris II 93
our progenitors I 606
regents of worlds, gods or I 99
seven classes of I 179; II 77, 89, 91-2, 97
take charge of planets I 442
twilight, issue fr sons of II 120-1, 163
two types of II 77, 89, 91
Pitṛis of the Demons, barhishads are II 89
Pivot, manas or II 241
Piyadasi [Piyadassī] (Pāli). *See* Aśoka
Placenta, Placental
earliest mammals have no II 166
Haeckel's views on II 649-50, 668
-mammal I 190n
umbilicus connected thru II 461
various types of II 713-14 &n
Placitus philosophorum. See Plutarch, *Moralia*
Plagiarism(ized) II 472n, 481-2
by anticipation I 401-2; II 476
fr *Book of Enoch* II 229, 482-3, 484-5
by Brahmins fr Bible I xxxi
de Mirville on, by ancients I 400-3
Sepp, Wilford on, Hindus I 654-5; II 619
Plaksha (Skt) fig tree II 404n
dvīpa, globe II 320-1
Plane(s) (cosmic)
diagram of I 200 &n
each atom has seven I 150
each, real to its denizens I 40, 296
energy on spiritual & physical I 644
everything conscious on its own I 274

Fall of Angels on every II 268
Fohat operates on all seven I 110-12, 328
fourth globe on lowest I 192
how to communicate w higher I 605
immortal ego acts on seven II 632-3
laya-centers & passage between I 148
light on our, darkness on higher I 450
manas irrational w/o ātma-buddhi I 242n
man related to, of his upādhi II 157
mental, almost endless gradations I 175
midway halt betw astral & physical II 736
our consciousness limited to one I 20
principles correlated to I xxxv, 633
seven, & man's consciousness I 199
seven angelic, 7 suns II 240-1
seven, called Seven Heavens II 273
seven globes on 4 lower I 152, 166; II 608
seven, of ideality II 335
subjective, objective I 176n, 189, 570, 603n
thickening of veil betw two II 281
three higher I 152
three higher, explained to initiates I 199
three higher, inaccessible to man I 200n
two poles on every I 41
visibility of globes & I 166
Zohar on I 239-40
Planet(s) I 21. *See also* Earth, Planetary
    Chains, Sacred Planets, Spheres
active, living (Aristotle) I 493
Agni-Vishnu-Sūrya source of II 608
Aletae were the seven II 361
all, comets or suns in origin I 103
all, septenary I 152-70
ancient knowledge re I 574 &n, 576
angels or regents of II 83, 89n
are born, grow, change, die I 609
aspects, nodes I 320
astral rulers of, create monads I 577
battles fought by growing I 101-2
biographies of, in Tārakāmaya II 45
chariots & steeds of II 31
conjunctions of I 656, 662; II 63, 76
creative powers, zodiac & I 213
day same on 4 inner II 707
death of, discussed I 147
Dev chained to each II 538
development of, around Sun I 595
did not evolve fr Sun's mass I 101, 588-9
distance fr Sun & status of I 602
each race under a II 24
elements differ among I 142-3 &n
ethereality of inhabitants of, (Kant) I 602
every, can evolve life (Littré) I 502n
every, has 6 fellow globes I 158-9

evolution of life on II 153-4
evolved fr primal matter I 625
fire common element of I 101
Flammarion believed, inhabited II 45, 699, 707
fourth, only seen I 163 &n
genii or stellar spirits of I 198
Gnostic geniuses of I 577; II 538 &n
Heavenly Snails I 103
how could astral Earth affect II 251
human stocks on I 166
incipient rotation of I 505
informing spirits of I 128
inhabited I 133; II 701, 706-7
initiates knew of more II 488n
intact during minor pralayas I 18n
Lares regents of II 361
life germs fr other II 158
life on other worlds? II 33 &n
limbs & pulses of solar system I 541
man's faculties fr I 604
many more, in Secret Books I 152n
Mars & Mercury mystery I 163-4
Mars or 6-faced II 382
matter differs among II 136-7n
Mazdean diagram of II 759
Moon &, cause catastrophes II 699
movements, positions of II 76
Music of the Spheres & I 433; II 601
never-erring time measurers II 621
nine, in *Vishnu Purāna* II 488-9n
older & younger II 251
orbital perturbations of I 503
origin of I 101, 103, 500-6, 601
other, better adapted for life II 706-7
polar compression of I 593
pralayas of I 12n, 18n, 149, 172n; II 660n
Purānas on rotation of I 442
rational intelligences (Kepler) I 493
rectors move, (Plato, Kepler) I 479, 493
regents of I 152, 576-7; II 22-3, 83
Sabean dance & motion of II 460
secret relation of, to Earth I 163-4
self-moving, queried I 670
seven II 22, 293
seven, & 7 races I 573 &n
seven, & terrestrial things II 361n
seven, & 12 zodiacal signs I 79, 573 &n
seven mystery gods & II 22
seven, or 7 circles II 488
seven sacred I 99-101 &nn, 152, 167, 573 &n, 574n, 575; II 602n
seven sons of Aditi I 448
seventy, explained I 576, 654 &n

small size of, near Sun I 500n
stars & II 83
Sun giver of life to I 386
Sun, Moon substitutes for I 575 &n
Sun's brothers, not sons I 449, 588-9
temples of gods I 578
theoi (θεοι) or gods, called I 2n
three sacred, unnamed I 575 &n
twelve gods or, 7 seen I 100
undiscovered I 102n, 576
uninhabited (science) II 699
upper globes of, invisible I 163
vary in orbits, axes, size I 593
wheel symbolizes I 40n
will be absorbed by Sun I 596
world bibles refer to II 703
Planet (Earth). *See also* Earth, Globe
ball of fire-mist once II 153
Fetahil creates I 195
Kabbala on birth of II 240
Planetary
almost all, worlds inhabited II 701
attraction &, motion I 529
conjunctions, importance of I 656
dissolution or pralaya I 159
gods, Agni-Vishnu-Sūrya head of II 608
gods gravitate to Sun II 361
life-impulses & evolution II 697
motion & spirits (Kepler) I 499
orbits puzzled Newton I 498
powers, 2 aspects of I 633
round & globe round defined I 160
seven, creators Gnostic symbols I 73
Planetary Chain(s) I 158-70. *See also* Earth Chain, Planets
age of I 205-6
architects of I 128, 442
ātyantika pralaya & II 309-10n
common belief in II 606-7
Days & Nights of I 154-5
death & energy transfer of I 155-6
destruction of, symbol for II 505
emerge fr cosmic monad II 311
evolution of I 231-2, 250 &n
failures fr previous II 233n
Fohat force that built I 139n
fourteen manus preside over II 321
in *Isis Unveiled* I 231-2n
karshvares 7 globes of II 384n
major manvantara one round of II 309
man-bearing globes of II 77
many, in our solar system I 654n
Mars, Mercury each a I 152-3, 164
new sun rises in each new I 655-6

nirvāna for monads betw two I 172-3
other, in our system I 575; II 699-709
our, described in world bibles II 703
principles of man & globes of I 153-4
second class of builders & I 128
septenary, all are I 152-70
seven dvīpas or II 320, 758-9
seven globes on 4 lower planes I 152
seven, in our solar system II 311
Seven Sons creators of I 60
"seven wheels" refer to I 144
starts as nebula I 22
three-, 6-fold II 616
upper globes of, invisible I 163
Uranus, Neptune guard other I 575
why teaching of, kept secret I xxxv
Zend Avesta on II 384-5, 606-7, 757-8
Planetary Spirits
Buddhists believe in I 635
each nation its own I 10, 576
highest, know our solar system II 700n
principles in man fr II 29
regents of planets or I 104; II 22
represented as circles II 552
rule destinies of men I 128
seven, of Christian mystics II 97
seven, or rishis II 318n
souls of heavenly orbs I 602; II 552
of stars, planets I 128
Planetoids, man's influence on II 700
Planet-tower of Nebo II 456
Planisphere(s). *See also* Dendera Zodiac
Carnac & West Hoadley are II 343
Plant(s) (kingdom). *See also* Botany, Vegetable
animals &, interdependent II 290n
bisexuality in I 320; II 133, 659
born fr bosom of the stone II 594
created before there was Earth I 254
dwarfed by climate in 3rd race II 329
force which informs & seed described
I 291
growth of, & Moon I 180
hard, that softened II 15
human embryo a I 184
intermediate hermaphroditism & II 167
Kabiri taught use of II 364
link Europe, America, SE Asia II 781
majority are hermaphrodite II 659
Moon (Soma) god of II 384n
nerves of I 49
New & Old World, similar II 792
not physical before animals II 290n
occult powers of, (Lévi) II 74
orders, classes of, in Purānas II 259n

seed must die to live as I 459n
seventh emanation of Mother & I 291
Plasm. *See also* Cells
immortal part of our bodies I 223n
spiritual, key to embryology I 219, 224
Plastidular Souls
Haeckel's, discussed II 650, 670-1 &n
spurious speculation II 663n
Plato
Atlantis account of, compressed II 760-1
Atlantis of II 147, 221, 263, 314, 322, 323-4n,
395, 408, 429
Atlantis of, Indian legend II 223, 407
best of Pythagoreans (Syrianus) II 599
bound by oath of secrecy II 763
chaos became soul of world I 338, 343
circular motion, on I 201
could not believe in personal God II 554
deductive method of II 153
defines genuine philosophers II 554-5
Deity cannot create, taught II 159
divine dynasties in II 367, 370-1
divine Idea moves the aether I 365
divine thought of, & lipikas I 104
elements, stoicheia of I 123, 338n, 461
embraced ideas of Pythagoras I 348
in error *before* initiation I 588
fifth rounder, explained I 161-2
God geometrizes II 39, 41
Hesiod's *Theogony* history to II 765
hints Pelasgians Atlanteans II 774
initiate-philosopher-adept I 2n; II 88, 266,
395, 554
innate eternal ideas of I 281
island of II 8, 141, 250n, 322, 352, 395, 407,
693
Logos of I 15n
Mayas coeval w Atlantis of II 34-5n
Mysteries, discipline, virtue I xxxv
Poseidonis or Atlantis II 265, 314, 407-9
&nn, 765, 767-8
Poseidon of, substitute name II 323-4n
principles & elements in I 491-2
science regards, as lunatic II 589
Secret Doctrine known to I xxxv
Solon's story of Atlantis II 221, 371, 395, 436,
781, 786
soul's faculties fr planets II 604
source of wisdom of II 530-1
spoke cautiously II 268
Sweden Atlantis of, (Rudbeck) II 402
taught all pledges would allow II 765
tetrad animal of, (Taylor) II 599
universal method of II 573, 584

—— *Banquet* or *Symposium*
androgyne race II 96, 132-4, 177
early races II 133, 264
—— *Cratylus*
Anaxagoras on nous I 451
Golden Age II 264, 372, 373
Koros as pure intellect I 353
theos, derivation of I 2n; II 545
Zeus not highest god I 425-6
—— *Critias*
Atlantis larger than Lybia II 761
island fragment only II 8, 324n
island of II 221, 266
Neptune divides Atlantis II 765
Plain of Atlantis described II 767-8
power of names II 767
sinking of Atlantis II 314, 394
source of Atlantis story II 743n
war of nations II 394, 743
—— *Laws* (*De Legibus*)
origin of wheat, wine, fire II 373
planets moved by rectors I 493
Saturn's Golden Age II 264, 372-3
—— *Parmenides*
One, reflection of Deity II 555
Taylor's Intro on chaos I 425-6 &n
—— *Phaedo*
mind cause of all things (Anaxagoras) I 451
—— *Phaedrus*
rectors of planets I 493
winged races II 55n, 96, 264
—— *Philebus*
infinite & finite I 426 &n
—— *Protagoras*
Prometheus gave man wisdom II 412
—— *Republic*
immorality of pantheons II 764 &n
—— *Statesman* (*Politicus*)
fertile & barren periods II 74
rulers & the ruled II 373
—— *Timaeus*
Atlantis described II 743n, 761 &n, 767-8
cross in space I 321n; II 561, 589
definition of soul II 88
destruction of Atlantis II 314, 395
Divine Thought, matter, kosmos I 348
elements or irrational daemons I 567n
on four elements I 460
God lighted the Sun I 579-80 &n
island a fragment II 8, 147, 266, 768
Jupiter or Father-Aether I 465
"man must not be like one of us" II 94-5
mundane macrocosmic tree II 97 &n
Phoroneus father of mortals II 519

secretion of elements I 568 &n
shapeless infants of early races II 132 &n
sinking of Plato's island II 250n
Solon on Greek history II 743
universe a dodecahedron I 340 &n, 344
world conflagrations, deluges II 784
Platonist, Alexandrian
compiled *Pymander* II 267n
Platonist, The, T. M. Johnson, editor
q Thomas Taylor on Jews I 426 &n
Platyrrhine (anthropoid)
apes & man II 171
fr late Atlantean times II 193
Pleiades II 549-50. *See also* Kṛittikās
Alcyone of, & age of Gt Pyramid II 432
Atlantides have become II 768
central point of universe II 551
connected w renovation of Earth II 785
connected w sound I 648n
cycle based on, & Virgo II 435
Hindus observed rising of I 663-4
Kārttikeya (Mars) & II 551, 619
mentioned in *Job* I 647-8
Niobe daughter of II 772
poussinière (Fr), Pillālu-kodi (Tamil) or
I 663
seven & I 648n; II 618-19
seven daughters of Atlas II 618, 768, 785
six of, then seven II 551
summer 'colure' passed thru II 407
Sun orbits Alcyone of I 501
"sweet influence of," (*Job*) I 648
Virgo inseparable fr II 785
when pyramids were built I 435
wives of 7 rishis II 549, 551
Plenum, the (Lat)
absolute container of All I 8
all matter connected in I 615
of Descartes I 623
fullness of the universe I 671
gods, genii within I 569
nothingness of science is I 148
science, vacuity, ether & I 495
Pleroma (Gk) fullness, completeness
astral light &, of Church I 196
downfall of I 416
fifth & 3rd states of II 79
Gnostic ogdoad & I 448
Logos reflected in II 25
planes of I 406
Satan's lair? II 506-18
scholiasts turn, into Satan II 511
Plesiosaurus(i) II 258
extinct w 3rd race II 206-7

law of dwarfing & II 733
man contemporary w II 206-7, 676, 713
paintings of, in China, Babylon II 205-6
Plexus(es), Nervous, 7, radiate 7 rays II 92
Pliny, *Natural History*
   Chaldean astron observations II 620
   circular meditation posture II 552
   Druid priests called magi II 756
   Earth kind nurse & mother I 154
   Earth's sphericity defended I 117n
   Egypt covered by sea II 368
   Egyptian year of 30 days II 620
   the Euxine II 5 &n
   giant Orion II 278
   giants II 336
   moving rock at Harpasa II 346-7
   Persians consulted the Oitzoé II 346
   rocking stones in Asia II 342 &n
   Saros cycle I 655n
   Saturnian Sea II 777n
   six-month polar day, night II 773
   stone which "ran away" II 342, 345
Pliocene II 254, 675-6, 690, 710, 714
   apes & men in II 676
   European man of, Atlantean II 790
   man existed in II 688n
   man immigrated to Europe in II 740n
   man's origin in, (Haeckel) II 680
   man's origin in, (Huxley) II 288
   portions of Atlantis sank in II 314n, 395
   scientists disagree on II 698
   temperate climate in II 738n
Plongeon, A. Le. *See* Le Plongeon, A.
Pluralité des mondes. See Flammarion, C.
Plurality of Worlds. See Maxwell, A.
Plurality of Worlds. See Whewell, Wm.
Plutarch II 336
—— *Lives (Vitae)*
   Caius Marius
      Cimmerians' long night II 773
   Numa
      Egyptian year of 30 days II 620
      May, Maia, Vesta I 396n
   Sertorius, tomb of giant Antaeus II 278
   Sylla, on the Great Year I 650; II 784, 785
—— *Moralia*
   De animae procreatione
      the double quaternary II 599
   De E apud Delphos
      stood for number five II 580
   [*De fraterno amore*], Castor & Pollux II 123
   De Iside et Osiride
      the elements I 125n
      father, mother, son in Plato I 348

      "ingress of Osiris into Moon" I 228
   De placitus philosophorum
      duad, mother, evil I 614
      Ecphantus on Earth's rotation [I 117
         &n]
      giving form to matter I 622
      Magnus Annus II 785
      Stoics on thunder II 526
      tetrad root of all things II 601
   Quaestiones Romanae et Graecae
      Castor's tomb in Sparta II 122n
      May, Maia, Vesta I 396n
   [*Quaestionum convivalium* or *Table Talk*]
      Pindar's *Hymn to Minerva* I 401
Pluto (Gk). *See also* Hades
   -Aidoneus or Aerial Jove I 464
   Atlantean islands sacred to II 408
   Axiokersos, Hades or II 362
   Dodonean Jupiter & I 463
   Earth, Yama or I 462-3
   fire-flame of helm of I 338n
   healer, enlightener II 26n
   in Pit, carries off Eurydice II 785
Pneuma (Gk) breath, spirit
   human soul or mind II 113
   spirit, soul or gas (Grove) I 465
   symbolized by wind or air I 226n, 342; II 113
   synthesis of 7 senses I 96
Πνεύματα (pneumata, Gk)
   spirits of the elements I 395-6
Pneumatics, kabbalists & esoteric I 242-5
Pneumatologie. See Mirville, J. E. de
Pococke, Edward, *India in Greece*
   myths are truths, not fables I 339
Poetica Astronomica. See Hyginus, G. J.
Poets, initiate-, preserve the wisdom I xlv
Poimandres. See Divine Pymander
Point(s). *See also* Sephīrāh
   Aristotle omitted I 615
   atoms of Leibniz mathematical I 628
   Avalokiteśvara, Verbum or I 429
   central I 635; II 612
   central, in crucifix II 556
   in circle I 1, 4, 11, 19, 91, 327, 426, 429, 613-16
   circle & "Golden Egg" II 553
   circle, triangle, etc & I 320-1; II 36
   emanates noumenal triangle I 614
   in En soph [Ain-sōph] II 111
   every, in infinity animated II 513
   fructifies the line I 91
   genesis of gods & men fr II 24
   germ or, in mundane egg I 57
   indivisible, limitless I 346
   knows only mūlaprakriti I 432

monad or I 426
mūlaprakriti conceals I 346
one, becomes triangle, cube II 612
one, is everywhere, nowhere I 11
the One or Logos I 426, 429
primordial, or Sephīrāh I 354
retires into the circle I 614
fr, to solid figures I 616
ten, & Pythagorean triangle I 612, 616
visible to eye of adept I 489
world fr the indivisible I 355
zero, or laya-centers I 551
Poitou (France), enormous stones at II 752
Polar, Polar Lands, Regions. *See also* Antarctic,
    Arctic, Hyperborean Continent
compression of planets I 593
continent prevails during round II 400n
first of 7 cradles of humanity II 324
magnolia blossomed in II 326
north of Meru II 326
occult commentaries on II 400-1 &n
opposite, forces II 84
periodically rise & sink II 325n, 360
Phaethon legend & II 770n
"pigmies" of II 331
semi-tropical climate at II 329, 356, 423
seven, circles of ancients I 204
shape of II 326
spoken of in *Avesta* II 291-2
Sun, Central Sun & ātma II 241
three, remain fr beginning II 776
tomb of Lemurian mankind II 324
Polar Dragon I 407; II 274, 770n, 771n, 786
Polaris. *See* Pole Star
Polarity
of cells II 117
death a change in I 526n
evil is, of matter & spirit I 416
of Fohat I 145
gravity caused by I 513
monadic principle fr passive to active II 669
opposite forces aspect of I 604
of spirit & matter II 84, 527
Pole(s). *See also* Hyperborean, North, South
    Pole
ancient names of, given II 274
beneficent & lethal influence of II 400n
celestial, as Meru II 785
changes of II 785-6
in constellation of Harp (Egy) II 360n
continents at North II 6-7, 12, 400n, 401, 785
dwarfed races of II 331
Earth's, &, of ecliptic II 332, 356-8, 431
Egyptians on ecliptic & II 332, 357

Fohatic forces at both I 205
"heavenly measure" II 363
imperishable Sacred Land & II 6
inverted 3 times II 353, 360, 368, 432-3, 436
moved for 4th time (Atlantis) II 350
negative, positive, of nature I 257
North, & first cataclysm II 138 &n
North, as Meru I 204
North, represents ātma II 403
North, symbolized as serpent II 356 &n
once pointed to Ursa Minor II 768
Seneca's prophecy re II 757
serpent w hawk's head II 357, 360n
South, abode of elementals II 274
South, as the Pit II 274, 357, 785-6
storehouse of vitality I 205
Sun dies for 6 months at II 769n
terrestrial, or Jupiter-Bacchus II 362
Pole of the Heavens
angle of, causes seasons II 356
hawk-headed serpent in Egypt II 356 &n
N Pole of Earth inverted to S II 360
Pole Star II 785. *See also* Alpha Draconis,
    Dhruva
Alpha Draconis, pyramid & II 432
Dhruva, Dhruvatārā or II 401n, 489n, 612n
Draco once was II 32n
founders of races linked w II 768
Meru metaphorically II 785
planets attached to II 488-9n
serpent symbol of, & seasons II 356
seven winds connected w II 612
in tail of Ursa Minor II 612n, 768
watches over Sacred Land II 6
when pyramids built I 435; II 432
Polier, Marie E. de, *Mythologie des Indous*
birth of Brahmā I 345
Pollux (& Castor)
born fr Leda's egg I 366
Dioscuri or II 122, 361n, 362
immortal man, demigod II 123
Polo, Marco, travels of, laughed at II 441
Polygenetic, Polygenesis(ism)
esoteric philosophy a modified II 249
fewer scientific problems w II 610
origin of races II 77, 168-9, 249-50
Polyhistor. *See* Alexander Polyhistor
Polynesia
Jacolliot on common myths of II 222-4
remains of Pacific continent II 222, 223
Polynesian(s)
dying out II 780
islands II 327
legends of sunken continent II 788-9 &n

Pacific continent &, (Haeckel) II 328
  skulls of, larger than French II 168n, 522
  taller than average II 332
Polynesian Researches. See Ellis, Wm.
Polyphemus (Gk)
  Titan, one-eyed Cyclops II 766
  Ulysses put out eye of II 769
Polyps, reproduce by budding II 177
  present fr primordial times II 712
Polytheism(ists)
  belief in powers of nature not II 592
  Greeks & nature forces I 466
  Hindu, reveals profound knowledge
    II 107n
  more philosophical I 575
  occultists are not II 194
Pompeii II 793
  declared fiction, myth II 236, 441
Πονηροῦ (ponērou, Gk) evil
  good (agathou) &, (de Mirville) II 515
Pontiffs-piromis
  statues of, shown to Herodotus II 369
Pope(s)
  Gregory & figure on cross II 587
  heliocentric theory banned by I 441
  infallibility of II 237-8, 316n
  literature banned by I 387
  named Lucifer II 33
  personates Peter & Jesus II 466n
  some early, were initiates I 311
[Pope, Alexander, *Essay on Man*] q II 189
Popol Vuh
  four men, 4th creation II 213
  man created of mud or clay I 345
  Noah in II 222
  race that saw any distance II 55n, 96, 221
  second & 3rd races II 160
  sevens II 35
  tzité tree & 3rd race II 97 &n, 181n
  Votan in snake's hole II 379
Popular Astronomy. See Newcomb, S.
Popular Science Monthly, confirmed Audubon's
    yellow water-lily II 440
Popular Science Review
  Hunt on Sun I 530-1, 538n
  Pengelly on "Ice Age Climate" II 695-6
  Richardson on "Nervous Ether" I 508,
    530-1, 537-9, 603; II 298n, 654
  Richardson on "Sun Force, . . ." I 508,
    524-7
  Seeman, Crotch on Atlantis II 781-2
  Seeman on Australia, Eocene II 779
  Seeman on Australia, Europe II 333
  Slack on the sciences I 588, 600

Woodward on axial changes II 726
Population, Moon's influence on I 228-9n
Popul Vuh. See Popol Vuh
Pores
  form oozing out of, & mediums II 86
  men born fr, of parents II 68
  Raumyas born fr Vīrabhadra's II 68, 182-3
Porphyriōn (Gk)
  scarlet or red Titan II 383n
Porphyry (Neoplatonist)
—— [*Concerning Images*]
  "Egg is the World" I 360
  Hermes as Creative Word II 542
—— *Peri apochēs empsuchōn [De abstinentia]*
  do not address the One w words I 425
—— *De vita Pythagorae*
  Pythagorean monad, duad I 426, 618
  Pythagorean numbers I 361
Porphyry (stone) II 530
Porpoise (Śiśumāra, Skt) constellation II 612n
Porta Pia, Gnostic sarcophagus of I 410
Port-au-Prince, Voodoos of II 209
Poseidon (Gk). *See also* Neptune
  dolphin vehicle of, -Neptune II 577
  dragon II 356
  five ministers of II 578
  god of the horse, (Homer) II 399n
  Neptune, Idaspati, Vishnu or II 765n
  -Neptune ruled over sea I 464
  sensual, vindictive (Gladstone) II 766
  spirit of 4th race II 766, 775
  took many forms to seduce II 775
  trident of II 390
Poseidonis (Gk). *See also* Atlantis
  Atlantean island II 265
  descendants of, built pyramids II 429
  existed in Purānic times II 407
  island of, not continent II 767-8
  not real name of Atlantis II 323-4n
  Plato's island or II 8-9, 265, 314, 324n, 395,
    407-8, 751n, 761
  Proclus on II 408-9
  sank 12,000 years ago II 124, 765
  Śankha-dvīpa & II 408 &n
  third step of Idaspati II 765 &n
Positive, awakens negative in minerals I 291
Positivism I 9n, 479
Positivists, Svābhāvikas called I 4
Post-diluvian II 356, 394, 406, 609
Postel, Guillaume
  saw *Genesis of Enoch* II 267-8n
Posthumous Humanity. See d'Assier, A.
Post-mortem States I 411; II 496

Postulant. *See also* Candidate
  symbolized Sun, resurrection II 462
Potency(ies)
  of all beings in Brahma I 450-1
  spiritual, guiding embryo I 219
"Potency of the Pythagorean Triangle"
    II 592n. *See also* Ragon, J. B. M.
Potential & Kinetic Energy
  sleeping atoms, life-atoms & II 672, 673n
Πόθος (Pothos, Gk) yearning
  desire or, principle of creation I 110
  union of spirit & chaos I 340
Potter, clay man fashioned on wheel of,
    I 366; II 213n, 291
Pottery, among primitive men II 716, 722, 724
Pouillet, estimates Sun's heat I 484n
Poussinière, French name for Pleiades I 663
Power(s). *See also* Śaktis
  celibacy, chastity & occult II 295
  creating, in animal man II 98
  an entity heads each yogi- I 293
  five & 7, of initiate II 580
  generative, symb by certain gods II 43n
  incarnating II 88-90
  intellectual, psychic, spiritual II 319
  magic II 427
  man's creative, gift of wisdom II 410
  messengers & 7, of Logos II 359
  misuse of, & 3rd eye II 302
  of plants, animals, & minerals II 74
  senses impediment to II 296
  seven, & the elements II 359
  seven vowels & the forty-nine II 564
  sidereal, awakened by man I 124
  superhuman, of siddhas II 636n
  used for selfish purposes II 319
Powers (cosmic). *See also* Cosmogony, Gods,
    Theogony
  assist Christian creator I 440
  astral light abode of I 196
  awakened by sound I 307
  belief in, personified II 592
  cosmo-psychic I 86
  creative, & unborn Space II 487
  creative, not the One Principle I 425
  divine & terrestrial, struggle II 495
  divine, born in mind of Logos II 318n
  divine, shape universe I 22
  forty-nine, & 7 vowels I 411
  given divine honors I 424
  hierarchy of creative I 213-15
  intelligent active, & blind inertia I 520
  intelligent, rule univ I 287, 499n, 554;
    II 502

invisible, or noumena II 517-18
  labeled unscientific I 424
  lower, make Earth ready II 242
  fr providence or divine light I 350
  seven elemental, & Great Bear II 631
  seven, of nature & noumena II 273
  subordinate, worshiped I 44
  fr Sun meet every 11th year I 290
  twelve subordinate, & Sun II 23
Prabhavāpyaya (Skt)
  manifested deity I 46; II 107-8
Prachetas (Skt) observant or wise
  name of Varuṇa II 578
Prāchetasas (Skt)
  fathered Daksha by Mārishā II 176-7
  five ministers of Gnostics II 578
  rishis of Aryan race II 495
  solar portion of manas II 496
  ten (exoteric), 5 (esoteric) II 578
Practical Lessons on the Occult
  re the Unknown I 581n
Pradhāna (Skt) primordial matter. *See also*
    Aether, Ether, Protyle
  Alaya & I 49-50, 50n
  Brahma-Pums &, in the beginning I 445
  Brahmā superior to I 370n
  efficient, material causes & I 55
  first form of prakriti I 582
  Mahat 1st production of I 216n
  matter is, or eternal I 545
  mūlaprakriti & akāśa I 256
  presided over by kshetrajña I 284-5
  purusha-, kāla & creation I 451-2n
  some schools call, illusion I 62
  Universal Mind 1st product of II 58
  unmodified matter I 176, 582
Prādhānika Brahma Spirit [Puṃs] (Skt)
  Mūlaprakriti-Parabrahman I 256, 445
Praelectiones Theologicae. See Peronne, G.
Praeparatio evangelica. See Eusebius
Pragna. *See* Prajñā
Prahlāda (Skt), son of Hiranyakaśipu I 420n
Prajāpati(s) (Skt). *See also* Lords of Being,
    Rishis
  advanced spirits fr lower planet II 611
  ātivāhikas or, aid jīva I 132
  Bhrigu one of II 76n
  Brahmā creates the II 176n
  Brahmā is, collectively I 81, 94-5; II 60
  create on Earth, not Brahmā II 163
  creators in *Rig-Veda* I 346, 426
  Daksha chief of II 82, 247n
  dhyāni-buddhas, mānasaputras or I 571
  dhyāni-chohans or I 375

fathers of various beings II 259n
first male & mother's husband I 91
flames or, incarnate in 3rd race II 247-8
forefathers of man I 445
informing intelligences II 34
Jyotis one of II 766 &n
led on by Adam Kadmon II 129
located along tail of tortoise II 549
lower, fathers of man's body I 457
Manu Svāyambhuva synthesis of II 704n
mind-born sons of II 140n
Nārada one of the II 82
Osiris as chief I 437
pitris &, seed-manus II 164
pole star & the seven II 768
pre-human period, belong to II 284
produce 7 other manus I 449
rishis become 7, 10 of I 442
rishis or I 346, 349
sephīrōth or, 7 of I 89-90, 355
seven builders or I 436
seven, 14, 21 of, explained I 235n; II 259n
seven, of this round II 614n
seven, origin of I 433; II 253-4
seven, progenitors, races I 248; II 611
śishtas &, throw seed of life II 150
speech & mind consult, (*Anugītā*) I 94-6
spiritual self in man fr I 457
ten & seven I 355; II 176n, 365, 573-4
ten, produced I 449; II 308n
ten semidivine I 349
ten, 6, 5 of I 90
twenty-one I 90; II 40
Vāch &, in creation I 137, 431
Vaśishtha-Daksha's sons are II 78
Zohar on II 624-5 &n
Prajñā (Skt) intelligence, wisdom. *See also*
    Consciousness
chinmātra is potentiality of II 597n
seven aspects of I 139; II 597n
seven states of II 29n, 636, 641
Prākrita [Prākritika] Creation I 427
first 3 creations called I 446, 453
Tairyagyonya creation & I 455 &n
Prakriti(s) (Skt) nature, primary substance
ākāśa, ether confused w I 255
ākāśa noumenon of I 508
alone is senseless I 247
astral light on low plane of I 255
bore Brahmā in its womb II 527
Brahmā & I 19, 542
Brahman is spirit & I 421
discrete & indiscrete I 373
illusion (Advaitī philosophy) II 598

irrational without purusha II 42
Kantian soul & I 602
in laya or sūkshma state I 522
localized matter II 65
mineral kingdom aspect of I 178
mūlaprakriti root of I 62; II 65
not the immortal spirit I 255
Padma &, creations I 427
positive aether I 508
pradhāna 1st form of I 545, 582
at pralaya I 255, 257, 373
purusha &, 2nd Logos I 16
purusha blind without I 247; II 123n
-purusha produce all things I 284
Sānkhya philosophy re I 256n, 335; II 42
seven, or protyles I 328
seven principles of I 257 &n
seven, purushas & principles I 335, 373 &n
three-faced prism of II 635
web of universe & I 83
Prākritika (elemental) Pralaya
described I 370-1; II 69n
at end of Brahma's life I 371-2
universal pralaya II 309n
Pralaya(s) (Skt) dissolution. *See also* Manvan-
    tara, Nitya, Obscuration
absolute & minor I 12n
beginning of, & 7 suns I 290
Berosus figured, by zodiac I 649-50
builders latent during I 88, 104
cosmic deluge or II 69n
cosmic ideation ceases in I 328-9; II 598
cyclic, are but obscurations II 660n
described I 172n, 368-78; II 307n
Deus implicitus or I 281n
duration equal to a manvantara I 240
fate of various beings during I 571-2
First Logos sleeps during I 429
follow manvantaras like nights & days
    I 373-4
after 14 manvantaras I 245, 370
gnatha [jñata] latent during I 428
great & minor I 18 &n
hinted at in *Revelation* II 565 &n
kalpa interval between minor II 307
matter undifferentiated in I 328
monad loses name in I 570
motion during I 497n
Night of Brahmā or I 240; II 307n
Noah's raven & I 443
after 1,000 periods of 4 ages I 370
Parabrahman the one ego in I 428-9
Parāśara's purānic account II 757
partial, after Day of Brahmā I 552

planetary dissolution or I 159, 172 &n
primeval matter during I 69
reduces bodies, egos I 265
Seneca quoted on II 757
seven sabbaths are seven II 747
seven terrestrial II 329-30
Siphrah Dzeniouta on II 504
solar I 172n, 371-2
Stanza I describes I 21
by submersion II 324-5
universal or mahā- I 172n, 371-3, 552
various I 53, 172n, 370-3; II 69n, 309-10n
Pralīna (Skt) reabsorbed, withdrawn I 372
Pramantha (Skt)
  Agni born to Arani & II 101, 526-7
  celestial fire &, Baudry on II 526
  friction of, degraded II 101
  Prometheus & II 413n, 520, 524-5
  tool for kindling fire II 413n, 524
Pramatha (Skt), signifies theft II 413n
Pram-gimas [Pramžimas] (Lithuanian)
  advised couple saved fr Deluge II 270
Pramlochā (Skt) a nymph
  Hindu Lilith II 175
  Kāmadeva & II 175-6
  perspiration fr pores of II 171n, 175
  story of Kandu & II 174-7
  symbol of nascent physical man II 411
Prāna(s) (Skt) breath II 242
  apāna, etc, life winds II 566-8
  atoms of, never lost II 671-2
  breath of life (Massey) II 632
  corresponds to globe five I 153
  expirational breath I 95
  inert without matter I 526n
  life, corresponds to oxygen II 593
  life essence II 596
  life principle I 157-8
  lowest subdivision of I 262n
  not jīvātman I 226n
  pervades body of man I 526n
  rudras, 10 vital breaths or II 548
  second principle, male, active I 525n
  second principle of dhyānis I 224
  speech, apāna & I 95
Prāṇamaya Kośa (Skt) I 157. *See also* Astral
  Body
Pranava (Skt) sacred syllable Om
  called Vāch I 138
  mystic term like Om I 432 &n
Prāṇāyāma (Skt) breath control
  acquiring of II 568
  dangers of, in yoga I 95-6
  regulation of vital winds I 96

Pranidhāna (Skt) persevering devotion
  yogi's 5th observance II 88
Prasaṅga Mādhyamika (Skt)
  teachings of, on time I 43
Praśraya or Vinaya (Skt) modesty
  mother of affection II 528
Pratisamchara (Skt). *See also* Pralaya
  incidental dissolution I 372
Pratisarga (Skt), secondary creation II 106
Pratt, Henry
  kabbalist-positivist I 226n
—— *New Aspects of Life & Religion*
  Central Sun II 240
  elemental spirits, matter I 234n
  fallen angels I 194n
  Jehovah Spirit of Earth II 508-9
  kingdom of spirits, souls II 242
  space & First Cause I 9-10n, 342, 615
  spirit called "deprived" II 246n
  triangles & pyramids I 616-17
  units I 617
Pratyagātma (Skt), Jīvātman as Logos II 33
Pratyāhāra (Skt) withdrawal
  elemental pralaya I 257, [373]
  restraint, regulation of senses I 96
Pratyayasarga Creation (Sāṅkhya) I 456
Pravaha (Skt) wind
  regulates course of stars II 612
Prayag (Allāhābād)
  built on subterranean cities II 221
  lunar kings reigned at I 392
Prayer(s)
  Christians & pagans both use I 466-7
  Council of Constantinople & II 279n
  for destruction is black magic I 416, 467-9
  of Earth Spirit II 28
  to Father in secret I 280n
  of gods to Devakī II 527-8
  of gods to Vishnu I 419
  Jewish liturgy of Pentecost I 618
  Mazdean & Lord's II 517
  Nemesis not propitiated by I 643
  of Rabbi Ben Gebirol I 439n
  Sabean II 361-2
  to Virgin of the Sea I 468
Pre-Adamic (-Adamite) Races II 172, 252,
  289n, 747
  Bible skips II 252
  Chwolsohn on II 452-7
  earth & alkahest I 345
  Figanière on II 289n
  implied in Genesis II 394
  kings II 83-4
  Kings of Edom I 375; II 705

period of divine man II 284, 285n
[of Reverend Gall] I 324-5
seven manus were, men II 311
Simorgh fr last, deluge II 397
third race men II 172
Preadamites. See Winchell, A.
Pre-animal Races, were "angels" II 650
Preceptors. *See* Divine Kings
Precepts for Yoga, on life & tree of life I 58
Precession of the Equinoxes. *See also* Equinoxes, Sidereal Year
Aldebaran & II 785
Babylonian dates fixed by II 693
beginning of kali-yuga & I 663
Bentley on II 550
climate changes &, (Croll) II 314
cyclic, sidereal years or I 439n
Egyptian records of I 650
great tropical year or II 505
Herodotus & data on, (Egy) I 435
movement of apsis, equinox & II 330n
recession of tropics & II 331
Precious Things, 14, & 4th initiation I 67 &n
Précis élémentaire de physiologie. See Magendie
Pre-Cosmic
ideation & substance I 15, 58, 452
theogony II 94n, 144-5, 147
Predestination
Calvinist II 304 &n
in history of globe, races I 641, 645
Preexistence
of every creature II 618
of universal consciousness II 490n
of universe I 278
Pre-Existing, evolves fr Ever-existing I 278
Pre-Glacial man II 71-4, 715-30
Prehistoric Ages
calculated by seers II 67
myths contain realities of I 304n
Prehistoric Congress (Brussels, 1872)
doubted Bourgeois' findings II 751-2
Prehistoric Europe. See Geikie, J.
Prehistoric Man. See Wilson, D.
"Prehistoric Man." *See* Lubbock, Sir John
Préhistorique antiquité. See Mortillet, G. de
Pre-Homeric Greeks II 11-12
Pre-human Period II 165n
first race up to 4th race II 315
genealogies embrace II 322
monsters II 115, 634
Pre-Matter, or protyle I 328n, 598 &n. *See also* Crookes, Wm. A.
Presence I 618
the All- I 46

ever incognizable I 1, 2, 239, 280, 629
kārana or I 280
Present. *See also* Duration, Time
cross section in time, space I 37
eternal, Divine Thought & I 61
generations & occult truths I 298
past & future alive in I 105
past, future & I 37, 43-4; II 446
past helps us grasp I xlvi
"Present Position of Evolution." *See* Haeckel
Preserver(s)
divine fire is II 114
rākshasas in allegory II 165n
Vishnu as I 286, 459n, 526n; II 313
were builders, fashioners, rulers II 514
President (US), Indian petition to II 439
Presidential Address. *See* Crookes, Wm. A., "Elements & Meta-Elements"
Prevision, & cyclic events I 646
Priam (King of Troy)
son of Laomedon II 796
Priapic Deities I 358
Priapus(ian,ic) (Gk) I 6n
celestial, or Agathodaemon II 458
Jewish God euhemerized II 543
Pride II 237, 271, 274, 514n
Priest(s)
ancient, moved stones by will II 342n
-architects I 208-9n
assume names of gods II 379-80
Atlantean, addressed gods I 464
grihastha, of exoteric ritual II 499
high, & revelation II 455
initiated, could read Dracontia II 346
-initiates II 494, 517, 529, 542
kept reincarnation secret II 552
lost teaching of rounds, races II 618
man's good actions the only I 280
responsible for materialism I 578
six Zuñi, & 1 priestess II 628-9
Priestess
-Mother, speckled corn & II 629
six Zuñi priests & one II 628-9
Priestley, J., "discoverer" of oxygen I 623
Prima materia. See Primordial Matter
Primary Age (geology) II 160, 710. *See also* Primordial-, Secondary-, Tertiary-, & Quaternary Age
compared w theosophy II 712 &nn
rocks of, 42,000 ft thick II 709
two & ½ races in II 712
Primary Creation I 454-5. *See also* Creation
creation of light or spirit I 450
darkness to profane II 59

elemental kingdoms dominant II 312n
evolution of worlds fr atoms II 731
forces self-evolving in I 446
found in *Genesis* I 450
gods & rudiments of senses in I 446-7
Hindu I 450-2
precedes all cosmogonies II 59
Secondary Creation & II 53n, 107, 113, 312n
of self-born gods, elohīm I 450
Primeval Age, divine men in II 712
Primeval Man Unveiled . . . See Gall, Rev J.
"Primeval Race Double-Sexed." *See* Wilder
Primordial Age (geology). *See also* Primary-,
    Secondary-, Tertiary-, & Quaternary Age
compared w theosophy II 712 &nn
marine fossils of, 3rd round II 712
rocks 70,000 ft thick II 709
Primordial Matter. *See also* Daivīprakṛiti,
    Pradhāna, Prakṛitis, Protyle
direct emanation of universal mind I 602
homogeneous I 601
Kant's, & ākāśa I 601-2
mind ordered, (Anaxagoras) I 595
Mother or Prima materia I 291-2
motion in I 97-8n
not hot or cold I 82
nucleus of, & the Sun I 540-1
sixth principle or I 594
sons of I 82
soul of, is aether I 341-2
upādhi of 7th principle I 594
various names for I 283
Ymir (Örgelmir) or I 427
Primordial Seven I 88, 106, 108
Primordial Substance. *See* Substance
Prince of the Air
an everlasting principle II 515
St Paul's, explained by Lévi II 485
Prince of Waters
St Michael called, in *Talmud* II 505
Principalities (of Christian hierarchy)
copy of archaic prototypes I 92
Powers of St Paul & I 632n
fr providence or divine light I 350
Principes, genii of Nazarenes I 195-6
Principia. See Newton, Isaac
Principia Rerum Naturalium. See Swedenborg
Principle(s) (cosmic)
ākāśa 5th universal I 13n
animating, of stars I 117
astral light 6th & 7th, of space II 511-12
daivīprakṛiti or unmanifested Logos I 216
divided variously I 110
elements & I 334-5

fifth, or mother & dhyāni-chohans I 293
fourth, animal soul of nature I 111-12
of globes transferred I 172
God the Father or 7th I 74n
& human principles II 596
indiscrete, Wilson, etc on I 521-2
informing, enter laya-center I 147
Kwan-shi-yin form of 7th I 471
lower, māyāvic I 17-18
Plato on elements & I 491-2
primordial light is 7th I 216
septenary in Purānas II 616
seven, & 7-headed serpent I 407
seven creations, rishis, etc II 612
seven, in Bible II 747-8
seven, purushas & prakritis I 335
seventh & 6th, in cosmogony I 594
seventh, in man, cosmos I 74n; II 593, 596
seventh, of mother substance I 289-90
seven, variously given I 335, 342; II 58n, 108
six, all come fr 7th I 17
sixth, or Brahmā I 17-18
solar system has seven I 110
spirit, soul-mind & life I 624 &n
three, & mūlaprakriti I 620
three, & 3 strides I 113 &n, 122
vital, of Sun I 591; II 105
world-stuff or 5th & 6th cosmic I 101
Principle(s) (human). *See also* Kāma, Manas,
    etc
analogy of, & root-races II 254n
in animals II 196n, 255, 267
body & two lower, die II 235
Brahmanic & theosophic II 640-1
buddhi is 6th, passive II 231n
buddhi-manas is higher self II 230-1
cannot be separated I 158
& cosmic principles II 596
derivation of 5 middle I 222
development of, in races II 254 &n
development of, in rounds I 259-60; II 167
divided variously I 110
each, fr hierarchy of spirits I 133; II 273
elements & II 593
emanate fr prism of prakriti II 635
esoteric & kabbalistic I 243-4
fifth, hypostasized II 275
four lower I 122n
four lower, 4 flames II 57n
four sacred animals symbolize I 363
globes, upādhis & I 153-4 &n
Gnostic II 604-5
of the gods I 633
God the Father 7th, in man, cosmos I 74n

how man obtained his 5th I 247
indiscrete, & buddhi I 453
Lévi's, & theosophists' I 242-5
man's lower, re-used next life I 173
Massey, Boehme on II 630-5
middle, most gross I 260
physical, not grossest I 260
saptaparna or I 236
seven II 635-41
seven, & gods, men I 226-7
seven, & 7-headed serpent I 407
seven, called 7 souls (Massey) II 631n
seven, developed in 7th round II 167
seven, fr *Kabbalah, Bk of Dead* II 633-5
seven Hindu & Egyptian, given II 632
seven, in Bible II 747-8
seven, in esoteric schools I 122; II 603-4
seven, in *Pymander* II 491-2
seven letters used for II 57n
seven, not in *IU* I 197, 231n
seven, or 7-eyed stone II 627
seven rishis symbolize II 139, 313
seventh, loaned to man I 224
seven, under 7 planets II 29 &n
six, given lay chelas I 122
source of II 241
three, & their garments II 315
three, & 3 strides I 113 &n, 122
three higher, 3 fires II 57n
three middle, more material I 225
two connecting, & agnishvāttas II 79
union of 5th & 6th II 247
wheat symbolizes II 374 &n
Principle(s) (primordial or philosophic)
   Absolute I 6; II 167
   Boundless I 14
   Brahmā as fructifying I 333
   female generative, & ark II 139
   First, of Plato II 554
   fundamental, of Secret Doctrine II 536
   Infinite, cannot create I 7
   of life may kill I 539
   moyst, of Poimandrēs II 236, 591n
   never-resting, & cosmic monad II 311
   Unknown, present everywhere I 481
   unseen, in nature, humanity II 555-6
Principles of Biology. See Spencer, H.
Principles of Geology. See Lyell, C.
Principles of Human Knowledge. See Berkeley
Principles of Psychology. See Spencer, H.
Principles of Science. See Jevons, W. S.
Principles of Zoology. See Agassiz, J. L. R.
Prithee [Prithī, Prithu] (Skt)
   milks Earth of grains II 259n

pursues the Earth I 398n
Wilford believed, was Noah I 654
Prithivī (Skt) I 237
   divided into 7 principles II 616
   as Earth greets Vishnu I 18
   six worlds above II 385n, 608
Privation(s)
   germ concealed in I 219
   prototypes (Aristotle) I 59; II 489
Priyavrata, King
   divides 7 dvīpas II 320, 326, 369n
   seven, 10 sons of II 320, 369n, 406n
Prjevalsky (or Przhevalsky), General N.
—— *From Kiakhta to the Sources* . . .
   Tchertchen ruins I xxxiii-iv
Probabilities, Law of I xlvi-vii
Proceedings of Royal Society (London), Reade, T.
   M., on sedimentary strata II 11
Proceedings of the Royal Institute
   Crookes on genesis of elements I 581, 621-6;
      II 105 &n
   Huxley on persistent forms II 256-7
Proclus, *Commentaries on Euclid's Elements*
   visible & invisible circles II 552
—— *Commentaries on the Timaeus*
   Arkite Titans II 143
   Iamblichus on Assyrians I 409, 650
   Marcellus on Atlantis II 408-9
   Rhea is monad, duad, heptad I 446
   Tetraktys II 603
—— *On the Theology of Plato*
   highest principle I 426
   Tetrad II 599
Procreation. *See also* Oviparous
   ancients venerated I 209-10
   animal, painless II 262
   change in, described II 415
   desecrating, caused curse II 410-11 &n
   by egg, vapor, vegetation, pores, womb
      II 183
   five evolutionary stages of II 166-7
   necessary pangs of incessant II 475
   occult evolution of II 657-60
   seasons of animal II 412n
   sexual, will disappear next root-race I 406
   variety of modes of II 168, 172-8, 183
   by will I 192; II 183, 766
   yod (Heb) or ten & II 574
Proctor, Richard A.
   "coincidences" of I 314-15, 324
   on Great Pyramid & pole star II 432
—— *Knowledge* (periodical)
   date of Egyptian zodiac II 435
   date of Great Pyramid II 431

Dragon constellation at pole II 352-3
refutes Smyth pyramid figures I 314
—— *Myths and Marvels of Astronomy*
　accurate astronomy 2400 BC I 650; II 435
"Proem to Genesis." *See* Gladstone, W. E.
Profugis, De. See Philo Judaeus
Progenitor(s). *See also* Pitris, Prajāpatis
　androgynous II 130
　are ourselves (1st personalities) II 88
　became gods before becoming men II 349
　created 7 races II 77
　creators of our bodies II 88, 110
　details about, contradictory II 138
　divine builder of men II 194
　highest, gave man mind II 92
　men in Mazdean ark are II 291
　merged w own astral bodies II 138
　mindless, & primeval man II 80
　monad used astral body of II 660 &n
　pitris, pitar I 456n; II 58-9, 88, 110
　projected shadowy men II 95, 138, 164
　prototypes of 1st root-race I 456n
　seven, & 7 races II 611
　seven degrees of II 712 &n
　seven, or pillars II 293
　seven, or prajāpatis II 611
　shadows of, dominate 3½ races II 110
Progress of Religious Ideas. See Childs, L.
Progymnasmata. See Brahe, *Astronomiae*
Προμανθάνειν (Promanthanein, Gk) to learn
　beforehand, name Prometheus fr II 521
Pro-Mater, divine fire II 114
Promati [probably Pramati] (Skt)
　son of Fohat II 413-14n
Promenades au Musée . . . See Mortillet, de
Prometheus (Gk) II 411-22, 519-28. *See also*
　Lucifer, Pitris (Solar)
　agnishvāttas became II 79, 411
　allegory of, explained II 103
　Athena &, create new race II 519
　Azāzēl is the Hebrew II 376
　boons of, to mankind II 523
　chained on Mt Caucasus II 414
　champion of mankind II 411-12n
　crucified on Mt Kajbee II 44
　crucified Titan explained II 413, 561
　derivation of name II 413-14n, 420n, 521
　divine soul II 419
　evil fire, lightning, etc II 526
　Fetahil [Pthahil] of Nazarenes I 195n
　fire of, inner not physical II 523-4
　forty-nine fires & II 521
　found in every theogony II 420-1
　gift of, became curse II 420

Jupiter is II 269
Loki same as II 283n
Lucifer another version of II 237n
molded & enlightened man II 519
myth fr Āryāvarta II 524
myth misunderstood II 525-7
myth older than Greeks II 413
Norse prophecy & II 100
phallic slant given to II 526
pitris or I 195n
prophecy of, & mysteries II 419
son of Asia, brother of Atlas II 768-9
son of Titan Iapetos II 525
spiritual man & II 95
steals divine fire II 244, 525
Sun-god, hero II 44
symbol of, degraded II 100-1
taught man civilization II 526
thunderbolt &, myth II 522
Titan-, rebelled against Zeus II 280n
Titans-Kabirim symbolized by II 363
transforms perfect animal II 244
Zeus cursed, sent to Hades II 244, 412
Prometheus Bound, Prometheus Vinctus. See
　Aeschylus
Promised Land, nirvāna or I 568 &n
Proof(s)
　history & tradition are II 336
　20th-century disciple may give I xxxviii
"Proofs of Evolution." *See* Haeckel, E.
Propagation. *See also* Procreation, Reproduc-
　tive
　by will before the Fall I 192
Propatōr (Gk) Forefather. *See also* Bythos,
　Depth
　existed before Bythos I 349
　periodical I 214
　ray fr Ain-sōph I 349
　unmanifest Logos I 214
Prophecy(ies)
　adepts taught Balaam II 409
　alleged, about savior I 653
　based on cycles & math I 646; II 621
　re chemistry as new alchemy I 622-3
　re deathblow to materialism I 612
　disciple may be sent I xxxviii
　door wider each century I xxxviiin
　Dracontia used for II 347
　re European nations I 644, 646; II 266, 435
　Figanière, re man's future II 289n
　Frankenstein, homunculi are II 349
　re future subraces II 444-6
　re kali-yuga I 377-8, 644-5
　re Kalki avatāra II 483

re modern nations II 330-1
re Moru [Maru] & solar dynasty I 378
Norse, of 7th race II 100
re priority of man II 690
prognostication is not I 646
re Prometheus & Sabasian Mysteria II 419
recording, beforehand explained II 621
re vindication of Asiatic philosophy II 334
volumes I & II of, described I xliv
zodiac & I 649, 653
Prophet(s) II 469
  Adam, of Moon II 468
  adepts of right-hand path II 211
  Hecate & jealous God of I 395
  initiates or II 492
  of Israel & Bath-Kol II 107
  leaping, of Baal II 460
  persecution of right-path, by left II 503
  secret colleges of II 533
Proportion
  laws of, taught at initiations I 208n
  lost canon of I 208-9n
Propositions I 272-82
  Three Fundamental I 14-18
  three new, re mankind II 1
Προσελήνοι (proselēnoi, Gk) prior to moon
  Arcadians called themselves II 352
Proserpine(a) (Lat). *See also* Persephone
  lunar goddess I 396
  seven Atlantis islands sacred to II 408
Prosimiae
  critique of Haeckel's II 649-50, 668-9
Protagoras. See Plato
Protamoeba, primitive protoplasm II 164n
Protein, protoplasm &, (Huxley) I 637n
Protesilaus, on skeleton at Sigeus II 278
Protestant(s) I 226
  faith of I 612
  link brazen serpent w Christ I 364 &n
  lost sight of Michael II 479
  slander Dragon of Wisdom II 377
Proteus
  Hindu, of 1,008 names I 349
  hypothetical, of science I 326
  light the great I 579
  primordial substance I 330
  superior wisdom of II 762
  Toum [Tum] the Egyptian I 673 &n
Protista(ic) (unicellular organism)
  germ of apperception in I 455
  Haeckel traces consciousness to II 650
  moneron passes fr, to animal II 153 &n
  not an animal II 594n
Protogenes, primitive protoplasm II 164n

Prōtogonos(oi) (Gk) firstborn
  called *dis* by Damascius I 70, 343 &n
  firstborn form & idea II 25
  firstborn gods II 43, 490n, 703n
  firstborn light I 70, 343
  manifested Logos II 592
  not yet mirrored in chaos II 704 &n
  produced fr spirit & chaos I 70
  "unknown Light" reflected in II 703n
Protologos(oi) (Orphic) II 107
  Brahmā same as all I 335
  spirit of nature II 108
  totality of prajāpatis I 356
Proto-organisms
  animals & man once ethereal II 184
  of Naudin II 120
Protoplasm II 730
  defined by Haeckel II 164n
  homogeneous I 46
  laya-center & I 204
  man's body began as II 255
  origin of II 158-60, 164-5n
  potentialities of, discussed II 653-4
  protein &, Huxley on I 637n
  sarcode or II 153 &n
  speck of, (moneron) II 151, 189
Prototype(s). *See also* Adam-Kadmon,
    Chhāyās
  astral, become physical II 68n, 660n, 712,
    736, 737, 738
  astral, of 3rd round II 186, 256-7, 712
  Christian angelology fr archaic I 92
  each human has spiritual I 235n
  mammalia fr, 4th round man shed II 684
  of mankind I 224
  monad requires a spiritual I 247
  present in ideal form I 63
  "privations" of Aristotle I 59; II 489
  reincarnation & celestial I 639
  senses fr astral II 295
  Silent Watcher or divine I 265
  spiritual beings objectivize I 282
  spiritual, in the ether I 282 &n, 332
  spiritual, of all things exists I 58
  Vaivasvata, of Noah II 306
  Venus is Earth's spiritual II 31
Protyle(s) (primordial substance). *See also*
    Elements, Ether, Ilus, Pradhāna
  atoms & I 582
  atoms evolve fr laya to I 522
  basic line of Pythagorean triangle I 617
  cooling of I 625
  corresponds to planes of matter II 737
  differentiates into elements I 130

elements become, again I 240
ether of science I 339
hydrogen nearly allied to II 105
invisible, of science I 58
is our layam II 105
mediate phase I 328 &n, 598n
next neighbor to mūlaprakriti I 582
original primal matter I 581
science returns to I 553
seven, or prakritis I 328
six, basis of objective universe II 737
Subba Row on Crookes' I 620-1
Sun & planets evolved fr I 625
undifferentiated matter I 60, 240
yliaster ancestor of Crookes' I 283
Proverbs [or *Proverbs of Solomon*]
wisdom & understanding II 134n
wisdom's house w 7 pillars I 356; II 641
Providence
analogy of ant, sin, & I 133
astral light material of active I 421
chief cause of "ways of" I 643
cruel, degradation of Deity II 305-6n
karma cannot be called I 634
proceeded fr the Word I 350
punishes evil to 7th rebirth expl I 643
Pruner-Bey, Franz
fallacies re man & ape II 681
Prytanea [Prytaneum]
& self-moving stones II 345
Psalms [or *Psalms of David*]
androgynous mankind II 134n
angels made spirits, etc I 92n
breaking heads of dragons II 505
evils come fr north & west I 123
God's ministers, a flaming fire I 107
"He placed his Throne in the Sun" I 493
"I know not Thy numbers" I 115n
Jehovah a god among other gods II 508
Kadush I 463
Kadushu (priests) II 460
Sōd II 212n
verses 25:14, 89:7 retranslated II 212n
Psammites. See Archimedes
Psellus, M. C. *See Chaldean Oracles*
Pseudo Berosus. *See* Berosus, *Antiquitates*
Pseudographs
palmed off on credulous II 442
Psyche, Psuchē (Gk)
butterfly Greek emblem of I 74
lower anima mundi I 194, 197n
manas or human soul II 275n
nous & II 134n, 377
in quaternary II 599

Psychic
astral light & the I 196
ātman warms inner man on, plane II 110
chief factor in, phenomena II 59n
civilization & the II 319
connects matter & spirit I 197n
craze described II 349
dhyānic group &, man I 559
evolution physical & II 62, 87, 109, 294, 365
faculties & 49 fires I 521
force as a weapon II 56n
force (Sergeant Cox) & Archaeus I 338n
form of primitive man II 154
guided by the animal is sin II 413
hallucination, delirium & II 370-1n
higher pitris our, & spiritual parents II 171
influence of Moon on, phenomena I 180
key to symbolism I 363
nature of man, origin of II 275
nature of Moon secret I 156
passions, powers & misuse II 302
power of, over physical II 192
prognostication is not I 646
prototype of, function II 92
struggle between spiritual & II 272
struggle on, plane II 64
"Psychic Force and Etheric Force." *See*
Bloomfield-Moore, C. J.
Psychism, is not psychology II 156n
Psychode of Thury I 338n
Psychologist(s)
Hume regarded as a II 156n
modern, are materialists I 620n
modern, ignores buddhi II 81
Psychology II 107n
Aryan & Egyptian, not understood I 226
deals only w false personality II 254
Eastern I 54
esoteric, septenary II 632-3
fifth element & II 135
"laws of association" I 292
in lunar worship I 398
monism, materialism & negative I 124 &nn
sees man as evolved animal I 636
shifted to crass materialism II 156n
spiritual vs materialistic I 620n
Psychometry
aspect of jñānaśakti I 292
physicists & I 201n
Psychopaths, & "spirits" II 370n
Ptaḥ, Phta, Phtah (Egy). *See also* Asklēpios
Ammon & I 675
carries mundane egg I 365
deity concealed by II 553

Egyptian creative intellect I 353
Khonsoo confused w II 464
original god of death like Śiva I 367n
Osiris-, creates his limbs I 231
proceeds fr world egg I 367
-Rā aspect of Archaeus I 338n
seventh Kabir II 365n
various names for I 353
Ptahil, Pthahil. *See* Fetahil
Pterodactyl(i)
    extinct w 3rd race II 206-7
    flying dragons & II 387
    flying saurian II 205-6
    genesis of II 151
    man contemporary w II 206, 218-19, 676
    paintings of China, Babylon II 205-6
Ptolemy [Claudius Ptolemaeus]
    Asuramaya &, Weber on II 49-50, 326
    calendars of I 663
    calls Arabs noble tribe II 200 &n
    Champollion vindicated II 367
    geocentric system of II 150n
    Hindu epoch & I 658-9
    observations of, & Hermes I 664
Ptolemy Philadelphus
    had Jewish laws transl into Greek II 200n
Ptomaine(s) I 261-2, 262n
Pueblos, secret meetings of II 181n
Pūjā (Skt) worship
    to Jesus in woman's clothes I 72n
Pulaha (Skt), mind-born son II 78
Pulastya (Skt)
    father of serpents, nāgas II 181
    mind-born son II 78
    missionaries link, w Cain I 415
    Parāśara & I 456n
    prajāpati II 232n
    progenitor of rākshasas I 415; II 232n
    Rāvana, Dattoli & II 232n
Pulomā (Skt) mother of Dānavas II 381-2
Pulse
    solar I 541
    Stratton on cycles of II 623n
    universal I 84, 216
Puma, & lion II 792
Puṃs (Skt) spirit I 256
    Brahma, pradhāna & I 445
    eternal all-pervading I 373
Punarjanman (Skt) rebirth I 293
Puṇḍarīkāksha (Skt) lotus-eyed II 108
Punjab, finest men physically in II 411n
Punjcaure. *See* Panjkora
Purāṇa(s) II 36-7, 58, 121, 137, 181. *See also*
    Vishṇu Purāṇa

Āgneyāstra II 629
allegorical & historical II 323
anticipated modern discoveries I 623
astronomy of, conceals II 253
Asuramaya in II 50
authors of, knew forces of science I 521
bhūtas in II 102n
Bible & I xxxi, 316; II 126, 251-2
bipeds before quadrupeds II 163, 183
Brahmā as a boar II 75
Budha, wisdom, Mercury II 498
chronology of I 316; II 225
commentary on, re Vishṇu, Śesha II 505
compiled fr "very old book" I xliii
confirm old teachings I 307
continents, islands II 263-4, 402-9
days & nights of Brahmā I 368-78
dead letter of, a fairy tale II 320
deal w causes II 252
decad, dual system in II 573
deluge (Atlantean) II 140
details of, contradictory II 138
disfigured by translation I 115n
dual creation II 81
dualistic, not evolutionary I 256n
esoteric keys in, for searcher II 585 &n
esoteric works at one time I 423
ether produced sound I 587
exaggerations in II 67, 252, 585
exoteric II 378
exoteric symbols used in II 455
expressed 5,000 years ago II 527
fallen gods II 232, 283
four vidyās in I 168-9
geometrical figures, numbers I 66
giants, Titans, Cyclopes in I 415; II 293
hide esoteric meaning II 148, 175n
history of our monads I 284
incongruities in I 420-1
Indra in, & *Rig-Veda* II 378
initiates knew meaning of I 423, 520; II 320
Kapilas, several in II 572
kings, rishis II 94
lunar, solar year, day II 621
Mahat inner boundary of universe I 257
Mahat-prakriti I 602
man 7th Creation I 217
many meanings in II 402-3
maruts sons of Diti II 613
material pole of Vedas II 527
more mythical than Stanzas II 23
must not be taken literally I 369; II 585
names allegorical, geographical II 403n
Nārada in II 47-9

north polar region II 326
occult secrets in II 571-2
older than Phoenicians II 406
older than Plato's island II 407
orders, classes, animals, plants II 259n
personnel of, pre-human II 284
physical, metaphysical worlds II 402-3
pitris described II 91, 121
pradhāna aspect of Parabrahman I 256
pralaya, Parāśara's account of II 757
primeval perfect cube I 344
primordial voice, light in II 107
rishi-yogis II 78-9n
rotation, revolution of planets I 442
scientific when read esoterically II 251-3
sea that never freezes II 12
serpent oracles II 381
Śesha I 407; II 505
seven creations I 21
seven human, cosmic principles II 616
seven manus II 3
sevens in II 35, 611, 616
son of Moon legend II 45
spiritual man independent of body II 254
Śveta-Dvīpa II 6
Tārakā War in all II 497-8
treat the pre-cosmic, pre-genetic II 252
twice-born II 70
two or more creations II 53
undying race II 275 &n
universal myths II 97
universal truths in II 409-10
universe as an egg I 360
Vaivasvata as Noah II 290-1
Vaivasvata Manu, one only in II 251
on various races II 173-7
Venus story II 30
Vishnu 1st, Brahmā 2nd Logos I 381n
war of asuras II 63
wars in heaven I 202, 418-19
weapons in II 629-30
wisdom in I 336
written emblems I 306-7
"The *Purāṇas* on the Dynasties of the
　　Moryas . . ." *See* Rao, D. B. R. R.
Purgatory, Kabbalistic I 568n
Purohita (Skt) "appointed," chief priest
　　Brahmanaspati is, to the gods II 45n
　　Gauramukha, to King of Mathurā II 323
Purūravas (Skt), legend of I 523
Purusha (Skt) man, cosmic or ideal Man
　　atom inseparable fr I 582
　　blind without prakriti I 247-8; II 123n
　　born fr Eternal Cause or non-being I 344

Brahmā & I 81, 542
divine spirit I 461
Heavenly Man II 703-4 &n
immutable, unconsumable I 582
male astral light I 196
manifested deity II 108
Nārāyana or I 231
only reality II 598
-pradhāna-kāla & creation I 451-2n
prakriti & I 16, 81, 284, 542, 582; II 42, 598
prakriti &, aspects of One I 51, 552
on prakriti's shoulders I 248
pure, created waters pure I 458n
sacrificed for production of universe II 606
seven logs, 21 layers of fuel & II 606
seven, principles, prakritis I 335
seventh principle II 574
Subba Row on I 428
Supreme Spirit absorbs I 373
various names for II 704n
Virāj born fr, or heavenly man II 606
web of universe & I 83
world soul born of, & matter I 365
Purushasūkta (Skt)
　　hymn of *Rig-Veda* II 606-7
Purushottama (Skt) Supreme Spirit
　　Achyuta or I 542
　　infinite spirit, Kapila or II 570
Pūrvaja (Skt) firstborn, pregenetic
　　name given Vishnu II 107
　　spirit of nature, protologos II 108
Pūrvāshāḍhā (Skt) a constellation
　　kali-yuga & II 550
Pushkara (Skt) blue lotus flower
　　America, North & South II 403, 407
　　described II 404
　　globe, loka, etc II 320-1
　　Pātāla or antipodes of India II 407n
　　seventh dvīpa II 319, 403
　　yet to come II 404-5
Pushkara Māhātmya (of the *Harivaṃśa*)
　　Daksha converts to female II 275-6
Putah (Egy), buddhi corresponds w II 632
P'u-to, Chinese island, temple I 72, 471
Putra (Skt) son, child II 163
　　ascetic son of Priyavrata II 369n
　　Daksha creates II 183
Pu-tsi-k'iun-ling [P'u-chi-ch'un-ling]
　　Kwan-shi-yin or I 471
Pygmalion(s)
　　fails to animate his statue II 150
　　first creators were, of man II 102
Pygmy(ies)
　　dwarf races of Poles II 331

glacial epoch or age of II 715n
good & bad giants & II 70
hippopotamus, elephant II 219
modern men are II 194
Pymander. See Divine Pymander
Pyramid(s). *See also* Great Pyramid
  adepts dwelt under II 351-2
  Alpha Draconis & I 407
  antedates Bible I 115n
  Atlantean descendants built II 429
  Aztec, discussed (Humboldt) I 322
  became pillars at Tyre I 347n
  of Cheops, initiation in II 462, 558
  Cholula, built by giants II 276n
  constellations, deluges & II 352
  cube &, or matter & form II 599-600
  decad found in I 321
  derived fr shape of fire II 594
  described II 352, 575
  each consecrated to a star II 362
  embody sacred name I 439
  four sides of, 4 cardinal pts I 125-6, 347n
  gallery of, & golden cow II 469
  "I am that I am" & II 468
  indestructible cement of II 430
  Kephren builder of 2nd II 226
  menhirs & nuraghi copies of II 352
  not exclusively Egyptian II 352
  perfection of, (Kenealy) I 208-9n
  quaternary is, (Ragon) II 575
  Seth, Enoch & II 361-2
  subterranean passages in II 429
  symbol of Mysteries, initiation I 314-15
  tabernacle of Moses based on I 347n
  third, 4th race initiates & II 353
  triangles & I 616-17
  units of measurement & II 226
Pyramidalists, figures of, "biased" I 315
Pyramid of Cheops. *See* Great Pyramid
Pyramids & Temples of Egypt. See Petrie, F.
Pyramis (Gk), Reuchlin on II 599-600, 601
Pyrolithic Age (Laurentian)
  oceans condensed in II 159
Pyrrha (Gk), escapes deluge in ark II 270
Pythag. See Stanley, T.
Pythagoras. *See also* Pythagoreans
  adept I xxxv; II 530
  Aristotle dwarfed ideas of I 615
  brought decad fr India II 573, 582
  brought symbols fr East I 612, 616
  called Venus "Sol alter" II 31
  circle of, & golden egg II 553
  circular meditation posture II 552
  contemporary of Confucius I 440

corpuscular theory of I 484, 507
decimal notation & I 361
duad of I 426, 618-19; II 575
focus of secret wisdom I xlv, 611-13
forces are spiritual entities I 492, 495
"fragments of," (Oliver) II 640-1
harmonic doctrine based on seven II 601
knew secret wisdom II 534
kosmos of II 599
monad & duad of, & Plato I 426
Monad of I 64, 426-7, 433, 440-1, 619; II 575
music of the spheres I 432; II 601-3
Mysteries, discipline, virtue I xxxv
oath of II 603
Plato embraced ideas of I 348
point, line, triangle . . . I 612; II 24
Porphyry on Plato & I 426-7
proceeded fr universals downward II 153
school of I 433-4, 616
seven of II 35, 582
sources of wisdom of II 530-1
studied in India I 433
Sun guardian of Jupiter I 493
taught heliocentric theory I 117 &n
ten perfect number w II 463
Tetrad sacred to II 599
Tetraktys, triad, decad of I 440-1
triad, triangle of I 344
Venus of II 31, 592
vouched for ancient legends II 217
Zeus not highest god I 425-6
zodiac & dodecahedron I 649
Pythagorean(s). *See also* Tetraktys
  abacus I 361
  all globes rational intelligences I 493
  chaos or soul of world I 338, 343
  corpuscular theory I 507
  decad I 321, 616-18; II 553, 573
  decad or all human knowledge I 36
  full numbers known to I 361
  hated the binary II 574
  initiates & deductive method II 153
  key to 365-day year II 583
  metempsychoses & human embryo II 188
  monad in darkness I 63-4, 427
  monad, Logos, or point I 614
  musical notation II 600
  numbered hierarchies of gods I 433
  number 4 called key-keeper by II 600-1
  number symbology I 361; II 573-6, 580-1,
    599, 601-3
  Plato best of, (Syrianus) II 599
  six & 1 among II 582
  Tetraktis, Logos becomes II 24

triangle symbolizes sephīrōth II 111 &n
triangle, 10, 7 points of I 612-13, 616
zero & 1 among I 361
Pythagorean Triangle. See Oliver, G.
Pythian Odes. See Pindar
Pythius, name of Apollo II 106
Python

attacks Apollo's mother II 383 &n, 771n
dragon serpent oracle II 381
equivalents of II 379, 516
falling demon of Greece II 486, 516
North Pole or, chasing Lemurians II 771n
red dragon of *Rev* II 383 &n, 771n
Sun conqueror of II 208

Q

Qabbalah. See Myer, I.
Qādēsh Qedēshīm (Heb), holy ones, Holy of
   Holies II 212n, 460, 463
Qādōsh (Heb), Sun, Adonāi, El-El or I 463
Qādoshō (Heb), holy place (*Ps* 24:3) II 460
Qai-yin II 315. *See also* Cain
Qaniratha. *See* Hvaniratha
Qedēshōth (Kadeshuth in tx)
   female, same as Nautchnis II 460, 463
Qedoshīm, Qedōshīm (Heb, Kadeshim in tx)
   far fr holy II 212n
   galli or, lived by the temple II 460
Quadrature (of circle)
   four-faced Brahmā is I 344
   Parker on I 315-16
Quadrigemina, Corpora. *See* Corpora Quad-
   rigemina
Quadrumana (four-handed). *See also* Anthro-
   poids
   descent of man fr, fiction II 193
   extinct before 7th race II 263
   man fr, (science) II 255, 258, 348, 661
Quadrupeds, Daksha made II 163, 183
Quaestiones et Solutiones. See Philo Judaeus
Quaestiones Graecae. See Plutarch
Quaestiones Naturales. See Seneca
Quaestiones Romanes. See Plutarch
Quain, Jones, *Elements of Anatomy*
   on the pineal gland II 297
Quarterly Journal of Microscopical Science
   Haeckel on monera II 153n
Quarterly Journal of Science
   Ward on temperature of Sun I 484n
Quartiles (astronomy) I 320
Quaternary I 221, 242n, 436
   Brahmā & I 213
   emanates lower triad II 595
   energizing light of Logos makes up I 428
   father, mother, son & I 614
   fire root of II 114
   first solid figure (Ragon) II 575
   has to be terrestrial or celestial II 604
   Heavenly Man symbolized by II 595
   Jehovah & I 618
   manifested, fr Mother alone I 88
   Marcus on I 351

Noah, 3 sons & II 597n
noumenal root of all numbers II 582
pyramid or II 575
Pythagorean double II 599
symbol of immortality II 575
Tetragrammaton & I 73n, 438n; II 625
triangle, trinity & II 35, 591, 612
unity & I 59
Quaternary Age (geology) II 710. *See also*
   Primordial-, Primary-, Secondary-, &
   Tertiary Age
   antiquity of man & II 288
   balmy spring of II 738n
   compared w theosophic periods II 715-17
   Europe in, described II 740
   man before the II 206
   man's origins placed in, (science) II 157, 686
   no human skeletons found before II 723
   rocks of, 500 feet thick II 709
   savages of II 749
Quatrefages de Bréau, Jean L. A. de
   an agnostic II 645
   gave blow to Darwinism II 56n, 681
   man-ape likeness exaggerated II 87n
   monogenesis of, criticized II 195-6
   reservations of, about Darwinism II 662
   right in his own way II 426
   scientific fallacies I 487
   theosophists respect II 651
   unbiased, honest, earnest II 645
   upsets Darwinism II 654, 711
—— *Les crânes des races humaines . . .*
   Canstadt & Engis men human II 744
—— *Histoire générale des races . . .*
   apes likely descend fr man II 287-8
   fallacy of evolutionists II 681
   man helpless without mind II 56n
   man lived before mammals II 155
—— *The Human Species*
   apes fr man II 682, 687n
   Cro-Magnon & Guanches II 678n, 740, 790n
   descent of Aryans, Semites II 426
   disposes of Haeckel's man-ape II 745n
   on Haeckel's prosimiae II 649-50, 668-9
   life rules inanimate forces I 540, 603
   man in Miocene & earlier II 746

man in Secondary Age II 10, 157, 219, 288, 686, 687n, 714n
milieux or environment II 736
new races come fr crossings II 444
Quaternary man intelligent II 749
q Naudin on 1st man II 119-20
race extinction II 780
rapid & gradual evolutionists II 646 &n
why man not fr apes II 646 &n, 666-7
Quatremère, Étienne M.
 Nabathean Agriculture a copy II 453
Queen of Heaven I 400-3
 Mary, Moon or I 403
 Mout (Mut) called the II 464
Quetzalcoatl (Quetzo-Cohuatl in tx)
 de Bourbourg on II 380
Quiché (Maya). *See also Popol Vuh*
 Egyptians & I 267n; II 34
Quiché MSS II 96. *See also Popol Vuh*
Qui circumambulat terram (Lat) [Cf. 1 *Peter* 5:8], human egos & II 485, 515
Quiescence, preceding creation II 488-90

Quinames (Quinametzin, legendary giants)
 built Cholula pyramid II 276n
Quinary (fivefold)
 found in double triangle II 592
 man a, when bad II 575
Quinquepartite (fivefold)
 division of man (Vedānta) I 226
 explains relations of gods, man I 226
Quintessence I 508; II 114-15
 universal, or fluid of life II 576
Quinto Libro, Euclid. *See* Proclus, *Commentaries on Euclid . . .*
Quintus Curtius, [*History of Alexander*]
 speaks of 15-day month II 620
Quis ut Deus (Lat) who is as God
 St Michael II 479
Qū-tāmy (Babylonian adept scribe) II 453
 doctrines of, & early 5th race II 457
 a fraud (Renan) II 454
 instructed by Moon idol I 394-5
 madonna & idol of Moon I 401

R

"R," signifies moving man II 574 &n
Rā (Egy) Sun-god. *See also* Amen, Amen-Rā
  Apophis enemy of II 588n
  contemporary w Haroiri I 366n
  defunct as Horus assimilated to I 228
  divine Universal Soul I 231
  father of Osiris I 437
  the generator I 367
  gestates in universal egg I 359-60
  issued fr the Deep I 231
  is the egg of Seb I 364-5
  as the "One God" I 675
  Osiris-Ptah or, creates limbs I 231
  Shoo personification of II 545
  Tum, Fohat & I 674
Rabbi(s), Rabbin(s). *See also* Jews
  angel, companion, adept II 626n
  blinds created purposely by II 388, 536-7
  in Book of Al-Chazari II 40
  Brahmans &, re lingam symbol II 471-2
  concealed meaning of Ain-sōph II 386
  enormous bird of, fr Simorgh II 618
  God-name of, despoiled II 388
  hated Christianity II 537
  Hecate predecessor of God of I 395
  initiated, purposely confused II 252n
  knew esoteric meanings II 127
  later, made Jehovah Adonai II 465
  later, not sincere II 126-7, 459n, 461
  numbers 10, 6, 5 sacred to I 90n
  phallicism of II 85
  revenge of, against Christians I 11
  secrecy of II 126
  seven souls of II 632
  sleight of hand of I 462
  taught 7 renewals of globe II 397n, 565, 618
  two accounts of *Genesis* II 252n
  two tetragrammatons II 626
  wisdom of, materialistic II 247
Rabmag (Chald), chief of magi II 213
Raca [Rēgā'] (Heb), fool I 578
Race(s). *See also* Humanity, Man, Mankind,
    Root-Races, Subraces
  Adamic, our II 6
  androgynous II 96, 134
  astral, & environment II 157
  astral doubles, were II 115

Bamian statues record II 339-40
black, brown, older (Winchell) II 695
w bones & Adamic rib II 193
born fr gods, universal concept I 323
born, grow, die II 443-4
cataclysms &, transition II 500n, 703
complexions of II 178, 227 &n, 249-50, 282
condensation of II 151
creation of II 86-108
cycles & I 642; II 330-1, 780
destroyed by fire, water II 725-6
differences betw II 103, 249-50, 607n
divine, our, sprang fr II 365
dying out of II 779-80
each, has its deva II 538
each, under a planet II 23-4
earliest, needed no elements II 160
early, boneless, ethereal II 149
early, had no egos II 610
early Lemurian, roots of mammals II 736
early, sinless, karmaless II 610
early, understood Moon I 386
effects of isolation on II 425
elect, & highest dhyānis II 276
ethereal, incorporeal II 194
ethereal to material & back again II 697
every, adapted to surroundings II 46
every, exalts its deity II 507
evolution of, & embryo II 187-9, 659
evolution of, performed in Mysteries II 419n
extinct, near Tchertchen I xxxiii-iv
fifth, humanity & *Mahābhārata* II 139
first, & Manu II 307, 311
first & 2nd, not physical II 108
first, had 3 elements II 107, 113
first, origin of II 86-7
first, or "self-born" II 164, 198
first, sexless II 134
first speaking, or Ad-i II 452
first 3, & 3 orders of mammals II 713-14
first 2, disappeared in progeny II 609n
first 2, knew no death II 609
first 2, many-shaped II 635
first, were created, destroyed II 704
first, without fire II 107, 113
five, & 4 Adams II 457, 503-4

five [in *Vishnu Purāna*] II 322
four, of Hesiod II 271
fourth developed speech II 198-200
garments of, (*Zohar*) II 315
giant II 754-6
of half-human monsters II 192
hermaphrodite (separating) II 134
human, can breed together II 195
hybrid, left by 3rd II 714
Indo-European, height of II 749
inferior, explained II 162, 249n, 425
inferior, not always older II 721
initiates know history of II 133
initiates veil info re early II 715n
inner senses atrophied in early II 294
intellect dormant in early I 210
intermediate, evolved II 275
Kings of Edom or II 2, 704
Lemuria's accursed, lived in jungles II 319
many, disappear without trace II 437
Massey misunderstood II 634-5
Mediterranean, Winchell re II 695
mindless, some early, remained II 161-2
mixture of, makes new races II 444
more ancient than mammals II 56n
once an organism without organs II 154
our, has reached 5th subrace II 471n
overlap each other II 433n
oviparous even now II 131
phoenix stands for, -cycle II 617
Plato's winged II 55n, 96, 264
polygenetic origin of II 168, 249
pralaya of a II 404
pre-Adamic, & sinning angels I 324
predestination in history of I 641
primeval, huge, filamentoid II 151
primitive, may be old, relapsed II 721-2
primitive, was boneless I 583n
procreation of 1st, described II 116-17
red & blue, destroyed II 192
relics of distant, will be found I 609
rise & fall of, & writing II 442
Rudra-Śiva patron of II 502n
savage & civilized, in all ages II 716
self-, sweat-, & egg-born II 30, 68, 116-17,
    172-3
Seth-Enos of 4th II 134
seven, & 7 rays II 191n
seven, born simultaneously II 1-12, 77, 329,
    611
seven, in Bible II 747-8
seven, in *Revelation* II 565, 748
seven, in various religions II 617-18
seven, kept secret I xxxv

seven kings or seven I 241; II 748
seven, on Babylonian Tree II 104
seven rishis are II 139
seven zones & II 77, 91, 249, 607n
sterility of, explained II 195-6, 780
superior & inferior, a fallacy II 425
Talmudists lost sense of forty-nine II 618
that never dies II 67
three ethereal II 669
three-eyed men of 3rd & 4th II 669
three great, only remain II 471n, 780
Rachel, mandrakes, magic & II 27n
Radiant Matter
    Crookes', & 4th son of Fohat I 562
    substance of occultist & I 514n, 545
    true nature of light & I 621n
Radiation(s)
    formless arūpa, & bodies I 632-3
Radicals
    comets or I 503
    forms of cosmic magnetism I 145
    six, of Simon Magus II 569n
Radiometer of Crookes I 514
Radius, of circle, triangle I 315-16
Raghunāthāchārya, Chintāmaṇi
—— *Tirukkanda Pañchānga*
    calendar of kali-yuga II 50-1 &n, 67, 68-9
Ragon de Bettignies, Jean-B.-M.
    European initiate I xxxvi
—— *Le cours philosophique* . . .
    number 3 & triangle discussed II 575
—— *Orthodoxie Maçonnique suivie de la
    Maçonnerie occulte* . . .
    believed in univ mystery language I 310
    Greek aspirated vowels II 576
    Greek "Z" a double seven II 582
    Hiram Abif a solar myth I 314
    keys to symbols, dogmas I 363
    meaning of Masonry II 795-6
    ogdoad II 580
    Pater Zeus, etc II 574
    St Germain re solar year II 583
    senary (6-fold) & physical man II 591
    six sacred to Venus II 592 &n
    Sun or Uranus w ancients I 99-100n
    tau, terminus (end) II 581
    triangle symbol explained II 575-6
    triple ternary II 580-1
    two spirits II 580
Rahasya (Skt) secret doctrine
    Upanishads or, & Gautama I 271
Ra'hmin [Raḥamīn] (Aram) compassion
    corresponds to Seth II 315
Rāhu (Skt), story & symbol of II 381

Rain
  no herbs until coming of I 345
  Rudra breathes I 370
Raivata (Skt)
  manvantara II 89
  root-manu, 3rd round II 309
Rāja (Skt), impenetrable or adbhutam II 621
Rājagriha, initiation cave in I xx
Rajāṃsi (Skt) worlds
  six, above Earth (globes) II 384-5n, 608
  three, discussed II 621-2, 622n
Rajarishi [Rājarshi] (Skt) II 225n
  class of royal rishis I 502
Rajas (Skt) activity, passion
  active aspect of ego I 335n
  one of the trigunas I 348
  sattva, tamas, &, in *Anugītā* I 535
Rājasas (Skt)
  incarnating dhyāni-chohans II 90
  kumāras, asuras, etc II 89
Rāja-Yoga (Skt) kingly union
  hatha-yoga alone cannot lead to I 95
  Tāraka, re man's principles I 157-8; II 603
Rāja-Yogin (Skt)
  every adept has to become I 158
Rākshasas (Skt)
  "adversaries" of gods II 164
  Atlantean giants II 70, 227n, 232n, 276
  become saviors (*VP*) II 163
  created by svabhāva I 571
  early Atlanteans later became II 323
  giants of Ceylon II 336
  gibborīm of Bible or I 415; II 273-4
  identified w asuras II 163
  incarnated in man II 164
  of Lankā & Rāma II 276, 752
  missionaries link, w Cainites I 415
  not demons II 232n
  preservers II 165 &n
  of *Rāmāyana* or devs (Pers) II 394
  regarded as demons II 165n, 288
  fr the 7th climate II 319-20
  Sinhalese & II 407-8
  tempters, devourers of man I 415
  tombs of, at Malabar II 347, 752
  war w Bharateans II 776
Rākshasī Bhāshā (Skt)
  Atlantean language II 199
Ram
  head & horns a symbol II 182
  -headed god makes man (clay) II 291
  horns on Moses II 213n
  on Phoenician coin II 546
Rāma (Skt). *See also Rāmāyana*

conquered rākshasas of Lankā II 276
  first Aryan divine dynasty & II 495
  Hanuman advisor of I 388
  Rāvana &, historical II 224n
  slew Rāvana II 225n
Rāmānujāchārya [or Rāmānuja] (Skt)
  founded Viśishtādvaita Vedānta I 522
Rāmāyana (Skt)
  battle between good & evil II 495-6
  Figanière & monkeys of II 289n
  Garuda, Anśumat, cycles II 570
  Hanuman, monkey god in II 680
  Kapila's eye destroys I 563; II 570
  Lakshmī in I 379-80 &n
  male & female manus in II 143
  maruts, sons of Diti in II 613 &n
  must be read esoterically II 496
  Pulastya & Rāvana II 232n
  rākshasas II 163, 394
  seven aspects of II 496
  weapons or sons of Kriśāśva II 629
Ramses or Rameses (Egy)
  Bait-Oxly tomb in reign of II 559
  heroical traditions of II 368
  many crosses on throne of II 559
Rao, Devān B. R. Ragoonāth
—— "The Purānas on the Dynasties of the
    Moryas . . ."
  Katāpa (Kalāpa) in Tibet I 378n
Rao, T. S. *See Subba Row*
Rao, T. V. K., calendar of kali-yuga II 50-1 &n
Raoul-Rochette, D.
  Moon goddess of Athenians I 400
  Palaemonius Tyrian Hercules II 345n
—— "De la Croix ansée"
  Phoenician Venus sign I 546
Rapa-Nui. *See also Easter Island*
  Lemuria extended beyond II 324
Rapes, prior to 5th race II 276
Raphael (archangel)
  denounced fallen angels II 382n
  dragon, the (Ophite) I 127n; II 115n
  speaks to Adam (Milton) I 622
Rash, B'rash [Rē'sh, Berē'shīth] (Heb). *See also
  Berēshīth*
  numerical 1st words in *Genesis* I 443-4
Ra-shoo [Rā-shu] (Egy) solar fire I 311
Rāśi (Skt), Virgo or 6th I 292-3
Rāśi-Chakra (Skt), zodiac I 376
Rasit [Rē'shīth] (Heb) wisdom, oldest, chief
  Greek Ἀρχή (Archē) (Parkhurst)
    II 313, 460
Rāta (Zend), sacrificial offering II 517
Rational Refutation. See Gore, N.

Rātri (Skt) night II 58
Rauchya (Skt) II 309. *See also* Manus
Raumyas, Raumas (Skt) demigods
  born fr pores of Vīrabhadra II 182-3
  strife between gods & II 182
  sweat-born race II 68
Rāvaṇa. *See also Rāmāyaṇa*
  carries off Sītā II 570
  giant King of Lankā II 224, 232n
  Hiraṇyakaśipu reborn as II 225n
  Pulastya grandfather of II 232n
  slain by Rāma II 225n
  symbol of Atlantean race II 495
Raven II 2
  number values of I 443-4; II 466
  Odin's I 443; II 100
  returned not to the ark I 444
Rawlinson, George
  Aryan (Vedic) influence on Babylon II 130
  —— *The Antiquity of Man* . . .
  primeval savage II 722
  —— *History of Herodotus*
  Egy civ before Menes II 432
  —— *The Origin of Nations*
  mythology of early man II 722
Rawlinson, Sir Henry
  Hea or Hoa (Chald) II 26n
  on two races at Fall II 5
  vedic influence in Babylon I xxxi
Ray(s)
  atom becomes seven I 635
  buddhi vehicle of solar I 216
  chaos ceases thru the I 231
  differentiates Waters of Space I 231
  divine, falls into generation II 231n
  divine, fr the One I 222
  divine, or Father I 70
  dropped into cosmic depths I 71
  of enlightenment II 231
  Father- II 592
  first manifest, of unknown ALL I 106
  flashes into the germ I 57
  Hansa-Vāhana is the I 80
  impregnates chaos I 64
  Logos emanates seven I 130
  Logos or, contains seven I 80, 572n, 573-4
  monad spark fr uncreated I 571
  omnipresent spiritual I 69
  penetrates mundane egg I 80-1
  Primordial Seven I 88, 106-9
  seven I 80, 571-4 &nn
  seven, & ether of science I 515n
  seven, & 7 principles II 635
  seven, & 7 races II 191n

  seven, & sushumna or solar I 523n
  seven, form 7 new suns I 290
  seven mystic I 515 &n
  seven, of Chaldean heptakis I 227n
  seven, of Osiris II 141
  seven, of 7 plexuses II 92
  seven, of solar lion's crown II 564
  seven, of the Sun I 290, 370, 515 &n, 524n,
    525n, 574; II 25, 69n, 605, 608, 611-13,
    772n
  seven, of time & THAT II 612
  seven, or dhyāni-chohans I 130, 573
  seven worlds of being hang fr seven I 120
  solar, & ascent of Jīva I 132
  triple, & unmanifested kosmos II 24
  unites w the soul I 119
  white, & 7 colors II 492
Reade, T. Mellard
  —— "Limestone as an Index . . ." II 11
  sedimentary strata II 694
Real, the
  is at the 7th depth I 628
  nothing on Earth is I 287
  as opposed to ideal I 55-6
  universe is invisible I 278
  universe is, to beings in it I 274
Reality I 273, 328, 619n
  ātman or the One I 181
  dual nature of I 327n
  eye of seer beholds I 617
  illusion & I 295-6
  māyā & I 39-40, 145-6
  mūlaprakriti & I 629
  "not on Earth" I 287
  one absolute I 14-17, 54n, 295, 629
  ONE, or Nameless Deity I 119
  Purusha the only, (Advaitīs) II 598
  Pythagoras, Plato on I 281, 617
  realities & I 59n
  transcendental, of occultists I 281-2
  unity of units (Leibniz) I 629-30
Reason
  "creation of," (Bacon) I 481
  governs world history (Hegel) I 641
  language & II 199n
  3rd race endowed w II 248, 363
Rebekah, 2 nations in womb of II 705
Rebel(s). *See also* Adversary, Asuras, Elohīm,
    Lucifer, Pitris (Solar)
  adepts, yogis fr past II 94
  against Kronos or immovable Duration
    I 418
  arūpa pitris II 94
  chose curse of incarnation II 246

Codex Nazaraeus re I 194-6
  described II 93-5, 489-92
  doomed to be reborn II 585
  ferouers (Pers), 7 hosts or II 489
  Fire Angels called II 243, 246
  hurled into space [*Rev*] I 202
  Lords of Spheres made into I 577
  sacrifice of II 246-8
  saviors of mankind II 103
  some incarnated, some quickened II 103
  would not create will-less men II 243
Rebellion. *See also* War in Heaven
  of angels II 94, 489-92
  of oldest & highest angels II 103
Rebirth(s). *See also* Reincarnation
  after 3,000 years (Egy) I 386n
  Druids' belief in II 760
  endless series of cosmic II 80
  initiation meant spiritual II 470
  karma & I 643; II 302-6
  karmic, cyclic II 232, 234
  kundalinī-śakti & I 293
  man may escape devachan & I 39
  providence punishes to 7th I 643
  of same individuality II 303, 306
  symbols of I 365, 385-6 &n; II 543, 617
  of the world II 757
Recapitulation of Embryo. *See also* Embryo,
    Foetus
  Aesculapius & Hippocrates knew of II 259
  dog & man (6 weeks) II 258-9
  Isis Unveiled on II 187-9
  kabbalists knew of II 259
  man passes thru kingdoms II 258-9
  man preceding mammals & II 255-63
  mirrors history of race II 187-9, 659
  relates to shell of man II 255
  seven rounds & 7 months of II 257
"Recent Researches on Minute Life." *See*
    Slack, H. J.
Recherches expérimentales. See Hirn, G. A.
Recherches pour servir . . . See Milne-Edwards
Recollection(s) II 311
  collective, in divine soul II 424
  lost, of monad's divine origin I 267
Record(s) I 271n, 409, 610-12; II 23, 335
  accessible to initiates only II 437
  astral I 105
  astronomical, beginning w 4th race II 353
  Atlantean II 436, 692
  Babylonian, esoteric II 691-2
  Book of Enoch resumé of history II 535
  of buddhas on palm leaves II 423-5
  cup marks, of oldest races II 346n

  destruction of II 692, 763n
  kabbalists tampered w II 457, 473, 560
  oral, of 4th race preserved II 530
  of past & future in zodiac I 646-7; II 332,
    353, 368, 431-2 &n
  of prehistoric past II 67, 251, 314
  primitive, copied & concealed II 530
  recorders of karmic I 104, 128-9, 132; II 529
  Rig-Veda oldest known II 606
  of serpents of wisdom preserved II 352-3
Rector(s). *See also* Regents
  become Samael, Schemal I 417
  cosmocratores & I 124, 440
  Fall of I 417
  Kepler's I 498
  magi must know wisdom of I 409
  mahārājah or I 124
  planetary, & humanity's monads I 575
  planets moved by, (Plato) I 493
  progenitors, sephīrōth or II 293
  St Michael "most powerful" II 479
  seven, in *Pymander* II 97
  seven, or pillars II 293
Rectores Mundi (Lat). *See also* Creator
  assist Christian Creator I 440
  host of, creative Logos II 237
Red. *See also* Dragon, Indian (American)
  -Adam, Semites, Jews fr II 426
  blue &, races destroyed II 192
  -brown face on column II 178
  color of "1st man" II 43n
  dragon II 93-4n, 379, 513, 771n
  earth or Adami II 454
  -hair-covered monsters II 184
  Śiva reborn as 4, youths II 282
  some, men remained (Stanzas) II 351
  third race was, (Stanzas) II 227
  Topinard on black, yellow & II 249n
  -yellow, Atlanteans became II 250
Redeem(er)
  celestial yogis sacrifice & II 246
  Egyptian prophecy & I 399n
  mankind its own II 420-1
  mind is our II 513n, 515
Redemption
  of man fr his "coats of skin" I 642
  of the pilgrim man I 268
  Satan cornerstone of II 515
  sin &, (Prometheus) II 420-1
Red Sea I 410
  Exodus story of, Atlantean II 426-9, 494n
Redskins. *See* Indians (American)
Rees, Abraham, *New Encyclopaedia* II 392
Reformers II 358-9

Regeneration. *See also* Initiation
  crucifixion & II 561
  initiation is II 470
  no, without destruction I 413
  occult teachings bring I 299
  serpent symbol of I 65, 73
  Śiva is, & destruction II 182
  winged globe & man's spiritual I 365
Regent(s), Ruling Intelligences I 152, 394, 448.
  See also Planetary Spirits, Rectors
  every world has its I 99
  four cardinal points & I 122-3, 126
  Lares as planetary II 361
  of Moon pulling on Earth II 325
  planetary, & humanity's monads I 575
  seven, & national, tribal gods I 421
  seven, of planets II 22, 23, 210n, 488
  seven, of *Pymander* II 488
  seventy planets blind for I 576
  supervise creation of Earth II 23
  various names for I 99
  of Venus incarnated as Uśanas II 32-3
  of zodiacal signs minor gods II 358
Regnard, Jean-François
—— *Voyage de Laponie*
  Laplanders call corpses *manee* II 774n
Règne des dieux. See Boulanger, N.
Regulus. *See* Cor Leonis
Reichenbach, Baron Charles von
—— *Physico-Physiological Researches*
  Od or vital fluid of I 76n, 338n
Reincarnating Ego(s)
  ātman imparts immortality to II 110
  principle in Egyptian religion I 220
  race sterility & II 780
Reincarnation(s) II 459. *See also* Incarnation,
  Rebirths
  of animals II 196n
  of avatāras II 358-9
  Buddhas, Christs do not escape I 639
  centuries between II 303
  Confucius on I 440 &n
  among Druids II 760
  ego wins way thru many I 17
  Egyptians kept, secret I 227; II 552
  Essenes, Jesus believed in II 111n
  of fallen gods or nirmānakāyas II 232, 255n
  is to be dreaded (Hīnayāna) I 39
  karma &, discussed II 302-6
  Krishna, Buddha on II 359
  man's divine soul remembers II 424
  necessity for I 171, 182-3
  racial II 146n
  same monad throughout I 175, 265

scarabaeus symbol of II 552
tenet of, fr Atlanteans II 760
voluntary, are nirmānakāyas I 132n
Reindeer II 741
  hunters of Périgord II 749n
  Paleolithic portrait of II 717-18, 720-3
Religio Laici. See Dryden, John
Religion(s). *See also* Church, Esoteric, Exoteric, Mysteries, Worship
  allegory & metaphor in every II 98
  all, fed fr wisdom-source I xliv-v
  all fr one center (Faber) II 760n
  ancient concept of II 106
  Babylonian II 691
  based on force called God I 397
  Carlyle on 2 kinds of II 470
  conflict of science w I 668-9
  cyclic rise & fall of II 723
  degraded by sexual mysteries II 471
  dhyānis original priests II 605n
  dogmatic, & sexual element I 381-2
  dogmatic, will die out II 415
  every, but a chapter I 318
  exoteric, & left-hand path II 503
  exoteric, anthropomorphic, phallic II 654-8
  exoteric, described II 281
  exoteric, gradual spread of II 527
  heliolatrous II 378-9
  Lemurians & II 271-6
  mystery language in I 310-11
  of nature vs human-born II 797
  oldest, are Indian, Mazdean, Egy I 10
  once a universal I 229, 341; II 760n, 774n
  one ennobling, described I 381n
  origin of modern II 272-4
  pagan, dreaded by Christians I xl
  primitive, nature of I 463
  reverence, piety, oneness in II 272-3
  science &, on Earth's age II 796
  sexual, & astronomy II 274
  students of ancient, dogmatize I xxviii
  superstitions of dogmatic II 104
  there is no new I xxxvi
  universal truth in all I xiii; II 489, 514, 516,
  610
  Vedic seed of old II 483
  wisdom-, in Central Asia I 376
Religions of India. See Barth, A.
Religio Persarum. See Hyde, Thomas
Rémusat, J. P. Abel, *Tao-teh-king*
  I Hi Wei means Jehovah I 472
Renan, J. Ernest
  on cradle of humanity II 204
  Egy civ had no infancy II 334

ignores annals of divine kings II 367
—— *La Chaire d'Hébreu . . .*
the supernatural II 194
—— *The Life of Jesus* I xlvi, 454
—— *History of the Origins of Christianity*
treats Adam-Adami w contempt II 457
—— "Sur les débris . . ." in *Revue Germanique*
derides *Nabathean Agriculture* II 452, 454-6
"Render unto Caesar . . ." [*Luke* 20:25] I 296
Renouf, Peter Le Page
—— *Religion of Ancient Egypt*
mythology a primitive disease I 303, 398
no Greek, Hebrew ideas fr Egypt I 402
Nouter [Neter], "god," generic not personal
I 675
Rephāīm (Heb)
first 2 astral races II 279
giants in *Job* (*IU*) I 345; II 496
Reproductive Process. *See also* Conception,
Generation
age of present, unknown II 118
arani & pramantha more than symbol of
human II 101 &n
bisexual II 133
budding II 116-17, 132, 166
fourth Adam had power of II 457
modes of, unknown today I 190 &n
oviparous II 132, 166, 181, 659, 735
ovoviviparous II 166
of polyps II 177-8
primitive human hermaphrodites II 118-19
progressive order of II 166-7
sexual & asexual II 116, 132, 658
stages in man II 659
third race II 171, 183-4
variety of modes of II 168, 658-9, 735
by will, sight, touch, yoga II 183
Winchell on I 607-8n
Reptile(s) II 55, 153, 656. *See also* Dragons,
Serpents
fr amphibians II 256-7
amphibious, age of II 201
atrophied 3rd eye in II 296
birds descended fr II 183, 254, 734
bisexual before mammalian age II 594n
foetus assumes shape of II 188
forms of, fr 3rd round II 684, 712
giant, described II 218-19
giant man lived w giant II 219
giant, now dwarfed II 733
Kaśyapa father of II 253-4, 259n
man lived in age of II 157
man preceded II 274
Mesozoic age of II 204

most, preceded man in 4th round II 594n
ovoviviparous II 166
preceded bird & mammal I 404
third eye covered in present II 299n
use man's 3rd & 4th round relics II 290
Republic. See Plato
Repulsion
Archaeus of Paracelsus & I 538
attraction, heat & I 103
force of attraction & I 102, 293, 497, 604
gravity vs attraction & I 497, 529, 604
Kepler & Empedocles on I 497-8
Sun fluids are attraction & I 529-30
Rēqā' (Heb), fool I 578
Rerum Natura, De. See Lucretius
Researches on Light. See Hunt, Robert
Resha Trivrah [Rě'shā' Ḥivvārā'] (Aram)
White Head in *Zohar* I 339; II 84
Responsibility, & free will II 255n, 412, 421
Rest, activity & I 62, 116, 134n, 240, 374, 377;
II 240, 281, 310-11, 545, 705n, 726, 747.
See also Motion
"Restes de l'ancienne . . ." *See* Rougemont
Resurrection, Resurrected
Apollo, every 19 years II 770
Egyptian I 312, 386n
frog symbol & idea of I 385-6 &n
Holy of Holies & II 459-62
initiation & II 462
of Jesus II 542
Norse version of II 100
origin of Christian I 310
phoenix & II 617
sarcophagus symbolized II 459, 462
serpent emblem of I 472
sound &, of man I 555
various gods of I 472-3
Retardation II 64. *See also* Retrogression
Australia affected by law of II 197
hermaphroditism & law of II 172n
law of II 260n
progressive development & II 260 &n
Retribution
dhyāni-chohans & I 188
exacting divinity or karma II 555n
karma unerring law of I 634
law of, vs blind faith II 304-5
lipikas & I 103-4
Retrogression of Form (Figanière) II 289n.
See also Retardation
Retzius, Anders
—— ["Present State of Ethnology . . ."] in
Smithsonian Report
linked American Indian w Guanches II 740

peoples of America, Africa linked II 792
Reuben (Jacob's son), man or Aquarius I 651
Reuchlin, Johannes, *De arte cabbalistica*
　q on heptad, etc II 599-601
Revealer(s)
　in every round, race I 42
　Logos of man is, of God II 589
　nature & character of I 317
　of truths faces moral death I 299
Revelation(s)
　Christian, discussed II 708
　fr divine yet finite beings I 10
　Jewish scriptures not divine I xxvi n
　of language explained I 309, 317
　mankind inspired by same I 341
　Marcus, re deity I 351
　mythology & I 304 &n
　Nabathean Agriculture a II 455
　no religion a special II 797
　Pentateuch not a II 3n
　primeval I xxx, 52, 356
　SD not a I vii
　seven, explained I 42
　Upanishads & I 269-70
　various sources of, listed I 10
Revelation. See Marcus
Revelation (St John's) I 452n; II 208-9
　Apollo's mother & red dragon of II 383 &n
　Babylon, mother of harlots II 748
　ch 12 fr Babylonian legends II 383-4
　Christ as the Morning Star II 540
　cubical city descending II 75
　divine, mortal years & II 619
　dragon of, Atlantean II 355-6
　fallen angels & 7th seal II 516
　Fall verses fr *Bk of Enoch* II 484
　four animals of II 533
　Latona legend in II 771n
　Logos w female breasts I 72n
　marriage of the lamb II 231
　Michael fights dragon II 382n
　Pistis Sophia older than I 410
　plagiarizes *Bk of Enoch* II 229, 482-3, 497, 506
　red dragon & arūpa pitris II 93 &n
　Secret Doctrine key to II 536
　seven-headed dragon II 484
　seven kings, 5 have gone II 565n, 748
　seven rounds, races II 565, 618
　seven stars II 355, 633
　seven thunders II 563
　stamping the forehead II 557
　virgin & dragon I 657
　War in Heaven I 68, 194, 202; II 103

　white horse & fire I 87
　woman w child II 384n, 771n
Revel [Reuel]-Jethro
　Midian priest-initiator II 465n
Reversion to Type
　giants, monsters & II 56, 293n
　not puzzling to theosophists II 685
"Review of Kölliker's Criticisms." *See* Huxley
Revolution(s)
　critique of theories re I 501-2
　Earth's, calculated by ancients I 117
　inverse, of satellites I 575
　of meteor swarms I 672-3
　perfect accord of mutual I 594
　physical, spiritual I 641
Révolutions du globe . . . See Cuvier, G.
Revue archéologique
　Central Asian changes (d'Eckstein) II 356
　day of "come to us" (de Rougé) I 134n
　rocking stones (Henry) II 344-5
　strife betw good & evil (Maury) II 497
Revue de Deux Mondes
　Littré on de Perthes' Memoir II 738-9
　Littré on matter I 502n
　Littré on skulls of Europeans, etc II 790
　Thierry on legends & real history I 675-6;
　　II 182
Revue Germanique
　Baudry on fire by friction II 524
　Baudry on lightning II 526
　Humboldt on Solar System I 497n
　Renan on Chwolsohn II 454
Reynaud, Jean
　——— *Philosophie religieuse: Terre et Ciel*
　changes in planetary orbits I 503
　incipient rotation I 505
Reynolds, Professor James Emerson
　classification of elements I 585 &n
　zigzag curve of, (Crookes) I 550
Rhea (Gk) goddess of Earth, matter
　monad, duad, heptad (Proclus) I 446
　Titans sons of, & Kronos II 142, 143, 269
Rhine River
　skulls found by, like skulls of Caribs II 739
Rhinoceros II 735
　fossils II 751, 773n
　Paleolithic man lived w woolly II 721
Rhizomata, roots of all mixed bodies II 599
Rhodes (Isle of)
　Colossus of II 338
　sank & reemerged II 391
　Telchines iron workers of II 391
"Rh Ya." *See* Erb ya
Rhys Davids, T. W.

criticizes *Esoteric Buddhism* I 539n
great Pāli & Buddhist scholar I 539n
—— *Buddhism* . . .
  on Avalokiteśvara I 471
Buddha's celestial counterpart I 108-9
Ṛibhu(s) (Skt) skilled artist II 55n
  Kumāra in *Sānkhya Kārikā* I 457n
Riccioli, G., [*Almagestum novum* . . .]
  mean motion tables of I 667n
Riccius, Augustinus
  Lyra, Hydra, etc, & Ptolemy I 664
Richardson, Dr Benjamin Ward
  favors solar magnetism I 498
  intuition of I 508-9
  original & liberal thinker I 526
—— "Sun Force & Earth Force"
  describes Metcalf's "caloric" I 524-7
—— "Theory of a Nervous Ether" I 634
  Archaeus or "Nerve-Force" II 654
  described I 531-3, 537-9
  nerve aura of occultism II 298n
  vital principle substantial I 603
Richardson & Barth. *See* Barth & Richardson
Richet, Charles
  Charcot &, vindicate Mesmer II 156
  "Do not deny a priori" I 640n
[Rigg, James M.]
—— "Notes on Aristotle's Psychology . . ."
  history, ancient, modern II 286
Right-hand Path
  adepts of, or prophets II 211, 503
  left &, began in Atlantis I 192n; II 494
  persecution of, by left II 503
Rigor mortis
  liquor vitae or vital principle & I 538
Rig-Veda (Skt)
  Aditi I 99
  Aja is Logos in II 578
  Apsarasas II 585
  asuras divine in II 59, 500
  begins w Hiranyagarbha I 426
  Brahmanaspati I 120n; II 45n
  Brahmā not in I 346, 426, 445
  Brihaspati I 120n
  Budha & II 498
  compiled by initiates II 451, 606 &n
  corroborates occult teaching II 605-11
  Daksha & Aditi II 247n
  "Deluge" not in I 67-8
  "desire first arose in It . . ." II 176
  Gandharvas of fire of Sun II 585
  globe chain referred to by II 384-5n
  Idā, Ilā II 138
  Indra in, & Purānas II 378, 614

kāma & II 176, 578-9
Lord arose in Hiranyagarbha I 89
maruts II 613
mirror of eternal wisdom II 484
"Nor aught nor nought . . ." I 26
not understood today I xxvii
occult ages in II 52n
occult volume of Aryanism II 378
older than Hesiod II 450
oldest known record I xxvii; II 606
poetry of, (Barth, Müller) II 450-1
rishis credited w I 442
seven paths or rays II 191 &n
seven rivers, rishis, races II 605-6
six worlds, 3 planes II 608
Sūrya's 7 rays & 7 globes II 605
10,580 verses, 1,028 hymns I xxvii
three Earths in II 758
three strides (rajāmsi) I 112; II 38, 622n
two deluges in II 270
universe divided into 7 regions II 611n
Unknowable I 128
Vāch I 427n; II 418n
Vaiśvānara (Agni) II 381
Viśvakarman II 101n
world divisions of II 622
Rig-Vidhāna (Skt)
  efficacy of Vedic mantras I 436
Ṛikshās (Skt) Pleiades, 7 Ṛishis I 227n, 453;
    II 631. *See also* Constellations, Great Bear
Rimmon (Heb), god of storms II 353
Ring(s). *See also* Planetary Chains, Rounds
  dvīpas form concentric II 758
  lokas or seven I 204
  luminous around moon I 590
  symbol of One I 11
Ring "Pass-Not" I 90, 129-35 &nn
Riphaeus, Mt, Hyperborean land II 7
Ṛishabha (Skt) bull, musical note
  quality of sound I 534
  Taurus II 408
Ṛishi(s) (Skt) seer. *See also* Dhyāni-Chohans,
    Prajāpatis
  Agnihotri descendants of II 499
  arūpa pitris appear as II 93-4
  Bhrigu one of the II 76n
  birth of the seven II 624
  Brahmā creates, spiritually II 44
  canons of proportion fr I 208-9n
  classes of I 436; II 501-2
  classes of, appear by sevens II 611
  creators I 442
  elohīm, cherubs, etc II 85
  fathers of various beings II 259n

flames or, incarnate in 3rd race II 247-8
forty-nine agnis (fires) or II 85
gods & men II 211
of Great Bear I 213n, 227n, 357n, 453; II 489, 549-50, 631, 768
highest dhyānis I 207, 208n
horses of Agni II 605
incarnated in man II 373n
informing intelligences II 34
initiates who recorded Vedas II 606n
initiation caves of II 381
invisible deity or I 114
Kaśyapa 1 of seven II 382n
kings & sages doubles of I 442
mānasaputras, dhyāni-buddhas I 571
manus & II 310, 359, 614-15n
mark time & periods of kali-yuga II 550
men in prior cycles I 107
milk the Earth I 398
named in various scriptures I 436
Nārada a I 413; II 47, 82-3, 275n, 502, 585
-Nārāyana, Krishna & II 359
nirmānakāyas II 93-4
no longer appear in India II 178
our races sprang fr pitris or II 365
patriarchs or II 129
planetary angels I 198
prajāpatis, manus, or I 346, 349, 355, 442
prehuman period, belong to II 284
fr previous manvantara I 207
rebellious & fallen gods II 232
reborn as mortals II 775n
reborn on Earth in various races II 318n
regents of worlds, gods I 99
saptarshi or seven II 318n
seven, Brahmā's mānasaputras II 625
seven, creations, zones, etc II 612
seven divine I 349
seven, 14, twenty-one I 235n, 433, 442
seven, in each root-race II 614n
seven, mark time of events II 549-50
seven, marry Krittikās II 551
seven principles II 313, 715n
seven races or II 139, 140
seven, saved fr deluge II 35, 139, 715n
seven swans or, & Great Bear I 357n
seven, 12 hierarchies of I 436
sons of, & progenitors of man II 614-15n
stellar, lunar spirits I 198
symbolized cycles I 641
ten or 7, sired man II 365-6
Titans, Kabiri same as II 142
Vāch entered into the I 430; II 107
Vaivasvata Manu & seven II 69n, 425

various equivalents of I 92, 442
Vedas arranged by II 146n
word, "to lead or move" (Kunte) I 346
worshiped as planetary regents II 361
Year of the Seven II 307n
Ṛishi-Prajāpati(s) (Skt)
Bhrigu the great II 32n
born again & again I 571-2
builders or primeval I 127
every race has 7 & ten II 365
first mind-born entities I 127
sources of man's revelation I 10
ten semi-divine I 349
Ṛishi-Yogis (Skt)
more powerful than gods II 78-9n
Rishoun [Rishōn] (Heb), Adam or II 315
Ṛitu (Skt, Roodoo in tx)
two solar months make a II 620
Ritual(ism)
Apollo & church II 383n
Brahmans concerned w II 567
Buddhistic & Catholic I 539n
Egyptian I 312, 359
husks of, & smoke II 566
inaugurated by left-path adepts II 503
now harmless farce II 748
origin of exoteric II 273
self-worship, phallicism & II 273
yogis oppose I 415
River Gods, ancestors of Hellenes I 345n
Rivers, 7, of Heaven & Earth II 605-6
Rivers of Life. See Forlong, J. G. R.
Rivett-Carnac, John Henry
—— *Archaeological Notes . . .*
cup-like markings on stones II 346n
RO, Cypriote & Coptic II 547
Road, "winds uphill" [Rossetti] I 268
Robes, Invisible, mystic root of matter I 35
Roc (Pers), or Simorgh symb cycles II 617
Rochas d'Aiglun, A. de
—— *Les Forces . . .*
Bouilland & Edison's phonograph II 784n
spirits that move matter I 645-6n
Rochester Cathedral II 85
Rock(s), balanced, in Harpasa (Pliny) II 346-7
Rock-cut Temples (Hindustan)
decad found in I 321
many vihāras in II 338
Rocking or Logan Stones
called "Stones of Truth" II 346
discussed II 344-5
found in Old, New Worlds II 342n
largest, Atlantean II 347
of natural origin (geologists) II 343

Rocks of Destiny
oracle rocks read by priests II 346
Rohanee [Rūhānī] spirit-knowledge
Sufi I 199
Rohiṇī (Skt)
embryo of Krishna conveyed to II 527
Rohit (Skt) hind, Vāch took form of I 431
Rolleston, Professor George
—— "On the Brain of Man . . ."
man's intellect, morals II 728
Romaka-pura (Skt) "in the West"
Asuramaya lived in II 67-8
last part of Atlantis II 50
Romakūpas (Skt) hairpores II 68
Raumas or Raumyas created fr II 183
Roman(s)
allegories of, convey truths II 410
ancient, fr Atlanto-Aryans II 436
astronomy fr Hindus I 658
Atlantis civilization higher than II 429-30
chronology of, fr India II 620
Five Years of Theosophy on II 743n
foot & Parker ratio I 313
initiated, view of Moon I 396
institutions fr Miocene (Donnelly) II 746n
punished by crucifying II 560, 586n
sevens in thought of II 612
succession of worlds taught by II 756-7
used 5 vowels symbolically II 458
Roman Catholic(s). *See also* Church, Roman
Church
associate Satan w Venus II 31-2n
astrolatry of I 402
Balaam &, scholiasts II 409
Christ, angels in II 237
demonologists, Satan reality to II 510
disfigured serpent story II 230
disfiguring of old concepts II 38
equate Satan w Ahura Mazdā II 476
faith as old as world I 402
faith of, blind I 612
idol worship & II 341
link Prometheus & Christ II 413
misunderstood the Fall II 93-4n
phallicism among II 85
prophecy of Christ & Jacob's dream I 649
religion of sensualism II 85
term lower double evil I 235-6
theology, Satan, Behemoth II 486
use duality as a tool II 479
Romance of Natural History. See Gosse, P. H.
Roman Church. *See also* Church, Roman
Catholic
anathematizes all other gods II 479

angels linked w planets II 89n
Anna, Virgin Mary in I 91
believes in 2 types of Titans I 417-18
borrowed earlier symbols II 481-2
Cain & Ham linked w sorcery by II 391
calls Jehovah creator I 440
canonized Confucius I 441n
carnalized virgin birth I 399
continues pagan teaching I 401
cross is phallic w II 562
devil or Satan reality for II 510
discussed II 377
dogma of hell lever of II 247
exoteric Northern Buddhism & I 539n
filioque dogma, Greek Church & II 635
finds Satan in other religions II 475-6
Greek &, idolatrous II 279
haughty, unscrupulous II 209
kyriel (litany) of working forces in I 440
legends of sorcerers, magicians in II 272
Lévi subservient to II 510-11
marriage ceremony in I 614-15n
Mercury, Aesculapius devils II 208
de Mirville defender of II 481-2
Mother of God idolatrous I 382n
Neptune, Uranus lead Hosts I 101-2
pagans plagiarized by "anticipation" II 476
persecuted occultism, Masonry I xliv
plagiarized II 472n, 481-2
slanders dragon of wisdom II 377
speaks of 70 planets I 576
teaches 2 immaculate conceptions I 382n
Romanes, George John
difficulties proving Darwinism II 681
—— "Physiological Selection"
vs natural selection II 426, 647
Ronororaka [Rano Raraku] crater
Easter Island statue quarry II 337
Roodoo. *See* Ṛitu
Root(s)
daivīprakriti as, of nature I 136
immaculate, fructified by ray I 65
-life as germ of solar system II 148
plane of circle or, is cool I 12
primary circle & II 113
pure knowledge or sattva I 68
rootless, of All or Oeaohoo I 68
undifferentiated cosmic substance I 75
undying I 237
Unknown, & Oversoul I 17
Root-base. *See also* Wondrous Being
arhats of 7th rung one remove fr I 207
Rootless Root. *See also* Be-ness, Boundless,
That, Unknowable

of all that is, was, or will be I 14
causeless One Cause I 15n
Oeaohoo is the I 68
Tree of Life has roots in I 406
Root-Manu(s) (Skt)
 become 14, twenty-one I 235n
 dhyāni-chohan or II 308
 each round starts w II 308
 prime cause or I 235n
 progenitor of our 5th race II 309
 seed-manus & Noah II 597
 table of II 309
 Vaivasvata, globe A, 1st round II 146-7
Root Matter
 first differentiation of I 246
 spirit or, & the elements I 543
Root-Race(s) II 443-6. *See also* Arc, Races,
  Rounds, Subraces
 age of 1st 2½ II 148-9, 250-1
 arhatship in 6th & 7th I 206-7
 Bamian statues record II 339-40
 bodhisattvas sent to every I 42
 Book of Enoch résumé of II 535
 cataclysm ends every II 307n, 309, 325
 column depicting four II 178-9
 complexion of II 249-50
 develop w the 4 elements II 135
 dhyānis watch over I 42
 diagrams symbolizing II 300, 533
 distinct & different II 443
 each, adds to senses of prior II 107-8
 early, not affected by climate II 135
 early, sexless, shapeless II 132
 Esau a race between 4th & 5th II 705
 every, has its revealers I 42
 figures for 1st 2⅔, guarded II 693
 first 3, described II 610
 first 3, followed failure II 312
 first 3, in *Genesis* II 124, 181
 first 2½, in Primary Age II 712
 first 2½ mindless II 261
 five, & 4 Adams II 457
 five, nearly completed II 443
 forms change w every round & I 183-4
 forty-nine, in each round II 309
 four ages of every II 198
 geological changes & II 47, 150
 geological strata & II 249
 intellect dormant in early I 210
 length of 1st 2½, secret II 312
 mankind same in each II 146n
 Manu for each II 140n, 309
 millions of years between II 128
 new forms every II 262

new, will form in Americas II 444-6
pentacle symbolizes the five I 125
physical origin of II 165n
Roman, Gnostic, Greek, symbols II 458
science can't ignore 3rd, 4th, 5th II 685-6
seven, among rabbins II 397n
seven, & 7 rays II 191n
seven, called globe round I 160
seven-headed snake, dragon I 407
seven, in *Genesis* II 252n
seven, on Babylonian tree II 104
seven subraces in every II 434
sexless, hermaphrodite, bi- & 2-sexed
  II 132, 134
sin of mindless II 191
size of, decreased II 728
start in the North II 768-9
survivors of II 445-6
teaching of, fr Mysteries II 435
three divisions of II 249-50
three earliest, sexless II 104
Vaivasvata seed for every II 146-7, 309
Root-Race–1st ("Self-born")
 Adam of *Genesis* 2 is II 46n
 age of II 46, 156
 astral shadows I 183; II 110, 121, 138, 164, 705
 ātma-buddhi (passive) II 254n
 barhishads & bodies of II 94-5
 born on 7 zones II 1-4, 29, 35n, 77, 329, 400,
   732
 born under influence of Sun II 24
 chhāyā birth (sexless) II 174
 chhāyās or shadows I 181; II 173
 colossal form of II 249
 continent never destroyed II 371-2 &n
 created 2nd race by budding II 132
 disappeared in 2nd race II 84, 121
 early Secondary or Primary Age II 156-7
 equator covered w water during II 400
 evolved fr pitar II 329
 evolved 2nd race unconsciously II 116
 first Adam or II 457-8
 had neither type nor color II 249
 had no history II 264
 Kandu symbol of II 175
 Kings of Edom symb I 375; II 705
 largest Bamian statue records II 339-40
 fr lunar ancestors or pitris I 160
 manus create creators of II 311
 mindless I 183; II 46n, 84, 164, 198
 monads entered shells of II 303
 needed no elements II 160
 never died II 121, 138
 no fire in II 107, 113

no kāma-rūpa in II 116
not affected by climate II 135, 150, 157
only Earth of, was at arctic pole II 329
progenitors prototypes of I 456n
Rephaim or II 279
reproduced by fission II 166
second &, moon-colored II 351
self-born II 164, 198
sexless II 116, 125
fr shadows of dhyāni-chohans I 183; II 242
Sons of Yoga, astral II 198
speechless II 198
spiritual & ethereal II 46, 298-9n, 685
too ethereal to be physical II 289
vegetation appeared before II 290n
Root-Race – 2nd ("Sweat-born") II 109-24
asexual II 116, 125
astral progenitors of marsupials & II 684
ātma-buddhi (passive) II 254n
Bamian statue & sweat-born II 340
belongs to Primary Age II 712
bisexual potentially II 2-3
born under Jupiter II 29
continent of II 401-2
did not die II 609n
emanation fr 1st II 164
endowed w germ of intelligence II 165
equator covered w water at time of II 400
fathers of sweat-born II 116-17
first race disappeared in II 84, 121
gigantic semi-human monsters II 138
had no history II 264
inactive androgynes II 134
intellectually inactive I 207
intermediate hermaphroditism & II 167
Lords, progenitors merged w II 103, 138
lower principles of, fr 1st race II 121
mammalia thrown off during II 684-5
Mārishā symbol of II 175-7
moon-colored II 351
Northern Asia as old as II 401
not affected by climate II 135, 150, 157
in *Popol Vuh* II 160
product of budding II 116-17
psychospiritual II 298-9n
Rephaim or II 279
reproduced by budding II 166
second Adam, androgyne or II 457-8
semi-astral II 685
seven groups of bodies in II 303
seven stages of reproduction & evolution of
    II 117-18
shadows of the shadows II 109, 112
"sound language," vowels alone II 198

submergence of continent of II 313
sweat-born II 68, 131, 138, 148, 164-5, 173,
    340
too ethereal to be physical II 289
Uranus ruled over II 765
yellow like gold II 227
Root-Race – 3rd. *See also* Lemurians, Ovip-
    arous
adepts dwelt under pyramids II 351-2
Ādi-Varsha (Eden) of II 203
agnishvāttas incarnated in II 91
analogy of principles & II 254n
androgyne II 165, 172, 177, 197
animalistic, last portion of II 254n
animal man descended fr I 650
animals 2-sexed during II 184
ape-like, but thinking & speaking I 191
ape's ancestor fr man in I 190 &n; II 184-5
    &nn, 187, 262, 729n
architecture fr rishis of I 208-9n
arūpa pitris incarnate in II 93-4
asuras, rudras incarnated in II 164
Atlantean conflicts w II 227n
Atlantean giants fr, females II 275
Australians descended fr II 199n, 328
awakening of mind in, karmic II 198
babes walked when born II 197
Bamian statues & II 340
began in northern regions II 329
begat its progeny II 267
bisexual II 135, 197
w bones II 172, 183, 193
bright shadow of gods II 268
built boats before houses II 399n
civilization drowned II 426
civ higher than Gk, Rom, & Egy II 429-30
climate semitropical II 329
colored light yellow II 250
continent II 7, 8, 328
cross in circle or I 5
cyclopean structures of II 317
Daksha & II 183
deluge not a curse II 410
deluge story applied to II 140 &n
demigods of II 319
description of, at zenith II 171-2
destroyed twice I 439n
deva-man of, & 3rd eye II 302
dhyānis incarnated in I 188; II 47n, 165, 228
disappeared at end of Secondary Age II 714
divine instructors & kings of II 194, 198,
    201, 318, 359
divine ones of, & kriyāśakti II 636-7
Dragons of Wisdom adepts of II 210

Earth's waist, navel appeared for II 400
Easter Island statues & II 340
Eastern Africa submerged in II 327
egg-born (oviparous) II 116, 123, 165-6, 173, 177, 181, 197
endowed w mind II 47n, 89, 248
"eternal spring" ended w separation II 201
Eva (Heb) & II 129-30
fallen "Serpent" (wisdom) descends on II 230
fell in North & Central Asia II 763n
fell into generation II 609
fell into pride II 271-2
first intellectual race II 211
first lands frozen over at time of II 201
first physical race II 46, 156-7, 789
first really human race II 329
fought giant monsters II 9
generation of bronze (Hesiod) II 97
Genesis 3 & II 46n, 410
geological deluge ended II 313
giant, ape-like, astral II 688n
giants, monsters produced in II 192-3
gods of, male & female II 135
hermaphrodite (separating) II 30, 134, 167
hybrid races left by II 714
Idā legend refers to II 147-8
intermediate race produced by II 275
Jared symbol of elect of II 597n
Jurassic, appeared in II 156
Kabiri, etc, incarnated in elect of II 360
knew death only toward close II 609
kriyāśakti used by II 173-4, 181
last remnant of II 220
last semi-spiritual race II 134
late, fell into sin II 319
lunar pitris build bodies of II 110
male, female born fr shells II 197
male Moon sacred to I 397
mammals fr man in II 186
man an animal intellectually until II 161
mānasa pitris awakened I 180-1, 539n; II 525n
man's spiritual origins in II 165-6n
mānushyas created woman II 140
mid-, 18 million years ago II 156-7
mind awakened in mid- I 180-1; II 254-5
mind-born & will-born II 156
mind-born sons of II 204
mindless at separation I 190; II 267
mindless, bred w animals II 184-5, 191-3, 201
Mysteries revealed to II 281
nephīlīm or II 279
nirmānakāyas & II 94, 201

nomads, savages of II 318
oral records of 4th race fr II 530
origin of culture II 782n
perished before Eocene II 313
Popol Vuh re II 160
pre-tertiary giants II 9
produced unconsciously I 207
psychospiritual mentally II 298-9n
religion of II 272-3
reproduction, 3 methods of II 132, 197
Secondary Age & II 713
secrets of nature public in II 319
semihuman during 1st half of II 685-6
Senzar fr 2nd race devas I xliii
separation ended satya-yuga II 201
Seth, Adam's 3rd son symbol of II 469
sexes separated before mind I 207; II 191, 198, 228
sex fr hermaphrodites II 177-8
sexual in later II 3, 125, 132, 167, 182, 609
sight at beginning of II 299
Sin of Mindless among II 184-5, 191-2, 683
solid after midpoint & Fall II 250
Sons of Will & Yoga among I 207; II 163, 173, 181, 199, 220
speech developed w mind II 198
sweat-born & II 67-8, 131-3, 148, 172, 177, 198
tau symbol of, up to Fall I 5
third Adam, man of "dust" or II 457-8
third eye of II 288-302, 306
third round & I 188-9, 190
thought transference II 199
three aspects of II 254n
transformation of sexes during II 147
two sexes during 5th subrace of II 715n
Vaivasvata Manu & II 148-9
Vaśishtha-Daksha's sons in II 78
vehicle of Lords of Wisdom II 172
Venus under influence of II 24
Wondrous Being descended in I 207
Zeus divides, man (Plato) II 177
Root-Race–4th. *See also* Atlantis(ean), Cyclopes
acme of materiality II 534
adepts of II 210, 351-2
agglutinative language of some of II 199
anthropoids fr late II 193, 195
arrogant & full of pride II 271-2, 760
astronomy imparted to, by divine king II 29
Atlas' daughters 7 subraces of II 768
Atlas symbolizes II 493
black w sin, became II 227, 250, 319
born in Secondary Age II 714

brown & yellow giants II 227n
catastrophe thinned II 309, 724
causes of destruction of, (*Enoch*) II 534
children of Padmapāni (Chenresi) II 173
civilization of, greater than ours II 429-30
conflicts of, w 3rd race II 227n
continent of, belonged to Eocene II 693
cosmic gods & 4 elements I 464
cross out of circle symbol of I 5
cyclopean civilization gave way to II 769
daityas, giants of II 31, 151, 183, 276
deified men of 3rd race II 172
deluge destroyed II 140, 144
deluge not a curse II 350, 410
descending arc ends at middle of II 180
destroyed in its kali-yuga II 147n
developed fr 3rd race men II 334
developed speech II 198-200
door into human kingdom closed in I 182
duration of II 10
early, worshiped spirit alone I 327
Easter Island statues II 224-5, 316n, 326-7,
   331
eleven buddhas only belong to II 423n
ethereal prototypes of II 9
Eye of Śiva in II 302
first "truly human" race II 715n
fled to high mountains II 724
fourth Adam "fallen" II 457-8
fourth continent of II 8
Genesis 3 refers to early II 410
gibborīm or II 279
golden-yellow race II 319
Hanokh (Enoch) gave wisdom of, to Noah
   II 532
height of, early Eocene II 433n, 710
inherited wisdom fr 3rd race II 530
initiates made Bamian statues II 339
instructors of II 359
intelligence of, earthy & impure II 134
Kabiri incarnated in elect of II 360
karma gradually changed II 411
language is perfected in I 189
last of, invade Europe II 743-4
lion symbolizes II 533
magicians of, called dragons II 280n
Mahābhārata re end of II 146
male heroes of, we worship II 135
mankind mostly fr 7th subrace of II 178
mated w lower beings II 284-5
middle of, man & globe grosser II 250-1
Neptune symb titanic strength of II 766
Nereus rules II 766
Noah symbol of II 597n

oral records of II 530
physical origin of later races in early II 165n
pioneers of, not Atlanteans II 323
pyramids & adepts of II 351-2
Rakshasī Bhāshā language of II 199
records since beginning of I 646
red-yellow II 250
resorted to body-worship II 279
semi-demons of II 319
Seth-Enos II 134
seventh subrace of, mixed w Aryans II 743
shadows of pitris dominate to midpoint of
   II 110
siddhas of, & 5th race sages II 636
Sons of Wisdom & II 228
sorcery & androgyne Moon I 397
spirits of giant tabernacles of I 225
third eye & II 294, 302, 306
third subrace of, & records II 353
three-eyed in early II 294
transmitted 4 elements to 5th race I 342
two eyes perfected at beginning of II 769
two sexes in II 125, 173
Ulysses hero of II 769
unique I 182
Vaivasvata & II 140, 309, 313
Venus story in Purānas & II 30
war between, & 5th race initiates I 419
white & black magic began in I 192n; II 211
wisdom only thru initiation in II 134
Zeus reigns but Poseidon rules II 766
Root-Race—5th. *See also* Aryan Race
adepts of II 210, 351-2, 384
adepts vs Atlantean sorcerers II 384
age of II 10
animal propensities in I 610
anthropoids will die out in I 184
arhatship at end of I 206-7
Aryan incorrect name II 434
in Asia II 280n
Atlantean deluge & II 144
Atlantean karma of II 302
Atlantis sank in infancy of I 650-1; II 147n,
   350, 714
Bamian statue records II 340
bull symbolizes II 533
China one of oldest, nations II 364
colors of II 249-50, 351
continent of II 8-9
cradleland of II 204
decrease in stature of I 609; II 279
deified man of 3rd race II 172
deluges in II 353
deluges of barbarians in II 742n

destruction of, (2 *Peter*) II 757
divine kings of II 351, 353, 359, 436
early, greeted Venus-Lucifer II 759
earthly spirit of 4th strong in I 224-5
earthquakes & eruptions in II 307n
Epimetheus & II 422
family races of 4th subrace of II 433
fifth element (ether) & II 135
fifth subrace I 319, 471n
first appearance of II 395
first deluge of, cosmical II 353
first glacial period & II 144
first, 2nd races & II 300
first symmetrical race II 294
fourth subrace of I 319; II 433
hearing limited at beginning of I 535n
history mostly of I 406; II 351, 444
idolatry, anthropomorphism in II 503
inflectional language of II 200
initiates wrote *Rig-Veda* II 606
intellectual replaced spiritual I 225; II 300
knowledge of writing & II 442
led away by preconceptions I 298
lunar-solar worship divided I 397
magicians called dragons II 280n
Mahābhārata prologue to II 139
mānasa period of races II 300
man helpless, scrofulous II 411
midpoint of *subrace* I xliii, 185, 610
mode of procreation will be altered I 406
Mysteries reestablished by II 124
not entirely Aryan II 429
now in kali-yuga II 147n
reincarnation tenets fr 4th race II 760
rescued fr last cataclysm I 273
Roman, Gnostic, Greek symbols of II 458
sages of, & 4th race siddhas II 636
Sanskrit & I 23; II 200
serpents redescended & taught II 355
skeletons 9-12 ft explained II 293
some of, have reached adeptship I 206
sorcery in II 503
Tau cross & I 5
third race spirituality coming to I 225
tribes of, fought Atlanteans II 225
twenty-four buddhas in II 423 &n
Vaivasvata saved II 140, 309, 310, 313-14
Vaivasvata seed of, man II 146-7, 249-50
volcanic conflagrations will end II 307n
war between, & 4th race sorcerers I 419
we are now in II 140n, 434
White Head or, (Kabbala) II 705-6
will gradually change II 445-6
will overlap 6th race II 444-6

will transmit ether to 6th race I 342
wisdom dictated to, in Senzar I xliii
Root-Race–6th
abnormal forerunners of II 445
anthropoids' fate in I 184; II 262-3
Book of Numbers on I 241
dawning of I 558
dhyāni-buddha will come in I 108
esoteric philosophy acceptance I 298
faculties to be developed in I 206-7
fifth race will transmit ether to I 342
fossil man like ape to I 184n
fossils of quadrumana in II 263
new continent of, (2 *Peter*) II 757
no sexual procreation in I 406
parallels 2nd race I 537
Pistis Sophia on II 618
preparation for II 445-6
sixth cosmic element in I 12
three racial stocks by dawn of II 780
Vishnu will appear in II 483
will appear silently II 445-6
will grow out of matter, flesh II 446
Root-Race–7th II 49
adepts will multiply in II 275, 531
dhyāni-buddha will come in I 108
fate of anthropoids in I 184
Kwan-shi-yin will appear in I 470
man perfected in 7th round II 167
mind-born sons in II 275
monad matter-free in, & 7th round II 180
Norse prophecy about II 100
race of buddhas II 483
seven cosmic elements & I 12
Simorgh & hidden continent II 399
will revert to astral II 263
Root-types
bar man-animal union II 688-9, 736
differentiation fr astral II 737
physicalization of animal II 649, 730
seven physico-astral II 736
"Rope of the Angels"
separates phenomenal, noumenal I 90
Rosary
of Mary II 38
on statue of Padmapāni II 178-9
Roscellin [or Rousselin, Rucelinus]
materialist views of I 3n
Rosenroth. *See* Knorr von
Rosetta Stone
god name IOH & II 464
Trismegistus of I 675
Rosetti, estimates Sun's heat I 484n
Rosicrucian(s)

creation due to War in Heaven II 237
cube unfolded of II 601
defined fire correctly I 121
Jehovah w Christian- I 438
light, darkness identical I 70
mystic fire of, fr Persian magi I 81n, 121
Paracelsus a great I 283n
pelican symbol of I 19-20, 80 &n
philosophy I 6-7
pregenetic symbol of I 19
St Germain's cypher, MS II 202
sidereal light of I 338n
Western heirs to I 611
Rosicrucian MS, Count de St Germain
  describes Babylon II 202
Rosicrucians . . . See Jennings, H.
Ross, W. S. (pseudonym Saladin)
—— *God & His Book*
  ascension of Christ II 708n
[Rossetti, Christina G., *Uphill*] q I 268
Rossi, Giovanni Battista de
  swastika used by early Christians II 586
Rossmässler, E. A.
  mistaken assumptions of I 640
Ro-stan [Re-stau, Egy] the otherworld
  mysteries of I 237
Rosy Cross, Rosecroix. *See* Rosicrucians
Rotae (Lat) wheels
  assist Christian Creator I 440
  moving wheels of celestial orbs I 117
Rotary Motion, Rotation. *See also* Motion
  ancient views of, (atomic) I 568-9
  critique of scientific theories of I 501-2
  heat fr collision produced I 250
  intelligences & I 601
  Master & Laplace q on I 592-4
  origin of I 505-6, 529-30
  origin of nebular I 97-8n, 500, 505-6
  pantheists taught Earth's I 569
  planetary I 593
  reverse I 150n, 575, 593
  of Solar System I 499-506
  39 contradictory hypotheses I 504-6
Rotation (of Earth)
  in *Book of Enoch* II 145, 314
  changes in axis of II 314, 534
  effects of slowing, described II 324-5
  taught by ancients I 117n
  Thor's Hammer symbolizes II 99
  in *Vendidad* II 292
  in *Vishnu Purāna* II 155
Roth, Professor R. von
—— *St. Petersburg Dict.* [*Wörterbuch*]
  ādityas II 489

āngirasas II 605n
Rouchya. *See* Rauchya
Rougé, Vicomte O. C. Emmanuel de
  Ammon-Rā & immaculate conception
    I 398-9
  Egyptians prophesied Jehovah I 399n
—— "Études sur le rituel funéraire . . ."
  day of "come to us" I 134n
—— "Examen de l'ouvrage . . ." in *Annuals de
  philosophie . . .*
  reign of gods & heroes II 367-8
Rougemont, Frédéric de
—— *Fragments d'une histoire de la terre . . .*
  Negro giants in Austria, Liège II 278
—— *Le Peuple primitif . . .*
  Chinese Holy Island II 372
  warring Atlanteans II 371
—— "Restes de l'Ancienne Lit. . . ." in *Ann. de
  philosophie . . .*
  opposes Chwolsohn II 454
Round(s). *See also* Cycles, Kalpa, Manvantara
  analogy of races & II 615n
  ape image of 3rd- & 4th-, man II 728-9
  Atlantean deluge after 3½ II 534
  blind wanderings of 1st three I 184
  bodhisattvas sent to each I 42
  development of Earth in I 158-60, 259-60
  development of elements in I 250-2
  development of kingdoms in I 175-6, 246-7;
    II 185-7
  development of monads in I 173
  dhyānis watch over each I 42
  each, has its own architects I 233
  each, has its revealers I 42
  Earth convulsed each new II 730
  Earth destroyed after each I 241
  elements not now as in prior I 253
  every, a rebirth II 46-7
  every descending, more concrete I 232
  evolution of principles in II 167
  first 3½, in *Genesis* II 181
  first 3, semi-ethereal II 149
  forms of each, cast off II 290
  forms of, improved in next I 187; II 730
  forty-nine root-races in each II 309
  genealogies embrace 3½ II 322
  geological convulsions in every II 46-7
  Great Day (*Jude*) at end of 7th II 491
  intellect & spirituality in II 167-8
  Isis Unveiled on I xliii
  Kings of Edom & II 704 &n
  length of kabbalist, a blind II 564
  life evolves thru seven I 159

life-forms fr man in 3rd & 4th II 683
man during 1st three I 188-9; II 185-7, 254, 260, 659-60
man passed thru all forms in early I 159; II 254, 260, 659-60
manus, root- & seed- II 308-9
maruts born in every II 613
materiality of past & present II 68n
monads thru all forms in every II 256-7
new forms every II 262
number of monads in, limited I 171
obscuration betw I 159, 161; II 47, 704-5, 713n
older wheels or past I 199
passage fr globes A to Z I 167-8, 232
phoenix symbol of seven II 617
planetary, & globe, defined I 160
Sacred Land lasts throughout II 6
seven among rabbins II 397n
seven, & 7 month embryo II 257
seven, in *Genesis* II 252n
seven, in *Leviticus* II 618, 747-8
seven, in *Revelation* II 565
seven, is manvantara II 180, 307-8, 434
seven, of Talmudists II 618
seven, or 7 worlds of māyā I 238
Stanza VI on early I 22
teachings of, fr Mysteries II 435
two more periods after seven II 257
wheels or I 40n, 232
Zohar II 704 &n
Round, First
ākāśic element developed in I 259
animal & man in 4th round & I 455
animal creation precedes man in I 455
building of globe in I 259
commentary on II 46-7
developed one element (fire) I 250
Earth a foetus during I 260
first human races of II 307
first monads reach humanhood in I 173
globe fiery, cool, radiant I 252n
highest pitris human in I 174, 182
human monad & mineral kingdom in II 185
Kings of Edom & I 375
man ethereal lunar dhyāni in I 188
man passes thru lower kingdoms in I 159-60; II 635
man prototype in, globe A I 175n
"one dimensional" space in I 250
Root- & Seed-manus of II 309
Vaivasvata & Root-Manu of globe A in II 146-7, 307-10 &nn
Round, Second

developed 2 elements I 251, 260
Earth in I 260
evolution different in I 159-60
fire, earth, & air in I 251-2
globe luminous, more dense in I 252n
human monad & vegetable kingdom in II 185
lunar gods' activities in I 174
man gigantic, ethereal I 188
manifests 2nd element (air) I 260
man passes thru human shapes in I 159
manus of II 309
second monadic class human in I 173
some pitris human in I 182
two-dimensional species in I 251
Round, Third
animals fr man in II 186-7, 684-5
ape image of, man I 180, 190; II 728-9
ape-man of, & anthropoid II 730
astral relics of, used in 4th round II 730
developed fire, earth, water I 251-2 &n
developed 3rd element (water) I 252
fossils fr II 68n, 684, 712
globe watery in I 252n
human monad & animal kingdom in II 185
insects & birds created in II 290
latest human arrivals fr II 168
lunar fathers human at end of II 115
lunar gods lead humans in I 174
man huge & apelike I 188-90; II 57n, 185, 261-2, 688n
man passed animal stage in II 299
man's changes in, parallel 4th II 257
man's stature decreases I 188
manus of II 309
perception of water in I 252
relics of, objectivized II 731
shadowy man of, & 4th I 233
some pitris human in I 182
third race repeats, man I 188-9
types formed 4th round types II 257
Vasishtha-Daksha's sons in II 78
Round, Fourth
animals of, consolidated fr 3rd round II 186-7, 730
anthropoids' monads will pass into astral human forms I 184
apes reached human stage before II 262
appearance of vegetation in II 290n
astral man in beginning of II 170
buddhas appointed to govern in I 108-9
cataclysms most intense II 149
crustacea, fishes, reptiles preceded physical man in II 594n

Rudimental Kingdoms / 327

developed fire, air, water, earth I 251-2
diagram of root-races in II 300
door to humankind closes I 173, 182, 184-5
Earth settles, hardens I 159
Earth's existence prior to I 252-3 &n
equilibrium betw spirit & matter I 106, 192;
  II 300-1
ether visible toward close of I 12, 140
fifth & 6th round men in I 161-2; II 167
first speaking race of II 452
forms of, fr 3rd round II 257, 684
four lower principles developed in II 167
four only of 7 truths given in I 42
humanity as 2 sexes 18 million yrs old I 150n
humanity develops in I 159
intellect develops in I 189
latest arriving monads in II 168
mammals fr man in I 455; II 168-9, 186-7,
  635, 683-4
man an animal up to mid- II 161
man 1st mammalian in II 1, 155, 187; II 288
man on Earth fr beginning of II 254
man physical in II 310
man ready for mind in mid- II 161-2
man's frame ready at beginning of II 660
man storehouse of seeds for II 289-90
manus in II 309, 321
materialization in II 68n
Matsya avatāra & Vaivasvata in I 369
matter spiritualizes at mid- I 185-6, 232
mid-, ends descending arc I 232; II 180
mind link betw spirit & matter in I 182
minerals receive final opacity in II 730
minerals, vegetables before man I 159
Noah story & beginning of I 444n
pitris evolve shadows on globe A I 174
pitris ooze apelike forms I 180
polar continent lasts entire II 400n
pre-septenary manvantara II 308n
primordial vegetable life II 712
produced hard material sphere I 260
SD volume 2 deals w I 22; II 68n
sedimentation 320 million yrs ago II 715n
seven pralayas in I 172 &n; II 329
seventh stage of materiality II 308n
shadowy man in, as in 3rd I 233
sixth sense & permeability I 258
those who refused to create in I 191
turning point I 182, 185-6
Vaivasvata Seed-Manu on globe D II 146-7
vegetation of, & soft minerals II 730
veiled record of, in Purānas II 253
we are now in I 232; II 47, 301, 307, 434
Round, Fifth. *See also* Fifth Rounders

anthropoids & men in I 184; II 261-2
ether familiar as air in I 12, 140, 257-8
field of resurrection (Norse) II 100
higher senses will grow in I 258
manus for II 309
men have been incarnating I 161
mind fully developed in II 162, 167, 301
permeability of matter in I 258
Rounds, Sixth & Seventh. *See also* Sixth
  Rounders
dying out of globes I 155
Earth after I 240, 260
globes, monads in I 171-3
Great Day after, (*Jude*) II 491
higher elements appear in I 12
hinted at in *Revelation* II 704n
laggard pitris (human) in I 182
mankind in I 159
man perfect septenary II 167
manus of II 309
men will inform laya-centers I 181
monad free fr matter in II 180-1
One Unknown Space known in I 344
Revelation on II 565
Round Table, & Morgana II 398 &n
Round Tower of Bhangulpore II 85
Round Towers of Ireland. See O'Brien, H.
Routers, rocking stones called II 345
Row, R. B. P. Sreenivas
chronology of II 69-70
Row, T. Subba. *See* Subba Row, T.
*Royal Institution. See Proceedings of the
Royal Masonic Cyclopaedia. See* MacKenzie, K.
Ru (Egy) II 547-9
third eye symbol II 548
Ruach [Rūah] (Heb) spirit
buddhi or I 242; II 633n
correlated w Ab Haty (Lambert) II 633
divine spirit I 225
garment of II 315
Gnostics get, fr yetzīrāh II 604
fr Hoa II 83
Michael, Samael proceed fr II 378
must unite w nephesh (soul) I 193
spiritual, not animal soul I 243-5
wind or I 226n
Ruach-Hajan [Rūah-Ḥayyāh] (Heb)
west wind I 466
Rudbeck, Olof
Bailly disproved theories of II 402
——— [*Atlands eller Manheims*]
Delos called Osericta II 773
Sweden was Plato's Atlantis II 402
Rudimental Kingdoms. *See* Elementals

Rudimentary Organs, human, expl II 683
Rudra(s) (Skt) howler, destroyer. *See also*
  Rudra-Śiva, Śiva
  "adversaries" of gods II 164 &n
  both qualities & quantities II 585
  Brahmā-, & kumāras I 458
  chose curse of incarnation II 246, 255n
  classes of II 182
  creates kumāras I 457
  as creator I 455-8
  destroys universe II 69n
  developed intellectuality II 585
  eleven, of Vedic Tridaśa I 71n
  Fohat &, fr Brahmā I 145
  four preceding manus & II 318n
  half gentle, half ferocious II 548
  highest dhyāni-chohans II 585
  identical w elohīm, cherubs II 85
  identified w fire god II 280n
  incarnated in man II 164
  incarnations of Śiva II 249
  Kārttikeya son of II 382n
  -kumāras & nirmānakāya II 255n
  kumāras or Kabiri II 106, 249, 318n, 613n
  Nīlalohita, kumāras & [*VP*] II 106, 192n
  Nīlalohita (Śiva) or II 106
  not direct creators of man I 445
  our paternal grandfathers II 164n, 248n
  production of 1st principle I 455n
  pure comp w other Hindu gods II 174
  rebellious or fallen gods II 232, 246, 613n
  sacrifice of II 246
  -Śankara (War in Heaven) II 498
  septenary character of I 460
  as Śiva I 459n, 526n; II 282, 382n, 502n, 548,
    550, 615
  sons of, in *Rig-Veda* II 613 &n, 615n
  tempting demons II 174-5
  Vishnu as I 370; II 69n
  wept 7 times, given 7 names II 615n
Rudra Sāvarni (Skt, Savarna in text), Seed-
    Manu, planet G, 6th Round II 309
Rudra-Śiva (Skt). *See also* Rudra, Śiva
  destroyer I 526n; II 164n
  forefather of all adepts II 502n
  grand yogi II 164n
  healer & destroyer II 548
  Kārttikeya son of II 550
Rūḥānī. *See* Rohanee
Ruins of Empires. See Volney, C. F.

Rulers. *See* Divine Kings, Regents
Rules of Initiation [Agruchada-Parikshai. *See IU*
    II 40], on secrecy I 299
Runes (Norse)
  cup-like writing & II 346n
  Sigurd became learned in I 404
Rūpa(s) (Skt) form(s) II 52-3, 57, 65. *See also*
    Pitris
  blending of, & arūpa I 118
  body (Massey) II 632
  destroyed II 65
  dhyāni-chohans both, & arūpa I 197
  divine kings, material or, spirits II 222
  Earth's I 259; II 52
  evolved fr pitris I 183; II 102
  highest of, 4th order of beings I 218-19 &n
  physical body is a I 242
  seven, classes of dhyān-chohans II 318n
  spirit without, nāman & jāti I 373
  spurned by some gods I 192
  Vishnu, of whole universe I 420
Rūpa & Arūpa (Skt) I 53, 118, 122, 129, 197,
    219n, 373, 420
Ruppel, Wilhelm P. E. S.
  found *Book of Enoch* II 531
Rush-light I 604
  flame of, could light universe I 85n
Russia(n)
  giant tombs in II 752
  mystics went to Tibet I xxxvi
  rocking stones in II 342n
  stones in, brought fr vast distances II 343
  tall people in II 277
  teems w legends of giants II 754-5
  will not eat pigeon I 80-1n
Ruta (Skt) Atlantean island-continent
  Egyptian zodiac fr II 436n
  giant magicians of II 428
  part of Atlantean continent I 650
  peoples of, called Rutas II 222
  sank 850,000 yrs ago II 141, 147, 314n, 433
  sank in later Pliocene II 314n, 710
  Solon's island &, [Plato] II 436
  still remained in Miocene II 740
Rutilius, Claudius N., [*De reditu suo*]
  q on Jewish race II 358
Rütimeyer, Ludwig
  Schmidt's charts based on II 735
  on sunken Southern continent II 789
  on Swiss cattle II 287

S

Sa, or Hea, Babylonian god II 5
Sabaean(s)
  Bedouins worship fire, light II 514n
  beliefs of II 361-2
  critics thought Nabatheans were II 452-3
  Henoch (Enoch) of, origin of II 366
  invoke Host of Heaven II 514n
  Seth & Edris gave language to II 366
  symbolic dance II 460-1
Sabaeanism
  disfigured Chaldean remnant I 10, 320;
    II 453-6
  Roman Catholicism & I 402
  Schemal or Samael in I 417
Sabaeorum Foetum (Lat) Sabean rubbish
  Maimonides termed Nabathean lit II 455
Śabalāśvas (Skt) Sons of Daksha
  dissuaded fr procreating II 275n
Sabao(th). See Tsebā'ŏth
Sabasian [Sabazian] Mysteries
  Epaphos or Dionysos in II 415
  festival II 419
  Serpent of Wisdom in II 416
Sabasius [Sabazios] (Gk)
  Bacchus, Dionysos or II 415, 419
Sabbath(s) I 407
  eternal, or light of spirit I 481
  generative Jehovah, moon or I 392
  of *Genesis* & Purānas II 624
  goat of Witches' II 510
  Hesiod on II 603
  Jewish, & lunar month I 387
  means rest or nirvāna I 240
  not a day but equals 7 days I 240
  St Michael, Saturn & I 459
  "Secret of Satan" on II 235
  seven, & rounds, races (*Lev*) II 565 &n
  seventh, end of 7th round I 240; II 491
  various meanings of I 447; II 395, 747-8
Sabbatical Week & Year, cycles II 395
Śabda-Brahman (Skt) Sound-Brahman (Un-
    manifested Logos)
  Avalokiteśvara or Word I 428
  Īśvara called Verbum or I 137-8
Sabhā, Mayasabhā (Skt) assembly hall
  knowledge fr Atlanteans & the II 426

Sabines, rapes before the II 276
Sacea. See Sakas
Sacerdotal(ism). *See also* Senzar
  castes & left-hand adepts II 503
  Chaldean I 655n
  Christian, lost key to cross II 560-1
  college, Java-Aleim of II 215, 220
  colleges & Sacred Island II 220
  Egyptian II 432
  hierarchy of Zuñi Indians II 628-9
  Theban, class I 311
Sacr. *See* Zākhār (Heb)
Sacrament(s,al) I 614-15n; II 467n
  dogma of the 7, origin of I 310-11
  loaf & serpent II 214
  fr *sacr*, phallic symbol I 5n; II 467n
Sacra Scrittura. See Lanci, M. A.
Sacred. *See also* Mysteries
  agnishvāttas *not* devoid of, fire II 77-8
  fire & the swastika II 101 &n
  fire of later 3rd race II 171
  fires or Kabiri, kumāras II 106
  number seven II 35
  phallic orig of word I 5n; II 465 &n, 467
  records of the East II 314
  science, ancient origin in II 794
  seven, islands (dvīpas) II 326
  spark given man II 95
  tree on Babylonian cylinder II 104
Sacred Animals I 362
  associated w Jehovah I 441-2n
  of Christians I 363, 440-2 &n
  emanated fr Divine Man I 89, 353
  of *Genesis* 1 zodiacal signs II 112n
  of Hebrews I 355
  meaning of I 442
  Mexican & Egyptian II 399n
  plants change into I 238
  refer to primordial forms I 442
  of Zodiac I 92, 446n; II 23, 181n, 625n
Sacred Four
  remain to serve mankind II 281-2
  swastika emblem of II 587
  Tetraktis or I 88, 99; II 621
Sacred Island(s) I 471; II 3, 637, 760-77. *See also*
  Gobi, Shamo Desert

Central Asian oasis today II 220, 503
instructors went to inhabit II 350
Isis Unveiled on I 209; II 220-2
Śambhala II 319
seven II 326, 349-50
"Sons of God" & II 209, 220-6
"war" betw initiates of, & sorcerers I 419
Sacred Land. *See also* North Pole
Imperishable II 6
Sacred Mysteries. *See* Mysteries
Sacred Mysteries . . . See Le Plongeon
Sacred Name II 126
biblical II 536
Hebrew I 385
Sanskrit & Hebrew I 78
seven letters of I 438-9
Sacred Numbers, Figures, Signs I 60, 66, 89, 114, 168, 384, 649; II 34-5, 57n, 410, 553, 580, 598-604, 622. *See also* Numbers
Sacred Planets
connected w Earth I 573n, 575; II 602n
four exoteric, 3 esoteric I 575
ruled by regents, gods I 152
seven, all septenary I 167
seven, only I 99-101, 152, 573n
Sun & Moon substitutes I 575 &n
why seven II 602 &n
Sacrifice(s, er, ial) I 276, 416, 422
animals or zodiacal signs II 625n
Atlanteans, to god of matter II 273
butter purified by II 101n
of Dakṣa II 68, 182-3
to elements by pagans, Jews, & Xtians I 466
of fiery angels II 246
of four virgin men II 281-2
great, of self & Self I 268
great, of Wondrous Being I 208
"himself to himself" I 268; II 559
man a, animal to the gods I 446n
myths & divine ancient II 450
Nārada on II 566-7
to Nemesis I 643
Parāśara's, sorcery II 232n
pitris collectively the One II 605
Purusha's, for the universe II 606
to Queen of Heaven II 462
fr *sacr*, phallic symbol II 467n
self-, of nirmānakāyas II 94
self-, of rebels II 243
triform II 527
Vedic ceremonial I 422-4
Yima his own II 609
Sacy, de. *See* Silvestre de Sacy

Sadaikarūpa (Skt) essence, immutable nature II 46, 108
Saddharmālaṃkāra (Skt), canon of Southern Buddhist Church I xxvii
Sadducees
angels rejected by II 61
guardians of laws I 320-1n; II 61, 472-3
high priests of Judea I 320-1n
most refined Israelite sect II 472-3
present generation of I xxii
spurned Pentateuch, *Talmud* I 320-1n
Zadokites or, fr Zadok II 541
Sādhu(s) (Skt) sage, saint
rākshasas are II 165n
third age, fr higher regions II 320
Sādhyas (Skt)
divine sacrificers, pitris II 605
one of 12 gods II 90
Sadic. *See* Tsaddīq
Sadu [Sedu], Chaldean spirits II 248n
Safekh (Egy), speaks to Seti I as Lunus I 228
Saga (Norse goddess)
ravens whisper past & future to I 443
sacred scrolls of II 283n
Sāgara (Skt)
name of ocean, Bay of Bengal II 572
Sagara, King
given Āgneyāstra weapon II 629
60,000 sons of II 570
sons of, personify passions II 571
Sagardagan. *See* Sakṛidāgāmin
Sagdiani [Sogdiana in *Vendidad*]
Aryan magi emigrated to II 356
Sage(s). *See also* Adepts, Initiates
actualities visible to I xxxvi
fifth race, inherit fr 4th II 636
great, disappear II 639
kriyāśakti of II 181
Purānas & I 415-16, 423, 457
searching w their intellect II 176
seven primordial II 267n
silent on higher teachings II 589
Sons of Wisdom became II 167
spiritual dhyānis were II 167, 181-2, 267n
taught 5th race II 359
teachers, philosophers II 133
of 3rd race I xliii
words of a, on past & present II 446
Saggitarius [Sagittarius], Joseph & I 651
Saḥ (Skt) "he," A-ham-sa or "I-am-he" I 78; II 465. *See also* Haṃsa
Sahagun, Bernardino de
on 7 families that accompanied Votan II 35
Sahara. *See also* Gobi

Atlantis fr, to Caribbean II 424
former sea of II 8-9n
Northwest Africa & II 793
ocean, continent, ocean, desert II 405
Quaternary sea washed basin of II 740
sea in Miocene (Crotch) II 405, 781-2, 787n
trilithic raised stones of II 346n
Saharaksha (Skt), fire of the asuras I 521
Saint. *See* given name (e.g., Paul, St)
Sainte-Claire Deville, Henri-Étienne
on chemical combinations I 544n
estimates sun's heat I 484n
St Elmo's Fire (Elmes in tx)
aspect of all-pervading Archaeus I 338n
Saint-Germain, Count de I 611
Babylonia described by II 202
classed a charlatan II 156
had copy of Kabbala, Vatican MS II 239
MS left by II 202, 582, 583
on number seven II 582
on number 365 II 583
Saint-Hilaire. *See* Geoffroy Saint-Hilaire
St Marc, de, & changes in *Pymander* II 491-2
Saint-Martin, Louis Claude, Marquis de,
astral light of Martinists I 348; II 409, 511,
513
St Petersburg
Russian mystics, Tibet & I xxxv-vi
St Prest, human & extinct animal remains of
II 751
Saints, Rome filled w blood of II 231
St Vincent, Australians & Gulf of II 196n
St Yves d'Alveydre, *Mission des Juifs*
terms kali-yuga golden age I 470-1; II 549n
Saïs (Egypt)
famous inscription at I 393
goddess Neith of I 399
Mysteries at, (Herodotus) II 395-6
priests of, describe Atlantis II 371, 743
Saitic Epoch (Egy)
Khnoum & lotus symbol in I 385
statue of Isis suckling Horus II 464
Śaiva Purāṇas
kumāras as yogins in I 458; II 576
Śaivas I 405, 456n, 458; II 576
Śaivas vs Vaishnavas I 675
Saka (Skt), the One I 73
Śāka-dvīpa (Skt)
"beyond the saltwater" II 323
early Atlantis II 322
globe, locality, etc II 320-1, 404 &n
Lemurians, Atlanteans & II 584
Magas of, forefathers of Parsis II 323
yet to come II 404-5 &n

Śakas (Skt), Yudhishthira king of I 369
Sakkarah, Sothiac cycle inscriptions at I 435
Śakra (Skt) Indra I 376
Sakṛidāgāmin (Skt, Sagardagan in tx)
grade of initiation I 206
Śakti(s) (Skt) generative power
Aditi, Eve & I 356
cow, woman or I 390 &n
daivīprakriti represents all six I 293
energy or, essence of trinity I 136
hierarchies of dhyāni-chohans & I 293
Lakshmī (Venus) white side of II 579
Logos & I 473
science & 6, of nature I 293
Shekhīnāh (fem) or I 618
six, described I 292-3
Śaktidhara (Skt) spear holder
Indra, Kārttikeya II 382 &n, 619
Śākyamuni II 423. *See also* Buddha, Gautama
Śākya Thub-pa (Tib). *See* Buddha, Gautama
Sal, Mater, Sanguis II 113
"Saladin" [Stuart Ross]
on Christ ascending & Sirius II 708n
Śālagrāma (Skt), a holy place II 321
Salamander(s) (reptiles)
giant II 352
man's saliva & venom of I 262n
Salamanders (fire elementals). *See also*
Undines
derided today I 606
Salisbury Plain, hinging stones of II 343
Saliva, of man & cobra I 262n
Śālmali-Dvīpa (Skt) silk-cotton tree island
II 320-1, 404 &n
Salt, crystals of, cones & pyramids II 594
Saltations (evolutionary jumps)
scientists' & occultists' views on II 696-7
Salts, spirits of the II 114
Salvation
egg symbol of I 367-8
personal god, damnation & I 613
Son of Righteousness & I 656
of spiritual humanity II 79, 281
story of Kwan-yin as I 471
Virgin as star of II 527-8
Vishnu & II 313
Salverte, Eusebe, *Sciences occultes*
winged serpents II 205
Samādhi (Skt) concentration, oneness
bodhi or I xix
Buddha in posture of II 339
jayas lost in II 90
man loses self in I 570
man quits body during II 569 &n

turīya, state or nirvāna I 570
Samael (Heb). *See also* Satan
  Angel of Death (*Talmud*) II 111, 385, 388
  Cain generated by II 389
  chief of demons in *Talmud* I 417; II 409
  concealed wisdom or II 378
  dark aspect of Logos II 216n
  fall of, draws down Titans I 417
  fell & caused man's fall II 112
  god-name of one of the elohīm I 417
  Kin son of Eve by II 388
  -Lilith, apes descend fr II 262
  Lucifer-Venus abode of II 31
  Satan or II 235, 378, 385, 388-9
  seat of passion I 242
  serpent of, kind of flying camel II 205
  Simoom, Vritra or II 385
  Uranides & I 417-18
  will be dethroned II 420
Samāna (Skt) same, equal, middle
  discussed II 567-8
  "at the navel" I 95
Samaria, giant race at II 755
Samaritan(s)
  alphabet of II 129, 581
  disciples not to go to II 231n
  pronounced Jehovah Jahé II 465
Sāmba (Skt) reputed Son of Krishna
  builds temple to Sun II 323
Śambhala (Skt, Shambhalah in tx)
  heart of Earth beats under II 400
  refuge of Lemurian elect II 319
Sambhūti (Skt), daughter of Daksha II 89
Samkhya. *See* Sāṅkhya
Saṃnati (Skt), daughter of Daksha II 528
Samoans
  stature of II 332
  sunken lands & II 222-4, 788
Samothrace(ian)
  colonization of II 3
  Electria or II 3
  flood legends II 391
  Hermes in Mysteries of II 362
  Kabiri, Titan story taught in II 390
  Mysteries II 3-4, 360n, 362
  Noah story II 4-5
  overflowed by Euxine II 4-5
  rites on British island (Strabo) II 760
  secret of fires in II 106
  seven & 49 fires worshiped in II 362
  volcanic origin of, (Decharme) II 391
Samuel, Books of (Bible)
  David danced "uncovered" II 459-61

David lived w Tyrians II 541
David moved to number Israel II 387n
God hurled thunderbolts I 467
God riding wings of the wind I 466
Goliath 6 cubits tall II 336
Jehovah tempts King of Israel I 414
Samuel, Rabbi
  on Adam, 2 faces, 1 person II 134n
Saṃvarta (Skt) a minor kalpa I 368; II 307n
Saṃvṛiti (Skt) false conception I 44 &n, 48 &n
Saṃvṛitisatya (Skt) relative truth
  only on this plane I 48 &n
Saṃyama (Skt), defined II 309-10n
Sana (Skt)
  esoteric name of a kumāra I 457
  every kumāra has, or sanat prefix I 459
Śanaiśchara (Skt) slow moving
  planet Saturn (Śani) I 459
Sanaka (Skt) I 457n; II 319
  Axiokersos & II 106
  exoteric name for a kumāra I 457
  one of 4 chief kumāras I 89, 372 &n
  prototype of St Michael I 372 &n
  refused to create I 372 &n; II 140n
  visited Śveta-dvīpa II 319, 584
Sanakādikas (Skt)
  seven kumāras visited White Island II 584
Sananda (Skt)
  Axiokersa II 106
  exoteric name for a kumāra I 457
  one of 4 chief kumāras I 89
  refused to create II 584
  visited Śveta-dvīpa II 319, 584
Sanandana (Skt) I 457n
  becomes kumāra II 579
  forced to incarnate in men II 176n
  mind-born son II 140n, 579
  one of the Vedhas II 78, 173, 176n
  refused to create II 140n, 173, 176n
Sanat (Skt)
  Adi-, primeval ancient I 98
  "Ancient," title of Brahmā I 459; II 625
  every kumāra has, or sana prefix I 459
Sanātana (Skt) eternal, primeval
  Camillus II 106
  exoteric name of a kumāra I 457
  a kumāra I 457n; II 319
Sanat-kumāra (Skt) eternal youth
  Aschieros II 106
  exoteric name of a kumāra I 457
  mind-born son of Prajāpati II 140n
  one of 4 chief kumāras I 89
  refused to create I 457-8n; II 140n, 584
  visited Śveta-dvīpa II 319, 584

Sanat-sujāta (Skt)
  called Ambhāmsi I 460
  chief of the kumāras I 459-60
  esoteric name of a kumāra I 457
  mind-born son of Prajāpati II 140n
  prototype of Mikael (Michael) I 459
Sanatsujātīya (Skt)
  sattva is antahkarana, buddhi I 68-9n
Sancha-Dvipa. *See* Śaṅkha-Dvīpa
Sanchoniathon (Phoenician historian)
—— *Cosmogony*
  Aletae or Titans II 141-2, 142n, 361
  animated stones of II 342
  Atlanteans II 761
  birth of universe by I 340
  copied older documents II 440n
  disfigured by Eusebius II 692-3
  Javo, Jevo II 129, 465
  Kabiri sons of Sydic II 392-3
  Lemuria, Atlantis confused in II 768
  Phoenician El Elion II 380
  pothos, desire to create I 110
  record of Phoenician religion II 692-3
  "time the oldest Aeon" II 490n
Sanctuary. *See also* Adytum, Sanctum
  "Anointed" entrusted w key of II 234
  arts & sciences preserved in II 572
  Egyptian II 432
  Hellenic II 7
  Holy of Holies II 234
  Plato & veiled language of II 395
  unbroken traditions & records of II 443
  womb of nature II 234
Sanctum Sanctorum. *See also* Holy of Holies
  curtain of, & elements I 462
  discussed II 459-74
  Holy of Holies, Adytum or II 459, 460
  stooping at entrance to II 470
  Williams approaches, of occult I 585
  womb & I 382
Sand, figures of, on vibrating plate I 112n
Sandhi(s) [Saṃdhi] (Skt) junction. *See also* Sandhyā, Sandhyāṃśa
  intervals between manus II 70
Sandhyā [Saṃdhyā] (Skt) dawn or evening, twilight. *See also* Sandhi, Sandhyamsa
  boker (Heb) II 252n
  Brahmā's body became II 60
  Brahmā's twilight I 206, 431, 530
  described II 58, 308n
  during, central sun passive II 239
  interval preceding any yuga II 308n
  laws of motion designed in I 529-30
  one-tenth of age it precedes II 308n

period of, symb in swastika II 587
Vāch or, Brahmā's daughter I 431
Sandhyamsa [Saṃdhyāṃśa] (Skt)
  interval following any yuga II 308n
Sands, the spirit of I 217
Sandwich Islands II 223-4, 788
Sangbai-dag-po (Tib) concealed lord
  one merged w Absolute I 52
Sanguis, Sal, Mater (chart) II 113
Sangye Khado (Buddha Ḍākinī in Skt)
  chief of Liliths II 285
Sanhedrin. See also Talmud
  two thaumaturgists I xliii n
Śani (Skt) Saturn I 459
  fourth race, globe under II 29
Sanjānā, D. D. P.
  ignores Zor incongruities II 758
  transl Geiger's *Civilization* II 758n
Sañjña, Saṃjñā (Skt)
  example of chhāyā-birth II 174
  leaves chhāyā w husband II 101, 174
Śaṅkara, Śaṃkara (Skt) blessed
  a name of Śiva I 286; II 498
  one of 3 hypostases I 18, 286
Śaṅkarāchārya, Śaṃkarāchārya, Śaṅkara, Śaṃkara (Skt) Hindu avatāra
  abandoning illusive body I 570
  Buddha &, closely connected II 637
  Buddha's successor I xliv
  Buddhism & I 47 &n
  fire-deity presides over time I 86
  greatest historical initiate I 86, 271
  Īśvara & ātma in I 573-4
  on knowledge of Absolute Spirit I 6
  Moon, Sun, mind II 639n
  one of the greatest minds I 522
  paraguru of I 457n
  sattva I 68n
  secret wisdom taught by I 539n
  on the sheaths I 570 &n
  some treatises of, kept secret I 271
  spirit & non-spirit I 573
  termed a 6th rounder I 162
  "THIS" explained by I 7
—— *Viveka-chūḍāmaṇi* ("Crest-Jewel of Wisdom") I 569-70, 573-4
Śaṅkha-Dvīpa (Skt, Sancha Dwipa in tx)
  existed in Purānic times II 407
  Hindu version Plato's Atlantis II 405-8
Śaṅkhāsura (Skt) Indian king
  described II 405, 407, 408
Sāṅkhya, or Sāṃkhya (Skt) school of philos
  beings born fr elements I 284

on intellectual creation I 456
Kapila founder of I 284; II 42, 571-2
man is spirit, matter II 42
a most perfect philos system II 253
pradhāna as a cause I 55
pradhāna in I 256 &n, 370n
purusha impotent I 247
seven prakritis in I 256n, 335
written down by last Kapila II 572
Sāṅkhya-Kārikā (Skt)
    kumāras (Vaidhātra) I 457n
    Pratyayasarga Creation I 456
    seven prakritis I 256n, 335
Sāṅkhya-Sāra (Skt)
    Mahat first appears as Vishnu I 75
Sannaddha [Saṃnaddha] (Skt)
    one of 7 mystic solar rays I 515n
Sanskrit [Saṃskṛita] (language)
    Ahura (Pers) is Asura in II 608
    Babylonia seat of, learning I xxxi
    decimal notation fr I 360-1
    disappearance of, works I xxxiv
    every letter has cause, effect I 94
    first lang of 5th race I 23; II 200, 204
    influence on Hebrew II 130
    invented by Brahmans (Stewart) II 442
    language of the gods I 269
    monads of Leibniz found in I 623
    mother of Greek II 200
    MS on astronomy II 551
    Mystery tongue II 200
    names used, not Senzar I 23
    not spoken by Atlanteans I 23
    once called Greek dialect I xxxviii
    origin of, & Hebrew I 73
    origin of, (Jacolliot) II 222
    primordial creation in I 450-1, 454
    D. Sarasvatī, authority on I xxx; II 214n
    Semitic languages fr II 200
    words have concealed meaning I 78; II 576-7
    works, Atlantis & Lemuria in II 326
Sanskrit Dictionary. See Goldstücker, T.
Sanskritists
    criticized I 456n, 647; II 50, 225, 450, 567, 585, 629
    ignorant of inner meanings I xxi-ii; II 451
    Sarasvatī greatest, of his day I xxx; II 214
Sanskrit Literature, Hist. of. See Müller, F. M.
Santhathi [Santati] (Skt) progeny, lineage
    each race the, of a manu II 140n
Saoshyant (Zor, Soshiosh in tx)
    Pers version of Kalki avatāra I 87; II 420
Sap. [Liber sapientiae]. See Book of [the] Wisdom of Solomon

Saphar (Heb). *See* Sephār
Sapta (Skt) seven
    four take on 3 becomes (Stanzas) I 71
Saptaloka (Skt) seven worlds
    Earth globes, Hades to Hindu II 234
Saptaparṇa (Skt) 7-leaved
    born fr soil of mystery II 574
    cave & Buddhist initiations I xx
    man-plant I 200, 236; II 574, 590-1
    seven principles or I 236
Saptarshi(s) (Skt) Seven Ṛishis
    angels, spirits & I 198
    constellation II 89n
    described I 436-7; II 318n, 549-50
    given various names I 436
    kali-yuga & I 407; II 549, 631
    seven Aeons & I 442
Sapta-Samudras (Skt) seven oceans
    minor gods fashion chaos into II 704n
    symbolize 7 guṇas I 348
Saptasūrya (Skt), & kab 7 Suns of Life II 239
Saqquarah Bronzes, Saitic Epoch I 367n
Sar (Bab), or circle I 114
Sarah, Sarai (Heb) Abraham's wife
    Moon cycle & II 76-7
    parallel story in Purānas II 174-6
    tempted Pharaoh I 422; II 174
    womb, Eve or II 472
Saramā, Sārameyas (Skt)
    related to Gk Hermes-Sarameyas II 28
Sāraph, Serāphīm (Heb)
    angels, archons, etc I 363, 604
    architects or I 16 &n
    brazen, fiery serpents I 364n
    cherubim same esoterically II 501
    Christian sacred animal I 363
    copy of ancient prototype I 92
    defined II 63, 501
    fiery serpents I 126, 364n, 442; II 212n, 387n
    Hindu sarpa or II 501
    knew well, loved more II 243
    "know most" (Jennings) II 238n
    Lucifer, Satan or II 243
    -Mehopheph II 206n
    Moses builds brazen II 387 &n
    one of the Holy Four I 92
    rule over 9th world (Syrian) I 435
    St Michael called II 479-80
    six wings of II 387n
    three in *Sepher Jezirah* I 92
    winged wheels, avengers I 126
Sarasvatī (Skt)
    dwelt between prāna & apāna I 95

goddess of hidden wisdom II 199n
goddess of speech I 95
universal soul I 352-3
wife of Brahmā II 76n, 77
Saraswati, Dayanand. *See* Dayānanda
Sarcode (protoplasm)
of Haeckel's monera I 542
name given by Beaumetz II 153n
Sarcophagus
baptismal font, not corn bin I 317n
of giants at Carthage II 278
Gnostic, of Porta Pia I 410
initiation II 462, 558
meant regeneration II 470
symbolic of female principle II 462
symbol of resurrection II 459-60
unit of measure (Smyth) I 317n
Sardinia(n), tombs, nuraghi in II 352, 752
Sargon, King
conquered Babylon II 691
Moses' story fr I 319 &n; II 428, 691
Śarīra (Skt)
attribute I 59n
body or form I 334-5, 522
Sarīsripa (Skt) any creeping animal
insects & small lives II 52
moneron of Haeckel & II 185
Sarku (Bab), light race II 5
Saros(es) (Chald) cycle
Berosus on I 655n
circle symbol & I 114
each, equals 6 naroses I 655n
smaller cycles within I 641
Sarpa (Skt) serpent
derivation of word II 181-2n
differ fr nāgas II 182n, 501 &n
flying II 183
produced fr Brahmā's hair II 181-2
Sarpa-Rājñī (Skt) queen of serpents
Earth or I 74; II 47
Sarvaga (Skt) all-permeant
soul-substance of world I 582
supreme soul is I 451
Sarva-maṇḍala (Skt)
Egg of Brahmā or I 257, 373
Sarva-medha (Skt) sacrifice
Viśvakarman performed II 605
Sarvātma (Skt) all self
Seven Lords lie hidden in I 90
Sarvāvasu (Skt) sunbeam
one of 7 mystic solar rays I 515n
Sarveśa (Skt) lord of all
devoid of name, species, body I 373

Śastra (Skt) edged weapon
not Astra or fiery II 629n
Śastra-devatās (Skt)
gods of divine weapons II 629
Sat (Skt). *See also* All, Boundless, That
absolute Non-Entity I 143n
asat &, key to Aryan wisdom II 449-50
Be-ness, Reality or I 14-17; II 310
immutable eternal root II 449
manifested things cannot be I 119-20
One ever-hidden or I 542
Parabrahman the esoteric II 58
threshold to world of truth I 119
unconditioned reality I 69
Universal Soul or II 58
universe, Divine Thought I 61
unknowable absoluteness of I 556
unmanifested I 289
Sat or Thoth, Seth, the later Sat-an II 530
Śata(s) (Skt) hundred(s)
Vedas into, of branches II 483
Satan (śātān, Heb) adversary II 231-9, 337-90.
See also Adversary, Angels, Asuras, Devils,
Fallen Angels, Lucifer
adversary to Jehovah II 243
agent of karma II 478
Angel of Death same as II 385
angel of God II 477
anointed identified w II 234
anthropomorphized I 412; II 507
Atlanteans prototypes of II 272
Baissac on II 245-6, 509
became a fallen angel I 194-5; II 506
became a savior I 193
Cain generated by II 389
Celestial Pole as II 358
Christ & Antichrist I 612
creator of Divine Man I 193
derivation of word II 387
Deus inversus I 411-24
door keeper II 233
as dragon crushed by Virgin I 403
dragon of wisdom miscalled II 94n, 234
Ea disfigured into Thallath or II 61
esoteric view of II 233-6
Fallen Angel II 60, 229n, 475-505, 489, 515
father of spiritual mankind II 243
fell as lightning fr heaven II 231 &n
fifth class of demons II 389n
a Frankenstein monster II 508
God forbids cursing II 477
God in *Talmud* II 478
God in the manifested world II 235
god of wisdom II 237, 530

Hermes or II 380
highest divine spirit II 377
horns, cloven foot, claws of II 230, 507
Jehovah &, one II 387n
Jehovah upside down II 510
killed by Michael, St George II 385
King of Darkness II 509n
kumāras degraded into I 458
Lévi on II 238n, 506-7
Logos firstborn brother of II 162
Lucifer &, is our mind II 513
Lucifer or II 30-1, 111, 230-1, 243, 283n
made grotesque by theology II 476, 508
made terrestrial man divine I 198
magistrate of karma II 234
Manichaeans on II 509n
manifested, bound, fallen II 235
Merodach or II 53
Milton on II 484
"Monkey of God" II 476
no reality to II 209
Ophiomorphos or II 244, 389
origin of pagan saviors II 482
personification of abstract evil II 478
plagiarist by anticipation II 476
Pleroma & II 506-18
prince of pre-Adamic world I 324
pure spirit originally I 413
reality to Roman Catholics II 510
rebellious angel I 193-4, 196
refused to create I 193-4
scapegoat for God's blunders I 412
scholiasts impose belief in II 776-7
secret of II 235
seducing serpent II 111
serpent (*Genesis*) not II 388
shadow of God II 510
Shamael [Samael] the supposed II 205
slandered by theologians I 415
Son of God [*Job*] I 412, 414, 422n; II 376, 378, 477, 489
stood up against Israel II 387n
tempter & redeemer II 513
tempts David to number people I 414
thou shalt not revile II 477-8
Venus-Lucifer or II 30-1, 45n
"War in Heaven" II 62-3
wisest of gods, archangels II 60
Satanians, sect of, degraded II 389
Satanic I 222, 325; II 228, 341, 390n, 482, 641
Satanism
hypnotism will soon become II 641
of idols (de Mirville) II 341
Satan ou le diable. See Baissac, J.

Śatapatha Brāhmaṇa (Skt)
Brahmā created thru daughter I 431
Brahman radiated gods, rests I 447
fourteen precious things I 67n
Idā (Ilā) II 138, 140, 147-8
Kaśyapa, account of II 253
no life after Flood II 146
Sarva-medha ceremony II 605
Seven Rishis in I 436
Śatarūpā (Skt) hundred-formed
daughter, wife of Brahmā I 431
Vāch is named I 94; II 128
Satellite(s). *See also* Moon(s)
Jupiter's, denser than planet I 593; II 137n
Mars has no right to its I 165
Mercury, Venus have no I 155n; II 32
Moon, of Earth physically I 180
of Neptune, Uranus, retrograde I 149-50n, 575, 593
planes of Neptune, Uranus, tilted I 101
theories of origin of I 596-7
Sati (Egy), triadic goddess I 367n
Satires. See Horace
Sattā (Skt) sole existence
Supreme Spirit is, in pralaya I 373
Sattapaṇṇi (Pāli) Cave (in *Mahāvaṃśa*)
Buddhist initiations at I xx
Sattva (Skt) purity, truth
dual monad or I 69n
one of the triguna I 348
quietude I 335n
rajas & tamas I 348, 535
understanding or antahkarana I 68n
Saturday, Saturn's day I 652
Saturn (god). *See also* Kronos, Saturn-Kronos
Agruerus, Kronos are II 142n, 341n
ate his progeny I 674n
Dāgōn, Kronos [Vallencey] I 642n
fr duration became limited I 418
Egypt, Greece, Phoenicia fr II 768
father of the gods I 418, 449n
god of time II 390n
Golden Age of II 372-3, 421, 777
Jewish Moon-god II 63
Kronos, & Noah II 391-2
Kronos or, governed Lemurians II 765
Kronos-Sadic & II 360n
Lemuria or kingdom of II 765, 768, 777
Plato's Golden Age under II 264
Sabaoth, Israel & I 576
Samothracian mysteries & II 360n, 391
serpent swallowing tail not I 253n
swallows Jupiter lapis II 341 &n
Saturn (planet)

building of Earth & II 23
conditions on II 137n
conjunction of planets & I 656, 662; II 63
evil-eyed, the dark II 29
fourth human group under II 29
Ialdabaōth-Jehovah genius of I 577n; II 538 &n
Jehovah &, glyphically same I 417, 578
Jews evolved under II 127
Mars, Jupiter, conjunction w, rare I 656
Moon, Jupiter &, high triad II 462
Moon, Qū-tāmy & II 453, 455
nations born under I 577
polar compression of Mercury & I 593
psychic relation to Earth I 575
rings of II 235
"ruler" of I 435, 459
Śanaiśchara is I 459
Satan astronomically II 235
septenary chain I 153
Uranus more dense than I 593
Saturn (7th world of Syrians)
thrones rule over I 435
Saturnine. *See* Hyperborean
cradle of race became II 777
great sea north of Asia called II 777n
Saturn-Kronos. *See also* Kronos, Saturn
Rudra-Śiva is II 502n
Samael, Schemal symbolic of I 417
Third Race Titans & II 766
Titans as, mutilated Uranos II 766
Satya (Skt)
absolute being or *esse* I 48n
unconditioned reality I 69
Satya-loka (Skt), one of seven II 321
"Satyān nāsti paro dharmaḥ" (Skt) "There is no religion higher than truth"
motto of The Theosophical Society I xli; II 798
Satyas (Skt), one of 12 gods II 90
Satya-Yuga, or Kṛita-Yuga (Skt) II 308n. *See also* Golden Age
always the 1st age I 377
astronomical signs for beginning of I 378
Eden or II 493
fifth race in, when Atlantis sank II 147n
first flood at end of II 146
Kapila of, a generic name II 572
length of II 69
manus & I 235n
occurs in Bhārata (Varsha) II 322
Ocean of Milk & I 67-8
separation ended, of 3rd race II 201
sixth race will be in II 147n

third root-race & II 520n
Vishnu as Kapila gives wisdom in II 483
"Watchers" & I 266
Satyr(s)
Church Fathers "saw" II 755
described (Commentaries) II 287
extinct race animal-men II 262
nephīlīm later made into II 755, 775
symbol of Atlantean bestiality II 775
Saul
armies of, scattered I 467
divination by II 455
Sauria(ns)
flying II 219, 258
genesis of II 151, 205
ibis saves Egypt fr I 362
third eye developed in II 299n
Savage(s)
abject, explained II 744
ancestors are serpents, belief of I 404
anthropoid fr, (Haeckel) II 171
Aryans & II 421n
civilized &, races side by side II 317-18, 522, 716-17, 722-3
complicated mythology, customs of II 721
do not imitate apes II 676n
Ice Age immigration of II 738n
of India II 676
inferiority of II 249n, 421n
latest human monads II 168
may be old, relapsed races II 721-2
moral discernment of I 423
Paleolithic, & civ man II 317, 686n, 716
primeval, never existed II 722
some of 3rd race were II 318
sterility in crossings w II 195
superior & inferior, discussed II 425
there have been, in all ages II 715
Savagery, isolation brings on II 426
Savahi (Pers), globe F, Earth chain II 759
Savarṇā (Skt)
mother of the Prāchetases II 578
Sāvarṇa, Sāvarṇi (Skt)
Seed-Manu, globe G, 4th round II 309
Savior(s) II 222
Agathodaemon, the Gnostic II 458
Chenresi called II 179
Christian, & Taurus I 656
cyclic II 415
holy seed-grain of future II 173
last, will be fr Sacred Island II 350
man his own I 644
mind is our II 513
no new, in Black Age I 470

periodical births of world I 657
personified in Prometheus II 411
Pisces symbol of I 653
rākshasas future, of humanity II 163
rebels are our II 103
Satan a I 193; II 243
satanic origin of pagan, (Sepp) II 482
spiritual Sun sends forth I 638
Vaivasvata, of our race II 140-1
Sāvitrī (Skt), Vāch or, mother of gods II 128
Saxon (races)
  God of, fr Heb yōdh or jōd I 347
Sāyaṇa (Skt) commentator on *Rig-Veda*
  makes Ilā goddess of Earth II 138
  makes Mania goddess of Earth II 143
Sayce, Archibald Henry
—— *Hibbert Lectures . . .*
  Babylonian astronomers II 693
  Babylonian religion II 691
  beneficent, maleficent gods II 477
  on Chaldean chronology I 320n
  Damti [Tamtu] the sea II 463
  Eridu foreign city II 203
  Eridu, Tel'loh II 226, 693
  evil servant of good II 477
  gods of Chaldea II 248n
  library at Nineveh II 692
  Moon created monsters II 115
  Nebo, god of wisdom II 456
  "Observations of Bel" II 693
  Sargon, Akkad, library II 691
  Seven Kings II 2
  statues at Tel'loh II 692-3
  two creations II 54
Scandinavia(n). *See also* Eddas, Norse, Wäg-
  ner, W.
  America settled by I 297
  Ases, oracles, runes of II 97, 346 &n
  cosmogony before Vedas (Müller) I 367
  dragon, swastika in II 486, 557
  legends begin w time & life I 427
  Loki, falling god of II 486
  mythology of II 754, 774
  Odin of, one of 35 buddhas II 423
  skull size of II 523
  wars in heaven among I 202
Scapegoat
  Azāzēl, of Israel II 387, 389n, 409
  Jewish, for the Fall II 510
  Satan as the I 412
Scarab(aeus)
  symbol II 552
  winged, symb of devachan I 365
Schamo. *See* Shamo

Schelling, Friedrich W. J. von II 461
  Absolute of, & Vedānta I 50
  accepted periodical avatāras I 52n
  believed many worlds inhabited II 706
  derivation of word Osiris II 114
  nature divinities of ancients I 463-4
  serpent is evil II 209
—— *Ideen zu einer Philosophie der Natur*
  illusion of matter I 510
Schemel. *See* Shemal
Scheo (Egy). *See* Shoo
Scherer, C., saw a dragon II 207n
Schesoo-Hor [Shesu-Ḥeru] (Egy) "Sons of
  Horus," settled & built Egypt II 432
Schibb. *See* Ragon
Schiller, Johann Cristoph Friedrich
  skull of II 523
—— "The Veiled Image at Sais"
  poem re veil of Isis II 654-5
Schilling. *See* Schelling, F. W. J. von
Schindler, V.
—— *Lexicon Pentaglotton*
  defines Sōd as Mysteries II 212n
Schlagintweit, Emil
—— *Buddhism in Tibet*
  commentators justify dogmas I xxvii
  Nāgas II 26-7n
Schlegel, Dr Gustaf
—— *Uranographie Chinoise*
  Chinese astronomy 18,000 yrs old I 658
Schliemann, Dr Heinrich
  proved Troy existed II 236
—— *Ilios*
  found prehistoric idols II 723
  inscriptions in unknown languages II 440
  swastika discs at Troy II 101, 586
Schmidt, Edward Oskar
—— *The Doctrine of Descent & Darwinism . . .*
  American & African fauna alike II 792
  ape grown more bestial II 646
  Darwin & our human ancestors II 667n
  difficulties of Darwinism II 734n
  Gerland on Australians II 779 &n
  hermaphrodite man II 172n, 184
  language & Darwinism II 662
  on Lemurian continent II 789 &n
  man grows more human II 646
  man's kinship w apes II 666n
  North Africa peninsula of Spain II 8-9n
  Paleolithic man not Pithecoid II 716n
  root of ungulates unknown II 735-6
  various types of reproduction II 166
Schmidt, J. F. J.
  discovered star in Cygnus I 596

Scholia in Apollonium Rhodium
on Kabiri II 362
Scholia in Aristotelem. See Simplicius
Scholia in Euripides "Orestes" (Dindorf). *See*
Euripides
Scholia Vaticanum ad Euripides Troades. See
Euripides
School(s)
Buddhist: Mahāyāna, Hīnayāna I 39, 47-9
&nn
catechism of inner II 281-2
esoteric I xxn, xxiii, xliv, 94, 306
secret Buddhist, trans-Himalayan I xxn, xxi,
xxiii
six Indian I 47n, 269, 278
war between initiates of two II 497-8
Schopenhauer, Arthur I 96n
agnostic I 19n
echoes *Zohar* II 528
pessimism of II 156n, 304n
Schöpfungsgeschichte. See Haeckel, *History of
Creation*
Schott, Wilhelm
—— *Entwurf einer Beschreibung . . .*
Confucius a transmitter I xxxvii &n
Schöttgen, Christian, *Horae Hebraicae . . .*
Adam not living soul II 162
Schwartze, Moritz Gotthilf
discovered & transl *Pistis Sophia* II 566n
Schwegler, Albert, *A History of Philosophy*
self-consciousness & Absolute I 51 &n
Schweinfurth, G. A., *In the Heart of Africa*
African giants, dwarfs II 754
chasm between man & beast II 655n
Science(s). *See also* Chemistry, Physics, Scientific, Scientists
adepts solved problems of II 451
aether, ākāśa, cannot analyze I 487
ancient, anticipated modern II 253
ancient nations pursued II 334
antagonism betw metaphysics & I 485n
approaches occult I 124, 548-9, 551-4, 600,
625-8
Atlantean II 49
Bible, Purānas & II 251-63
in Brahmanical chronology II 66-70, 73
calls Atlantis Lemuria II 314-15
can't answer what a man is I 636
compelled to accept ether I 485
conceit of our age I 133
contradictions in I 482-3
corroborates physical only I 164
could profit fr ancients I 586-7
denies violent axial changes, Atlantis II 314

dicta not necessarily proven I 279
dogmatic assertions of II 349
Donnelly put aside by II 334
esoteric & orthodox, on life II 711-15
esoteric figures & II 156
esoteric, profane, & astral body II 149
ever becoming like universe I 516
evolution thru blind force I 139
exoteric II 124
faithful to its ape ancestor II 329
fallibility of theories II 316n
fears to make man ancient II 347-8
force-matter unknown god of I 509-10
forces, effects of elements I 342
foundation of, Grecian, Indian I 579
Genesis &, (Gladstone) II 252n
geology & evolution not exact II 656
Grove demanded reform of I 495
honeycombed w metaphysics I 485, 544
inductive I 298
inertia in I 511
infallibility of I 520
Kabiri taught man II 364
on Keely's work I 555-6
laws of, self-guiding I 506-7
laya zero point of I 148-9
Lemuro-Atlantean II 285
life an aspect of matter in I 602-3
ludicrous mistakes of II 439
on man as 1st mammal II 155
man's size & II 277
materialism of, & divine spirits I 276
materialism often miscalled I 279
mathematical abstraction basis of I 670
may ignore first 2½ races II 685-6
men of true, defined I 514
metaphysics &, (Slack) I 588
modern, fr ancient I 507, 579
must study causes II 592
mystery is the fatality of I 670
mystified by fire I 121
mythology man's most ancient I 304
nature purposive & I 640-1
needs the spiritual & psychic I 588
new, hidden in old gods II 130
nothingness of, is a plenum I 148
occult & modern II 322n, 348, 449
occult, changeless traditions of I 516
occultism & I 477-81, 496, 636-7
occult, key to world problems I 341
occult teachings & I 506-7
one name for all substance I 510
"organized common sense" I 477
real, not materialistic I 518-19

recognizes only physical man II 315
rejects special creation II 731
relation betw mind & matter in I 124 &n
religion &, on Earth's age II 796
ridicules intelligent universe I 287
secure only in solar system I 601
seven liberal, & 7 accursed II 641
sophisms of I 279
space, force, matter I 615
Stonehenge "explained" by II 344
studies effects, not causes I 262, 464-5
studies 4 elements only II 592
takes nothing on trust I 669
taught to man by gods II 366
theories of rotation I 500-6
theosophist realizes value of I 296
traces proximate causes I 515
true, described II 663-4
truth should be sole aim of I 509
turned fr theology to matter II 689
universal life & I 49
uses many things it does not know II 655
Vishnu as Kapila taught man II 572
walls of modern Jericho I 298-9
"Science and the Emotions." *See* Clodd, E.
Science occulte. See Salverte, E.
Science of Lang., Lectures on. See Müller
Science of Language, The. See Hovelacque, A.
Science of Rel., Intro. to. See Müller, F. M.
Science of Serpents (Upanishads)
  science of occult knowledge II 26n
Science of Thought. See Müller, F. M.
Scientific. *See also* Science, Scientists
  conclusions fallible II 316n
  confirmation of Lemuria II 324-34
  data taken on faith II 438
  discoveries & occult teaching I 546, 623
  fictions on life on other worlds II 701
  hypotheses unverifiable phantoms I 617
  imagination of Tyndall I 483
  must follow Hermetists I 625
  teachings & occult compared II 348
Scientific American
  USS Dolphin's findings II 793
Scientific Arena
  A. W. Hall on force & energy I 146n
Scientific Letters. See Butlerof, A. M.
Scientific Religion. See Oliphant, L.
Scientist(s). *See also* Science, Scientific
  anticlerical enthusiasm of II 645
  attack spiritual beliefs II 664
  blind force, mechanical nature of II 298
  blind theories of, "miraculous" II 664
  confirm periodic submergences II 325-6

deride metaphysics II 664
do not believe in Atlantis II 429
do not know Earth's ages II 66
failure of, due to materialism I 600
fallacies of I 487-8
future, will discover marvels I 297
know matter only skin deep I 147
modes of motion confuse I 491
mysterious help given a few I 612
often as bigoted as clergy I 509
restate ancient ideas I 117-18
see only what they wish II 752
75% evolutionists II 645
some great, referred to I 517-20
unable to understand Svābhāvikas I 3-4
will be driven out of materialism I 620
will not become anti-Cartesian I 627
worship force-matter I 509-10
Scinde. *See* Sind
Scintillas. *See also* Sparks
  souls of gods, monads, atoms I 619
  sparks, worlds or I 98-9
  of 3 upper & 4 lower worlds I 618
  worlds that came & died II 704
Sclater, Philip Lutley
  invented name Lemuria II 7, 171
  opposed by Wallace II 8n
Scorpio
  Aries, Mars &, (Skinner) II 392
  desert rains &, (*Job*) I 648
  heart of, & beginning of kali-yuga I 663
  reproductive organs, sign of II 129
  Virgo becomes II 129
  Virgo-, or Dan I 651
  Virgo-, separated II 502n
Scorpion, ref in Egy *Bk of Dead* II 588n
Scotland
  cup-like markings on stones in II 346n
  sinking II 787n
Scribe(s)
  lipika means I 103-4, 128-9n
  Thot is sacred, of Amenti I 385
Scripture(s)
  all allegorical II 77, 409-10
  astronomy, cosmolatry & II 77
  Chaldean, mutilated by Eusebius I xxvi &n
  chanted, rationale of I 94
  double origin of Hebrew II 202-3
  every, has 7 aspects II 496
  exoteric I 165, 278, 306-7
  great, convey truth II 409-10
  impudence of modern translators II 537
  man once luminous, incorporeal in II 112
  man's parent-gods in every II 358

national, for exoteric use I 229
no, contains the whole I 318
numbers, figures in every I 320-1
old, constantly altered II 657-8
prove antiquity of teachings II 449
seven primeval races in all I 248
sevens in biblical II 747-8
tree, sacred knowledge, or I 128n
Scrolls of Wisdom (Norse) II 100
Scythia(ns) II 7
  of Herodotus II 416
  Hyperborea beyond II 11
  one-eyed race of II 769n
Scyths
  descend fr Atlantean subrace II 774
  Mongolians should be called II 203
Sea(s). *See also* Ocean, Space
  chalk deposits on, bottom II 325
  dragon of, (Tiamat) I 357; II 503
  of fire or noumenal light I 75
  glacial, gloomy in tradition II 398
  inland, of Gobi II 5, 220, 502-3, 637
  of milk & Lakshmī I 380
  N Asian, called Saturnine II 777n
  Polar II 12
  of sorrow or Earth life II 505
  of Space, Akkadians, Babylonians II 477
  Thalatth, Thalassa & II 65n
  Venus-Aphrodite personifies I 458n
  of wine, butter, curds II 321
  Zohar on serpent of II 504
Sea Anemone, reproduces by budding II 166
Seang of Wai [Hsiang of Wei] (Chin)
  Bamboo Books & II 302
"Sea of Knowledge"
  once on Gobi Desert II 502-3
Sea Serpent II 207, 477
Seasons
  angle of pole causes II 356
  Arab year of six II 621
  eternal spring in 3rd race II 201, 356
  on Jupiter & Venus II 706-7
  Kabiri & the I 642n
  no changes greater than I 441
  procreation & II 412nn
  Titan-Kabirim regulate II 363
Seb (Egy). *See* Keb
Sebakh or Sevekh (Egy) seventh
  defunct man, crocodile, dragon I 219-20
  Kronos or I 408
Sebti (Egy), Kep, Kepti & I 408
Secchi, Father Pietro Angelo, *Le soleil*
  estimates Sun's heat I 484n
  on sunspot activity I 541 &n

Second Adam, septenary, 7 races II 1-2n
Secondary Age (geology). *See also* Primordial-,
  Primary-, Tertiary-, & Quaternary Age
  age of reptiles II 713
  animals bisexual at end of II 594n
  cataclysms destroyed 3rd race in II 714
  civilization back to II 266n
  mammalia of II 684
  man in II 10, 157, 219, 288, 687n, 714n, 734
  reptiles preponderated in II 254
  rocks of, 15,000 ft thick II 709
  science denies man in II 713
  strata of, twice the Tertiary II 715n
  table II 710
  third race appeared in II 713
  third race Titan of II 9
  Wealden river bed Lemurian II 333
Secondary Creation
  atoms issue fr laya-center in I 453
  begins I 449-50
  cataclysms of II 312 &n
  of darkness, matter I 450
  dhyāni-chohans, rishis in I 453
  Earth grew opaque in II 312 &n
  every cosmogony begins w II 59
  first elemental differentiation I 452
  Hindu I 452-3
  manifested universe emanates I 446
  mineral, vegetable in II 312
  Primary & II 53n, 107, 113, 312n, 446, 447
  second hierarchy of manus in I 453
Second Birth (Skt). *See also* Dvija
  janna signifies I xxn
Second Continent. *See also* Hyperborean
  Continent
  destruction of II 138
  eternal spring of, became Hades II 138
Second Logos. *See also* Adam-Kadmon
  Ampsiu-Ouraan (Gnos) or II 569n
  androgyne dual force I 437
  creative subordinate powers II 544
  demiurge II 22, 478
  First &, or Avalokiteśvara I 72n
  first begotten ogdoad I 448
  First Cause manifests thru I 214
  manifested Logos I 448; II 25
  Microprosopus I 240
  purusha-prakriti I 16
  role of II 478
  Sephīrōth, Adam Kadmon II 544
  spirit-matter I 16
  Sun, Mārttānda, 8th son of Aditi I 448
  Tetraktys of Greeks II 599
  Vajrasattva I 571

Second Race. *See* Root-Race–2nd
Second Round. *See* Round–2nd
Secrecy. *See also* Secret
  about life & death II 451
  re certain symbols I 306, 363
  Egyptian priests pledged to II 763
  esoteric catechism on I 299
  except to pledged chelas I 164
  fear of desecration II 124
  of initiates II 586
  millenniums of, re Secret Doctrine I xxii
  re mysteries of nature II 518
  Neoplatonists bound by oaths of II 763
  Plato pledged to II 266, 763
  reasons for I xxxiii-v; II 451
  reticence in giving truth I 167; II 571
  rules on, strict I 163-4, 168, 170
  Sepher-Jezirah I 299
  since Plato's Atlantis sank II 124
Secret(s)
  Asuramaya confirmed in, records II 50
  Atlantean, cycles II 49
  books about man II 444
  books in temple libraries II 529
  catechism of Druses II 27
  complete, record of Lemurians II 334-5
  data fr generations of adepts II 700
  description of, Lemurian records II 334-5
  documents hidden, knowledge not I xxxv
  dual power of, wisdom II 364
  figures kept I 163-4, 168, 170; II 251
  Kabbala's secret of II 282n
  knowledge confined to temples II 532-3
  "Mirror of Futurity" one of, records II 49
  of nature II 319
  records & 7 keys to man's genesis I 323
  sciences, history of II 503
  teachings, portion only given I 480
  works & esoteric cycles II 70
  works unknown in Europe II 439
Secret Doctrine. *See also* Esoteric, Occultism
  accumulated wisdom of ages I xxii, 272-3
  avoids miraculous, materialistic II 153
  basis & source of all things I 46
  Buddhism, Upanishads rest on I 47
  choice betw, & Darwinism, Bible II 157
  Church Fathers tried to destroy I xl
  common property of mankind II 794
  on cosmogenesis (*IU*) I 4
  dates incompatible w science II 794
  defined & described I 272-3
  difficulties in describing II 794-8
  of the East II 127
  esoteric Zoroastrianism same as II 356

  found in 1,000s of Skt MSS I xxiii
  generations of seers checked I 272
  Hermetic fragments part of I 287
  Hindu philosophy older than Egy I 387
  intelligent powers rule universe I 287
  interprets archaic symbols II 96-7
  key to theogonies & sciences II 767
  looked upon as hoax II 441-2
  loses caste II 275
  manus, races, etc II 307
  millions of beings around, in us I 604-5
  more given each century I xxxvii-viii n
  Nabathean Agriculture & II 455
  New World, before Buddhism II 424n
  preserved in Vatican I xliv
  proofs of its diffusion I xxxiv, 307
  Rosicrucian pelican symbol fr I 19-20
  state the, & bear consequences I 323
  synonyms of Hindu gods in I 92
  teaches no atheism I 279
  teaches progressive development I 43
  teaches reliable history I 267
  three fundamental propositions I 14-18
  three fund prop re evolution II 1, 274-5
  univ diffused rel of mankind I xxxiv
  Word: one number fr no number I 94
Secret Doctrine, The. *See* Blavatsky, H. P.
Secretion(s)
  fr divine bodies & atoms I 568
  spiritual, of alchemists I 509
"Secret of Satan." *See* Kingsford, *The Perfect Way*
Secret Science. *See also* Gupta-Vidyā
  dual power of II 364
  Gandharvas instructors in II 584
  known to initiates, adepts I 611-12
  new teacher of, in 20th cent I xxxviii
  not a fairy tale II 795
  portions of, concealed I xxxv
  works on, destroyed I xxiii-iv
Secret Work (of Chiram or King Hiram)
  perfect man culmination of II 113
Sedimentation(ary)
  animal evolution & II 325n
  carbonic acid & II 157
  first, 320 million yrs ago II 710, 715n
  preparation for, 4th round II 715n
  var scientists on beginning of II 694
Sedu (Sadu in tx)
  Chald class of spirits II 248n
Seed(s)
  becomes a golden egg I 333, 350
  brought by 1st "Seven" II 590
  design of future evolution in II 653-4

every, a potential god I 201
force which informs I 291
ideal prototype within I 63
Incomprehensible drops a I 350
latent potentialities of II 653
lotus, symbol of II 472
man storehouse of all II 289-90 &n
must die to live as a plant I 459n
Mysteria Specialia, of anything I 283n
preserved in an ark II 307n
racial II 444
self-existent Lord cast a I 333
serpent's, & woman II 411
of undying wisdom II 282
world germ or I 200-1 &n
Seed-Manu(s)
divine śishta II 164, 308
each round closes w II 308
Noah symbol of root- & II 597
table of II 309
twenty-one manus explained I 235n
Vaivasvata, root-manus & II 321
Seeman, Prof B., "Australia & Europe . . ."
Australian race & Eocene man II 779
confirms horseshoe continent II 333
floral evidence of Atlantis II 781
relegated man to Eocene II 288
Seer(s). *See also* Adepts, Initiates
Apollo god of II 770
can commune w higher beings II 281n
catastrophe predicted by I 646
cosmic forces seen by I 633-4
Dangma or I 46n
data fr generations of II 700
eye of, sees pregenetic protyle I 46n, 617-18
flashing eye of I 272
generations of, checked SD I 272
generic names of II 361-75, 529-35
life on other stars & II 703
observe interstellar shoals I 633-4
of the open eye, Enoïchion or II 530
perceive mysteries of motion I 116n
physiological purity of II 295
recorded the soul of things I 272
Śiva eye of II 284
spiritual eagle eye of I 605; II 67
sushumna ray & trance of I 515
trace sound beyond matter I 633
vision limited to solar system II 700n
visions of, checked I 273
Seer of Patmos. *See also* John, St.
sought to improve *Bk of Enoch* II 510
Sefekh Abu (Egy) I 408
Seiffarth. *See* Seyffarth, G.

Seket (Egy, Sokhit in tx)
cat sacred to II 552n
Sekhem (Egy)
devachan or I 220-1, 237
mysterious face concealed in I 220
Seldenus [John Selden], *De Diis Syriis*
divination by the terāphīm I 394
Select Specimens of the Hindu Theater. See
Wilson, H. H.
Selenic, Selenognosis, Selenography I 305, 396
Seleucus of Seleucia
taught heliocentic theory I 117 &n
Self. *See also* Ātman, Egos, Higher Self
divine, perceived by human I 471
divine, wisdom of II 569
-guidance longed for II 484
higher I 266, 445, 610n, 638-9; II 95, 103, 109-10
higher, & dreamless sleep I 266
higher, crucified by man II 36
higher, goaded by personal II 109
humanizing the II 246
memory generates notion of I 292
merging the, w the II 639 &n
must emancipate, fr 7 senses I 87, 534
paralyzing the lower I 276
parent-source of ego I 129
passions of terrestrial II 268
sacrifice of II 94n, 243
seat abiding in the, (*Anugītā*) II 495
voice of, within II 640
which is & is not I 333-4
-worship leads to phallicism II 273
yoga inhalation & higher I 96
Self-born I 203, 450
beings born thru will II 120-1
chhāyās II 120, 138, 164, 198
first race called II 198
Kaśyapa the I 366; II 382n
Logos I 363; II 355
materialists reject II 151
Sons of Wisdom rejected, (boneless) II 171
Svāyambhuva or II 311
Self-conscious(ness). *See also* Agnishvāttas, Asuras, Kumāras, Lucifer, Man, Prometheus, Root-Race—3rd
absolute, not the Unconscious I 50-1
ahamkāra or I 335 &n
animals lack I 234
atoms are potentially I 107
becomes egoism, selfishness II 639n
buddhi plus, is Christos II 231n

development of, in mindless II 79-81, 103, 167
dhyāni-chohans endow man w II 233n
efforts toward divinity II 93
evolution I 416
Fallen Angels key to II 274
instinct & I 210, 234
lunar men had to become II 45
Mahat, manas & I 75
Mahat root of II 58-9
makes human evolution different I 175
manas springs fr I 334
man is a brute without II 163
no, in early races I 210, 539n
no, in pure spirit II 80
organizing principle or ego II 654
paramārtha or I 48n
spirit becomes, explained I 192-3
tortures of, (Prometheus) II 421
unconscious becomes, (Hegel) I 106
voice of self within II 640
won thru experience I 106
Self-existent. See also Svāyambhuva
absolute divine essence I 56
angelic spiritual essence II 242 &n
Ātma-bhū or the II 176, 578
eternal in essence only I 88
Heavenly Man & II 128
Ibn Gebirol on the I 439n
Lord I 52, 85, 333
not the universal One I 88
One, Reality I 2, 18
projected their shadows II 242-3
Svāyambhuva or I 80-1
Selfishness
intellect &, dangerous II 163
moves lower man II 422
of personality II 110
pride chief prompter of II 237
Semelē (Gk)
ascends to heaven I 400
had Bacchus by Jupiter II 362-3
Semite(s), Semitic. See also Arabs, Jews
Adam of, fr Aryans II 452
age of, empire II 691
ancient, language II 755
Aryan &, cosmogony II 241
Aryan &, on initiation II 470-4
belong to 5th race II 266
borrowed their theology II 203
branchlet of 4th & 5th subraces I 319
chasm betw Aryan &, religion I 383
common religion before separation I xxix
creation not emanation II 54

creation story sinful II 53
descend fr red Adam II 426
exalt God over all others II 507-8
family race II 147n
-Hebrews 8,000 yrs old II 470-1
introduced phallicism II 54
invented temptation of flesh I 383
Kabbala &, on God & man I 444-5
language fr Sanskrit II 200
later Aryans II 200
Moon once masc & Sun fem w I 397
obsessed w procreation II 543
orig unity of, & Aryans (Bunsen) I 115n
paradox of the, mind I 383
Seth primitive god of II 82n
sin, esoteric & exoteric view of I 383
triadic deities of II 54
womb Holy of Holies w II 457n
Senā (Skt) spear, army
fem/male aspect of Kārttikeya II 619
Senary (six) II 580
discussed II 582-3
hieroglyphical (Ragon) II 591
Seneca, Epistles
Earth shall return to chaos II 757
—— Hercules Oetaeus
dissolution, birth of worlds II 757
—— Quaestiones Naturales
Berosus on cataclysms I 649-50
dissolution of worlds II 757
Senectute, De (On Old Age). See Cicero
"Senior occultatus est . . ." I 214-15
Sensation
animal lives life of II 525n
every atom has, (Haeckel) II 673
mind ultimately rests upon I 2n
nerve molecules & 134n
space & I 555n
Sense(s). See also Hearing, Sight, Smell, Taste, Touch
Aindrī personified evolution of II 614
barrier to spiritual development II 296
beings w more or less I 608n
buddhi is 7th II 639
came in 3rd creation I 453
characteristics of matter & I 251
developed w physical man II 298
die before the body I 459n
evolution of outer II 294
evolved fr astral prototypes II 295
fire (self) burns lower 5, away II 639
five, & illusion I 329-30
five, born fr elements II 106-7
five, 6, 7, explained I 535n

freedom fr thralldom of I 329-30
inner, atrophied in early races II 294
jñānaśakti & I 292
knowledge fr 5, & 4 elements I 462
laborious knowledge of I 279
loss of physical II 370n
organs of, originate fr elements I 284-5
pentacle symbol of five I 125
physical, of a lower creation II 106
rudimentary, produced 1st I 447
Self beyond perception of II 568
seven, & causes of action I 535 &n
seven, & 7 priests I 87, 96; II 630
seven, in older Upanishads I 268 &n
seven spiritual & physical I 534
sixth, & permeability I 251, 258
Vedic Aryans & double set of I 534
Sensitives, hallucinations & II 370n
Senzar (secret sacerdotal language)
catechism on Space I 9
early, hieroglyphic cipher II 439
origin & universality of I xliii
used betw master & chelas I 23
Separation of Sexes. *See also* Root-Race—3rd,
Sexes
animals separated first II 184
began in egg stage II 197
in Bronze Age (of myth) II 520n
circle w vertical line or I 5
Daksha allegorized II 275
diagram II 688
early mankind & II 2-3
gradual II 84, 132, 197, 201
history begins w II 312
in mammals before man II 736 &n
man astral before II 736
man generated sexually after II 173
monosyllabic speech after II 198
Naudin on II 119-20, 181
Noah story & I 444n
part of natural evolution II 217, 275
"polar cells" & II 117
Pymander on II 96
rib of Adam legend & II 193
Schmidt on II 172n, 184
Tahitian myth of II 193-4
in 3rd root-race II 132, 135, 147, 177, 248,
715n
third round Indra & II 615n
Virgo-Scorpio separated w II 502n
Sephār (Heb, Saphar, S'phor in tx). *See also*
Sephārīm
one of 3 seraphim [sephārīm] I 92
Sephārīm (Heb, sephrim in tx)

ciphers, numbers, letters I 361n; II 39-40,
234
Sēpher (Heb). *See also* Sephārīm
implies numeration II 39
one of 3 seraphim [sephārīm] I 92
Sepher Jezirah. See Sēpher Yetsīrāh
Sepher M'bo Sha-arim [Sēpher M'ro Sheārim]
Superior emanates into inferior II 116
Sēpher Yetsīrāh (Heb, *Jezirah* or *Jetzirah* in tx)
air, water, fire I 447
alhim, sephrim II 39-40
compiled fr "very old book" I xliii
cosmic elements I 338 &n
cosmogenesis I 337
Divine is eternal Boundless I 447
dual light II 36-7
incomplete now II 536-7
miracles performed w I xliii n
occult work (Lévi) II 536
q by Rabbi [Halevi] in *Al-Chazari* II 234
rules of secrecy in I 299
sacred animals, Holy Four I 92 &n
spirit of the elohīm I 130n
Word of I 94
Sephīrā[h] (Heb, sing). *See also* Sephīrōth
Adam Kadmon & I 98, 137, 215-16n, 337,
430-2
Ādi-Sanat, Brahmā I 98 &n
Aditi I 53n, 357; II 43
becomes androgyne I 246n, 354-5
Chaldean I 357
emergence of I 354-5
-Eve or Aditi-Vāch I 355-6
first, the Crown I 215n; II 39
Hindu Vāch anticipated I 137
Hokhmāh, Bīnāh & I 98n
Kether or I 215n
light or I 337
mother in all religions I 215-16 &n
mother of sephīrōth I 53n, 355
Point or II 111
sephīrōth & I 89-90
sephīrōth later II 111
Shekīnāh or I 53n, 355, 430
shown as a woman I 352
Tiamat, Aditi or I 357
universal soul I 352-3
Vāch, Kwan Yin, etc I 431n
wife, daughter, mother I 430
Sephirah Djenioutha. See Siphrā di-Tsenī'ūthā'
Sephīrōth. *See also* Sephīrāh
Adam Kadmon synthesis of I 427, 432; II 2n,
544, 704n
Alhim created six I 342

architect generic name for I 579n
become creators, patriarchs I 355
builders of physical universe I 375
circle w diameter is ten I 391
creative secondary powers II 544
dbrim [debārīm] or the ten I 432
deity manifests thru ten I 239
dhyāni-chohans or I 339, 579n
elements stand for I 339
elohīm or I 230; II 388
fourth in descent I 614
heavenly man synthesis of I 337; II 704n
host of, first Adam II 46n
Jehovah one of lower I 197-8, 438
Jehovah 3rd of, or Bīnāh I 6n
Kabbala rests on II 37
later than Sephīrāh II 111
led on by Adam Kadmon II 129
man created by II 44
metaphysical, not Jehovah I 438-9
not abstractions I 632n
Osiris as chief I 437
prajāpatis or I 355
Pythagorean Tetraktys symb II 111
relation of, to man (Kabbala) I 230
second & 3rd of, or Microprosopus II 626
Sēpher Yetsīrāh on II 39-40
sephrim [sephārīm] & I 361n; II 39-40, 234
seven & upper triad I 98n, 128, 130; II 97
seven centers of energy I 604n
seven, channels of intelligence I 239
seven creative hosts I 72
seven limbs or I 239, 352
seven lower, or 2nd Adam II 1-2n, 595
seven, or builders I 128
seven, or pillars II 293
seven, or prajāpati I 89-90
seven splendors or II 603
six, of construction (builders) I 375
ten, & kingdoms I 176
ten & 7 classes of I 90, 215, 239, 352, 355, 361n, 391, 432; II 111
ten, limbs of heavenly man I 215, 239
Tetragrammaton head of 7 lower I 344
three II 39-40
three attributes of II 234
three orders of I 438
various names for I 375
Zohar on I 241
Sephīrōthal Tree II 25
Adam Kadmon is I 352; II 4, 293, 625n
Brahmā or universe I 352
four unities, 3 binaries of I 237n
seven, 10 & 12 parts II 36

Tetragrammaton, IHVH or II 625n
Tree of Life I 619; II 97
two triads & quaternary form II 595
universe sprang fr II 625n
Sephīrōthal Triad, Triangle I 619
emanates quaternary II 595
Fiery Breaths same as upper I 213
first II 269n
Sephīrāh, Hokhmāh, Bīnāh or I 98n
Sephra Dzenioutha. See Siphrā di-Tsenī'ūthā'
Sephrim. *See* Sephārīm
Sepolture dei Giganti
prehistoric Sardinian tombs II 752
Sepp, Dr J. N., *Vie de Notre-Seigneur* . . .
dwarfing of Hindu yugas I 655; II 619-20
Hindus borrowed fr Christians I 655
Messiah born in lunar year 4320 I 654
plagiarized Wilford I 655
satanic origin of pagan saviors II 482
Septarshis. *See* Saptarshis
Septempartite, Earth is, explained II 758
Septenary. *See also* Hebdomad, Septenate(s), Seven(s)
anima mundi is a II 562
arrangement infallible I 586n
cosmic & human principle II 616
cycle a law of nature II 623
diagram of kosmos I 200
discussed II 582-3, 622-30
division of solar forces I 290
division of stars, men, once esoteric I 168
division preceded fourfold I 408 &n
Earth must become II 312n
evolution I 267-8
highest triad, quaternary & II 595
Jah-Noah lowest II 596
law governs sound II 628
law of periodicity II 627
man clue to, powers I xxxv
man's principles II 79, 592-3, 604, 627
matter, in esotericism I 10n
meaning of dragon II 208
nature of life, disease II 622-3 &n
Oeaohoo six in one I 68
pre-, manvantara II 308n
principle universal I 241; II 628-30
refers to our world only I 333
system best for occultism II 592-3n
teaching ancient II 604, 640
teaching in Egypt I 236n; II 632-3
"Septenary Division in Different Indian Systems." *See* Subba Row

"Septenary Principle in Esotericism." *See* Blavatsky, H. P.
Septenate(s). *See also* Septenary, Seven(s)
  abstract nature a II 595-6
  Bartlett on, in nature II 595
  every man a II 29, 603-4
  Second Adam as a II 2n
  sidereal II 551
  stands for physical realm II 603
  the universal II 598-9
  various II 616-18
  in Vedas II 605-6
Sept leçons de physique générale. See Cauchy
Septuagint (Gk version Old Testament)
  disagrees w Protestant Bible I 576
  Jewish law in Greek II 200n
  rendering of *Joshua* (8:29) II 558
"Sépulture des Tartares." *See* Tooke, Wm.
Serapeum, Temple of Serapis
  Khnoum enshrined in lotus at I 385
Seraph, Seraphim. *See* Śáraph
Serapis (Gk-Egy)
  healer, enlightener II 26n
  serpent or sarpa II 501
  temple of II 396
Sermon 160. See Augustine, St
"Sermon on the Holy Virgin." *See* Bernard, St
Serpent(s). *See also* Ananta, Dragons, Kála, Nágas
  adored & cursed II 209-10
  Apap, Aker are II 213
  associated w darkness II 32n
  on Babylonian cylinders II 104
  Balaam learned fr II 409
  "Be ye wise as," *Matthew* I 74
  brazen I 253n, 364 &n, 414, 472-3; II 206n, 208, 364, 387, 473
  w camel's neck II 205
  Chenresi holds a II 178-9
  Christians borrowed I 410, 442n
  Christians made devil of I 442n
  Church made, into devil I 344; II 98
  coiled within Tiphereth II 214
  cosmic, born of Kaśyapa-Āditya II 382n
  cosmic, 370 leaps of II 505
  cosmological interpretation of II 386
  described II 132, 204-19, 377-90
  divine symbol not evil II 505
  dragons &, North & South poles II 274
  of Eden same as Lord God I 414
  egg &, univ symbol I 65, 364n; II 756
  emblem of logoi I 363
  of eternity, macrocosmic I 344, 411; II 98, 377-8

  of evil II 25-6, 213
  falling fr on high II 230
  fiery I 364, 442; II 206, 212
  first light fr the abyss I 407
  flying I 364; II 183, 206n
  Fohat as a hissing I 76
  of *Genesis* II 234-6, 243, 377-8, 388
  giants &, demons (Clement) II 280
  glyph of immortal being I 406
  Gnostic I 73, 410; II 386-7
  Gnostic Logos or I 364
  good & evil I 73-4, 404
  good & perfect, Messiah II 356
  hatched fr egg of incense I 363-4
  hawk-headed, explained II 357
  Hercules killed, at his birth I 403
  hierophant, initiate I 404; II 213
  Hindu, & Ophite cherubim I 127
  -holes, Adepts came fr II 748
  hypnotizes birds I 409
  the initiator II 355
  of Jesus II 364, 386
  kabbalists' spiritual sun II 214
  Kaśyapa father of II 253-4, 382n
  lion standing on, (Dendera) II 433
  magicians called dragons & II 280n
  of man, microcosmic, manas II 98
  mystery of II 504-5
  Náhásh symbolized as a II 246n
  North Pole in *Vendidad* II 356
  not evil or of the devil II 214
  Ophio-Christos or I 364
  Ophiomorphos, Jehovah II 243-4, 389
  Pulastya father of II 181
  redescended, taught 5th race II 355
  sarpa & nága, 2 kinds of II 181-2n
  as savior II 214-15
  scapegoat for Jehovah II 387
  sea-, may exist II 207
  seduces woman & man II 104, 364
  septenary meaning II 208
  Śesha thousand-headed II 49, 98
  seven-headed, & races I 407
  seven-headed, of space I 342
  seven voweled, of Gnos I 410-11; II 280n
  souls of ancestors are I 404
  swallowing tail I 253n, 291; II 504-5, 552
  symbol of, & Jod of Kabbala II 246n
  symbol of eternity, regeneration I 65, 73
  symbol of evil (Christian) II 208
  symbol of time (kála) I 404; II 756
  symb of wisdom I 65, 73, 363; II 26n, 364, 386
  tail of, & Ráhu II 381

two, nodes of Moon I 403
various symbols of I 65, 73 &n, 407-11; II 356
Vishnu &, -race I 420
Vishnu rests on I 379; II 98, 505
voice of reason in man II 98
winged, killed by Ibis I 362
woman & matter are II 202
worshipers or Naasenians II 355
Zeus a II 419-20
Serpent(s) of Wisdom. *See also* Adepts, Initi-
　ates, Nāgas
　Amshaspends, dhyāni-chohans or II 328
　connected w the Sun II 210n
　Dānavas, giants or II 381
　dragons or II 215
　Great Dragon (deluge) respects II 351, 355
　Kapila an initiate or II 572
　records of, preserved II 352
Serpents of Darkness
　reflection of univ Logos I 411
　seven heads of, 7 logoi I 411
Sertorius, Life of. See Plutarch
Śesha, Śesha-Ananta (Skt). *See also* Dragon,
　Serpent
　Ananta-, form of Vishnu II 505
　Ananta is II 49n, 98
　contains germs of universe I 73n
　infinite time I 73 &n, 371; II 49 &n
　Lord sleeps on, at pralaya I 371
　manvantaric cycle II 98
　seven pātālas, Nārada & II 49
　thousand-headed, & Vishnu I 407; II 381
　vehicle of Krishna I 73
Sesostris, greatest king of Egypt I xxixn
Sesquialtera (ratio 1½ to 1, or ³⁄₂) II 600
Sesquitertia (ratio 1⅓ to 1, or ⁴⁄₃) II 600
Set, Seth (Egy). *See also* Seth
　biblical patriarch (Bailly) I 648
　called 7th son II 213
　degradation of, (Bunsen) II 36n
　Edris &, taught astronomy II 366
　founder of Sabeanism (Soyuti) II 360-1
　god of time II 390n
　Hermes or II 380
　later became Typhon II 32n, 213, 366, 380,
　　385
　murders Osiris II 385
　mutilated by Horus II 283n
　once great god, later debased II 32n
　planetary god (Sabean) II 361-2
　Sat-an or II 530
　various names of II 530
Seth (Heb). *See also* Set
　Adam begat, in his likeness II 125

Adam's 3rd son or 3rd race II 469
borrowed & disfigured by Jews I 361
Cain, Chium, Saturn & II 390n
Enos &, new race fr II 127
-Enos, 4th race II 134
Enos son of, 1st sexual race II 715n
genealogies of Cain & II 391n
Hermes son of, (Sabeans) II 361
Jewish travesty of Hermes II 380
Ka-yin, Habel &, 3 races II 397
mankind hermaphrodite before II 125
Mercury or, pillars of II 530
Ra'h-mim- II 315
represents later 3rd race II 125-6
Sabean language established by II 366
semi-divine ancestor of Semites II 82n
serpent &, (Wake) II 26n
Set (Egy) & II 366, 380, 530
son of Adam exoterically II 127
son of Cain & Abel II 127, 134
two-sexed race II 125
Typhon & II 32n, 82n, 231, 366, 380
Seti I (Egy)
　renewed as Lunus when a babe I 228
Set-Typhon (Egy)
　Apophis or II 380, 385
　as 7th son II 213
Sevekt [Sevekh] (Egy), Kronos, 7 or I 408
Seven(s). *See also* Hebdomad, Septenary,
　Seventh
　adopted on this plane II 312n
　ages of man II 117, 312n
　in *Anugītā* II 637-8
　Apollo patron of II 772n
　astral phenomena & II 627
　became 8 (ogdoad) II 358n
　Bible, prominent in I 387; II 4
　in *Book of the Dead* (Egy) I 674
　born fr upper triangle II 574
　bright Sravah or Amshaspends II 516
　chemical elements governed by II 627-8
　in Christian dogmas I 310-11
　churches, Sodalian Mysteries II 633
　circles II 80
　classes of pitris II 77, 89, 91-2
　colors fr 1 ray II 492
　columns, *rectores* around tree II 293
　creations I 21, 217, 445-60; II 53n, 612, 624
　cross, circle & oldest symbols II 582
　crucifixion, esoteric meanings of II 560-1
　dialects of Mystery language I 310
　dvīpas & planetary chain II 320
　earths, heavens, seas I 447-8
　elements, cosmic I 137, 140, 347, 460

elements of man (Gnos) II 604-5, 632
every scripture has, aspects II 496
eyes of the Lord II 22, 626
feminine number of generation II 581-2
-fold division secret I xxxv
forces, powers, planets II 602 &n
forms, colors, sounds, taste & II 622
forty-nine &, fires II 363
forty-nine &, in Skt texts II 611
found in all religions II 34-7
four lower, 3 higher II 92, 581-2, 598
generative number w Hebrews I 114
Gnostic vowels of St John II 565
governors of dhyāni-chohans I 601
Greek, fr Hindus II 408
-headed serpent of space I 342
heart, skin plexuses & II 92
heavens, dhyānis of II 273
heavens, vowels (Gnos) II 563
Hebrew word for week II 624n
hosts build world II 489
initiators linked w II 529
keys I 310, 318, 325; II 291n, 335, 471, 538,
    632-3
keys to meaning of swastika II 99
keys to symbol language II 471, 538, 584, 765
kings, rishis I 376
Laycock on cycles of II 622-3 &n
letters of Jehovah's name I 335
Logos, -voweled sign I 79
magic number II 629-30
manifested universe II 626
master of the Moon II 601
modes of interpretation I 374
not confined to any nation II 603
number of divine mysteries I 36
number of present manvantara II 590
occult virtues of, (Hippocrates) II 312n
pass fr India to Christians II 612
Philo on I 407
planes, keys, sciences II 335
planetary spirits II 318n
point, triangle, quaternary became II 612
powers of, & cycles I 36
powers of nature, angels of II 273
powers of the Logos II 359
primeval gods II 514
principles, states of matter II 29, 92, 491,
    631-2
properties of nature (Boehme) II 595
in Purānas, *Esoteric Buddhism* I 348
Qabbalah (Myer) re various I 347-8
races, continents II 1-12, 77, 91
real scale of natures I 656n

regents of Pymander of elohīm II 488
root nature-number present cycle I 460;
    II 621
sacred in every nation I 114
sacred islands II 326
senses & 7 hotris (*Anugītā*) I 87, 96
sins, virtues, sacraments I 310-11
-skinned, space called I 9
son of 7th son II 213
sons of Priyavrata II 320
sound, color & II 627-9
spheres of action II 621n
Spirits of the Presence I 312
spring, summer & II 583
states of consciousness I 96
three, 4, 10 & II 564
triad emanates the I 427
truths, 4 only given in 4th round I 42
various, -fold symbols II 529-30, 612-18,
    637-41, 771-2n
virgin men (kumāra) II 281
vowels & 49 powers I 410-11; II 564
Seven Against Thebes. See Aeschylus
Seven Angels of the Face I 352n
Seven Angels of the Presence I 104, 312, 335;
    II 237
seven manus or II 573-4
Seven Capital Sins (Christian, Gnos)
    born fr astral soul I 195
    Christian scheme of, & Gnos II 641
Seven Circles of Fire
    higher angels break thru II 80, 275n
Seven Cities, Antilles, Heroes, Caves
    stand for zones, races II 35n
Seven Eternities
    length of I 144n
    periods of manvantara I 36, 53, 62
Sevenfold
    classification of kosmos II 29n, 92, 574
    division of anima mundi II 562
    occult forces I xxxv
Sevening I 408
Seven Precious Things (Japan) I 67n
Seven Primeval Gods
    builders, rulers of the world II 514
    kings, instructors of men II 514
Seven Principles. *See also* Principles
    diagrams of I 153, 157
    in nearly every school I 335
    Seven Rishis & II 139, 313, 715n
    teaching in all religions I 238-9, 241; II 491
    three-tongued flame & 4 wicks I 237 &n
    three upādhis & I 158
Seven Rays. *See* Rays

Seven Rishis. *See also* Saptarshis
　consorts of Krittikā (Pleiades) II 55!
　dhyāni-chohans (*Gītā*) II 318n
　of Great Bear II 318n, 488-9, 549, 550
　kali-yuga when, in Maghā II 550
　on line w Agni II 550
　mark time, events II 549
　mysterious constellation of II 549
　primal races & II 35, 97, 139, 365
　saved in ark II 139, 142, 290-1
　seven principles & II 313, 715n
　Vaivasvata Manu & II 146, 290-1, 313
Seven Rivers II 603, 605-6, 616
Seven Senses. *See* Senses
Seven Sons (Hermetic Logoi)
　creators of planetary chain I 60
　seven laya-centers & I 138
Seven Sons of Fohat
　preside over 7 cold, hot lokas I 204
Seven Sons of Light I 575
Seven Sons of Sophia
　Light of Logos or I 430 &n
"Seven Souls of Man . . ." *See* Massey, G.
Seventh. *See also* Seven(s)
　Creation I 217, 376, 445-6, 456; II 162-3,
　　233, 516
　day as 1st day of Creation II 488
　eternity, paradox of I 62-3
　fourth &, in series important I 586n
　sabbath or pralaya, nirvāna II 491
　son of 7th son II 213
　"thousand" various meanings of I 376
Seventy Planets, a blind I 576
Seven Vowels, & Gnostic Ophis I 73n
Sex(es), Sexed. *See also* Separation of Sexes
　ancient veneration for I 209-10, 358
　androgyne separated into II 147
　a bacterium can be both II 116
　Chaldean account of II 104
　evolved fr androgyne stock II 119, 132-5,
　　165-7
　first race without II 2
　Hebrew & Gnostic views of II 457-8
　involution of II 289n
　neutralized in animals II 412n
　passing phase I 415-16
　procreation by, not sudden II 182
　separated before mind awakened II 191, 198
　separated 18,618,727 yrs ago I 150n
　separated gradually II 84, 132, 192, 197, 201
　separation of, & man's curse II 516
　vast problem of, & procreation II 415
Sexless, or Asexual
　fr, to bisexual to sexual II 197

race becomes sexual II 2-3, 132, 165 &n
Sextile(s), quartiles &, in astronomy I 320
Sexual, Sexuality
　abyss betw Old & New Testament I 382n
　action & the spinal cord II 296
　Daksha started, intercourse II 182, 375, 658
　element in lotus symbol I 381-2
　exoteric religion, fr beginning II 657
　function as basis for symbol I 210, 381-3
　generation & occult knowledge I 228n
　intercourse betw man & animal II 192,
　　200-1, 688-9
　man &, procreation II 262, 458
　man 18 million years old II 157
　procreation disappears 6th root-race I 406
　relations & Moon phases I 228-9 &n
　separation 1st in animals II 184, 262, 736n
　in symbol spoils moral beauty I 381
　true, union (3rd race) II 167
Sexual Selection
　factor in variation II 738
　secondary cause only II 648-9
Seyffarth, Gustav
—— *Beiträge zur Kenntniss . . .*
　ancient zodiacal signs II 502n
　Cedrenus q on Mars II 143-4n
　Moon as cycle of time II 464
Seyn [Sein] & Daseyn [Dasein] (Ger)
　Fichte on I 281n
Shaddai. *See* Ēl Shaddai
Shadga [Shadja] (Skt) quality of sound
　I 534
Shadow(s). *See also* Astral Body, Chhāyās
　amānasa (mindless) called II 91
　annihilated after death I 227
　astral bodies or II 46, 86, 105
　astral, or early races II 105, 110, 138, 164
　bodhisattvas of dhyāni-buddhas I 572
　chhāyās or II 90, 101-2, 487, 503
　deity's, passive II 25
　devas cast no II 112
　each w own color II 97
　everything is, of eternal light II 268, 512
　form oozing fr medium II 86-7
　four Adams & II 503
　lords "threw off," for man II 86, 109, 112
　not evil but necessary I 413; II 214, 510
　of past & future events II 424
　of progenitors, 1st root-race II 138, 167
　real universe, on a screen I 278
　Satan or devil, of God I 413; II 510
　seven primeval men were, of 1st hebdomad
　　I 449
　of the Silent Watcher I 265

-son or body II 241
spirits of Earth clothe I 225; II 110
third race a bright II 268
Shaitan [Shaiṭān] (Arab)
  genii, djin or I 295
Shakespeare, William II 674
  Aeschylus & II 419
  Moon favorite theme of I 386
  some hold name *nom de plume* II 761
—— [*As You Like It*]
  seven ages of man II 117, 312n
—— [*Henry IV*]
  counterfeit of a man I 191
  thought father to the wish I 413
—— [*Henry V*]
  gently to hear, kindly to judge I xvii
—— [*Measure for Measure*]
  the ignorant are most assured II 655
—— [*Romeo and Juliet*]
  shrieking mandrakes II 27n
Shākya Thub-pa. *See* Buddha, Gautama
Shamael. *See* Samael
Shamballah. *See* Śambhala
Shamo (Gobi Desert) II 405. *See also* Desert,
  Gobi, Sacred Islands
  ancient India extended into II 327
  oasis in, Sacred Island relic II 502-3
  part of Arghya-Varsha II 416n
  sea in Lemurian times II 324
  "Sea of Knowledge" in II 502-3
Shānāh (Heb) lunar year
  connected w name Jehovah II 561
Shan-Hai-King (Chuang Tzu)
  Chuang q fr II 219
  information about II 302
  men w 1 head & 2 faces II 302
  monsters described II 54n
Shatana [Śaṭān] (Heb) adversary
  origin of name Satan II 387
Shaw, on pyramid sarcophagus I 317n
She. See Haggard, H. Rider
Sheaths (kośas, Skt)
  in man I 570-1n
  principles & I 157-8
Shebā (Shebū'āh] (Heb), oath in II 603
Sheba Hachaloth [Sheba' Ḥeikhālōth] (Heb)
  seven zones of our globe II 111
Shekīnāh, Shekhīnāh (Heb). *See also* Mūla-
  prakriti
  Adam Kadmon knows only I 432
  Ain-sōph emanates I 433n
  Ancient of Days, Ain-sōph & 109
  chaos, great deep or I 109; II 527
  Devamātri, Aditi & I 53 &n

divine voice, light II 107
divine wisdom or grace II 293
female Aranī, Aditi, or II 527
first Sephīrāh or I 355, 430
four forms of I 433n
Hokhmāh, Bīnāh & I 618
metatron &, become tree II 215-16n
mūlaprakriti or I 629
śakti (fem) or I 618
same as Sephīrāh I 53n
sexless in Chaldean Kabbala I 618
Tiphereth issues fr II 214
veil of Ain-sōph II 215n
way to Tree of Life II 216
Shell(s) (astral body)
  of early 3rd race II 165
  emanated by pitris II 303
  empty, devoid of manas II 80
  inhabit 7 zones of globe II 111
  kāma-loka abode of I 244
  kāma-rūpa II 111n
  man's body a II 255
  monads entered, of 1st race II 303
  our Moon as a II 115
  prenatal, of 3rd race II 197
  senseless, & pitris I 181
Shell(s) (Crustacea)
  gelatinous, of mid-Atlantis II 250
Shelley, Percy Bysshe
—— [*Adonais*]
  radiance of eternity I 238
—— [*Epipsychidion*]
  describes Moon I 386
Shelley, Mrs (Mary Wollstonecraft)
  Frankenstein of II 349
Shem (Heb) Noah's son
  Arkite Titan (Faber) or myth II 343n
  children of, & Kabiri II 393
  Sydyc &, (Cumberland) II 393
Shemal, Sabaean alter ego of Samael I 417
Shemesh (Heb) (of Moabites)
  same as Sun-Jehovah, Baal I 397n
Shemite(s). *See* Semite(s)
Shepherd(s)
  Mercury patron of II 541-2
  parable of the good, & *Enoch* II 482
Shepherd Kings. *See* Hyksos
Shetland, dolmens found in II 752
Shewbread, 12 cakes of I 649
Shibboleth in Masonry II 575
Shield, of Achilles & Gian-ben-Gian II 394
Shih Huang Ti, Emperor
  destroyed countless books II 692
Shiloh, dance of daughters of II 460

Shimon, Rabbi, *Nuctemeron* [*Nuchthēmeron*]
   according to the Hebrews
   man shaped in 2nd hour I 450
Shimon ben-Yohai
   angels in *Zohar* II 487
   Midrash before Kabbala of II 704
   mystery of serpent II 504
   teachings of, not in Rosenroth I 391
   Tetragrammaton II 626
Shinto (Japanese religion) I 241
   anthropo- before cosmogenesis I 213-19
Shistas. *See* Śishṭas
Shittim Wood
   horns of, & Jewish temples II 418n
Shiva. *See* Śiva
Shlomo del Medigo, Rabbi
—— *Novelōth Hokhmāh*
   Ain-sōph's delight in creating II 126
Shoo, Scheo [Shu] (Egy)
   appears as great cat II 545
   dragon of darkness I 364
   god of creation I 75n
   Haroiri contemporary w I 366n
   personification of Rā II 545
   solar force I 312, 360, 364
   Tefnut, Keb, devachan & II 374n
Shuckford, Dr, on Kabiri II 264
Shu-king [*Ching*], *Book of* I 366n
   compiled fr "very old book" I xliii
   Earth cut off fr heaven II 280-1
   Miaotse (giants) in II 337
   religion of Confucius founded on I xxvn
Siam (Thailand) II 327
   Buddhism declined in I xxi
Siamek (Pers), son of Kaimurath-Adam
   murdered by giant brother II 396
Siamese
   distort their ears II 339
   egg symbol among I 366
   lunar tables predate European I 666-7
Sib. *See* Keb
Sibac (Quiché) reed or egg II 181n
Siberia
   East & West, & 2nd continent II 402
   East, West, & Atlantis II 402
   giants' tombs in II 752
   stones in, fr vast distance II 343
   Śveta-dvīpa & II 327
Sibyl (Gk)
   fire that gives eloquence to I 339
Sibylline Books
   death penalty for revealing II 396
   inspired Virgil I 658
Sibylline Oracles II 454

Sicanus, deified Aretia (Lat q) II 144
Sicily
   fire (Kabiri) worship in II 363
   joined to Africa once II 751
Siddha(s) (Skt) perfected
   astronomical meaning of II 401n
   great, of 4th race II 636
   of janarloka I 372
   nirmānakāyas or II 636n
   sleeping Brahmā glorified by I 372
   Vidyādharas & I 539n
   yogis in heaven, sages on Earth II 549
Siddhānta-Śiromaṇi (Skt astron work)
   Golādhyāya of II 321
Siddhapura (Skt), "White Island" II 408n
Siddha-Sena (Skt)
   leader of siddhas II 382 &n, 549
Siddhis (Skt) powers
   arhats & laws governing I 97n
Sidereal
   birth of, bodies I 147, 158-9, 203-5, 590, 602
   bodies, animals of *Genesis* II 112n
   bodies fr cosmic substance I 569
   bodies, septenary constitution of I 168
   flood, & cosmic II 146
   geological &, phenomena II 314
   jelly speck II 160
   kalpa II 307n
   motions regulate events on Earth I 645
   phenomena model for Earth II 502
   science & proof of giants II 278
   sun king of, orbs II 123
   world, powers of I 124
Sidereal Light of Paracelsus I 255
Sidereal Virgin
   astral light w alchemists II 511
Sidereal Year (precessional cycle)
   Berosus, cataclysms & I 649-50
   circle of, called serpent II 356
   cyclic year or precession I 439n
   Earth's climates alter during II 770
   ends in 16,000 years II 331
   Great Pyramid & I 314-15; II 432-3, 435
   human history & II 330-1
   initiations & I 314
   length of I 314, 439n; II 330, 770
   Plutarch on I 650
   zodiac & II 332, 357
Siderites, star stones II 341
Si-Dzang [Hsi-Tsang or Tibet] (Chin)
   mentioned in MSS at Fo-Kien I 271n
Siemens, Dr Charles William
—— "On the Conservation of Solar . . ."
   gas absorption & Sun's heat I 102n

Sien-Tchan(g). *See* Hsien-Chan
Sigalions (images of Harpocrates)
  fingers to lips (secrecy) II 396
Sigē (Gk) Silence
  angle of Gnostic square II 573
  unknown universal soul II 574
Sigeus (Sigeum, now Yeniṣehir)
  giant skeleton at II 278
Sighru [Śīghra] (Skt)
  Moru [Maru] son of I 378 &n
Sight
  double set of I 533-4
  inner II 294n
  man's spiritual, blinded II 74
  procreation by, will & yoga II 176
  related to fire II 107
  third eye & II 298-9
  in third race II 299
  unlimited in some of 4th race II 221
Sigillae, magical symbol of I 306
Sign(s). *See also* Ideographs, Symbols, Zodiac
  (signs of)
  divine instructors taught in II 391, 439
  esoteric cosmogony described in I 272
  occult virtue of thing & its I 93-4
Signatura rerum. See Boehme, J.
Signs of Zodiac. *See* Zodiac, Signs of
Signum Thau (Lat) mark of Tau
  Ezekiel stamped foreheads w II 557
Sigurd, ate dragon's heart I 404
Silence
  Gnostics on II 569n, 573-4
  neither sound nor I 54
  reasons for II 451
  of sages re higher themes II 589
  on secret invisible things I 95
  worship in I 280
Silent Watcher I 207-8. *See also* Watchers
  & his shadow I 264-5
Silenus, Midas &, on Atlantis II 760
Silik-Muludag, Akkadian highest God II 477
Silliman's Journal. See Amer. Journal of Sci.,
  Hunt (E.B.)
Siloam, sleep of II 558
Silo River, flows fr Lake of Dragons II 204
Silurian Age II 71-2 &n
  astral fossils physicalized w II 712
  chronological placement of II 710-11
  corals like today's millepores II 257
  living matter of, less gross II 256
  man in, unknown by geology II 71n
  oceans of II 160
  pre-, & natural selection II 259-60
  races 1 & 2 & II 150

seas of II 685
Silver Age. *See also* Tretā-Yuga
  every race & subrace has its II 198
  Golden &, 1st & 2nd races II 270-1
  of third race II 520n
Silvestre de Sacy, A. I.
  astronomy of *Book of Enoch* II 533
Simeon (Son of Jacob) II 211
  Levi &, or Gemini I 651
Simeon, Rabbi, expl "Fiat Lux" I 215-16n, 356n
Simeon, Rabbi. *See* Shimon, Rabbi
Simeon ben Iochai. *See* Shimon ben-Yohai
Siṃha (Skt) lion
  man-lion, Garuda or II 564-5
  Persian Simorgh & II 618
  Sinhalese descended fr II 407-8
  tail of, & inverted poles II 432-3
Simian(s). *See also* Apes, Monkeys
  characteristics in man II 315n
Simon de Sienne (Simone Martini)
  painted Petrarch's dragon II 207n
Simon Magus
  six radicals of, & aeons II 569n
Simoom (hot desert wind)
  Samael, Vritra, devil & II 385
Simorgh, Simurgh (Pers)
  numerical mysteries of II 564
  symbol of 7 Earths, races II 617-18
  various names of II 617-18
Simorgh-Anke (Persian Phoenix)
  cycles, symbol of II 397, 617
  manvantaric cycle II 399
  polyglot steed of Tahmurath II 397-9
Simplicius, *Scholia in Aristotlelem*
  antiquity of Egyptian astronomy I 650
Simpson, Sir J.
  copied symbol of 4 quarters II 546
  cup-like markings on stones II 346n
Sin (Bab) I 238
  Chaldean Moon I 248n, 263, 264
  Chaldean worship of I 388
  fish, & Soma (Moon) I 238, 263-4
  linked w Anu, Jehovah II 62
  lunar god (Chaldean) II 23, 139n
  male Moon I 395
  occult relation to Moon I 248, 396
  Sinai, mt of Moon or II 76-7
  Soma &, parents of Earth II 23
  son of Mulil II 139n
Sin(s). *See also* Original Sin
  Atlantis called land of II 322
  black w II 227n, 319, 408 &n
  comes in w manas (Gullveig) II 520
  creative powers not gift of II 410

eating the fruit a II 215
fall of spirit into matter I 264
of 1st parent & the ant I 133
of ignorance & Satan I 198
of the mindless II 180, 185, 191-2, 683, 688-9
physical body does not II 302
redemption of, (Prometheus) II 420-1
Scorpio emblem of, & matter II 129
seven capital I 195, 310-11; II 641
Sinai. *See* Mt Sinai
Sinaitic Peninsula
   influence of Eridu II 226
Sind, Scinde
   East Ethiopians, Nile River & II 417
   Jews sought refuge in II 200
Sindhu (Hindu) Muslin
   known in Chaldea II 226
Sinful Intentions
   only sacrificial victims I 280
Singh, Singha. *See* Siṃha
Singhalese, Singalese. *See* Sinhalese
Singing Stones II 341-2
Sinhalese
   heirs to giants of Laṅkā II 407-8
   regard Veddhas as animals II 286-7
Sinless, of Śāka-dvīpa were early Atlanteans
   II 323
Sinnett, Alfred Percy. *See also* Mahatma Letters
   HPB had copies of letters to I 163n
   HPB's estimate of I 160-1
   Masters not always allowed to answer I 168
—— *Esoteric Buddhism* I 122, 155, 168, 185,
      306; II 8, 325, 598, 672, 756
   Alps, elevation of II 751n
   Aryan race II 714
   astral prototypes II 186 &n
   Atlantis I 439 &n; II 156 &n, 433n, 717
   Australians Lemurian remnant II 328, 779
   Budhism, not Buddhism I xvii-xviii, 539n
   Chinese civilization II 280n
   cosmology not systematic I 168
   critic of, & *Isis Unveiled* II 496
   Day of Judgment II 617
   dhyāni-buddhas I 108 &n
   Egyptians Atlanto-Aryans II 750
   on eighth sphere I 156
   fifth principle not developed II 318n
   figures remain secret II 251
   first attempt I 231-2
   Greeks, Romans, Atlanto-Aryans II 436
   Haggard seems to summarize II 317n
   "invented" by HPB I xlv
   Lemuria II 313 &n

Lemuria not Atlantis II 334, 779
Lemurian relics II 196n
life-impulses & globes I 176, 177
life-waves on globe A, 1st round I 175-6
majority of men 7th subrace II 178
man & animal separate kingdoms I 186
man not fr ape I 186-7, 191
re Mars-Mercury I 163-70
Massey's criticism re 7 races II 634-5
mistakes in I 151 &n, 152, 153, 163-70,
   189-90; II 640
monads on the globes I 170
neither esoteric nor Buddhism I xvii
no European knew secret science I xviii
Nordenskiöld's fossil finds II 773n
perplexity re monads I 169
Poseidonis II 265
reluctance re cosmogony I 170
revealed merely esoteric lining I 165
Rhys Davids criticizes I 539n
root-races II 434
rounds defined, explained I 231-2
seven principles II 633
sevens I 348
sinking of Atlantis I 439 &n; II 778
sinking, rising continents II 332-3, 433n
śishtas II 308n
third race drowned II 426
third root-race II 156 &n
traditional methods of teaching I 162, 164
—— *The Occult World*
communication in color, sound I 514n
giant human & animal bones II 293n
on thought & matter I 124
Sin of the Mindless (in 3rd root-race)
   defined II 184-5, 191-2
   involved 1 race II 191
   produced semihuman monster II 683
   sexes separated before II 191
Siphrā' di-Tsenī'ūthā' (Dzeniouta in tx)
      (Heb) "Book of Concealed Mystery"
   Adam Kadmon & II 4
   Alhim created 6 sephīrōth I 342
   biblical *Genesis* & II 624
   Book of Numbers key to II 626n
   compiled fr "very old book" I xliii
   destruction, evolution, serpent II 504
   disfigured II 624
   elohīm formed worlds 6 by six I 239
   first race imperfect, destroyed II 2
   kings of ancient days dead I 676; II 705
   Kings of Edom I 375-6
   Microprosopus I 214-15
   Myer quotes fr I 374-5

number 7, Sephīrōthal Tree II 4
oldest Hebrew document I xlii
on opening lines of *Genesis* I 374-5
serpent of 370 leaps I 339; II 505
sparks fr flint are worlds II 83, 99
spirit breathes over chaos II 505
tree w birds, nests II 292
two creations II 54
Sippara
    Akkad near, on Euphrates River I 319n
    Zipporah or, Moses' wife I 319n, 385n
Sippor, Sipur [Sippūr] (Heb) II 41
    one of 3 seraphim [sephārīm] I 92
Sire, Pers anthropomorphic god II 602
Sirius (Dog Star)
    dwarfs our Sun II 708
    Mercury, Budha, instructor II 374
Śishṭa(s) (Skt) remains
    divine, is Seed-Manu II 164
    in *Esoteric Buddhism* II 308n
    incarnate in man I 248
    "King," in Purānas II 307n
    Noah was a human II 596
    prajāpati &, seed Earth w life II 150
    preserved in the ark II 307n
    a sacred land II 6
    seed humanity I 182
    Sons of Light, 7th race adepts or II 531
    "surviving fittest" II 308
Sister(s)
    every world has its, planet II 33
    seven, or Pleiades II 619
    six, of Bhūmi (our Earth) I 250
Sistrum(a) (musical instrument)
    Isis holds, w cat on top I 387
    used in religious dancing II 461
Śiśumāra (Skt) porpoise [constellation]. *See also* Kūrma, Tortoise
    avatāra of Vishnu, II 549
    potent stars in tail of, (Ursa Minor) II 612n
Śiśupāla (Skt), Rāvana reborn as II 225n
Sītā (Skt) (Rāma's wife)
    Rāvana carries off II 570
Śiva (Skt). *See also* Logos, Rudra, Śankara, Trimūrti
    Angiras guru of Śankara II 498
    Baal, Bel, Saturn & I 459
    Brahmā, Vishnu & I 437n; II 115
    bull of, or man I 390 &n
    burned Brahmā's fifth head II 578n
    destroying, regenerating deity I 358, 459n, 538; II 182, 249, 313, 548
    Devi-Durgā & I 91
    fire principle of II 591

Gaurī (Śrī) bride of II 76n
god of war born of sweat of II 43n, 124n
hurled asuras to Earth II 246
hurled Brahmā into abyss II 515
hurled Mahāsura down to Pātāla II 237n
Ilā & II 147-8
Īśvara or II 114
kumāras progeny of I 458-9
Mahat & 75
maruts children of II 613
Meru personated I 341
patron of yogis, adepts II 282
Ptah & I 367n
reborn each kalpa (race) II 282
Rudra becomes II 282, 548-9
-Rudra creates Vīrabhadra II 182-3
Rudra or I 370; II 502n, 576, 613
Śankara or I 286; II 498
savior of spiritual man I 459n
seed of, generated Mars II 619
Śukra & II 32
supports Brihaspati in war II 498
as Śvetalohita II 249
unknown name in Vedas II 548, 613
as Vāmadeva II 249
-worship, lingam & yoni of II 588
Śiva-Eye, Eye of Śiva. *See also* Third Eye
    atrophy of, explained II 302
    on brow of Chenresi II 179
    burned Brahmā's fifth head II 578n
    opened eye or I 46 &n
    seers w, perceive Purānic history II 284
    tri-bochana [trilochana] or II 295
Śiva-Gharmaja[la] (Skt) perspiration
    Kārttikeya, Earth & II 43n, 124-5n
Śiva-Kumāra (Skt)
    represents human races I 324
Śiva-Rudra (Skt) I 370
    creates Vīrabhadra II 182
    forefather of adepts II 502n
    maruts sons of II 615
    regenerator I 459n
Sivatherium (of Himalayas) II 218-19
Siwalik (mt range, India & Nepal)
    pass of Hardwar near II 571
Six (senary) II 580, 582
    derived fr a seventh II 628
    directions of space I 118
    emblem of physical nature II 591
    naros cycle & II 619
    no stability in, alone II 628
    principles in man II 616
    sacred to Venus II 592
    666 & Beast I 655n; II 619

symbolizes animating principle II 583
symbolizes Earth II 581
symbolizes swastika II 587
world created according to I 407
Six-pointed Star. *See also* Double Triangle
dual nature of man, symbol of II 533
first emanated Logos I 215
Fohat center of I 216
six powers, planes, etc I 215
snow crystals & II 594
Six Schools of Indian Philosophy
all teach 6 principles fr 7th I 278
occult doctrine & I 269
Sixth Round. *See* Round, Sixth
Sixth Rounder, Buddha a I 161-2
Skanda (Skt) (or Kārttikeya)
described II 382
refused to create I 457-8n
Skanda-Purāṇa
no longer procurable I 367n
Skeletons (human)
American, 9-12 ft fr 5th race II 293
Atlantean, may be discovered II 674
in Cro-Magnon cave II 678
57,000 years old (Dowler) II 352
giant, at Carthage II 278
giant, found by ancients II 753
of Haute Garonne ancient II 739
man's, unchanged II 720, 725, 734
no, before Quaternary II 723
older, larger II 278
pagans spoke of giants' II 336
Paleolithic, superior to present II 257-8
why no giant, in dolmens II 753-4
Skepticism I 479-80, 676; II 74, 443
Skin
Earth's, cast off each round II 47
seven layers of II 92
Skinner, James Ralston
acute scholar, mystic II 388
discovered 2 of the keys I 315
esoteric measurements of II 465
great services of I 308
—— "The Cabbalah"
Ain-sōph & great circle I 429
Alhim & sephīrōth II 39-40
Alhim, Jehovah, light I 91; II 37-8
Cassell & kabbalistic trinity II 38
our perceptions of light II 41
sephīrōth, dbrim [debārīm], etc II 37
seventh day, conjunctions, etc II 76-7
—— "Hebrew Metrology"
elohīm, dhyāni-chohans same number

I 90 &n
—— *Key to the Hebrew-Egyptian Mystery in the Source of Measures*
ansated cross, etc II 36
Ararat & Arath II 597n
candlestick & cross II 581n
confirms *Isis Unveiled* I 318n
creation basis of Jewish religion II 543
on crucifixion II 36, 542, 558-61, 600
cube unfolded, man I 321
Easter Island, Aztecs, etc I 322
Hermes as a cube II 542
Hindu knowledge concealed II 499n
"I have gotten a man" (*Gen* 4:1) II 127
immaculate conception I 59-60
Jehovah derivation II 125
Jehovah male, female II 125, 467
Jehovah's measure II 38
Jod (Yod) & Havah-Eve II 467
King's Chamber, Holy of Holies I 264
language based in number II 560
Mars & conception II 43-4n
Mars, Melchizedek II 392-3
men call themselves Jehovah II 388n
Moses, Jehovah, "I am" II 468
nails of cross II 561
numerical analysis of "raven" I 443-4
origin of measures I 313
pagan basis of Jewish religion II 465
Parker ratio I 313
Parker's key to Kabbala II 544
π (Pi) & alhim same numbers I 90-1
sacr, sacrament, sacrifice I 5n; II 467n
tau cross II 543
Tree of Knowledge & cross II 215-16
Tree of Life & ansated cross II 216-17
Vulcain II 392-3n
—— MSS (unpublished)
ancient symbolic language I 308-9
androgynous goddess I 392
bull, cow, Moon etc I 390
cube unfolded I 321
Holy of Holies I 383, 391
IOH, Moon, Jehovah II 464
Jewish & Aryan esotericism I 115n
lotus as symbol of generation I 381-2
Moses & Lord's Glory (*Exodus*) II 539
Nile River, Isis, etc II 583
Old Testament number values I 444
Parker ratio I 313-14
secret of ancient symbol I 389
solar year & Moon cycles I 392
symbology of the womb I 382

Skrymir (Norse) giant. *See also* Ymir
  sons of gods fought against II 754
Skull(s). *See also* Neanderthal Man
  comparison of II 523, 677-8, 687, 792
  enormous, found on Thera II 278-9
  judging intellect by, capacity II 168n, 193,
    522-3, 686n, 721
  old, of Europe like Caribs II 738-9, 790
  old, of Negro type II 278
  old, of very tall men II 278
  prehistoric & modern, compared II 522-3
  variety of European, (Littré) II 738-9
Sky, Egyptians divided, into 7 parts II 631
Slack, Henry James
—— "Recent Researches in Minute Life"
  metaphysics & science I 588, 600
Slaughter, Reverend Wm. B.
—— *The Modern Genesis*
  rationale of nebular rotation I 97n
Slavonia(ic, ian)
  chiton (coat) became, word II 202
  deluge in, mythology II 270
  God of, fr Gk Bacchus I 347
  legends of giants in II 754-5
  Leibniz of, descent I 628n
  red Easter egg of I 368
  Russian &, "R" is Latin "P" II 547n
Sleep(ing)
  Atlanteans did not dream in II 761
  dreamless I 47, 266
  dreamless, of 1st 2 races (Adam) II 181
  ideation ceases in deep I 38
  laya or, center I 147
  matter during universal I 69
  mental, of early man II 194
  profound, too deep for dreams II 701
  sushumna ray during I 537
Sleep of Siloam
  initiated adept plunged into II 558
Sloth II 733
Smaragdine Tablet (of Hermes)
  as above, so below . . . II 113
  disfigured by Christian hands II 113
  Isarim, an initiate, said to have found II 556
  seven keys to meaning of II 109
  swastica in II 99
Smārta, Smārtava Brahmans
  founded by Śaṅkarāchārya I 271
  head of, sometimes a real initiate I 272
Smell I 251
  Anugītā on I 535 &nn
  Earth rudiment of I 372
  evolution of II 106-8
Smith, George, *Assyrian Discoveries*

evil gods II 61-2
evil principles emblems of chaos II 386
Hea-bani raised to heaven II 531
King Sargon's date II 691
story of Moses fr Babylonia I 319n
War in Heaven II 386
—— *Chaldean Account of Genesis*
Adam (mankind) II 4
Chaldean gods, genii II 248n, 383-4
corroborates teachings II 5
cosmogenesis described in I 357
creations, 2 or more II 53, 54
Curse & the Fall II 282
dragon of Chaldea II 354
evil gods II 61
monsters II 52
proves forgeries of Eusebius I xxvin
Sargon's story I 319n
seven races (kings) II 2
Sun & Moon II 145
tablets written before Moses II 3n
war between gods, dragons II 383-4
War in Heaven & Fall II 104
Zu & Umsimi II 283-4n
—— *Transactions of Society of Biblical . . .*
Sargon-Moses story I 319n
Smithsonian Contributions to Knowledge
Alexander on nebular theory I 588
Stockwell on glaciations II 141, 144
Smithsonian Reports
Retzius on Guanches, Caribs II 792
Smoke
  baptism by, Holy Ghost II 566-9
  clouds of, are Montanist heresies II 485
  stood for exoteric religion II 566-7
Smyth, Charles Piazzi
  Astronomer Royal of Scotland I 317n
  Hebrew language divine I 316-17
  height of Grand Gallery II 466
  King's Chamber & sarcophagus I 317n
  Mosaic origin of measures I 313
  pyramid figures I 314, 315
  Solomon's temple I 115n
Snails II 659
  intermediate hermaphroditism & II 167
  Sons of Light or Heavenly I 103
Snake(s). *See also* Dragons, Nāgas, Serpents
  blind, atrophied eyes II 296n
  cosmic, -gods born of Kaśyapa II 382n
  great, of the Pueblos II 181n
  hole or initiation passages II 379-80
  initiate called I 408
  king-, or nāgas II 381
  Kneph, emblem I 353

Nagpur city of II 346n
Ophites revered a living II 386
tortuous, of the Jews II 230
Sochoniston. *See* Sanchoniathon
Society of Antiquaries [*Archaeologia*] II 380
Socrates
  believed in higher beings I 611
  daimon of II 419
  would not argue about Being I 4
Socrates [Scholasticus]
  calls Eusebius forger I xxvi
Sod, Sodalian (Heb)
  arcanum, mystery(ies) I 463; II 212n, 626
  calculations of II 395
  Mysteries of Baal, Adonis, Bacchus II 212
  mysteries of the 7 stars II 633
Sodales
  members of priest colleges II 212n
  Moses chief of II 212
  of right-, left-hand paths II 211
Sōd-Ihoh, Mysteries of Ihoh II 212n
Sōd, the Mysteries of Adonis. See Dunlap, S. F.
Sōd, The Son of the Man. See Dunlap, S. F.
Sogdiana (Sagdiani in text)
  Aryan Magi emigrate into II 356
Soham (Skt), "he (is) I" I 78; II 465. *See also*
    A-hamsa, Haṃsa-vāhana, Kalahaṅsa
Soirées de St. Petersbourg. See Maistre, J. de
Sokhit. *See* Seket
Sol (Lat) II 575. *See also* Sun
Sol alter
  Śukra-Venus called II 31
Solar. *See also* Solar System, Sun
  body & 7 rays I 525n
  dynasty, Moru [Maru] will restore I 378
  extinctions of, fires I 84, 552
  fire & the gandharvas I 523 &n
  life part of universal life I 591
  lunar &, beliefs of Christians I 388, 395
  lunar &, cycles II 620-1
  lunar &, deities I 362, 397; II 427
  lunar &, influences & "Wind" II 105
  mythos I 303-4
  vortex of Kepler I 623
  year interpreted by St Germain II 583
Solar Boat
  Osiris & 7 rays enter II 141
  soul coeval & disappears w I 227
  Thoth, solar discus & II 529
Solar Devas. *See also* Pitṛis (Solar)
  brought mind to humans I 181
Solar Lhas (spirits) II 105, 109-10. *See also* Lhas

Solar System(s) II 148. *See also* Manvantara,
    Pralaya
  anima mundi of II 672n
  becomes ocean at pralaya I 371
  birth of I 110-11, 289
  central & other suns in I 13; II 240
  cosmic evolution refers to II 68 &n
  cosmic monads progenitors of II 311
  critique of evolution of I 501-2
  dhyān-chohans limited to I 13; II 700-1 &n
  elements differ in planets of I 142-3
  enormous age of, (Laing) II 72
  fabricated by Kosmocratores II 23
  failures born into new II 232-3n
  fire septenary in I 87
  formation out of nebular rings I 149-50n
  heart, brain, circulations of I 541
  Humboldt on other, like ours I 497n
  intelligences regulate laws of I 530-1
  invisible worlds of I 605-6
  is a monad I 21
  knowledge of previous I 369
  kosmos may refer to our I 199n
  lifetime of II 68 &n
  many planets in I 654n
  matter different outside I 601
  nebular theory of I 595-9
  other intellectual beings in I 133, 164
  pralaya of I 53
  rotations, revolutions in I 501
  science secure only within I 601
  Secret Doctrine deals mostly w our I 60
  seven conditions of matter in I 139; II 597n
  Sinnett's mistakes re I 163-5
  starts as nebula I 22
  sūkshma form of I 138
  Sun-fluids impart motion to I 529
  Sun heart of I 540-2
  vital principle of I 530-1; II 311n
  young, old, dead planets in II 251
Soleil, Le. See Secchi, Father P. A.
Solids, liquids, gases & I 526; II 136-7n
"Solids, Liquids, and Gases." *See* Williams,
    M. M.
Soliman's Ring. *See also* Suliman
  brings one to fountain of life II 398
Solinus, Gaius Julius ("Polyhistor")
—— [*Collectanea rerum memorabilium*]
  Hyperboreans sow, reap in one day II 773
Solomon, King. *See also* Temple of Solomon
  biblical, fr Persia II 396n
  on circuits of the spirit II 553
  did not recognize Moses or Law II 541
  left pillar in temple of II 461

never really existed II 314
Seal of I 118; II 591
seventy-two of, (Herbelot) II 396
Solon
  Atlantis story & II 221, 371, 395, 436, 743
    &n, 781, 786
  Egyptian dynasties related to I 266
  giant intellect II 217
  knew power of names II 767
  one of Grecian 7 sages II 743n
Solstice(s) I 363, 639; II 533, 546, 576. *See also*
    Equinox
  Northern & Southern in *Gītā* passage I 86
  symbols of living verity I 639
Solus (Lat). *See also* Sun
  later became Sol, the Sun II 575
Solvent
  hydrogen & occult II 112-13
  motion, the alchemical I 258
  universal I 260
Soma (Skt) Moon. *See also* Deus Lunus, Moon,
    Soma Juice
  born fr churning of the Ocean I 398
  Brihaspati, Tāra, Budha & I 228n; II 45 &n,
    138, 456, 498-500
  as Earth's calf or Moon I 398
  embodies Trimūrti power I 398
  fish, sin, & I 238
  fourth race & globe under II 29, 44-5
  fruit of Tree of Knowledge II 499n
  gandharva force of I 523n
  generative, creative god II 466
  illegitimate father of Budha I 288n
  Indra & his, drinking II 378
  King, masculine Moon I 386, 395
  lunar god I 392, 396-8; II 23, 29, 139n, 386,
    495
  makes alliance in solar portion II 496
  moon-plant I 210, 523n; II 45n, 101n, 378,
    384n, 498-9, 590
  occult potency of Moon I 396
  our globe under II 29
  parent of esoteric wisdom II 500
  rays of, mature Mārishā II 175
  regent of visible Moon I 45
  second race & II 175-6
  sidereal Don Juan I 228n
  Sin &, parents of Earth II 23
  sons of, not immortal II 44
  War in Heaven story & II 45
Soma Juice
  Akta anointed w II 101n
  fr *Asclepias acida* II 498-9
  experiences of drinker of II 499n

of Moon-plant I 210
real, & the reborn initiate II 499
Rig-Veda, Purānas on II 378
sacred II 45n
Soma-Loka (Skt) region of the Moon II 44
Somapa Pitris (Skt)
  worshiped by Trisuparna Brahmans II 590
"Some few whose lamps . . ." *See* Dryden, J.
"Some Things the Aryans Knew." *See*
    Brahmachāri Bawa
Somniis, De. See Philo Judaeus
Son
  above is kosmos, below is mankind I 60
  becomes own father & mother I 398
  Father &, equivalents of II 492
  Father &, meaning of II 231n
  fatherless, & immaculate Mother I 256
  Father, Mother, & I 40
  Heavenly Man is Logos or II 236n
  kosmos is, w Plato I 348
  Logos or, various names of II 703-4n
  of Mahat II 103
  mother's husband I 614
  one w the Father II 113
  only begotten, is Brahmā I 349
  right side of triangle I 614
  seventh, of a seventh II 213
  by whom God made worlds II 703
Sonata of Beethoven
  cannot play itself II 348
Son of Kriyāśakti. *See also* Sons of Will & Yoga
  Mundane Tree compared w I 211
Son of Righteousness I 656
Son of the Morning. *See* Lucifer
Son(s) of the Serpent, Dragon
  hierophants of Egy & Bab II 378-80, 530
  sheds old skin, has new body II 380
Son(s) of Wisdom II 52
  Atlantean survivors led by II 428
  became Sons of Darkness II 272
  becoming a, described II 380
  Chinese teachers, adepts I 271n
  deferred incarnation II 161, 228, 286
  dragon mystic name for II 280n
  entered those who were ready II 167, 185,
    286
  failed karmic duty II 185
  first mind-born sons II 204
  give rise to adepts II 167
  incarnated in Aryan ancestors II 318
  incarnated in early buddhas II 423
  incarnated in Sons of Will II 199
  legendary names for II 269-70
  mānasa or II 171

produced Sons of Ad I 207
seed of iniquity carried by some II 228
serpent of *Genesis* & II 236
sin of mindless & II 185, 191, 228
some, refuse to create II 191
Sons of Night II 161
warned re forbidden fruit II 267
will enlighten humanity II 167-8
Son of Yered (Jared) or Enoch II 532
Sons of Ad. *See also* Sons of the Fire Mist
produced by kriyāśakti I 207
Sons of Atri, barhishads reborn as II 89
Sons of Brahmā I 88-9, 116, 236, 413, 436,
457n, 521, 571; II 44, 78, 82, 89, 91-3, 121,
132, 161, 173, 176 &n, 249, 253, 284, 374,
382n, 548, 613n, 624-5 &n, 775n. *See also*
Asuras, Dhyānis
kumāras or, refused to create I 236
were sons of Vasishtha II 146n
Sons of Cycles, Cyclopes I 208n
Sons of Darkness
asuras called II 487-8
human failures became II 272
Sons of Dark Wisdom
archangels or II 248
Atlantean adept sorcerers II 495
"fallen," pure, divine II 248
Sons of God. *See also* Asuras, Bnēi Elohīm,
Elohīm
Aryan adepts II 495
assist Christian creator I 440
Bamian statues depict II 224
became fallen angels I 412
brahmaputras or I 209
could live in water, fire, air II 220
destroyed sorcerers II 772
as dragons, serpents II 274
fallen angels in *Genesis* II 61, 229, 284
founded civilizations I 208 &n
four, of Egyptians II 213
hierophants of King's Chamber II 470
history begins w, marrying II 284
immaculate virgin legends fr I 61
initiated Brahmans descend fr I 209
instructed hierophants II 221
lower, had sexual connection II 375
not punished in *Genesis* II 491
prototype of Enoch's angels I 523n
of Sacred Island II 221, 495
Satan as one of II 378, 489
seventh race will be II 483
Sons of Light are II 489
taught arts, sciences I 208 &n; II 572
Titans progeny of II 501

various, described II 374-6
Vedas on II 605
War of, & Sons of Darkness II 495, 500
Wondrous Being guided I 208
Sons of Jacob
allegory of black & white II 211-12
story of, & 5th race II 428-9
Sons of Joseph, Afghan tribe called II 200n
Sons of Kriśāśva
gods of legendary weapons II 629
Sons of Kriyāśakti I 211
Sons of Light. *See also* Ahriman, Asuras,
Elohīm
are Sons of Darkness II 489
battled Sons of Night II 772
described I 481
formless fathers of dhyānis I 572
root of spiritual man I 106
self-generated in infinite ocean I 481
seven, & sacred planets I 575
seven, born fr conscious life I 572
śishtas of 7th root-race II 531
those who conquered joined II 272
Sons of Manasseh, Afghan tribe II 200n
Sons of Marīchi
agnishvāttas reborn as II 89
Sons of Necessity, universes I 43
Sons of Night II 161, 772
Sons of Passive Yoga
Daksha's will-born progeny II 275
early 3rd root-race I 207; II 165, 275
Sons of Rebellion (Egypt)
dragons, serpents were II 386
Sons of the Dragon
hierophants II 379, 380, 530
Sons of the Fire, Fire-Mist I 86-7
Chinese teachers, adepts II 271n
did not fall into sin II 319
first to evolve fr fire I 87
not fiery serpents II 212
Sons of Ad or I 207
Sons of the Flame of Wisdom
saviors, agnishvāttas II 411
Sons of the Shadow. *See also* Black Magic
war w Sons of God II 500
"Sons of the Sorceress" (*Isaiah*)
phallic practices of II 588
Sons of the Sun, war w Sons of Night II 772
Sons of Twilight
pitris II 91, 120-1, 138, 163
Sons of Will & Yoga II 163, 771
adepts &, 7th race II 275
ancestors of arhats, mahātmas II 173
body gnawed at by time I 211

born before separation of sexes II 181
created by kriyāśakti II 172, 181, 228
did not fall into sin II 319
divided into sexes I 209
early 3rd root-race II 181
first to have mind II 199
four sacrificed themselves II 281-2 &n
pitar were called II 394n
remained apart fr mankind I 207
remnants of, & inland sea II 220
roots of, & Mundane Tree I 211
seed of future saviors II 173
Sons of Wisdom incarnated in II 199
third race created II 173
warred w Atlanteans II 227n
Sons of Yoga II 109
first race called II 198
forms created by fathers II 115
seven stages of evolution of II 117
zodiacal calculations fr II 436n
Sōpatros (Sopater of Apamea)
unchained the winds I 469
Sophia (Gnos) Wisdom
ākāśa or I 197
Mother, Holy Ghost I 72n, 197, 618; II 512
serpent symbol of II 386
Seven Sons of I 434; II 210n
universal soul or I 353
Venus & II 512, 540
Sophia-Achamoth (Gnos)
Aditi is II 43
daughter of Sophia, wisdom I 197, 449
Divine Mother (King) II 570n
lower astral light or ether I 197
mother of Ialdabaōth (demiurge) I 197 &n, 449; II 243
rescued fr chaos by Christos I 132n
spiritual principle of 1st couple fr II 215
Sophocles II 674
Sorcerer(s, y). *See also* Black Magic, Dugpa
African, & Irish stones II 343-4
astrology & II 179
Asuramaya a II 67, 70
Atlantean II 93n, 224, 272n, 286, 371, 762
Atlantean, destroyed II 93-4n, 147, 350, 493, 495, 636, 772
Atlantean, memory of, lingers II 503
Cain, Ham &, (Roman Church) II 391
died after passing the Word I 404
Easter Island statues of II 224
followed beginning of Christianity I xl
giant races of II 285
holy, survived II 350
Institutes of Justinian & I 469

Jews acquainted w I 230
Lords of the Dark Face or II 427
Moon friend of I 156
Mysteries deteriorate into II 281
reverse 5-pointed star symbol of I 5
reverse side of Magic II 179
Roman Catholic legends of II 272
serpent or II 26
seventh son of 7th son is II 213
sex during some lunar phases is I 228-9n
Sons of God victorious over II 224n
war betw initiates & I 419; II 384, 492-5
Soret, estimates Sun's heat I 484n
Soshiosh. *See* Saoshyant
Sothiac Cycles (Egy)
five, observed in Egypt I 435
Soul(s). *See also* Animal, Human Soul
animates every atom I 51, 567
ascends fr lowest to highest I 17
atom, genius, angel or I 569
blending w spirit II 639n
butterfly symbol of, (Gk) I 74
cell, evolves into human, (Haeckel) II 670
Christian view of I 106, 182-3, 570; II 302-3
cosmic, or astral light II 113
could die while body lives I 234 &n
descends first as astral mold II 728
descent of spirit into I 113n, 226n
distinct fr spirit I 568-9
divine, or buddhi I 216
divine, Prometheus aspires to II 419
divine, remembers all past II 424
divine, symb by water, Moon II 113
"Doctrine" of Buddha I xxi
each, born fr boundless light I 577
evolution of, (Stobaeus) II 137-8
faculties fr planets (Plato) I 604
human, & earth, water II 43n
human, symb by wind, air II 113
identity of all, w oversoul I 17
influence on evolution II 728
intracosmic, no beginning or end I 3
is number four II 575
journey of, & moksha I 132
Kantian, & prakriti I 602
latent in monad II 150
Luciferian, Lucianist views on II 239n
mahātma a purified, I 46n
matter, spirit, life, & I 49
māyāvic vehicle of, -mind I 624n
monads are atomic I 619, 629
Odin gives man, & life II 97
Paul on man's (Adam's) II 513
physical intellect & I 225

pineal gland seat of, (Descartes) II 298
Plato's definition of II 88
psyche or I 194
purified in Amenti, reborn I 365
scintillas & I 619
separation of, fr body I 234-5 &n
spirit &, or Father & Son II 231n
spiritual, or anima mundi II 573
struggle betw spirit & II 377
thread-, or sūtrātman I 17n, 610n
-voice II 424
whirling, or atoms I 568
will pass into new bodies II 760
of the World (Plato) I 338, 343
Soulless Men I 234-5 &n
Soul of the World. *See also* World Soul
    ākāśa, divine astral light or I 140
    Alaya or I 48, 49
    born of purusha & matter I 365, 461
    female, or "Great Deep" I 353
    primordial substance, chaos, & I 338, 343
    various names for I 365
Soul of Things, The. See Denton, Prof & Mrs
Sound(s). *See also* Communication, Lan-
    guages, Logos, Voice, Word
    ākāśa & Ether cause of I 296n
    ākāśa & touch, color & I 205, 372
    ākāśa the Mother-Father of II 400n
    Anugītā on I 534-6
    apex of ladder of life I 539
    atoms called, in occultism I 633
    bell-, in space I 557
    bhūtādi devours, in pralaya I 372
    collective Demiurgos or I 372
    commanding forces by, & color I 514n
    described, explained I 554-5
    disturbs atomic equilibrium I 565
    effect of equal, waves meeting II 489
    ether produced, [*VP*] I 587
    Fohat & I 139, 145
    Gandharva & causes of I 523n
    Keely's occult ideas on I 564-5
    language of 2nd race II 198
    noumenal & phenomenal I 145-6
    occult power of I 93-5, 464, 534-7, 555,
        564-5
    odor &, real substance I 564
    opens door betw mortals & immortals I 464
    related to elements & senses I 307; II 107
    rhythm &, related to elements I 307
    Second Logos or I 563
    septenary law governs II 613, 622, 627, 628
    seven II 613
    speech &, ether of space II 107

subjective or sensational I 633
Tyndall has traced physical I 633
ultimate causes of I 514-17
Vāch magic potency of I 137
in *Vishnu Purāna* I 521
"Source of Heat in The Sun." *See* Hunt, R.
Source of Measures. See Skinner, J. Ralston
South (direction)
    red corn depicts, (Zuñi) II 629
    Yama guards the I 128
South Africa
    arrowheads of Bushman of II 522
    mere fragment of Lemuria II 333
Southall, Dr J. P., *Epoch of the Mammoth* . . .
    Paleolithic man came to Europe II 740n
South America(n)
    beaches rose 100-1,300 ft II 787n
    bird-eating spider of II 440
    esoteric schools in I xxiii
    fossils linked w Europe, Africa II 791
    India &, connected once II 327
    man on cross carvings in I 322
Southern Cross
    Alpha Draconis of Pyramid I 407
    three & 4 shown in I 321
Southern Fish, & kali-yuga I 663
South Pole
    abode of cosmic elementals II 274
    fohatic forces, ākāśa & I 204-5
    lethal influences fr II 400n
    nether pole, demons, hells II 404, 785
    passing of North Pole to II 360
    Pātāla associated w II 357
    Pit, Hell or II 274, 357, 785
South Sea Islander(s) II 168, 421n
Soyuti, on Seth, Enoch, pyramids II 361-2
Sozura
    entirely unknown to science II 669, 745n
    Haeckel's mythical amphibian II 652, 656,
        745n
Space. *See also* Duration, Motion
    abode of Ea, wisdom II 53
    Absolute transcends time & I 1-2n; II 158
    abstract, generator, female II 43
    all born in, & time must die II 549
    always part of larger increment I 87-8
    aspect of Be-ness I 14-15
    aspect of the Absolute I 43
    astral light (ākāśa) is II 511-12
    Bain on, & time I 251n
    body of limitless extent I 342
    boundless, infinite I 99, 113
    boundless, of divine Plenum I 148
    boundless void (science) I 587, 615

Brahmā-Vishnu is infinite I 8n
bright, son of dark I 71-2
chaos is, (Aristotle) I 336n
chaos or unmanifested Deity II 269
chaos-theos-kosmos aspects of I 344
chaos, void, Ain-sōph or I 109
cosmic, or devamātri I 53 &n
Crookes on I 550-1, 581n
dimensionless in every sense I 55
duration, matter, motion & I 55
of East not understood in West I 496n
eternal substance, boundless II 239n
every point in, animated II 513
female or chaos I 431; II 84
filled w atoms (Leucippus) I 2, 64, 117
first Mother, then Father-Mother I 18
Fohat divides I 674
force, matter &, (Pratt) I 615
fullness & void I 8, 35
good & evil progeny of, & time II 96
gravity as force pervading I 511
Hari as Brahmā sleeps in I 371-2
incomprehensible deity I 35, 336n
Kronos beyond, & time I 418
Māqōm stands for II 612
measurability of, absurd I 251
Parabrahman infinite cosmic I 6
perpetual motion & limitless I 2
potential & abstract I 4
Pratt on, & First Cause I 9n
realm of divine knowledge II 502
ruling intelligent powers in II 502
six directions of I 116, 118
spirit 1st differentiation in I 258
there is no empty I 289, 527 &n
thick w molecules I 150
time &, forms of Deity II 382n
unborn & undecaying II 487
unknowable living entity I 615
unknown container of all I 342
vacuum betw celestial bodies (Newton) I 491
whole finite kosmos called I 277
Spagyrisation (alchemy) of matter II 592
Spain, Spaniards
    dolmen of Anteguera in II 752
    joined to Barbary once (Joly) II 751
    met savage chiefs II 744
    NW Africa once extension of II 8n, 740,
        751-2, 793
    rocking stones in II 342n, 793
Spark(s)
    animate all kingdoms I 103, 246
    extinguished by bestiality II 318
    hangs fr the Flame I 238

identical w devas, rishis II 85
immortal, reflecting divine flame I 275
individualities in lower spheres I 275
monad a homogeneous I 571
sacred, in man II 421n
some sons projected a II 161, 286
term for atoms I 108
universes called, of eternity I 16
will rebecome the Flame I 265
worlds like I 99, 199, 246n; II 99, 704
Sparśa (Skt) touch, in pralaya I 372
Sparta, Castor's tomb shown at II 122n
Speaking
    Ad-i name of 1st, race II 452
    animal, beast (automata) II 427-8
    stones II 341-2 &n
Spear-holder. *See* Śaktidhara
Specialization, Specialized
    gradual human, missing II 716
    man & lower genera exceptions to II 256
    man's skeleton not II 720-3
Species
    all, change w every root-race II 697
    all, once hermaphrodite II 299
    continuance of, (Kabbala) II 457
    crop of, after physicalization II 736
    designers, builders & growth of II 732
    differentiation of II 737
    different rates of evolution for II 256
    gradual transformation of II 347-8
    growth & decline of II 733-4
    human, can breed together II 195
    interbreeding of II 184-5, 191, 201, 267, 287
    law of retardation on II 260 &n
    now stereotyped II 697
    progressive development of II 260
    relapse to ancestral types II 697
Species Immateriata
    Kepler's planetary forces I 479
Specimens of the Hindu Theatre. See Wilson, H.
Spectroscope(ic)
    analysis of nebulae I 595-9
    Crookes q Maxwell on I 143n
    findings of, limited I 142, 543-4n
    no use beyond visible matter I 543n
    seven colors & II 627-8
    shows Sun's outer robes only I 528
Spectrum, of the stars I 595-6, 598
Speech I 464; II 563. *See also* Sound
    development of II 198-201
    Ilā goddess of, (Dowson) II 148
    inflectional in Atlantis II 199
    Logos both reason & II 199n
    māntrika śakti & I 293

Mercury symbol of II 542
  noiseless, superior to noisy I 95
  not evolved fr animal sounds II 661-2
  origin of, & occult properties I 93-4
  Sarasvatī goddess of I 95
  third race, monosyllabic II 198-9
  Vāch goddess of I 137
Spencer, Herbert II 671
  agnostic I 19n
  on environment & unity of types II 736-7
  evolution of chemical atoms I 622
  internal & external relations I 293
  John Fiske's master II 787
  monism & I 124-5n
  more dangerous than Büchner I 528n
  pale copyist I 96n
  positivist II 156n
  will-o-the-wisps of II 451
—— *First Principles*
  First Cause I 14-15 &n
  matter affected by motion I 12n
  motion I 496
  unknowable of I 19n, 54n, 281, 327 &n, 675
—— "Nebular Hypothesis"
  implies a First Cause I 600 &n
—— *Principles of Biology*
  evolution fr a preexisting being II 348-9
  worthlessness of Darwinism II 730
—— *Principles of Psychology*
  evolution as a dream II 490n
  ideas vs absolute thought II 490
Spencer, Johann (Joannes)
—— *De Legibus Hebraerum*
  Abarbinel on Nabatheans II 455-6
  Azaz(y)el sent to Mt Hermon II 409
  derives Azazel fr *Ajal, El* II 376
Spenta Armaiti (Zor) Spirit of Earth
  Ahura Mazdā father of II 385
  helped Yima enlarge Earth II 609-10
Speucippus, followed in Plato's steps II 555
Sphere(s). *See also* Globes, Planets, Stars
  "above, higher," & invisible I 605
  Ain-sōph a boundless I 429
  astral rulers of, create monads I 577
  of being numberless II 33
  beings of other, live in & thru us I 605
  builders, watchers of the seven I 53
  chain of, beyond Earth II 701
  Earth contains 6 other II 111
  egg symbol of our I 65, 89, 359
  eighth I 156, 163, 227n
  emblem of infinity & eternity I 65
  every, called dragon's head II 505
  of expectation II 57 &n

gyratory movement of, & atoms I 117
  human prototype in, spiritual I 235n
  Lords of, now rebellious angels I 577
  music of the I 167, 432-3, 445-6; II 601-2
  seven, in Hindu scriptures I 112
  seven, of action II 621n
  "Wheels" gradually become I 116-17
Sphericity
  of Earth among ancients I 40n, 117 &n, 441
  primordial form of everything I 65
Spheroidal Form
  drop assumes, I 97-8n
Sphinx(es) I 643
  Aeschylus, Shakespeare were II 419
  narthex must be wrenched fr II 518
  recalls androgynous race II 124
  riddle of the II 403, 516-17, 540
  Simorgh or II 618
Sphinx (magazine)
  Lambert diagram, 7 principles fr II 633
Sphinxiad. See Mackey, S. A.
Spider, bird-eating, disbelieved II 440
Spiller, Philipp, *Der Weltaether . . .*
  incorporeal matter of I 493n, 508
Spinal Cord
  sexual action connected w II 296
Spinoza, Baruch
  Leibniz & I 628-30
  opposed Descartes' ideas I 629
  subjective pantheist I 629
—— *Chief Works of: Letters*
  face of universe ever the same II 1
Spiral
  lines traced by Fohat I 118-19
  motion, cycles, ogdoad & II 580
Spirit. *See also* Body, Purusha, Soul
  ākāśa is ideation or I 326
  all things originate in II 190
  astral is vehicle of I 624n
  Bacchus or II 458
  blind without matter II 123n
  breath of life confused w I 225-6
  chief, of 7 planetary genii II 22-3
  cosmic ideation or I 16; II 24
  directs the elements in ether I 343
  disembodied, or future man I 277
  divine, & divine substance one I 337n
  divine, symb by Sun, fire II 113
  divorced fr matter is chaos I 640
  evolution of, into matter I 550-1
  evolves forms out of aether I 332
  fecundates germ in space II 84
  female, evil w Nazarenes I 194n
  fire, male or, & water I 341

first differentiation fr THAT I 35, 258
first human principle, not seventh I 153n
force, matter & I 341
higher, or male astral light I 196
history realization of, (Hegel) I 640-1
is & is not (*Manu*) I 447
latent in matter II 42
lipika separate pure, fr matter I 130
Logos is II 25
of love (Ragon) II 576
manas link betw matter & II 98
man's, sole mediator I 280
matter & I 327-8
matter &, aspects of Parabrahman I 15, 51
matter &, inseparable, interdependent
    I 247, 416
matter &, latent in chaos I 64
matter &, māyā I 633
matter &, psyche & nous II 134n
matter &, reconciled I 623
matter &, struggle of II 64
matter &, 2 poles same subst I 247, 542
matter is, & vice versa I 179, 633
nature &, illusory universe II 36
Noah is, vivifying matter II 145
no name, species or body I 373
one w paramātman I 265
permeates every atom I 338, 449, 567-9
plunges into matter, redeemed II 88
the, Principle I 5
pure, lost in absolute Non-Being I 481
root-matter or I 543
Śankara on not-spirit & I 573
soul &, or Son & Father II 231n
soul distinct fr I 568-9
soul united w, is monad I 119
struggle w soul & II 377
supreme, alone remains I 373
swan & good symbols of I 357-8
swastika, matter & II 99
three hypostases of I 18-19
unconscious purposiveness of I 328
Vishnu Purāna on I 284
wind, air &, synonymous I 342
worshiped by 4th race I 327
Spirit-Guardian, of our globe II 22
Spirit History of Man. See Dunlap, S. F.
Spiritismus, Der. See Hartmann, K. R. E. von
Spiritistic Revelations
    about Moon, stars, planets II 701
Spirit-Kings, ruled Atlantis II 222
Spirit-Matter
    evolution of, or cosmogony I 277
    infinite depth of I 628

Second Logos, life, or I 16
symb as white pt in darkness I 327-8
Spirit of God
    aetherial winds are, (Müller) I 365
    Ain-sōph, Parabrahm II 128
    breathes over chaos II 505
    lived in sea of space (Bab) II 477
    spiratus or, (Ragon) II 576
Spirit of the Sands (Jap) I 217
"Spirit of the Supreme Spirit"
    Prithivī greets Vishnu as I 18
Spirits (angels, elementals, etc)
    animated man of clay II 273
    broke thru circles of fire II 275n
    degradation of II 275n
    described II 370n
    drawing down powers of II 455n
    Egregores or, of energy & action I 259n
    elementals guided by high planetary I 278
    elementaries or nirmānankāyas I 233n
    elementary I 234n, 620; II 632
    of elements & divinations I 395
    of elements of primary creation I 218n
    evil, at war w gods II 232
    Fall of the I 192-8
    Gobi desert protected by II 372
    of heaven & then of Earth II 248
    hosts of, surround man II 370 &n
    incorporeal beings II 87
    of light & darkness II 162, 512
    materialization of II 737
    of mediums not higher principles I 233n
    must attain self-consciousness I 193
    nature, or elementals I 221, 461; II 102
    personating, or demions (dimyōn, Heb)
        II 508-9
    planetary I 128, 278, 602; II 22-3, 29, 318n
    science, spiritualism on I 276
    seven divine & 6 lower orders of I 133
    seven invisible II 488
    seven planetary, (rishis) II 318n
    three, explained (Ragon) II 576
    were or will be men I 277; II 370n
Spirits of the Earth II 23, 109-10
    clothed the shadows I 224-5; II 110
    lowest dhyānis were I 224
    Spirits of Heaven then became II 248
Spirits of Heaven then became II 248
Spirits of the Elements. *See* Yazatas
Spirits of the Face
    seven, all in Jehovah's image I 197-8
    seven, or builders I 128
Spirits of the Presence (Christian)
    Egyptian counterparts of I 312

Spirits of the Stars (Christian)
  suspiciously like gods I 123n
Spiritual
  civilization & the II 319
  fire of agnishvāttas II 79
  higher pitris man's, parents II 171
  iniquity & loss of, 3rd eye II 302
  intellectual has replaced II 300
  intelligences must pass thru human stage
    I 106
  involution & evolution II 348
  key to symbolism highest I 363
  lives are a māyā (Buddhism) I 635
  man in Purānas II 254
  oldest subraces at, apex II 301
  rock that followed Israel II 341
  senses barrier to, development II 296
  sight, pineal organ of II 299
Spiritual Ego(s). *See also* Egos, Higher Self,
  Self
  drawn to rebirth by lower selves II 109
  experiences of, in initiation II 558
  higher self II 230
  man's, dwells in unseen worlds I 234n
  one w Viśvakarma II 559
  reemerge w mother-source I 237
Spiritual Fire
  hydrogen is, in alchemy II 105-6
  makes man divine, perfect II 105
  man's higher self II 109
  noumenon of "Three in One" II 113
Spiritualist(s, ism)
  believe in spirits of dead I 287
  Butlerof defended I 520
  facts of, & man's origin II 86-7
  ignorant of matter I 276
  limitations of I 288
  materializations of II 86, 87
  Pember on II 229n
  phenomena will be recognized II 156n
  possessing entities of I 233 &n
  regard kriyāśakti as phenomenal II 652
  Wallace, Crookes, Zöllner & I 520
Spirituality
  ascending arc & II 110
  cycles of I 175-7, 620; II 300-1, 446
  intellect &, discussed II 167
Spiritual Monad
  of early man II 154
  needs 4th & 5th principles II 79, 242
Spiritual Soul
  buddhi (in man) I 157 &n; II 596
  universal ideation (cosmic) II 596

Spiritus (Lat) breath, wind I 226n
  begets 7 evil spirits I 195-6, 217, 248
  elementorum, spirit of elements I 395
  female astral light I 196
  flamma, sulphur & II 113
  ventus (Lat, wind) &, synonymous I 342
Spiritus Vitae, Spiritus Mundi (Lat)
  former originates in the latter I 532
Spitzbergen II 398, 677
  continent fr, to Dover II 324, 326
  Nova[ya] Zemlya & II 398
  part of pre-Lemurian continent II 775
  second race continent & II 401-2
Spleen, little understood II 296
Spoëren, estimates Sun's heat I 484n
Spontaneous Generation II 189, 718-19
  esoteric philosophy teaches II 150-1, 157-8,
    286, 719
  existed in nature II 116
  Haeckel on II 164n
Spores, reproduction by II 167, 171n, 659
Sport, creation of world a II 53, 126
[Sprenger, Jacob, *Malleus Maleficarum*]
  on Hoppo & Stadlein I 469
Spring
  equinox & origin of zodiac II 435
  eternal II 135, 201, 356, 400, 738 &n
  eternal, of 3rd race II 135, 201, 356, 777 &n
  seven symbol of, & summer II 583
Spring, Professor
  q by Littré on human bones II 739
Square(ing) II 573-5
  within circle I 99
  circle & initiation II 450
  formless I 98-9
  four is Tetraktys or Sacred I 89n
  four sacred powers or I 134n
  Gnostic gnosis rested on II 573
  Hindus know how to, circle II 544
  Macroprosopus is perfect II 626
  Parker's premises on I 315-16
  second figure in nature II 594
  triangle & II 24, 36, 596
Śraddhā (Skt) faith
  Kāma son of Dharma & II 176
Śramaṇa (Skt) religious ascetic
  Akbar & the I xxivn
Sravah (Pers)
  seven bright, or Amshaspends II 516
  spirits of manifested powers II 385
Śrī (Skt)
  is Lakshmī, Sarasvatī II 76n
  Moon, water & II 77
  rising fr waters (Williams) I 380

wife of Nārāyana, Śiva II 76n
Srī Antara (yantra) (Skt)
    double triangle or I 118-19
Śrīdhara (Skt) commentator
    on hiranyagarbha I 406
    Ulūpī daughter of Nāga king II 214 &n
Śriṅga-giri (Skt)
    monastery of Smārta-Brahmans I 272
Srip (Skt) to creep
    sarpa or serpent fr II 182n
Śrī-Yantra (Skt), double triangle or I 118
Srotāpanna, Srotāpatti (Skt)
    degree of initiation I 206
Śruti (Skt), revealed knowledge I 269
Ssabier und der Ssabismus, Die. See
        Chwolsohn, D. A.
St. *See* Saint
Stadlein, magic arts of Hoppo & I 469
Stained Glass, tints of II 430
Stallo, John B., *Concepts & Theories . . .*
    actio in distans I 487-8
    antagonism betw sci & metaphysics I 485n
    contradictions in science I 482-3, 485, 487-9
    critique of vortical theory I 488-9
    defines Avogadro's Law I 512n
    disagrees w Spiller I 493n, 507-8
    errors of ontology I 544
    ether discussed I 486-7, 488n
    force & mass I 510-11
    force an independent entity I 512
    gravitation & ether I 490-1
    on idealism I 556n
    Kepler on the Sun I 493
    mistaken re matter & force I 510
    physics & metaphysics I 544
Stanley, Thomas, *History of Philosophy* [ch IX,
        Pythagoras]
    quaternary is female & infernal II 600-1
Stanzas (of Dzyan). See also Book of Dzyan
    VOLUME I:
        First I 20-1, 27, 35-52
        Second I 21, 28, 53-61
        Third I 21, 28-30, 62-85
        Fourth I 21-2, 30-1, 86-105
        Fifth I 22, 31-2, 106-35
        Sixth I 22, 32-3, 136-52, 191-212
        Seventh I 22, 33-4, 213-68
    VOLUME II:
        First II 15, 23-51
        Second II 15-16, 52-74
        Third II 16, 75-85
        Fourth II 17, 86-108
        Fifth II 17-18, 109-30
        Sixth 18, 131-60

        Seventh II 18-19, 161-79
        Eighth II 19, 180-90
        Ninth II 20, 191-226
        Tenth II 20, 227-315
        Eleventh II 20-1, 316-50
        Twelfth II 21, 351-436
    anthropogenesis II 15-21
    cannot be verified by scholars I xxii, xxxvii
    conflict w modern science I 478
    cosmic evolution I 27-34
    cosmogony only of our planetary system I 13
    described I 13, 20-4; II 1, 22n, 23
    elucidation requires proofs II 354
    Fohat & world germs (VI) I 672
    gap betw 7th & 51st I 478
    less mythical than Purānas II 23
    portions only given I 23; II 15n
    sequence of, & Commentaries II 12
    speak for themselves II 56
Star(s). *See also* Five-, Six-pointed Star; Great
        Bear; Pleiades
    abodes of archangels II 455n
    acting & living bodies (Aristotle) I 493
    become suns, planets I 206
    of Bethlehem II 619
    Church made devils of I 331
    condensation of a nebula I 595-6
    distances betw, incalculable II 708
    dragon's head, called II 505
    each man has his I 572-3
    each pyramid consecrated to a II 362
    each world has a parent II 33
    elements of, may not be Earth's I 583, 589
    evolve fr ethereal substance I 590
    five-pointed I 5, 219; II 464, 576 &n
    Flammarion believed, inhabited II 45
    genii of I 294
    goddess of the seven II 547
    history written in the II 438
    humanity &, bound together II 352
    influence on man I 532
    informing spirits of I 128
    inhabited II 701-3
    intelligences rule the II 352
    Kant's view of I 601-2
    of Magi in Pisces I 654
    manifesting incessantly I 16
    materials of, differ I 589
    motionless, in motion, self-moving I 500,
        670
    nebulous (Hindu astronomy) II 253
    NT Epistles, not known as worlds in II 704
    occult influence of I 647
    our destiny written in the I 639

Pantomorphos prince of I 672
of salvation I 471
seven, of Great Bear (Rishis) I 407; II 318n
seven, of *Revelation* II 355, 633
Seven Sons of Light called I 572
six-pointed I 215, 224, 375; II 533, 594
-stuff or curds I 69, 673; II 321
that have disappeared II 486n
triple force in, (Brahe) I 493
Star, Ely (pseudonym of Eugène Jacob)
—— *Mystères de l'horoscope*
influence of planets, signs I 79
rationale of horoscopy I 105
Star Angels I 574n
Starkad, Starkadr (Norse)
depicted carrying runes II 346n
Star of Bethlehem
"confirmed" by Dr Sepp II 619
Star-Yazatas (Zoroastrian)
angels of stars are II 358
Statesmen (Politicus). See Plato
Statius, P. Papinius, *Silvae*
harp & trident II 390n
Statue(s). *See also* Bamian, Easter Island
Babylonian, of green diorite II 692
black & white stone, (Egy) II 360
four-armed, 3-eyed II 294-5 &n
Lemuro-Atlanteans built huge II 316
Mahadeva destroying Tripurāsura II 591
of Sulimans (Pers) II 396
340+, of Egyptian kings II 369, 750
200 ft Buddha in S India II 224 &n
Statue of Liberty
compared w Bamian Statues II 338 &n
Stauridium (a polyp)
sex evolved fr hermaphrodite II 177-8
Stauros Cross & Gnostic Christ II 587
Steenstrup, Johann, on flints II 752n
Stella del Mare (Lat)
Venus, "Star of the Sea" I 392
Stella Matutina (Lat) morning star
Hathor called I 400
Stella nova . . . , De. See Kepler, J.
Stellars, 7 (planets) I 195
Stellar Spirits I 449
genii of 7 planets, globes I 198
Stellar Systems, run down? [entropy] I 149
Sterile, Sterility
between animals & men imposed II 192
differentiation &, (Romanes) II 647
karma, cyclic law & II 196, 780
lunar phases & I 229n
nature makes certain unions II 195-6
among women of old races II 779-80

Sterling, J. H. *See* Stirling
Steropē (Gk, Asterope in tx)
daughter of Atlas II 768
Stevenson, Robert Louis
Dr. Jekyll and Mr. Hyde I 416; II 317n
Stewart, Prof B. & Tait, P. G.
theosophists respect II 651
—— *The Unseen Universe*
fr ether have come all things I 462
matter is passive I 485n
Stewart, Dugald, denied Skt as a lang II 442
Sthāvara (Skt) standing still
contrasted w jangama, moving I 454
Sthūla (Skt) gross, material
differentiated condition I 522
Sthūla-Śarīra (Skt) physical body II 242
of ākāśa II 615
of ākāśa, manas & I 619
charts w I 153n, 157, 242; II 596
corresponds w globe 4, Earth I 153
corresponds w Mt Ararat & Earth II 596
external body I 222
molded over linga-śarīra II 593
not grossest principle I 260
visible kosmos is the I 598
Sthūlopādhi (Skt), basis of principle I 157
Stirling, J. H., *As Regards Protoplasm*
believed in vital principle I 634
points up Huxley's admissions I 637n
Stobaeus, *Eclogae*
evolution of souls II 137-8
τίμιον (timion) honored one II 555
—— *Florilegium*
idea of God I 286
Stockwell, John N. & Croll, Dr James
—— "Secular Variations . . ." in
Smithsonian Reports
deluges, glacial periods II 141, 144
Stoic(s) I 76-7
catastrophes of 2 kinds II 784
knew 3 phases of Hecate I 395
Στοιχεῖα (stoicheia, Gk) elements
Aristotle's principles I 123
elements of Plato, Aristotle I 461
terāphīm positioned by I 394
Στοιχειωματιχοί (stoicheiōmatikoi, Gk)
diviners (astrologers) I 394
Stone(s). *See also* Baetyl, Dolmen, Rocking
Argonaut, described II 345
in ark phallic JHVH II 473
becomes plant I 107, 197, 246; II 186, 188,
258, 590
betyles (baetyl) II 342
circle at Malabar II 347

circle of Galilee II 755
consciousness in I 274
cup-like markings on II 346n
Dracontia as rocking II 346-7
equipoise of ancient II 343-4
hinging, of Salisbury Plain II 343
huge, universally distributed II 752-4
incandescent celestial I 440
Irish circular, fr Africa II 343
Lemurian cities of, & lava II 317
life energy dormant in II 673n
magic, moving, speaking II 341-2, 342n
men are lively, (I *Peter*) II 627
Mona, described II 345
moved by will II 342n
particles of, constantly moving I 507-8n
plants born fr bosom of II 594
in profound lethargy I 626n
rocking, Atlantean relics II 343, 347
science of, fr Atlantis II 426
w sculptured symbols II 790
w 7 eyes explained II 626-7
soft, that hardened II 52, 593-4
twelve, "mysteries of the elements" I 395
twelve precious I 649
virtues of precious II 426
Stone Age Man
larger brain capacity than modern II 168n
Miocene civilization upsets II 786n
no, in Egypt II 786n
writing unknown to, (Evans) II 442
Stonehenge II 70, 752
called dance of the giants II 342
form of Dendera planisphere II 344
giants & II 341
gods of, like Delphi, Babylon II 379
pre-Druidic symbolic record II 754
relic of last Atlanteans II 343
stones of, fr Ireland II 344
traveling initiates built II 750, 754
Stonehenge. See Petrie, Flinders
Stone of the Ordeal II 342n
Storm(s)
genii & I 294
-gods or maruts II 498, 613
-Hammer or Mjölnir II 99
Stotra (Skt) prayers I 421
Strabo, *Geography* II 390n, 781
Egypt covered by sea II 368
Euxine overflowed Samothrace II 4-5 &n
Samothrace rites on Brittannia II 760
Strachoff, N. N., *Fundamental Conceptions*
spirit clothes itself in matter II 654
Straits of Dover

continent fr, to Spitzbergen II 324, 326
Stratification, in 4th round II 715n
Stratton, Dr, cycles in human pulse II 623n
Straws, divining, of Confucius I 356, 441
Strides, Steps
Fohat takes 5, explained I 122
Vishnu, Fohat take three I 112-13 &n, 122;
II 38, 622n
Strobic Circles II 589
Stromata. See Clement of Alexandria
Struggle
betw inner man & man of flesh II 269n, 272
betw Sons of God & Darkness II 495
there is no merit without II 95
Struggle for Life, Existence I 154
birds in, turned on reptiles II 254
in cosmic evolution I 201-3
natural selection & II 299n, 648
de Quatrefages accepted II 662
Sub-astral Sphere of Action II 117, 621n
Subba Row, Tallapragada
—— "Brahmanism on the Sevenfold . . ."
dual meaning of Vedas I 270n
primary prakriti is ākāśa I 256
—— "Constitution of the Microcosm"
sevenfold man & logos II 635-6
—— "Idyll of the White Lotus" (review)
seven classes of adepts I 574
—— *Notes on the Bhagavad Gita* I 15n
Crookes's birth of elements I 620-1
daivīprakriti, light, Logos I 136 &n
energy behind Fohat I 139
equates ātman w Logos I 110 &n
Fohat instrument of Logos I 137n
force & mūlaprakriti II 25 &n
four aspects of Vāch I 432
gods & devas II 90
infinite number of logoi I 134n
Īśvara & Śabda-Brahman I 137-8 &n, 428
Īśvara or Logos I 351n
Logos as 1st center of activity I 130n
manus & root-races II 140n
mūlaprakriti I 10n, 349n
on the nature of Krishna II 318n
One Logos & mūlaprakriti I 273-4
Parabrahman, Logos I 428; II 310n
purely metaphysical esotericism I 431
—— "Personal & Impersonal God" (*Five
Years of Theosophy*)
on the One II 598
Parabrahman & Unconsciousness II 598
seven aspects of prajñā I 139; II 597n
—— "Septenary Division of Different Indian
Systems" (*Five Yrs. . . .*) I 157-8

—— "Twelve Signs of the Zodiac"
history of creation I 269
kriyāśakti II 173
Makara (Capricorn) II 576-80
six primary nature forces I 292-3
Sub-elements
numberless I 12-13, 460, 621, 624, 673
Subhāva (Skt)
svabhavat, yeu (Chin) or I 61
Sublunary World (or Earth, Syrian)
watched over by angels I 435
Submersion(s), Submerge(d). *See also* Atlantis,
Axis (Earth's), Continents, Lemuria, Upheavals
of Atlantis II 124, 140, 141, 250, 265-6,
313-14, 493-5
of Boeotia & Eleusis II 270n
British Isles, 4 times II 746n
Easter Isles &, continent II 316n, 328
eclipse of spiritual sun & II 250n
fifth continent & II 445-6
Garden of Eden locality now II 494
geologists &, continents II 316
influence of tides upon II 325
Lemuria not, but was sunk II 266
men on, continents II 316-17
north polar lands II 328, 360
periodical II 325n
of Plato's island II 8, 141, 250n, 314
pralayas by II 324-5
successive, of continents I 650
third eye &, of Atlantis II 306
Subrace(s)
Atlantean, & their descendants II 743, 774
Atlantis destroyed during 4th II 147n
born, mature, die II 443-4
cycling upward, downwards II 301
each, has a manu II 614
each root-race has seven II 198n
Europeans fr early Aryan II 743
every, has 7 branches II 434
every, repeats root-race cycles II 301
fifth, or European II 445
first, of 5th race II 351-2
follow footsteps of mother races II 768
fourth, of Atlantis & beauty II 319
fourth, of 5th race II 433
lives 210,000 years II 435
man's size less after Aryan 3rd II 753
most men are of 7th, of 4th root-race II 178
nascent simplicity of first II 784
oldest, at spiritual apex II 301
our history is of 5th, only II 351
our own special I 417

our race has reached its 5th II 471n
of 2nd race II 117
seed-manus of II 308-9, 321, 597, 614
seven daughters of Atlas were II 493, 768
seven, in every root-race II 434
seventh, after 25,000 years II 445
seventh, of Atlanteans Aryanized II 743
sixth, & America II 444-5
subject to cleansing process II 330
third Atlantean, & records II 353
third Atlantean, & 3rd eye II 306
third of 5th root-race & divine dynasties
II 436
tropical year & II 446
we are at midpoint of our I 610
"Subsistence and Elevation . . ." *See* Gardner, J. S.
Substance(s). *See also* Matter, Prakriti, Protyle
abstract potential in pralaya I 328-9
ākāśa is the primordial I 326
all, endowed w force I 627
astral light or ether is cosmic I 326
becomes gods, monads, atoms I 624
cause of light, heat I 514-15
correlation of forces or I 566n
cosmic, & Fohat I 16, 328
cosmic, eternally homogeneous I 569
creation out of preexisting II 239n
divine, one w divine spirit I 337n
entirely unknown to us I 607n
eternal boundless space, is II 239n
ether a principle of primal I 326, 339
imponderable, fills space I 587
infinite divisibility of I 519
informed by divine breath I 520
laya as noumenon of cosmic I 148
on many planes I 510
matter &, defined I 329
mūlaprakriti is primordial II 24
no inorganic I 280-1, 626n; II 672
not matter in metaphysics I 508
noumenon of matter is primal I 601
of occultist most refined I 514n
Parabrahman w Vedāntists I 59n
perpetual motion of I 525-6 &n
pradhāna as undifferentiated I 62
precosmic, or mūlaprakriti I 15
primordial, & our senses I 330
primordial, evolution of I 58-9
primordial, is divine I 594
same each manvantara I 145
science has but one name for I 510
sevenfold I 289, 624
sixth principle upādhi of I 594

supersensuous but atomic I 82
triune 1st differentiated I 614
undifferentiated, normal condition I 567
various names of primordial I 330, 510
Substance-Principle I 273
Substantialists(ism) I 194n
    American, use wrong terms I 146
    views of, on force, substance I 566n
Śuchi (Skt) solar fire
    called "drinker of waters" I 521 &n
    fire of passion, animal instincts II 105
    fire of the gods & II 57n
    one of 3 fires II 247
    Pāvaka &, made animal man II 102
Sudden Leaps. *See also* Saltation
    evolution by, (Naudin) II 120
Śuddhasattva (Skt) pure sattva
    bodies of gods made of I 522
    essence of Īśvara's body I 132
Sudyumna (Skt)
    becomes Idā II 143, 148
    is also goddess Ilā II 135
Suffering
    needed to reach nirvāna II 81
    pain &, value of II 475
Sūfi(s)
    ancient zodiac owned by a II 431
    initiates preserve Chaldean works I 288
    mystics II 244
    rohanee [rūhānī] of, & Ātma-vidyā I 199
Suggestion mentale . . . . See Ochorowicz, J.
Suhhab, Babylonian god II 5
Suidas, *Greek Lexicon*
    on animate stones II 342
    cited by Dr Sepp I 655n; II 619-20
    Hermetic fragment q by I 286
    Orpheus taught man zoomancy I 362-3
    universe created in 12,000 yrs I 340 &n
Śukra (Skt). *See also* Venus
    is Earth's primary II 31
    male deity, son of Bhrigu II 30, 32n
    mother of, killed by Vishnu II 33
    third race under II 29, 30
    Uśanas-, is Lucifer, Satan II 45 &n
Sūkshma (Skt) subtle, intangible
    latent undifferentiated state I 522
    solar system exists in, form I 138
Sūkshma-Śarīra (Skt) subtle body
    clothes inferior dhyānis I 132 &n
Sūkshmopādhi (Skt)
    mind-desire body I 157
Suliman [Sulayman] (Pers)
    ring of II 398
    seventy-two wise kings II 396

Sulla, Lucius C. (Sylla in tx)
    augurs in the day of II 518
Sulla. See Plutarch
Sulphur, in alchemy II 113-14
Sumati (Skt) son of Bharata II 321
Sumatra
    legends of II 788
    once part of Lemuria II 324
    remnant of sunken continent II 222
Summer
    7 symbol of Earth in Spring & II 583
Sun(s). *See also* Central Sun, Solar, Solar Systems, Sūrya
    Adonai or, (Gnostic) I 577; II 538n
    all Earth's elements in I 583
    Apollo, Phoebus or II 770
    born, grows, changes, dies I 609
    bright god of light I 479
    Brothers of the I 271n
    central mass of, gaseous I 530 &n
    chief of 12 constellations II 23
    -Christ lives in thee (Bernard) I 401
    combustion, not in I 149, 541, 591
    Commentary on I 289-92
    conjunction of, Moon, & Earth II 76, 435
    connection w cross II 559
    contains many unknown elements I 583
    contraction & expansion of I 541-2
    creation of, (Chald) II 145
    creation of life by I 294
    creation of 7 new I 290
    crocodile & II 577
    deviated fr course, (Phaethon) II 535
    divine spirit symb by fire or II 113
    dragon symbol of II 380
    eclipses of, & allegories II 380
    eleven year cycle of I 541 &n
    evolution of I 101-2
    evolved fr primal matter I 625
    explosion of, & planets I 500
    eye of Odin or I 402
    "eye of Osiris" II 25
    Father II 462, 540
    father of man II 105, 109
    father of pneuma, human soul II 113
    Father of the 7 fathers I 575n
    fed on "Mother's refuse & sweat" I 102
    feminine to Semites once I 397
    fire, air, &, 3 occult degrees of fire II 114
    first race under II 29
    -fluids awaken life, motion I 529
    focus, lens of primordial light I 580
    formation of, & stars I 595n, 602
    generation, Moon & I 229

gives life to planets I 386; II 23
glowing, not burning I 149, 541, 591
gods called Archagetos II 463n
guardian of Jupiter I 493
has no nucleus (Williams) II 136n
has no polar compression I 593
heart of solar world I 540-2
heat of I 102, 149, 484n, 528, 591
highest god II 361, 538
incandescent, a fallacy I 149, 591
initiation of II 381
inner man drawn to Parent- I 639
jīva (soul) goes to I 132
Joshua stopped II 535
kāma-rūpa of ākāśa I 527n
Kant's theories on I 602
larger than Earth (1300 times) II 708
legend of Rāhu & II 381
legend of Sanjñā & II 174
as the Logos I 134n, 428
luminosity of, (science) I 528n
as a magnet I 497-9, 501
manas, kāma-rūpa fr II 241
Mercury & II 28
Mercury Messiah of II 541
Messiah, Christos II 23
Metcalf's caloric flows fr I 524 &n
millions of I 576n
Mithra, Iaō & II 474
Moon &, affect man's body I 229
Moon &, cycles discussed II 620-1
Moon &, Son & Father I 229
Moon as eye of I 304-5
neither rises nor sets I 290n; II 155
not a planet but fixed star I 448
not cause of light, heat I 580
noumenon of electricity I 531
occult influence on 7 planets I 575n
path of, called serpent II 356
perturbing influence on planets I 503
planets &, time measurers II 621
planets brothers not sons I 101, 449, 588-9
planets did not evolve fr I 101, 588-9
at pralaya I 370, 376; II 69n, 611
rebirth of northern, & Ankh II 547
reflect concealed primaries I 289
regulates manifested life II 595
revolves round Alcyone (Mädler) I 501
rises & sets once a year, (*Avesta*) II 291
rising, setting of, (*VP*) II 155
rose in the south II 535
rotates w the planets I 100 &n
Sabasius, called II 419
self-moving, queried I 670

seven I 179
sevenfold I 290 &n
seven(fold) ray(s) I 290, 515 &n; II 25, 69n
seventh planet, ancients called I 99-100n
as 7th principle I 527n
in ship on back of crocodile I 409-10
solidity of, repudiated I 591
source of vital force I 531
spectroscope shows outer, only I 528
spectrum of I 143n, 528, 595-6
spheres of action of II 621 &n
spirit of fire resides in, (Kepler) I 493
spirit of light, life giver I 481
spirits oversee, (Kepler) I 499
spiritual, & avatāras, saviors I 638
spiritual, enlivens kosmos II 23
spirit under the, (*Zohar*) II 553
substance of all I 289
substance of, immaterial I 499
substitute for sacred planet I 575 &n
surface described I 530, 531
swallow comets I 204
symbol became phallic II 584
symbolizes resurrection II 459
in Taurus (Druids, Magi) II 759
Thomson on age of I 501; II 10n, 258n
threatened younger brothers I 102
understanding II 639n
unknown rays in spectrum of I 143n
Uranus, Neptune, & I 575
various names for I 463; II 540
vehicle of a god I 479
Venus "the other" II 24, 31
Vishnu becomes II 38
visible, a māyā or reflection I 179
vital electricity of, & man II 105
warmed sweat-born egg II 131
zodiacs & II 431
Sun (Fourth World of Syrians)
  mightiest gods in I 435
Sun-Abrasax, central spiritual sun II 214
Sunda Island II 327
  sank w 80,000 Malays II 787n
Sun-day
  should be Uranus-day (Ragon) I 99-100n
Sunday School, & astrology I 228-9n
Sun Fluids, or emanations I 529
"Sun Force and Earth Force." *See* Richardson
Sung-Ming-Shu (Chin)
  Tree of Knowledge, Life II 215
Sun-God(s). *See also* Avatāras, Christ, Saviors
  allegories of, agree II 381-3
  connected w Taurus I 656
  creative powers of II 386

Dragon of Wisdom & II 507
in Egy mysteries I 353, 366n, 379n, 385;
II 462-4, 466, 633
Horus-Apollo the I 367
Krishna, the bright I xliii
male gods first become II 43-4
many names of II 379
Phta later classed as I 353
supreme deity everywhere II 139n
turned into Satan II 507
-worship fr India to Pharaohs II 379
Sung Period (China)
sages of, used circle symbols II 554
Sun-Initiate, crucified II 543
Sunlight, tiny beings visible in I 608
"Sun like blood . . ." [Byron's *Childe Harold*]
I xli
Suns of Life II 239-41
Suns of Righteousness
Sun-gods become II 43
Sun-Sons I 100, 103
Sunspots
ascent of jīva after death & I 132
contraction of solar heart I 541-2
cycle of 11 years I 541 &n
Sun-Wolf, or Mercury II 28
Śūnya (Skt) empty, void
nought & Arabic ciphron (cipher) I 361n
Suoyatar [Syöjättären] (Finn)
Serpent of Evil born fr II 26
Superhuman Intelligences II 194
Supernatural(ism)
adepts living in astral not II 531
Christian theology & II 41
vs dead letter of Bible II 3
early humanity & II 319
rejected by wise men II 631n
term a misnomer I 555n
Superstition(s, ous) I 479
Christian & alleged pagan I 466-70
emotionalism & II 41
many, based on ideas now lost I 466
Upas trees of II 797
used to sway men's minds II 517
"Suppressio veri" (suppression of truth)
II 663
Surabhi (Skt)
cow of plenty I 67
parent of cows, buffaloes II 181
Surādhipa (Skt), one of Indra's names II 614
Surārani (Skt), Aditi called II 527
Suras (Skt) gods. *See also* Asuras
became asuras I 412, 418; II 57n, 59, 86, 93,
227n, 237, 500, 516

Surārani matrix of II 527
various equivalents of I 92
Surasā (Skt), mother of dragons II 381
Surgal. *See* Suryal
"Sur [De] la distinction des forces." *See*
Jaumes, A.
["Sur l'origine des monuments . . ."] *See* Henry
Surtur [Surtr] (Norse), fire giant II 99
Survival of the Fittest II 648
blind force, chance & II 475
in cosmic evolution I 202-3
among nations II 330
shows nature is conscious I 277-8
strongest often not fittest II 475
takes place after variations II 299n
taught by ancients I 203; II 254
Sūrya (Skt). *See also* Solar System, Sun
Asuramaya pupil of II 67
cures Sāmba of leprosy II 323
Fohat connected w, & Vishnu I 112
Manu as son of II 141
one of Vedic Trimūrti I 90, 100-1
reflection of spiritual sun I 100
Sanjñā wife of II 101
seven rays of II 605
Vedic god II 114
visible expression of 1st principle I 289
Viśvakarman & II 559
Suryal (archangel)
denounces fallen angels II 382n
Sūryamaṇḍala (Skt), region of the Sun I 132
Sūrya-Siddhānta (Skt) I 667
Atlantis & Lemuria in II 326
Meru described II 404
oldest astronomical work II 326
place of no latitude II 401-2n
real names of Atlantis, Lemuria II 323-4n
Sūryavaṅśa (Skt) solar dynasty
Chandravaṁśa I 397
war of, w Indovanśas I 397
Sushumna (Skt)
adept under, sees higher states I 515
affects sleeping man I 537
connects heart w Brahmarandhra I 132
furnishes Moon w light I 515n, 516, 537
highest of 7 rays I 523n
mystic ray of Sun I 515 &n
vegetation largely affected by I 537
Sushupti (Skt) deep sleep
human ego latent in I 429
Sūtrātman (Skt) thread self
discussed I 236
life-thread I 222
personalities of higher ego on II 79-80, 513

thread linking all principles I 610 &n
thread of immortal monad I 16-17n; II 513
Svabhāva (Skt) self-becoming
  prakriti or plastic nature I 571
Svabhavat (Skt) self-existent
  active condition of essence I 3-4
  Buddhistic mūlaprakriti I 61
  Devamātri & I 53
  dual root of all things I 46
  emanates noumenon of matter I 84
  Father-Mother I 60, 83, 98n
  gods generated by I 571; II 115
  manifested work of, is karma I 634-5
  noumenon of ether I 671
  plastic essence of all things I 61, 98 &n
  purusha-prakriti I 83
  secondary stage I 46
  sends Fohat to harden atoms I 85
  Svayambhū & I 52
  various names for I 98 &n
Svābhāvikas (Skt) Buddhist school
  called atheists I 3-4
Svāhā (Skt)
  mother by Brahmā of Abhīmānin II 247
  one of Daksha's daughters I 521; II 52
Svapada (Skt) one's own abode II 52
Svara (Skt), intonation of Vedas & light I 270n
Svarāj (Skt), 1 of 7 solar rays I 515n
Svarga (Skt) heaven
  Indra's, & Eden II 203
  war in II 498
Svar-loka (Skt)
  described II 404
  inhabitants of, at mahā-pralaya I 371
  Meru is II 404
  one of 7 dvīpas II 321
  in sacred utterance (vyāhriti) I 432n
Svarochi or Svārochisha (Skt)
  second manu II 765-6
  Seed-Manu, Planet G, 1st round II 309
Svasaṃvedana (Skt)
  paramārtha or I 44n, 48n, 53-4
Svastika. *See* Swastika
Svayambhū (Skt) self-produced
  Nārāyana or, penetrates egg I 80-1
  universal spirit, svabhavat or I 52
Svayambhū-Nārāyana (Skt)
  Manu Svāyambhuva sprang fr II 128
Svāyambhuva. *See also* Manus
  Adam Kadmon II 128
  cosmic monad II 311
  dhyāni energies or I 452
  Earth's calf I 398n
  father of Priyavrata II 326

first manu is II 310-11, 321
as 14th manu I 375
Manu I 398n
manus create humanities I 248; II 311
Manu, son of I 307
manvantara of II 322
Nārāyana or I 80
planetary chain energies fr II 311
pre-nebular cosmogony I 452
root-manu, Planet A, 1st round II 309
synthesis of the prajāpatis II 704n
ten sons of II 369n
union w Vāch-Śatarūpā II 148
universal spirit, highest svabhavat I 52
Śveta-Dvīpa (Skt)
  denizens became black w sin II 408 &n
  described II 327
  divine instructors fr II 366 &n
  early Lemuria II 264, 327, 408
  of Mt Meru II 6, 366n
  Pañchaśikha visits I 236
  replaced by Śambhala II 319
  seven kumāras visit Vishnu at II 584
  sons of, became corrupted II 319
  Tāradaitya, demons & II 404
  White Island or II 319, 322, 402n, 404, 408
  Wilford mistaken re II 402n, 404
Śvetalohita (Skt) white-red
  Śiva as, root kumāra II 249
Śvetāśvatara Upanishad
  on Mūlaprakriti I 10n
  siddhas, nirmānakāyas II 636n
Swabhava. *See* Svabhāva
Swan(s). *See also* Duck, Goose, Kalahansa
  air-water symbol I 358
  caduceus & wings of I 549
  dark, or goose I 20, 79, 80
  divine, & Zeus II 122
  Egyptian sacred bird I 353
  Kalahansa or I 77, 359; II 122 &n
  Leda as, bears an egg II 122
  of Leda, Jennings on I 358
  magical properties of I 362
  man-, of later 3rd race II 131
  of Myorica II 772n
  Seven, Rishis & Great Bear I 357n
  symbol explained I 357-8
Swanwick, Mrs Anna, *The Dramas of Aeschylus*
  Arrian & Virgil on Alexander II 417
  character of Zeus II 419
  Io's wanderings inconsistent II 416n
  Kuhn on word Prometheus II 413n
  man's lower passions II 412-13
  role of Prometheus II 411-18

Swastika [or Svastika] II 29
born among early Aryans II 99-101
on brow of Kārttikeya II 619
circle & I 433
cross & II 29, 30n, 31, 558
crucifixion, cross I 321n
described II 99-101, 586-7
Eastern symb univ known II 585-6
emblem of Fohat II 587
figure 6 symbolizes II 587
found at Troy II 101
four-footed cross II 546
initiation & II 558
kindles the sacred fire II 413n
Mackenzie on II 556n
macrocosmic motion II 99
Masonry & II 98, 100
meant "10,000 truths" II 585
π (pi) number of circle & I 90-1
placed on hearts of initiates II 586
Pramantha, Arani & II 101
seven, on crowns of serpent I 411
tau, Jaina cross & I 657
Thor's hammer or mjölnir II 99
Wan of Buddhist Mongols II 556
within circle I 5
Sweat-Born. *See also* Root-Races–2nd & 3rd
Commentary II 121, 164-6, 170, 180
corroboration fr Purānas II 174-5
evolution of II 131-4
hermaphrodites of 3rd race fr II 30
mānasa spurned the II 171
men born fr pores of parents II 68
most, animals destroyed in 4th race II 349
produced egg-born II 172, 197, 198
in Purānas, *Mahābhārata* II 182-3
second Bamian statue & II 340
second race as II 146, 148, 164, 173
second race fathers of II 116-17
third race was II 67-8, 131, 177, 198, 329
tilting of Earth's axis & II 329
transition fr, to oviparous II 177, 197
Ūrdhvasrotas were evolvers of I 456
Sweden
ancient records (runes) of II 346n
dolmens (gånggrifter) of II 752
has risen 200-600 ft II 787n
part of Lemuria, Atlantis II 402, 775
Plato's Atlantis (Rudbeck) II 402
Swedenborg, Emanuel
Adam a church II 42n
first races of men II 33n
great seer of past century II 797
human beings on other planets II 701-2

intuition re ancient ideas I 118 &n
truths of I 622
—— *Principia rerum . . .*
vortical theory of I 117, 118n, 623
Swiss Cattle
descended fr fossil oxen II 287
Switzerland
Neolithic lake-dwellers of II 716
reindeer portrait in grotto in II 717-18
Sword, Flaming, symbol of animal passions II 62
Sybil. *See* Sibyl
Sydyk. *See* Tsaddīq
Syene, walls of, reflected Sun at summer solstice I 209n
Sylla. *See* Sulla, Lucius C.
Sylphs (air elementals)
salamanders, etc, derided today I 606
Symbol(s). *See also* Myths, Symbology
ancient, adopted by Christians I 402-3
ancient use of I 466
Church Fathers disfigured II 98, 481-2
Confucian, & esoteric I 440-1
cosmic, astrological, religious I 229, 241
of cosmogenesis I 4-5
cruciform, of *Dii Termini* II 542
emblems &, compared I 305-6
esoteric meanings of I 443-5
exoteric, & creeds II 194
Fohat key to many I 673
heirloom fr Atlantis II 431
Hindu & Chaldean II 383
history contained in II 437
initiates' knowledge of II 439
Jews killed spirituality of II 459n
levels of I 407
many-faceted diamond I 305
many meanings to every I 359
Massey on importance of I 303-5
most, archaic I 320-1
occult II 335
Ophidian II 355
origin of, older than Egypt II 630 &n
phallicism reigns supreme in II 273
Pythagorean I 618-19
rationale of I 81
religion & esoteric hist in I 272-3, 307
Renan ignorant of pagan II 457
revelation of the godlike, (Carlyle) I 303
serpent a divine, not evil II 505
seven meanings to every I 363; II 22n, 335, 357, 538, 547, 584, 765
sources of error in I 119
of symbols II 547n

Talmudic Jews profaned II 471
of 3rd, 4th races II 30
universal language II 469
years of Patriarchs are II 426
Symbolik . . . . *See* Creuzer, G. Fr.
Symbology, Symbolism. *See also* Symbols
  Bible, Indian, Chald, Egy I 320-5
  Christian fr Heb, Heb fr Chald II 354
  discussed I 303-9
  fourth stage of, & generation I 36
  Hebrew-Egyptian I 308-9, 364n
  Hindu I 667
  history of world found in II 438
  interpretation of II 335
  kabbalistic II 457
  of marriage ceremony I 614-15n
  of Meru & Pātāla II 357
  Mosaic, became crude under Ezra I 319
  Mystery language or I 309; II 124
  & origin of evil II 274
  of Pentateuch & New Testament I 115n
  power of occult I 272
  representing abstractions I 615
  seven departments of I 305
  seven keys to universal I xxxviii, 310-11, 363;
    II 335
  spirit & value of II 469

of temple curtain I 125
Symposium. See Plato (*Banquet*)
Synagogue, influence in modern *Zohar* II 462
Syncellus, Georgius
  calls Eusebius a forger I xxvi
Synchronistic Tables
  of Abydos II 367
  of Manetho & Eusebius I xxvi; II 368, 392,
    692-3
Synesius, initiated into Mysteries I xliv
Synodical Month, Saroses I 655n
Synoptics (1st 3 Gospels)
  Egyptian & pagan symbols in I 384
Synya. *See* Śūnya
Syria(ns)
  acquainted w Indian figures I 361
  egg symbol among I 359
  esoteric school in I xxiii
  gods of I 435; II 42n, 43
  initiates of II 558
  Nabatheans came to, fr Basra II 455
  seven lower & 7 higher worlds of I 435-6
Syrianus, on Plato (q Thomas Taylor) II 599
Système nouveau. See Leibniz, G. W.
System of Logic. See Mill, J. S.
Systolic & Diastolic, property of universe II 43

T

Taaroa (Tahitian Creator) II 194
Tabernacle
    curtain hiding, explained I 125
    of man designed for a god II 302, 420
    of Moses identical w Egy I 125, 347n, 391
    priests of, & revelation II 455
    Solomon's Temple based on I 314-15
    square form & Cardinal pts I 125, 347n
    symbol based on Great Pyramid I 314-15
Tables. *See* Diagrams
Tables of Stone of Moses II 530
Tablets. *See* Babylonian, Chaldean
Tabor. *See* Faber, G. S.
Tabula Smaragdina II 109. *See Divine Py-
    mander*, Smaragdine Tablet
Tad (Skt) That. *See* Tat
Tadpole, foetus assumes shape of II 188
T'Agathon. *See* Agathon
Tahiti(an)
    creation of man fr dust II 193-4 &n
    legends of Pacific continent II 223-4, 788
    taller than average II 332
Tahmurath [Teimūraz] (Pers)
    legend of II 397-9
Taht [Taat]-Esmun (Egy) Moon-god
    eighth sphere or I 227n
    seven souls of I 227n; II 633
al-Taifāshī, Ahmad ibn Yūsuf
—— *Book of the Various Names of the Nile* . . .
    on the nature of Seth II 366
Tail(s)
    in caduceus I 549
    of comet I 203, 504, 606
    dragon's, or moon's nodes I 403
    Great Dragon's II 351, 484-5
    in human foetus II 685
    peacock's, or sidereal heavens II 619
    rudimentary, of man II 681
    serpent swallowing I 65, 74, 253n, 291, 642;
        II 504-5
Taimuraz. *See* Tahmurath
Taine, H. A., *History of English Literature*
    antiquity of civilization II 334
Tairyagyonya or Tiryaksrotas (Skt) Animal
    Creation
    archebiosis begins in I 455

both primary & secondary I 455n
creation of animals & monsters II 162
fifth or sacred animal creation I 446, 455-6
Tait, P. G. *See* Stewart &; *also* Thomson &
*Taittirīya Brāhmaṇa. See also Aitareya Brāh-
    maṇa*
    asuras fr Brahmā-Prajāpati (*Aitarêya* in tx)
        II 500
    Kāma son of dharma II 176
Taittirīya Upanishad
    intelligence, ether, air, elements I 330
Taka-mi-musubi-no-kami (Jap)
    offspring of Heaven & Earth I 214
Talbot, M. G.
    Bamian statues pre-Buddhist II 339
Tales of Derbent
    Simorgh & the good Khalif II 397
Taley [Dalai] (Tib) II 502n. *See* Dalai Lama
Taliesin (Cymric Bard), serpent, Druid II 380
Talisman(s)
    porcelain, (Mackey) II 436
    preparation of, (Nabatheans) II 455n
    primitive cross II 557, 588
    serpent I 410
Tallies (Nallies in tx)
    show writing among early men II 729
Talmud
    age of II 454
    Angel of Death is Satan II 385
    axiom fr II 118
    degraded Jewish symbols II 459n, 618
    describes Lilith as charming II 262
    dragon Prince of Waters in II 505
    forbids cursing Adversary II 477-8
    highest deity not a creator I 439 &n
    Lord rebuking Satan II 478 &n
    Macro-, Microprosopus I 350
    Mikael, Prince of Water I 459; II 505
    Paul (Saul) "little one" II 504
    St Michael called God II 478
    Samael, serpent, demon I 417
    Satan, Samael, evil spirit II 388
    spurned by Sadducees I 320-1n
    thaumaturgists mentioned I xliiin
Talmudic Jews, Talmudists
    altered Jewish faith I 320

lost rounds, races teaching II 618
Midrashīm &, differ re Enoch II 532
non-initiated II 618
profaned nature's symbols II 471
Tam (Tamil), same as Thomas, Athamas II 135
Tamas, Tāmasa (Skt) darkness, inertia
dullness, insensibility I 330
Hindus called elements I 332
one of the trigunas I 348
sattva, rajas & I 535
spiritual darkness I 373
stagnant I 335n
Tāmasa (Skt, Thamasa in tx), a Manu II 309
Tamaz [or Athamaz]
same as Adam Kadmon II 44
Tamial [Tamiel]
taught astronomy (*Enoch*) II 376
Tamil
edition of *Bagavadam* [*Bhāgavata Purāṇa*]
II 620
works on Atlantis, Lemuria II 326
Tamil Calendar, *Tirukkaṇḍa Pañchāṅga* II 51n,
67-70
Tāmrā (Skt), wife of Kaśyapa II 181
Tamtu (Assyr, Damti in tx) the sea
Belita, Eve or II 463
Tanais River [now the Don] II 773
Taṇhā (Pāli) thirst for life
of lower, personal selves II 109-10
Tanjur (Tib Buddhist canon)
225 volumes of I xxvii
Tanmātras (Skt) rudimentary elements
five, Mahat & ahankāra I 256n, 335; II 639
noumenoi of elements I 536n, 572n
rays of the Logos I 572n
rejected by Hopkins I 334
release from, leads to highest goal I 572
in Sāṅkhya I 335
Second Creation & I 452, 454
Tannaim (Heb), initiated teachers I 202; II 469
Tantalus (Gk)
revealed secrets, punished II 396
Tantrik[c] (Skt), five makaras II 579
Tāntrika(s) (Skt)
of Bengal & Moon I 156
mahāvidyā now degenerated into I 169
Tao (Gnostic). *See* Iaō
Taoists
seven jewels of I 173
used circles as symbols II 554
Tao-sse. *See also* Lao-tzŭ
sacred scriptures of I xxv
Tao-teh-ching. See Lao-tzŭ

Tapas (Skt) heat, devout exercises
Sañjñā practiced II 174
Taphos (Gk) tomb, placed in adytum II 459
Tapirs, prehistoric bones of, in France II 277
Tapo-Loka [Taparloka] (Skt)
1 of 7 dvīpas II 321
Tārā, or Tārakā (Skt)
Budha son of II 45, 138, 456, 498
"Helen of Hindus," causes war II 498-9
initiation of, by Soma II 499
prefers esoteric truths II 45n
War explained II 497-500
wife of Brihaspati II 45, 138
Tāradaitya (Skt)
demon II 404
lived on 7th stage II 407n
white devil of Purānas II 403
Tāraka (Skt)
demon & his austerities II 382 &n
slain by Kārttikeya II 382-3, 549n, 619
Tāraka-Jit (Skt) title of Kārttikeya
vanquisher of Tāraka II 382, 619
Tārakāmaya (Skt)
War in Heaven I 418; II 45, 63, 384n
Tāraka Rāja-Yoga (Skt)
division of man's principles I 157-8
three upādhis enough for II 592-3n, 603
Tārāmaya. *See* Tārakāmaya
Tāraṇa (Skt), Hindu year 1887 II 68
[Tardy, Joseph], *Cosmographie . . .*
could the Earth fall I 502
Targum of Jonathan
King of Ai crucified II 558
Targum of Onkelos
crucified against the Sun II 558
Tarija (Ecuador)
giants of, warred w gods & men II 754
Tarim (Turkestan desert)
once many cities in I xxivn, xxxii
subterranean libraries in I xxivn
Tartars [or Tatars], astron tables of I 658-9
Tartarus (Gk) lowest hell. *See also* Hades
Atlas legend & II 762
imprisoned giants in II 776
Prometheus hurled into II 525
Tashi (Panchen) Lama (Tib, Teschu in tx)
Chenresi incarnates in II 178
incarnation of Amitābha I 471
Tasmania(ns)
became sterile II 196
descend fr Lemuro-Atlanteans II 195,
195-6n
lost continent fr India to II 221, 324
now extinct II 332

race apart (Broca, Virey) II 725
Taste I 96, 251, 535-6. *See also* Senses
related to senses & elements II 107
Tat, Tad (Skt) That. *See also* Boundless,
Kalahaṅsa, Parabrahman, That
all that is, was, or will be I 545
unrevealed abstract Deity I 77
Tat (Egy). *See also* Thoth
Apophis bound on, or tau II 588n
emblem of stability II 557
Seth, Thoth (Hermes), or II 380, 530
Tathāgata (Skt) "thus gone," epithet of Buddha
Lord, & Bamian statues II 339
Tatoo [Tattu] (Egy), erection of Tat in II 588n
Tattva(s) (Skt) principles of matter
five, 6, 7 elements II 574
Mahat-, creation I 446, 450-2
Tau, Tau Cross (Egy)
borrowed by Christians I xli
called γαιήιος (Gaiēios), son of Earth
II 591n
closed Jewish alphabet II 581
couch in form of II 558-9, 573
cube unfolded becomes I 321; II 542, 600n
desc & explained I 5; II 546-8, 557, 581
Egyptian II 30, 36, 542, 557
formed fr figure "7" II 590-1
found at Palenque II 557
initiation connected w II 543, 558
Inman & Knight degrade I 405
Jaina, Christian &, same I 657
mahāyogi w Ru on II 548
phallic symbol II 214, 542
stands for androgynous man II 30
stands for generation I 365
supports Egyptian egg I 364n
or Tat II 588n
three & 4 in I 321
Tau-ists. *See* Taoists
Tauris [in Crimea]
human sacrifice to Artemis in I 395
Taurus (constellation)
Aldebaran looks down fr eye of II 785
Aleph of, & Christ I 656-7
Eridu & Sun in II 693
eye of, & beg of kali-yuga I 663, 665
in Issachar I 651
Pleiades in neck of II 551
sacred in every cosmogony I 657
Sun-gods connected I 656
Sun in, understood by Druids II 759
symbol of II 551
when vertical to Atlantis II 407-8

Taurus Draconem . . . II 133
Taut. *See* Thoth
Taygetē (Gk) a Pleiad, daughter of Atlas II 768
Taylor, Thomas. *See also* Plato
knew less Greek but more Plato I 453n
most intuitional Gk translator I 425
—— "Introduction" to *The Parmenides*
"Chaos was generated" (Hesiod) I 425n
the One never creates I 425-6
—— *The Mystical Hymns of Orpheus*
on nature of Dionysos I 335
—— "On The First Principle"
Jew's concept of artificer of univ I 426n
—— *On the Theology of Plato* [by Proclus]
ref to, by Oliver on Tetrad II 599
Tchandalas. *See* Chaṇḍālas
Tchan-gy. *See* Chan-chi
Tchengis-Khan. *See* Genghis Khan
Tcheou. *See* Chou
Tchertchen. *See* Cherchen
Tchoon-Tsieoo. See Ch'un Ch'iu
Tchy-yeoo. *See* Khih Yu
Teachers I 159-60. *See also* Adepts, Initiates,
Mahatma Letters, Masters
HPB had Sinnett's letters fr I 187
on cometary matter I 597
forbidden to speak on some subjects
I 163-5
inhabit Snowy Range I 271
Mahāguru guides I 208
various names for I 271n
Teachings. *See also* Occultism
qualifications for secret I 164
Rig-Veda corroborates occult II 606
SD, old as the world II 449
Teakwood, Babylonians used, fr India II 226
Teapy[i]. *See* Easter Island
Tectum (Lat) roof, Ragon on tau & II 581
Tefnant [Tefnut] (Egy)
inhabits devachan II 374n
Tehung & Lhy [Li] (Chin)
two lower dhyāni-chohans II 280-1
Teimūraz. *See* Tahmurath
Telang, Kashināth Trimbak
on *Anugītā* II 566n
Buddhism not taught in *Gītā* I 419n
on fire symbol in Vedas II 567
Gītā passage puzzles I 86
on life-winds II 567-8
meanings of sattva I 68-9 &n
transl *Anugītā* II 496n
Telchines, Kabiri, Titans, Atlanteans II 391
Telepathic Impacts
science now considers II 156

Telescopes
  cannot see outside matter world I 166-7
Telesphoros (Gk) bringing to fulfillment
  name for heptagon II 602
Tell, Wm., some say, never existed II 761
Tel-loh
  monuments at, 4000 BC II 226, 691-2
Temperature
  differs on other planets I 142
  theories of solar I 484n
Templars, serpent symbol of Christ w I 472
Temple(s). *See also* Initiations, Pyramids, Temple of Solomon
  body of man is a I 212, 327, 574n; II 470, 651
  bulls in old Hindu II 418n
  curtains in ancient I 125, 462; II 459
  Dracontian, grandeur of II 380
  gods are, of God I 578
  -libraries II 529
  planetary, in Babylon II 456
  rock-cut, of India I 126
  sacred to Sun, dragon II 378-9
  in universe & in us II 651
  Vitruvius gives rules for Greek I 209n
Temple, Bishop Frederick
  —— *The Relations between Rel. & Sci.*
  "primal impress" of Logos II 24, 645
  supported Darwinism II 645
Temple de Jerusalem. See Villalpand, J.-B.
Temple of Pachacamac (Peru) II 317
Temple of Solomon II 233. *See also* Solomon
  based on pyramid symbolism I 115n, 314-15
  Holy of Holies of I 391
  left pillar of, or Boaz II 461
  like that of Hiram II 541
  Masonry &, (Ragon) II 795
  measurements of, universal II 465, 543
  never had any real existence I 314
  planets, elements, zodiac I 395
Temptation
  of flesh in Eden I 383
  two kinds of, defined I 414
Tempter. *See also* Jehovah, Naḥāsh, Rākshasas,
  Satan
  in Garden of Eden I 383, 422; II 387
  mind is redeemer & II 513
  Zeus as the II 419
Temurah, T'murah [Temūrāh] (Heb)
  interchange of Hebrew letters, I 78, 90n; II
  40
Ten. *See also* Decad
  born fr matter, chaos, female I 90n
  described & explained I 94-6, 392; II 581
  double womb I 391-2

dual, 1 & circle I 94, 391, 398
  esoteric in India I 360
  esoteric rendering of I 433
  five &, sign of Makara I 221
  four, 7 & II 603
  full number of Sephīrōthal Tree II 595
  Jehovah, androgyne or II 416n
  Jod is, male & female I 347; II 126n, 574
  mother of the soul (Hermes) I 90n
  number of all human knowledge I 36
  one & 9 or I 98 &n
  part of sacerdotal language I 362
  perfect number I 98n; II 564, 573
  phallic number I 391; II 463
  Pythagorean decad I 36; II 553, 573, 603
  seven proceeds fr II 573
  three plus 7 or I 98n, 427
  three plus 3 & 4 or II 564, 603
  twelve & II 36
  universal only w Ain-sōph II 596
  universe contained within I 94, 360-1, 427;
    II 573
Ten-brel chug-nyi (Tib) I 38n. *See* Nidānas
Tenerife (Mt)
  Asburj & II 408
  Atlantis & II 727, 791
  once 3 times higher II 763
  relic of 2 lost continents II 763
  Sun sets at foot of II 407
Tennyson, Alfred, *The Idylls of the King*
  temptation of Merlin II 175n
Ten-shoko-daijin [or Ten-Sho-Dai-Jiu] (Jap)
  1st of 5 gods (races) of Earth I 241
Tephireth. *See* Tiphereth
Terāphīm (Heb) nourisher, oracle
  mode of divination II 455
  Seldenus describes I 394
Tereti, power of Chald gods II 283-4n
Termini (Lat) II 542
Terminus & Tectum (Lat)
  Ragon on tau & II 581
Ternary
  animals are, only II 575
  divine creation & II 128
  spiritual & physical man are II 575
  symbol of 3rd life I 384
  three spirits or II 576
  triangle & I 616
Terra (Lat), Gaia (Gk) Earth-goddess
  Cyclopes sons of, by Coelus II 769
Terra del Fuego. *See* Tierra del Fuego
Terrestrial. *See also* Cataclysms, Earth, Sub-
  stance
  cosmic &, forces I 205, 291, 554, 594, 604

laws begin w physicalization II 736
life no gauge for stellar life II 703, 707
Tertiary Age II 688n. *See also* Mesozoic, Pri-
    mary Age, Secondary Age, Quaternary
    Age
age & size of animals II 733
Atlantean apex & destruction II 710
axis change began early in II 314
beginning of II 751
brilliant civilization in II 679
Croll's figures re II 10 &n, 685, 715n
endured 5-10 million years (Laing) II 676
flora in II 727, 790
Lemuria perished before II 313, 433n
mammals appear in II 258
man & ape date back to I 190; II 87n
man existed before II 206, 288, 751
man fr ape in late, (Haeckel) II 680
man lived in II 56n, 155, 751
NE Asia, America united in II 322n
pre-, giant man in II 9
rocks of, 5,000 ft thick II 709
science on man in II 288, 713-15 &nn
term Age of Mammals misleading II 713n
uncertainty as to periods of II 10-11, 693-5
Tertullian
Devil "Monkey of God" II 476
existence of, some doubt II 278 &n
—— *On Baptism*
great fish saves many fishes II 313n
—— *On the Resurrection . . .*
giant skeletons in Carthage II 278
—— *The Prescription against Heretics*
Basilidean teachings I 350
World Holders, Dominations I 331
Teshu, Teschu Lama. *See* Tashi Lama
Teth. *See* Set, Thoth
Teth (9th letter of Hebrew alphabet) I 76
Tethys (Gk) wife of Oceanus
is & is not Gaia or Earth II 65
magi &, [should be Thetis] I 467
Tetrachord
in ancient musical notation II 600
Tetractis. *See* Tetraktys
Tetrad. *See also* Four, Tetraktys
animal of Plato, (Thomas Taylor) II 599
four elements & I 448
Microprosopus is, male-female II 626
root of all things (Plutarch) II 601
Supreme, appears to Marcus I 351-2
unfolded makes hebdomad II 599
Tetragram
interpreted II 128-9
Isis Unveiled on II 557

Tetragrammaton (YHVH)
Adam Kadmon or I 99n; II 596
Ancient of Days becomes I 60
androgynous I 72 &n
cherubs (2) on sides of II 361n
equivalents in other faiths II 601, 625
esoteric interpretation II 601, 625-6
firstborn I 344; II 25
four letters of I 438n; II 57n, 312n, 625n
head of 7 lower sephīrōth I 344, 438n
"Heavenly Man" or II 25, 625n
host of builders I 344
invented to mislead profane I 438
is Jehovah I 618; II 601
Jah-Noah was II 596
Logos in Kabbala I 99n
Malkuth bride of I 240
manifested kosmos II 24
Microprosopus or I 240
Ophis & I 73n
Protogonos or II 25
secondary perfection II 582
Second Logos II 599
Sephīrōthal Tree II 625n
seven, essence of II 626, 628
six-pointed star & I 215
Tetraktys & II 312n, 463 &n, 599, 621
triangle, Tetraktys & II 312n
two of, discussed II 626
universe emanates fr II 625n
YHVH or I 438n, 618
Tetraktys (Pythagorean) I 616
dhyāni-chohans & I 197
eternal in essence only I 88
four or sacred square I 89n, 134n
heptagon & II 598-602
lower, root of illusion II 599
Macroprosopus in circle II 626
musical notations & II 600
mystery of I 344
oath on the II 603
Reuchlin on unfolding of II 601
Second Logos II 599
self-existent one or I 88
symbolizes the sephīrōth II 111 &n
symbol of man II 36
Tetragrammaton II 312n, 463 &n, 599, 621
three becomes II 621
triad becomes I 60, 99
triangle in square II 24
triangle, quaternary & I 614; II 582
Teut, Egyptian 4-letter god II 602
Teutobochus (Teutonic chief)
spurious bones of, found II 277

Teutonic Peoples, & giants II 754
Text-book of Physiology. See Foster, M.
T.G.A.O.T.U. (Masonic) The Great Architect
  of the Universe I 613
Thābit ibn Qurrah (Thebith in tx)
  oscillatory theory of I 664
Thackeray, Wm. M., soul part eternal II 424
Thaingen Grotto (Switzerland)
  reindeer portrait in II 717-18, 720
Thalamencephalon (interbrain)
  in Quain's *Anatomy* II 297
Thalami, Optic. *See also* Third Eye
  pineal gland & II 297-8, 301
Thalassa (Gk). *See also* Thalatth
  deep sea, Moon II 115
  Greek goddess II 65n
Thalatth (Chald). *See also* Thalassa
  Bīnāh, Elohīm, Tiamāt or I 394
  Chaldean feminine element I 394; II 54, 115
  gave birth to sea monsters II 65n
  sea dragon, Satan II 61
  signifies beginning of creation II 135
Thales (Gk philosopher) I 330
  universe evolved fr water I 77, 345 &n, 385
  on water element I 385; II 591n
Thalia. See Herodotus
Thamasa. *See* Tāmasa
Thammuz [Akkadian Tammuz, Sumerian
  Dumuzi]
  son, father, husband I 396
Thartharaoth, mule, Uriel & II 115n
That I 373-4. *See also* Ain Sōph, All, Boundless,
  Parabrahm, Sat
  the Absolute All II 158
  abstract Deity or I 77
  alone was I 445
  Be-ness, not a being II 310
  can never be at rest II 80
  cause of spirit & matter I 35
  First Cause & I 391n, 426
  golden womb & I 89
  illusory dual aspect of I 545
  is Non-being to finite beings I 7
  is the One Life I 258
  neither asleep nor awake II 310
  "One Prādhānika Brahma Spirit" I 256
  Parabrahman or I 7
  precedes manifestation I 450-1
  Rabbi Barahiel on I 618
  space & time as incognizable II 612
  "Thou art," or Brahman I 572
  unfathomable darkness I 77, 373-4
  of which all things are made I 371
Thaumaturgists

two mentioned by Franck I xliiin
Thavatth. *See* Thalatth
Thayngin Grotto. *See* Thaingen Grotto
Thebes, Theban (Egy)
  Ammon at I 367, 675
  catacombs of, described II 379
  heroes who fell at II 271
  now dated 7,000 years old II 750
  sacerdotal class conceptions I 311
  temple of Kabirim at II 363
  triad discussed II 464
Thebith. *See* Thābit
Θέειν (theein, Gk) to run
  theos, theoi derived fr (Plato) I 2n, 346;
  II 545
Theists I 147, 414, 421, 634
Themis (Gk)
  kept man within nature's limits II 305n
Thenay, Miocene flints of II 740n, 748 &n
Theocritus, *Idylls*
  Castor & Pollux, dual man II 122 &n
Theodolinda, crucifix of II 587
Theodoret, *Quaest. xv in Exodum*
  Jehovah or Yahva (Samaritans) II 129, 465
Theodosius I 312
  Bossuet on II 485
Theogony(ies) II 147. *See also* Hesiod
  all, have divine rebels II 79, 94n
  beginning of I 231
  connected w zodiac I 652
  of creative gods a key I 424-45
  future, concealed in divine thought I 1
  Gk & Lat appropriated fr India II 143-4
  key of, re Moon not phallic I 390
  key to all II 23, 767
  key to symbols I 363
  manifest, begins w Brahmā-Vāch I 434
  metaphysics of, & elements II 359 &n
  old primitive II 248
Theogony. See Damascius
Theogony. See Hesiod
Theogony. See Mochus
Theoi (Gk). *See* Theos
Theologian(s)
  compress Hindu chronology I 654
  craft & deceit of I 423
  dated man 6,000 years old II 675
  degraded kumāras into Satan I 458
  distorted ancient ideas II 475-6
  Hindu genealogies & II 248
  slander Satan I 415
  symbols confused by II 476
  take everything on blind faith I 669
  took God, angels, Satan fr pagans II 475-6

Theological
  historical facts become, dogmas II 776
  religions stand for dead letter II 377
Theology
  absurd fictions of materialistic II 149
  anthropomorphism of I 3n
  antiquity of man & I 323; II 194-5
  astronomy &, linked I 320
  biblical II 9, 194-5
  Christian, enforces belief I 287
  cruel & pernicious dogma II 231
  dead-letter sense of II 94n, 95n
  disfigures truth II 451
  distortions of Christian I 414-15, 417, 458;
    II 475-6, 485
  dogmas of, based in fact II 776
  dogmatic assertions of II 349
  every, sprang fr Mystery language I 310
  followed twisted paganism II 507
  materialism & I 323
  materialistic II 149
  occultism differs fr II 449
  rejected doctrine of emanations II 41
  sees every occultist as evil II 70
  western, holds copyright to Satan II 231-2
Theon (of Smyrna)
—— *Mathematics Useful for . . . Plato*
  Pythagorean musical canon II 600
Theophanē (Gk)
  Poseidon as a ram deceived II 775
Theophania (Gk)
  & astrological magic I 652
Theophilus, & cruciform couches II 559
Theophrastus II 760. *See also* Theopompus
—— *De Ventis* (Weather Signs)
  Moon a feebler Sun II 124n
Theopompus of Chios, *Meropis*
  on Atlantis [q by Aelianus] II 371, 760, 764
"Theorie der Materie, Die." *See* Wundt
Théorie du monde. See Huygens, C.
Théorie mécanique . . . See Hirn
Theory(ies)
  anthropology & geology II 71-2
  can never excommunicate fact II 715n
  given out as facts II 662-3
  short-lived, one-sided I 637
  speculation, not law II 665
"Theory of a Nervous Ether." *See* Richardson
Theos, Theoi (Gk) God, gods I 288n
  chaos-, -kosmos I 342-9
  derivation of, (Plato) I 2n, 346; II 545
  evolves out of chaos I 344
  four-letter god II 602
  messengers of the law I 346

planets are I 2n
Plato's conception of II 554
Theosophical Publication Society [*Theosophical Siftings*]
  Moore on Keely's work I 560-1
Theosophical Society
  first rule of I 296
  interlaced triangles & II 591-2
  motto of I xli; II 798
  mysteries of spiritual procreation & II 415
Theosophist(s)
  arraigned by public opinion I 298
  Brahman 7-fold classification & II 641
  God no-being, no-thing to I 352
  Massey vs II 630-1 &nn
  no true, claims infallibility II 640
  q on avenging angel I 644
  reception of *SD* volumes (I & II) II 798
  recognize value of science I 296
  some, transl karma as nemesis II 305n
  take nothing on trust I 669
  taxed w insanity I 676
Theosophist, The I 306, 570n
  HPB on higher states of matter I 560
  HPB on manus II 307-10
  HPB on Pacific Lemuria II 788-9
  on *Esoteric Buddhism* I xviii
  Figanière article II 289n, 290
  Mitford on War in Heaven II 244-5 &n
  Row, B. P. S. on yugas II 69-70
  Row, T. S., *Notes on Gita* I 10n, 428; II 25n,
    90, 140n, 318n
  Row, T. S. on cosmic vital principle II 311n
  Row, T. S. on evolution of elements I 620-1
  Row, T. S. on forces of nature I 292-3
  Row, T. S. on history of creation I 269
  Row, T. S. on mūlaprakriti I 10n
  Row, T. S. on 7-fold man I 157-8
  Row, T. S. on 7-fold nature II 635-6
  Śankara on Īśvara, ātma I 573-4
  Wilder on bisexuality II 133-4
Theosophy. *See also* Esoteric, Occult, Secret
    Doctrine
  essence of Buddhistic, (King) I 668
  not limited to Buddhism I xvii
  Pember on II 229n
Thera (Isle of), giant remains on II 278-9
Theraphim. *See* Terāphīm
Thermochemie [*Grundriss der*]. *See* Naumann
Thermuthis (Egy)
  crown formed of an asp II 26n
Thesmophoriazusae. See Aristophanes
2 Thessalonians
  Lord (Christos) as flaming fire I 87

Thessaly
  deluge of, confused w Atlantis II 776
  sorcerers of, called down Moon II 762
  witches of, & Moon I 156
Thetis (Gk, Tethys in tx), sea deity
  Xerxes' Magi sacrificed to I 467
Theurgist(s). *See also* Alchemy, Neoplatonists,
    Paracelsus
  Emperor Julian on II 35
  Fire & the Magi I 81n
  "living fire" of I 311, 338, 344
Thevetat, evil Atlantean king II 222
Thierry, Augustin, *Revue des deux mondes*
  legends as history I 675-6; II 182
"Thieves, all . . . before me are" [*John* 10:8]
    II 482
Third Creation. *See* Indriya Creation
Third Eye. *See also* Dangma, Pineal Gland,
    Śiva-Eye
  acted no longer II 227, 271, 288
  active into Atlantean times II 306
  ascetic must acquire II 615
  ascribed to early man I 46n
  atrophied II 294-5 &n, 302, 306
  atrophy of, & Ulysses-Polyphemus II 769
  connected w karma II 302
  embraces eternity II 298-9n
  expands during visions II 294
  Eye of Śiva I 46n; II 284, 295
  holy Atlantean sorcerers & II 350
  laid aside for future use II 299
  location of II 294 &n
  loss of, evolution not Fall II 302
  many animals have atrophied II 296
  odd, primeval, or Cyclopean eye II 299
  originally seeing organ II 299 &n
  origin of II 295-302
  pineal gland relic of II 295
  retreated within II 294-5
  simple gland after Fall II 301
  Śiva's, is Egy Ru on Tau-cross II 548
  Śiva's, spiritual insight II 179
  spiritual intuition I 46n; II 299
  window, mirror of soul II 298
"Third Letter to Bentley." *See* Newton, I.
Third Logos. *See also* Amshaspends, Brahmā,
    First Logos, Jehovah, Logos, Prajāpatis,
    Second Logos
  Man regarded as II 25
Third Manvantara
  can mean 3rd root-race II 94
Third Race. *See* Root-Race–3rd
Third Round. *See* Round, Third
Third Stage of Cosmic Manifestation

all personal gods belong to I 437
ray separates into 7 Forces I 437-8
Third World (Yetsīrāh, *Zohar*)
  sephīrōth inhabit II 111
Thirteen, & 13 forms I 374-6
This, or manifested universe I 7
Thlinkithians, in *Popol Vuh* II 222
Thomas, or Adam, Athamas, Tam II 135
Thomas, Prof
  man has no connection w monkeys II 729
Thomas Aquinas I 582n
  prototypes of Michael were devils II 478
Thompson, Charles Wyville
—— "Geographical Distribution . . ."
  Old, New World fauna, flora II 792
Thompson, Prof S. P., strobic circles II 589
Thomson, Sir William
  age of vegetable kingdom II 154, 694
  ether continuous I 482
  incrusted age of world II 149n, 694
  life came via meteorites I 366n, 488; II 158,
    719
  man product of matter II 719
  nebular matter dark, cold I 505
  predicts death of universe I 552
  primitive fluid & chaos I 579
  tidal action of II 64
—— "On the Dynamical Theory of Heat"
  life span of Sun I 501; II 149n, 258n
—— "On Geological Time"
  age of Earth 400 million yrs II 258
—— "On Vortex Atoms"
  vortical atoms I 117, 488, 492, 579
—— *Philosophical Magazine* (article in)
  perfect elasticity of atoms I 513-14
Thomson, Sir Wm. & P. G. Tait
—— *Treatise on Natural Philosophy*
  age of Earth & Sun II 10n
  cooling of Earth I 501 &n; II 694
  matter resists outside influence I 485n
Thor (Norse)
  four-footed cross weapon of II 546, 588
  swastika, mjölnir, hammer, & I 5; II 99, 588
Thorah. *See* Torah
Thor's Hammer. *See also* Mjölnir
  fylfot II 546
  genesis of II 99, 588
  sparks fr, become worlds II 99
  swastika in circle I 5
Thot[h] (Egy) Hermes. *See also* Hermes, Mer-
    cury, Set, Thoth-Hermes
  authenticity of *Book of* II 506
  biblical Patriarch, (Bailly) I 648
  caduceus & II 364

chief of 7 planets (Gnostic) II 538n
divine instructor II 365
in earliest trinity II 462, 464
Edris became II 529
escaped fr Typhon I 362
explained II 267-8n
generic name of initiates II 210n, 267n
god of wisdom II 558
has retreat in Moon I 403
Horus, Set & II 283n
Ibis-headed god II 558
Ibis sacred to Mercury or I 362
invented Egyptian alphabet I 307; II 581
Khonsoo confused w II 464
Osiris &, initiate candidate II 558
scribe of Amenti I 385
Seth a Jewish travesty of II 380, 530
seven-rayed solar discus of II 529
sitting on lotus I 385
symbol of Virgin Mother I 403
Taut or, serpent symbol II 26n
various names of II 380, 529-30
Wednesday sacred to II 366-7
Thoth-Hāpi (Egy), Lord of Horizon I 674
Thoth-Hermes (Egy) I 353, 675; II 359, 540
Budha, Mercury or I xxxii
chief of the rectors I 577
generic name II 210n, 211, 267n
hides in Moon I 403
Osiris reappears as II 359
represents secret wisdom I 403
sacred volumes of I xliii
secretary to King Saturn I 459
Thoth-Lunus (Egy)
Budha-Soma, Mercury-Moon I 396n
Khonsoo becomes II 464
occult potencies of Moon I 396
septenary god of 7-day week II 529-30
Thotmes, Pharaoh
shown worshiping Hathor I 400
Thot-Sabaoth, bear in alchemistry II 115n
Thought(s). *See also* Divine Thought,
Ideations, Mind
Descartes on I 629
divine I 1 &n, 3, 16, 39, 44, 61, 64, 74, 325-41,
348; II 158, 488-9, 536-7, 649n
divine, becomes kosmos I 43
divine, or boundless darkness I 327
divine, or Logos I 58
exists eternally I 570
Fohat & I 108, 137n; II 649n
freedom of, in Upanishads I 270
ideas vs absolute II 490
impressed on astral I 93, 104; II 199n

infinite gradations of I 627
karma & I 644
kriyāśakti power of I 293; II 173
language & II 199n
nerve molecules & I 134n
passions stimulated by II 244
without phosphorus no II 244
product of molecular change I 124 &n
reflection of univ mind I 38, 280, 617
seven modes of II 335, 569n
subjective side of nervous motion I 124-5n
unrelated to intellection I 1n
Voltaire on what produces II 88-9
"Thought father to the wish" (Shak) I 413
Thought Transference
once common to mankind I 537; II 199
Thrace
fire (Kabiri) worship in II 363
Orphic priests of, & Druids II 756
Thraëtaona (Pers)
war betw, & Azhi-dahaka II 390
Thread
analogy the Ariadne's, to mysteries II 153
of immortal monadship II 513
of life I 222
of radiance II 80
betw Silent Watcher & shadow I 264
-soul or sūtrātman I 16-17n, 222, 236, 610
&n; II 79-80, 513
Three
becomes the Sacred Four II 621
-eyed man II 744
Father, Mother, Son I 58
first came, or triangle II 594
five, 7 &, in Masonry I 113n
four &, female & male I 321
four, 7 &, explained II 582-3
gamma or Gaia (Earth) II 583
higher grades of initiation I 206
male, spirit or I 36; II 592
seven & divine, or ten II 564
-tongued flame I 237
transformed into four I 58
Three Fires II 57n, 247
Three Fundamental Propositions I 14-20
Three in One
ātma-buddhi-manas II 113
higher triad II 595-6, 597n, 599
spirit, soul & mind II 113
Three New Propositions II 1-12
Three Strides (of Vishnu) II 38, 622n
body, soul & spirit or I 113 &n, 122
Thribhujam. *See* Tribhuja

Throne(s)
abode of pure spirits II 111
of the Almighty II 63
b'ne-aleim 10th subdivision of II 376
copy of ancient prototype I 92
Dominions & I 92, 435
firstborn, 1st to fall II 80
monad as the, (Masonic) I 613
Saturn governed by I 435
Thummīm. *See* Ūrīm & Thummīm
Thunder(s)
Jove, Agni, fire & I 462
seven of *Revelation* I 410; II 563, 565
Thursday, Jupiter's Day I 652
Thury, psychod & ectenic force of I 338n
Thyan-Kam (Tib)
power guiding cosmic energy I 635
was not, Stanza One I 23
Ti, China's demon who fell II 486
Tiahuanaco, ruins of II 317, 337
Tiamāt (Bab) sea dragon
Bīnāh, Elohīm, Thalatth I 394
chaos, sea, mother I 357
Ea disfigured into II 53, 61, 477, 503
female power I 394
female, womb II 104
slain by Merodach II 53, 503
spirit of chaos, Abyss II 104, 384
struggle of Bel w II 477
war betw gods & II 384
Tiaou (Egy) infernal region
conception, Osiris, Moon & I 227-8
Tibet, Tibetan(s). *See also* Dalai Lamas, Tashi
Lamas
ancient civilizations in I xxxii
Buddhism declined in I xxi
Chenresi protector of II 178
dorjesempa, mahātma, etc I 52 &n
esoteric schools I xxiii
high tablelands once submerged II 608-9
Kwan-yin patron deity of I 72, 471
Lhassa, derivation of II 63
Little, or Baltistan II 204, 416n
meaning of Dalai Lama II 502n
Od of von Reichenbach a, word I 76n
Russian mystics traveled to I xxxvi
sea in Lemurian times II 324
seat of occult learning I 271n
seventh subrace, 4th root-race II 178
square form of tabernacle & I 125
swastikas on hearts of, buddhas II 586
tradition of White Island II 408n
Zampun, mystical tree of II 97
Tidal Waves, due to Moon, planets II 699

Tides(al)
axial changes & II 52, 64, 325
effect on Earth life II 595
influence on continents II 325
Moon & the I 180; II 669, 699
physical cause of I 292n
T'ien (Chin) sky
dropped egg (man) into waters I 366
first teacher of astronomy II 766
heaven or I 356
T'ien-hoang [huang] (Chin)
kings of Heaven II 368
twelve hierarchies of dhyānis II 26-7
Tien-Sin [T'ien-hsin] (Chin)
"Heaven of Mind" I 139
Tierra del Fuego
portion of sunken continent II 789
Ti-hoang [huang] (Chin)
kings on Earth II 368
Tikkoun, Tikkun [Tīqqūn] (Aram)
firstborn, Protogonos, idea II 25
not yet mirrored in chaos II 704n
Timaeus. See Plato
Timaeus, Commentary on. See Proclus
Timaeus the Locrian, on Arka II 463n
Timaus, alleged cradle of humanity II 204
Time. *See also* Chronos, Duration, Kāla,
Kronos
Absolute above space & I 1-2n; II 158
abstraction of deity (Coleridge) I 645
always part of larger increment I 87-8
aspect of Ain-sōph I 350
aspect of Brahmā I 19
Bain on, & space I 251n
based on number seven I 408
beginning of, in *Book of Concealed Mystery*
I 239
best test of truth (Laing) II 662
boundless circle of I 113-14; II 233, 488, 549
Chium (Egy) god of II 390n
described I 36-7, 43-4
duration & I 37, 43-4, 62
eats up works of man (Haggard) II 317n
eternity brought forth II 233
eternity is, whose ends are not known I 354n
evolution of I 407
fire deity presides over I 86
form of Vishnu II 307n
genesis: coming out of eternal into II 24n
Goethe on I 83
good & evil progeny of, & space II 96
Great Bear mother of, (Egy) I 227n; II 631
infinite, or Kāla I 407
Kronos beyond divided, & space I 418

Kronos or II 142 &nn, 341n, 420
limitless, in eternity & circle I 113
man is the "Eternal Pilgrim" in space &
    II 728
a Master's words on I 44
measures of, were secret II 396
Moon as cycle of II 464
nature, man &, (Cicero) II 451
never-erring measures of II 621
no, without consciousness I 37, 43-4
Old, of Greeks w scythe I 459
origin of, -periods w ancients I 389 &n
Ormazd firstborn in boundless II 488
perception of, is one of first occupations
    I 389-90
pitiless devourer of events II 743
prakriti, spirit & I 545
rishis mark, of kali yuga II 550
Rudra-Śiva god of II 502n
St Michael a son of, or Kronos I 459
Saturn or II 341n
secondary creation born in & out of I 427
septenary cycles of I 392
serpent symbolizes II 756
Śesha or infinite II 49
seven rishis mark II 549
space &, are one II 612
space &, forms of incognizable Deity
    II 382n
space &, forms of THAT II 158
space &, infinite, eternal II 154
succession of conscious states I 37, 44
swastika & cycles of II 99
truth the daughter of II 571
Vishnu enters circle of II 549
"was not . . ." I 27, 36-7
will cease at end of 7th round II 565
Times, The (London)
    Max Müller on myth in, (Massey) I 303
    review of Laing's *Modern Science* I 669
Τίμιον (timion, Gk)
    reflection of Deity (Plato) II 555
Timoor [Timur or Tamerlane]
    hordes of II 338
Tiphereth (Heb)
    one of the sephīrōth I 200
    symbol of grand cycle II 214
Tiresias, Greek soothsayer II 381
Tīrthankaras (Skt) Jain adepts
    buddhas identical w II 423n
Tirukkaṇḍa Pañchāṅga, Tamil calendar for kali-
    yuga II 50-1 &n, 67-9, 551
Tirvalour [Tiravalur]
    Brahmans of, & Hindu epoch I 661-2, 666

Tiryaksrotas (Skt)
    monsters slain by Lords I 446; II 162
Tiryns (Greece)
    cyclopean structure at II 345n
Tisalat, Ea disfigured into II 61
Tishya (Skt), lunar asterism I 378
Tismat. *See* Tiamāt
Tit. *See also* Tityus
    the Deluge (Faber) II 361
Titaea, Titea, Tythea (Gk)
    bosom of Earth II 269
    mother of Titans (Diodorus) II 143
Tit-ain, Titan possibly derived fr II 142
Titan(s)
    Aletae, Kabiri or II 141-2 &n
    anthropological fact II 154
    Atlantes called II 360-1
    belong to 4th race II 293
    biblical giants I 416-18; II 70, 154, 236, 265,
        273-4, 390-1, 755, 775
    crucified, is Prometheus II 413
    daityas or II 501
    Dānavas or II 183, 501
    derived possibly fr Tit-Ain II 142
    divine, or Prometheus II 363, 411, 422
    dragons of wisdom & II 381
    fallen angels, not demons II 516
    fell into physical procreation II 766
    giants, mentally & physically I 416
    giants of ancient days II 154, 236, 775-7
    giants of *Genesis* II 236
    giants of Greece II 336
    gibborīm became II 273-4
    Hesiod's I 202, 418; II 63, 269-71 &n, 293,
        525, 777n
    Kabiri & II 142-3, 360, 363-4, 390
    man will rebecome the free II 422
    Michael a divine, (de Mirville) I 418
    Mt Atlas last form of divine II 493
    mutilated Uranos II 766
    Noah an Atlantean II 265, 390
    one of 3 dynasties II 369
    Orphic, Ephialtes II 70
    π (pi), circle & I 114
    Porphyrion the red II 383n
    -Prometheus rebelled against Zeus II 280n
    Purānic, called devils I 415
    real men, not mere symbols II 755
    rebelled against the gods II 525
    rebelled against Zeus II 776
    rebellious, were fallen angels II 525n
    Rhea mother of II 144, 269
    seven divine, or Kabirim II 141
    sons of Kronos II 142n

spiritual creators or II 422
Telchines or II 391
theologians link, w devil II 354
third race II 9
Titea mother of, (Diodorus) II 143-4
two types of, in Latin Church I 417-18
various names of I 114
Venus-Lucifer & II 31
War of the I 202; II 63, 269n, 493, 498, 500-1
Titanic Age, close of 1st, described II 411
Titanidae. *See also* Titans
  heptad, sevenfold (Proclus) I 446
Tit-an-Kabiri, or Manes II 144
Titanosaurus Montanus II 218
Tityos, Tityus (Gk), son of Earth II 591n
  or Tit-theus, divine deluge II 142
T'murah. *See* Temūrāh
Toad, man's saliva & venom of I 262n
Tod, Colonel James
—— [*Annals . . . of Rajast'han*]
  re name Morya I 378n
Todd, Prof James Edward
  oscillatory movements on earth II 325
Tohū-Bohū (Heb) without form & void
  the Deep of *Genesis* II 477
Tōledōth (Heb), generation II 134
"To live is to die, to die is to live" I 459n
Tolla. *See* Olla
Tollner. *See* Zöllner, Prof J. K. F.
Toltecs, Senzar known to forefathers of I xliii
Tomb(s). *See also* Dolmens
  contained ashes of giants II 753
  giant, of Sardinia II 352
  placed in adytum II 459
  Stonehenge & Carnac not II 754
Tones, 7, in music of spheres II 601
Tonga Island, relic of Lemuria II 223, 332
Tongshaktchi Sangye Songa (Tib MS)
  described II 423
  quoted II 424, 427-8
Tooke, William, "Some Account . . ." [*Sépulture des Tartares*]
  rocks not native II 343
To On (Gk) the One II 105, 113. *See also* On, Plato
Tò πᾶν (to pan, Gk) the All I 353-4
Topinard, Paul, *Anthropology*
  color of the races II 249n
Torah [Tōrāh] (Heb, Thorah in tx) law. *See also* Pentateuch
  allegory of heavy load I 393-4
  Zohar &, dogmatic II 462
Torpor, mental, of 1st two races II 181
Torquay, Kent's cavern in II 724

Torquemada, Tomás de II 70
Torricelli, Evangelista, vortices of I 623
Tors (West England)
  natural origin (geol) II 343
Tortoise. *See also* Kūrma, Śiśumāra
  Brahmā as II 75
  Kaśyapa means II 253
  mystery of I 441-2 &n
  sacred, of Confucianists I 441
  Vishnu as, -avatāra II 549
Totmes III (Egy), fragment fr hall of II 559
Touch I 96, 535. *See also* Senses
  ākāśa, sound, light, color & I 205
  procreation by II 176
  related to senses, elements II 107
  sparśa or, in pralaya (*VP*) I 372
Toum. *See* Tum
Tower of Babel. *See* Babel, Tower of
Tower of Bhangulpore. *See* Bhangulpore
Toyāmbudhi (Skt) (Sea of)
  England identified w, (Wilford) II 402n
  northern parts of II 319
T.P.S. *See* Theosophical Publication Society
Traces de Bouddhisme en Norvège. See Holmboe
Tractates de Anima . . . . See Cordovero
Tradadhafshu. *See* Fradadhafshu
Tradition(s)
  ancient, convey truths II 224, 235, 410
  based on soul's memory II 424
  corroborated by esotericism I 646
  history &, are proofs II 336
  living II 351
  more reliable than history I 676; II 136-7, 349, 424
  myths are I 425; II 235
  proofs afforded by, rejected I 317
  prove prehistoric civ (Bailly) II 742-3
  unbroken, of sanctuaries II 443
  universal, safest guide II 349
  universal, scientific weight of II 136-7, 217, 340
  universal, supports occultism II 194
Tragos (Gk) goat, Azāzēl, *Genesis* & II 387
Traité de l'astronomie indienne . . . See Bailly
Trance
  on cruciform couch II 558-9
  initiate & 3 days' II 580
  samādhi or mystic II 569n
  seer & sushumna ray during I 515
  third eye active in II 294
Trans. of the Geol. Soc. of Glasgow. See Thomson, Sir Wm.
Trans. of the Royal Soc. of Edinburgh. See Thomson, Sir Wm.

Trans. of the Soc. of Biblical Archaeology. See
Smith, George
Transcendentalists, Hegel & German I 50
Trans-Himalayan. *See also* Cis-Himalayan
arhat esoteric school I 157
esoteric doctrine & 7 principles II 636
esotericism & Stanzas II 22n
Transmigration. *See also* Reincarnation
doctrine of I 261, 293, 440
gilgoulem [gilgūlīm] or I 568
of life-atoms II 671-2n
of souls & kundalinī-śakti I 293
"Transmigration of the Life Atoms." *See*
Blavatsky, H. P.
Träume eines Geistersehers. See Kant, I.
Treatise concerning The Principles of Human Knowledge. See Berkeley, G.
Treatise on Colour. See Newton, *Opticks*
Treatise on Electricity . . . . See Maxwell, J. C.
Treatise on Optics. See Brewster, D.
Tree(s). *See also* Aśvattha, Sephīrōthal Tree,
Yggdrasil
of Ahura Mazdā II 97
armies of Assyria called II 496
of Bodhi II 589
of evolution II 259n
ferns larger than California giant II 733
w golden fruit given Jupiter I 128-9n
have souls (Hinduism) I 454
initiates, sorcerers or II 494-6, 560
Jesus called, of Life II 496
Jewish, & cross-worship phallic II 588
meaning of, symb II 587-9
on Mt Meru, serpent guards I 128-9n
mundane I 211; II 259n
savage tribes live in II 676
serpent, crocodile &, worship I 403-11
seven, or senses, mind II 637-8
symbolize secret knowledge I 128n
withering, or left-path adepts II 496
"Tree is known by its fruit" (*Matt* 12:33) I 421
Tree of Being (Universe), triple seed of II 589
Tree of Eden I 114; II 97
initiates or II 494
Tree of Knowledge
Adam Kadmon II 4, 293
Adam tasted of, received intellect II 175
becomes Tree of Life II 587
dragons guard I 128-9n
esoteric or Secret Doctrine II 202
Eve, Juno, & fruit of I 128-9n
fourth race had tasted of II 134
fruits of, give life eternal II 588

of good & evil I 247; II 4, 124, 214-15, 293,
626n
fr India II 215
Metatron-Shekīnāh become II 215-16 &n
Ophis represents II 214-15
serpent, apple &, interpreted II 354-5
soma is fruit of II 499n
suffering generated under II 124
various II 215-16
Tree of Life. *See also* Aśvattha, Yggdrasil
Adam driven fr, expl II 216
Babylonian II 104
Christians borrowed I 410
described I 405-6; II 216-17
Ennoia represents II 214-15
glyph of immortal being I 406
on Gnostic gems II 458
initiate crucified on II 560
kabbalistic I 614
life known only by I 58-9
microcosmic in macrocosmic II 97
Persian, & androgynes II 134
roots of, in heaven I 406
serpent connected w I 405
symbol fr India II 215
Tree of Knowledge becomes II 587
various II 97
Venus sign & II 30-1
Tree of the Hesperides
golden apples of I 128-9n
Tree of Wisdom (Eden), eating fruit of II 272
Trees of Righteousness
initiates called, in Asia Minor II 494
Trent, Council of II 209
Tretā, Tretāgni (Skt)
sacred triad of fire I 523
Tretā-Yuga (Skt) II 308n. *See also* Dvāpara-
Yuga, Kali-Yuga, Satya-Yuga, Yugas
Brahmā sacrifices to open II 625n
length of II 69
occurs in Bhārata (Varsha) II 322
of 3rd race II 520n
Vishnu as Chakravartin in II 483
Triad(s). *See also* Pyramids, Sephīrōthal Triad,
Triangle
Agni, Vāyu, Sūrya (Vedic) I 90
Akkadian II 54
Aristotle's, misinterpretation I 615-18
arūpa I 213-14
becomes the Tetraktys I 60, 99
Chaldean II 26n
crocodile symb of human I 220 &n
diagram of I 242
emanates 7 other numbers I 427

Father, Mother, Son I 18
  female II 463
  first II 80
  firstborn, or O_2, N_2, H_2 I 623
  Gnostic I 351
  higher, emanates quaternary II 595
  higher, lower, & planets II 462
  immortal, spiritual I 237
  initial, manifested, creative I 278
  intelligible & intellectual II 599
  kabbalistic I 352, 354-5, 384
  lower, emanated by quaternary II 595
  monad evolves, & retires I 427, 573-4
  planetary I 574 &n
  Pythagorean I 440-1; II 599-600
  root of manifestation I 15, 18
  Theban, explained II 464
  three in one I 278
  Trimūrti or II 591
  upper Sephīrōthal I 130
  which disappears at death I 122n
Triangle(s)
  becomes Tetraktis I 60
  in a circle I 613-14
  circle, point & I 320-1
  cube, circle & I 612
  Deity is abstract, (occultism) I 19
  double, & races (IU) II 533
  double interlaced I 118; II 36, 533, 591-2
  equilateral, Parker on I 316
  Father-Mother-Son II 582
  fire in possession of II 79
  first came 3 or the II 594
  first of the geometric figures II 575
  first One or I 131
  Gnostic I 351
  kabbalistic I 354-5
  kosmic, explained I 614-15
  lower line of II 80
  manifested, & hidden Tetraktys II 312n
  marriage ceremony & I 614-15n
  mysterious 7 born fr upper II 574
  point becomes, & quaternary II 612
  pyramids & I 616-17
  Pythagorean I 612; II 24, 111n
  quaternary &, septenary man II 591-3
  quaternary, Tetraktys & I 614
  side lines of II 57
  space, matter, spirit II 612
  in the square II 36, 626
  symbol of Deity I 113n
  symbology of, (Ragon) II 575
  ten dots & 7 points I 612; II 111n
  vehicle of Deity II 582

Triassic Period
  marsupial fossils II 684
  third race & mammals in II 713
Tribe(s), Tribal
  cycles within national I 642
  every, exalts its deity II 507
  or karmic cycles I 642
  savage, live in trees II 676
Tribes of Israel
  disappeared during captivity II 130
  ten lost I 651; II 130
  two, Judah & Levi II 130
  zodiacal signs & I 400, 651; II 200n
Tribhuja (Skt), triangle II 576
Tri-bochana. See Trilochana
Tricephalos (Gk), 3-headed Mercury II 542
Tridaśa (Skt) thrice ten
  Vedic deities I 71n
Τριδυνάμεις (tridunameis, Gk) 3 Powers
  lower triad in *Pistis Sophia* II 462, 512
Trigonias, fossil shells II 196
Trigonocephalus (of Portugal)
  man's saliva & venom of I 262n
Trigram(s) (of Fo-He)
  ciphers known before II 554
Triguṇas (Skt) 3 qualities I 348. See also Rajas,
    Sattva, Tamas
Trilithic Raised Stones
  in Asia, Europe, Etruria, etc II 346n
Trilobites
  not result of gradual change II 697
  in oceans of Primary Age II 160
Trilochana (Skt) 3-eyed
  Rudra-Śiva called II 502n
  three-eyed II 295
Τρίμορφος (trimorphos, Gk) 3-formed
  Diana-Hecate-Luna I 387 &n
  three moon-phases or I 395
  various equivalents of I 396
Trimūrti (Skt) having 3 forms
  Brahmā, Śiva, Vishnu II 313
  hypostases of I 571
  Sephīrāh, Hokhmāh, Bīnāh is I 355
  Soma embodies triple power of I 398
  three kabbalistic heads or I 381
  triad or II 591
  Vedic, or Agni, Vāyu, Sūrya I 90
Trinité Chrétienne dévoilée. See Lizeray, H.
Trinity(ies). *See also* Logos, Triad, Trimūrti
  Christian, purely astronomical II 358, 540
  Diana-Hecate-Luna I 387
  double mystery of I 58
  dragon, 2nd person of II 355
  Egyptian II 462

esoteric & Christian I 18-19, 574n
Greek, Chaos-Gaia-Eros I 109
highest I 429-30
Hindu, Christian, & Brahmin forgery
    I xxxi &n
Kabbala on, (Skinner) II 38
kabbalistic I 337, 343, 346, 384, 447
kosmos emanated fr I 337
Kwan-yin & I 136
light, heat, moisture I 2-3
matter-force-chance I 505
Moon prototype of our I 387, 396
origin of Christian I 113n
perfect cube among Christians I 19
personal, of Christians II 236n
primordial cosmic II 107
Reuchlin on II 601
St Michael just below II 479
spirit, soul, & matter I 49
Sun, Mercury, Venus II 540
in *Tao-teh-ching* (Amyot) I 472
Theban II 464
three aspects of universe I 278
three steps of Vishnu & I 433n
triangle symbol of (occult) I 19
unified in supersensuous world I 614
unity & quaternary I 58-9
Voice-Spirit-Word or I 337
Trinity College (Cambridge) II 132
Trinosophists (Masonic order)
    founded by Ragon II 575
Tripartite, Earth is II 758
Tripiṭaka (Buddhist "Three Baskets") I xxxviii
Tripurāntaka Śiva (Skt)
    statue of, in India House II 591
Tripurāsura (Skt)
    Kārttikeya slayer of II 549n
    statue of Mahādeva destroying II 591
Trismegistus. See Hermes Trismegistos
Tristan da Cunha Island
    Atlantic ridge extends to II 333
Triśūla (Skt) trident of Śiva II 548-9
Trisuparṇa (Skt), Brahman whose forefathers
    drank Soma I 210; II 590
Triteye [Tṛitīya] (Skt)
    3 rajāṃsi or worlds II 621-2
Tritheim, Johannes, or Trithemius
    on astral light II 512n
—— *Concerning the Seven Secondaries*
    seven spiritual intelligences I 453n
Triton (Gk) son of Poseidon
    Man-Fish or Matsya avatāra II 578
Triune
    man, limiting influence of I 225-6

nature of differentiated substance I 614
Triyuga(m) (Skt) 3 ages
    plants came in, before the gods II 52n
Troad (region around Troy)
    fire (Kabiri) worship in II 363
Troglodyte (cave dweller)
    gap betw man &, (Huxley) II 315n
Trojan(s). *See also* Troy
    ancestors pure Āryans II 101
    origin of, religion II 796
    War closer to 6000 BC II 437n
Tropical Year II 76. *See also* Sidereal Year
    circle of, called serpent II 356
    length of, & 370 "leaps" II 505
    subraces & II 446
Tropic of Cancer
    Atala on same degree as II 403
Tropics(ical)
    Fohat & I 204
    Poles once had, climate II 11-12, 726
    recede 4 deg fr poles each sidereal year II 331
Troy
    end of, foretold by Ophite stone II 342
    founding of, interpreted II 796
    regarded as myth II 236, 440, 441
    Schliemann proved existence of II 236
    skeleton of giant killed at II 278
    swastika uncovered at II 101, 586
True Intellectual System. See Cudworth, R.
Trumholdt, Prof. *See* Humboldt, F. H. A. von
Truth(s). *See also* Paramārtha
    absolute I 48, 53
    always has its champions I 297
    ancient, disfigured II 515-16
    can never be killed I xl
    described as a woman I 352
    esoteric, never change I 312
    Four (Buddhist) I 45
    is the daughter of time II 571
    love it, aspire to it II 640
    Master unable to give whole I 168
    moral death to revealers of I 299
    no religion higher than I iii; II iii, 798
    not exclusive property of West I 279
    occult, tabooed I 297-8
    preserved thru initiation I xxxvi
    primeval, killed by dogma II 797
    relative I 48
    rests on facts II 711
    reticence concerning I 167
    satya age of II 146
    search for, endless II 640
    should be sole aim of science I 509
    spiritual, taught man I 267

there is no new I xxxvi-vii
time best test of, (Laing) II 662
of today, yesterday's falsehoods II 442
tradition based on II 264, 777
universal in antiquity I 285
visible to eye of seer xxxvi
Tsaba. *See* Tsebā'āh
Tsaddīq (Heb, Sadic, Sydic, Zedek in tx)
  Agruerus, Saturn are II 142 &n
  Kabiri, Titans, sons of II 142, 392
  Melchizedek, Father Sadik II 392
  Noah was II 391-2
Tsaidam, Western (China)
  hidden libraries in I xxiv
Tsan (Stanza) fraction I 140
Tsanagi-Tsanami [Isanagi-Isanami] (Jap) I 217, 241
Tsang (Tib), Alaya or I 48
Ts'an t'ung ch'i. See Wei Po-yang
Tsāphōn (Heb, Tzaphon in tx)
  north wind I 466
Tsebā'āh (Heb, Tsaba, Saba in tx; sing) II 366, 501. *See* Tsebā'ōth (pl)
Tsebā'ōth (Heb, Sabao, Sabaoth in tx) hosts.
  See also Iaō
  genius of Mars I 577; II 538n
  Iaō-, the 10-lettered god II 603
  Jehovah & I 438, 576
  Saturn or I 459
  stellar spirit I 449
  thirty-two paths & II 39
  Thoth-, or the Bear II 115n
Tselem (Heb, Tsala, Tzelem in tx) image
  Adam the, of the elohīm II 137
  four Adams & II 457, 503-4
  reflects Michael & Samael II 378
  several in Kabbala II 633
Tsien-Tchan. *See* Hsien-Chan
Tsin Dynasty. *See* Ch'in Dynasty
Tsin She Hwang-ti. *See* Shih Huang Ti
Tsi-tsai (Chin), self-existent or the Unknown Darkness I 356
T'sod Olaum. *See* Yesōd 'Ōlām
Tsong Kha-pa
  avatāra of Amitābha Buddha I 108 &n
  —— "Aphorisms of *Tson-ka-pa*"
  workers received Thyan-kam I 635
Tsu-no-gai-no-kami (Jap)
  male being (Shinto) I 217
Tsūrāh (Heb)
  prototype of 2nd Adam II 457
Tuan ying t'u (Chinese classic)
  describes Yellow Dragon II 365
Tuaricks [Tuaregs], Berber nomads II 792

Tubal-Cain (Heb) legendary craftsman
  Kabir, metal arts instructor II 390
  mineral kingdom symbolized by II 575
  Vulcan, Viśvakarma or II 384n
Tum (Egy)
  creative force in nature I 312
  divider of Earth or Fohat I 674
  Fohat or I 673 &n
  primordial creator II 580
Tumuli (of Norway, Denmark) II 352
  like mounds in USA II 424n, 752
Turamaya
  Indian "Ptolemaios" (Weber) II 50
Turanian(s) I 113
  Aryans & II 200, 203
  borrowed Aryan terms II 452
  common religion before separation I xxix
  effects of isolation upon II 425
  forefathers in Central Asia II 425
  Mongolo- I 319
  Negro-, & Canstadt Man II 744
  races II 421n
  religion not new I xxxvi
  Shemites or Assyrians & II 203
  typified as dwarfs II 754
Turin Papyrus
  vindicates Manetho, Ptolemy II 367
Turīya (Skt) 4th state of consciousness
  man loses self in I 570
  samādhi, nirvāna or I 570
Turkestan
  lost cities in Tarim district of I xxivn
Tuscan sages
  on Great Year, Plutarch's *Sulla* I 650
Tuscul. Quaest. See Cicero
Tushitas (Skt)
  12 gods in 2nd kalpa II 90, 182
Tvashtri (Skt). *See also* Viśvakarman
  divine artist & carpenter II 101
  family of, among maruts, rudras II 615
  father of gods, creative fire II 101
Twan ying t'u. See Tuan . . .
Twelve. *See also* Dodecahedron, Zodiacs
  classes of creators I 213; II 77
  gods, apostles, tribes, zodiac signs I 400, 651
  great gods created by Brahmā II 90
  -legged horse of Huschenk II 397-9
  nidānas I 39
  relation of, to Zodiac I 649
  transformations symb by day's "hours" I 450
"Twelve Signs of the Zodiac." *See* Subba Row
Twelve Tribes of Israel I 400, 651; II 130, 200n
Twentieth Century
  disciple may give final proofs I xxxviii

Michelet on I 676
nineteenth & I 378
proof of man's priority to ape in II 690
SD will be vindicated in I xxxvii; II 442
Twice-Born. *See also* Dvija, Initiate
Brahmins I xxi, 534, 542; II 111
cycles known to II 70
invasion of India by I 270
Twilight(s). *See also* Sandhyā I 289
Hilasira [Hilaeiro] or, & Phoebe (dawn)
II 122
pitris issue fr II 163
of a planet II 660n
seven, & 7 dawns II 308
Sons of II 18, 91, 120-1, 138
time betw I 144
Twin Souls, esoteric meaning of I 574
Two Brothers (Egy tale) II 270n
Two-Horned, term explained II 398
Tycho. *See* Brahe, Tycho
Tyndall, John I 528n
atmospheric vibrations of sound I 633
on atom & force I 510n
atoms instinct w desire for life I 249
called metaphysics "fiction" I 584n, 669
can we grasp ultimate structure? I 670-1
molecularist I 637n
"scientific imagination" of I 483
—— *Faraday as a Discoverer*
Faraday & Aristotle I 507
—— [*Fragments of Science*]
chasm betw brain & consciousness II 673
on spontaneous generation II 150-1, 719
Tyndareus (Gk)
father of Castor & Pollux II 121-2
Tyndaridae (Gk)
Castor & Pollux as day & night II 122
Types
basic, thrown off by man II 683
cast off human, & lower beings II 263
diversified in post-Atlantis II 425
human repertory of all II 187n, 256-9,
289-90, 659-60, 682, 685, 736n
persistent, in evolution II 256, 257, 259
tend to revert to original II 277

three great human II 780
Types of Mankind. See Nott & Glidden
Typhoeus (Gk). *See also* Typhon
winds sons of, (Hesiod) I 466
Typhon (Egy & Gk). *See also* Typhoeus
becomes power of darkness II 93
brother of Osiris II 283n, 380
cosmic war betw Osiris & I 202
cuts Osiris into pieces II 93, 385
Diana escapes, as a cat in moon I 387-8
Dragon of Eden (de Rougé) I 399n
equivalents of II 379
fallen angel II 283, 516
falling god of Egypt II 486
of Great Bear & ankh II 547
Hermes or II 380
once great god, later debased II 32n
Osiris & II 379
Pan, goat & II 579
pictured bound to cross II 588
Seth & II 32n, 82n, 231, 366, 380, 385
Seven Rishis, Great Bear & II 549
Thoth as Ibis escapes fr I 362
will be dethroned II 420
Tyre
pillars at, & elements I 125-6, 347n
Tyrian(s)
David brought name Jehovah fr II 541
Jews &, kin in Bible I 313n
purple II 430
Tyrrhenian Cosmogony (Suidas)
Creation took 12,000 yrs I 340
Tyrus, King of. *See* King of Tyrus
Tythea (Gk). *See* Titaea
Tza [Tsādēi] (Heb) fishing hook
male Hebrew letter I 114n
Tzabaoth. *See* Tsebā'ŏth
Tzaphon. *See* Tsāphŏn
Tzelem. *See* Tselem
Tzité Tree (of Mayans)
3rd race created fr II 97, 181n
Tzon-kha-pa. *See* Tsong Kha-pa
Tzure. *See* Tsūrāh
Tzyphon (Heb)
genius of doubt (Lacour) II 215-16n

U

Udāna (Skt) to breathe upwards
　physical organs of speech I 95
　principal life-wind II 567-8
Ueber die Auflösung . . . See Wiegand, J.
Ueber die Grenzen. See Du Bois-Reymond
Ugrasena, King of Mathurā II 323
Uhlemann, Rosetta Stone of II 464
Ulom. *See* Ōlām
Ultramontanes
　patriarchs & 12 signs of zodiac I 651
Ulug-Beg [Ulugh-Beg] (Arab)
　tables of, (1437 AD) I 658
Ulūpī (Skt), Arjuna married II 214 &n, 628
Ulysses, story of, interpreted II 769
Umā-Kanyā (Skt) light-virgin
　Anaitia, astral light & I 91-2
Umbilicus, connected thru placenta II 461
Umsimi (Chald)
　ideal creative organ II 283-4n
Unconsciousness
　cannot know self-consciousness I 51
　consciousness &, discussed I 56
　esoteric school rejects idea of I 453
　of Hegel becomes self-conscious I 106
　of von Hartmann & Hegel I 1-2n, 50, 51,
　　106; II 649, 662, 670
Underground Region (Zuñi)
　black coin depicts II 629
Underworld, various deities of I 463
Undines (water elementals)
　sylphs &, derided today I 606
Undulatory theory of light I 483, 486, 495,
　528, 579-80
Unger, Professor Franz
—— *Die Versunkene Insel Atlantis*
　believed Atlantis theory II 783
Ungulate(s) (hoofed mammals)
　diagrams of II 735
　root of II 736
Unicorn, Gould on credibility of II 218
Unicorn, The: A Mythological Investigation.
　See Brown, R.
United States
　artificial mounds in II 424n
　flora of East Asia & II 781
　germs of 6th subrace in II 444-5

　Miocene, Tertiary flora II 727, 790
Unity. *See also* One
　absolute I 58-9; II 239, 545
　ALL & I 8
　of all nature I 120, 276
　boundless, infinite II 42-3, 553
　in diversity I 285; II 310
　divine, as a circle I 1; II 553
　divine, Egy idea of I 675
　of divine names II 39
　dual in manifestation II 24
　ever unknown I 347
　Fohat the binding I 111
　is no number (Pyth) I 433
　kosmos is a unity in all its parts I 480
　of mankind & exceptions II 195-6
　One, & manus II 322
　original status of all beings II 545
　plane of illusion & I 582
　pulsating great heart II 588
　reabsorption into I 266
　spirit & matter aspects I 16
　of structural plan II 737
　systolic, diastolic nature of II 43
　in thought & action I 644
　universal, during pralaya I 613
　universal, 1st occult dogma I 58
　zero &, symbol of Deity II 581
Unity of Nature, The. See Campbell, G. D.
Universal
　agent or lapis philosophorum II 113
　belief in man's origins II 492
　Deity has naught to do w form I 492-3n
　element I 75
　events preconcerted II 500n
　history & Chinese moon-periods II 621
　tradition safest guide II 349
　tradition, testimony of ages II 194, 340
Universal Mind. *See also* Ideation, Mahat,
　Mind (Cosmic)
　collective dhyāni-chohanic minds I 579n
　comes into action I 38
　Demiurgos or I 110; II 704n
　dhyāni-chohans reflect ideation of I 279-80
　directs divine thought into chaos II 704n
　earliest adepts & II 215

Father & Son are II 492
Fohat impresses ideas of I 85
intellectual process not akin to man's I 1n
is not a being I 285n
lipikas objectivize plans of I 104
Mahat or I 216n; II 58-9, 79
matter is upādhi for I 280-1
reflection of, or cosmic ideation I 110
self-consciousness & I 51
surrounds ahamkāra II 616
various names of I 110
was not (pralaya) I 38
Universal Oversoul
aspect of Unknown Root I 17
identity of all souls w I 17
Universal Soul
ākāśa or II 511-12
Alaya, anima mundi I 49-50
astral light material aspect of I 421
ether breath of I 102
mahā-ātma, Brahmā I 365 &n
Mahat, Mahābuddhi or I 420-1
mind of the Demiurge I 352
Mother, female I 352-3
Plato's, & Ptah I 353
Rā, Nārāyana or I 231
upādhi or basis of I 101
vehicle of spirit I 420
Universal Spirit I 257n; II 596. *See also* Spirit
ātma, anupadaka [aupapāduka] & I 52, 571
Christos, Fravashi, or II 478
Paramātman or I 265
waking, sleeping of I 372
Universe(s). *See also* Cosmos, Kosmos
& all in it māyā I 274, 329-30
anupadaka [aupapāduka], was I 52
birth of I 110-11, 337
birth of, as spider & web I 83
blind forces could never build II 348
bounded by pentagons II 576
as Brahma & Brahmā I 17-18
Brahmā expands to become I 83
breathes as does man I 541
casts off skin periodically I 74
cause of its successor I 43
condition of, during pralaya I 54-5, 69
creation of, needed intelligence II 239
disintegration of visible I 4
divine thought & I 61
dodecahedron, built as a I 340, 344; II 36
dreamless sleep of I 47
Earth born in, like foetus II 188-9
effect of predecessor I 43
egg in the beginning I 359-60

elements & I 92n, 461
Essence is life & light of I 6
an eternal becoming II 449n
eternity of, as boundless plane I 16
everything in, is conscious I 274
evil a necessity in manifested II 389
evolution of, mere phallicism? II 544
evolved fr sun, point, germ I 379
evolved out of ideal plan I 281, 340
expanding, contracting of I 83-4
figures for birth of I 340
fire or intelligence moves I 77
Fohat in the unmanifest I 109
guided fr within outwards I 274
Hegel's I 51
hierarchies explain mystery of I 89
ideal, & manifested kosmos I 614
incessantly appearing, dying I 16-17; II 43
invisible, throughout space II 25
in Japanese cosmogony I 217
lipika spirits of I 128-9
lives in & returns to Brahma I 8-9
lotus symbol of I 379-86
made of ether-matter-energy I 669
manifested, is Secondary Creation II 59
manifested, pervaded by duality I 15-16
manifested, reflected in monads II 186
manifests only what is there I 570
mechanical origin of I 594-6
mechanicians in, necessary I 594
metaphysical abstractions become I 45
mind-born Son of Virgin I 399
mirrors the Logos II 25, 186
monads the expression of I 629-30
Moon & fire make up II 639n
more than what is perceived I 421n
Mundane Egg contains II 616
not separate fr the All II 384n
our, one of infinite number I 43
periodical manifestation of I 273
periodical, or Son I 41; II 492
periodical renovations of I 637-8
perpetual motion of I 2
phenomenal, an illusion I 145-6, 329
plenum or a fullness I 671
point in mundane egg & I 1
pralaya of I 41
real to the beings in it I 274, 329-30
reawakening of, in 3rd Stanza I 21
represented in the monads I 632
requires elastic atoms I 519
rests on inter-etheric point I 556-7
revolves around Pleiades II 551
ruled by intelligent powers II 502

Sephīrōthal Tree is I 352
septenary state of II 598
seven & 4 principles of I 18; II 58n
seven heads of Śesha support II 505
"Son of Necessity" I 42
Son or, springs fr point, Logos I 614
three aspects of I 278
Trithemius on actuating of I 453n
fr unconscious to self-conscious I 106
unfolding of, (*Manu*) I 333-5
unknown absolute essence of I 273
Vāch, Voice, calls, out of chaos I 137
various modes of procreation in I 406
visible, is sthūla-śarīra I 598
whole, lit fr one rush-light I 85n
will live 49,000 yrs (Pers) II 618
L'Univers expliqué . . . *See* Chaubard, L. A.
Unknowable, Unnameable. *See also* First
    Cause, God, Reality, That
absolute divine essence I 56
Ain-sōph I 113; II 41, 128
circle symbol of I 113
Crookes on I 581 &n
God, not God of Israel I 327
ideas opposed to, (Spencer) II 490
karma one w II 306
materialization of 1st Principle II 503
not the creator I 346
Parabrahm II 128
source & cause of all II 43
of Spencer I 14 &n, 54n, 281, 327 &n, 496,
    675
spirit of God moving on waters II 128
various names for I 113
Unknown
    Aditi, chaos in 1st remove fr the II 527
    darkness & I 134n, 333, 356, 365, 425
    Hellenes had altar to, god I 327-8
    light reflected in Firstborn II 703n
    power & motion II 551-2
    Zeruana Akerne is Persian II 488
Unmanifested
    the Absolute or I 88
    Heavenly Man is I 215
    motion eternal in I 97n
Unpublished MS. *See* Skinner, J. R.
Unpublished MSS. *See* Mathers, S. L. M.
Unseen Universe. See Stewart & Tait
Upādāna (Skt), material cause I 55, 370n
Upādhi(s) (Skt) base, vehicle
    ākāśa, of divine thought I 326, 515n
    ātma may work in each I 158
    basic human mold I 282
    can be separated by adepts I 158

conductor of nervous ether I 538n
consciousness must have I 15 &n
cosmic ideation focused in I 329n, 330
devas have affinity w human II 90
first, of solar system I 289
four, 3, of Brahmans II 592-3n
globes, principles & I 153-4
hydrogen, of air & water II 105
inorganic, of mineral atom II 255
manas the, of buddhi I 101
man related to plane of his II 157
matter, of universal mind I 280
mind needs an II 670
mūlaprakriti the, of all phenomena I 35
one absolute II 34
seven rays, of ether I 515n
six sephīrōth as I 375
three fires & II 247
three periodical I 181
of Universal Soul I 101
Upadvīpa(s) (Skt)
    dry lands in general II 404n
Upanishads (Skt)
    Anugītā's original one of oldest I 94n
    based on Secret Doctrine I 47
    correlation of senses & elements I 534-6
    described I 269-72
    esoteric glossaries of Vedas I 270; II 484
    explain the noumenon I 522
    full of secret wisdom II 590
    Gautama popularized I 271
    once 3 times size of Vedas I 271
    over 150 of, known I 270
    pantheists echo the I 7
    passed into Gnostic literature II 566
    seven senses in I 268n
    show scientific knowledge I 522, 534
    treatise on serpents in II 26n
    Vāch & I 138
Upas Tree of Superstition II 797
Upheaval(s). *See also* Submersions
    of Alps II 751n, 778, 787n
    of Americas II 407
    of Andes II 745
    caused by inverted poles II 360
    depend upon moon & planets II 699
Upsala, Ancient (Sweden)
    capital of Atlantis (Rudbeck) II 402
Upward cycle. *See* Arc, Ascending
Ur (Mesopotamian city)
    Abraham came fr I 376; II 139n
    Moon-god worshiped at II 139n
    teakwood at II 226

Uraeus (Gk) asp or snake symbol
  astral body destroyed by I 227
  defunct is devoured by I 674n
  emblem of cosmic fire I 437
  manas & ātma-buddhi or I 227
  serpent, naja, or I 437, 674n
Ural (mts & river)
  Arismaspi inhabited, (Newman) II 416-18
Urania's Key to the Revelations. See Mackey
Uranides (Gk) heaven dwellers
  theology reversed role of I 418
Uranographie . . . See Francoeur, L.-B.
Uranographie Chinoise. See Schlegel, G.
Uranos. *See* Ouranos
Uranus (planet)
  ancients knew of I 99 &n
  discovered in 18th cent I 99n, 103
  more dense than Saturn I 593
  not one of sacred planets I 575
  plane of satellites tilted I 101-2
  Ragon on, & Sun I 100n
  receives 390 times less light I 575
  satellites apparently retrograde I 101,
    149-50n, 575
Urd, Fountain of (Norse)
  waters Yggdrasil II 520
Ūrdhvasrotas (Skt)
  divinities created after man I 446 &n
  happy celestial beings II 162
  prototypes of 1st race I 456
  third, 6th creations I 446, 453, 456
Urea
  analogous to venoms I 262n
  in blood during strangulation I 249n
Uriel (Heb)

  denounces fallen angels II 382n
  Enoch & I 609; II 483n, 533
  mule, bull, & I 127n; II 115n
  Ophite bull, ox or I 127n
Ūrīm & Thummīm (Heb)
  Kab &, or Kabirim (Mackey) II 362n
  twelve stones of I 651
Ūrjā (Skt) strength, progeny of II 146n
Ursa Major. *See also* Constellations, Great Bear
  Seven Rishis once linked w II 768
  Ursa Minor &, 2 cherubs symb II 361n
Ursa Minor. *See also* Constellations, Śiśumāra
  four potent stars in tail of II 612n
  70,000 yrs ago pole pointed to II 768
  Ursa Major &, 2 cherubs II 361n
Urschleim (Oken), origin of II 158-60
Uśanas (Skt) Venus
  ally of Soma II 498
  degraded into an asura II 45
  gives laws to Earth II 32
  host of planet Venus II 501
  Satan, Lucifer of Catholics II 501
Uśanas-Śukra (Skt) Venus
  associated w Lucifer, Satan II 45n
  Earth & II 31-3
  War in Heaven story of II 45
Ush [Osch, Asch in tx] (Skt) to burn II 114
Uttama [or Auttami] (Skt) most excellent
  second round manu II 309
Uttara-Mīmāṃsā (Skt), & Buddhism I 46-7
Uxmal (Cent Amer)
  ruins at, & Palenque II 430
Uzza ['Uzzā] (Heb)
  Azāēl &, twitted God II 491

V

Vāch (Skt) Voice. *See also* Aditi, Logos, Voice
  Aditi or I 431, 434; II 43, 107
  Bath-kol & II 107
  Brahmā separates into Virāj & I xv, 9n, 89,
    137; II 128, 143, 472
  calls universe out of chaos I 137
  daughter of Brahmā I 431; II 128, 418n
  described & explained I 137-8, 430-3
  equivalent of Logos II 199n
  female Logos of Brahmā I 9n; II 107
  four aspects of I 138, 432, 433n
  goddess I 95, 434
  hidden power of mantras I 354
  Idā (Ilā), Mania & I 523; II 143
  identical w Eve II 128, 147
  Kwan-yin & I 136n, 137, 431n
  Lahash similar to I 354
  light, sound, ether & I 431-2
  magic potency of sound I 137
  "melodious cow" (*Rig-Veda*) I 137, 427n,
    734; II 418n
  mother of the gods I 430, 434
  mūlaprakriti & I 430
  mystic speech, occult knowledge I 430
  Sarasvatī (speech) form of I 95, 353
  Śatarūpa or I 94; II 128
  Universal Soul I 352-3
  various names of I 137, 430, 434; II 128
Vāchaspatya (Skt), on Katāpa (Kalāpa) I 378n
Vāch-Śatarūpa (Skt), Manu w II 128, 148
Vacuum, Vacuity
  caloric & I 524
  does not exist anywhere I 527
  inter-etheric, & bell sounds I 557
  Keely motor & I 556-7, 565
  of Leucippus is latent Deity I 343
  plenum, ether & I 495
  betw sidereal bodies (Newton) I 491, 494-5
Vadukku, Chaldean genii or spirits II 248n
Vāhana (Skt) vehicle I 39, 73, 80, 153
  buddhi is II 241
  buddhi the, of ātman I 265
  Fohat as a I 108
  Garuda the, of Vishnu II 564
  of Lords of Wisdom II 172
  Makara the, of Varuna II 577

matter, of spirit II 58n
Merkābāh, chariot of Ain-sōph or I 214
physical forces are, of elements I 470
soul the, of spirit I 153
spark, of the Flame I 265
Sun, of ākāśa I 527n
Vyāvahārika used as a I 356
yāna or I 39
Vaidhātra (Skt)
  patronymic name of kumāras I 89, 457n
Vaidyuta (Skt), electric fire I 521
Vaikharī-Vāch (Skt)
  kosmos in its objective form I 138, 432
  lowest form of Vāch I 434
  that which is uttered I 138
Vaikrita (Skt) secondary
  origin of gods fr Brahmā was I 455n
Vaikuntha-loka (Skt)
  heaven of Vishnu I 522
Vaikunthas (Skt), 1 of 12 gods II 90
Vairāja-loka (Skt, Virāja-loka in tx) II 89n
Vairājas (Skt) sons of Virāj
  seven classes of pitris called II 89-90
Vaishnava(s) (Skt) followers of Vishnu
  Brahman interpolators II 550n
  God of the I 421
  haters of Nanda II 550 &n
  mahā-buddhi & I 451
  śaivas & I 675
  of the Vaśishthā[Viśishta]-dvaita or I 55
  Wilson re system of I 456n
Vaiśvānara, Vaiśvāna (Skt)
  blazes within the body II 496
  described II 311 &n, 381-2
  elements spring fr I 621 &n
  often denotes the self II 496n
  sevenfold fire II 568
Vaivasvata (Skt) belonging to Vivasvat (Sun)
  manvantara & 18 million years II 310
  manvantara or round I xliii, 456
Vaivasvata (Manu). *See also* Deucalion, Noah,
    Xisuthrus, Yima
  ark of II 290-1, 313, 610
  Brahmā-Vishnu-Śiva preceded II 144
  connected w 5th race II 140-1
  date of II 250, 310

Deluge & 4th race I 68, 369; II 69n, 146,
    310
Deva-Manu or II 715n
    four axial changes during II 330
    fourth human wave, manu of II 309
    generic character of II 145, 251, 306
    gods called Ādityas during, cycle II 90
    Hindu Noah I 444; II 35, 140, 222, 306-7,
        309, 314, 774
    humanity II 251, 313, 693
    Idā, wife, daughter of I 523; II 138, 140
    Ilā, Sudyumna, progeny of II 135, 138
    Kaśyapa father of II 253, 382n
    lives even now II 250
    manvantara or round I xliii, 456; II 69 &n,
        310
    Matsya avatāra & I 369; II 69n, 139, 307, 313
    more than one II 251
    name contains story II 335
    Noah repeats I 444; II 265, 306, 597
    progenitor of 5th race II 249-50, 309
    rishis, Titans saved by II 142, 715n
    root-manu, 4th round II 309, 321
    saved germs of humanity II 715n
    saved our race in Deluge II 146, 309-10
    seed of life connected w II 140-1
    seven rishis saved w II 35, 69n, 290-2
    seventh manu II 308n, 309, 321
    son of Sūrya, the Sun II 140-1, 211
    story records Atlantis deluge II 4
    three attributes of II 146-7
    Vāch, wife & daughter of I 523
Vajradhāra (Skt) diamond holder
    First Logos, Supreme Buddha or I 571
Vajrasattva (Skt) diamond-hearted
    full mahātmas or I 52
    Second Logos I 571
Valentinus
    Bythos & Sigē primordial binary II 574-5
    on 1st Aion I 349
    good, evil, Logos, serpent of I 410
    Great Seven of I 446
    "Greek Kabala" of I 310
    light, heat, fire, particles I 568 &n
    pairs of Aeons of II 569n
    Pistis Sophia & II 512, 566n
    sevenfold nature of Logos I 446
    table of Aeons in II 458
—— *Esoteric Treatise on the Doctrine of Gilgul*
    I 568 &n
Valhalla (Norse), hall of the heroes I 427
Vallabhāchāryas (Hindu sect)
    distort Krishna symbols I 335
    phallic worship & II 588

Vallancey, Charles, *Collectanea . . .*
    on the Kabiri I 641-2n; II 264
    Morning Star of Irish, Chald II 759n
Vāmadeva (Skt)
    reborn white, red I 324
    Śiva as, became four I 324; II 249, 282
    symbolizes 4 racial types I 324; II 249
Vamadeva Modelyar [Modely]
    Night of Brahmā I 376-7
Vananin-Lamertade (Lamer in tx)
    androgynous Aeon (Gnostic) II 458
Vapor(y), transformation of globes I 205-6n,
    250, 439n
Vara (Skt), & avara II 163, 183
Vara, Argha (Pahlavi) enclosure, vehicle
    ark or, is man of 4th round II 291-2 &n
    built by Yima II 6n, 610
Varāha (Skt). *See also* Avatāra, Boar
    boar avatāra I 368-9 &n; II 53, 321
    Buddha born in, kalpa I 368n
    kalpa I 368, 457; II 179, 321
    marks one-half life of Brahmā II 179
Varia Historia. See Aelianus
Variations (evolution) II 677
    fortuitous, criticized (Mivart) II 697
    ideation reflected in matter II 299n
    reflects dhyān-chohanic wisdom II 649
    of species II 677 &n, 679, 696
    as transmitted by heredity II 738
Varṇa (Skt) color, orders (class) I 419
Varsha(s) (Skt) country
    Americas the, of Pushkara II 403, 407 &n
    Bhārata-, II 369
    dvīpas &, of kings expl II 320-2
    Meru north of all II 401n
    Purāṇic term II 264
Varshayantī (Skt), one of the Pleiades II 551
Varuṇa (Skt) ocean god
    an asura II 92, 500
    chief Āditya, Ouranos II 65
    chief of dhyānis, devas II 606
    five Prachetas(es) & II 578
    guards the West I 128
    imparts the Mysteries II 269n
    Laws of, or Vratāni II 606
    Makara vehicle of I 220; II 577
    reigns as Neptune II 65, 268n
    space or II 268n
    Uranos a modified II 268n
    Vaivasvata sacrifices to II 147-8
    water, Neptune or I 462
Vase of Election. *See* Araṇī
Vasishta-dvaita. *See* Viśishṭādvaita

Vasishtha (Skt) a rishi
  advises Parāśara I 415-16; II 232n
  curse of II 247
  sons of, 1st manvantara II 146n
  third round, 3rd race, sons in II 78
  Varuna imparted Mysteries to II 269n
Vassariddhi, Rājah
  & huge human bones II 347
Vastubhūta (Skt) substantial
  Vishnu not II 612n
Vāsudeva (Skt)
  even mlechchhas may know II 48n
  the liberator I 286
  seed of all things I 420
Vasu(s) (Skt) good, bountiful
  eight, of Vedic tridaśa I 71n
  our fathers were II 248n
Vatican
  Lanci, librarian of, q II 376
  preserves some esoteric doctrine I xliv
  St Germain & MS of Kabbala in II 239
  secret work "Bnēi Shamash" II 506
Vau (Heb) letter V
  crook, hook, nail (YHVH) II 460
  letter for Hokhmāh I 438n
Vaughan, Thomas [Eugenius Philalethes]
  correlations of sound, color I 514 &n
  no one has yet seen Earth I 260
Vāyu (Skt)
  god of air I 190, 462, 468
  Indra or, in *Rig-Veda* II 378
  one of Vedic Trimūrti I 90
  Pavana or, father of Hanuman I 190
  Vedic god II 114
Vāyu Purāṇa
  beginning of mahā-pralaya I 371
  birth of Janaka II 524n
  boar, Varāha I 368-9n
  Brahmā forces Nārada into birth II 82
  Dānavas, giants, dragons II 381 &n
  Kapila son of Kaśyapa in II 572
  lower pitris born as fools II 91
  Mahat, names for I 256
  Moru [Maru] comes in 19th yuga I 378 &n
  Nara, Nārāyaṇa I 457-8 &n; II 495n
  personified fires I 521
  pradhāna & prakriti I 50n
  rudras II 613n
  sacrifice of Daksha II 182-3
  Śankha-dvīpa II 405
  seven classes of pitris II 89
  seven rishis I 436
  seven times 7 maruts II 613
  sons of manus, rishis II 614n

three creations I 454n
three fires II 57n
twelve great gods in II 90
Veda(s, ic). *See also Atharva-Veda, Rig-Veda,*
    Vedic
  Aditi, ākāśa in II 42n
  Ambhāmsi synonym of gods in I 457-8n
  anticipated modern discoveries I 623
  barhishad, agnishvātta in II 77
  chanted, rationale of I 94-6
  chief gods of II 114
  date fr early Aryan history II 714
  divided in dvāpara age II 146n, 483
  dual meaning of I 270n
  Eternal Cause or That I 391n; II 80
  Europe has text of, (Müller) I xxiii n
  fire deities in I 101; II 567
  four, & 4 truths I 42
  greatest of all authorities II 616
  heavenly gandharvas taught man II 584
  of highest antiquity (Müller) I xxxviii
  influence on Babylon (Rawlinson) I xxxi
  initiates know meaning of I 520
  leaves of Hiranyagarbha I 406
  Mahādeva divine ego II 548
  maruts discussed II 613
  meaning of elements hidden in I 520
  "Mirror of Eternal wisdom" II 484
  Müller & Barth on II 450-1
  no idol worship in II 723
  not complete I 318
  once called modern forgery I xxxviii
  Orientalists differ on age of I xxx
  primary & secondary creations II 59
  Purānas human expression of II 527
  Scand cosmogony older (Müller) I 367
  secret commentary on I xxxiv
  Secret Doctrine antedates I xxxvii
  septenary element in II 605-11
  seven wise ones, 7 paths II 191n
  Śiva known as Rudra in II 548
  six earths born w our Earth II 616
  sole property of Brahmans I 271
  Sun called loka-chakshuh in I 100-1
  tens of thousands of yrs old II 527
  Tvashtri in II 101
  universal myths in II 97
  Upanishads esoteric glossaries of II 484
  Upanishads expound mysticism of I 270
  Vāch mother of I 430
  Vishnu divides, into four II 483
  Viśvakarma in II 269n
  went into every nation II 483
Vedānta (school) I 52n, 59n

Advaita, nearest esoteric I 55
on bodies w negative qualities I 584n
on cause I 55
discord betw 3 sects of I 451
division of man's principles I 157, 226
doctrine in Hermetic philosophy I 281n
esoteric teaching differs fr I 62
gives but metaphysical cosmogony I 269
Hegelian doctrine & II 449n
last word of human knowledge I 269
nimitta as an efficient cause I 370n
not fr Buddhism I 46-7
occultists & I 8
One Life, Great Breath I 226n
Parabrahm-mūlaprakriti I 46
prajñā, chinmātra II 597n
quinquepartite division of man in I 226
Spencer approaches I 14-15, 281
sūtrātman (thread self) I 610 &n; II 513
teachings of I 522, 569-70, 573, 610; II 597n,
    598
Vedas are mirror of wisdom II 484
Western philos echo, doctrines I 79n
Western scholars perverted I 295
Vedāntasāra. See Jacob, G. A.
Vedāntins I 8, 10n, 16, 17n, 51, 52n
divided man into 5 kośas II 603
idealists I 226n
Īsvara highest consciousness I 573
Mahat aspect of prakriti w I 62
nirvāni of, can never return II 80
not atheists I 7
Veda-Vyāsa
mentions Tchandalas [Chandāla] I 313n
Vishnu as, in dvāpara age II 146n, 483
Veddhas of Ceylon (Sri Lanka)
culture cannot raise II 421n
mixed Lemuro-Atlantean stock II 195-6n
Sinhalese regard, as animals II 286-7
weapons of, Paleolithic II 723
Vedhas. *See also* Asuras, Sons of Brahmā, Suras
agnishvāttas II 78-9
eldest, refused to create I 88
Sanandana & other II 78, 173, 176n
Vedic
calendar, Krittikā & II 551
deities I 71n, 90, 112; II 268-9n
hymns (Pañchadaśa), magic of II 579
influence on Babylon I xxxi; II 130
Nārada a, rishi II 47
sage, Kaśyapa II 132
treatment of women I 382
Venus a, sage II 30

Vega (expedition)
fossils on northern islands II 773 &n
Vega, Garcilaso de la
—— *Comentarios Reales . . . de los Incas*
on enormous human bones II 337-8
q on cyclopean works II 345
Vegetable (Kingdom). *See also* Plants, Vegeta-
    tion
appeared before 1st race II 290n
astral, & 3rd & 4th rounds II 730
bisexuality of II 133
early minerals &, luminous II 312
energy centers for each, species II 732
evolution of, in Mukhya Creation I 454
evolves thru man I 159
fruits & grains brought to man II 373
human monad passed thru II 185-7, 254, 260
individualization in I 178-9
lower principles of animals & I 267
lunar gods pass thru I 174
man storehouse of seeds for II 289-90
many in, reproduce by budding II 166
monad & I 174, 176, 246, 619; II 42, 180, 185,
    635
phase of foetus (Haeckel) II 685n
Schibb (Shibboleth) symbol of II 575
second side of triangle II 575
size of, & giants II 276
third round, astral prototypes II 186-7
Thomson on earliest of II 154
300 million years before man II 68n, 149,
    290n
Vegetarians, Atlantes were, (Herodotus) II 761
Vegetation. *See also* Plants, Vegetable
all, endowed w life (Wilson) I 454
belong to this (4th) round II 712
born fr bosom of stone II 594
changes w each root-race II 697
consciousness of I 277n
creatures born fr II 183
ethereal before primordial II 713n
has consciousness I 277n
man &, before animals II 112n
nervous ether in I 537
physicalized in Secondary II 713n
300 million yrs before man II 290n, 308n,
    712
Veil of Isis. *See* Schiller, J. C. F.
Vendidad. See also Zend Avesta
Fravashi (or Ferouer) II 480
karshvar of Earth II 607
volcanism in Central Asia II 356
Yima & 1st 3 races discussed II 609-10

Venezuela, Canary Islands, Africa, &, once
    joined II 791
Venice, Campanile of San Marco at II 85
Venoms, living tissues produce I 262n
Ventricles, 3rd eye & II 297
Ventus (Lat) breath or wind
    spiritus &, synonymous I 342
Venus (goddess). *See also* Lucifer
    Aditi identified w II 43, 458
    Amphitrite early form of II 578
    -Aphrodite, Argha & II 461
    -Aphrodite personified sea I 458n
    associated w Satan II 31-2n, 45n
    -Astarte & Kadeshim II 460
    Ashtōreth, Jehovah & II 462
    bearded I 72n; II 30n, 135
    born fr sea wave II 65
    celestial Priapus born of II 458
    w cow's horns II 31, 418n
    described II 29-33
    Durgā Kālī black side of II 579
    Hiram built temple to II 541
    Ishtar & II 62
    Isis or II 30, 43
    Jehovah-Bīnāh or I 392
    Kāma son of II 176
    Lakshmī or I 380n; II 76 &n, 77, 578-9
    leader of Dānavas II 498
    Lucifer-, war w Jupiter I 202
    origin of mythology of II 30
    passive generative power II 418n, 461
    six sacred to, (Pyth) II 592
    star of the sea I 392
    Uśanas or, aid Soma in war II 498
    Uśanas-Sukra is, & Lucifer II 45
    Virgin took over, worship I 400-1
    wife, mother, sister I 396
Venus (planet)
    adept's' knowledge of races on II 699
    adopted Earth II 32-3
    ansated cross symb of II 30, 31n
    called little sun II 24
    changes along w Earth II 32
    described II 29-33, 707
    Earth linked w II 30-1
    Friday the day of I 652
    hostile to human life II 707
    inclination of axis of II 32
    in last round I 165
    less dense than Earth I 593
    light-bearer to Earth II 33
    looking glass sign of II 546
    Lucifer or I 202; II 30, 31-2 &n, 45n, 501,
        512, 540

Mars, Mercury &, lower triad II 462
    men of, more gross I 602
    Mercury more occult than II 28
    Moon, water & II 77
    Morning Star II 540
    no satellites I 155n, 165; II 32
    one w Mercury & Sun II 542
    Orai genius of I 577; II 538n
    parent moon of, dissolved I 155-6n
    planetary chain I 164
    Principalities gods of I 435
    rulers, regents of I 435, 575
    Semele presides betw Mars & I 400
    sign of, expl I 5; II 29-30
    Sophia, Holy Ghost & II 512, 540
    superior globes of, invisible I 153
    third race under II 24, 29
Venus (3rd world of Syrians)
    Principalities rule over I 435
Venus-Lucifer. *See also* Lucifer, Lucifer-Venus,
        Morning Star, Venus
    descends to pit II 785-6
    Moon more influential than I 305
    sister, alter ego of Earth I 305
Verbum (Lat) II 542. *See also* Logos, Word
    Avalokiteśvara I 428
    Christ, Taurus or I 656
    daivīprakriti, mother, daughter I 136
    dhyāni-chohans form manifest I 278
    divine Christos, Logos I 130n
    dual aspect of II 515
    esoteric meaning of II 25, 237
    light, sound, ether & I 431-2
    Logos or Word I 93-4, 136, 431, 537
    Mercury, Logos, or II 25, 541-2
    of Parabrahman I 130n, 136
    of St John I 657
    St Michael & II 479, 481
    St Paul confused w II 481
    sound of the I 256, 629
    of Thought Divine I 72, 74
    various names for I 130n, 137
    vehicle of unmanifested Logos I 278
    vibrates thru mūlaprakriti I 629
Verbum Princeps
    head of angels (Catholic) II 237
Vermes (Lat) worms II 656
Vernal Equinox. *See* Equinox
Versunkene Insel Atlantis, Die. See Unger, F.
Vertebrate(s), Vertebrata. *See also* Animals
    blind, early 3rd race man II 299
    first, in Devonian II 254
    higher II 684 &n
    primitive germ of II 731

rudimentary sex organs in II 118, 184
separated before mammals II 184
sevens among II 595
third eye in lower II 295-6, 299
Vesica Piscis (Lat), in Catholic engraving II 38
Vesta (Lat) Earth goddess
  burning fire in temple of I 338n
  Horchia title of II 144
Vestal, serpent & II 209
Vestiges of the Spirit History of Man. See Dunlap
Vi, Vili (Norse; We, Willi in tx) Odin & I 427
Via Straminis (Lat) Milky Way
  tenth world of Syrians I 435-6
Vibhāvasu (Skt) fire
  absorbed by air I 372-3
Vibhūtayah (Skt) potencies
  manus & rishis, of Vishnu I 8n; II 611n
Vibration(s)
  atomic, in nature I 455, 633
  awaken corresponding powers I 307
  commanding forces by means of I 514n
  eternal, of matter I 118n, 507-8n
  imponderable substances cause I 587
  Keely & I 561, 564
  last, of 7th eternity I 62
  of light & sound I 554
  masters perceive causes of I 514
  of molecules I 515
  music, color, etc II 628
  patterns of, in sand on plate I 112n
  power of I 563
  in Stanzas I 62-3
  table of various I 562
Vibratory Theory
  correctness of, for Earth I 514, 524-5
  Keely's I 556, 558-9, 564
Vicaire, estimates Sun's heat I 484n
Vicinus, M. See Ficino, M.
Vidadhafshu Keshvar (Pers) II 759
Vídbláinn (Norse)
  globe F, Earth chain II 100
Vidyā(s) (Skt) knowledge
  ātma- I 199
  budh & I xviii
  esoteric, & Kabbala I 241
  four of 7 in Purānas I 168-9
  right- & left-hand paths of I 192n
  sacred science & II 439
Vidyādharas (Skt) lower pitris
  exoterically demigods, siddhas I 539n
  seven classes of pitris I 539n
  sound, ladder of life & I 539
Vie de Notre-Seigneur. See Sepp, J. N.
View of the Levant. See Perry, E.

Vignanamaya Kośa. *See* Vijñānamaya Kośa
Vigrid [Vígrídr] (Norse)
  Battle of Flames & I 202
Vihāra(s) (Skt)
  Buddhist caves, grottos II 338
  Miaotse grottos turned into II 339
Vijñāna (Skt), higher mind I 157
Vijñānamaya Kośa (Skt)
  higher mind I 157-8
  jīva &, water, blood I 570n
Vikāra(s) (Skt) deviation, perturbation
  buddhi destroys egotism & its I xix
Vikartana (Skt) Sun, Sūrya
  Rāhu & initiation of II 381
  Viśvakarman crucifies I 322n
Vili. *See* Vi
Villalpand, Jean-B., *Temple de Jérusalem*
  zodiac & 12 sons of Jacob I 649
Villars, Abbé Nicolas de Montfaucon de
  —— *Le Comte de Gabalis*
  on sylphs, salamanders I 606
Villiers, on venoms, alkaloids I 262n
Vimāna(s) (Skt) air vehicles II 427, 428
Vimāna-Vidyā (Skt) aeronautics
  Aryans learned, fr Atlanteans II 426
Vina-svata
  on origin of Jews I 313n
Vinatā (Skt) daughter of Daksha
  Garuda born fr egg of I 366
  wife of Kaśyapa I 366
Vinaya (Skt) decency, modesty
  Devakī, mother of, & affection II 528
Vine
  I am the true, (*John* 15:1) I 195n
  Isis & Osiris taught use of II 366
Viper, hatched fr egg of incense I 363-4
Vīrabhadra (Skt)
  destroys Daksha's sacrifice II 182-3
  Raumyas born fr pores of II 68, 183
  thousand-headed monster II 182
Virāj, Virāja (Skt) universal sovereignty
  born fr Heavenly Man II 606
  Brahmā & I 9n, 59, 81
  Brahmā creates, spiritually II 44
  Brahmā separates into Vāch & I 89, 137
  created Manu II 308n, 311
  is Brahmā II 90
  male symbol fr Brahmā-Vāch II 472
  Manu & I 449
  mortal man born fr II 606
  sons of, are all mānasa II 89
  Vāch as female II 143, 472
  Vāch becomes, to punish gandharvas
    II 143

Vaiśvānara or II 311
Virāja[Vairāja]-Loka (Skt) II 89 &n
Vīrasvāmin (Skt), father of Medhātithi I 333
Virchow, Prof Rudolph
  dolmens not built by giants II 753
  on flints II 752n
  links Basques w Guanches II 740, 792
  on spontaneous generation II 719
  takes Haeckel to task II 650, 651
  witnessed Trojan discoveries II 440
Virey, J. J., re today's lower races of men II 725
Virgil [Vergil]
  Sibylline books inspiration of I 658
—— [*Aeneid*]
  Eternal Mind diffused thru all II 594 &n
  Mercury evoking souls II 28
  mind agitating matter I 451n
—— [*Eclogues*]
  Moon Virgin Queen of Heaven I 401
  unequal numbers please gods II 602
—— [*Georgics*]
  confused Nile w Indus II 417
  Pater omnipotens Aether I 331
Virgin(s). *See also* Immaculate Conception, Virgo
  Abel, blood & II 388
  admitted to be the Moon I 401
  -angels or divine rebels II 246
  birth discussed I 399-400
  celestial I 60, 215, 458n; II 208, 486, 512, 572
  celestial, & mother or ākāśa I 332
  Ceres-Venus worship I 400-1
  Chinese had their celestial II 486
  cold, or hyle I 82
  dawn, morning star or II 527-8
  divine, -mother or arka II 463n
  egg I 64-5
  Eve, Mary or I 91, 384, 392, 399, 458n; II 463
  fifty, of Prometheus II 418
  immaculate I 60-1
  Kanyā the I 92
  kumāras II 249, 281-2
  of Light or Umā-Kanyā I 91-2
  Lion &, (Virgo) II 431, 432-3
  marriage of Heavenly Man w II 231
  Mother I 65, 88, 400, 403, 460; II 43, 463n
  Mout, mother or II 464
  Nārada & II 140n
  rosary of the blessed II 38
  shown w child (Dendera) II 433
  sidereal, or astral light II 511
  son of celestial I 60
  sons of god born of I 61
  universe mind-born son of I 399

Zeus the beautiful I 72n
Virginal Reproduction
  hermaphrodite or II 659
Virgin Ascetic(s)
  kumāras I 459
  Nārada as II 140n
Virgin Egg
  micro-symbol of Virgin Mother I 64-5
Virgin Mary. *See also* Madonna, Mary
  Anna mother of I 91
  Church disfigured II 38, 463
  discussed I 400-3
  Gabriel comes w lilies to I 379n
  Magna Mater & I 392-3, 400
  Mary or Mare, sea, water I 458n
  pagan origin of II 463
  seven children of II 527
  various terms for II 527-8
  water lily & I 384
Virgin Mother
  chaos or I 65, 460
  gods born fr II 463n, 527
  immaculate I 88, 399
  keynote to I 91; II 43
  overshadowed by univ mystery I 88
  prayers to, stay the waves I 468
  Thoth-Hermes & I 403
Virgin of The World. See Kingsford, A.
Virgo(s).
  Astraea is II 785
  descent of, to pit II 785-6
  Dinah or I 651
  inverted II 785
  kali-yuga & position of I 663-5
  Kanyā, Kanyā-Durgā & I 92, 292, 657
  linked w Leo, Pleiades, Hyades II 785
  lion & II 431, 433
  -Scorpio androgyne I 413
  separated becomes Scorpio II 129, 502n
  three, at Dendera II 368, 433, 435-6
Viribus Membrorum, De. See Paracelsus
Virtue(s)
  Confucianists love I 440
  of God I 437-8
  hidden, of stones II 426
  Jesuitical use of deceit as I 423
  personified attributes of God II 237
  seven, of Christians I 310-11; II 641
  seven, of Nazarenes I 196
Virtues (angelic order)
  angelic, & 4 Mahārājas I 123
  angelic, & terāphīm I 394
  copy of ancient prototype I 92
  rule over 5th world of Syrians I 435

Viś (Skt) to pervade
    Vishnu derived fr I 8n, 112
Visha (Skt) poison, evil
    latent in chaos I 348
Vishnu (Skt). *See also* Logos, Nārāyana, Tri-
    mūrti
    abstract divine principle II 313
    Achyuta ("not-fallen") avatāra I 19
    avatāra of I 18, 87, 263-4, 369, 394, 653;
        II 139, 307, 408n, 483, 549
    birth of, (universe) I 333-5
    both Bhūteśa & Viśvarūpa I 452n
    breath of, blows at pralaya I 371
    calling forth the kosmos I 348
    disk or chakra of I 114; II 546
    double-sexed, Lakshmī & II 31
    double triangle sign of I 118
    emerges fr egg w lotus I 366
    enters circle of boundless time II 549
    Fohat connected w, I 112, 673
    Garuda vehicle of I 366
    god of moist principle II 591
    gods' supplication to I 420-1
    of Hindu Trimūrti I 8n, 437n, 459; II 115,
        144
    ideal cause of potencies I 349, 381n
    imparts wisdom in krita age II 483
    is all that is II 612n
    kāla (time) or I 427; II 564
    as Kapila imparting wisdom II 572
    legend of Rāhu, Sun, Moon II 381
    lotus (Brahmā) fr navel of I 379; II 472
    Mahat appears 1st as I 75
    manifests the lotus I 381n
    many forms of II 146n
    Matsya avatāra of I 263-4, 394; II 139, 313
    mover on waters I 345, 348
    names of II 107
    Neptune, Idaspati, Nārāyana or II 765n
    not a high god in *Rig-Veda* I 112
    not direct creator of man I 445
    orders ark built II 139
    Pañchaśikha visits I 236
    pervades manus, rishis II 611n
    the preserver I 459n; II 313
    races of men & II 32-3
    Rajāmsi or 3 strides of II 621-2 &n
    regenerates I 459n
    rests on golden lotus (padma) II 578
    rests on serpent (Śesha) during pralaya
        I 344, 379, 381; II 98
    role of, in 4 yugas II 483
    as Rudra, the destroyer I 370; II 69n
    six-pointed star & I 215

    as the Sun I 290n; II 38
    svar-loka abode of II 404
    symbolized as serpent II 756
    three steps of I 112, 113n, 433n; II 38, 622n
    time only a form of II 307n
    trickery, deceit of, & Jehovah I 421-2
    triple hypostasis of I 18, 286-7
    two aspects of I 421, 545
    Vaikuntha-loka heaven of I 522
    visited by 7 kumāras II 584
    waters of space & navel of II 472
    White Island, lived on II 584
Vishnu Purāṇa
    referred to:
        events purposely blended in II 310
        heliocentrism in II 155
        kumāras hardly hinted at in II 577
        misunderstood II 320-1
        oldest MS of II 174n
        oldest of Purānas II 58
        secret meanings in I 423
        tampered w by Brahmans I 423
        Wilson & I 255, 257n, 419n, 423n; II 73
    quoted:
        Ādi-bhūta I xix
        ākāśa (ether), sound, color I 205
        asexual & other reproduction II 658
        asuras fr Brahmā's body I 218-19n
        beginning of cosmogony I 545
        in the beginning there was One I 256
        bhutas described II 102n
        Brahmā as cause of potencies I 55
        Brahmā creates anew II 58-9
        Brahmā, 3 aspects of I 19
        Brahmā wrathful at Vedhas II 78
        Budha born fr Tārā & Soma II 45 &n
        Chiti (chitti) I 288n
        creation of 4 kinds of beings II 625
        Daksha creates progeny II 183, 275n
        Daksha reborn every kalpa II 247n
        divine dynasties II 369 &n
        dvīpas listed, expl II 320-3, 404n
        Eighth Creation I 448
        elements, meaning of I 520-23
        elements, properties, creation I 521
        eternity, meaning of I 336n
        ether material cause of sound I 255
        forty-nine fires I 291 &n, 520-1
        "fragrance affects the mind" I 451-2n
        geography, geodesy, & ethnology
            II 320-2
        gods created & perish I 376
        gods' supplication to Vishnu I 419-22
        Hari (Vishnu) described I 421

immortality defined I 36n
kali-yuga described I 377-8
kalpas, yugas II 307n
Kandu, Pramlochā (sweat-born) II 171n, 174-5
Kapila's Eye destroys 60,000 I 563
karma of created beings I 456n
kumāras II 173
legend of Purūravas I 523
Mahādeva springs fr Brahmā II 548
mahāpralaya I 371
Mahat & matter are boundaries I 257
mānasa, rājasas II 89
manus, manvantaras, rishis II 614-15n
man was 7th Creation I 376
many forms of Vishnu & Brahmā II 146n
mind-born sons II 625 &n
Mt Meru described II 403-4
mundane egg I 65-6, 360
Nārada son of Kaśyapa II 47-8
nine creations in I 450-7
nine planets mentioned in II 488-9n
Parāśara II 232, 326
potency of every cause I 450
prabhavāpyaya defined I 46
pradhāna, prakriti I 50, 545
pralaya & prakritis I 257
pralayas (various) I 370-1; II 309-10n
primeval creatures II 162-3
primordial subst, all comes fr I 284-5
Priyavrata & 7 dvīpas II 319-22, 326
Pushkara II 403-4
rākshasas II 165n
rishis destroy trees (sorcerers) II 495
rotation of Earth II 155
Sāgara I 563; II 572
sandhyā, sandhyāmsa in II 308n
sarpa, Ahi fr Brahmā's hair II 181-2n
seven creations I 445-6 &n
seven rishis, 14 manus II 624
sevens in I 348
Seventh Creation (man) I 445
size of Earth II 616-17n
Śrī, various names of II 76n
Sun neither rises nor sets I 290n; II 155
Sun reflection of Vishnu I 290n
Surasā mother of dragons II 381
undying race in II 275 &n
universe one w divine knowledge I 421n
Vishnu creates at play II 126
Vishnu pervades all II 611-12 &nn
Vishnu, triple hypostasis of I 286-7
Vision(s)
adepts', confirmed by others I 273

Enoch's II 229, 482-3, 533-5
exuberance of nervous fluid II 370 &n
Ezekiel's I 126-7; II 134n, 552-3
inner, awakened (initiation) II 294 &n
of insane persons I 295; II 370n
panoramic, of the soul I 266
St John's I 72n; II 93n, 497
of seers I 633
symbolic, pillars of Xtian theol II 497
Viśishṭādvaita(ins) (Skt) qualified non-dualist (Vedanta school)
describing moksha I 132
logic higher than Christianity I 522
Mahat divine mind in action I 451
on Parabrahman I 59n, 233n, 522
pradhāna called illusion in I 62
Vaishnavas & I 55
Viśishṭādvaita Catechism I 132. *See Catechism of the Viśishṭādvaita*
Viśvakarma(n) (Skt). *See also* Logos, Purusha, Tvashṭri
architect of world II 269n, 559
carpenter, builder II 101n, 345n, 542-3
crucifies Sun-initiate I 322n; II 543
highest, oldest of gods II 101n
Kronos &, (Bréal) II 269n
Logos I 470
made "fiery weapon" II 559
one of mystic rays I 515n
patron of initiates II 615
potencies of space I 9-10n
represents mankind II 607
sacrifices himself to himself I 268; II 559, 606
Sanjñā daughter of II 174
Tvashṭri synonym of II 615
universal sacrifice or sarvamedha of II 605
Vulcan, Tubal-Kain or II 384n
Viśvāmitra (Skt)
Egypt settled in days of II 746
Viśvānara (Skt)
elements spring fr I 621 &n
son of the Sun II 568n
Viśvarūpa (Skt), title of Vishnu I 452n
Viśvatryarchas (Skt)
1 of 7 principal solar rays I 515n
Vis Viva (Lat) living force
Ganot & Huxley on I 669-70
Vita Apollonii. See Philostratus
Vital. *See also* Archaeus, Caloric, Life Principle, Nervous Ether
circulating of, solar fluid I 541
fluid of cat curled up II 552n
Fohat is, fluid, solar energy I 111-12

force in man & nature I 538-9 &n
force, never-dying breath II 589
force no objective reality I 296
forces of globe fr Sun II 29
no, principle (science) I 538, 602; II 720
phenomena septenary II 622-3 &n
principle discussed I 603-4
principle not of *our* matter II 672
principle of solar system I 591; II 311n
principle, pro & con I 634
Vital Electricity
    invisible, all-pervading life I 338 &n
    Sun's, feeds entire system I 541, 602
Vital Fire(s) II 109
    in all, latent in some II 267
Vita Pythagorae. See Porphyry
Vit. Pythag. See Diogenes Laertius
Vitatha (Skt), Kapila son of II 572
Viṭhobā (Skt, Wittoba in tx)
    crucified in space I 321n; II 560-1
Vitruvius Pollio, Marcus
    an initiate I 209n
—— [*De architectura*]
    laws of proportion esoteric I 208n
Vivasvat (Skt)
    the Sun or Sūrya II 211
    Vaivasvata Manu son of II 211, 253
Viveka-Chūdāmaṇi [*Crest-Jewel of Wisdom*]
    on Īśvara, ātma I 573-4
    soul, spirit in I 569-70
Vivien, tempting Merlin, parallel story of
    II 175n
Viwān. *See* Vimāna
Viwān Vidyā. *See* Vimāna-Vidyā
Vixanghat [Vivanghat or Vivahant] (Pers)
    Yima son of II 609
Voḍhu (Skt), a kumāra II 319
Vogt, Karl C. II 646, 652
    ape theory of II 665, 679
    brain of apes & aborigines II 193n, 661, 682n
    derides vitalist "fallacy" I 540
    man fr New World apes II 171
    man orig in Asia & America II 679
    missing link betw reptile & bird II 183
    a molecularist I 637n
    opinions not respected by theos II 651
    Paleolithic & Neolithic man II 716n
    places man among primates II 667
    thought is molecular motion I 134n
Vohu-Mano (Pers), good thoughts II 517
Voice. *See also* Bāth-Kōl, Logos, Vāch, Verbum, Word
    Bāth-kōl & Hebrew divine I 431n; II 107
    calls universe out of chaos I 137

described I 94-6
divine, as Kwan-yin I 72, 136, 137, 431n
gandharvas the, of nature I 523n
inner, in man or chit I 288n
of SELF WITHIN SELF II 640
spirit & word, kab trinity I 337, 447
still small, of consciousness I 280
that speaks to initiate I 431n
Vāch, Śatarūpa or I 94
of the Will (*Zohar*) I 346
Word or Logos I 99 &n
Void, Voidness. *See also* Abyss
    Alaya & I 48
    chaos, space, Ain-sōph or I 109
    container & body of universe I 342-3
    darkness & non-ego I 42
    full of bodies (Hermes) I 671
    Ginnungagap or I 367
    no, space in universe I 289
    space is a, to science I 587 &n
Volcanic
    action destroyed Lemuria II 141n
    conflagration & 5th race II 307n
    energies & Titan-Kabiri II 363
    eruptions in Central Asia II 356
Volcanoes(ism)
    destroyed Easter Island II 326
    destroy evidence of past II 311
    earthquakes, & continents II 776n
    fifth continent & II 445-6
    Metcalfe's solar caloric & I 524
    Moon, planets cause II 699
    Plato's Atlantis & II 408
    submarine, or ecpyrosis II 784
    twice destroyed races II 725-6
Volcanoes of Greece, The. See Pègues, Abbé
Völcker, K. H. W., *Mythische Geographie . . .*
    Hyperborean continent II 7
Volga River
    Io crosses, in wanderings II 416
Volger, on age of strata II 154
Volney, Constantin François Chasseboeuf
    Comte de
—— *The Ruins . . . of Empires*
    age of Greek zodiac I 658; II 436n
Voltaire [François-Marie Arouet] II 702
    attracted to Indian Brahmans II 742
    believed Hesiod factual II 777
    did not know Secret Doctrine II 742n
    "Ezour Veda" a precious gift II 442
    what produces our thoughts II 88-9
Völuspá (poem in Elder Edda)
    on mundane egg I 367
Von Buch, Leopold. *See* Buch, L. von

Von Hartmann. *See* Hartmann
Von Schelling. *See* Schelling
Voodoo(s), revered serpent II 209
Vormius [Wormius] & Olaus Magnus
  oracle rocks elected kings II 346
Vortex-Atoms
  Stallo on theory of I 488-9
  Thomson on I 117, 492
  Thomson's, & early atomists I 488, 579
Vortical Movement, Theory
  aether & I 487
  Greek concepts of, traced I 117
  in primordial matter I 117-18
  Stallo on I 488-9
  Swedenborg on I 118n
Vortices
  of Descartes, & stars I 206n, 492
  elemental, & Universal Mind I 623
  initiates taught of atomic I 569
  systemic, of Kepler I 623
Voru Barshti (Pers)
  globe G, Earth chain or II 759
Voru-Zarshti (Pers). *See also* Earth Chain
  globe A, Earth chain or II 759
Vossius [Gerrit Jansz Vos]
—— *Theologia Gentili . . . Idolatriae*
  Angelic Virtues oversee I 123n
  Aristotle's view of planets I 493
  Mercury, Sun are one II 28
  Michael is Mercury II 480-1
Votan (Mexican demigod)
  Quetzalcoatl, Ham, Canaan II 380
  seven families & II 35
  son of the snakes II 379
Vowel(s)
  "All-in-all" & ONE ALL I 20
  five, AEIOV, & root-races II 458
  five mystic, & creation II 579
  -parent of monosyllabic languages II 199
  potency of I 94
  seven, & 49 powers I 410-11; II 564
  seven, heavens, logoi II 563
Voyage dans le Comté de Cornouailles . . . See
  Halliwell, J. O.
Voyage de Laponie. See Regnard, J.-F.
Voyages dans la basse. See Denon, D. V.
Voyage to Siberia. See Chappe d'Autroche

Voyageurs anciens et modernes. See Charton
Vrata (Skt) law or power
  Indra's, most powerful II 606
Vratāni (Skt) active laws
  Varuna's laws or II 606
Vriddha-Garga, on yugas II 624n
Vril
  of Bulwer-Lytton I 563
  of Keely kept secret I xxxv, 563
Vritra (Skt)
  cosmic serpent II 378
  demon of drought II 385
  killed by Indra I 202; II 382, 384
Vritra-Han (Skt) slayer of Vritra
  title of Indra II 382, 384
Vritri, or Ah-hi [Vritra or Ahi] serpents
  I 202
Vul (Assyr) atmospheric god
  same as Hindu Indra II 386
Vulcan, Vulcain (Lat)
  Cain, Saturn, Jehovah & I 578
  father of 4 Kabiri II 106
  Kabir, instructor of metal arts II 390
  Lemnos sacred to II 3
  Mars, Cain, Vul-Cain or II 390n, 392-3n
  power over fire I 464
  Sepp in error re II 619-20
  Viśvakarma, Tubal-Kain or II 384n
Vulgate (Latin version of Bible)
  Protestant Bible disagrees w I 576
  on Reuben I 651
Vulture, Promethean II 413, 422
Vyāhritis (Skt) declaration
  bhūr, bhuvar, svar I 432n
Vyakta (Skt) II 46
  matter as, conditioned I 10n
Vyāna (Skt), one of the "Life Winds" II 567
Vyāsa(s) (Skt)
  Vishnu is all 28, of Vedas II 146n
Vyāvahārika (Skt), ray manifested in I 356
Vyaya (Skt) perishable
  Purusha-pradhāna & I 582
Vyse, Colonel Howard
—— *. . . The Pyramids of Ghizeh*
  Arabs, Sabeans, Pyramids II 361-2
  q var authors on Seth II 366

W

Wagner, Prof, believed in 4th dimension I 251 &n
Wägner, W., *Asgard and the Gods*
  battle of the Flames in I 202
  black ravens of Odin I 443
  common orig of rel concepts I 424
  first creation described I 427
  hammer, mjölnir II 99
  honey dew or astral light I 344-5
  Loki fr "liechan" [liuhan] II 283n
  Mundane Tree I 211
  Nidhögg gnaws World Tree I 407
  Niflheim or chaos in I 367
  Odin, Mimir in I 402
  pillars of the world or Ases II 97
  prophecy of 3 goddesses II 100
  Starkad described II 346n
  wars in heaven II 386
  Yggdrasil, Norns, story of II 520
Waite, A. E.
  —— "Biographical & Critical Essay" in Lévi's
    The Mysteries of Magic
  in error re *Book of Enoch* II 506
  Lévi's ideas on astral light I 253-4n
Wake, C. Staniland
  —— *The Origin & Significance* . . .
  age of Egypt (Wilkinson) II 432
  age of Great Pyramid II 431-2
  astron knowledge in Great Pyramid I 314
  Bunsen on Seth II 82n
  Deluge & pyramids II 352
  Great Dragon (Dupuis) II 32n
  Hermes son of Seth II 362
  Proctor on Great Dragon II 352-3
  on Sabaeans II 361-2
  sacred Mysteries in Gt Pyramid I 317-18n
  serpents & wisdom II 26-7n
  Seth, Hermes II 362, 366
Waking State, & spiritual sight I 289
Walhalla. *See* Valhalla
Wallace, Alfred Russel II 646
  believed in spiritualism I 520
  on evolution of plants I 585
  last glaciation 70,000 yrs ago II 778n
  man's origins complicated II 729
  theosophists respect II 651
  —— *Contributions to the Theory* . . .

  "higher intelligences" I 107, 339; II 677n
  man speechless ape-creature II 661
  natural selection not enough II 696
  —— *Geographical Distribution* . . .
  Lemurian continent II 7-8, 8n, 193n
  —— *Island Life*
  criticism of, by Gardner II 782-3
  Lemuria II 7-8, 8n
  —— *The Malay Archipelago* . . .
  sunken Pacific continent II 789
Wan, Buddhist Mongolian swastika II 556
Wanderers. *See* Comets
Wandering Jew
  man would be, without "Rebels" II 243
War(s)
  adepts vs sorcerers II 384, 501, 503
  disease &, fr North & West winds I 123
  betw divine & terrestrial self II 268
  first, for man in 4th race II 276
  betw gods & dragon II 384, 503
  betw good & evil II 225
  planetary I 101
  Skanda, Kārttikeya, Mars & II 382
  among stars, planets, moon I 202
  struggles or, during evolution I 193
  betw Tiamat & Bel II 503
War between Gods & Giants
  Atlas assisted giants in II 493
  described II 222-3
  solar eclipse 945 BC &, (Bentley) II 76
  submersion of Atlantis ended II 222
Ward, Robert, ["On Heat and Light"] I 484n
War(s) in Heaven. *See also Revelation*
  betw adepts of left & right II 501-2
  allegorized in *Rāmāyana* II 495
  Assyrian, (G. Smith) II 386
  astronomical phases of I 201-4
  Brahman ecclesiastics disfigured II 502
  Christian version of, transformed II 390
  Codex Nazaraeus on, (*IU*) I 194-6
  creation due to, (Rosicrucian) II 237
  expl I 194-8, 201-3; II 103-4, 384-90,
    492-505
  first, discussed I 419-23
  of gods vs asuras II 390, 498
  human phase of II 501-2

fr India via Persia, Chaldea I 198
of Michael & dragon I 202
origin of Christian I 68, 193; II 497
pagan in origin I 198, 418
repeated on every plane II 268
[*Revelation*] story of I 194
secret of, in initiation crypts II 379
betw sons of god & of shadow II 495, 500
betw spirit & matter II 268, 269n
struggles for candidate for adeptship II 380
Tārakāmaya or I 418; II 45, 63, 497-8
Theosophist article on, (Alee Beg) II 244-5
third, betw adepts & sorcerers I 419 &n
betw Thraētaona & Azhi-daksha II 390
three, in every cosmogony I 418
triple meanings in var religions I 202
"War in Heaven, The." *See* Mitford, G.
War of the Titans (Hesiod) II 63, 500
Wassilief [V. P. Vasilyev], *Der Buddhismus* . . .
    nidānas, etc I 39 &n
    time I 43 &n
Watcher(s). *See also* Silent Watcher
    Amshaspends are our II 358
    descended to teach early man I 267
    each globe, race has its I 233
    each nation has its I 576
    higher dhyāni-buddhas or I 267
    lipikas are the four I 103-4 &n
    same as builders I 53
    watch over man until 3rd race I 266
Water (element). *See also* Cataclysm, Deluge
    in alchemy, radical moyst II 542
    around Egg of Brahmā II 616
    blood of Earth II 43n, 400 &n
    combines hydrogen, oxygen I 121
    connected w messiah, baptism I 385
    "critical," on Jupiter (Williams) II 137n
    Demiurge became, (Egy) I 311
    earth &, female, passive II 130
    fr earth, fire, heat & mist I 250
    female element I 457-8n; II 65
    female, passive, & fire I 341
    fire &, or Father & Mother I 70
    fire &, produced matter II 65
    fire finds refuge in I 402
    fluid animating Earth II 400n
    great deep, chaos or I 460
    fr heat, heat fr air I 330
    hydrogen base of II 105
    Jesus a fish in midst of II 313n
    Kārttikeya born of, & fire II 550
    letter "M" a glyph for I 384-5
    liquid fire II 114
    lotus product of, & fire I 57, 379n

man made of, & earth I 344-5
Metis as II 130
Mimir drew wisdom fr I 402
more complex on higher planes I 542
mother-substance regulates I 291-2
primordial form of I 254
principle of all things (Thales) I 345, 385
production of Nara II 495n
progeny of electricity I 81-2
progeny of Moon II 66
races twice destroyed by II 725-6
related to taste II 107
represents matter, female II 64
St Matthew, angel-man, & II 114
sign of II 179
swallowed by fire (pralaya) I 372-3
symb divine soul II 113
symb lower steps of initiation II 566n
symb matter, exotericism II 566 &n
universe fr air, fire, & I 92 &n
Varuna, Neptune as god of I 462
Water Lily I 385
    air-water symbol I 358
    Audubon's yellow, doubted II 440
    Gabriel holds, (Christian art) I 379n, 384
    symbol of, & lotus I 379-80
Water Men
    produced in early eras II 52-3, 634
    fr remains of early rounds I 55
Waters. *See also* Flood, Space, Waters of Space
    ākāśic ocean or I 457-8n
    Apām-Napāt son of the II 400n
    basis of material existence I 64
    displacement of Earth's II 138
    Ea, Dāgōn, Oannes & II 495n
    firmament created in midst of II 75
    of the flood or deep, chaos II 145
    of grace (Christian) I 458n
    great flood of, in chaos II 144
    important in all cosmogonies I 64
    Rudra drinks up, of universe II 69n
    scientists misunderstood word I 64
    Sea of Space became, of Earth II 477
    spirit moves on face of II 128, 145
    turbid, dark II 57, 63
    of wisdom II 495n
Waters of Space
    chaos, great deep I 431
    dry I 625
    explained I 62-3, 64
    fiery II 400n
    primordial I 431, 437
    ray differentiates the I 231
    sea, ocean & II 477, 758

symbols of I 365, 625-6
Vishnu's navel & II 472
Waterston, on Sun's heat I 484n
Watery, nature of 1st dhyāni-chohans I 82
Watery Abyss (or Space)
  abode of Ea, wisdom II 53
Water-Yazatas (Pers)
  ether, not the water we know II 400n
Watson, Dr John
  rocking stones & Celts II 344
Watts, Isaac
  Earth footstool of God I 154
Wave
  carrying man to 6th race I 558
  of sound & light II 489
We. *See* Vi, Vili, & Odin
Wealden
  bed of Lemurian river II 333
  iguanodon of II 348
Weapon(s), 7 & principles II 629-30
Weather, Moon, planets & II 699
Web
  symbol I 60, 83-5, 639; II 614
  weaving of, expansion & contraction I 83-4
Weber, Prof Albrecht
  blunders w oriental symbol of II 570
  misunderstood *Vishnu Purāna* II 320
—— *Akad. . . . Vorles (Hist. of Indian Lit.)*
  age of Indian zodiac II 50
  on Asuramaya II 49-50, 67, 326
  darśanas show Gk influence I 47n
  date of *Rig-Vidhāna* I 436
  in error re āngirasas II 605n
  Hindu arts fr Greece II 225
  Hindu zodiac fr Greece I 647
  Indo-Germanic before Vedic race II 166n
  purusha in *Katha Upanishad* I 461
  world soul fr spirit & matter I 365
Webhāra (Mount Baibhār of Pāli MSS)
  Buddhist cave initiations near I xx
Webster (dictionary of)
  definition of evolution II 653
  "empirical" II 664-5
  "fire" I 121
Wednesday
  Mercury day I 652
  sacred to Hermes, Thoth II 366-7
Week(s). *See also* Septenary, Sevens
  applied to life of embryo I 389
  of creation in Kabbala II 623-4
  days of, same in var nations I 652
  each lunar, has its influence I 409
  Hebrew word for, is "seven" II 624n
  man's life a, of decades II 623

Sabbath equals I 240
septenary cycles & II 624-5n
Thoth-Lunis god of II 529-30
used for various cycles II 395
Weight. *See also* Atomic Weight
  caloric without I 525
  no, of bodies in space (Tardy) I 502
  pregenetic matter had no I 590
Wei Po-yang, *Ts'an t'ung ch'i* II 554n
Weismann, August
  ex-evolutionist I 223n; II 711
—— [*Studien zur Deszendenztheorie*]
  germ plasm theories of I 223n, 224
Welcker, F. G., *Griechische Götterlehre*
  Kabeiron fr Gk "to burn" II 363
  Mars, derivation of II 392n
Well of Knowledge, & Moses II 465n
West (direction)
  blue corn depicts, (Zuñi) II 629
  evil, epidemics, wars fr North & I 123
  Varuna guards the I 128
West(ern)
  consciousness by-product of matter I 327n
  Eastern &, metaphysics I 79n, 149, 169, 171,
    225-6, 295, 327 &n
  hearsay unacceptable to, scholars I xxxvii
  metaphysics & triune man I 225-6
  mind subject to conceit I 161
  mystics start w 3rd creation II 544
  repudiated pagan wisdom I 642
  scholars & Secret Doctrine II 449
  truth not exclusive property of I 279
West Hoadley
  ruins of Atlantean monoliths in II 343
West Indies(ian)
  West African &, fauna alike II 792
Westminster, talking stone at II 342
Westminster Review
  Spencer on nebular hypothesis I 600
  Thompson & Atlantis II 792
Westropp, Hodder M.
  no race of dolmen builders II 753
"What is Matter & What is Force?" *See*
  Blavatsky
Wheat
  brought fr other lokas II 373
  defunct given, (Egypt) I 221
  Dendera Virgo holds ear of II 433
  Kabiri revealed by producing II 364
  mysteries of II 374n
  sacred to Egyptians II 374
Wheat Ear of Virgo [Spica] II 433
  kali-yuga & I 665; II 435
Wheel(s). *See also* Chakra

centers of force I 116-17, 144
of Ezekiel's vision I 127; II 128, 134n, 552-3
older, globes of previous rounds I 199
Rabbi Parcha's II 397n
small, or Earth chain I 205
symb of world, globe, round I 40n, 199, 205,
  232, 440; II 27, 52
winged, or seraphim I 122, 126
of world or ōphannīm I 440
Wheva, bone (Maori) II 194n
Whewell, Dr William
—— [*Philosophy of the Inductive Sciences*]
sevens & color, sound, taste II 622
—— *Plurality of Worlds*
disputes idea of other worlds I 607;
  II 149-50n
Whirlwind I 77
birth of heavenly bodies & I 103
Deity becomes a I 117
Fohat or fiery I 106, 108
nebulas, 1st stage of I 22, 97-8n
One Life, Great Breath or I 226n
Whiston, William, *Old Testament*
re human chronology II 395
White
brown-, race II 250
children of, Mother (Stanzas) II 109
Head, Resha Hiv'rah [Rēishā' Hivvārā'] or
  II 84
race(s) II 249
region, dhyāni fr (Stanzas) II 55
Śiva reborn as 4, youths II 282
Whitechapel Murderer (Jack the Ripper)
  II 507n
White Devil
Div-sefid of White Island II 403, 407 &n
other names for II 403
of Wilford II 147, 402-3
White Head, 5th race or II 705-6
White Island. *See also* Śveta-Dvīpa
became black w sin II 67, 408 &n
[Mackey] II 406-7
not Atlantis or Śankha-dvīpa II 408n
rākshasas, daityas of II 288
Ruta, was II 147
seven kumāras visited Vishnu at II 584
seventh zone of Purānas II 402
Śveta-dvīpa or II 319, 322, 402-4, 408 &n,
  584
veiled its face II 319
white devil (Div-sefid, Tāradaitya) of II
  403-4, 407 &n
Wilford mistaken re II 402n, 404, 407
White Magic

lords of II 427
Rāmāyana struggle betw black & II 495
White Swan. *See also* Haṃsa, Swan
Leda as a II 122
overshadowed egg II 131
White Yajurveda, & Mahādeva II 548
Whydah, Africans of, revered serpent II 209
Wicks, four, or 4 lower principles I 237
Widblain. *See* Vídbláinn
Wiegand, Julius, *Ueber die Auflösung . . .*
ape evolved fr man I 185n
Wigred. *See* Vigrid
Wilder, Dr Alexander
dianoia & logos defined II 25
Gan-duniyas name of Babylonians II 202
genesis defined II 24n
—— "The Primeval Race Double-Sexed"
Madagascan legend II 177
man androgyne II 134 &n, 135
vegetables, insects, bisexual II 133
Wilford, Col F. (in *Asiatic Researches*)
deceived by forged MSS I xxx-i
Hindus borrowed fr Christians I 655n
mistakes of, described I xxxi; II 402n
misunderstood *Vishnu Purāna* II 320
saw relation betw Hebrew & Hindu I 654
—— ["An Essay on the Sacred Isles . . ."]
Atlas & Meru II 401n, 404
confused Gades, Spain, Atlantis II 406n
dwarfed Hindu chronology I 655
kumāras II 319
seven dvīpas I 409
theories on England & dvīpas II 402-9
White Devil II 147
—— "On Egypt & The Nile"
Atala & the 7 dvīpas II 404
I't & peace in Śankha-dvīpa II 406
Śankhāsura II 405
—— "On the Chronology of the Hindus"
Prajāpatis are manus, rishis II 142
—— "On the Kings of Magadha"
the "Great War" I 369n
Yudhishthira I 369-70
Wilkins, Charles, & univ phil tongue I 310
Wilkinson, J. G., Egy civ before Menes II 432
Wilkinson, Rev Wm F., *Modern Materialism*
Newton's use of "Subtle Spirit" I 490
Will(s)
absolute, & law II 164
aggregate of cosmic, & atoms I 632-3
animals have II 671n
atoms have memory, sensation & II 672
Deity 1st manifests as I 343
faith without, is barren II 59n

Fohat & I 111
human forms born of I 211
incarnating host preferred free II 421
Itchasakti [īchchhāśakti] as, -power
    I 292-3; II 173
it is the, of Deity that acts II 528
procreation by I 192
rebellious angels & free- I 193-4
result of, on our actions I 639
Sons of, & Yoga II 163
voice of the, (*Zohar*) I 346
Will-Born
    kumāras & jayas called II 584-5
    lords propelled by Fohat II 86
Willi. *See* Vi, Vili, & Odin
William of Salisbury
    saw Mona stone in 1554 II 345
Williams, W. M., *The Fuel of the Sun*
    critical state of Sun II 136n
    Sun, ether, heat I 102, 585
—— "Solids, Liquids, and Gases"
    critical matter in Sun, Jupiter II 136-7n
Willow Leaves (Nasmyth theory)
    colleagues derided Herschel re I 590-1
    Herschel on I 541, 591
    shapes on Sun desc by Nasmyth I 530
    source of solar vital energy I 541
Wilson, Dr A., "The Evolution of Man"
    all living forms not fossilized II 674
    evolution a young subject II 152
—— "Letter" to *Knowledge*
    replies to queries by "G.M." II 152
Wilson, Daniel
—— [*Archaeology & Prehistoric Annals . . .*]
    on giant Scottish skeleton II 749
—— *Prehistoric Man*
    writing known to earliest man II 729
Wilson, Horace Hayman
    birth of Rudra fr the Śaivas I 456n
    blundered re Hindu symbols II 570
    confused Brahma & Brahmā I 453n
    confused Buddhists & Chārvākas I 419n
    contradictions re 7 prakritis I 257n
    creation I 452n
    dating of *VP* ridiculous I 419n, 423n
    did not enjoy modern advantages I 453n
    did not understand "Waters" I 457-8n
    on egg symbol I 360
    on *Garuda Purāna* II 565n
    has Buddha teaching Daityas in *VP* I 419n
    Hindu chronology fiction II 73
    indiscrete principle of I 521-2
    lived w Brahmins, pandits I 420
    misunderstood Hindu chronology II 321

sarpa (ahi) fr Brahmā's hair II 181-2n
spirit acts thru intermediaries I 451-2n
—— [*Essays . . . on Sanskrit Literature*]
    Buddhism in *Bhagavad-Gītā* I 419n
—— *Medical & Surgical Sciences . . .*
    all vegetable bodies alive I 454
—— *Select Specimens of the Theatre . . .*
    āgneyāstra (fire weapons) II 427n, 629-30
Winchell, Alexander, "The Cycles of Matter"
    essay [in his *Sketches of Creation*] I 638 &n
—— *Pre-Adamites*
    Egypt civilized before Menes II 334
—— *World Life . . .*
    all elements fr 1 element I 542
    ancients on Earth's rotation I 117n
    beginning of sedimentation II 715n
    beings w dif corporeality & senses I 608n
    Charles's Law, ref to I 84
    Croll on geological eras II 9
    declared Kepler's ideas fanciful I 499
    dissociation of matter I 543n
    ethereal medium I 528 &n
    generation of rotation I 500
    gravity & unexpl phenomena I 497-8
    heat of the Sun I 102 &n
    heat thru contraction I 84-5
    magnetism & gravity I 498
    mistakes of Laplace I 592n
    Moon cooled faster than Earth I 155n
    nebular theory I 505, 544
    periodical submergences II 325n
    q Faye I 496
    q Laplace I 498
    q Lecouturier I 494
    q Mädler I 501
    q Newcombe II 149n
    q Newton I 494-5
    q Whewell I 607
    science on age of life II 694
    scientific divination I 638
    sedimentary age of globe II 695
    sunken northern continent II 323-4 &n
    Swedenborg's vortical theory I 118n
    Thomson on Earth's cooling II 694
    unknown substances I 607n
    what nebular theory is not I 599-600
    years required for evolution II 72
Wind(s). *See also* Four Winds
    aethereal, impregnate divine egg I 365, 461
    agent of transmission, nurse II 105
    air, spirit &, synonymous I 342
    Athenians invoke, (Boreas) I 467
    carries man in his bosom II 109
    evil, at South Pole II 400

fed sweat-born egg II 131
fiery, incandescent cosmic dust I 107
four kinds of, explained I 123
of Hebrews I 466
Jesus rebukes the I 468
in *John* 3 should be spirit I 226
life, (prānas, *Anugītā*) II 566-9
man nursed by II 113
seed sprang fr, & chaos I 340
seven principal II 612
Sopatrus unchained the I 469
spirit or I 340, 461
symbol of human soul II 113
Toum [Tum] North & West (Egy) I 673
Typhoeus, Aeolus, Boreas & I 466
Vāyu god of I 190, 468-9
Wind (the hot, destroying)
related to dragon story II 384-6
various religions on II 384-5
Wine
god of, & terrestrial Poles II 363
origin of, (Plato) II 373
Wing & Shadow II 121-4
Winged Globes
became the scarabaeus II 552
form of egg symbol I 365
Four Mahārājahs or I 126
Winged Races
in Plato & *Popol Vuh* II 55n, 96, 264
Winter
eternal Lemurian II 777 &n
six symbol of, & Autumn II 583
Sun in Cancer in, (Egy) II 431
Wisdom. *See also* Budha, Wisdom Religion
absolute, mirrored in ideation I 328
absolute, transcends time & space I 1-2n
Apollo god of oracular II 106
birds of I 443; II 292-3
black birds symbols of primeval I 443
budhism or II 100
Chochmah [Hokhmāh] II 84-5, 134n
divine, & earthly, struggle II 377
dragons of I 657; II 26, 94n, 210, 379, 381, 384n, 507
dual aspect of II 364, 489
Ea god of II 53, 61, 115, 139n
early magic meant science of II 319
earthly, sensual, (*James*3:15) II 134n, 275n
falling like lightning II 230-1
first emanation of Deity II 489
flows fr Deity (*Zohar*) I 239
follower of true Eastern II 588-9
intelligence &, described II 134 &n
knowledge & I 165

light symbol of esoteric II 94n, 162
Mercury (Budha) Lord of II 27, 28, 44, 498
-Ocean, Dalai Lama symb name II 502n
Samael & Michael aspects of II 378
Sarasvatī goddess of I 95
secret, acquired by Self I 534
of self-consciousness II 113
serpent(s) of II 98, 386-7
serpent symbol of II 214, 351, 377, 386, 552
seven forms of divine I 574; II 29n
Soma parent of esoteric II 500
Sons of II 16, 18, 52
spiritual, is buddhi II 275n
Tārā, Budha & birth of II 499
thirty-two paths of II 39
understanding heart & II 134n
of universal tradition II 133
West repudiates pagan I 642
Wisdom Eye. *See* Cyclops, Pineal Gland, Third Eye
Wisdom of Solomon. See Book of Wisdom
Wisdom Religion
in Central Asia I 376
Druids, Persians had II 756
Gautama & I xx
inheritance of all nations I xviii, xx, xliv
Jews once possessed II 469
seven main branches of II 636
Wise, Thomas A., *History of Paganism* . . .
on giant bones (India) II 347
on Stonehenge II 343 &n
Wiseman, Cardinal Nicholas P. Stephen
plural worlds in OT & NT I 607n
—— [*Twelve Lectures* . . .]
other worlds alluded to II 704
Wise Men. *See also* Adepts, Dragon(s), Initiates, Mahātmas, Masters, Serpents
of 5th race verified the SD I 273
Witches, Witchcraft
incantations & I 469
Sabbath of, goat & Pan II 510
Satan head of II 389n
of Thessaly & the Moon I 156
Witness(es)
one & 3, John & Śankara I 570-1 &n
Wittoba. *See* Viṭhobā
Woden. *See* Odin
Wogan, on divine Providence I 634
Wolf
mates w dog II 287
"who comes out of Darkness" II 386
Wolf, C. J. E., *Les Hypothèses Cosmogoniques*
endorses Kant's esotericism I 601
every star is in motion I 500, 596

how did chaos produce stars? I 599
Kepler's moon rings I 590
nebulae & nebular theory I 596-602
Wolf, F. A., [*Prolegomena ad Homerum*]
   on Fate or Μοῖρα (Moira) II 604n
Woman(en)
   ark, navel, Moon & II 461
   w child (in *Revelation*) II 383, 384
   created fr Adam's rib II 129
   creation of, in *Genesis* II 387
   creation of, (Tahitian) II 193-4
   curse on man came w, (Kab) II 216
   early Aryan, free as men I 382-3
   a "fatal gift" (Pandora) II 270 &n
   formed subsequent to man II 135
   inferior to man in popular religions I 136n
   lunar influence on reproductive cycles I 264, 389
   mānushyas created, by kriyāśakti II 140
   procreation painful to II 262
   sterility among, of old races II 779-80
   treatment of I 136n, 382
   Truth as a naked I 352
   when, knew no man II 415
Womb
   ark symbolizes II 139, 461
   circle w diameter double I 391-2
   desecration of symbol of I 382-3
   effulgent, or golden egg I 89
   Eve, Sarah or II 472
   Holy of Holies w Semites I 264, 391; II 457n, 466
   human, a reflection II 84
   lotus symbol of I 385
   Māqōm (Heb) or II 84, 457 &n
   of nature I 373n; II 234, 462, 466
   nether world, of life I 364n
   sarcophagus symbol & II 462
Wonders by Land and Sea. See Shan-Hai-King
Wondrous Being. *See also* Watcher
   "ever-living-human-Banyan" I 207
   Great Sacrifice & I 208
Woodward, Dr H.
—— "Evidences of the Age of Ice"
   axial changes & glacial ages II 726
Word. *See also* Logos, Sounds, Vāch, Verbum, Voice
   Ahura Mazdā & II 358
   basic property of ākāśa I 372
   born fr mind I 350
   called image of God II 479-80
   of central sun I 231
   Fohat is, made flesh I 111
   of God I 87; II 107

Logos, Spirit, Voice I 79, 99, 103, 337, 384, 431-2, 447, 470, 472, 614; II 25, 36
   Māthra Spenta or II 480
   Mēmrah or I 346
   Mercury or II 541
   motion, number & I 67
   names in various religions II 704n
   "one number fr no number" I 94
   passing on, by initiates I 404; II 220
   syllables & letters of I 351-2
Word(s)
   five, of Gnostics expl II 580
   last, cannot be given II 310
   ten, or *dbrim* of Kabbala II 37, 39-40
   unknown potency of spoken I 307
Word on Atlantis, A II 371. *See* de Mirville
Wordsworth, Bishop Christopher
   King of Ai hung on tree II 558
   transl of *Genesis* 4:1 II 127
Worker's Hammer (in *Book of Numbers*)
   swastika is II 99
Working Powers. *See* Builders
Workmen, 7, in *Pymander* II 97
Works and Days. See Hesiod
Works by The Late H. H. Wilson. See Wilson
Works of Sir Wm. Jones. See Jones, Wm.
World, The (NY), criticized HPB I 317n
World(s). *See also* Earth, Globes, Planets, Universes
   ākāśa soul of I 13n
   appearance & disappearance of I 16-17
   believers in plurality of II 706
   billions of, every manvantara I 143n
   born fr one another I 203-5
   communication betw other, & ours I 133
   consciousness key to knowing II 701
   creative, formative, & material I 98-9
   destroyed, renewed II 704-5
   destruction of, many meanings II 705-6
   deva of each portion of II 538
   dhyāni-chohans "created" II 510
   "dragon's head" symb name of every II 505
   elohīm formed, 6 by six I 239
   every atom becomes a I 85
   every, has parent star & sister planet II 33
   evolved fr the One Element I 540-3
   Fohats as many as there are I 143n
   formation of, (Stanza 5) I 22
   formed of preexisting material II 84, 510
   fourfold destruction of II 311
   fourteen, of Syrians expl I 435-6
   Hermes on building of I 436; II 489
   higher & lower, blend w ours I 604-5
   higher by essence not location I 221n

history in zodiacal signs II 431
hostile conditions surround new I 203-4
invisible, peopled I 583n, 606, 611; II 700, 702
"Kings of Edom" does not mean II 705
Kliphoth (Qelīppōth) is our, (*Zohar*) II 111
laya-centers & I 145
like sparks fr a hammer II 704
a living organism I 281
Malkūth lowest I 239
matter of various, differs I 143 &n, 589
new, patterned on former I 144-5
objective symb of One & many I 129
often needs repair (Newton) I 503
old, conquered by new I 202-3
once "of one lip," knowledge I 229-30
orientalists & Vedic divisions of II 622
other inhabited II 699-709
outbreathing & inbreathing of I 4
plurality of I 607-9; II 699-709
plurality of, implies many gods II 538
progressive development of I 43
rulers & regents of I 99
scintillas, sparks or I 99
Seven Agents contain material, (Egy) I 436
seven times depopulated II 617
seven, (globes) in Hindu lit I 112
some primordial, died soon II 704 &n
-Soul, or Deity (Plato) II 555
Space is real, ours, artificial I 615
stars not known as, to Epistles eds II 704
succession of, widely taught II 756-7
tenth, of Syrians our quaternary I 436
three, or rajāmsi II 621-2
within worlds I 133
World Egg I 64-5. *See also* Egg
World Germs
   primordial, & Fohat I 672
   spiritual particles I 200-1
World Life. See Winchell
World of Action (Asiatic ['Aśīyyāh] World), our Earth, our world II 111
World of Emanations (Atzilatic ['Atsīlōth]) gives birth to 3 worlds II 111
World of Formation (Jetzira, Yetsīrāh) habitat of the angels II 111
World Soul. *See also* Anima Mundi
   connected w all phenomena I 10
   differentiated I 140
   homogeneous element I 203
   Mahat or Mahā-buddhi I 16
   plane of a circle & II 555
World Stuff
   Anaxagoras on I 595

curds in cometary stage I 206
eternally homogeneous I 569
fifth, 6th cosmic principle I 101
first ignition of I 84
now called nebulae I 595
pre-protyle I 598
of science vs ancient chaos I 579
Sun, planets evolved fr I 101
World Teachers, Reformers. *See also* Avatāras, Initiates
   described II 358-9
   transmitters I xxxvi-vii
   truths of, not new I xxxvi-vii
World Tree. *See also* Aśvattha, Tree of Life, Yggdrasil
   described I 406-7
Worms, hermaphroditism & II 167
Worsaae [J. J. A.], on flint remains II 752n
Worship. *See also* Faith, Religion
   ceremonial, profitless II 93
   degeneration of II 273-4
   essential meaning of II 34 &n
   exoteric, a materialization II 498
   fourth race resorted to body- II 279
   idol- II 279, 723
   Lemurians had no outward II 272-3
   lunar & solar I 387, 397, 402; II 139n
   man should, in his soul I 280
   phallic I 264n; II 469-73
   sacrificial II 230
   sexual- & body- II 285
   of shells I 578
   silent, of nature I 381n
   tree, serpent & crocodile I 403-11
Wraie or Wraith
   or will-o'-the wisp II 206n
Wren, Sir Christopher I 426
Writing
   ancient methods of II 346n
   in China & India II 226
   discussed II 439-40, 529
   invented by Atlanteans II 439, 442
   known to earliest man (Dawson) II 729
   known to Phoenicians II 440
   Pānini & II 225, 439-40
   refused to some ancient nations I xxxii
   unknown in Stone Age II 442
Wuliang-sheu [Wu-liang shu] (Chin) Boundless Age or I 356
Wundt, Wilhelm M., *Die Theorie der Materie*
   on physical atomism I 513
Wu Wang, Emperor of Chow Dynasty II 302

XYZ

Xanthochroics
  fr anthropoids (Huxley) II 315n
Xanthocreatinine I 262n
Xenocrates, followed Plato II 555
Xenophanes
  condemns Homer, Hesiod II 764n
  "Sun turned toward another land" II 535
Xenophon, *Cyropaedia*
  Cyrus' death & signs in heaven I 652
Xerxes, winds destroyed fleet of I 466-7
Xisuthrus (Chald)
  Atlantean catastrophe & II 774
  Babylonian, Vaivasvata, Noah II 309
  Chaldean Noah II 4, 141, 222, 314, 397, 454
  Dāgōn (Matsya avatāra) & II 139
  Great Father (*Popol Vuh*) II 222
  Israelites repeated story of II 265
  Mulil, Flood & II 139n
  name contains story II 335
  saved & translated alive to heaven II 141

Yāh. *See also* Jāh
  Bīnāh & I 355, 394; II 85
  feminine I 438n, 618
  Kether-Bīnāh or, female I 438n
  same as Jah (Lord) II 126
  term not used before David II 541
Yāh-Ḥavvāh (Heb, Yāh-Hovāh in tx)
  androgyne Jehovah, Adam I 18, 60, 113; II
    125-8, 134, 388 &n, 469
  Jehovah or, same as chaos I 394
  male-female II 388 &n, 469, 601
  as mankind II 388
  mind-born son of Adam Kadmon II 126
  one of the elohīm of Saturn group II 127
Yaho, Yaho-Iah
  Jaho-Jah or Jaho is Jah II 129
  mystery name II 541
  pronunciations of II 129, 465
Yahoudi [Yahūdi]
  Afghans resent being called II 200n
  name given Jews II 127
Yāhweh. *See also* Jehovah, YHVH

Jehovah or II 388, 464
  male, female II 388
  other deities & II 514n
Yāhweh Elohīm (Heb, Java-Aleim in tx)
  hierophant I 346; II 202
  knew of sacred island II 220
  taught men to be like themselves II 215
  took Enoch II 532-3
Yājñavalkhya-smṛiti (Skt) I 432n
Yajña-Vidyā (Skt) I 168-9
Yajur-Veda, White (Skt)
  Śiva (Mahādeva) 1st appears in II 548
Yakshas (Skt)
  demigods (Purānas) II 90, 211, 369n
  demons created by Brahmā II 165n, 182n
  of Lankā II 70
Yama (Skt) god of the dead. *See also* Yima
  Earth, Pluto or I 462-3
  god of death II 44
  guards the South I 128
  heart of defunct read before I 105
  lord of underworld I 463
  Pitri-pati, king of the pitris II 44
  son of Vaivasvata Manu II 609
  various equivalents of I 105
  Yima or II 609
Yamabooshis [Yamabushi] (Jap)
  seven jewels, mysteries I 173
  seven precious things I 67n
Yamyad (Zamyad) Yasht (of *Zend Avesta*)
  Amesha-Spentas (Amshaspends) II 358
Yāna (Skt) vehicle (vāhan) or I 39. *See also*
  Vāhana
Yang (chin) & Yin I 471; II 554
Yang Sun (of Ming Dynasty)
  on *Shan-Hai-King* II 54n
Yao (Chin)
  ark of, contained human seed II 141
Yard, derivation of term II 597n
Yared, Jared (Heb)
  British yard, literally II 597n
  Hanokh (Enoch), son of II 366, 532, 597n
  son of Mahalaleel II 391n
  "source, descent" or, & Nile River II 583
  third race, esoterically II 597n
Yasna (Pers) [litanies of *Avesta*]

Atlantean sorcerers drowned II 772
Earth septempartite II 758
"Mystery of the Law" II 517
Yāthās (Pers) Gāthās or Mazdean hymns
Brāhmanas, Purānas, same origin II 409-10
Yati(s), Atlanteans 9, high II 331, 336
Yātudhānas (Skt), as gods & men II 211
Ya-va, Yave [Yāhweh] (Heb)
Yava Aleim. *See* Yāhweh Elohīm
Ieve pronounced as II 129
Jehovah or II 464-5
Yazatas (Zend)
Aryan forefathers met w II 356
celestial spirits of elements II 356
Fohat betw fire-, water- II 400n
Star- II 358
Year(s). *See also* Seasons, Sidereal Year
ancient lunar, solar II 620-1
calculating mean solar I 392
divine I 419 &n; II 619-21
each, a day of the gods II 620
great tropical II 505
lunar I 36, 654-6; II 38, 76, 391n, 464, 466,
539, 561, 583, 619
of Patriarchs are cycles II 426
solar, interpreted by St Germain II 582
Thoth, solar discus & II 529
tropical II 76-7, 356, 446
tropical, sidereal, & initiation I 314
twelve thousand divine I 450
used for various cycles II 395
Year(s) of Brahmā. *See also* Brahmā
creation of universe & I 340
length of I 36; II 69-70
one hundred I 206; II 70
Year of Dhruva, kalpa of 9,090 yrs II 307n
Year of the Seven Rishis
kalpa of 3,030 mortal yrs II 307n
Yeast, lives without air I 249n
"Yeast." *See* Huxley, T. H.
Yehīdāh (Heb, Jeshida in tx)
man's divine spirit II 633
Ye-hou-vih (Heb)
Gibbs suggests Jehovah is II 129
Y(e)H(o)V(a)H. *See also* Jehovah, YHVH
meaning of II 460
Yellow
Adams, Aryans fr II 426
Caps (Tibet) I 108n
children of, Father (Stanzas) II 109
dragon (Chinese) II 365
face of column II 178
-gold, 2nd race (Stanzas) II 227
-hued race forefathers II 425

light, color of 1st solid race II 250
race(s) II 199n, 249-50, 780
second race II 178, 227
Śiva reborn as 4, youths II 282
third race was II 198
wars betw black &, races II 223
Yered. *See* Jared
Yesōd, Yesōdōth (pl, Heb) foundation(s)
globe C, Earth chain (Kab) I 200, 240
series of, (*Genesis* 2:4) I 346
Yesōd 'Ōlām (Heb, T'sod Olaum in tx)
Foundation of the World II 583
Yetsīrāh (Heb, Jezirah in tx)
kabbalistic rūah fr, (King) II 604
sephīrōth inhabit II 111
Yeu (Chin) being, subhāva, svabhavat or I 61
Ye-yeva, Sabah [the elder]
Rabbi on hokhmāh II 85
Yezidīs (Persian tribe)
Nabatheans & II 455
worship "Lord Peacock" II 514n
Yezōd. *See* Yesōd
Yggdrasil (Norse). *See also* Tree of Life, World
Tree
ash tree of Aryans II 520
bees of, & honey dew I 344-5
Nidhögg gnaws roots of I 211
Norse Tree of Life II 97
tree of time & life I 427
YHV, Kether-Bīnāh-Hokhmāh are I 438n
YHVH (Heb, also IHYH, JHVH in tx) II 39,
76. *See also* Jehovah, Tetragrammaton,
Yāhweh
bisexual symbol II 460
four letters expl I 438n; II 460, 473
Israelites used Adonai for II 452
Jehovah, Tetragrammaton I 393, 438n, 618
not in use before King David II 541
"Secret of Secrets" II 282n
Sephīrōthal Tree II 625n
Yih-shu-lu-kia-lun [Yi chou lou kia louen]
Chinese transl of *Ekaśloka Śāstra* I 61
Yeu & svabhavat in I 61
Yi King. See I-Ching
Yima (Pers). *See also* Noah, Yama
builds ark (vara), makes man II 6n, 291
guardian of 1st 3 races II 609-10
human races under rule of II 270 &n
progenitor of 2nd race II 609-10
uncreated, created lights & II 290-1
Yin (Chin) binary, expl by É. Lévi II 554
Yin, Chung Ku carries books to II 54n
Yin-sin, Yih-sin (Chin) I 23, 635
Y-King. *See* I-Ching

Yliaster (of Paracelsus)
  ancestor of Crooke's protyle I 283-4
Ymir (Norse). *See also* Giant, Skrymir
  Ases create world fr body of II 97, 99
  formed fr 1st creation I 427
  Heavenly Man or I 367
  Örgelmir or I 427
Yo (Jap) male aethereal principle
  heavens or I 216-17, 241
Yod, Yōdh (Heb, Jod in tx) letter "i" I 60; II 40
  Adam symbolized as II 129, 468
  forefinger symbolizes II 126n
  God of Saxons fr I 347
  Heh &, make Bīnāh II 85
  -He, Jehovah personates as II 509
  holy, within ark II 518
  later than elohīm symbols II 473-4
  letter of Kether is I 438n
  membrum virile II 125, 460, 467, 574
  perfect letter II 551, 603
  phallic hook I 347; II 574
  phallus II 473
  serpent preferable to II 246n
  ten or perfect number I 347, 392, 394; II 39,
    551, 574, 603
Yodcheva [Yōd-ḥavvāh] (Heb)
  Jehovah or II 127-9
  leads prajāpatis, sephīrōth II 129
  offspring of Adam Kadmon II 127
Yoga (Skt) I 47n; II 176, 371n
  described II 115
  hatha, discouraged I 95
  -powers of Tāraka, story of II 382 &n
  powers, senses barrier to II 296
  propagation by II 183
  regulation of breath in I 95-6
  Sons of II 109, 198
  Sons of Passive I 207; II 165-6
  Sons of Will & II 172-3, 181, 199, 220, 275,
    281n, 319, 394n
  supreme wisdom of, freed soul I 132
Yogāchārya (-chāra) School
  Alaya personifies voidness in I 48
  Āryāsanga of II 637
  made paranirvāna esoteric I 42-3
  Mādhyamika vs, re paramārtha I 44n, 48
  "Vedantins in disguise" II 637
Yoga Shāstra [*Yoga-Śāstra*] (Skt)
  yogis & pranidhāna in II 88
Yoga-siddha (Skt), Viśvakarma son of II 559
Yogel, Rabbi, 1065 explains kosmos I 90n
Yogi(n, s) (Skt). *See also* Yoga
  arūpa pitris were formerly II 94
  beguiled by Indra II 614

Brahman-, claim to see highest I 426n
  celestial, sacrifice for humanity II 246
  Fire Angels, rebels are called II 243
  great, fr Advaita School I 522
  Hindu demons were often I 415
  know subterranean passages II 221
  may merge soul w Alaya I 48
  Moon deity of mind w I 516
  must control kundalinī-śakti I 293
  numerous powers of I 293
  oppose clergy, ritual I 415
  pranidhāna 5th observance of II 88
  rākshasas are II 165n
  resist temptations II 614
  Śiva patron of II 282
  some, die in personalities II 532
  traditional grihastha becomes II 411n
  uses ichchhāśakti & kriyāśakti I 292-3;
    II 173
Yoginī (Skt) female yogin
  made into prostitute by Jennings I 472
Yojana(s) 4-9 miles (Skt)
  Earth 50 crores of, in extent II 616n
Yom [Yōm] (Heb) day
  series of foundations I 346
  six days of creation expl II 252n
Yong-grub (Tib) parinishpanna
  absolute bliss or I 42
Yoni(c) (Skt) womb II 465 &n, 548
  cherubs on "Ark" form a II 460
  degenerated symbol II 125, 588
  Hindu, comp w rabbinical II 469
  n'cabvah [neqēbāh] or II 467
  numerical value of II 125
  phallus & I 392
  stone in Ark, linga & II 473-4
  symbol of Holy of Holies I 264
Young, on sunspots I 541n
Young, Edward, *Night Thoughts*
  angels superior men I 276
  stars are religious houses I 578
Youssoufzic [Yusafzai] sons of Joseph
  Afghan tribe II 200n
Yttrium (rare earth)
  complex of 5 or more parts I 625
  fractionation of I 141n, 624
Yu, Emperor
  initiate, mystic I 271n
  knowledge fr "snowy range" I 271n
  nine urns of II 54n
  Shan-Hai-King & II 302
Yudhishthira (Skt) I 369-70
Yuga(s) (Skt) cycles II 198. *See also* Dvāpara-
    Yuga, Kali-Yuga, Satya-Yuga, Tretā-Yuga

bearing on human life I 637
Brahmā opens, by creating II 58
doctrine of I 655-6
double & triple meanings of II 147n, 307n, 308n
dwarfed by Dr Sepp, Suidas II 619-20
four, in Jambu-dvīpa II 322
-kalpas descend by 4, 3, 2 II 307n
length of various II 69-70, 147 &n
no figures more meddled w II 73
three, during 3rd race II 520n
total of, is mahā-yuga II 308n
various lengths of, (Colebrooke) II 624n
Yurbo-adonāi (Jurbo in tx)
    Jehovah in *Codex Nazaraeus* I 463
    var names for I 463
Yuyuje (Skt) yoga-like II 58

Z (letter), double 7 (Ragon) II 582
Zablistanee (Zebulon), Afghan tribe II 200n
Zabulon [Zebulūn] (Heb)
    son of Jacob, Pisces I 651
Zachar va Nakobeh [Zākhār ūNegēbāh] (Heb)
    male & female II 127, 467 &n
    phallus & yoni I 390
Zadok [Tsādōq] (Heb) righteous
    made high priest by David II 541
Zadokites, or Sadducees II 541
Zākhār (Heb, sacr in tx)
    phallus, lingam I 5n; II 465n
    tau cross & I 5; II 467n
Zalmat-Gaguadi, Babylonian dark race II 5
ZAMA ZAMA ΩZZA ΠΑΧΑΜΑ ΩZAI (Gnos) II 580
Zampun, Tibetan Tree of Life II 97
Zamyād Yasht (Pers)
    re Amesha Spentas II 358
Zanoni (Lytton character)
    faces his Augoeides I 573
Zaō (Gk) "I live" II 582
Zarathustra, Zarathushta (Pers). *See also* Zoroaster
    Amshaspend called II 6n
    became ruler of 4th race II 610
    dialogue of, w Ahura Mazdā II 292
    first, fr Atlantean Magas II 322-3
    grotto of, & 4 cardinal pts I 464
    invokes his fravashi II 480
    invokes the Amesha Spenta II 384-5
    septenary chain taught by II 757
Zarpanitu (Bab)

Moon deity II 456
Nebo son of Merodach & II 210n
Zebulūn. *See* Zabulon
Zechariah, Book of
    seven eyes of Tetragrammaton II 626
Zedec or Melchizedek. *See* Tsaddīq
Zenana [Zanāna] (Hindi)
    women's quarters or penetralia I 382
Zend Avesta (Pers)
    Ahriman becomes devil II 93
    ahura fr Vedic *asura* in II 92, 500
    change of poles II 356
    confirms old teachings I 307
    on the elements I 125n
    the Fall described in II 516
    ferouer or fravashi in II 480
    fire giving knowledge of future I 339
    Fohat is Apām-Napāt in II 400n
    holy tree II 97
    Mazdean Noah in II 290-2
    sacred land in II 6
    St Michael story in II 384-5
    serpent w camel's neck II 205
    sevenfold chain in II 757-9
    sevens in II 35, 92
    three-thirds of Earth explained II 757-8
    Yima's rule II 270
Zen-Do (Jap, Dzenodoo in tx)
    seven jewels I 173
Zeno (Gk philosopher)
    nature a habit II 159
    universe fr fire, air, water I 76-7
Zero
    boundless circle or I 99
    cipher of Arab origin I 360-1
    egg-shaped, or kosmos I 91
    laya state or I 545, 551
    number 1 & II 114
    unity within, symbol of deity II 587
Zeroana Akerne [Zervān Akarana] (Pers)
    boundless time I 113; II 488
    circle, chakra of Vishnu I 114
    ever unmanifested principle II 233
    Ormazd issues fr I 113
    various equivalents of I 113
Zero Point. *See also* Laya
    a condition or state I 145
Zeus (Gk). *See also* Jupiter, Kronos
    Astraea allegory & II 785
    "beautiful virgin" I 72n
    bisexual I 72n; II 135
    born in & out of Kronos (Time) I 427
    changed Niobe into fountain II 772
    commands creation of new race II 519

creates 3rd race of Ash tree II 181n
cruelty towards Prometheus II 411-12n
curses Prometheus II 244
deity of the 4th race II 776
desired to quench human race II 412
dethrones father Kronos II 269-70, 421
Deus among Boeotians II 582
disrespectful god (Hesiod) II 269-70
divides man in two II 134, 177
dual nature of II 419-20
"Father of all living" II 582
father of Castor & Pollux II 122
Greco-Olympian Don Juan II 420
host of primeval progenitors II 421-2
Kronos curses II 421
not highest god I 425-6
not perfection II 413
Pater, not phallic II 574
Prometheus rebelled against II 280n
reigns over 4th race II 766
reverences night (*Iliad*) I 425
of secondary creation I 427
as serpent, begat Dionysos II 415, 419-20
son of Kronos-Saturn I 72n
supreme being of heaven I 672
wanted man animal-like II 414
Zeus-Belos [Bel (or Marduk)] (Gk-Bab)
    II 210n
Zeus-Kataibatēs (Gk) Zeus descending
    aspect of Archaeus (Pausanias) I 338n
Zeus Triopios or Triopis
    3-eyed colossus II 294n
Zeus-Zēn (aether)
    Chthonia & Metis wives of I 340-1
    double-sexed creator II 130
Zi, Babylonian god II 5, 54
Ziku, Babylonian god II 5
Zipporah (Heb)
    Jethro's daughter II 465n
    & Sippara (shining) I 385n; II 465n
    town of Sippara (Bab) & I 319n
    wife of Moses I 319n, 385n
Zodh (Cain), slew his female brother II 43-4n
Zodiac(s). *See also* Dendera Zodiac, Zodiac
    (Signs of)
    ancient, discussed II 66, 431
    antiquity of, (Bailly) I 648-9
    Aryan initiates built II 750
    Bailly re Hindu II 332, 435
    Chinese, divided into 24 parts II 620-1
    clearly mentioned in 2 *Kings* I 649
    discussed I 647-8
    Egy & Hindu, immensely old I 650
    Egy, antiquity of II 332, 431-2, 435-6

Egy, fr India II 435-6
    Greek, age of II 436 &n
    heirloom fr Atlantis II 431-3
    Hindu, fr Greeks (Müller) II 225, 332
    Hindu, older than Greeks I 657-8
    history contained in II 438
    Indian, fr Greeks (Weber) I 647; II 50
    Indian, not fr Greeks I 650; II 50
    lords of, now rebellious angels I 577
    Old Testament ref I 649
    reddened w solar blaze II 357
    sidereal prophecies of I 653
    traces to Argonauts (Newton) I 652
    universality of I 648-9
    Volney re origin of I 658; II 436n
Zodiac (Signs of)
    animals of *Genesis* are II 112n
    archaic nations knew I 320
    on body of Kārttikeya II 619
    descend, ascend (expl) I 658; II 357
    "Fiery Lions" & Leo I 213
    kumāras connected w II 576
    Makara (Capricorn) I 384; II 268n, 576-80
    man's past, future in II 431-3
    mentioned in Homer I 648
    Mother of God surrounded by I 400
    patriarchs connected w I 651
    reflected on Earth II 502-3
    regents of, minor gods II 358
    sacred animals of II 23, 181n
    seven planets & twelve I 79
    ten, 12, among ancients II 502 &n
    tribes of Israel & I 400, 651; II 200n
    twelve great orders & I 213
    twelve rulers, kings or I 651
    twelve, 7 planets & races I 573 &n
    twelve, cakes, stones (Philo) I 649
    two mystery II 502 &n
    when, vertical to pole II 357
    world builders II 23
    worshiped (2 *Kings*) I 649
Zodiacal
    allegory is historical II 353
    Aryan, calculations II 436 &n
    records (Atlantean) cannot err II 49
    ring, relic in Gobi II 503
Zohak, Persian usurper II 398
Zohar (Heb) II 2, 215n
    Ain-sōph I 349; II 290
    allegory of man w heavy load I 393-4
    antiquity of II 461n
    astral 1st race II 137
    astral light, Magic Head I 424
    Balaam's birds were serpents II 409

birth starts w a point I 337
black fire in II 162
b'ne-aleim, Ischin II 375-6
book of Hanokh & II 532 &n
Chaldean *Book of Numbers* & I 214, 230
Christian Gnostics influenced II 461n
circle w point found in I 19
cosmogenesis in, described I 214-15
creation of man II 490-1
creations, several in II 53, 54
creator delighted in creation II 126
divine beings, descending order II 111
Earth 7th globe I 241
Eden called bird's nest II 292
edited by Gnostics, Christians I 214, 352
elements, forces form Word I 346
elohīm called Echod or one I 112
everything shadow of divine II 268
fall of the angels II 487
first Adam II 503-4
flying camels II 205
fountain of life I 356
garment of man II 315
Iachin chained to mountain II 376
indivisible point, world fr I 355
key to, in the names II 536
light II 39
Lord rebukes Satan II 478 &n
man emanated fr septenary group I 230
modern views of, mistaken II 461
more occult than Bks of Moses II 626n
Moses de Leon, Ibn Gebirol & II 461n
Moses de Leon re-edited I 214
Nahash (the "deprived") rebels II 247
occult work (Lévi) II 536
phallic, cruder than Purānas II 625n
quotes *Book of Enoch* II 535
real man is soul, not body II 290
repeats Purānic expressions II 126
roots of human race II 315
rotation of Earth II 28n
St Michael called Jehovah in II 479
Sephīrāh, Shekhīnāh or Aditi in I 53n
seven seas, mountains II 603
Shekhīnāh II 293
six-month night, day in II 773
soul put on earthly garment II 112
spirit & matter II 528
Sun moves in circuits II 553
on 10 sephīrōth I 239
three heads in II 25
Tree of Life II 216
Unknown Light I 356
visible types, invisible prototypes II 120

white hidden fire I 339
will of the king expl in I 356
Zöllner, Prof J. K. F., [*Transcendental Physics*]
    believed phenomena of spiritualism I 520
    on 4th dimensional space I 251 &n
Zone(s)
    globe divided into seven II 403
    seven, of indestructible continent II 400 &n
    seven, rishis, creations II 612
Zonoplacental Mammals II 668, 713n
Zoömancy
    Orpheus taught, (Suidas) I 362-3
Zoroaster. *See also Chaldean Oracles*, Zara-
    thustra
    addressed as "Son of God" II 772
    forbade killing of birds I 362
    the last II 6n
    the original II 6
    twelve, 14 of II 359
    "When you doubt, abstain" II 442
Zoroastrian(s, ism). *See also* Ahura Mazdā,
    Amshaspends, Mazdeans, Ormazd, *Ven-
    didad, Zend Avesta*
    Ahriman made devil in II 93
    antiquity of, scriptures II 356
    asura(s) & ahura II 59, 92-3, 500
    Catholic &, astrolatry I 402
    caves I 126
    Central Asian region of II 416n
    change of pole II 356
    did not believe evil eternal II 488
    dualism of I 196, 235, 239
    esotericism & SD II 356
    on ether I 331
    Hyde on Kabiri & II 363n
    "I am that I am" I 78
    living fire of I 338n
    made devils of Hindu devas I 73
    MSS on flying camel II 205
    Ormazd of II 358, 420
    septenary in II 607-10, 757-9
    seven Amshaspends I 127
    seven Devs I 577
    similar to Hindu tenets II 757-9
    star-yazatas of II 358
    Taurus sacred to I 657
    universal mind manifests as Ahura Mazdā
        I 110
ΖΩΤΙΚΩ ΖΩΤΙΚΗ (Zōtikō Zōtikē, Gk)
    life of life (Massey) II 586
Zū, Babylonian god II 283-4n
Zuñi Indians
    Cushing lived among II 629
    septenary principle among II 628-9

APPENDIX

Appendix

In this alphabetical listing of the foreign language quotations and phrases found in *The Secret Doctrine*, each entry is followed by the page(s) where it appears in the *SD* and a language designation in parentheses. An English translation is then given, followed when applicable by the source of the foreign phrase. Where the Greek or other foreign words in the *SD* are in obvious error, corrections have been made. Words and phrases not included in this appendix may be found either in the Index or in foreign language dictionaries.

Achath-Ruach-Elohim-Chiim ['Aḥāth rūaḥ 'elohīm ḥayyīm] I 130n (Heb) "One, the spirit of the living god(s)" (Westcott trans.) or "First, the spirit of the god(s) of the living" (Stenring trans.) — *Sēpher Yetzīrāh* I.9 & nn.

Actio in distans I 487, 488, 491, etc. (Lat) "Action over (at) a distance."

Addit Cedrenus (Salem I.3): Stella Martis ab Egyptiis vocatur Ertosi (plantare, generare). Significat autem hoc omnis generis procreationem et vivificationem, omnisque substantiae et materiae naturam et vim ordinantem atque procreantem II 143-4n (Lat) "Cedrenus says (Salmasius I.c): The planet Mars was called by the Egyptians Ertosi (to plant, generate). This implies the creating and generating of everything, the creating and determining of the nature and powers of all substance and matter."

ἀγαθαὶ καὶ κακαὶ δυνάμεις (agathai kai kakai dunameis) II 497, 515 (Gk) "Good and evil forces."

'Ahiye asher ahiyé ['Ehyeh 'asher 'ehyeh] II 539 (Heb) "I am that I am."

An lumen sit corpus, nec non? I 483 (Lat) "Is light a body, or is it not?"

Αντίμιμον Πνεύματος (Antimimon Pneumatos) II 604, 604-5n (Gk) "Modeled after the spirit."

ἀοιδῶν οἴδε δύστηνοι λόγοι (aoidōn hoide dustēnoi logoi) II 764 (Gk) "Those miserable stories of the poets." — Euripides, *Hercules Mad* 1.1346

ἀπρεπὲς τῷ θεῷ [ἀπρεπὲς ἂν εἴη θεῷ] (aprepes an eiē theōi) II 159 (Gk) "Still less becoming for a god." — Aristotle, *De Mundo* (On the Cosmos) 6.398b.7

Au spectacle de tant de grandeur opposé à celui de tant de misère, l'esprit qui se met à observer ce vaste ensemble, se représente je ne sais quelle grande divinité *qu'une divinité, plus grande et plus pressante* **encore, aurait comme brisée et mise en pièces en dispersant les débris dans tout l'Univers** II 554-5n (Fr) "At the sight of such immensity on the one hand, and so much misery on the other, the spirit which undertakes to study this great whole envisions who knows what great divinity *that a still vaster and more exacting divinity* had shattered, broken to pieces, and scattered the fragments throughout the whole universe." — de Montlosier, *Mystères de la vie humaine* 1.2.126, 1829 ed., Paris

αὐτουρνεῖν [αὐτουργεῖν] ἅπαντα (autournein [autourgein] hapanta) II 159 (Gk) "To execute everything himself." — Aristotle, *De Mundo* 6.398b.5

B'raisheeth barah elohim ath hash ama yem v'ath haa'retz [B'rē'shīth bārā' 'elohīm 'ēth hash-shamayīm v'ēth hā'ārets] I 374 (Heb) "In the beginning God created the heaven and the earth." (*Gen* 1:1, King James version); alternatively, "In a host the gods (elohīm) formed themselves into the heavens and the earth" (G. de Purucker, *Fundamentals of the Esoteric Philosophy*, 2nd ed., pp. 98-9).

Cadebat ut fulgar II 230 (Lat) "Fell like lightning."

Casta fove [fave] Lucina: tuus iam regnat Apollo I 401 (Lat) "Pure Lucina, be gracious: thine own Apollo now is king." — Virgil, *Eclogues* 4.10

Ce qui manque à tous les deux, c'est l'intuition du mystique I 496 (Fr) "What both lack is the intuition of the mystic."

Certus sum, scio quod credidi II 451 (Lat) "I am certain, I know what I have believed."

χρυσοφαὴς Ἑρμῆς (chrusophaēs Hermēs) II 28 (Gk) "Golden-colored Hermes."

Cogito ergo sum II 242 (Lat) "I think, therefore I am." — Descartes, *Principes* . . . 1.7

Credat Judaeus Apella II 451 (Lat) "Apella the Jew may believe that . . ." — Horace, *Satires* 1.5.100

De minimis non curat lex I viii (Lat) "The law does not concern itself with trifles."

Deliciae humani generis I 604 (Lat) "Delightful human creations."

Demon est Deus inversus I 411 (Lat) "The Devil is God inverted."

Deorsum fluens II 230 (Lat) "Flowing downwards."

Deus enim et circulus est II 552 (Lat) "And certainly Deity is circular." — Pherecydes' hymn to Jupiter.

Deus non fecit mortem II 422 (Lat) "God did not make death." — *Wisdom of Solomon* or *Sapientiae* (Apocrypha) 1:13

Dieu est devenu une hypothèse inutile I 498 (Fr) "God has become a useless hypothesis." — Laplace

Diva triformis, tergemina, triceps I 387 (Lat) "Goddess three-formed, threefold at birth, three-headed."

ἐγγὺς γὰρ νυκτός τε καὶ ἤματός εἰσι κέλευθοι (engus gar nuktos te kai ēmatos eisi keleuthoi) II 7 (Gk) "for the outgoings of the night and of the day are close together." — Homer, *Odyssey* 10.86

ΕΙΣ ΖΕΤΣ [ΖΕΥΣ] ΣΑΡΑΠΙ (Eis Zets [Zeus] Sarapi) II 474 (Gk) "Sarapis is the one Zeus"; *see* King, *Gnostics & Their Remains*, pp. 326-7

ἐν οὐρανίοις σημείοις (en ouraniois sēmeiois) I 652 (Gk) "In signs from heaven." — Xenophon, *Cyropaedia* 8.7.3

E pur se [si] muove! II 451 (It) "But it does move!" — Galileo

Ἑρμηνεύει δέ τὸ ᾠον κόσμον [ἑρμηνεύειν δὲ τὸ ᾠον τὸν κόσμον] (Her-mēneuein de to ōion ton kosmon) I 360 (Gk) "And the egg represents (symbolizes, interprets) the cosmos." — Porphyry

Ἤτοι μεν πρώτιστα χάος γένετ' (Ētoi men prōtista chaos genet') I 425n (Gk) "Chaos of all things was the first generated." — Hesiod, *Theogony*, line 116

Ex connexione autem ejus spiritus prodidit [prodiit] Mot I 451 (Lat) "Out of the union with that spirit has proceeded Mot."

Ex oriente lux II 42 (Lat) "Out of the East, light."

Facies totius Universi, quamvis infinitis modis variet, manet tamen semper eadem II 1 (Lat) "The face of the whole universe, though it varies in infinite modes, yet remains always the same." — Spinoza, *Correspondence of Spinoza*, Letter 64

Genitum, non factum I 399 (Lat) "Born, not made."

Il est impossible de découvrir le moindre trait de ressemblance entre les parties du ciel et les figures que les astronomes y ont *arbitrairement* tracées, et de l'autre côté, *le hasard est impossible* I 652 (Fr) "It is impossible to find the least trace of similarity between the segments of sky and the figures astronomers have *arbitrarily* assigned to them, while, on the other hand, *chance is impossible*." — C. F. Dupuis, "Zodiaque," *Origine de tous les cultes*

Il fallait éviter de paraître autoriser le dogme du double principe en faisant de ce Satan créateur une puissance réelle, et pour expliquer le mal originel, on profère contre Manes l'hypothèse d'une permission de l'unique tout Puissant II 509 (Fr) "It was necessary to avoid seeming to sanction the dogma of a dual principle by making this creative Satan into an actual power and, in order to explain the origin of evil, the theory of a divine authorization given by the Almighty One was adduced in opposition to Mani." — Jules Baissac, *Satan ou le Diable* . . . , p. 9

Il manque quelque chose aux géologues pour faire la géologie de la Lune, c'est d'être astronomes. À la vérité il manque aussi quelque chose aux astronomes pour aborder avec fruit cette étude, c'est d'être géologues I 496 (Fr) "The geologists are lacking what is needed to study the geology of the moon, and that is: they are not astronomers. Truly what astronomers lack for a fruitful pursuit of this study is to be geologists." — Hervé E. Faye (in Winchell, *World Life*, p. 379)

Il n'est plus possible aujourd'hui, *de soutenir comme Newton*, que les corps célestes se mouvent au milieu du *vide* immense des espaces. . . . Parmi les conséquences de la *théorie du vide établie* par ce grand homme, il ne reste plus debout *que le mot 'attraction,'* et nous verrons le jour ou ce dernier mot disparaîtra du vocabulaire scientifique I 494n (Fr) "Today it is no longer possible *to maintain, as Newton did*, that the heavenly bodies move in EMPTY space. . . . Among the consequences of the *theory of vacuum established* by that great man, all that remains unrefuted is *the word 'attraction'* and we expect to see the day when that last word will disappear from the vocabulary of science." — C. H. Le Couturier, *Panorama des mondes* . . . , pp. 47, 53

In adversum flumen I 169 (Lat) "Against the current."

In pluribus unum I 461 (Lat) "In many, one" or "one in many."

IΩ Ioh, Ægyptiis *Lunam* significat neque habent illi in communi sermonis usu, aliud nomen quo Lunam, designent praeter IO II 463 (Lat) "*IŌ, Ioh*, to the Egyptians signifies the Moon. They don't have in their everyday language any other word with which to denote the Moon except IO." — P. E. Jablonsky, *Pantheon aegyptiorum*, 2.3.1.6, 1752 ed.

Judaea gens, radix stultorum II 358 (Lat) "The Jewish people, a root of foolishness." — Rutilius Namatianus, *De Reditu Suo*, bk. I, lines 383, 389

Καλλίστα πολὺ παρθενῶν (Kallista polu parthenōn) I 395 (Gk) "Loveliest by far of the maidens." — Euripides, *Hippolytos*, line 66

Κοῖὸν τε, Κροῖόν τε μέλαν [μέγαν], Φορκύν τε κραταιὸν, / Καὶ Κρὸνον, Ὠκεανὸν δ', Ὑπερίοα [Ὑπερίον] τε, Ἰαπετόντε (Koion te, Kroion te melan [megan], Phorkun te krataion, / Kai Kronon, Ōkeanon d', Huperioa [Huperion] te, Iapetonte) II 143 (Gk) "Coeus, the great Croeus, the strong Phorcys, / Also Cronos [Saturn], Ocean, Hyperion, and Iapetus." — Cf. Proclus, *On the Timaeus of Plato*, 2.5.324 (Thomas Taylor trans.)

Lateras coctiles I 357 (Lat) "Burned tiles (tablets of clay)."

Le Jour de "Viens a nous" . . . c'est le jour où Osiris a dit au Soleil: Viens! Je le vois rencontrant le Soleil dans l'Amenti I 134n (Fr) "The Day 'Be With Us' . . . that is the day when Osiris said to the Sun:

Come! I see him meeting the Sun in Amenti." — Paul Pierret, *Le livre des morts* (The Book of the Dead) 17.61

Leontoid ὀφιομορφος (ophiomorphos) II 481 (Lat & Gk) "The lion-like serpent."

Liquor Amnii II 188 (Lat) "Amniotic fluid."

Malum in se I 413 (Lat) "Evil in itself."

μεγάλοι δυνατοὶ (megaloi dunatoi) II 363 (Gk) "Great and powerful."

Menses in quinos dies descriperunt [denos descripserunt] dies II 620 (Lat) "They have divided the months into periods of fifteen days." — Quintius Curtius, *History of Alexander* 8.9.35-6

Monstra quaedam de genere giganteo. II 375 (Lat) "Monsters that gave birth to giants."

Natura Elementorum obtinet revelationem Dei I 125n (Lat) "The nature of the elements contained the revelation of God." — Clement of Alexandria, *Stromata* (*Miscellanies*) 5.6, 2nd para.

Natura naturans I 412 (Lat) "nature begetting" (nature as a creative principle).

Natura non facit saltum II 287, 696 (Lat) "Nature makes no leaps."

Ni fallat fatum, Scoti quocumque locatum / Invenient lapidem, regnasse tenentur ibidem II 342 (Lat) "Unless the oracle fails, wherever the Scots find / This stone placed, they will hold sway." — J. de Cambry, *Monuments Celtiques*, p. 107 (1805 ed.)

Νοῦς [ἐστιν] ὁ διακοσμῶντε καὶ πάντων ἄιτιος (Nous [estin] ho diakosmōnte kai pantōn aitios) I 451 (Gk) "An ordering and disposing mind, which was the cause of all things." — Plato, *Phaedo* 97c

Oh, ma pensée, que s'ensuit il? car je désire grandement ce propos. Pimandre dict, ceci est un mystère celé, jusques à ce jour d'hui. Car nature, soit mestant avec l'hôme, a produict le miracle très mer-

veilleux, aiant celluy qui ie t'ay dict, la nature de l'harmonie des sept du père, et de l'esprit. *Nature ne s'arresta pas là*, mais incontinent a produict *sept hômes, selon les natures des sept gouverneurs* en puissance des deux sexes et esleuez. . . . La génération de ces *sept* s'est donnée en ceste manière . . . II 491n (Fr) "Oh, my thought, what is it pursuing? For I greatly desire to know. Pymander says, this is a sealed mystery until today. For nature, in man has produced a marvelous miracle, having that which I have told you, a nature in harmony with the seven of the father, and of spirit. *Nature did not stop there*, but unsatisfied, produced and reared *seven men, according to the natures of the seven governors* with power of the two sexes. . . . The generation of these *seven* happened in this wise . . ." — *The Divine Pymander* 1.16; *see also* Walter Scott, *Hermetica* 1:123

Οἱ δ'εν Αἰγύπτῳ ['Οἱ δ'οὖν Αἰγύπτιοι] μυθολογοῦσι κατὰ τὴν Ἰσιδὸς ἡλικίαν γεγονέναι τίνας [τινάς] πολυσωμάτους (Oi d'en Aiguptōi [Hoi d'oun Aiguptioi] muthologousi kata tēn Isidos hēlikian gegonenai tinas polusōmatous) II 344n (Gk) "Furthermore, the Egyptians relate in their myths that in the time of Isis there were certain creatures of many bodies [who are called by the Greeks giants"]. — Diodorus Siculus, *Bibliotheka* 1.26.6

Omnis enim per se divom natura necesse est [necessest] / inmortali aevo summa cum pace fruatur I 7n (Lat) "For the very nature of divinity must necessarily / enjoy immortal life in the deepest peace." — Lucretius, *De Rerum Natura* 2.646-7

Pareshu [yāḥ] guhyeshu, vrateshu II 622n (Skt) "remote and secret realms." — *Ṛig-Veda* 10.114.2, 3.54.5

Pater (omnipotens) Æther I 10n, 331, 488n (Lat) "Omnipotent Father Aether."

Περὶ ἀποχῆς ἐμψυχῶν (Peri apochēs empsuchōn) I 425 (Gk) "*On Abstinence from Animal Food*" (a work by Porphyry; in Latin, *De Abstinentia*).

Περὶ [τῶν πρωτῶν] ἀρχῶν (Peri [tōn prōtōn] archōn) I 425 (Gk) "*On First Principles*" (a work by Damascius).

περὶ χυμείας αργύρου καὶ χρυσοῦ (Peri chumeias argurou kai chrusoū) II 763n (Gk) "Concerning the mingling of silver and gold."

πνεύματα τῶν στοιχείων (pneumata tōn stoicheiōn) I 395 (Gk) "Spirit of the elements."

Princeps aeris hujus [principem potestatis aeris hujus] II 485, 515 (Lat) "Prince [of the power] of the air" — *Ephesians* 2:2.

πρωτόγονον διφυῆ τρίγονον Βακχεῖον Ἄνακτα / Ἄγριον ἀρρητὸν κρύφιον δικέρωτα δίμορφον (prōtogonon diphuē trigonon Bakcheion Anakta / Agrion arrēton kruphion dikerōta dimorphon) I 335 (Gk) "O firstborn, dual in nature, thrice begotten, Bacchic king / Rural, ineffable, cryptic, two-horned, two-formed." — "To Bacchus," *Mystical Hymns of Orpheus*, Hymn 30

Qui circumambulat terram II 485, 515 (Lat) "who circles the earth."

Qui fruges excantassent [excantasset] segetem pellicentes incantando I 469 (Lat) "Who draws away by incantations the fruits of one field to another." — Servius Maurus Honoratus on Virgil's *Eclogues* 8.99

Satis eloquentiae, sapientiae parvum I 349 (Lat) "Eloquence enough, too little wisdom." — Sallust, *Cataline* V

Σεμελῆν τρέμουσι δαίμονες (Semelēn tremousi daimones) I 400 (Gk) "Semele made the spirits tremble."

Senior occultatus est et absconditus; Microprosopus manifestus est, et non manifestus I 214–15 (Lat) "The Ancient One is hidden and concealed; the Microprosopus is manifested, and is not manifested." — Rosenroth, *Kabbala Denudata*, *Liber Mysterii* (Siphrā' di Tseniūthā, "Book of Concealed Mystery"); *see* Mathers, *Kabbalah Unveiled*, p. 91 (4.1)

Sicanus deificavit Aretiam, et nominavit eam linguâ Janigenâ Horchiam II 144 (Lat) "Sicanus deified Aretia and named her Horchia of the lineage of Janus."

Solaris luminis particeps II 28 (Lat) "Participating in solar light."

Spiritualia nequitiae [in] coelestibus I 331n (Lat) "Spiritual wickedness in heavenly regions." — *Ephesians* 6:12

Spiritus intus alit, totamque infusa per artus, / Mens agitat molem, et magno se corpore miscet I 451n, II 594 (Lat) "A spirit within sustains, and mind, pervading its members, / Sways the whole mass and mingles with its mighty frame." — Virgil, *Aeneid* 6.726-7

Taurus Draconem genuit, et Taurum Draco II 133 (Lat) "A bull has begotten a dragon, and a dragon a bull" (*see* A. Wilder, "The Primeval Race Double-Sexed," *Theosophist* (4:112–14, Feb 1883).

Tibi sunt Malchut [Malkūth] et Geburah [Gebūrāh] et Chassed [Ḥesedh] per Aeonas II 562 (Lat) "For thine is the Kingdom, the Justice, and the Mercy throughout the Aeons."

Totum corpus circumagimur II 552 (Lat) "All bodies move in a circle."

Tum virgam capit, hac animas ille evocat Orco [pallentis] II 28 (Lat) "Then he takes his wand; with this he calls pale ghosts from Orcus." — Virgil, *Aeneid* 4.242

Tu vestis solem et te sol vestit I 393 (Lat) "You clothe the Sun and the Sun clothes you."

Unum intra alterum, et alterum super alterum II 25 (Lat) "[Three Heads have been formed] one within the other, and the other above the other" — *The Lesser Holy Assembly* (*Idrā Zūtā Qadīshā*) 2.59 (Mathers, *Kabbalah Unveiled*, p. 265)

Verbum sat sapienti I 349 (Lat) "A word to the wise is sufficient."

Vinculum substantiale I 631 (Lat) "Substantial bond."

Virgo pariet I 399 (Lat) "Virgin brings forth."

Vis viva I 670 (Lat) "Living force."

Vox populi Vox Dei II 298 (Lat) "The voice of the people is the voice of God."